PERSONAL CARE MANAGEMENT

S.M. JHA

Ph.D., D.Lit.

Professor,
Department of Commerce and Business Administration,
L.N. Mithila University,
Darbhanga-846 008.
India

First Edition : 2012
Edition : 2018
Edition : 2019

Published by : Mrs. Meena Pandey for **Himalaya Publishing House Pvt. Ltd.,**
Ramdoot, Dr. Bhalerao Marg, Girgaon, Mumbai - 400 004
Phone: 022-23860170/23863863; **Fax:** 022-23877178
E-mail: himpub@bharatmail.co.in; **Website:** www.himpub.com

Branch Offices :

New Delhi : Pooja Apartments, 4-B, Murari Lal Street, Ansari Road, Darya Ganj, New Delhi - 110 002. Phone: 011-23270392, 23278631; Fax: 011-23256286

Nagpur : Kundanlal Chandak Industrial Estate, Ghat Road, Nagpur - 440 018. Phone: 0712-2738731, 3296733; Telefax: 0712-2721216

Bengaluru : Plot No. 91-33, 2nd Main Road, Seshadripuram, Behind Nataraja Theatre, Bengaluru - 560 020. Phone: 080-41138821; Mobile: 09379847017, 09379847005

Hyderabad : No. 3-4-184, Lingampally, Besides Raghavendra Swamy Matham, Kachiguda, Hyderabad - 500 027. Phone: 040-27560041, 27550139

Chennai : New No. 48/2, Old No. 28/2, Ground Floor, Sarangapani Street, T. Nagar, Chennai-600 017. Mobile: 09380460419

Pune : First Floor, Laksha Apartment, No. 527, Mehunpura, Shaniwarpeth (Near Prabhat Theatre), Pune - 411 030. Phone: 020-24496323, 24496333; Mobile: 09370579333

Lucknow : House No. 731, Shekhupura Colony, Near B.D. Convent School, Aliganj, Lucknow - 226 022. Phone: 0522-4012353; Mobile: 09307501549

Ahmedabad : 114, SHAIL, 1st Floor, Opp. Madhu Sudan House, C.G. Road, Navrang Pura, Ahmedabad - 380 009. Phone: 079-26560126; Mobile: 09377088847

Ernakulam : 39/176 (New No. 60/251), 1st Floor, Karikkamuri Road, Ernakulam, Kochi - 682011. Phone: 0484-2378012, 2378016; Mobile: 09387122121

Cuttack : New LIC Colony, Behind Kamala Mandap, Badambadi, Cuttack - 753 012, Odisha. Mobile: 9338746007

Kolkata : 108/4, Beliaghata Main Road, Near ID Hospital, Opp. SBI Bank, Kolkata - 700 010, Phone: 033-32449649; Mobile: 07439040301

DTP by : Sudhakar Shetty (HPH Pvt. Ltd., Mumbai)

Printed at : M/s. Aditya Offset Process (I) Pvt. Ltd., Hyderabad. On behalf of HPH.

PREFACE

Corporatisation another edition of westernisation has been successful in injecting new life and strength to the material culture which has made ourselves addicted to the opulent lifestyles for which we have no option but to earn as much as we can. Corporatisation has opened doors where the upcoming and budding youths are found nurturing optimism and high level of expectations vis-à-vis the zest for life. On the flip side, they of course invite stress and bid a goodbye to peace and pleasure. It is an age which is found full of wonders. It is an age which is globalised not only in terms of economy and markets but also in the context of fashion, culture and civilisation. It is an age which rewards you for your personal score. And, it is an age which also punishes you for not respecting the organisational culture. We cannot negate that enrichment is a brick-by-brick process. Our consistent and creative efforts, for the long time, make us potentially of world class. The most important thing is to identify the need of the hour and to shift our predilections or priorities and change our perceptions. Time cycle necessitates a change in our perception and we have no option but to respect the requirements of time. Look the wonders of the corporate world where it isn't the extraordinary who are grabbing the plush jobs; the new high-flier is your average boy-next-door. Of course, they are differentiator and consistently hone their leadership skills, logic, intuition, thinking, communication and mannerism. They have "zippy" attitude. They are creative leaders, possess poise and assertiveness and a rock star personality. They are visionaries who anticipate future changes, accept challenges and thrive on change. They are a problem-solver, adaptable and agile and nurture temptation to shape their personality rather than getting lost in books. The corporate world looks for people with all these properties and in the enrichment process, we have to make sincere, honest and professionalised efforts to conceptualise them in a right fashion.

The Business and Finishing Schools bear the responsibility of diagnosing the requirements and levels of expectations of the corporate world and to educate, train and develop people in such a fashion that they prove themselves to be productive. The potential managers need to switch on the enrichment process and to make it sure that they have all the properties and traits in tune with the changing corporate or business world. Since we find increasing heat of corporatisation sizably influenced by the MNCs, it is imperative that both of them make place for the perception that employees serving the business world are just an extension of the corporate brand; be it globally, nationally or albeit regionally. Of late, we find Finishing Schools mushrooming specially in the big towns and cities because a majority of the Business Schools have failed in gauging the changing mood and temperament of the corporate world. It is high time that we increase our sensitivity and conceptualise the faculties bearing the efficacy of making us nationally and globally productive.

The corporate world looks for a rock star personality and this makes it essential that the corporate strategists or potential corporate professionals assign a transcendental priority to the management of body. Healthy body engineers a sound foundation for the development of a healthy mind vis-à-vis an attractive personality. If we assign due weightage to our lifestyles, find ourselves sensitive to the quality of food and water, keep ourselves aware of the communicable and infectious diseases, show our temptation to the environment and ambience where we work and live and assign top priority to personal hygiene; a number of health problems are automatically arrested. Generally, we do not realise the importance of food in having a sound health. In one of the text of Yoga, i.e. Gherand Sahita, it is said that no amount of yoga can help us if we do not take suitable and balanced diet. This focuses our attention on the management of food for the sound management of our body. If we spend on foodcare, we save on medicare. It is an unvarnished fact that increasing the satiety value of food is the most important thing which requires our priority attention. We need to perceive that mindful eating helps us in regulating and preventing a number of diseases. We need to understand the significance of food for our body and cells. Mindful eating is about savouring each morsel we eat. In addition, water constitutes an important place in the sound management of our body and therefore we need adequate potable water. Sanitation is considered to be a basic requirement of a civilised society. Inculcating habits for exercises and aerobics may benefit us in many ways. For soundness of body, it is also pertinent that we do not welcome a stage of sleep deficit. Thus all the dimensions need due care to have a sound body.

Good hygiene practices not only protect health of an individual but virtually health of all those having a direct contact. Hygiene plays an effective role in attaining physical and emotional soundness. Activating the sensitisation process is urgently needed to make society aware of the standard of hygiene. The management of personal hygiene includes in its ambit a number of facets such as children personal hygiene, personal hygiene, education and training, personal hygiene guidelines and a number of allied problems directly or indirectly influencing the process of infection. It is not only related to the well-being of human beings but albeit also to the surroundings, atmosphere and ecology responsible for providing to us a healthy living condition. Washing our hands, trimming our nails, keeping our hair clean, good oral hygiene, disinfecting the clothes that we wear are some of the important dimensions necessitating due attention of ours.

Civic sense is nothing but social ethics. It is a school of thought. It is consideration by the people of a civilised and disciplined society. It is even more than that. The stinking public and even private toilets, scattered garbage on roads, unawareness of the traffic sense, insensitivity to personal hygiene, gross misuse of public water supply services and electricity services make us uncivilised. Of course, we have been successful in enriching our thematical competence but when we talk about the civic sensibility, we lag far-far behind. Our personal score come to zero, when we lack even some of the basics of a civilised society. The increasing cases of separatism, vandalism, intolerance, racism road rage, etc., are all results of lack of civic sense. Besides, we need to assign due weightage to aesthetic sense. Understanding the beauty of nature, receiving the beauty of art and enjoying the beauty of life are the three important considerations for the development of aesthetic sense. The ultimate focus we find on the zest for life which is possible when we are creative and optimistic. The corporate world looks for creative and optimistic people. The moment we start loving nature; our temptation for beauty starts gaining a rapid momentum and resulting from which we start loving ourselves. Cultivating aesthetic sense thus occupies a place of outstanding significance.

Healthy mind paves avenues for the development of a healthy body. In the world of hurry, curry and worry and hustle and bustle, it is difficult for us to have a healthy mind. This necessitates a scientific management of mind so that the purification process gains a rapid momentum. In a true sense, the accumulated complexes obstruct the process of development of mind and body. The accumulation of negative feelings and thoughts impact both mind and body in an adverse fashion. To be positive is a brick-by-brick process. Each and everyday, if we make place for some of the positive thoughts; the negative thoughts start going out and we find our mind fresh and body healthy. Of late, we find emotional challenges complicating our tasks. We hardly find even a single day when we do not experience some emotional challenges. This necessitates laughing and laughter. The different postures of Yoga may help us in purifying and managing the mind. The rise and fall are the properties of the corporate world. If we find the economy booming, we should keep ourselves mentally and potentially ready to counter the recession and depression. If we witness a pay hike; we should also keep ourselves ready for a pay cut. If we witness creation of new job opportunities; we should also keep ourselves ready for retrenchment. But the crux of the problem is that we never welcome the odds and find ourselves, tensed, irritated, stressed and depressed. The devices to combat stress are different postures of yoga, our participation in the spiritual sessions, sleep better, gardening, entertainment and laughter, pet-therapy and retail-therapy. A well managed clearing of stored complexes would be found after combating stress.

In the emerging cross-cultural society, the employees are considered an extension of the corporate brand and therefore social graces and polish can not be underrated. Our outward behaviour, etiquette and manners and soft skills need due attention to get the competitive advantages. When we talk about etiquette, it is concerned with the conventional law of courtesy. It is decorum in which we find place for polite and socially acceptable behaviour observed between the members of same profession. In the process, the employees are required to be courteous and their speech and action must be polite. When we talk about manners, our focus is on the outward behaviour or attitudes towards others. It is also personal style of acting or bearing or a way in which something is done. In every educated and civilised society, the etiquette and manners become a part and parcel of relationships.

Actually, professional excellence cannot be possible in absence of a professional growth and if we undermine corporate etiquette and manners, the professional growth is difficult.

Philanthropy comes from the heart of the people which makes place for desire. The focal point is not that you give back to the society rather than it is humility and your attachment with humanity that transforms your attitudes. Managing ethics is, of course managing yourself. The task of developing a holistic personality remains difficult if we fail in managing ethics and building character. In an age of societal globalisation, we find ethics and character emerging as major determinants of individual or organisational success. Ethics is a far-reaching concept and goes beyond the idea of making money legally. The use of company resources for personal interests and benefits cannot be ethical. Taking undue advantages of business resources cannot be ethical. Using the wealth of the business for personal reasons is not ethical. Using company funds for personal reasons is unethical. A thoughtful and a careful utilisation of the resources of the company is a part of the business ethics. When we find corporate people conceptualising business ethics, it is meant that they are successful in adding new dimensions in their personal score. Because they are ethical, we find their conduct good and character different from others. This proves to be his/her strength and originality. We need a prescription which may be effective in making an assault on the negative thoughts of corporate people who have started nurturing a dream of overnight trading and an easy walkover to have an opulent lifestyle.

What is pleasant to our eyes is found acceptable to our mind. Better-looking people are found creative, optimistic and productive. There is nothing more appealing than a man with a sense of wit and fun. There is nothing more paying than an aesthete. Shifting from relaxed mode to the professional mode makes a strong advocacy in favour of corporate looks. Better wardrobe, big bucks. The corporate world is found full of wonders. You are fired because your belt buckle has shifted three or four notches too high. You are promoted because you are good looking. Your looks can help or hinder your professional growth regardless of your qualifications. This focuses our attention on the management of looks. Powerful looking clothes impact our mindset and attitudes, we start believing in the professional mode. We are creative and optimistic and therefore start playing a big role in building and projecting the corporate image. Etiquette and grooming experts feel and corporate trainers advocate that we need a transformation in the whole package of attitude, body language, behaviour, communication and etiquette. In the process of grooming, we need to respect the organisational culture. A microscopic evaluation of our appearance is essential such as the dresses that we wear, the shoes and socks that we use, the ties that we select, the colour combination that we adopt and the hair style that we follow play an incremental role in climbing the corporate ladders. Our Business Schools need to educate, train and develop their products in tune with corporate requirements.

Honing leadership skills is found significant to counter the mounting volatility in the business world. We need strong management with strong leadership because strong leadership with weak management may be worse than the reverse. The leadership trait of an individual is essential for the development of professional mode. Around the globe, we find emergence of a new trend. The big city firms recruit from the top universities, they cherry-pick students with strings to their bows such as football captains and leaders of orchestra party. What impress recruiters today are the youngsters with leadership skills because, we find them having a high risk-bearing capacity. They try to lead, take a risk and learn from both triumphs and failures. They can adjust themselves with the changes and challenges. Hence, we need to develop leadership skills. Creating a culture of leadership is found significant in today's corporate world.

A journey of million miles begins with a single step. The personal care services are day-by-day becoming much more sophisticated and specialised. Actually, we find transformation of a prototype business into a big sector necessitating institutional support. The corporate users look for quality services and the personal care organisations of world repute can satisfy them. The marketing professionals need to study their requirements in the face of organisational culture.

The future of personal care business is found prosperous because the corporate culture has started influencing our lifestyles. Euromonitor Survey, 2011 reveals that in the demand of beauty products, there has been an increase of 17 per cent in the year 2011 as compared to 2010 and this trend will continue even in the coming years. Capitalising on the opportunities in a right fashion requires professional excellence vis-a-vis the technological and infrastructural support.

Synchronising different dimensions of personality in an optimal fashion is significant with the viewpoint of developing personality in totality. The educational institutions in general and the Business Schools in particular need to realise the crying need of the hour. They need to inculcate and cultivate different traits and properties which can make them hireable and promotable. They need to transform their attitudes. Be smart, get hired. Remain poised and be assertive. Cultivate confidence and keep up with reading. Cultivate skills, not knowledge. Display your leadership skills and get big bucks. Be doers and blend easily into a multi-cultural environment. Strengthen your perception, change your predilections. Your personality scores over any professional degree.

The present book attempts to throw light on the various dimensions of personality development specially in tune with the emerging corporate culture. The students in general and the potential managers in particular would immensely be benefited with the literature made available to them. In various chapters, concerted efforts are made to address everything from voice and accents to dining etiquette and dressing up basics. In an increasingly global competitive environment, you should realise the significance of personality in totality. India's first corporate trainer Sabira Merchant is not a hotshot CEO but she teaches CEOs something important for conducting their business.

I am grateful to all who directly or indirectly helped me in preparing a book helping all in developing a holistic personality to face life in totality.

Department of Commerce and Business Administration,
L.N. Mithila University, Darbhanga

S.M. JHA

CONTENTS

CHAPTER 1 : THE FOUNDATION OF PERSONAL CARE MANAGEMENT 1 – 44

Introduction – Personal Care Management: The Conceptual Exposition – Dimensions of Personal Care Services – Personal Scores for the Modern Corporate World – Personality: The Concept – Holistic Personality vs. Character Managing Mind, Yoga – Pranayam and Meditation – Managing Body – Managing Facial Appearance – Awareness of Personal Hygiene – Awareness of Sleeping – Behavioural Profile of Personal Care Users – Personal Care Management vis-a-vis Four Es of HR – Emergene of Personal Care Business – Summary – Key Terms – Expected Questions – Application Exercises – Back-up Materials.

CHAPTER 2 : MANAGEMENT OF BODY 45 – 82

Introduction – Basics About Our Body – Management of Diet – The Energy Requirements – A Balanced Diet – Foods Making a Balanced Diet – Food Triangle – The Key Indian Food Items – About Foods, you need to think Off-wise Regulation of Food – Awareness of Vaccination and Immunisation – Our Sensitivity to Diseases – Potable Water-Walk and Exercises – Sleeping – Top Priority for Rock Personality – Summary – Key Terms – Expected Questions – Application Exercises – Back-up Materials.

CHAPTER 3 : MANAGEMENT OF PERSONAL HYGIENE 83 – 108

Introduction – Personal Hygiene: The Concept – Dimensions of Personal Hygiene – Bath Daily – Hand Washing – Trimming of Nails – Haircare – Clean Clothes – Oral Hygiene – Home Hygiene – Bathroom and Toilet Hygiene – Water Hygiene – Laundry Hygiene – Food Hygiene – Medical Hygiene at Home – Workplace Hygiene – Excessive Personal Hygiene and its Effects – Personal Hygiene, Education and Training – Personal Hygiene Influencing Emotion – Activating the Sensitisation Process – Personal Hygiene for Corporate Professionals – Summary – Key Terms – Expected Questions – Application Exercises – Back-up Materials.

CHAPTER 4 : CIVIC AND AESTHETIC SENSE 109 – 140

Introduction – Civic Sense: The Concept and Percept – Dimensions of Civic Sense – Justifications for Developing Civic Sensibility – Cultivating Civic Sensibility – Education Your Child About the Civic Sense – Civic Insensibility to Bio-medical Waste – Civic Sense of the Rural Folks – Civic Sense of the City Folks – Civic Sense and the Corporate World – Aesthetic Sense – Cultivating Aesthetic Sense – Aesthetic Sense and the Corporate World – Summary – Key Terms – Expected Questions – Application Exercises – Back-up Materials.

CHAPTER 5 : MANAGEMENT OF MIND **141 – 177**

Introduction – Healthy Mind – Meditation and Mind Puriflcation – Yoga: A Conceptual Exposition – Yogic View on Human Personality – Yoga and Ethics – Karma Yoga: Understand the Perception – Yoga in Combating Stress – Yoga Postures – The Sun Salutation – Lotus Posture – Shoulder Stand Posture – Head Stand Posture – Fish Posture – Plough Posture – Accomplished Posture – Corpose Posture – Wind Release Posture – Cultural and Spiritual Forces Combating Stress – Participation in Spiritual Sessions for Combating Stress – Working Holiday for Combatting Stress – Sleep Better for Combating Stress – Gardening for Combating Stress – Entertainment for Combating Stress – Pet-therapy for Combating Stress – Retail Therapy for Combating Stress – Healthy Mind for Healthy Body – Summary – Key Terms – Expected Questions – Application Exercises – Back-up Materials.

CHAPTER 6 : ETIQUETTE AND MANNER **178 – 208**

Introduction – Business Etiquette and Business Ethics – Corporate Society vs. Etiquette – Social Graces and Polish – Etiquette for Facing Interview – Etiquette for Introducing and Paying Compliments – Workplace Etiquette – Dress Etiquette – Dining Etiquette – Disastrous Ravines – Etiquette for Corporate Success – Summary – Key Terms – Expected Questions – Application Exercises – Back-up Materials.

CHAPTER 7 : MANAGING ETHICS AND BUILDING CHARACTER **209 – 233**

Introduction – Ethics: the Concept – Business Ethics: the Concept – Why Business Ethics? Area for Unethical Practices – Factors Influencing Business Ethics – Unethical Practices in Business – Ethical Codes – Ethics Training Programme – Corporate Ethics vs. Corporate Image – Ethical Dilemma – Managing Ethics in Business – Building Character – Summary – Key Terms – Expected Questions – Applications Exercises – Back-up Materials.

CHAPTER 8 : MANAGEMENT OF LOOKS **234 – 309**

Introduction – Looks: the Concept and Percept – Globalisation and the Corporate Looks – Corporate Culture: Local and Global – The Dimensions of Looks – The Management of Wardrobe for Corporate Men – The Management of Wardrobe for Corporate Women – Select the Right Professional Business Suit – Tips for Corporate Women Professional – Investment Dressing – Saree as Corporate Wear – Grooming – Accessorising – Leveraging Colour – Manage Your Hair – Manage Your Shoes – Your Make up – Your Wrist Watch – Tie as a Sense of Pride – Spectacle Frame for Your Face and Personality – A Great Looking Briefcase – The Pen Reflecting Your Personality and Taste – Regulate the Body Odour – Promotional Corporate Apparel – Organisation Resposibility – The Wardrobe for Academics – Emerging Trends in the World of Corparate Looks – Summary – Key Terms – Expected Questions – Application Exercises – Back-up Materials.

CHAPTER 9 : LEADERSHIP SKILL **310 – 335**

Introduction – Leadership: the Concept – Managers vs. Leaders – Leadership: The Typology – Theories of Leadership – Learning Leadership – Leadership Skills – Emerging Challenges in Developing Leadership Skills – Responsibility Before the Business and Finishing Schools – Summary – Key Terms – Expected Questions – Application Exercises – Back-up Materials.

CHAPTER 10 : MARKETING PERSONAL CARE SERVICES **336 – 367**

Introduction – Marketing Personal Care Services: A Conceptual Frarmework – Organisational or Institutional Support for the Personal Care Business – Market Segmentation for Personal Care Organisations – Marketing Information System for Personal Care Services – Behavioural Profile of Corporate users – Synchronising the Mixes of Marketing – The Product Profile – Promoting the Services – Channelising the Services – Pricing the Personal Care Services – Processing of Personal Care Services – Physical Evidence – People – Marketing Personal Care Services in the Indian Context – Summary – Key Terms – Expected Questions – Application Exercises – Back-up Materials.

CHAPTER 11 : THE FUTURE OF PERSONAL CARE BUSINESS **368 – 388**

Introduction – Emerging Positive Trends in the Personal Care Business – Improving the Supply Position – Personal Care Business: The Strategic Areas – The Tactical Decisions for Personal Care Services – The Future of Personal Care Business is Prosperous – Summary – Key Terms – Expected Questions – Application Exercises – Back-up Materials.

BIBLIOGRAPHY **389 – 393**

1 THE FOUNDATION OF PERSONAL CARE MANAGEMENT

There is nothing more appealing than a man with a sense of wit and fun. There is nothing more paying than an aesthete. If you provide professional touch to your wardrobe, you get big bucks in the modern business world.

CHAPTER DESIGN

Introduction – Personal Care Management: the Conceptual Exposition – Dimensions of Personal Care Services – Personal Scores for the Modern Corporate World – Personality: the Concept – Holistic Personality vs. Character – Managing Mind, Yoga, Pranayam and Meditation – Managing Body – Managing Facial Appearance – Awareness of Personal – Hygiene – Awareness of Sleeping – Behavioural Profile of Personal Care Users – Personal Care Management vis-à-vis Four Es of HR – Emergence of Personal Care Business – Summary – Key Terms – Expected Questions – Application Exercises – Back-up Materials.

CHAPTER OBJECTIVES

Corporate looks need distinction and elegance. A look that generates a positive attitude; a look that brings optimism – a look that nurtures attractions and strengthens zest for life and a look that visualises professionalism cannot be possible unless we inculcate some of the personal traits found essential in the modern business world. Attractions in ambience and appearance need priority attention. What is pleasant to our eyes is found pleasant and acceptable to our mind. Our impressive looks make us hireable and promotable. For the development of personality in totality, a fair synchronisation of multi-dimensional attributes is essential. This chapter aims at engineering a sound foundation for the development or personality commensurate with the existent organisational culture.

THE FOUNDATION OR PERSONAL CARE MANAGEMENT

◈ Introduction

The increasing pace of corporatisation has paved copious avenues for aesthetic management and it is against this backdrop that we find corporate culture opening new vistas for the development of personality in totality in which internal and external attractions occupy a place of outstanding significance. Looking attractive, pleasant and impressive is now becoming a common choice. Corporatisation has opened doors where the upcoming and budding youths are found nurturing optimism and high level of expectations though we find them heavily stressed and distressed. They witness a whole array of opportunities found instrumental in enriching the potentials of job markets. The Indian Retail Survey 2010 clarifies that the current size of beauty care industry is about ₹ 10,000 crores and we expect the size of the emerging industry expanding at a high pace approximately at a robust 25 per cent each year. The way in which we find an attitudinal transformation amongst almost all sections of the society cannot obstruct the emergence of a big job market in the personal care sector in general and the beauty care sector in particular.

There is nothing more appealing than a man with a sense of wit and fun. There is nothing more paying than an aesthete. Of late, the different categories of organisations are found assigning due weightage to the physical attractions and facial appearance or look of the people working there which is significantly to increase the demand position. Of course, we cannot deny the instrumentality of world-class thematical competence of an individual in getting the productive results but the task of developing personality in totality demands something more. The corporate strategists need a new look and a new vision to be efficacious of anticipating the changes and challenges to emerge in future. A look that generates a positive image; a look that magnifies optimism; a look that bears the efficacy of attracting others and a look that visualises elegance. It is against this backdrop that we find personal care services taking a new shape in the face of situational and professional compulsions in addition to the changing socio-cultural requirements. The cine artists, corporate executives, technocrats, singers, players, dancers, medicos and academics do not prefer an identical look.

Like women, we find even men of today developing a temptation or a deep sense of fascination for using cosmetics or facial and preferring a beauty treatment. We find a majority of us now becoming very careful to the healthcare management. With a change in the lifestyles sizably influenced by the western culture, it is quite natural that we find each one of us becoming sincere to the development of our personality. There are a number of dimensions found effectively instrumental in the personality and physique development process. The first and foremost task before us is to be physically sound which requires priority attention on healthcare management and its different tracks helping an individual in the development of a sound health. The physical appearance is also an important dimension in the very context. This makes ways for yoga, pranayam and Meditation and in addition, the organisation of spiritual sessions. The personal care sector thus involves in it a number of devices helping an individual in having personality in totality.

For the development of personal care organisations, it is pertinent that leading brands in the personal care sector are innovative while developing the service profile based on customisation. A large number of users make use of the personal care services with diverse motives. It is essential that marketing professionals make use of their world-class professional excellence and with the help of creative promotional pleasures sensitise the potential users of different segments. In addition to other aspects, they also need to consider affordability which focuses on making the process of service generation cost-effective.

The users of services come from different tier of cities, no doubt, but a majority of them come from Tier 2 and Tier 3 cities. Making people conscious to beauty requires due attention of marketing professionals. This in a natural way would pave avenues for the development, of cosmetic industry which would be helpful in accelerating the pace of growth. The professionals need to consider the likes and dislikes of people of all ages. Since we find a basic change in the concept of beauty care during the yester decades, we cannot deny the impact of it on the requirements of customers or clients. The manifold developments in the personal care sector have increased the demand for smart, well-informed and trained professionals. In a true sense, we find a correlation between the requirements of customers and the delivery of service and by the personal care organisations. The leading brands need to manage information regarding the changing requirements of clients. They also need to develop their awareness of the innovative measures taken by the rival brands. We find scope for the development of small as well as the big players. They can develop as a speciality centre or even as a general centre. The main thing in the product development is quality bearing the potentials of satisfying the customers.

Managing different dimensions of personal care is significant with the viewpoint of developing personality in totality. We need to be physically sound and this necessitates due attention on different facets making us nutritionally sound. Our lifestyles also help us in keeping fit. Another stream where we need focus is our physical attraction. This necessitates, professional excellence in the field of personal care services which add additional attractions to our personality. The third dimension in this context is our mental health. In this respect, it is pertinent that we nurture positive feelings in our minds and find ourselves much more resistant to counter the stress, tension and depression. Orchestration of all the three properties help development of personality in totality. Externally impressive and internally fair people often prove to be productive. The development of personal care services as an industry makes it essential that we have world-class professionals to manage things in an excellent way. The most important thing in the changing scenario is to diagnose the emerging trends and to initiate and activate the steps in tune with the taste preferences of customers.

With the increasing heat of globalisation, we find the Indian economy thriving and becoming instrumental in changing the lifestyles of common people. How and in what way we capitalise on the opportunities would determine the magnitude of our success. A large number of brands have been found making the business environment much more competitive specially for the providers and users of the beauty care industry. The providers offering customised and personalised services establish an edge over others. We cannot negate that in the days and years to come the beauty care industry would witness multipronged qualitative-cum-quantitative improvement and therefore the upcoming youths would have lucrative job opportunities in the different areas of personal care sector such as beauty consultants, product analyst and assistants, beauty advisors, technical and managerial staff, pedicurists, manicurists, nail technical class, chemical engineers and people with management degree photo or movie stylists, Hair colour and Perm Specialist, Cosmetology Instructors, Image Consultants, product distributors *et. al.* We cannot deny that during the yester years, in the field of dermatology, we have witnessed multi-dimensional improvements. We find common people now aware of their looks and appearance and he/she has not only the capacity to spend but albeit the willingness or courage to spend much more on personal care. The Indian dermatologists need to study the Indian environment and Indian customers. The techniques of cosmetology are now in more developed form. The wellness boom and attitudinal transformation make it clear that personal care sector has a prosperous future.

The beauty brands need innovative strategy in the face of Indian business environment. On the one hand, they need to make it sure that the requirements and expectations of corporate and allied sectors are fulfilled while on the other hand, they also bear the responsibility of protecting and promoting the Indian culture by throwing positive imprints on the western culture with the help of a mix followed by the queens in the ancient India. Vulgarity is not beauty. Indeed, it is something more which touches the heart and soul. It lies in the hands of those who make use of their professional excellence. It lies in the eyes of the beholder. How to synchronise the hands of professionals and the eyes of beholders are the responsibilities before the domestic or global beauty brands.

Of course, looking impressive is significant but if we talk about development of personality in totality, it requires something more. It is pertinent that we have a sound physique, but it is also much more impact generating that we have a sound mental health. This make it essential that we nurture positive feelings in our mind because only normal behaviour and action cannot serve our purpose. Here it is also imperative that we have transformed our behaviour and made ourselves much more resistant to counter the stress due to tension and depression as the natural by-products of corporate culture based on and influenced by material culture.

Since we find the services day-by-day becoming much more innovative, it is pertinent that people working there develop expertise to deliver goods to the users. The professionals need to develop a package in tune with the changing requirements of different segments. On the one hand, we need focus on the hierarchy of needs while on the other hand, we also need to consider the interests and preferences of occasional users. Innovative services and creative promotion may be instrumental in tapping the tremendous opportunities. The sensitive points for the location of personal care centres are shopping malls, colleges and institutes, universities, residential areas of high profile people, where the potential users are available. The centres can be developed even in the rural areas or at the points close to fairs and exhibitions, of course, on a temporary basis. In the villages and small towns and cities, the centres can be developed on an unorganised basis even as a cottage industry where during marriages and festive occasions, we find demand for personal care services.

The markets are becoming wider and wider and now it is upon the personal care centres to capitalise on the existent opportunities by making use of their professional excellence and personalised services. The working ladies find it a professional compulsion because this is closely related with the image of the organisation where they serve. The increasing impact of cable culture has changed the lifestyles of even the housewives because they want to look attractive and impressive. The school and college-going boys, and girls have been found developing a craze for using the services like facial and hair dressing. The increasing demand of Jogging and Gym centres is due to health consciousness. Thus, men or women, teens or youths, grey or senior citizens are the potential users and the professionals have to transform them into actual or habitual users. We cannot negate that recent developments in the corporate sector have injected new life and strength to our lifestyles in which we find sufficient place for western culture. The new generation of technology used for innovative personal care services has been found defining and redefining quality and this may help tapping of not only the domestic markets, but even the overseas markets, because we find globe nurturing a positive opinion regarding the cultural heritage of India and the medical tourism.

With the increasing demand side, it is quite natural that supply side will also gain a rapid momentum which would increase requirements for trained professionals in the personal care sector which has witnessed multifold developments. What to talk of beauty conscious cosmopolitan towns and cities when we find this culture gaining popularity even in the small towns, and cities. It is due mainly to the fact that we find cosmetic industry expanding like wild fire. The upcoming youths have been found evincing keen interests in the beauty business. This makes it essential that interested persons have entrepreneurial excellence, a good sense of aesthetics and creativity and a liking for people of all ages. All of us need a friendly manner, an attractive well-groomed appearance, good health, the ability to stay on our own feet for long periods and a sense of hygiene and cleanliness. The personal care sector has the potential to fulfil the requirements of all the segments.

The important areas help in adding additional attractions to our physical appearance such as dresses, hair style, attractive face, dental care, quality of shoes. The beauty care industry plays an important role in the process of developing our personality. We cannot deny that beauty lies in the hands of those who have made it their business to make others look attractive, pleasing and more importantly, impressive. Since we find both men and women making use of the services, it has emerged as a multi-billion dollar industry.

People may be physically sound and albeit, sincerely caring their physical attractions but the process of developing personality in totality cannot be considered to be complete unless we find them, having a sound mental health. This draws our attention on regulating stress which necessitates focus on spiritualism. It is due mainly to the fact that this dimension of our personality enriches inner strength and inculcates faculties for the development of morality. It is high time that we have a temptation for spiritualism. This makes it essential that personal care organisations have a link with the religious organisation where organisation of sessions promoting spirituals would serve our purpose.

The gender, age, region, profession, culture, customs and traditions considerably influence our decisions. Since it becomes difficult for an individual to develop expertise in all the concerned areas, we find development of personal care centres even on an organised basis. We cannot negate that personality development is a combination of our multi-dimensional efforts and the multi-track decisions. All of us are well aware of the importance of our inner strength which helps us in enriching our career profile. On the one hand, we are supposed to look attractive while on the other hand, it is also pertinent that we are spiritually and morally sound. The corporate culture considerably influenced by western culture paves avenues for the development of material culture and with the increasing domination of material culture, we find even common people developing a craze for looking attractive and impressive. The emergence of niche markets in almost all the areas and regions makes it essential that marketing professionals capitalise on the opportunities is an optimal fashion.

For making people physically sound, it is imperative that our health care measures are of world class. The professionals engaged in the process need an attitudinal transformation. The important strategic areas in the development of a sound physique are beauty care measures, healthcare measures and Yoga, Pranayam and Meditation, Gym, Jogging, personal hygiene such as bathing, showering, hair washing, maintaining the calories required for maintaining good health and continence management or controlling movements of the bowels and bladder such as toilets, stoma care, catheter, skin care, laundry, bed changing. The awareness of nutritional value is also an important dimension for the development of a sound health. Only external attractions cannot serve our purpose and therefore, we also focus on our internal strength.

The personal care centres working in the Indian setting need a new vision which will make ways for creativity. Clubbing different dimensions in an optimal fashion is considered significant. We find creative centres developing both on formal and informal basis necessitating involvement of small and big players and therefore marketers have wider opportunities to cash on.

The people involved in the process need entrepreneurial as well as professional excellence to capitalise on the increasing opportunities in the personal care sector. How and in what way, the personal care organisations provide holistic treatment to body, mind and soul, and in what manner they add attractions to our look would require multi-dimensional efforts. The three-tier approaches are physical invigoration, mental elevation and spiritual rejuvenation which make a call in favour of a number of personal care services. Managing all the three in the changing scenario where we find discretionary income of people increasing very fast would require managerial proficiency. We find a significant increase in the spending power and behaviour and a number of people have been found developing their temptation to personal care. The increasing corporate culture has opened doors for the development of material culture and the deep seated spa culture has been opening new vistas because we find this gaining popularity in almost sectors and segments. It is an unvarnished fact that people with high discretionary income never mind the expenses on personalised beauty care. The mental pressure has been found increasing resulting into a high level of stress and therefore willingly or unwillingly, we find people showing their fascination to spiritualism. Attractions are the lifeblood of corporatisation and therefore, we find people specially serving the corporate sector spending huge money on their personal care. It is high time that we tap the existent opportunities in the personal care sector.

The emergence of a large market albeit in the Indian perspective makes it essential that small as well as the big players are found evincing their special interests. On the one hand, this sector is to create new job opportunities while on the other hand, we also find people in general developing consciousness to their physical fitness. We need to see the beauty in managing our bodies. How we gain and lose our weight is the real thing. Because despite of making incredible efforts for lowering our weight, we find a majority of us still overweight and unfit. Of course, we welcome to the fitness revolution and are hopeful that our efforts in this direction go through a natural process. How do we response to our stress that has been invited by ourselves. All of us have an innate fitness personality based on the inner feelings and therefore getting back in touch with yourself is the real thing.

Personal care management, thus requires multi-pronged efforts and we need to perceive things as a professional. We find emergence of a profitable market and it is upon us that to what extent, we are sincere and honest to our efforts. The most important thing necessitating due attention in the very context is Indianisation. Vulgarity has no place in the world of beauty. We need to strike a balance between the eastern and western devices so that we incorporate the best in the emerging personal care industry. Because all of us find it difficult to look attractive and impressive with the support of their own efforts, this sector is to be developed as a business in a right fashion. The observations of Indian Retail Survey, 2010 and Euromonitor, 2011 indicate the future of personal care business prosperous. We need professional excellence to cash on the opportunities.

◈ Personal Care Management: The Conceptual Exposition

At the outset, it is imperative that we go through the concept of personal care management, and focus on its changing perception which would help professionals in managing the different dimensions. With the passage of time, we have witnessed multipronged transformation in almost all the areas which has been increasing the functional areas of managers. Of course, the new generation of technology has been contributing to the development processes in a big way; however the quality of people has an edge over others. The corporate sector in particular bears the responsibility of receiving and perceiving the increasing levels of expectation of people in a right fashion. We need to develop quality people by managing the different dimensions of personal care which in a majority of the cases, remain neglected. The three dimensional efforts of managers would enrich the faculties of development of people serving an organisation in different capacities.

The first dimension focuses our attention on physical health of people so that avenues for the development of allied problems are sealed. We cannot decay that a majority of our population are not aware of the practices which can help them in remaining physically fit. Our unawareness of nutritional deficiency, potable water, food habits, communicable diseases or say the lifestyles become very much instrumental in inviting the diseases. We do not know even basics about the management of body. What to talk of the illiterate or uneducated segment when we find even educated segment in the same boat.

This dimension of personal care is found related with the tracks responsible for our sickness. Developing consciousness, sensitising masses and making general masses aware of the areas helping them in keeping fit need due attention.

The second dimension of personal care management is soundness of our mind. Our all efforts turn into a fiasco, if we are not mentally fit. Mental illness contracts our potentials and considerably impact our physical health. We start nurturing negative feelings in our minds and invite a condition where we are found mentally sick even resulting into madness. A stage of mental illness is invaded when we are sincere to the facets like Yoga, Pranayam and Meditation. These devices bring a stage of soundness where concentration is possible. In this context, we also focus on spiritualism instrumental in linking our minds with the soul. The religious centres can play here an effective role by developing temptation to these devices. The personal care organisations can also sensitise masses to the devices helping them in keeping mentally healthy. Thus managing all the devices also prove to be an important facet of personal care management.

The third dimension where we need focus is physical attractions. This is found related with the dresses, uniforms, shoes, hair style, skin, nails, teeth which are external attractions of our body. If we manage them in a right fashion, the process of adding additional attractions to our body gains a rapid momentum. We look attractive and impressive. The personal care organisations play here an important role.

Adding beauty to our personality is an important consideration for the development of personality. We find human beings developing a temptation for looking beautiful early in child development and the standards of attractiveness are similar across different genders and cultures. Of course, the style and fashion vary widely; however we find commonalities in people's perception of beauty where symmetry and proportion are found important. A strong indicator is averageness or Koinophilia where personal care organisations play an important role.

Professionalism becomes an important consideration while promoting the mixing process because establishing symmetry or proportion require expertise. Averaging of human faces with the motto of forming a compositive image may be considered to be an ideal stage where we look much more attractive. The personal care management focuses on classical beauty in terms of female human beauty which with minor changes may also be effective for male beauty.

The concept and perception of personal care management have been found considerably influenced by corporate culture in which we have witnessed emergence of a cross-cultural civilisation sizably influenced by globalisation because globalisation of economy has made the was for globalisation of fashion culture and civilisation. The foundation of corporate culture is based on attractions and therefore professionals need to manage the different dimensions of personal care services in such a fashion that individuals and institution develop temptation for looking attractive and impressive.

Managing mind of an individual, of course is an important consideration in the personal, care management which till now has not received due weightage. Expectations cannot remain static and with the increasing heat of globalisation, we have witnessed a galloping increase in the levels of expectation of common people. Expectations make the ways for frustrations and paves avenues for the generation of tension which extends invitation to stress and we find people in a depression. The increasing focus on Yoga, Pranayam and Meditation as ancient devices and Gym and Jogging as modern devices are developing as the areas of personal care. We cannot negate that these devices engineer a sound foundation for the development of spiritualism where we may be much more close to peace.

We find people developing temptation for health care and it is right to say that our lifestyles have witnessed significant changes where we find ourselves much more conscious to the quality of food and water we consume. We have developed consciousness related to the communicable diseases and are found ourselves sensitive to the immunisation and vaccination culture. These devices have been making personal care management much more efficacious. The increasing number of morning walkers, improving enrolments in the Gym and Jogging centres and strengthening realisation of common people to the Yoga of "Baba Ramdev" are a staunch testimony to this proposition that personal care management would gain popularity in the days and years to come and therefore it is high time that professionals promote personal care organisations related to the different tracks or streams.

The personal care management, thus is the management, of three streams or tracks helping us in achieving total health for the development of total personality. The following facts are composed to clarify its concept and perception:

- Personal care management is a managerial process where professionalised efforts are made to manage the different dimensions found helpful in achieving the total health for developing the total personality.
- It is concerned with the management of total body where internal and external factors are managed in such a way that physical soundness, physical invigoration and spiritual and mental elevation are made possible.

- It is an effort which may be manual or techno-driven. It may be developed individually or institutionally. Development of expertise is found essential for personal care management where professional excellence of people involved in the process determines the magnitude of service quality.
- Personal care management is the management of physical health which includes in its purview a number of areas such as quality of food and water that we consume, quality of sanitation services that we use, our awareness of nutrition and vaccination, time and duration of our sleeping, our awareness of communicable diseases, our awareness of healthcare, lifestyles which help us in keeping our physique fit.
- Personal care management also covers the management of mind for mental elevation which helps us in achieving blissful self where we find ourselves in a position to be normal though the environment at the workplace is found stress-friendly. The dimensions like Yoga, Pranayam and Meditation and our involvement in the spiritual sessions bring concentration and help development of mind. This helps inculcation of positive feelings where we learn regulating our behaviour and nurturing the positive feelings.
- Looking attractive and impressive is also concerned with the personal care management. Here, we focus on the management of dresses, uniforms, shoes, hair care, nail care, skin care, tooth care, manicure, pedicure, beauty care, management of perm, image, etc. Since we find masses developing temptation for looking beautiful, this dimension of personal care has resulted into the development of beauty care industry.

◈ Dimensions of Personal Care Services

Personal care services have wider areas. Looking impressive, of course, is found significant but when we find our health weak, it becomes difficult for us to manage even the small things. Physical soundness coils in its essence all the facets essential for having a sound physique. Nothing is possible, if we are totally ill. Hence, it is so imperative that we have a healthy mind where positive feelings are gently nurtured. If we start storing negative feelings in our minds, it starts harming the health and if we have a poor health, physical attraction, carries no meaning. It is against this backdrop that a number of components are included in the personal care services. If we synchronise all the facets of personal care services in an optimal fashion, we find scope for the development of personality in totality which appears to be an urgent requirement of the present society.

Physical soundness is the first dimension that we go through in a distinct way. With the multi-dimensional developments in the society, we find general masses heavily stressed. Almost all segments of society and particularly the budding youths are the worst affected. They have a high level of expectations and in a majority of the cases their expectations remain unfulfilled. It is also pertinent to mention that expectations and satisfaction move together. We find a majority of the youths hankering after the materialistic gains and this in a natural fashion affects their lifestyles. They do not have any time management. All the activities are mismanaged. They frequently take junk foods or unhealthy foods. With the development of corporate culture, we also find them very much fascinated to the pub culture and further even live-in relationships which ultimately damage their health. It is amazing that a majority of even the educated segment of society are unaware of food-prone, water-prone and communicable diseases. They do not have time and environment for uninterrupted or sound sleeping, really a state of rest in which the nervous system is inactive, the eyes are closed, the muscles are relaxed and the mind is unconscious the disturbing elements are the mobile phones, girl friends, boy friends and an overambitious career plan for the future. Can we expect a sound physique with this condition? Of course, we have an answer which is "No".

We cannot negate that lifestyles play a commanding role in regulating our physical vis-à-vis the mental health. Hence, this dimension of personal care services focus on management of life-styles such as our food habits and the food items, our sleeping schedule, our sensitivity to the role of potable water, our programming for entertainment, our awareness of health care and nutritional values, our awareness of quality sanitation services, the timing of our breakfast, lunch and dinner, etc. We cannot undermine the role of all the components mentioned earlier because our insensitivity to lifestyles engineers a sound foundation for the beginning of health problem.

The next dimension that we go through is our mental health. A large number of people today are found mentally ill. Of course, they are not mad but nurture negative feelings in their minds and in due course we find them heavily tensed, stressed and depressed. And finally, they are ill. It is in this context that we assign due weightage to the management of mind where we find openings for positive feelings.

Spiritualism bears the efficacy of transforming our attitudes and further makes the ways for the development of positive feelings. It is much more significant that we nurture optimism and this is to be possible when we develop our temptation to spiritual sessions. With the help of meditation we find ourselves in a position to concentrate our energy and developing the resistance power to regulate our behaviour. Today, if we find youths highly tensed, depressed and stressed, it is due mainly to the fact that they are highly fascinated to the materialistic gains. We find Yoga, Pranayam and Meditation, instrumental in linking our minds with the soul and thus purify our heart.

In the modern age of hurry, curry and worry, we find a majority of the people hankering after materialistic gains and this opens new vistas for the cropping up of multi-dimensional problems. It is high time that we are sincere to our mental health and make all possible efforts to have mental balance. It is Yoga that would help us in many ways. We cannot negate that yoga makes us realise that diseases affecting any specific part of our body is not really a disease confined only to that part but in fact, it is a manifestation of some disharmony in the body-mind complex of the whole personality. It is an unvarnished fact that mind plays a vital role in ensuring total health which is essential for the development of total personality.

The personal care services thus include one more facet and it is upon us that how and in what way we synchronise the physical attractions partially in our own interests and partially to safeguard the interests of organisations where we serve. In the changing business world, the organisations make a call in favour of people having a sound blending of all the properties for the physical and mental fit that we have gone through earlier.

The third dimension related to the development of a sound personality is physical attraction. This focuses our attention on the external look of an individual. We cannot negate that corporate culture is found based on attraction and in this context the attraction of people serving the organisation is considered significant. Of late, we find people less sensitive to price but much more sensitive to service quality. They mind the service quality not the service cost. They want to look impressive and for that they are ready to pay. This has resulted into the development of a large-sized beauty industry. It is against this background that we find Indian Cosmetic and Beauty Industry witnessing a galloping increase. Now we need to showcase cosmetic, skincare, haircare, beauty and hygiene products and accessories, professional care for salons, spa and wellness, fitness equipment, dental care, manicure and pedicure, to packaging raw materials interior design and furniture for beauty parlours, fashion accessories as well as training centres and publishers. With the increasing awareness of health, we find beauty and personal grooming gaining popularity both in men and women. Almost all the segments of society are now found interested in looking attractive and impressive.

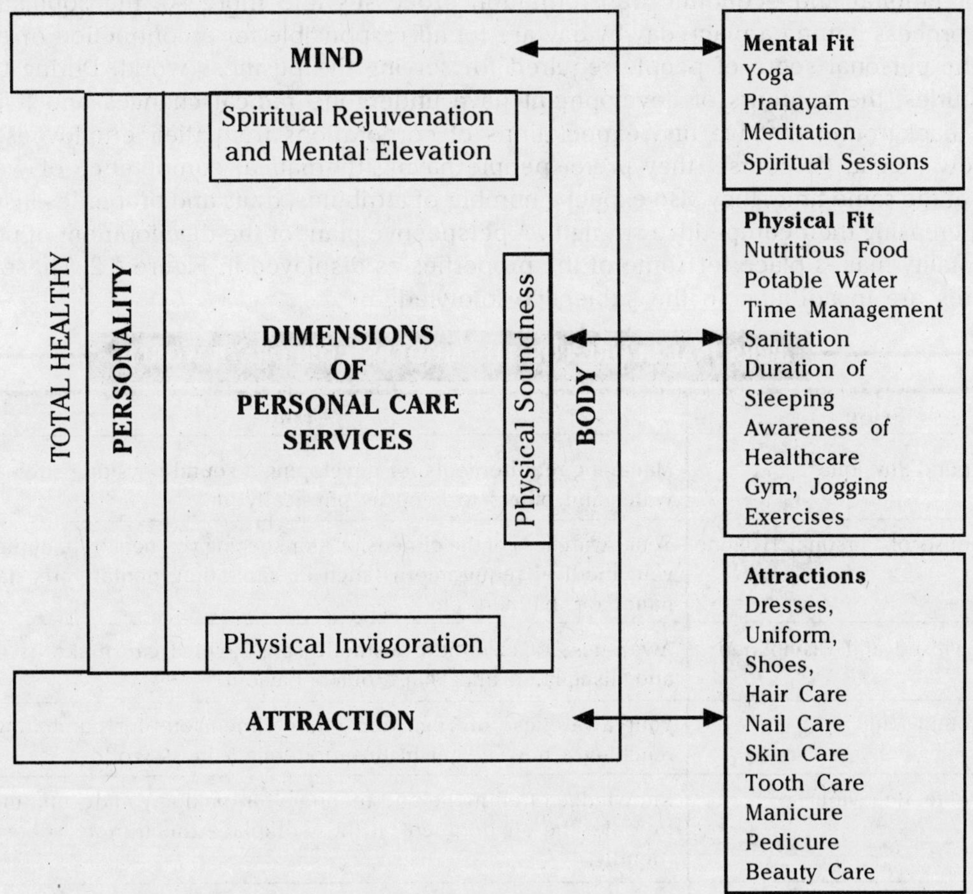

Fig. 1.1: Emerging Dimensions of Personal Care

All the three dimensions detailed in Figure 1.1 speak of the fact that total health results into total personality. Hence, how do we manage them is found to be important specially in today's context when we find ourselves heavily stressed and depressed. It is not possible that an individual develops expertise in all the related areas and therefore we find emergence of personal care centres in the concerned areas. Now we find development of personal care centres both in organised and unorganised sectors and it is in this context that the beauty care industry emerging as a sector has been attracting diverse segments of society. With the development of corporate culture, we find a significant increase in the demand side and with the emergence of personal care sector as an industry, the supply position is also required to be improved. Clubbing a number of tracks, the personal care sector is found full of potentials and it is upon the professionals that how and in what way they create and tap opportunities. When we have been facing the problem of unemployment, the personal care industry would create a number of job opportunities both for men and women.

◈ Score for Personality in Totality

The changing requirements of an organisation, the established brand image, the socio-cultural and economic transformation processes and more so, the sophistication in the process getting a place day-by-day are found responsible for a contraction or expansion in the personal score of people required for serving the business world. During the yester centuries, the contours of development have undergone radical changes and it is against this background that we find expectations of corporations from their employees touching a new height. Of course, they prefer people having thematical competence of world class but at the same time, they also expect a number of attributes, traits and properties instrumental in increasing their competitive strength. A perspective plan for the development of personality in totality makes place for some of the properties as displayed in Figure 1.2. These personal scores are in addition to the subjective knowledge.

PERSONAL SCORE FOR THE MODERN CORPORATE WORLD

Score	Trait
Sound Physique	Managing requirements for developing a sound physique such as food, water and others to keep us physically fit.
Sense of Personal Hygiene	Your awareness of the dimensions for keeping you healthy and minimising your medical requirements such as sanitation, dental care, nail care, handcare, bathing, etc.
Civilised and Disciplined	Awareness of civic and aesthetic sense which can make us civilised and disciplined and shape our behaviour.
Sound Mind	Your awareness of Yoga and other dimensions for combating stress reaching a new height in the modern business world.
Polite Behaviour	Knowledge of etiquette and manners for making you decent and polite to make the environment at the workplace much more cohesive and friendly.
Morality	Managing ethics and building character for making people ethically and morally sound. Developing character as a power.
Attractive Looks	Managing facial appearance to look attractive and impressive such as business attire and other dimensions of wardrobe management.
Leadership	Honing leadership quality to make people visionary to anticipate the emerging changes and challenges in the business world.

Fig. 1.2: Personal Score for the Modern corporate World

The personal scores can be developed individually or even institutional or organisational support may be required for getting the best results. These traits may be helpful in developing personality in totality in the face of changing requirements of the corporate world.

◈ Personality

With the development of corporatisation and increasing domination of corporate culture, we find an individual or an organisation very much sensitive and active to the development of personally. Of late, we find corporate sector sizably investing for the development of personality of people working there. In a true sense, they need a unique personality bearing the potentials of countering the challenges and threats in an effective fashion. On the one hand, the people serving the organisations need to be attractive and impressive while on the other hand, they also need to nurture positive feelings in their minds. This necessitates conceptualisation of the ideas and thoughts helping development of personality in totality. It is not only the privately managed corporations but we find such even in other organisations. A transformation in the perception of personality makes it essential that we focus on the different dimensions of personality development.

The yogic view on human personality makes a strong advocacy in favour of five different dimensions working as layers or tiers where absence of one dimension contracts the avenues of other dimensions. It is in this context that we find the concept of holistic personality gaining popularity. A fair synchronisation of physical self, energy self, mental self, intellectual self and blissful self helps in the development of a holistic personality. Almost all categories of organisations specially in the changing scenario need priority attention while developing personality of their staff, employees, people so that they have a strong team of corporate citizen. The holistic personality, if conceptualised in a right fashion, keeping in view the organisational, social and cultural requirements, resolve the multi-pronged problems.

The Physical Self is found concerned with the physical facilities demanding physical faculties. On the one hand, it represents the senses while on the other hand, we find it also related to our physical attractiveness. The Yoga is found considerably instrumental in enriching physical self. This focuses on a balanced diet and a healthy lifestyle. The Yama and Niyama of Yoga need due attention. Our people may be physically attractive and impressive if we find them wearing dresses and uniforms in tune with the requirements. Both the dimensions need due attention of professionals for having a holistic personality.

The Energy Self injects life and strength to the physical self. We need to perform which requires more vitality and intensity and if we are not sincere to the management of energy for maintaining an ideal flow of Prana (life); our efforts to enrich physical self are found not only ineffective but albeit dangerous. Assimilation of flow of life is essential for various parts of the body.

The Mental self focuses our attention on acquiring a strong mental capacity in which we find ourselves much more sound to stay calm and focused even in a rough weather. The working conditions vary from profession-to-profession and place-to-place. Working in a condition pro to tension cannot be easier. This makes it essential that we are potentially sound to regulate our mental self. The doctors and other staff working in a hospital and specially in an emergency ward are found heavily stressed and this is due to the nature of profession. Unless we find them calm and focused, they cannot deliver services of high quality.

The Intellectual Self is influenced by the concept of "Buddhi" or intelligence which provides us power to receive and transmit. How and in what way, we discriminate ourselves by showing high degree of intelligence and knowledge would determine the magnitude of our success. For acquiring intellectual knowledge and developing intellectual capital, we find formal education essential. Wisdom provides to us an opportunity to show our intelligence at appropriate time and opportune moment. This necessitates a continuous study so that we are in a position to enrich our knowledge bank which cannot be possible unless we form the habits of reading books and literature.

The Blissful Self is the ultimate goal to improve human personality. This invites a stage where we succeed in preserving happiness and avoid formation of negative thoughts in our minds. To show our excellence, it is also imperative that we regulate our emotions which may stand as a barrier. We cannot negate that struggles provide to us an opportunity to learn and enrich our behaviour. Emotional, physical or psychological struggles make us perfect because we get an opportunity to prove our excellence that how and in what way we can regulate deviation in a changed condition.

In the fast changing corporate world of today, we need a unique personality which is essential to establish distinction and prove uniqueness. It is right to mention that personality is innate in an individual and we enrich and nourish it by using various methods. Yoga is considered the almost effective device to produce a unique personality and it is against this background that we find corporate world and Business Schools of today focusing on formalising Yoga. The increasing heat of corporate culture would gain a rapid momentum in the days and years to come because we cannot regulate the mounting temptation of masses to the material culture. Hence, it is also natural that we cannot make the working conditions stress and tension-free. What we can do in the present condition is to develop our human resources in such a fashion that they learn the skill of becoming resistant to a condition which is found pro or friendly to tension.

The above mentioned five dimensions of human personality are in the face of Yogic view which may help us in producing unique personality to be efficacious of distincting their decisions for establishing an edge over the rivals The different layers of human personality need proper synchronisation and Yoga may help us in the process.

◈ Holistic Personality

The increasing heat of globalisation makes a search in favour of a personality found efficacious of countering the challenges and at the same time effectively resistant while facing the stress and diffusing the tension. It is against this background that we talk about holistic personality. This focuses our attention on personality in totality in which we find all the properties found in an individual to perform excellently. The perception of such a personality may be taken from Bhagvad Gita – Chap - 3:38. The three properties Rajas, Tamas and Satwic are the GUNAS helping us in identifying the threats and developing a personality which may serve both organisational as well as the social interests.

घमेनाप्रियते वाहनर्यथादर्शो मलेन च ।
यथोल्बेनावृतो गर्भस्तधा तेनेदमावृतम ।।३८।।

Dhumenaavriyate Vahirryathaadarsho Malen Cha
Yatholbensaavrito garbbastthaa tenddamaavritam.

As fire is covered by smoke
As mirror is covered by dust
As an embryo is covered by the womb
So is this covered by it.

TAMAS:

With this property, we get the worst lot of people almost dull and fit only for the ignorant organisations. People with such a personality find it difficult to differentiate between right and wrong, deeds and misdeeds and focus on all his interests, and attention upon self. They concentrate on their own actions, perceptions, emotions and thoughts and cash on the opportunities for their own welfare and interest. They are always stressed and depressed, discontended and disturbed and may throw the organisation not only in the wrong box but may also be instrumental in the image tarnishing and value erosion process.

RAJAS:

With this property, we find development of a passionate personality found fit only for the hot organisations. They are blessed or cursed with the habits of endless earnings and spending, racing and procuring, procreating and protecting and always thirsting for getting more and more. They are found involved in the process of generating sorrows and failures and trap themselves for getting the materialistic gains. We find them heavily stressed and depressed. The urges, desires, emotions and feelings, are found at the top but the organisations; national or global, cannot continue to remain hot in all the conditions and times and therefore the people with this personality cannot serve and subserve organisational and social interest on equal footing. People with such property and personality with such traits are influenced by material culture and we find them considerably influenced by the philosophy of earning more and spending more.

SATWIC:

We find people with this property much more productive. They nurture positive feelings in their minds and are influenced by creativity. Because they have a balanced personality and steady mind free from agitations, demonstrations and inertia; they are found productive to the society and the national economy. If we find agitations developing and becoming aggressive; the environment at the work place cannot remain conducive. An organisation bears the responsibility of developing and promoting Satwic personality.

How and in what way, the professionals identify people with three "Gunas" determine the magnitude of success in an organisation. Since we advocate in favour of people with Satwic features, it is significant that professionals educate and train people in a different way so that they develop their temptation to the satwic personality. Nurturing positive feelings in mind is found to be an essential consideration which makes the ways for creativity. In the changing corporate world, the ethical considerations are found gaining popularity. Character building is an important functional responsibility before corporate professionals and this task is considerably simplified, if managers succeed in nurturing ethical dimensions. We cannot develop character and morality with the help of regulations because attitudinal transformation is considered to be the most important thing in the development process and such an attitude requires Satwic personality.

Organising, Yoga, Pranayam, Meditation and spiritual sessions is significant and the corporate professionals need to move forward in managing all the streams in an effective fashion with the help of Saints, Dharmgurus, Prophets, Philanthropists which would engineer a sound base for the development of character and morality. The professionals while evaluating the efficiency level of employees need to assign due weightage to a number of properties. In this condition, it is also pertinent that they consider the morality level of employees in the evaluation process. The employees found to be dishonests play a very effective role in the value erosion process. Sooner or later, they create an image problem which opens doors for the movement of development graph of the organisation in the reverse gear.

Holistic personality thus focuses our attention on three important tracks. The employees have a sound physique. They assign due weightage to nutritional awareness and are sincere to their lifestyles. They need to be aware of the food habits and the food items. Because we find sound body essential for the development of a sound mind, it is pertinent that professionals also think about another dimension that is found concerned with physical attractions. There are a number of areas where we find tremendous opportunities for qualitative improvements. The employees need to look smart and impressive and for that we find a good number of beauty parlours, hair dressing centres, outlets for readymade branded garments, footwear show rooms and Gym, Jogging centres which keep them fit and impressive.

Personality in totality thus focuses our attention on body, mind and look. We need a sound or healthy body. We need to develop our temptation to spiritualism and further we need to look impressive.

Andocronologists feel that sound health helps in building character. The Yoga, Pranayam and Meditation have the potentials to develop value-based people required by the present corporate world.

We cannot negate that transformation of character makes the ways for the transformation of attitudes and the behavioural patterns. If we find people developing their temptation to these dimensions, they are virtually transformed. Good people are good, if they have a good character. If we find people hankering after the materialistic gains and adopting unfair and unethical practices for achieving them, it is due mainly to the fact that they are dissatisfied with their living condition, and status. Since they want to satisfy themselves, the only option left in their hands is to adopt unlawful practices because by doing such they find themselves in a position to satisfy in the short duration. If we find bad people showing their temptation to Yoga, they succeed in linking their minds with heart and soul and in the process, they get natural pleasure because here conditioning of an individual is based on mind and soul. Why do we find children experiencing natural pleasure that we do not get in others? Of course, it is on account of their conditioning which is not influenced by the materialistic gains. If they get food, we find them satisfied and gaining natural pleasure. Gradually, we find them witnessing everything happening in their families or society which is due to the materialistic gains and on account of that we find a change in their perception. New perception initially comes from the family where we find children witnessing everything done by their parents and other family members. Because we find children crossing the age of three gaining a new experience and whatsoever they witness, help a change in the perception of good and bad people. The galloping corruption in the Indian society is due to the fact that members of society are becoming insensitive to the problem of corruption. They believe in short-term gains and want to be the richest person overnight. This makes it essential that they engage themselves in the unfair and unlawful practices. It is imperative that we start the process when they are teens. The corporate sector and the Business Schools may adopt it as a continuous process. The educational institutions in general need to promote it as a part of their curriculum.

Feeling good, thinking positive and looking impressive are the results which we get by developing personality in totality. The people with such a personality may be productive to almost all the sectors. We cannot negate that all the dimensions of personal care services would create tremendous job opportunities. We cannot believe that even Yoga globally acceptable and preferred by Americans in particular has been creating a business of not less than 5 billion US dollar. In the Indian perseptive, we find wider avenues because Yoga, Pranayam and Meditation are the gifts of our ancient values. It is amazing to mention that even till now, we find high rate of insensitivity amongst all the sections and segments of society and therefore we need to make society much more conscious. The concept of total health cannot be practised failing these stress whose contributions are sizable to the development of personal care sector. The emergence of this sector as an industry is need of the hour.

◈ Personality vs. Character

At the outset, it is significant that we develop our awareness of the concept of Personality which by many of us is not taken in a right fashion. Personality by definition comes from the sufficient word of Greek origin "Persona" which is meant a mask. The actors make use of masks to depict the various characters they play. We try to appear and act as something by using mask actually that we are not. The modern connotation is a suspect word where we say, "He has a nice personality or he appears rich". We do not make use of these adjectives to a rich person. We say, "He appears educated but the same not to a man who is actually educated. This makes it clear that personality by definition is something we put on outside which in a true sense is something which we are not inside. Personality at the office, personality at home, personality at the club or personality with your children cannot be identical in nature and behaviour. We put additional properties at different places and in different capacities to justify the role we are supposed to play.

Intuitive judgement, of course, is the real thing that we find pertinent because the desires cloud our judgement and we commit mistakes. Our intuitive ability to judge is the real thing, that requires due care. The professional psychologists and the spiritual psychologists differ while making use of words. The former focuses on personality whereas the later emphasises on character. We cannot deny that personality is false and character is true. Character building is, no doubt, a difficult task which is made possible by the brick-by-brick process as we build a house in the process of building character, we do not think about personality.

Character is our internal property whereas personality is our external feature. It is not essential that a man of character also happens to be a man of personality and vice versa. Our activities and words reflect our character and such a reflection helps us in diagnosing a man of character or a man of personality. When we talk about the holistic personality our focus is on blending of character and personality and in this context we find the words of spiritual psychologists as well as the professional psychologists productive to the corporate world.

In the modern corporate culture, we find focus on personality whereas the property character remains uncleared. It is against this background that we find people having world-class professional excellence, proving themselves as star performer, looking attractive and impressive but not having character and resulting from which they are found instrumental in the value erosion process and make an invasion on the corporate image which ultimately harm not only their own interests but the interests of stakeholders in general.

The management of mind bears the efficacy of building character where people start realising the difference between right and wrong, good and bad and deeds and misdeeds. As and when we find integration of mind with the soul, the transformation process is switched on. The Yoga, Pranayam, Meditation and our temptation to the spiritual sessions cultivate the process and inculcate faculties for positive developments and as a gradual process, we start nurturing positive feelings in our minds, preserving happiness and nourishing ethics.

◈ Managing Mind

We cannot negate that management of mind occupies a place of outstanding significance because nothing is found looking good and impressive, if there is something wrong with the mind. Occupying much more sensitivity in its property, it affects almost all the organs of our body. This necessitates an effective control of mind even for a healthy body. Keep your mind healthy and only then it will be easier for you to keep your body healthy. Discipline of daily routines is a must. We agree with this view that agitated mind is unhealthy and our efforts in this respect should be to regulate those factors found instrumental in agitating human mind. Not getting what one desires, getting what one dislikes and uncontrolled emotions in the mind need due care while regulating agitations. Agitated mind cannot be healthy. If we find a continuous accumulation of such likes and dislikes we invite stress which agitates the mind, makes it indisciplined and stressed mind is found unhealthy. Hence, we need to regulate stress which is not to be possible unless we manage the mind to be a regulator. It is an unvarnished fact that stress-free mind is healthy and calm and if we feel ourselves calm and cool, it is found easier for us to regulate the mind. This focuses on de-stressing the mind and for that we need to seal doors for the accumulation of day-to-day complexes. The stored complexes need to be cleared. How and in what way, we can clear the stockpile of stored complexes need due care. It is found that non-reactive observation of oneself mitigates the strength of these complexes. Awareness proves to be an effective prescription in the very context as the continuous awareness makes this a continuous process resulting into clearing the stockpile of complexes.

The accumulated complexes complicate our task while managing the mind and therefore we need to be aware of the paths for the removal of complexes disturbing our mind. The three important paths draw our attention viz., adapting the path of service, path of intellectual analysis and path of devotion. The professionals managing affairs need to make it clear that if you start serving the interests of humanity and fulfilling the humanitarian commitments; the complexes accumulated in different forms start a reversal. Our temptation for the intellectual self also help controlling the complexes. And the last one, the path of devotee as an effective prescription needs creative promotion.

The path of meditation has been found much more effective while regulating and mimimising the accumulated complexes in different forms. If we talk about personality, we cannot underestimate body and mind. Healthy body needs a healthy mind and we can achieve healthy mind by preventing accumulation of complexes in mind. It is also found that non-active, self observation distresses the mind which is possible through path of service intellectual analysis, devotion or meditation. In the face of aforesaid facts, it is right to opine that in the changing scenario, the religious organisations can play a very positive role in regulating the stress found as a lever spring for the development of all the evils and problems. Of course, the task is found much more difficult because we find a majority of the people developing a temptation for materialistic gains, a smooth path for the destination "stress".

◈ Yoga, Pranayam and Meditation

The three dimensional approaches for managing mind are considered significant. Here, we go through the basics of all the three tracks.

◈ Yoga

In the increasing heat of globalisation and mounting domination of material culture, it is quite natural that we adopt the lifestyles which open doors for a number of problems. Hurry, curry and worry have been found getting important places in our lifestyle. We have a busy schedule and hectic time-table keeping us unnoticed of the problems coming in the natural process of acquiring the materialistic gains. Yogic Asanas and Pranayams are the two wings of Yoga. Practising Yoga and Pranayams can help us in improving the health of our heart and mind. If practised on a regular basis, it can prevent cardiovascular diseases. Yoga Postures can help us in the development of personality. By adding flexibility and strength to our body, we find Yoga postures improving our body circulation and injecting strength to our mind. This helps us in keeping ourselves physically fit. It helps us in thyroid and weight loss problems and feeling younger. It delays ageing and helps us in keeping active, having a perfect shape of our body and looking beautiful. It improves blood circulation and helps in balancing the harmones which provides to the skin a healthy glow. A large number of problems are resolved with the help of Yoga which we recognise at the later stages.

During the yester years, we have received and perceived the concept and perception of Yoga in a different way where we have witnessed misrepresentation and packaging specially by those who have done it for personal profit. Paradoxically, it has been reduced to the status of just another exercise programme available of videotape. It has been presented as a cult not as the way of life. This necessitates to re-define Yoga in the changing perspective so that we find people perceiving the right concept of Yoga.

Yoga is a science. It is a set of techniques to protect and promote the interests of human beings. It is a systematic, methodical and practical discipline and more so an experiential science of self study. It is also right to mention that Yoga does not contradict or interfere with any religion. Anybody coming from any religion can practise Yoga. Of course, we find concrete experiences of Indian sages and saints who have previously used these techniques to experience the deepest self. Even historical facts testify that Yoga has been practised both in the East and West. If we find its imprint on the Eastern Culture, it is due to the fact that cultural transformation has not obscured the origin of the science there and therefore an ongoing tradition is continuing and we find its roots in the East. In a true sense, we find Yoga as a living tradition dating back for centuries, codified by a scholar and teacher named Patanjali in the Yoga Sutras, written about the second century B.C.

The root is "yuj" which is meant unity or Yoke makes it clear that the purpose of Yoga is to unite ourselves with our highest nature.

The various disciplines of Yoga help the re-integration process. We feel ourselves incomplete and limited unless the re-integration process is completed which results into feelings of sorrow, insecurity, fear and separation. We cannot deny that in the modern age we have a number of amenities and facilities to lead a comfortable life and these external achievements through new generation of sophisticated technology have also been instrumental in the generation of tension, dissension, unrest and displeasure. We are silently witnessing the destructiveness of our powerful weapons. The yawning gap between the rich and poor, the mounting disparities, the misuse of our material and personal resources and above all the loneliness and violence of our modern world are the results of our wrong decisions. The economic achievements cannot be helpful in minimising the gap and dissatisfaction. The only solution to the self-generated problems is to make an invasion on the human problems. We need to diagnose that why we are making a search for inner peace tranquillity and wisdom within ourselves. Yoga bears the efficacy of completing our search and providing an effective solution by helping human beings, in developing their awareness of the ultimate nature.

All the methods of Yoga are found based on perfection which is essential state of all the human beings. The focus is on perfection of our personality which may help to create a new world order. Actually, the restlessness of our mind is the root-and-branch cause of any problem. It is also right that mind by its very nature is outgoing and unsteady. Here we find meditation effective and for that we do not need to give up our homes and society because we can achieve a state of peace, harmony and contentment even though daily meditation which may regulate our lifestyles. The meditative experiences inject new life and strength and we are in a position to carry out our defined duties and activities with the love and devotion. Irrespective of where we live and what we do, it is possible for us to make progress in Yoga even in the modern world.

The various paths of Yoga need our attention. Hatha Yoga, Karma Yoga, Jnana Yoga, Bhakti Yoga, Kundalini Yoga, Mantra Yoga and Raj Yoga are summarised below:

Hatha Yoga: It deals with body and breathing exercises found considerably helpful to students to sensitise them of the internal states. Making the body a healthy and strong resource for the students would be possible with the help of Hatha Yoga.

Karma Yoga: It is actually the Yoga of Action. This path focuses on our duties. It also shows our responsibility to society and the human beings. By practising Karma Yoga, we find a significant increase in our potentials. Besides, we also develop our temptation to sacrifice and contentment.

Jnana Yoga: It is considered to be the path of knowledge and wisdom. Here, we find intense mental discipline. This helps us in realising the difference between real and the unreal, transient and the everlasting and the finite and infinite. This necessitates our awareness of higher and subtler realities of life. Achieving a stage of intense mental discipline is difficult and so not possible for all.

Bhakti Yoga: We consider it as the yoga of devotion where we find ourselves at the stage of self-surrender. The ultimate reality is to be achieved by devoting and dedicating all human resources.

Kundalini Yoga: We consider it a highly technical science. This is done with the help of a competent teacher. A serpent-like vital force is found asleep in every human body. We need to learn the methods of awakening the force.

Mantra Yoga: This Yoga involves meditation where we make use of certain sounds known as 'Mantras' which are transmitted to the students and are used as objects of concentration. This helps in having self-purification concentration and meditation. The sages and saints have discovered these 'mantras' when they were in deep meditation.

Raj Yoga: We consider Raj Yoga as the royal path which is found scientific where we get an opportunity to learn refining our desires emotions and thoughts. This helps us in identify the inner reality. Attaining the eighth rung and samadhi are the objects of Raj Yoga. We also call it Astanga Yoga or the eighth-fold path. The eight steps of Raj Yoga help us in creating an orderly process of self transformation. The eight steps are Yama Niyama, Asana, Pranayam, Pratyahara, Dharana, Dhyana and Samadhi. The first four steps are the path of Hatha Yoga which we find essential for making preparations for the Raj Yoga. The fourth step of Raj Yoga is Pranayam which is also called the science of breath. We find Prana the vital energy sustaining body and mind where the greatest manifestation is the breath. These stages help us in concentration. The seventh step of Raj Yoga is Dhyan or Meditation which is found instrumental in eliminating the physical and psychological problems. Meditation is the result of continued unbroken concentration which makes the mind one-pointed and brings it to the stage of superconsciousness. It is the uninterrupted flow of mind toward one object or concept. A number of problems crop up due to conflicts, repression or emotional distress and meditation helps us in becoming aware of these conflicts.

The different tracks of Yoga need due attention to manage mind. In the modern corporate culture, we find copious avenues for the development of stress and complexities. It is utopian to think that managerial proficiency would make an invasion on the stress which is experienced by the working people. The only thing a professional can make possible is to sensitise the working people to the importance of Yoga and providing to them an opportunity to learn. It is in this context, that we find business organisations vis-à-vis the business schools assigning due weightage to Yoga.

Organising Spiritual Sessions: One way to keep the people stress free is organisation of spiritual sessions. The moment they start evincing interests in spiritual sessions, we find an attack on stress. The religious organisations with the help of saints, prophets, dharma gurus may organise such sessions. With the development of new generation of information and communication technology and increasing domination of satellite communication, we find different television channels promoting spiritual sessions. The most important thing is creating interests and involving them in the process.

Spirituality at workplace cannot be possible unless we motivate people to evince interests in the spiritual sessions.

The most burning problem in the corporate culture of today is high intensity of stress which makes the environment at the workplace unproductive because stressed mind invites irritation and depression. The scientific management of mind makes the ways for cheerfulness and we cannot negate that cheerfulness and warmth spread like viruses. Today, we find everyone asking about economic showdown and recession and everyday organisations either laying off people or thinking of other ways to cut costs. It is quite natural that amidst such working conditions, the people in general find it difficult to remain happy. We cannot deny that a happy employee is a productive one. A study by the Yale School of Management dwells on how one's mind or mood can affect the work environment. According to the study, emotions spread most easily almost like viruses. Cheerfulness and warmth spread most smoothly whereas irritability is less contagious and depression spreads hardly at all.

The most outstanding benefits of Yoga, Pranayam and Meditation are making minds stress-free which paves the avenues for keeping us happy. When we find ourselves happy, laughing is easier and nothing like a good laugh. Laughter is the most contagious in nature. Hearing laughter, our automatic response is to laugh too. It is also said that laughter involves highly complex neural systems that are largely involuntary. In a neurological sense, laughing represents the shortest distance between two people because it instantly interlocks limbic systems. Hearts and minds work together and impact each other to influence the conditions. If in an organisation, we hear sound of laughter, it signals that the working group is on an emotional high. Such a working condition where we find experiencing opportunities to be emotionally high, the rate of productivity is found at its peak.

In the face of emerging negative trends in the social, cultural, and economic environment around the globe, it is but natural that there is seldom a time in our life when we do not experience some sort of emotional challenges. This makes it essential that we share laughter along with the sadness. But the task of sharing is too much difficult unless we know the art of managing the mind. It is due mainly to the fact that management of mind emerges as the most effective dimension of personal care management. If we practise Yoga and keep on moving the practices of attending the spiritual sessions, our task of helping others to find something to laugh about is found easier. The professionals in today's context bear the responsibility of creating joyful experiences for their subordinates or albeit peers. It is pertinent that professionals form a group and provide to them an opportunity to go out to find something to laugh.

Everything is possible if we assign a transcendental priority to the management of mind. The traditional as well as the modern practices are to be promoted to keep mind creative. Nothing like a good laugh and nothing like a sound mind. Laughter is effective but unless we have a command on mind, it is difficult.

◈ Managing Body

Healthy body engineers a sound foundation for the development of a healthy mind. The emergence of a health-conscious society makes it convenient for the government policy makers to speed up the development process. If we have nutritional awareness, consciousness of vaccination and immunisation, sensitivity to food and water-prone and communicable diseases, temptation to the quality of environment; the doors are sealed for negative developments adversely affecting our body. This makes it essential that we are sensitive to the different facets of body management. In one of the text on Yoga in Bherand Sahita, it is said that no amount of Yoga can help if the person is not taking suitable and balanced diet. It is in this context that we find Mitahar i.e., less food recommended for everybody practising Yoga. The present corporate culture has considerably affected our lifestyles and has been increasing temptation for material culture sparing less time for taking food and rest. We find a majority of us leading a tensed and stressful life causing more damage to the heart. Faulty diet and specially junk food is found adding fuel to the fire. This focuses on the consciousness about our body requirements and our sustainable power helping us in protecting ourselves from the most fatal diseases of the recent times. We need to see beauty in managing our bodies.

Food plays an important role in managing our bodies. The quality, quantity or volume, timing and duration of taking food need our care to have a sound body. Weight, food and fitness are found interrelated. The first and foremost thing regarding the management of food is to change our perception of food. Let us perceive that food is for cells not me; we eat food, not ingredients. What to eat? How much to eat? Where to eat? These questions need a right answer. Our hunger for nutrients cannot be underrated. Our sensitivity to quantity cannot be underestimated. The crux of the problem is that a majority of the population are found unaware of the role of food for the management of body and therefore we find them inviting a plethora of problems for themselves and the coming generations.

If we find masses realising the fact that food is for the cells, a large number of problems related to food are solved. We need to be conscious of eating healthy, whole, quality foods, found rich in nutrients. When we find cells receiving proper nutrients, our desire for eating is found less. In this context, it is also imperative that we are well aware of the fact that we eat food not the ingredients. What we eat is food. If we start thinking in this direction, the whole process is found easier. When we talk of carbohydrates, proteins, fibre, vitamins and mineral, etc.; our perception of diet, is found confused. Conversely, if we think of the food itself that we eat, we find less scope for any confusion.

What to eat is an important question. We need to eat a balanced mixture of fresh vegetables, a variety of beans, whole grains, brown rice along with some fresh fruits and follow a time-table or schedule for each and everyday.

Beans or legumes are found loaded with nutrients and fibre helpful in improving our digestive system vis-à-vis an important source of protein. Brown rice or whole grains provide vitamins, minerals and fibre. While managing food, we need care on seasoning which focuses on the produces of different seasons to bring a change in our palate. A combination of spices is essential because some of the spices provide nutrient value. The healthy core foods requires priority attention while managing the food. In this context, it is also pertinent that we eat the good food first. The habits of starting day with a rushed breakfast need a shift. We should have first the better food. We should not forget the two important aspects such as nutrition and cleansing. Actually, we need to counter balance the two polarities. While making food choices, we should make it sure that food items that we take provide to us nutrition and at the same time are also facilitating cleansing. Subtraction is also an important aspect to be given due weightage in the management of food. When we find someone recommending us not to eat much fat or sugar, it is a recommendation based on the principle of substraction. Addition and substraction are the two important aspects, we need to remember. Try to add good things to your diet. Make it sure that you will eat certain foods each day such as fresh vegetables, fresh fruit, beans and whole grains. These items are to be taken without exception. In that case even the substractive stuff would start falling away on its own or this one in an easy way.

Water constitutes an important aspect affecting our health. We are supposed to drink a proper amount of water. Two full glasses in the early morning is essential which would clear out some of the toxins, will trigger peristalsis, movement of muscular which would clear the bowels. Then after some interval take the first food of the day. The flow of urine must be clear. If it is not like this, it may be that water taken by you is not adequate or you have some problem in the urinatory track. The quality of water requires your priority attention. Try to make it sure that water taken by you is not contaminated. The potable water in adequate quantity would keep you fit.

It is significant that we develop our awareness of the immunisation and vaccination culture. This will help us in minimising the possibilities of diseases and in addition will also increase our resistance power. A majority of us are found insensitive to the same and they invite problems which would have been controlled much earlier.

While managing our body, it is also pertinent that we develop our awareness of the communicable diseases, contagious or infectious diseases and adopt the necessary precautions. This will help us in regulating the complications.

In this context, it is also imperative that we are aware of the artificial exercises with the help of Gym and Jogging. Actually, we need to form a habit and maintain the schedule.

The above mentioned some of the aspects will help you in managing your body which will keep you physically fit. The most important thing in the management of body is our lifestyles.

The above mentioned facts make it clear that we need to be physically fit and this necessitates sound management of body. Fitness of body makes the ways for the soundness of mind. Everyone wants to be physically fit or to have a sound figure and it is not to be possible unless we have a proper and balanced diet with a regular schedule of exercise. Staying fit, slim, and trim requires due care. We have to cultivate a habit of taking right kind of food and have also to be careful that how and in what way we regulate our weight. We also need to be careful that how we gain and how we lose our weight.

Disciplining of daily routine is a must. Nutrition and personal hygiene need priority attention. Exercising cannot be underrated where we can practise both the traditional and modern methods. The Yoga, Pranayam and Meditation are the traditional methods whereas the Gym and aerobics are modern. In a true sense, we cannot think about body or mind in isolation because both of them affect each other. Managing body makes our task of managing mind easier and vice versa.

Personal hygiene involves bathing, showering, hair washing, shaving, oral hygiene and nail care. Continence management includes in its purview toileting, catheter and stoma care, skin care, incontinence laundry, bed changing. All of them are found significant to our health. We also need to develop our awareness of simple treatments such as assistance with medication, including eye drops, application of creams and lotions, simple dressings, oxygen therapy.

Of late, we find it essential to develop our consciousness of the environmental impact on the food that we take. The administration of pesticides on the vegetables or grains that we take have been found causing a number of diseases. This has been found to be a matter of grave concern specially in the developing countries like ours where the farm sector has not been approaching experts for right administration. The organic manures need due attention of agriculturists for minimising the intensity of side effects. Besides, we also need to make use of preventive devices to counter the harmful effects.

Water constitutes an important place in the management of body and all of us are aware of the problem due to contaminated water. While making water impure, we hardly think about its dangers. We frequently use detergent powder or cake but are unaware of the dangers. The supply position of potable water is required to be increased and in addition, we also need to be careful while drinking water.

Management of body thus requires multi-dimensional concerted efforts. Any institution or organisation cannot protect us if we are insensitive. Sensitisation is thus found to be an effective device to make an assault on the food-prone and water-prone diseases. We damage our body also due to our unawareness of communicable diseases. When we talk about, managing body, it is quite natural that we go through all the core and allied problems. Hygiene and nutrition can keep us safe. Small things generate big problems. It we care small things; the doors for dangers are sealed.

◈ Managing Facial Appearance

The corporate culture assigns a transcendental priority to physical attractions and this makes it essential that in the management of personal care, we also go through the problem of adding additional attractions to our personality. With the changing lifestyles and increasing levels of income; we find people showing their temptation to look beautiful, attractive and impressive. By and large almost all segments of society have been found fascinated to the external attractions of their facial appearance. We cannot negate that faculties of development rest on our personality. Creativity transgresses the limits of physical boundaries. For looking good, attractive, beautiful and impressive, it is essential that we take care of our health and it is in this context, that we find management of body and mind significant but at the same time, it is also pertinent that our focus is on matching nature's creation with our creative actions. An affluent desires something more than a poor. The beauty needs more than a beauty care.

If we make an anatomy of the development scenario in the field of dermatology during the yesteryears, it is found that innovative developments have taken place. We find people of today much more sensitive to their look and appearance. Well supported by the corporate sector, there has been a significant increase in their levels of income vis-à-vis, a transformation in their spending behaviour. In the foreign countries, the techniques of cosmetology are found in more developed form. We cannot deny that we still lag behind. However, we have witnessed multi-dimensional developments in the field of dermatologies during the first decade of 21st century and the positive trends are found existent.

In the face of emerging trends in the Indian beauty care industry, it is right to opine that spa culture has been gaining popularity and people today are not just concentrating on regular haircuts and facials but in addition, they have also been evincing their interests in aroma therapy, soothing massage, easy yoga and fat reduction techniques. The Beauty World India 2010 reflects a healthy market. It is in this context that we find Indian Cosmetic and Beauty Industry witnessing a rapid growth in the last couple of years. The expansion of this industry of course is influenced by a number of factors but the most important reason for such a positive development is the emergence of a cross cultural civilisation considerably influenced by the corporate culture which is found to be another edition of westernisation.

The important dimensions of physical attractions are management of hair, eyes, skin, hands, feet and nails. Healthy and glossy hair depend on nutritious diet because hair is made of protein. This necessitates a protein rich diet and minerals. The eggs, mango, liver, dark green leafy vegetables, carrots dried apricots, whole grain cereals, peas containing Vitamin A and B are needed for healthy hair. When we have good hair, the dressing and style are other areas for adding attractions. The beauty parlours have been found serving the users for an impressive hair style in tune with the structure of face and height.

Management of nail also occupies an important place. Strong, smooth and pink are the hallmarks of healthy nail. The formation of nail is from Keratin, a kind of protein Amino acids containing food, green leafy vegetables, fish, poultry, meat, liver, dried dates, raisins, bajra and jaggery are found important sources of iron and good for healthy and beautiful nails. Zinc containing foods are found excellent for brittle nails. Olive oil is good for sparkling nails and hair. We can prefer to add one teaspoon of olive oil in our salad for strong and healthy nail.

Teeth and bones cannot be underestimated while managing physical attractions. Calcium and phosphorus are needed for this which we can get from milk and milk products, fish, meat, ragi, leafy vegetables. Since we find human frames rigidity depending on the strength of bones, we cannot undermine it, and therefore mineral calcium requires due weightage.

Since we go through external attraction, it is imperative that we also manage our skill. We find skin as the largest organ of our body. It is quite natural that, most of us like to look beautiful and this draws our attention to healthy skin. To have an attractive and healthy skin, it is pertinent that we drink plenty of water which should be clean and safe or potable. When we drink plenty of water, the skin is found moisturised, soft and healthy. We need to avoid confectionery, chocolates, cakes, sweets and soft drinks found high in sucrose. The whole grains, fresh fruits and raw vegetables, zinc are found good for skin. The refined, fried and junk food are to be avoided. Rose oil is also considered good for healthy skin. Vitamin A, C and E help healthy and beautiful skin.

Rest and Relaxation cannot be underrated for proper maintenance of health. Sleep disturbances result into multi-dimensional problems, affecting our health and mind in an adverse fashion. Eight hours of sleep is important. If we are honest to our lifestyles, it is easier to have a sound sleep.

Dresses and uniforms add additional attractions to our physique. We look attractive and impressive. We find a fair match between our profession and dresses or uniforms. It is quite natural that professional, occasional and circumstantial considerations determine the types of dresses we need to wear. In this context, the most important thing is cleanliness. Since we find dresses and uniforms adding additional attractions to our personality, the personal care services cannot undermine it.

Keeping in view the protection and attraction of our feet, we also need to focus on the management of our feet. The pedicure refers to the treatment of feet. Incorporating the toenails and the softening or removal of callus are essential for a sound and attractive feet. We find nail salons offering pedicure services for this purpose.

The main theme in the management of physical attractions is adding beauty. We need a number of devices for massages, facials, manicure, pedicure with the motto of looking attractive and impressive. Physical beauty or outer beauty has been found gaining popularity today and the process will continue even in the days and years to come.

The increasing temptation of a majority of our population to the branded garments makes it clear that people are now becoming much more dress conscious. Of course, the management of beauty remains incomplete if we ignore quality and attractive dresses in tune with our profession, figure, height, age and gender. We have talked about the management of skin to add beauty; we have also focused on the management of hair to look attractive; we have considerably emphasised on the management of hands, nails and feet and we have significantly talked about the personal hygiene but in a civilised society and specially in the face of Indian culture; our deliberations and explanations remain incomplete unless we assign due weightage to the management of dresses and uniforms. With the increasing heat of globalisation of economy, we find globalisation of fashion culture and civilisation gaining a rapid momentum and it is in this context that fashion and designing has also impacted physical attractions. The increasing domination of corporate culture and the mounting impact of western culture on the eastern culture has redefined the concept of fashion and attraction. We cannot keep ourselves isolated particularly when we find emergence of a cross-cultural society.

The management of physical attractions also makes it essential that we turn our eyes on the management of feet and in this context in addition to their treatment; we also need to throw light on the footwear. During the yester decades, there has been a significant increase in the footwear industry and it has become an integral part of fashion vis-à-vis our personality. To be more specific when we talk about the corporate culture, it becomes imperative that our due attention is on the quality and matching of footwear with our personality, gender and profession. Hence, our deliberations about the management of external beauty also includes in its purview the quality and style of footwear that we use. In addition to attractions, it is also concerned with the safety and elevation of our feet. It is against this backdrop that we find footwear industry expanding very fast and a number of institutes developing quality people to improve the supply position.

If we talk about footwear and remain silent about the quality and matching of socks; the external beauty cannot be considered to be complete. This focuses our attention on the matching of socks with our footwear, the colour and its matching with the dresses and uniforms that we wear. The protection of feet is an important consideration and this focuses our attention on the type of socks to be friendly to our feet.

Believe it or not, but we find cases when the quality of your handkerchief and its availability in our pocket or purse is found significant. The colour and size depend on the gender. Neatness and cleanliness become essential considerations to protect us from infection. Often, we are found insensitive to the management and maintenance of handkerchiefs and therefore our due attention is needed.

We cannot deny that even small things count our physical or external attractions vis-à-vis our personality. It is pertinent that we manage them in a right fashion and keep into considerations the remarks of people. Directly or indirectly, we find it a form of "shringar" to add additional attractions to our physique.

Keeping in view the wider areas for physical attractions, it is difficult for us to manage all the dimensions based on our own skill and expertise. In addition, we find a majority of us facing the problem of time constraint. Hence, the emergence of a personal care sector on an organised basis is but natural. It is against this background that we find small as well as the big players cashing on the opportunities existent in the beauty care sector. Physical invigoration has gained popularity and even in the coming days, we expect positive signs of development.

The sudden wellness boom in the society mainly due to the increasing heat of globalisation is an important reason for the development of business of beauty. Actually, we find this sector giving a fillip to the beauty trade. The growth is found more in Tier 2 and Tier 3 cities compared to the smaller cities. In this context, it cannot be refuted that gradually we find its imprint even on the small cities. The cosmetic industry has been found witnessing a galloping increase. Thus, we expect positive developments in the field of beauty industry. This would also create new job opportunities in the beauty care sector. For those, who have a keen interest in the beauty business, it is essential to have a good sense of aesthetics and creativity and more so, a liking for people of all ages. They need a friendly manner, an attractive well-groomed appearance, good health, the ability to stay on their feet for long periods and a sense of hygiene and cleanliness. This makes a strong advocacy in favour of professional courses for beauty care industry.

It is right to mention that carving out a successful career is not difficult in this field if one has sufficient knowledge of the basic aspects of beauty in addition to the aesthetic sense. Apart from make-up tips, an indepth knowledge of cosmetology and the science of human anatomy are important. Since skin care, hair care, nail technology, massages cosmetology and therapies involving aromas, oils or light are important, it is essential that a professional has a thorough knowledge of all these tools and ingredients. We find a number of institutes both in public and private sectors offering professional courses for developing quality people for the beauty care industry.

With the increasing heat of globalisation, we find a number of foreign brands coming to the country and getting a positive response. Not only the big players but the small players are also to be motivated. It is significant that we engineer a sound foundation for the development of beauty care industry. We cannot deny the outstanding role of inner beauty but at the same time, it is also imperative that we make masses conscious of outer or external beauty. In addition to other influences of positive nature, we cannot deny its influences on developing optimism. When we stand before the mirror and feel that additional attraction have been added and actually we are looking impressive and attractive; the doors are opened for the development of optimism. Since by managing body and mind, we have increased our internal strength and later have made them attractive by adding attractions; we find and feel ourselves strong enough to face the challenges. The beauty care is an emerging sector and with the organised and systematic development; we can expect tremendous growth of personal care organisations in the different streams or tracks.

In view of the above, it is right to mention that professionals developing keen interests in serving the corporate sector have no option but to nurture and strengthen their feelings that projection of personal image must be on the foundation of an established organisational image. The moment we start bridging the gap between the two, we start witnessing a positive impact on business relationships. Since by managing our looks, we respect the feelings and honour the culture of organisation, it is quite natural that we are benefited. Commitments to self, engineer a sound foundation for showing commitments to others. Outfits portray personality and position of a person vis-à-vis culture of the organisation where he/she serves. Corporate outfits also speak of our dressing sense and success story. This also helps in attracting the clients or customers. Corporate clothes help uplift the business to earn more name and fame in the business world. Quality clothes give to the employees a sense of pride and belonging and make their looks more proficient and elegant. The management of wardrobe thus requires an in depth study of a number of aspects. We need to identify the benefit areas and to adopt them. We need to define the disaster areas and to remove them. Actually, we need to promote the organisational culture.

Local corporate culture and global corporate culture cannot move forward in the different directions and with a different culture. Naturally, the direction is one and it is in a true sense the corporate culture, not just locally but globally too. For adopting corporate culture, it is imperative that corporate brand is expressed uniformly. A situation like dress-culture-shock is witnessed when we start believing that dress culture is meant, only for the corporate offices found in the headquarters.

Powerful looking clothes virtually change our mindset and we start switching from relaxed mode to the professional mode. The impact of that positive change in our attitude is found on our body language and behaviour and we find better posture, firm handshake, eye contact and sticking to business, everything positive and productive. This strongly supports the instrumentality of looks in the larger interests of an organisation. Uniformity without relaxation or compromise with the dress code policy remains to be the only option because as and when they have been liberal to the dress code policy; a number of negative developments crop up which ultimately affect the work culture. Corporate culture has no place for the relaxed culture and the relaxed dresses bring an attitudinal change because clothing and behaviour are found interrelated.

The corporate culture sizably influenced by the wardrobe culture thus makes it essential that employees serving their organisation view things in detail. They have a temptation for looking attractive and they carefully mind even the small things. The dresses, hairstyle, shoes, hands and accessories need due attention. Thus management of looks or management of facial appearance requires focused attention on a number of things with the prime motto of attitudinal transformation. Looks and behaviour cannot be viewed in isolation. We need to view things in detail and to practise them with a professional touch.

◈ Awareness of Hygiene

In the management of personal care, we need to assign due weightage to the hygienic considerations which may keep us physically fit and mentally disciplined. Though all the segments of society lack awareness of hygiene specially in the Indian context, however our kids do not get proper care of their parents which become responsible for the formation of a vicious spiral of unhealthy living, sick body and unhealthy thoughts. This necessitates priority attention on personal hygiene. In this context, a daily shower is a must. Keeping ourselves clean, fresh and odour-free is an important consideration. It is not to be forgotten that the cleaning of body is found effective even in the protection of skin and other skin eruptions. It is amazing that in the Indian society, a majority of us are not sincere and habitual while washing their hands. We need to cultivate the habits of washing our hands before eating and after using those articles which carry dust or dirty elements or after handling garbage after coughing or sneezing, after handling pets or other items, where we find possibilities of infection through bacteria and viruses. We generally forget that nails are an important carrier of germs. This focuses on regular trimming of our nails and keeping them in good shape. The nail beds need due care for preventing infection. We need to trim them weekly and to brush them daily so that no dirt or residue remains beneath the nail.

In the context of personal hygiene, we need due focus on practising good oral hygiene. We need to remember that mouth is more prone to collecting harmful bacteria and generating infections. A majority of us are found unaware of the relationships and link between gum diseases and narrowing of the arteries which can lead to heart attack and stroke. Infection of gum is found through the bacteria which gradually enters the blood stream, activates the immune system and make the walls of artery inflamed and narrowed. This makes it essential that we wash our teeth regularly and also wash the toothbrush and replace them after three or four months. Maintaining good oral hygiene also makes it essential that we visit our dentists at least every six months.

Keeping our hair and scalp healthy cannot be undermined when we start talking about the management of personal hygiene. The problem of lice and dandruff need necessary action at earliest. We indeed to cut our hair and to shape them in tune with our professional requirements. A number of products are found for keeping our hair and scalp healthy and we need to select them commensurate with our requirements.

The dresses that we wear cannot be underrated while managing personal hygiene. We should not forget that dirty clothes are the source of contamination and may cause serious skin disorders. Washing clothes and linen on a regular basis need priority attention in the context of tips for personal hygiene. We cannot deny that good hygienic habits are easy to begin and maintain which protect ourselves and even others from the illness.

◈ Awareness of Sleeping

We cannot deny that sleeping is essential to keep our mind and body fit. Sleep is a state of rest in which the nervous system is found inactive, the eyes are closed and the mind is unconscious and in the process, the muscles are relaxed. It is in this context that we need to develop our awareness of sleeping to provide to our body and mind new strength. When to sleep, how to sleep and for how many hours to sleep depend on our age, physical and mental condition. Normally, eight hours of sleep is found important. For the proper maintenance of health, we cannot undermine the importance of rest and relaxation. The sleep disturbances strain the eyes and general health. The children and diseased persons need much more rest and relaxation. We find the same prescription even for the senior citizens or old people. How to get a good night's sleep is an important consideration. Getting enough sleep is essential to stay fit and healthy. In this context, it is pertinent that we are aware of some of the consequences which may create critical problems when the sleeping schedule and duration are affected. It can cause headache, fatigue, and disinterest in working. It can also lead to poor memory, concentration, constant yawning and bad mood. Besides, we may also face stress and tension due to lack of sleep. Right posture sleeping cannot be underrated to keep ourselves away from body pain, stress and tension. If the problem of sleep disturbances continue for the long time, it may also create a condition for madness. Refreshing our body and mind assume a place of outstanding significance and it is not to be possible unless we follow and maintain the schedule.

Sleeping is not meant taking sleeping pills and getting relaxation. In a true sense, it is a stage which should be based on a natural condition just when we go to bed for this purposes stress and tension are supposed to be the vital obstacles and for this, we need to change our life style vis-à-vis the way of life. We cannot deny the impact of our dietic discipline on our sound sleeping. Behavioural profile of an individual is also found instrumental in obstructing the process. It is not to be forgotten that accelerating the stage of happiness is considered to be the most effective prescription for having a sound sleep. Developing a passion for serving the mankind and nurturing healthy thoughts provide to us a conducive environment where we do not witness sleep disturbances and get enough sound sleep. Remembering almighty God is also found helpful in regulating sleep disturbances.

The most effective reason for aggravating the problem of sleep disturbances is stress which is a by-product of material culture for which each one of us is found hankering. Of late, we find a majority of upcoming and budding youths so much tempted to the material culture that they have a good number of sleepless nights and ultimately we find them sick. These facts make it clear that achieving a balanced mental condition is essential for good sleep and it is not to be possible unless we make place for positive thoughts in our mind. Taking sleeping pills cannot be accepted unless it is medically essential.

Our disrespect to sleep has been increasing fast and actually we find it spreading like a national epidemic. A majority of the Indian youths nurturing the dream of mounting the corporate ladders have forgotten the feelings of being rested. Today, they are medically ill and tomorrow they will find themselves physically misfit. They have been pushing their bed time back to fit in extra work and further we also find them waking up early for a jump start on the competition. In a true sense, the overambitious budding generations have been looking at sleep as expendable. Though almost all of us are well aware of the fact that not getting enough shut-eye can cause all sorts of health and behavioural problems. Increasing addiction to career, craze for leading an opulent lifestyle have virtually made the upcoming youths sick. Both men and women have a dream and to fulfil it they are doing and can do anything!

Let's have a look at the schedule that we find a majority of the corporate people following.

> "It's midnight and Mr./Mrs. A is clacking away or making a sharp sound on the keyboard of his/her computer. Although he/she is yawning and frequently we find him/her head hitting the pillow. May be that around 2 a.m., he/she forces herself/himself to go to sleep. We also find them during late night zipping-off e-mails to members of the non-profit boards where he/she sits on. Meanwhile, we also find him/her planning for their children or for presentation or for meeting the clients. He/she is willing to give up sleep to get more done. They push their bedtime back to fit in extra work. They wake up early again for a jump-start."

Unfortunately, it is not a schedule just for a couple of days rather than for the whole life. It is not a schedule for a few selected people but of the total new generation. We can easily imagine the future of our upcoming or budding youths. They are virtually not remembering the feeling of being rested.

An internationally acclaimed Psychologist, Diane Halpern of Claremont McKenna College in Claremont, California, author of the book "Women At the Top" opines that people look at sleep as expendable. In a working mother survey, a stunning 77% of the mothers said they did not get the shut-eye, they needed. A survey by Men's Health shows men are not doing much better. Indeed 62% said, they managed on less than seven hours of sleep a night.

Of course, we are well aware of the fact that not getting sound sleep can cause all sorts of health and behavioural problems but each one of us are found pushing back bedtime to get in more work. Too few zzz's or snoring can cause a host of problems, from being unable to focus at work to being susceptible to illness, moodiness, depression and even injury. It can elevate our cholesterol levels which can put a spare tyre around our waists, thin our skin and cause wrinkles. However we are taking the risk to cross one more items off our to-do lists. Consequently, we are tired at work. A March study by the National Sleep Foundation in the US found the average worker spend nine hours a day at the workplace, topped off by another several hours of work from home and decreasing total sleep time during the week. By 3 p.m. most workers hit an afternoon slump. We cannot negate that in the entire globe, we find the problem of sleep deficit.

Whatsoever the reasons are entailed behind but we cannot appreciate such a negative development in our lifestyles. One thing is very clear that our increased temptation to material culture considerably influenced by the techniculture has been playing a significant role in having sleeping deficit. Particularly, the new generation of Information and Communication Technology (ICT) has been found aggravating the magnitude of problem. It is essential to warn the upcoming or budding generations who have been found moving forward to the direction of sleep deficit. 28% of the iPhone users check or update Twitter before getting out of bed. With this, we can imagine that what lies ahead for the coming generation. Pew Research found that more than eight in 10 millennials sleep with a cell phone glowing by the bed, poised to dispatch texts, phone calls, e-mails and videos.

Dr. Mathew Edlund, author of the "Power of Rest" believes rest is as important as sleep. Adults typically need seven to nine hours of sleep each night, or enough to feel awake, aware and rested throughout the day. Here, people need to alternate physical activity with mental activity. Sometimes getting out of the office and walking will restore you. A study by medical researchers at the University of Pennsylvania concludes, it takes several nights of extra sleep to make up a severe sleep deficit.

Willingly or unwillingly, we have to accept the fact that the dominating corporate culture is primarily responsible for such sleep deficit because our career-addiction has been making us restless. We are becoming high-flier and are nurturing dreams and consequently our life-styles are unregulated. We have to earn much more as we can and for that we have to work for the maximum hours either at home or in offices and unfortunately, we have only 24 hours in a day. If we continue with a lifestyle making us restless and keeping us sleepless; there will be a significant increase in the number or stressed and depressed people.

The facts outlined above make it essential that we need to regulate our lifestyles.

- You have to reprioritise your life-style.

  Decide the task that you really need to get done.
- Figure out a time and place in your schedule early in the day to get it accomplished.
- Spend 15-30 minutes your priority without interruption. Staying focused helps shut out the stress harmones, doubles productivity and keep you away from wasting sleep time.
- Make your to-do list before bedtime and if possible write down problems and solutions.
- Eat a light dinner at least two hours before sleeping and consider walking after the meal.
- Keep your smartphone out of your bedroom.
- Shut-off your computer an hour before bed.
- Close your eyes, remember almighty God and enjoy the pleasure of sleeping.

◈ Behavioural Profile of Personal Care Users

Emergence of personal care sector as an industry makes it essential that providers of services are well aware of the changing levels of expectations of users for personal or institutional purposes. Gone are the days when we were insensitive to our personality. Today, we find a majority of the population developing high level of temptation for looking decent and impressive. The increasing heat of globalisation and the motivating impact of corporate culture are found making the society much more conscious to health and beauty. People living in the cosmopolitan towns and cities, no doubt, have a different culture and lifestyles but we find its impact even on the people living in small towns and cities. On certain occasions, we find even rural people making a call for beauty care. Hence, we find a large number of users such as corporate executives, cine and TV artistes, athletes, women attending offices and parties, tourists, brides and bridegrooms and even housewives developing temptation for looking impressive and attractive.

Creation, satisfaction and retention are the three key issues before the professionals for which they need to be fully aware of the changing needs and requirements of users. This necessitates an in-depth study of the changing levels of expectations of users. Some of the users are habitual whereas some of them are occasional. The professional engaged in different sectors, cine and TV artistes, front-line staff of the business happen to be the regular users but foreign or domestic tourists, brides and bridegrooms for wedding or attending reception parties are the occasional users. The recent emerging trends indicate that there has been a significant increase in the number of regular users of personal care services. With the increasing level of income and expanding avenue of beauty care, we find copious avenues for the creation of new customers.

Creation of customers makes it essential that providers are not only delivering them the innovative and cost effective services but are also making it sure that services delivered are in tune with their needs and requirements. At an age of new generation of information technology, it is quite natural that the levels of expectations do not remain static. Now we find users not only sensitive to the beauty care but even to skin care. The users are found sensitive even to the physical fit. The increasing cases of stressed and depressed people add to the demand side. These developments make it essential that professionals have an in-depth study of the changing behavioural profile so that they keep on moving the process of creating, satisfying and retaining customers.

With a significant change in the perception of people regarding the personal care services, it is quite natural that levels of attitudinal variations are identified. Now people have started understanding the differences between beauty parlours and beauty clinics, the differences between traditional and modern exercises and the variations between tasty food and nutritional food.

With the increasing domination of corporate culture, we find a galloping increase in the number of stressed people. Actually, we find people inviting stress just to have materialistic gains. Our increasing temptation to the material culture makes it essential that we change our attitudes.

The people serving the personal care organisations in different capacities bear the responsibility of making available to the users a peaceful and stable mindset, a sound health and an impressive personality. High level of stress and fatigue cannot be healthy for an individual or a family and society. It is to make an invasion on the operational efficiency vis-à-vis the organisational productivity. Particularly in the Indian society where we find people having a different family discipline and culture, it is essential that we develop awareness of people to the behavioural studies and provide to them an opportunity to join Behavioural Science Foundation's Psychological Resilience Training Programme which would help in minimising their stress and fatigue. Healthy people have an inner sense of control and therefore they know the art of regulating their attitudes. Hence, it is pertinent that professionals also think in favour of organising short term courses and refresher courses specially to enrich the mind of people. In a true sense, relearning attitudes appears meaningful. Smitha, an airhostess, who experienced chronic fatigue and stress due to the demands of looking after two children, home, odd work timings and flights across international time zones experienced it difficult to enjoy her children. The Psychological Resilience Training Programme provided to her relief and she felt less stressed and more energetic. The problem of backache which she experienced earlier inexplicably disappeared which had not responded to months of exercise, physiotherapy and painkillers. Behavioural Science Foundation Courses may provide to the people a number of benefits. In addition, the Yoga and spiritual sessions may also provide to them a considerable amount of reliefs.

We need to relearn attitudes because we have created a condition which we did not experience earlier. We have redefined the lifestyles which we did not prefer earlier. We have changed our priorities which we could not consider earlier. We have started taking pleasure in the materialistic gains which we underrated earlier. These recent developments make a strong advocacy in favour of regulating our behaviour. The professionals nurture a task of studying our priorities and delivering personal care services which help us in having a sound physique, a healthy and creative mind and an impressive and pleasing holistic personality which guide us how to be optimistic and productive in the present corporate world where at each and every step we witness a number of odds.

◈ Personal Care Management Vis-à-Vis Four Es of HR

The different dimensions of personal care may be helpful in transforming the human resources into human capital. Presently, we deliberate upon the four Es of HR such as Engagement, Empowerment, Excellence and Enlightenment.

The Engagement focuses our attention on leadership, hiring, training, cultural adoption, workplace, assignments, team building, reward systems, information and communication networking and we find all of them helpful in creating people.

The Empowerment throws light on transformational leadership, core competence identification, training and development, mentoring, coaching, climate and cultural designs where people are empowered.

The Excellence advocates in favour of visionary leadership, performance management, appraisal, rewards, motivation and counselling helping people in achieving professional excellence.

The Enlightenment talks about principled leadership, humanised leadership, stress management, spirituality at workplace, ethics and morals where people achieve perfection.

The four Es thus cover all the facets to be effective in getting the best from the available stock of human resources. How and in what way the three dimensions of personal care management can be effective in the process, the professionals managing the affairs need to understand.

If our focus is on the management of body, it provides to an organisation people having a sound physique. Since they are supposed to have the thematical competence, it is easier for them to be adaptive to the organisational culture. By managing physical attractions, we make them attractive and impressive. Our big task is concerned with the management of mind which makes them professionally excellent and morally and ethically enlighted. Since they are well aware of the skill of regulating stress, we expect from them to be mentally disciplined. Besides, it is also easier to promote participated and humanised leadership because they are in a position to practise spirituality at the workplace. The people working there start realising their defined responsibilities and because training and development activities have made them potentially sound, we expect from them the best quality of services, performance and behaviour.

In the Indian perspective, the available stock of human resources, of course, have world-class professional excellence but they fail in achieving perfection because they lack humanised and principled leadership. Spirituality at the workplace makes an invasion on stress and tension but because we find them not sincere to the management or body and mind, the task becomes much more difficult. They do not have the life-styles which may help them in becoming mentally disciplined. This results into making the environment at the workplace unfriendly to the available stock of human resources. Professional ethics have no place in the environment at the workplace which prove to be an important reason for a deceleration in productivity.

◈ Emergence of Personal Care Business

The changing faces of personal care services make it difficult for an individual to manage all the dimensions of services with the support of his/her own efforts and this engineers a strong foundation for the development of personal care business with the cooperation of national as well as the global small and big players. A large number of personal care organisations were established to balance the demand and supply position but till now we find a big gap existent both in quantitative and qualitative terms. Of course, we find emergence of personal care organisations even before 1990 but the development process could gain a momentum only during 1990s which was found gaining a high speed during the first decade of 21st century.

Of late, a majority of the people have been found concentrating on grooming themselves with not just regular haircuts and facials but also aroma therapy, soothing massages, easy yoga and fat reduction techniques as well. In a true sense, spas are becoming popular in the five star hotels where the concept of holistic treatment has been attracting guests in which they avail treatment of mind, body and soul. Just by providing a little extra space, the hotels are adopting a strategy of offering an attractive package and increasing the occupancy rate. Actually, we find emergence of a spa culture.

Mr. Amitabh Kant, CEO and MD, Delhi-Mumbai Industrial Corridor of Development Corporation, says, "Wellness — the world covers all aspects of mental elevation, physical invigoration, spiritual rejuvenation... when the mind and body is balanced, beauty comes from within, a glow will come from within and the mind will work better. "Messe Frankfurt, Organiser of Beauty World India 2010 has cited the promising market results of a recent Neilson Global Consumer Confidence Survey to launch trade show. The survey found that confidence (in some markets) has increased and has been the most promising in India, Hong Kong, China, Singapore and Brazil resulting in a rapid change of consumer spending patterns. With a growth rate of 8.5%, India may continue to be the second fastest growing economy in the world, thanks to the strength of domestic demand and domestic nature of its investment financing.

We cannot deny that it is due to its rapid growth and a significant increase in the discretionary income that Indian Cosmetic and Beauty Industry has witnessed a rapid growth in the last couple of years growing at a rate of around 15 to 20%. The concept and perception of beauty has been found changing. Earlier, we said that beauty lies in the eyes of beholders but today we say beauty also lies in the hands of those who have made it their business and make professionalised efforts to look us attractive, pleasing and more importantly, impressive. During the yester years, there has been a rapid increase in the awareness of health, beauty and personal grooming and hygiene amongst both men and women and it is an important reason for a massive increase in the demand position.

Today, we find beauty care sector emerging as an industry having a business of multi-billion dollar which has been offering a whole array of opportunities to youngsters in general and the budding youths in particular. According to the Indian Retail Survey 2007, the current size of the beauty care industry is about ₹ 6,000/- crores which is growing steadily at a robust 25% each year and therefore by 2010, we expect it to be around

₹ 10,000/- crores. It is right to mention that sudden wellness boom in society is giving a fillip to the trade. The growth is more in Tier 2 and Tier 3 cities.

The continuing positive trends signal a significant increase in the job markets and now we find youth segment of society interested in adopting it as a career. For the persons interested in the beauty business, it is essential that they have a good sense of aesthetics and creativity. Besides, they need a friendly manner and an attractive well-groomed appearance, good health and more so the ability to stand on their feet for long periods. Apart from the government affiliated vocational training institutes across the country, we find a number of private training centres and institutes offering specialised courses in different streams. We cannot negate that the demand for smart, well-informed and trained professionals has increased more than three folds. The International Coaching Institutes like Lakme Institute, L'Oreal, Conte International Desthetique Et De Cosmetology (CIDESCO) also run Certificate and Diploma Courses in aesthetics and beauty therapy.

Further, we also find a significant increase in the branded garments. A number of foreign companies have started their units and we find people showing their temptation to the same which has been making a strong foundation for the development of personal care sector. We cannot deny that globalisation of economy has made ways for the globalisation of fashion, culture and civilisation and it is in this context that we find fashion and designing emerging as an important business. Almost all segments of society have developed a craze for their products which has made a strong foundation for the development of readymade garments as an important business. During yester years, this sector has been successful in creating a big export market.

The footwear is a point of attraction and during yester years, we have found a number of foreign brands making this sector much more competitive. With the emergence of corporate sector, the footwear industry has been providing job opportunities to a large number of people in different positions. To improve the supply position, we have also seen a good number of institutions offering different courses keeping in view the recent trends.

Thus multi-dimensional areas of physical attractions have injected new life and strength to the beauty care business helping people in adding additional attractions to their personality and transforming national economy in different ways. In the face of emerging positive trends, we expect future of beauty care business to be much more prosperous.

Of late, we find masses developing health consciousness and assigning due weightage to the management of their physique. This has helped emergence of business even in this area.

The artificial measures like Gym and Jogging have been getting good business and attracting guests in five-star hotels where they avail a package. We find people becoming sensitive to the quality of food and this has been opening job markets in the field or dietetics. With the increasing nutritional awareness, we find a number of institutions developing quality dietician getting job in hospitals. Since we find people seeing beauty in managing their bodies, a number of areas have been emerging. With the increasing awareness, we find personal hygiene also emerging as a sector. Bathing, showering, hair washing, nail care, oral hygiene have been creating business. Both the big as well as the small players are found interested in getting business in the different areas of managing body. The immunisation and vaccination need much more sensitisation because in the Indian context, we find a majority of the people very insensitive to these healthcare measures, influencing the health of coming generations.

Of late, we find stressed people showing interest in adopting those measures which help them in getting peace. It is in this context that Yoga, Pranayam and Meditation have been found gaining popularity and emerging as a business. With the increasing work pressure and mounting levels of expectations, we have been making place for stress, tension and depression. The worst sufferers are the youngsters. The corporate sector has also been found promoting Yoga and in addition, a number of organisations have been adopting it as a business. We find it essential to promote Yoga by all the educational institutions which would develop people having high resistance power. In the changing scenario, it is impact generating that our approaches focus on the management of mind. The Yoga bears the efficacy of impacting the character building process. It helps development of value system in an individual.

The modern system of education is found one-sided and shallow. Of course, it has been successful in developing the thematical competence but, if we talk about ethical dimension or the value system, the results are disappointing. We know how to keep in our memory the equations and facts but fail to understand and develop our own inner life. Our minds remain scattered and our emotions persist to be negative. We fail in tapping the potentials we have. The meditation helps us to overcome these limitations. It is in this context that we make a strong advocacy in favour of managing our mind and Yoga may considerably help us in the process. A number of organisations big and small have been found engaged in the business and there is nothing wrong in it provided they have quality people to teach and guide. In this context, it is also significant that public and private institutions evince interests in developing quality people for Yoga. The medical science has also been realising the role of Yoga in managing our health and mind and therefore quality people may also be occupied there. The leading business organisations need to make it sure that Yoga is adopted as a part of their management development programme.

Emergence or Personal Care Sector as an industry paves avenues for personal care business which would bring to the nation multi-dimensional positive results. E.g. the pace of economic transformation would be accelerated, the creation of job opportunities would be wider, the process of human capital formation would gain a rapid momentum and what not, if we find people developing character and becoming ethically and morally sound. It is quite natural that the development process would make the ways for qualitative-cum-quantitative improvements which would make the business environment much more innovative and competitive. This would make it significant that world-class professionals and new generation of technology are used for excelling competition. The two important tasks before personal care organisations to make them nationally and globally sound are involvement of quality professionals and conceptualisation of innovative marketing.

The marketing of services related to the management of body need due care which has failed in attracting the attention of marketers. Of course, we find development of medicare services in a right way but the services like dietics, personal hygiene, vaccination and immunisation, Gym and Jogging as artificial exercises, awareness of lifestyles, etc., are yet to attract the attention of a majority of our population. Hence, it is imperative that the concerned services are developed as an industry and the services of world-class marketing professionals are used to make available to the users quality as well as the affordable services. It is not judicious that we develop our knowledge bank related to the transformation of economy and keep the human resources at the bottom. The public as well as the private sector organisations bear the responsibility of sensitising the general masses to the personal care services related to the sound management of body which would engineer a sound foundation for the development of this sector as an industry and business pari passu.

Another dimension of personal care is still found at the bottom which, of course, should remain at the top. Nothing is possible, if we find something wrong with our mind. On the one hand, we have opened all the doors for the generation of stress, tension and depression but what we needed to counter the same remained neglected. The educational institutions, business organisations, non-government organisations and the government departments underestimated this facet of personal care and resulting from which the youths considered to be the most productive segment were the worst affected. The increasing cases of depression specially amongst youths are testified from the records of hospitals located specially in the cosmopolitan towns and commercial cities; where we need priority attention. The Yoga needs a transcendental priority. We do not find anything wrong in developing yoga on an organised basis which would develop it as a business. In addition, the involvement of people to the spiritual sessions cannot be underrated. The religious organisations can successfully organise it as a part of their social responsibility where the TV channels may promote it to serve their business interest.

The management and marketing of physical attractions, of course, attracted the attention of business organisations but even in this area, we find a large number of opportunities which have remained partially tapped or untapped. Innovative and cost effective personal care services are to be marketed by the world-class professionals in all the concerned areas. The beauty care industry has tremendous opportunities and with the emergence of corporate culture; we find niche markets and the profitable opportunities.

The marketing professionals need to be innovative in the formulation of service mix. Since we find new generation of technology instrumental in improving the quality of services; they have to assign due weightage to the techno-driven services. Keeping in view the taste preferences of users coming from different segments and professions, the quality is to be defined and redefined. Of late, we find even some of the rural users nurturing temptation for personal care services, of course, occasionally and therefore, the professionals have also to explore that how and in what way they can make the services useful and affordable to the rural users.

Increasing intensity of competition, makes it essential that professionals, initiate creative and cost-effective promotional measures to sensitise the users. We find high level of unawareness regarding the various personal care services and this focuses our attention on the sensitisation process. It is right to mention that a majority of us lack awareness of personal hygiene, lifestyles and the role of modern and traditional exercises. We are also unaware of the role of vaccination and immunisation in keeping us healthy. Nutritional awareness is not found even amongst those segments who are found dress conscious. We also find a few of us aware of external beauty but fully unaware of internal beauty. A majority of us are not aware of food-prone and water-prone and communicable diseases. Thus the sensitisation process may be helpful in creating new markets by tapping new segment of users.

In a country like India, where we find domestic customers in a large number, it is significant that the professionals are sincere to affordability. Of course, we have witnessed an increase in the spending power and a transformation in the spending behaviour but our efforts for making the services cost-effective would attract those customers who are sensitive to price. The corporate sector, no doubt, has created a group of customers who are potentially and resourcefully sound to afford even the expensive services but at the same time a large number of customers find it difficult to afford. Hence, the pricing cannot be undermined while formulating a strategy.

In the personal care sector, we find involvement of small as well as the big players. What to talk of the domestic brands when we find even foreign brands developing their network. It is not possible that foreign brands reach to the customers belonging to Tier 1 towns and cities and therefore small players would have profitable markets in the smaller towns and cities. While placing the services, it is pertinent that our focus is on quality and availability in tune with our promises. It is also to be ensured that occasional customers are also benefited from the services.

Since we find technology instrumental in improving the quality and minimising the time, while processing the marketing professionals need to keep into consideration the operational flow. Particularly in Tier 2 and Tier 3 cities and towns where we find customers very much sensitive to time consideration, it is imperative that providers are successful in increasing the operational flow. The services of quality people and sophisticated technology may be preferred for them.

The personal care organisations also need to manage service ambience in the face of services delivered by them. The centres or organisations providing beauty care services need such an ambience that attracts users and influence their instinct to form a positive opinion regarding the service quality. The furnishing, lighting, air-conditioning, display of technology to be used in the process, the displays of the services to be delivered and the exteriors are some of the key aspects helping in making the ambience conducive. The personal care organisations providing services related to the management of mind such as Yoga, Pranayam and Meditation vis-à-vis the organisation of spiritual sessions need to focus on the environment to be instrumental in generating peace. The displays must be helpful in generating attractions amongst the potential users of services. Ambience bears the efficacy of influencing the prospects. The photographs, literature, paintings displayed must be effective in stimulating the prospects. The colour of light, intensity of light, positioning of light need due care. Of late, we find a number of organisations offering these services in a camp where potential users assemble. The professionals need due care on managing the ambience even we find it in the open air. The devotees or even others are found attending the spiritual sessions organised in almost all the religions. The service environment must be efficacious of generating the service culture where the saints, prophets, dharmagurus and philanthropists may play a positive role.

In almost all the dimensions, we find supply position of quality people significant to improve the service quality. Since we find a major change in the perception or people regarding the management of personal care services, it is imperative that people serving in different capacities are of quality. The Yoga may not deliver positive results if we find teachers or trainers not having an indepth knowledge. Like this, the people engaged for Gym also need to be well qualified and experienced. The different types of services are offered by the organisations providing beauty care services. Here it is essential that they are well educated and trained. The services related to the management of body make it essential that different streams or tracks of services are delivered by experts having adequate knowledge of the concerned area. They need to potentially excellent and behaviourally decent. The users, of late, are found mare conscious; and therefore providers need to make it sure that possibilities of a gap between services-delivered and services-desired is bridged.

Creating customers, satisfying them to the desired levels of expectations make our task of retention much more easier. Today, when we find the personal care sector becoming much more competitive, it is imperative that services are made innovative. We cannot negate that beauty also lies in the hands of experts and the associates who deliver the same to the customers. We need to strengthen the realisation of customers that they will get more than their expectations. Defining and redefining service quality need to be a continuous process.

SUMMARY

In this chapter, you go through the different dimensions helping the engineering of a sound foundation for managing the personal care services. Before starting another chapter, make it sure that the following facts are well versed.

Personal Care Management: the Concept: This is management of different traits for enriching the personal score in tune with changing requirements of the corporate world.

Dimensions of Personal Care Services: The various dimensions required for personal care services focus our attention on the management of mind, management of body, management of facial appearance or looks for spiritual rejuvenation, mental elevation and physical invigoration helping us in developing personality in totality.

Personal Score for the Modern Corporate World: The various traits considered as personal score are sound physique, sense of personal hygiene, civic and aesthetic sense, sound mind, polite behaviour, morality, attractive looks and leadership.

Personality: The Concept: The yogic view on human personality makes advocacy in favour of five different dimensions such as physical self, energy self, mental self, intellectual self and blissful self.

Holistic Personality: The Concept: Holistic personality focuses our attention on personality in totality in which we find a fair blending of all the properties found in an individual to perform excellently. This is the combination of Rajas, Taranas and Satwic.

Personality vs. Character: Personality is our external feature whereas character is our internal property.

Managing Mind: By managing mind, we focus on the management of those measures which may help us in combating stress. We find Yoga an effective prescription in this regard.

Managing Body: By managing body, we focus on the management of food, water and other aspects helping us in having a sound physique.

Managing Facial Appearance: By managing facial appearance or looks, we throw light on our dresses, ties, shoes, socks and other accessories enriching the grooming process.

Behavioural Profile of Personal Care Users: In the main group of users, we find businessmen and women who have no options but to respect the organisational culture. The management of wardrobe is found in tune with the changing requirements of the corporate world.

Personal Care Management vis-à-vis Four Es of HR: The management of personal care is found effective for managing the four Es of HR such as Engagement, Empowerment, Excellence and Enlightenment.

Emergence of Personal Care Business: The traits required for the management of looks or facial appearance and other areas have paved avenues for the development of personal care business. This has made it essential that personal care organisations manage the business in a right way so that the users of services remain satisfied. This requires managerial proficiency vis-à-vis the professional touch. With the development of personal care organisations we expect tremendous opportunities for the creation of job in different areas where technical, managerial and general people are absorbed.

KEY TERMS

Aesthetic	Synchronisation
Wit	Etiquette
Elegance	Morality
Fun	Leadership
Yoga	Personal Hygiene
Pranayam	Corporate Citizen
Meditation	Tamas
Hygiene	Rajas
Globalisation	Satwic
Orchestration	Persona
Customised	Intuitive Judgement
Craze	Yuj
Albeit	Hatha Yoga
Junk Foods	Karma Yoga
Physical Invigoration	Jnana Yoga
Spiritual Rejuvenation	Bhakti Yoga
Mental Elevation	Kundalini Yoga
Personality	Mantra Yoga
Holistic Personality	Raj Yoga
Sleep Deficit	Vaccination
ZZZ	Immunisation
Gym	Dietics
Jogging	Prophets
Aerobics	Philanthropists

EXPECTED QUESTIONS

1. What do you mean by Personal Care Management? Explain the relevance of personal care management in the present corporate world.
2. Discuss in brief the different dimensions of Personal Care Management to be effective in the development of personality in the face of changing corporate requirements.
3. Throw light on the facets helping corporate professionals is diffusing tension and combating stress.
4. Focus on the factors found helpful in keeping you mentally fit.
5. Discuss in brief the different measures helpful in keeping you physically fit.
6. Explain the measures to be adopted for physical attractions in the light of changing requirements of the corporate world.
7. What do you mean by Personality? Explain the role of holistic personality in the present corporate culture considerably influenced by the material culture.
8. Do you find personality of an individual considerably dominated by character? Defend your arguments.

9. Throw light on the measures helping you in cleaning the stored complexes complicating your task of making quality decisions.
10. Explain the role of Yoga, Pranayam and Meditation in the sound management of your mind.
11. Bring out the different types of Yoga and explain the role of Karma Yoga for success of corporate professionals
12. What do you mean by the Management of Body? Explain the dimensions for keeping you physically fit.
13. What do you mean by the management of facial appearance? Explain the measures helping us in adding attractions to our appearance.
14. Do you find Sleeping the most important dimension for the sound management of our body and mind? Justify your statement.
15. Explain the relevance of personal hygiene in keeping us physically fit.
16. Throw light on the changing level of expectations of personal care users in the present corporate world to help providers to improve the quality of services.
17. Write a reasoned note on the emergence of Personal Care Business mainly after globalisation.
18. Throw light on the development of beauty care sector in India.
19. Explain the role of personal care management in regulating Engagement, Empowerment, Excellence and Enlightenment.

APPLICATION EXERCISES

1. "There is nothing more appealing than a man with a sense of wit and fun. There is nothing more paying than an aesthete."

   In the capacity of a corporate professional, throw light on above mentioned statement.
2. "The Personal Care Management is the management of three streams or tracks helping us in achieving total health for the development of total personality. The three dimensions are body, mind and facial appearances."

   Do you agree with this statement? Defend your arguments.
3. "Spiritual rejuvenation and mental elevation, Physical soundness and Physical Invigoration help development of total personality."

   Comment on the statement outlined above.
4. In the capacity of a corporate professional and in the face of emerging trends in the corporate world focus on the physical self, energy self, mental self, intellectual self and blissful self helpful in the development of a holistic personality.
5. "Intuitive judgement is, of course, the real thing that we find pertinent because the desires cloud our judgement and we commit mistakes." In the light of this statement, focus on the personality and character emerging as two important powers in the modern business world.
6. "Nothing is found looking good and impressive, if there is something wrong with the mind. Occupying much more sensitivity, the mind affects almost all organs of the body."

   Do you agree with the above statement? Justify arguments in your favour.
7. Do you find Yoga, Pranayam and Meditation very much effective in the purification of mind? Defend your arguments.

8. "If we have nutritional awareness, consciousness of the vaccination culture, sensitivity to food and water-prone and communicable diseases, temptation to the improved quality of environment; the doors for negative developments are sealed." Comment on the above statement.
9. In the capacity of a corporate professional, throw light on the various dimensions for the management of facial appearance commensurate with the changing requirements of the business world.
10. Do you find sleeping helpful in the sound management of body and mind. Justify your arguments.
11. In the management of personal care, we need to assign due weightage to the hygienic considerations which may keep us physically fit and mentally disciplined. Comment on the above statement.
12. Do you find personal care business an emerging area in the 21st century? Defend your arguments in the face of recent developments in the corporate world.

BACK-UP MATERIALS

1. www.bplans.com
   www ehow.com
   www.ibisworlld.com
   Beauty-a world of Perfection
2. www spas.about.com
   Beautyworld India 2010
   Business of Beauty
3. www.hindu.com
   www.healthyeating world.com
   www.healthyforms.com
   Importance of having a Healthy Body
4. www.korencheng.com
   www.pierss.com
   Building a Wardrobe
5. www.mindtools.com
   www.sosuave.com
   www.askmen.com
   First Impression
6. www.frontntierlaw.com
   www.thehindubusinessline.com
   Corporate Personality
7. www.nos.org
   www.webhealthcentre.com
   Hygiene
8. www.statefunds.com
   Personal Hygiene

9. www.missattymaam.wardrobe.com
Wardrobe Essentials

10. www.indianetzone.com
www.yogaforums.com
Diet and Meditation

11. www.yogacards.com
www.yogajournal.com
www.yogawiz.com
Yoga Postures

12. www.search.4 beauty.blogspot.com
Goodness, Truth and Beauty

13. www.cithr.com
www.corporategurukul.com
Adapting to Corporate Life

14. www.wikihow.com
www.carryfitness.com
Business of Beauty Parlour

15. Jha, S.M. Services Marketing
HPH Pvt. Ltd., Mumbai, 2011.

16. Buy me beauty!: The Times of India,
July 10, 2011.

◆ ◆ ◆

2 MANAGEMENT OF BODY

Healthy body engineers a sound foundation for the development of a healthy mind vis-à-vis an attractive rock star personality. The quality food, potable water, proper vaccination and immunisation, walk and exercises or aerobics are some of the facets helping us in the sound management of body.

CHAPTER DESIGN

Introduction – Basics About Our Body – Management of Diet – The Energy Requirements Foods Making – A Balanced Diet – Taking a Balanced Diet – Food Triangle – The Key Indian Food Items About Foods, you need to think off-wise Regulation of Food Awareness of Vaccination and Immunisation – Our Sensitivity to Diseases – Potable Water – Walk and Exercises – Sleeping Top Priority for Rock Personality – Summary – Key Terms – Expected Questions – Application Exercises – Back-up Materials.

CHAPTER OBJECTIVES

This chapter aims at sensitising the masses to the various facets of healthy body. We do not forget to manage, maintain and decorate our houses. We are found very much sincere while managing our vehicles. We are found creative while adding additional attractions to our facial appearance. It is really amazing that we are very insensitive while managing our body through which we acquire everything. The motive of this chapter is to activate the sensitisation process specially in the face of maturing corporate sector and emerging corporate culture in which a rock star personality helps us in getting the big bucks.

MANAGEMENT OF BODY

◈ Introduction

Health is wealth, an old proverb that we still find relevant but fail to conceptualise and resulting from which the process of generating wealth is sizable affected. We do not forget to manage and maintain our house. We are found very much sincere while managing and maintaining our vehicles. We are found very creative while adding additional attractions to furnish and decorate our house. It is really amazing that we are very insensitive while managing our body through which we have acquired everything and plan to generate as long as the almighty God allow us to remain existent on this planet Earth. Actually, we fail to realise that all the physical problems that we face are the results of our own decisions. We cannot negate that unawareness or insensitivity leads to multi-pronged degeneration. Particularly in the Indian context, we find even educated segment of the society not well aware of the basics of healthcare devices then what to talk about the illiterate and backward segments. We may be particular in having a regular medical check-up of our body but surprisingly enough, we never realise and confess that all the health problems are the result of our own actions. A majority of us fail to understand instrumentality of food habits, nutritional awareness, sanitation, personal hygiene, lifestyles, potable water, etc., in keeping us physically fit. The policy makers often talk about accelerating the rate of human capital formation but they hardly mind the Gross Happiness Index. It is against this backdrop that all of us bear the responsibility of activating the sensitisation process so that high intensity of awareness and health consciousness bring the positive results.

Healthy body engineers a sound foundation for the development of a healthy mind vis-à-vis an attractive personality. If we accord a transcendental priority to our lifestyles, find ourselves sensitive to the quality of food and water, keep ourselves aware of the communicable and infectious diseases, show our temptation to the environment and ambience where we live and assign top priority to the personal hygiene; a number of health problems would automatically be arrested. We do not realise the importance of food in having a sound health. In one of the text of Yoga, i.e., Gherand Sahita, it is said that no amount of yoga can help us if we do not take suitable and balanced diet. This focuses our attention on the management of food to keep our body healthy. The present dominating corporate culture has been found adversely affecting our lifestyles and increasing and aggravating our temptation for material culture which appears to be the root-and-branch cause for the development of a number of health problems. The quality, quantity or volume of food and water play an incremental role in having a sound health. How do we manage our diet is found significant even with the view point of managing our body and regulating a number of diseases which may be proved to be hazardous. If we spend on foodcare, of course we save on medicare.

It is an unvarnished fact that increasing the satiety value of food is the most important thing which requires our priority attention while managing the diet. If we eat in haste, the satiety value is reduced and therefore our focus must be on mindful eating. Actually, we need to be compassionate and non-judgemental in the very context mainly to understand what, why and when we eat. Saveta Bhassin, Mumbai-based dietician and nutrition consultant says, "A human brain consumes a lot of energy to do the daily mental activities. This energy comes from the carbohydrates in its simplest form — glucose which is supplied by the food we eat or from the glycogen stored in our body. Glucose is also supplied from the protein stored

See the Beauty in Managing your Bodies

in the muscles. We cannot deny that eating small, frequent meals found full of good quality proteins and carbohydrates ensure a constant flow of sugar to the brain and minimise drop in the level of blood sugar. We need to eat patiently or to avoid eating in haste. We also need to avoid eating while standing, watching T.V., chatting on the internet or when we are mentally preoccupied because we find these conditions reducing the satiety value. The important aspects in the management of food are the colour, texture, flavour, taste and appearance of food imparting a sense of contentment. We cannot deny that even a simple but balanced meal provides to us the pleasure of the most exotic-looking food. We need to develop our awareness because the scientific knowledge of different nutrients and their functions are found important.

In view of the above, it is right to observe that, management at food is an important area for keeping our body and mind healthy. The most important thing is related to the activation of the sensitisation process so that general masses come to know the basics. A majority of us lack awareness and invite multipronged problems. Mindful eating focuses on how and why we do eat, where, what we do eat become less significant. We need to identify the exact moment where we feel ourselves satisfied and neither feel stuff nor starve. Eat more during the day and eat less during the night which would compensate the drop in metabolism. We need to remove the perception that fat-free is always healthy. We need to eat slowly and to savour our food. Regular meals are a must. Smaller meals eaten through the day are better than three larger meals.

Unless we are sincere to the management of food, the task of maintaining a sound health and having a sound mind would be difficult. We need to perceive that mindful eating is about savouring each morsel we eat. Mindful eating helps us in regulating and preventing a number of diseases. Preventing the release of stress harmones is significant which helps us in protecting the so called damage to our organ systems but here it is also pertinent to know that bringe-eating or sugar-cravings may lead to drop in the levels of sugar. For balancing the stree harmones, we may take help of Yoga, Pranayam and Meditation. Actually, we need to understand the significance of food for our body and cells. This would bring a change in our attitudes and behaviour.

Weight, food and fitness are found interrelated. While managing our body, it is pertinent that we bring a change in the perception and strengthen this realisation that food is for the cells which would help us in controlling the food-prone diseases. What to eat is an important question and in this context, we need to ensure a balanced mixture of different items making available to our body carbohydrates, proteins, fibre, vitamins and mineral, etc. Developing our knowledge bank is an important consideration for managing our body which a majority of us lack.

Water constitutes an important place in the sound management of our body. The quantity and quality of water need due attention to regulate water-prone diseases. The potable water in adequate quantity would keep us fit. This focuses on drinking quality water. Maintaining a balance is essential which is not to be possible unless we have a comprehensive knowledge of its role in keeping us fit.

Personal hygiene has often been found neglected specially in the Indian context which becomes instrumental in inviting a number of diseases. A majority of us do not know the role of taking bath and development of civic sense for the sound management of body. The quality of water and timing are important considerations. Of course, in the ancient India we find due importance of taking bath but in the modern India, the increasing contamination of water makes it essential that we think over this problem to minimise the problem of skin disease.

Sanitation is considered to be a basic requirement of a civilised society but it is amazing that in the Indian perspective, we find it very much neglected. Particularly in the rural India, we find the problem at a critical juncture where a very few of the population make use of the proper sanitation services. Of course, we find a number of schemes of government for the construction of subsidised latrines but a majority of us are insensitive to the problem and prefer to make use of the open air space. The public services for sanitation cannot be considered adequate both in the urban and rural areas. In a majority of the towns and cities, the drainage system is found neglected which creates numerous health problems before the population living there. How and in what way, we provide to our body the scientifically accepted norms for personal hygiene is a matter of concern which requires sensitisation.

Inculcating habits for exercises and aerobics is an essential requirement for a sound body. We find artificial measures to keep us healthy and fit. The aerobics or physical exercises if properly and regularly done improve the intake of oxygen and its movement around the body. The Gym, Jogging help in making and keeping our body physically sound. In the Indian perspective, we find people less aware of aerobic exercises. Walking requires due weightage to maintain a sound physique.

Our awareness of the vaccinisation and immunisation devices also need due attention for short and long term healthcare programmes. By promoting these programmes, the government keeps the future of upcoming generations physically sound. A number of diseases can be prevented if we find society much more sensitive to the immunisation and vaccination culture.

For providing energy to our body and keeping our mind fresh, it is pertinent that we sleep which is a state of rest in which the nervous system is found inactive, the eyes are closed, the muscles are relaxed and the mind is unconscious. It is significant that we are aware of the duration and time of sleeping which depends on age vis-à-vis the condition of our body. It is a part of our life-styles. It is found effective albeit in refreshing our mind. Since we find corporate people heavily stressed, they frequently take sleeping pills for having a sound sleep but it is not a normal condition. Except for medical reason, we should avoid taking sleeping pills.

Lifestyle or the way of living makes place for a number of items. Since morning when we wake up till late night when we go to our bed for sleeping and even sleeping in itself is a part of our lifestyles. The timing for wake up, breakfast, lunch and dinner is a part of our lifestyles. By reforming our lifestyles we can bid a good bye to a number of health problems. The multi-dimensional problems pertaining to our body crop-up because we do not realise the importance of lifestyles.

Developing fatigue cannot be a right condition because it minimises our energy and strength. This focuses on taking rest and keeping our eyes close and mind free for relaxation after an interval which depends on the use of our body and mind. The moment we feel ourselves tired, it is essential that we relax and for that the most effective and easy way is to close our eyes. In the process, we gain energy and after making use of our energy, it is imperative that we regain. If we break the cycle, the problems emerge in different forms. How many hours we need to work and for how many hours, we have to take rest are found interrelated. Gaining energy and making its right uses simplifies the process of avoiding and delaying fatigue.

Optimal utilisation of energy is an important consideration which requires our priority attention. Since we find a majority of the people serving the corporate sector working hard for earning more and reshaping the career, it is pertinent that we avoid such a strategy which minimises our potentials and become instrumental in developing stress. It is also significant that corporate professionals regulate the practices of assigning continuously such responsibilities which may agitate and irritate them. The process of gaining energy with the sound management of body is disturbed if we keep it continuously engaged.

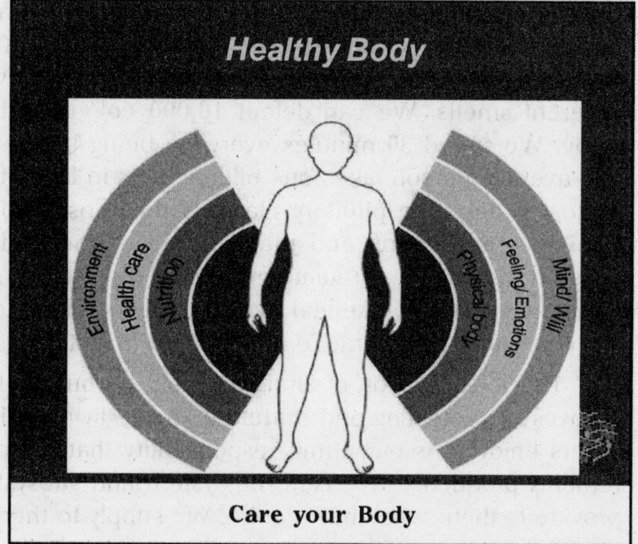

Care your Body

Thus we need multi-pronged efforts for having a sound management of body and all the dimensions require intensive and comprehensive efforts specially in the modern corporate world where a number of problems crop-up due to mismanagment or unawareness. On the one hand, the people serving the corporate sector need to assign due weightage to the management of their physique while on the other hand, the corporate professionals and specially the high echelon professionals need to make it sure that their decisions are not to motivate them for taking such steps which may harass and harm them.

In this chapter, we focus on the management of food considered as the most important dimension for the management of body. We need to change our perception of food for its sound management.

◈ Basics About Our Body

We find human body a very complicated system consisting of millions of cells organised uniquely and functioning dynamically. The human body is classified into eight systems such as the Skeleton, the Muscles, the Circulatory and Respiratory System, the Urinary System, the Glandular System, the Nervous System and the Skin. The body has 6,096 metres of small intestine and six of large with a surface area of more than 9.29 sq.m. It is also significant to know that 2.72 kg of skin cover the 1.85 sq.m of surface of an average adult. Babies are borne with over 300 bones and many of them fuse together as we grow up. Finally, we find 206 bones. The human brain consists of two parts such as the brain located in the skull and the spinal cord located in the vertebral column. The brain along with spinal cord constitutes the nervous system. The weight of the average human brain triples between birth and adulthood. There are about 96,000 km. of blood vessels in our body. The blood comprises plasma, red blood cells, white blood cells and platelets. The stomach produces 2 litres of hydrochloric acid daily. 5,00,000 cells of stomach's inner walls are replaced every minute so that the acid does not harm or damage the wall. The liver regulates hormonal balance, cholesterol, blood clotting and poisons. The liver is the only organ of our body which can be regenerated even if two third is removed, a whole liver can grow backs. There are 639 muscles which also account for 40% of the total body weight. Man breathes 13-17 times a minute at rest and 80 during exercise. On an average, we breathe 21,600 times a day. Our ears can detect 1,500 different tones and trace the direction of a sound within 3°. The nose can smell 2,000-4,000 different smells. We can detect 10,000 colours with our eyes and a lighted candle 1.6 km away. We spend 30 minutes everyday being blind, the time taken by blinking or annoyance. The average person takes one billion steps in his/her life. 1,25,000 hairs grow in the scalp with 45 lost a day. The pituitary gland is the most important organ of our body which controls growth, reproduction and the working of the endocrine glands. Life is a system and the subsystems are the circulatory system, digestive system, endocrine system, nervous system, respiratory system, skeletal system, muscular system, reproductive system, urinary system and the immune system. To get the best from the system, we need to manage the subsystems.

Precious creation of almighty God, the human beings are sent to this planet with defined motives of protecting and nurturing all the living beings so that they enjoy themselves and let others enjoy. It is our prime responsibility that we manage our body in such a fashion that it remains productive. We care the system and subsystems. We protect the different organs. We provide to them what they require. We supply to them the food, water and quality air. We make use of the organs with a sense so that we get the best possible from them not only in our own interest but also to protect and promote the interests of coming generations so that the cycle continues for the longer duration. We can do it well without institutional support. Of course, we need to be sensitive and to prioritise our habits and behaviour.

An English poet and writer, Samuel Johnson rightly says, "To preserve health is a moral and religious duty, for health is the basis or all social virtues. We can no longer be useful when we are not well." When we think of health, it is quite natural that we start exploring the ways to stay healthy, such as we practise good hygiene to prevent heart diseases, cancer and several diseases to obtain an optimum state of health. We cannot deny that our physical health is the most important consideration determining our physical or emotional or even mental feelings because only a healthy body can house a healthy mind. Good food is, of course, the greatest pleasure of life. Not only this, we also find good quality of food very much effective in protecting and nurturing our body. We do not find any sense in eating without mind and inviting numerous problems.

What food is very important and what make us good to eat is an important consideration that we are not supposed to overlook. To have a healthier diet, it is imperative that we prefer omega fatty acid, vitamins and fibre. Besides, we also care for the taste. We need to eat sensible amounts of nutritious food. Eating right makes possible proactive developments such as we feel good, control our weight and succeed imbalancing our body. A balanced diet shows a number of wonders that we cannot imagine. It is against this background that our focus here is on the dimensions which can keep us fit both in looking and feeling. If we are overweight, we neither look good nor feel perfect. We invite obesity and pave avenues for plethora of health problems. It is right to mention that a healthy mind equals the healthy body.

There are certain things which cannot be overlooked for having a sound body. You are supposed to include as much of raw foods in your diet as possible. The major food groups such as fruits, vegetables, grains, low-fat dairy products, lean protein meat sources (preferably only chicken and fish and avoid red meats) nuts and seeds. We need to keep our body perfectly hydrated and in this context, we find water very-very essential to smooth functioning of our body. We need to drink at least 8-10 glasses of water per day. We need to make it sure that our body get proper amounts of nutrients and calories to help us maintain a healthy weight. Prefer food easily available in your nearby area and to suit your budget and fit your lifestyles.

Avoid taking fried foods and fast foods, prepackaged foods and soft-drinks, excess alcohol and smoking. You are supposed to refrain yourself from unhealthy choices like taking hydrogenated oils, preservatives, emulsifiers, dyes and colouring agents and artificial flavours. Avoid drinking contaminated or polluted water.

To provide adequate strength to our body, we cannot undermine some of the basics as outlined above. Making our lives productive should be the motto of all of us which is not to be possible unless we sensitise ourselves at least to the basics. A majority of the problems crop up due mainly to our knowledge bankruptcy, managerial deficiency and inadequate support of family as an institution. In this context, it is pertinent that we bring momentum in the sensitisation process with the support of potentially sound individuals or institutions.

◈ Management of Diet

At the very outset, you need to, change your perception of food which in a true sense is for cell. Adjust your diet, take simple, wholesome, easily digestible, bland and non-irritating food. Give up hot, pungent curries and chillies. Rest the stomach and small bowels by taking recourse to partial fasting. If you can fast for a whole day, it is all the better. You need to remember that fasting eliminates poisons and thoroughly overhauls the system. The digestive system by and large influences all other subsystems of the life system. With minimum precautions and seriousness, we can get the maximum benefits of food management.

Food is for cells, not me. This is considered to be the most effective principle helping us in framing our mindset conducive or friendly to good diet. The medical experts estimate that there are 10-50 trillion cells in the human body. Whatsoever the nutrients that we find in food are for them not for our personality or identity. If we realise the significance of diet decisions in proper perspective, it is imperative that we believe in this perception that food is for cells. A number of foods lack nutritional value or nutrients and if we lack nutrients or our cells are not getting the sufficient nutrients, it is quite natural that the inner system forces us to eat more and more which results into overweight when we literally starve, desire to eat more and the process of gaining weight keeps on moving and we face the problem of obesity. This necessitates that we are sincere to the foods that we eat. In this context, our focus is on eating foods containing nutrients.

While managing our diet, it is also pertinent that we are aware of the ingredients taken by us such as carbohydrates, proteins, fibre, vitamins and minerals, etc. Actually, we do not eat ingredients and therefore what we eat is food. The focus must be on the management of diet and our sensitivity to the ingredients that we get from foods. A nice mixture of fresh vegetables, a variety of beans and whole grains, brown rice along with some fresh fruits makes available to our cells the ingredients required.

It is important that a surprising number of physical problems and diseases are caused by foods producing acid after digestion. Almost all the developed countries or a majority of the populace in industrialised nations suffer from the stress of acidosis because we find the modern lifestyle and diet promoting acidification of the internal environment of body. We find typical western diet containing acid-forming foods (proteins, cereals, sugars) and the alkaline producing foods such as vegetables are eaten in smaller quantities. The stimulants becoming essential for the modern population such as tobacco, coffee, tea and alcohol are extremely acidifying. They are found heavily stressed and keep themselves less involved in physical activities which also adds strength to the acidification process. A number of foods are found alkaline-producing by nature but we find the manufactured and processed foods mostly acid-producing. Hence, it is pertinent that we are aware of the foods producing alkaline and acid and in this context our focus is on the alkaline diet strategy which shows wonders for the sound management of our body. We need to consume at least 605 of alkaline-producing food and 40% acid-producing foods. For getting recovery after illness, the alkaline-producing foods may be increased to 80% and the acid-producing foods may be reduced to 20%. It is significant to clarify the alkaline which focuses on a substance with particular chemical properties that include turning litmus blue and neutralising acids and in this context, we find a pH greater than 7. When we talk about acid, it is a substance with chemical proportion including turning litmus red, neutralising alkalis and dissolving some metals. In this context, we find a pH of less than 7. The pH is potential of Hydrogen, considered as a measure of acidity or alkalinity. The human body rests on the balancing process that how with the help of our diet strategy, we balance pH.

In order to maintain a sound health, we need plenty of fresh fruits and specially vegetables which are found alkaline-producing and balance our necessary protein intake which is acid-producing. It is imperative that we avoid processed, sugary or simple carbohydrate foods because on the one hand they produce acid while on the other hand, they also raise blood sugar level too quickly and lack nutrients. In addition, we may also find them toxic. An imbalanced diet found high in acidic-producing foods such as animal protein, sugar, caffeine and processed foods put pressure on our regulating system and we fail in maintaining pH neutrality. If we find an imbalance, the alkaline minerals such as sodium, potassium, magnesium and calcium are borrowed from the vital organs of the body and we are found prone to chronic and degenerative diseases.

This makes pH balance very much significant because if we do not maintain the balance whatsoever the measures we adopt to take care of our health are found ineffective because we fail in having an effective assimilation of minerals and food supplements. The acidosis decreases the ability of our body to absorb minerals and other nutrients which decreases the production of energy in our cells and we feel helpless in repairing the damaged cells and the fatigue and illness become very common. It is pertinent to mention that the acid-forming diet, emotional stress, toxic overload may result into acid pH. This focuses on following the alkaline diet strategy by developing our awareness of the end-products of food found after digestion. As for example, we find lemons very acidic but the end-products after digestion and assimilation are alkaline and therefore lemons form alkaline in our body. Just reverse, the meat will test alkaline before digestion but it leaves acidic residue in the body and therefore we find meat helpful in the formation of acid.

ALKALINE PRODUCING FOOD CATEGORY

Food Category	High Alkaline	Average Alkaline	Low Alkaline
Beans, Vegetables, Legumes	Vegetable Juices, Parsley, Raw Spinach Broccoli, Colery Garlic Barley Grass	Carrots, Green Beans, Lima Beans, Beets, Lettuce, Zucchini, Carob	Squash Asparagus, Fresh Corn, Mushrooms, Onions Cabbage, Peas, Cauliflower, Turnip, Beetroot, Potato, Olives Soyabeans, Tofu
Fruit.	Dried Figs. Raisins	Dates, Blackcurrant, Grapes, Papaya, Kiwi, Berries, Apples, Pears	Coconut, Sour Cherries, Tomatoes, Oranges, Cherries, Pineapple Peaches, Avocados, Grape fruit, Mangoes, Strawberries, Papayas, Lemons, Watermelon, Limes
Grains, Cereals	–	–	Amaranth, Lentils, Sweetcorn, Wild Rice, Quinoa, Billet, Buckwheat
Meat	–	–	–
Eggs & Dairy		Breast Milk	Soya Cheese, Soya Milk, Goat Milk, Goat Cheese Cream, Ice-cream
Nuts & Seeds		Hazelnuts Almonds	Chestnuts Brazils. Coconut
Oils			Flax Seed Oil, Olive Oil, Canola Oil
Beverages	Herbal Teas. Lemon Water	Green Tea	Ginger Tea
Sweeteners, Condiments	Stevia	Maple Syrup, Rice Syrup	Raw Honey Raw Sugar

Fig. 2.1

ACID PRODUCING FOOD CATEGORY

Food Category	Low Acid	Acid	High Acid
Beans, Vegetables Legumes	Sweet Potato, Cooked Spinach, Kidney Beans	Pinto Beans, Navy Beans	Pickled Vegetables
Fruit	Blueberries Cranberries, Bananas, Plums, Processed Fruit Juices	Canned Fruit	
Grains, Cereals	Rye Bread, Whole grain Bread, Oats, Brown Rice	White Rice, White Bread. Pastries, Biscuits, Pasta	—
Meat	Liver, Oysters, Organ Meat.	Fish, Turkey, Chicken, Lamb	Beef, Pork, Veal, Shelfish Canned Tuna, Sardines
Eggs & Dairy	Whole Milk, Butter, Yogurt, Cottage Cheese, Cream, Ice-cream	Eggs, Camembert Hard Cheese	Parmasan, Processed Cheese
Nuts & Seeds	Pumpkin, Sesame, Sunflower Seeds	pecans, Cashews Pistachios	Peanuts Walnuts
Oils	Corn Oil, Sunflower Oil, Margarine, Lard	—	—
Beverages	Cocoa	Wine, Soda/ Pop	Tea (black) Coffee, Beer, Liquor
Sweeteners, Condiments	White Sugar, Processed Honey	Milk, Chocolate, Molasses, Jam, Ketchup, Mayonnaise, Mustard, Vinegar	Artificial Sweeteners

Fig. 2.2

The above Diet Chart would be effective in developing awareness of general masses that what diet mixture would be helpful in maintaining a sound health. Of course, it is a scientific analysis but even common people may receive it in a right fashion. What to eat and how much to eat; if we come to know it, a majority of the health problems mainly due to food can be regulated. Making a balance of alkaline-forming foods and acid-forming food is significant. Some of the food items provide high alkaline whereas some of them average and less. Like this, some of the food items generate high acid whereas some of them average and low. Let's have a view of the diet-chart and follow it to have a sound health.

◈ Know About the Energy Requirements

In the management of body, it is of paramount importance that you develop your awareness of the energy required by your body which depends on your age and gender. It is in this context that we focus on a chart which would sensitise you in the concerned area. Not only the illiterate segment but even educated and highly educate segments lack knowledge of the level of energy required by them for a normal lifestyle. We cannot negate the incremental role of food items taken by us in increasing and decreasing the level. With the increasing domination of corporate culture, we find a basic change in our food habits and we find specially the upcoming or budding generations nurturing a special temptation for junk food, fast food or fat food responsible for creating the imbalance. Because, we do not find a single food group providing to as the required nutritions, it is imperative that a mix is developed when we would be required to make it sure that food groups such as fruits, vegetables, cereals and pulses, dairy and poultry, fish and meat products are optimally included in our diet chart. Cereals like rice or wheat do not supply to our body the required nutritional support. We need to supplement minor quantities of a number of vitamins and minerals to make our diet-chart balanced. Carbohydrates, fat, water minerals and vitamins are the different nutrients found in food stuff and we are unaware.

The following chart may develop your awareness.

Category	Age Years	Height cm	Weight kg	Energy Allow Kcal	Protein gms
Infants	0-5	60	6	650	13
	5-1	71	9	850	14
Children	1-3	90	13	1300	16
	4-6	112	20	1800	24
	7-10	132	28	2000	28
Males	11-14	157	46	2500	45
	15-18	176	66	3000	59
	19-24	177	72	2900	58
	25-50	176	79	2900	63
	51+	173	77	2300	63
Females	11-14	157	46	2200	46
	15-18	163	55	2200	44
	19-24	164	58	2200	46
	25-50	163	63	2200	50
	51+	160	65	1900	50

Fig. 2.3

◈ A Balanced Diet is Essential

Eating healthy food promotes good health and conversely, the unhealthy food habits lead to a diseased body. This focuses on taking a balanced diet which is the combination of diverse and healthy foods. We are aware of the fact that foods containing nutrients provide strength to the metabolic function of our body. If we do not take nutrients, this results into an accumulation of toxins within the body found responsible for chronic diseases in different forms if not in short run, of course, in the long run. Hence, we make a strong advocacy in favour of a nutritious diet which ensures overall well-being, maintains healthy Body Mass Index (BMI), reduces the risk of a number of debilitating diseases like cancer, cardiovascular ailments, diabetes, osteoporosis and stroke. Thus both as preventive and even as a curative measure, we find a nutritious and healthy or balanced diet essential. How to form a habit of taking a balanced diet appears to be the real thing for having good health which a majority of us fail to receive in a right perspective.

It is also right to mention that we do not find even a single food group which can nourish our body with all the vital ingredients required and therefore, we have no option but to consume a variety of healthy foods to make available the required nutrition to our body. The five main food groups need our due attention such as fruits, vegetables, cereals, pulses, dairy and poultry, fish and fat products. A fair mix of these five food groups ensures essential vitamins, minerals and dietary fibre. Here, it is to be made clear that various factors like age, activity level, body size and gender determine the quantity. Here, we also need to remember that to the extent it is possible, we should get the maximum number of recommended nutrition from the food group because some foods from within a particular food group provide more nutrients than others.

The type, nature and mixture of the five food groups vary if we take them with certain defined motives.

Diet for Weight Loss: Excessive weight is found to be a major problem. A sedentary lifestyle or say problem of over or excessive weight due to excess sitting, unhealthy eating habits result into an increase in our weight. There is a general tendency of crashing diet for reducing the weight which cannot be advisable. In a true sense, a restrictive diet-chart for weight loss is found unhealthy. In this context, it is significant that we have a daily-diet-chart which shows wonders. The physical activity level of an individual cannot be undermined in the very context which may show positive results because this will demand more calories. A sedentary lifestyle creates numerous problems and therefore, it is imperative that even those persons who have no option but to go with continuous sitting involve themselves in the physical exercises. Inclusion of healthy snacks (a small quantity of food eaten between meals or in place of a meal) in our daily diet charts may also be preferred. But in no case, we should go through weight loss by crashing diet.

We cannot negate the impact of our figure on the personality and facial appearance but it is not meant that just to look attractive you adopt harmful devices. The most important thing is cultivating the habit of maintaining a balanced diet and if you make it possible a number of problems would automatically be resolved. Particularly, the corporate people and the cine artistes for increasing the span of their attractions are found crazy and follow dieting or restrict themselves to the diet schedule for losing their weight which ultimately affect their body and make the ways for the development of numerous health problems. You should not forget that a healthy balanced diet leads to a slimmer and healthier body. We need to strengthen our realisation that food is our medicine which would help us in maintaining a healthy lifestyle.

Diet for Diseases: Food we eat are the strong force responsible for the health conditions. The food we eat are also responsible for the diseases we have or we nurture. Conversely, we find food also helping us in resolving the health problem. We can adopt food both as preventive and curative measures. This focuses our attention on nutritious diet with an adequate amount of high fibre foods. It is simplest to draw a balanced diet chart which may be helpful to us while keeping a track of nutritional diet requirements. A personalised diet plan is an answer to the food-prone problems for which we can also take help of dieticians.

Heart Diseases: We need to develop our awareness that coronary heart diseases, a very common health problem is caused or aggravated by the food we eat. Diet containing unhealthy fats need to be removed from our diet chart and in addition fatty and fried foods are required to be restricted for preventing heart diseases. For the people having heart problem, a balanced diet chart provides to the body an adequate amount of fibre foods. Raw fruits and vegetables are found rich in fibre.

Diabetes: A diet plan containing high-fibre and low-fat acts like an effective prescription specially for the people found to be diabetic. They are required to take a minimum amount of saturated fats. This focuses our attention on a Vegan diet or say vegetarian diet which could be very effective in resolving the problem.

Anaemia: Nutritional deficiency results into the problem of anaemia and it is found most commonly associated with low-iron diet. In this case, it is advisable to take foods found to be rich in iron such as green leafy vegetables.

The above mentioned diseases can be prevented if we are sincere to the foods that we eat. In addition, the cases related to high cholesterol, high blood pressure, gout and even cancer are affected by the diet taken by us. This focuses on adopting the diet plans which may be helpful in resolving the problems such as Alkaline Diet Plan, the Low Glycemia Index Diet Plan and the DASH Diet plan. The specific conditions are to be studied before adopting a particular diet plan.

A 2009 study by the National Diabetes, Obesity and Cholesterol Foundation (N-DOC) found that 35.5% of children in the 14-18 age group mostly reading in private schools of repute and coming from affluent segment are overweight or obese. NDOC's study covered 20,537 school children in six cities and found 25.3% overweight and 8.6% obese in both private and government schools. This makes it clear that we find development of a pudgy generation addicted to empty calories. We also find increasing cases of nutritional transition specially in the urban India. It is meant that a wide variety of affordable convenience foods, high in fat and sugar are increasingly available and there is a perceptible decline in the consumption of traditional foods found low in fat, rich in fibre and micro nutrients. We cannot deny that the coming and existing generation is moving to a sedentary lifestyle and the results are very alarming. We find creation of a Pudgy Young India. The big fat problem is found at a critical juncture. We Indian have a poor metabolic rate. It is to be made clear that high metabolic rate provides an opportunity to burn the undersigned or extra calories and therefore find less accumulation of calories and the piling up of extra calories around the waist is not found. But when the metabolic rate is low, we find less burning and therefore high accumulation. The metabolic rate is found associated without lifestyle. When we keep ourselves engaged in physical exercises and work, the possibility of burning extra calories is high. The increased problem of obesity is due mainly to the lifestyles we are promoting where sitting for more and more hours becomes a professional compulsion. The present is problematic but the future is alarming. Of course, we find facts in favour of a win-win situation and a tom-tom India due to our demographic dividend that more than a third of our population is below 18. But other side of the coin presents a very gloomy picture when we find that a significant proportion of the budding generation may face the problem of obese, particularly when they will enter their middle age.

The corporate men and women of even the present generation have been found tempted to the sedentary lifestyle. Of course, this is due to the organisational requirements, and professional compulsion but at this stage if we avoid and delay physical exercises for burning the extra calories; our task would be much more complicated. It is not only significant that we get calories. It is much more significant that we are very much careful to the burning of extra calories. We do not find wisdom in creating a condition to be prone to the serious health problem. Dr. Priyali Shah of NDOC says the adolescent waistline is expanding across urban India which may be considered as a snow-balling crisis. It is high time that we realise the instrumentality of traditional foods found low in fat, rich in fibre and micro nutrients. Corporate culture has injected new life to urbanisation which has been responsible for the emergence of a new lifestyle and increasing pudginess is the by-product of new urban living conditions.

A change in the lifestyle is imperative without which the demographic dividend would not be socially and nationally productive.

◈ Foods: Making a Balanced Diet

We cannot negate the instrumentality of food in the existence and development of our body. In a true sense, we consider food as chief of the essential materials which the body needs for its well-being. The essential materials required by body are nutrients. At all the stages or life, we need quality food for satisfactory growth during infancy, childhood, adolescence and adulthood. Wholesome food in adequate quantities is no less important for pregnant and nursing women who undergo a severe nutritional stress. To get more from our body, it is pertinent that we have a diet schedule which supplies all the required nutrients necessary for the growth and development of the body. It is in this context that we talk about a balanced diet. It is our responsibility that we make available to cur body a variety of foodstuff in appropriate quantities. This focuses our attention en the properties or different food stuff in the mixed diet chart.

BALANCED DIET

Food Group	Food Stuff	Amount per day (gm)
I	Rice, Wheat and Millets. Oil, ghee, butter, etc. Sugar & Jaggery	350 35 40
II	Milk, Curds, etc. Pulses, dried beans, nuts Meat, Fish, Egg	225 45 60
III	Fruits Green leafy Vegetables Other Vegetables	30 150 125

Fig. 2.4: Quantity of food varies in the face of age and the type of work

◈ The Nutrients

The supply of nutrients to our body is significant which is found in different forms such as Protein, Fat, Carbohydrates, Vitamins and Minerals and Water.

Proteins: We find proteins as the chief substances of the cells of body responsible for the formation of different constituents of muscles and other tissues and vital fluids like blood.

Fat: It is an important ingredient found in diet which is a concentrated source of energy and supplies per unit weight more than double the energy furnished either by protein or by carbohydrates. The vegetable oils provide essential fatty acids, linoleic and archidenic acids to the body.

Carbohydrates: We find carbohydrates including every kind of starch and sugar; active in the formation of the main source of energy. The grain foods are largely composed of starch and foodstuffs like sugarcane and glucose are pure carbohydrates.

Vitamins and Minerals: We find them comprising micro nutrients something different to proteins, fats and carbohydrates which we call macro nutrients. The vitamins can be fat-soluble and water-soluble. The vitamins A, D, E, K are fat soluble whereas Vitamins C and B are water-soluble. In the metabolism, we find vitamins as necessary auxiliaries which combine with specific proteins. They are found involved in the mechanism which releases energy, carbon dioxide and water as the end product of metabolism.

◈ Food Triangle

In the food triangle, we find everything required by our body. The above mentioned food triangle throws light on the mix that we need to follow to have a healthy body. The first combination is found of cereals such as Rice, Idly, Poori, Bread, Yoghurt out of which we can

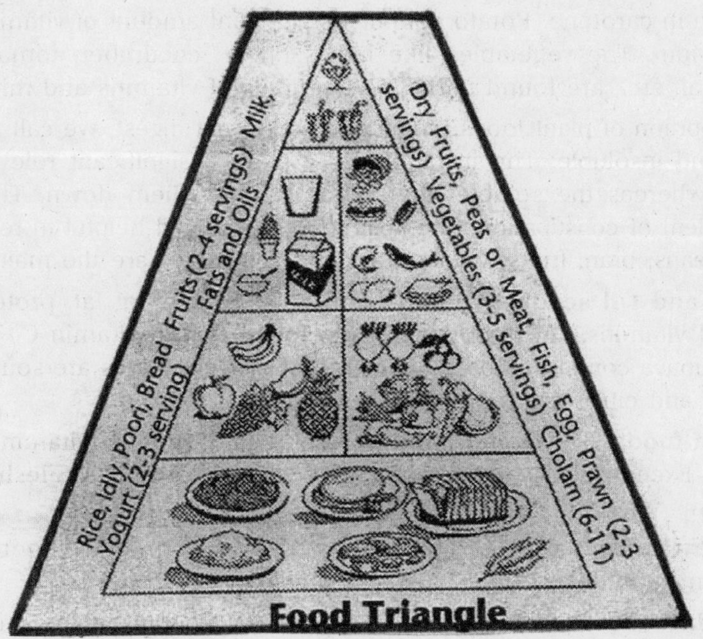

Fig. 2.5

serve two or three. The second combination that we find of fruits and milk and out of which two to four, we can serve. The third combination we find of dry fruits, peas or meat, egg, prawn and out of which two to three, we can serve. The fourth combination is of vegetables and out of which three to five, we can serve. The motive is to provide to our body a balanced diet which contains everything that we need. Since we get all the nutrients necessary for the growth and development of our body, it is possible for us to maintain a sound physique.

During the yester decades, we have witnessed a significant change in our lifestyles which has been found impacting our food habits. The changes are faster now and we are not sure that even in the days to come there will be a fall in its speed and behaviour. The "fast food" or "junk food" has been found harming the present and budding or upcoming generations. In this context, it is also right to say that directly or indirectly, it is due to the domination of material culture on the economic systems. The corporate sector is now turning into the corporate culture which has been sizably impacting our lifestyles vis-à-vis the food habits.

◈ The Key Indian Food Items

Cereals: The cereals like rice, wheat and millets, ragi, cholam and bajra form the main food in India. We find cereals rich in carbohydrates. They generally contain 6 to 12% protein. The proteins found from the cereals are found deficient in lysine except rice which is found richer in lysine. Most cereal grains are found poor in mineral content, except ragi which is rich in minerals.

Pulses: We find pulses or legumes rich in protein. Of course, we find pulses of low biological value because of some deficiency but we find them rich in lysine. The pulses are not rich sources of minerals but rich in B-vitamins.

Vegetables: Most of the leafy vegetables are found rich sources of calcium, iron, carotene, vitamin C and folic acid. The roots and tubers are found rich in carbohydrates. But roots like carrot are also rich in carotene. Potato contains significant amount of vitamin C and tapioca also contains calcium. The vegetables like lady's finger, cucumber, tomato, bitter gourd, snake gourd, brinjal, etc., are found fairly good sources of vitamins and minerals.

Fiber: That portion of plant foods which bodies, do not digest, we call them fiber which may be soluble and insoluble. The insoluble fiber plays a significant role in activating the digestive system whereas the soluble fiber tends to slow them down. The fiber helps in removing the problem of constipation. The soluble fiber is found helpful in reducing the blood cholesterol. The beans, bran, fruits, whole grain and vegetables are the main source of fiber.

Nuts, Fruits and Oil seeds: We find them good sources of fat, protein and minerals are fair sources of vitamins. Fruits in general are found rich in vitamin C. The yellow fruits like mango and papaya contain carotene and dried fruits like dates are sources of iron. The gooseberry, guava and citrus are found rich in vitamin C.

Fish and Sea foods: These are found rich sources of protein, vitamin B and minerals, specially calcium. Except liver, we find them deficient in vitamin A. Fleshy foods are rich sources of protein.

Egg: Egg is a rich source of all nutrients except vitamin C. The protein value of egg is found of high magnitude.

Milk and Milk Products: Milk is found to be an ideal food for infants and young children and a good supplementary food for all. It contains all vital nutrients except vitamin C and iron.

In addition to the foods outlined above, we find even others in these categories and it is upon us to identify the properties and to make a diet chart considerably supplementing to our cells. Our dietary chart should have a correlation with our energy requirements which depend on age, gender, profession and our physical conditions. We need calories which in a true sense are food energy. While designing a diet sheet, we need to consider a number of factors which may confuse an individual and therefore, it is safe to take the help of dietician.

◈ About Foods, many things you need to think off

Prevention is better than cure. A majority of us are unaware of the fact that foods can be helpful in preventing a number of diseases which we invite due to our wrong food habits. We find people spending their health for gaining wealth and again spending their wealth for regaining health. Prevention is the key to good health which we need to practise. What food is very important and what make them good to eat? We lack awareness. We need to know about the nutrients and to develop a mix found to be effective in keeping us fit. To get a healthier diet, it is pertinent that we eat foods found to be rich in omega fatty acid, vitamins and fiber. Outlined below, we find some of the healthy foods to eat everyday.

Canned Tuna: Canned tuna is packed of so many proteins but with low fatty content. A tuna is found in the category of healthy foods in which we do not find concentration of an omega fatty acid just like in fresh tuna.

Any of Whole Wheat's: You should not forget that a carbohydrate of whole wheat keeps the level of insulin stable instead of starchy white carbohydrates. The level of insulin determines how foods are processed to fatty cells. Shifting from white bread to a wheat type of bread makes, a big difference.

The Plant Oil: The plant oil is found great in Omega 3 and Omega 6 fatty acid. The different types of oil are the safflower oil, the soyabean oil the flax seed oil, the sesame oil, the pumpkin seed oil.

Fresh Veggies and Fruits: It is essential that we assign due weightage to the veggies and fruits. Fresh fruits and fresh veggies need priority instead of frozen because we find them containing lots of nutrients and even much more tasty. Each and everyday, we need fruits and veggies. The eating of vegetables and fruits improves the digestive activities and at the same time also reduce the risk of stroke or related conditions such as cancer, lower pressure of blood and a lot more. It may also be found effective in improving the vision.

Fig. 2.6: Spend on Foodcare on Medicare

Herbs and Spices: The herbs and spices are found important for our health because it provides to us an opportunity of becoming creative on foods. Of course, it is pertinent that you are sincere to have healthy food but it is not meant that you eat boring. The herbs and spices have zero calories but add flavours to our foods to change the taste. There is no doubt in it that we find some of the negative effects of spices in particular but whatsoever the positive effects we find have an edge over the negative provided we maintain a balance.

All of us should assign due weightage to the consideration that healthy meals help protect our family from major health problems and besides, we also find meals for enjoying and celebrating.

From the early morning to the night when we go to our bed for sleeping, a schedule in the face of our professional requirements vis-à-vis the situational compulsions need priority attention of each one of us to provide to our body much more vigour. Since we find the people serving the corporate sector over-pressed, it is imperative that whatsoever the diet schedule they adopt do not stand as a barrier while performing and discharging their assigned responsibilities.

From the facts narrated earlier, it is almost clear that an optimal mix of different food groups is essential. Actually, we need to strengthen our realisation that we eat for our cells. If they are not getting the required nutrients, the sub-systems would adversely be affected which would make an invasion on the strength of our body. Since we find body and mind closely linked, the physical deficiency may question the mental efficiency resulting into irritation, agitation, tension and depression. Thus, we find management of diet not only a source of enjoying the pleasure but even a compulsion to make our body and mind much more active. Carefully and scientifically designed diet schedule is a must.

What to eat and what not to eat; when to eat and how much to eat are considered essential to have a sound body and a sound mind. The increasing temptation for junk foods and fast foods, especially amongst the corporate people cannot be allowed to continue if we are really interested in getting the best from our body and mind. If we spend on healthcare, we save on medicare. Let your food habits act as a preventive force to regulate and control the food-prone diseases. This necessitates a high degree of awareness and for that we remain to be much more conscious. On the one hand, we are supposed to be responsible for a poor knowledge bank regarding the diet management while on the other hand, we also make organisation responsible for its failure in the sensitisation process. We provide to them a routine and a target which is required to be achieved within a time frame but we hardly ensure that they are physically and mentally capable of responding to our directives and guidelines. Ignoring diet is making our cells unproductive and in the long run damaging the subsystems of our body vis-à-vis banning the vital organs.

The earlier outlined facts make it clear that if we take care of ourselves, we feel better. The important aspects in the very context are eating healthy foods and avoiding junk foods. We have to make it sure that vegetables and fruits, whole grain foods like bread, pasta, cereal and rice and protein foods like chicken, fish, cheese, cottage cheese and yogurt get due place in our diet chart. A diet-chart with the help of dietician would benefit you. Besides, it is also essential that you move your body to feel better and improve your self-esteem. You also need to arrange a time everyday or as often as possible for some exercises. You can run, ride a bicycle, play a sport and climb up and down stairs several times. The focus is on physical labour which corporate people cannot do. Hence, the solutions are walking and exercise to be effective in the process of optimising the sources.

◈ Wise Regulation of Food

We cannot negate that the food that we eat has a telling impact on our body, mind and emotions. This necessitates that we are aware of some of the aspects which regulate our food habits.

Food is for Cells: At the outset, we need to strengthen this realisation that food is for cells not for me. This will considerably help us in regulating our diet. There are 10-50 trillion cells in the human body. Whatsoever the nutrients that we get from food are for the cells. This will help us in making right diet decisions.

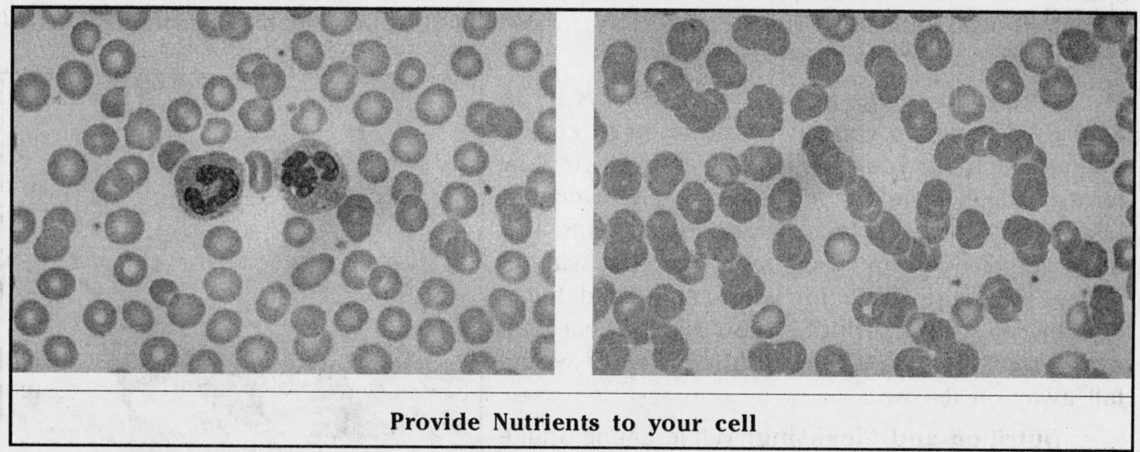

Provide Nutrients to your cell

Thought pattern guides us: When I want to eat something, it is not I but the thought pattern or the desire itself. Our all the inner wants are influenced by the thought pattern or desire. In a true sense, we find desire as a motivator. Thus, the two companion principles guide us such as the food is for the cells and the thought pattern that is expressed desire for consumption. It is the individual thought pattern itself that guides us.

We starve for nutrients: We are aware that food is for cells and if we do not eat the foods having nutrients, we starve. It is due to the fact that cells do not get the required nutrients. Of course, we eat more and more but the nutrients requirements remain insufficient. The nutritionally deficient foods would, no doubt, increase our weight but we would starve. This necessitates healthy eating or say eating foods found rich in nutrients. When our cells get proper nutrients, we feel ourselves satisfied and we find less desire for eating.

We eat food, not ingredients: Actually, we do not eat the ingredients such as carbohydrates, proteins, fiber, vitamins and minerals, etc., rather than what we do eat is food. The moment we start thinking that what we do eat is food all the confusions that we nurture in our minds disappear. Of course, we need to develop our awareness of the ingredients but in addition, we also need to think of the food itself. We need to educate and train our mind that we need to eat fresh vegetables. If we eat vegetables it is quite natural that we get all the nutrients that we find in the vegetables.

What to eat? We are supposed to eat a nice mixture of fresh vegetables, a variety of beans and whole grains, such as brown rice along with some fruits and cultivating a habit to eat in the same fashion.

Vegetables: A mixture of green, yellow and other vegetables makes available to us a lot of nutrients. We can formulate a mix in tune with our requirements.

Beans/legumes: We find beans full of nutrients and a lot of fiber. This activates the digestion process. Besides, we also find them an excellent source of protein.

Brown rice or equivalent: Whole grains such as brown rice or basmati rice provide vitamins, minerals and fiber.

Seasoning: May be that you are not enjoying your foods and getting bored by eating the same everyday. You can make a choice for seasoning packages or a combination of spices. The creative mixing would make your foods much more tasty besides the nutrients would also be available. The healthy core foods would neutralise the harmful effects of spices that you eat in huge quantity.

Add good things in your diet: Always try to add good things in your diet. You need to ensure that certain foods you eat each day and you virtually form a habit. Be sure that you eat vegetables everyday. Like this fresh fruits, beans and whole grains also need due place in your food items everyday without exception. Make place for what to do and bid a goodbye to what not to do. Know what to eat then even you have taken the subtractive stuff would fall away on its own.

Mindful eating increases the satiety value

Nutrition and Cleansing: While eating, make it sure that your food choices provide full nutrition and in addition, they also facilitate cleansing. Actually, nutrition and cleansing work together. Avoid eating foods hard to digest and which blocks cleansing and dextofying.

Eat the good food first: You need to start the day with a rich breakfast. First have the better food. Breakfast like a prince, lunch like a king and dinner like a pauper. In a true sense, we need to educate our mind to eat the good food first. Start the day with healthy food and have healthy snacks early.

Useful or not Useful: Make use of your wisdom and ensure that your foods are useful to your body. Let the inner wisdom guide your preferences, you will get the answer. Eat useful and avoid eating not useful.

Plenty of Potable Water: You are required to drink plenty of safe drinking water. Morning water practice is essential which will help you in cleaning the bowels. Avoid drinking water just after the meal which is against the established law of nature. At least after twenty minutes of eating, you should drink proper amount of water.

The facts outlined above provide to you some guidelines. Since we find food very much important to the sound management of our body, it is imperative that we provide due attention to the diet schedule to be followed by us. A transcendental priority to foodcare is essential to minimise the risk of medicare. If we honestly honour the wise regulation of food, the body is sound which makes ways for the soundness of mind and emotions. There are so many things to think off. In the plain words, we need to observe that foods containing large amount of nutrients are healthy and therefore we need to rank them at the top whereas the foods containing low degree of nutrients need to be ranked at the bottom. Almost all the studies observe that foods containing omega fatty acid, vitamins and fiber are healthier and therefore it should be our first choice.

The words of wisdom expressed by Reb Materi need due attention. "So many people spend their health gaining wealth and then have to spend their wealth to regain their health. "We find wisdom in spending foodcare and saving on medicare. Each one of us bear the responsibility of managing the body which cannot be possible unless we manage our diet, the corporate people are found over pressed. They do not get time even for eating. A majority of them frequently eat junk food or fast food. They prefer to eat questionable snacks. One after another they eat too much but are found nutritionally deficient. Eating with a sense is significant to all the segments of both the genders to keep them fit.

◈ Awareness of Vaccination and Immunisation

With the increasing heat of environmental pollution, we find much more scope for the development of a number of diseases. Polluted air, contaminated water, ecologically-unfriendly atmosphere and our contracting resistance power sizably aggravate the magnitude of problem. If we are sensitive to the preventive devices, we succeed in regulating the possibilities of a number of health hazards. It is in this context that we talk about vaccination and immunisation. Vaccination is a treatment with the help of a vaccine in which a substance is injected into the body to cause it to produce antibodies for providing immunity against a disease. The educated and conscious society are found much more sensitive to the vaccination culture and therefore, they succeed in controlling a number of health hazards which in the developing countries like ours create plethora of problems. Both for the present and coming generations, it is pertinent that vaccination culture gains a rapid momentum which is not to be possible unless the government and NGOs, the hospitals and healthcare centres and even the business organisations come forward to make an assault on the emerging problem. Sensitisation for vaccination needs to be adopted as a mission so that we succeed in eradicating the health problems.

In a true sense, we need a revolution on the vaccinology front. A reduction in infant mortality rate is the result of child immunisation. The Universal Immunisation Programme aims at a healthier 21st Century. An intensive use of polio vaccine has led to the elimination of polio in most of the countries. Another important disease in the very context is leprosy. Cholera is still around and often appears as an epidemic. The old cholera vaccine is no longer used because it gives only a short duration immunity and had many side-effects. Tuberculosis is a major disease in India. Of course, we have Vaccine like BCG in the immunisation programme but it is not found effective against pulmonary tuberculosis. Typhoid is another problem and an oral vaccine developed in Switzerland is available in the market.

The very sense in promoting immunisation programme is to minimise the intensity of problem due to some vulnerable diseases and till now, we have not been successful in eradicating diseases like polio, cholera, typhoid, tuberculosis which very often trap us and we find loss of lives even due to these diseases. The most important task before the government and healthcare centres is to develop mass awareness. The welfare agencies and NGOs involved in the process have to activate the sensitisation process. What to talk of others when we find even Malaria yet to be eradicated.

The vaccination and immunisation thus need priority attention specially in the rural India where intensity of problem is high but the level of sensitivity is very low. We need to care our children vis-à-vis we need to protect ourselves. If we talk about healthy India, it is of paramount importance that we promote vaccination considered to be the most cost-effective agent for control of communicable diseases in particular.

◈ Our Sensitivity to Diseases

Awareness makes the ways for low diseases profile. Insensitivity paves avenues for a number of food-prone, water-prone and communicable diseases which can easily be regulated and prevented just by managing our lifestyles. We find disease a condition which impairs the proper functioning of our body. The human beings are supposed to be much more conscious and manage their lifestyles and behavioural patterns in such a fashion that avenues for a number of diseases are sealed. If we are sincere to the food items that we eat, quality of water that we drink, remain sensitive to the behaviour responsible for infectious and communicable diseases and food and water-borne diseases; the task of minimising the intensity of problem is considerably simplified. Each one of us are responsible for something wrong in the body and this focuses our attention on developing sensitivity. Of course, the task of detection is on the shoulders of doctors but our awareness may be much more effective in resolving the alarming problem. Every disease has a cause which doctors detect but our task is to seal doors for the development of such cause which is possible by managing our lifestyles.

Communicable or Infectious: We find communicable diseases from one person to another such as by means of airborne droplets from a cough or sneeze. The organics like viruses, bacteria, fungi and worms produce infectious diseases. We also find cases of silent transmission when the infected person is found unaware of the problem. We need much more precautions to regulate their transmission and to take help of doctors.

Non-infectious or Non-communicable: The non-infectious diseases are caused by multifunction of the body. Erratic growth of cell, degeneration of tissues or organs and faulty blood formation and flow are the key reasons responsible for non-communicable diseases. Besides, the disturbances found in the urinary and reproductive system, stomach and intestine, diet deficiencies, lapses in the body's power of resistance and poorly operating nervous system are also responsible for the non-communicable diseases.

Diseases due to deficiency: The deficiency found in the diet or nutritional deficiency is also responsible for diseases and in that case, it is significant that we ensure the supply of missing nutrients. The deficiency of protein, mineral, vitamins make the ways for the development of a number of diseases.

Degenerative diseases: Due to malfunctioning of some organ or organ system, we find degenerative diseases such as heart attack, diabetes and arthritis.

Viral diseases: The diseases caused by virus are known as viral diseases such as, AIDS, BIV, Chicken Pox, Measles, German Measles, Rabies.

Eye Diseases: Since we find it a vital organ, it is pertinent that we are aware of cataract, glaucoma, hypermetropia, strabismus and trachoma.

In cataract, the normal vision is hampered which may also cause to blindness. For treatment, lens is removed and artificial lens is used. In Glaucoma, we find an increase in pressure or tension which may also result into blindness. In Hypermetropia, the distant objects can be seen clearly but the near objects cannot be seen clearly. This is due to formation of image behind the retina. The use of Bifocal lens is found useful. In Satrabisrmus, the eye ball turns to any of the side. In Trachoma, we find redness in the eye and sensation for foreign body in eye.

Aizhelmer's disease: It is a progressive degenerative disease of the brain in which brain cells die and are not replaced which results into impaired memory, thinking and behaviour. It strikes equally among both the genders of all races. Eventually, the patients become totally incapable of caring for themselves.

By regulating diet and balancing lifestyles, it is possible for us to keep our body sound which may also increase our resistance power. As and when you have some health problem, it is safer to go through medical treatment for having a right diagnosis and proper treatment. During the yesteryears, we have witnessed a significant increase in the medicare services. You should be aware of the fact that every disease displays a cycle of onset, or beginning, course or time span of affliction and end when it disappears or it partially disables or kills its victim. The early treatment provides you relief when the delayed treatment complicates your problem.

In this context, you also need to know that most of the diseases take their origin in overeating, sexual excess and outbursts of anger and hatred. This makes it essential that you need to keep yourself cool and calm at all times. Of course, this has a far reaching impact on your body because you will have wonderful health, vigour and vitality. The cells and tissues of your body would function in a right way. Actually, the cells and tissues are filled with morbid or say poisonous material, when one loses his/her temper. This may also result in various kinds of diseases. Excessive loss of the seminal energy may result in nervous diseases.

In the prevailing conditions, we need to develop the power of endurance and resistance. We need to strengthen our body and mind. We need to take plenty of open air exercises, substantial nutritious food, plenty of rest, mental and physical recreation and adopt a well-regulated life. We need to assign due weightage to personal hygiene. We need to be moderate in food, drink and enjoyments. We need to strengthen this realisation that nothing like happiness. Let all micro organs of your body die and this is possible when your vitality, vigour and strength are at a flood tide. This necessitates regulating your diet, life-styles and behaviour. You can do it when you are well known with the positive and negative conditions affecting your body.

◈ Potable Water

We find water a vital constituent of diet. Altogether 70% of the weight of our body is contained by water. The cells contain almost two-third of the total water contained by our body, *i.e.,* 45 litres. Three litres are in the plasma of the blood where the suspended cells make a total volume of blood up to 5 litres. The remaining 12 litres fill the space between groups of cells. Water is absolutely necessary for digestion and absorption of the foods taken by us. It is the great solvent and neutraliser in the body. We find it a substance in which bodily chemical reactions take place. It is carrier for all nutrients and body substances. It regulates the temperature of our body and keeps skin fresh and works as a stimulating agent in the body that removes the waste material in different forms such as tear, perspiration, urine and faeces. In a true sense, the watery substances act as lubricants in the body specially the joints. The body obtains water mainly from the fluids we drink, from the solids we eat and also from the oxidation of energy foods. Fats and carbohydrates are oxidised in the body to carbon dioxide and water.

Keeping in view the importance of water for our body, it is pertinent that we drink safe water or potable water but on account of increasing contamination of water, it is becoming much more difficult to have the potable water in adequate quantity. This makes it essential that we are very particular to the availability of safe drinking water to our body. There are different devices to clean the polluted water and if we cannot afford the bottled mineral water, we should adopt the methods to clean it. The most important, thing that we find here is initiating the disinfection process. The bleaching powder or lime is found helpful in the disinfection process. Even through boiling and filtering the water, it is possible to get the safe drinking water.

Adequacy of water is also an important factor to be considered by all of us which we generally fail to mind. A gap between demand and supply aggravates the magnitude of problem particularly in the urban areas of the country. This necessitates due attention of all of us so that we succeed in bridging the qualitative as well as the qualitative gap. A majority of us lack awareness that contaminated water is to harm them in different ways. The germs like bacteria, viruses protozoa need to be removed.

WTO data confirm that 21% of all communicable diseases in India are water-borne. The magnitude of problem is found at its peak because all the 14 major rivers and tourist-generating lakes are found contaminated to the point of no return. Even the ground water is now not safe and in most of the cases the contamination has reached to a critical stage. Almost all surface water is found unfit for human consumption and much more sensitive to water-borne diseases. It is estimated that 30.5 million lives are lost every year due to poor water quality, sanitation and hygiene. "Potable water for all" should not be perceived as a programme but in a true sense as a mission that necessitates a new vision. This would help us in making an assault on the water-borne diseases.

Water is a vital constituent of diet. An average man in the Indian condition consumes much less than the required quantity and this invites numerous health problems. Since we find water a great solvent and neutraliser in the body, its inadequacy results into major health problems. Besides, it is also to be ensured that we are very particular in maintaining quality of water that we drink. Since we find water acting as the carrier or transporting medium for all nutrients and body substances, instrumental in regulating the temperature of our body and very much active in improving the digestive system because it acts as a purifying agent, it is imperative that we do not drink water found contaminated, polluted and carrying worms. The increasing heat of industrialisation has been found aggravating the intensity of water pollution as a good number of industries throw polluted water into rivers and seas without making any treatment. In addition, the lifestyles adopted by us has also been fuelling the contamination problem because detergents cakes and powders and even soaps, found in common use, mix up with water and get it polluted.

The most important thing to resolve the problem is to sensitise the masses. We are not sincere to the management of safe drinking water and do not follow the precautions. The agencies or government departments responsible for supplying the safe drinking water are found insensitive to the managerial problem. The sewerage and drains are found mismanaged. The tanks and supplying pipes are never cleaned. Hence, the only remedy is to be careful on an individual basis and to adopt the practices to ensure quality. The social advertising, may be instrumental in the sensitisation process. Ensuring the supply of safe drinking water is not a programme rather than a mission. Hence, the attitudinal transformation becomes a must.

Our prime theme is sound management of body. We have talked about different dimensions of food management which can keep us healthy. But unless we are sincere to the adequate quantity of quality water, our body cannot remain healthy. We should not forget that it is to affect our survival because we can live without food but not without water. Its inadequacy is to affect our efficiency and its absence is to cause our lives.

Hence drink a proper amount of water. To take two full glasses (total of about 1 litre or 1 quart) of room temperature water in the early morning is very useful. If you are not accustomed to this, it might take a few days to get used to. Just drink down the water somewhat quickly, though not causing bloating. You should not forget that morning water practice will clear out some of the toxins in the systems, trigger peristalsis, movement of muscular and clearing the bowels. After some gap, you should take first food of the day. It is also to be ensured that you do not take water just after meal but after a gap of twenty minutes or more. If you feel flow of urine slow, it is due to inadequacy of water. Hence, you need to realise the importance of water and to drink sufficient potable water which keeps you fit and assists your subsystems to function in a right fashion.

In the face of paramount importance of potable water for the survival and existence of almost all the living beings, it is quite natural that quality and availability factors assume a place of outstanding significance. People living in rural or urban areas witness a big gap between demand and supply of potable water and resulting from which we find a significant increase in the water-prone diseases. We need to clean the water tank regularly, medicate water as and when the circumstances necessitate so and make the supply system one hundred percent leak-proof. A minor mistake at one stage complicates the entire process. Hence, it is a crying need of the hour that governmental agencies in particular are sincere to the problem and bring managerial reforms to resolve them. To the extent it is possible, we need to minimise our dependence on the ground water specially to protect the interests of coming generations. The concerned agencies need to ensure Zero incidence of Guinea worm disease. Besides, they also bear the responsibility of finding solutions for other bacteriological and chemical problems such as fluorides and salinity and iron in water sources.

An important problem complicating our task specially in the urban areas is poor management of drains and lack of underground sewerage system. A number of functional responsibilities need due attention of water supplying agencies such as removing the leakages, replacing the old and depleted pipes and technologies and concreting of the spots, specially in the small

Jogging keeps you fit

towns and cities where sewerage systems are almost all dismal. Sewerage treatment facilities and discharge of filtered water by the concerned industries into rivers or seas would be effective in minimising the problem of water contamination. Of course, we also need to think in favour of promoting capital intensive projects for collecting and cleaning the water. Using the rain water assumes a place of outstanding importance. We need to preserve rain water in a scientific way. The rivers, ponds, lakes may also add to the supply side.

It is amazing that at least 31 million lives are lost every year due to poor water quality, sanitation and hygiene. WHO data confirm that 21 per cent of all communicable diseases in India are water-borne. All the 14 big rivers of the country are heavily polluted to the point of no return. Actually, our efforts for cleaning the water of rivers have been turning into a fiasco. This makes it essential that we realise gravity of the problem and ensure supply of adequate potable water to all the segments of society because it is not possible for a majority of the population of the country to afford bottled mineral water. On the other hand, it is also essential that we regulate misuse of water.

◈ Walk and Exercise

When we move at a fairly slow pace using our legs, we call it walk. We consider "Exercise" an activity requiring physical effort carried out for the sake of health and fitness. Both the dimensions play an effective role for the sound management of our body. Particularly for those persons who have no option but to adopt a lifestyle in which a continuous or a regular sitting becomes a must, it is imperative that the concerned people engage themselves in walking and physical exercises in order to keep themselves fit. For walking, we find period before sunrise much more suitable because this provides you an opportunity to get fresh air. Though there is nothing wrong in evening walking. Medically or spiritually, walking

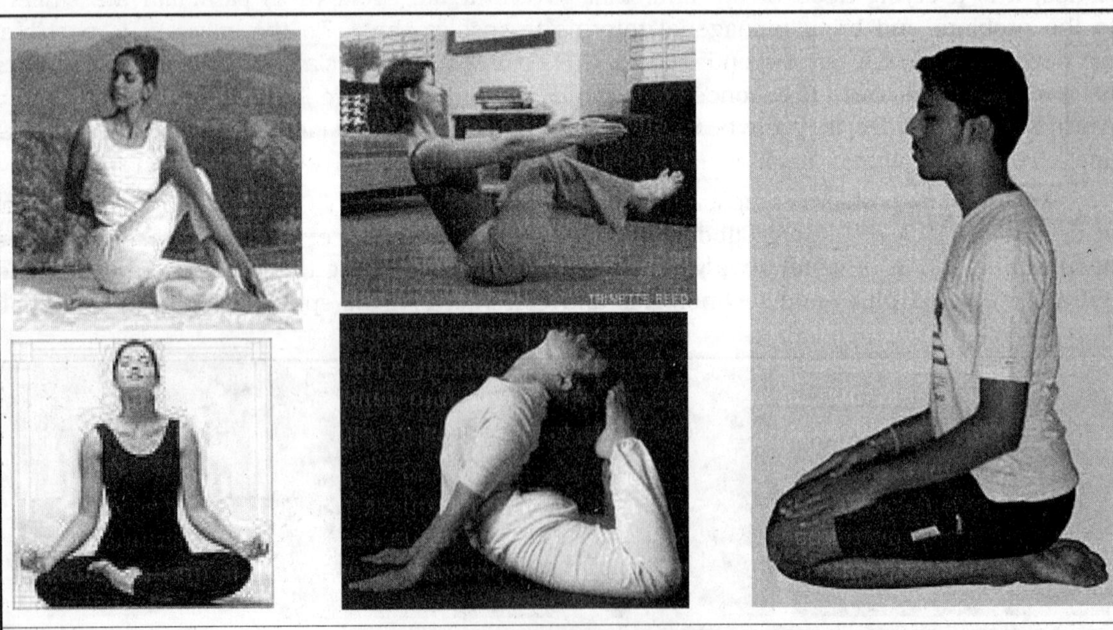

Exercise protects your Body, Mind and Nerves

in morning has an edge and therefore we should walk both in morning and evening which would keep our systems active vis-à-vis would fresh our mind. The increasing heat of atmospheric and environment pollution in a true sense make it a compulsion for the sound management of our body and mind. The duration of walking may be from half an hour to full one hour which keeps all the subsystems active and allows the organs of our body to act and move in the right directions.

For getting the best from our system and subsystems, it is essential that we keep on moving the practices of injecting additional strength to our body, mind and nerves. Taking plenty of open-air exercises helps us in the process and keep us fit. We need to identify an open place for walking where we get fresh air and peaceful environment. It is also significant to perceive that functioning of mind and body is found interrelated and therefore if we find something wrong with our mind, its direct impact on our body cannot be denied. The fresh and peaceful environment or ambience or eco-friendly place, help us in keeping our mind fresh in which right thoughts can be nurtured. We cannot negate that right thoughts and feelings also become instrumental in injecting new life and strength to the organs of our body. The nervous system digestive system and circulatory system function in a right way, if we activate them and walking helps us in this direction.

We cannot deny that exercise is probably the most important tip to stay fit and healthy. Doing exercise on a regular basis can keep you stay healthy and strong and in addition would also keep many health problems at bay. In this context, we should indulge in strength building exercises or cardiovascular exercises to stay fit and maintain a good body shape. To be more specific when we talk about a corporate professional, it appears to be an essential criterion. Maintaining a balanced healthy weight is also very significant to stay fit and healthy. Meditation may also be effective in the very context which would help us stay healthy and relaxed. Believe it or not, but it is right that if we meditate for half an hour, we are able to engage ourselves with peace and spiritual strength in the battle of life at least for one week through the force of meditation. Besides, you will have a magnetic and charming personality, sweet voice, powerful, presentation, lustrous eyes, strong healthy body, etiquette and manners, virtuous qualities and what not.

Everyone wants to have a beautiful figure and a strong body. This draws our attention not only on the balanced diet but in addition also on a regular exercise schedule. Staying fit, slim and trim is significantly needed in the corporate world and you have to make it sure that how and in what way, it is to be possible. You are supposed to know the secrets of looking young, active and healthy. In this context, proper and balanced diet is considered as a key to a healthy and fit body. But, we cannot underestimate the role of walk, exercise and yoga. This will help you even in balancing your weight. The corporate people are not required to gain weight which makes their figure disproportionate. Believe it or not but in today's corporate world, your over weight may also be a consideration for your firing.

You may go for swimming which would help you in many ways. You may also go for cycling. You may even go for "samba" which is a Brazilian dance of African origin. These devices would considerably help you in balancing the weight and making your figure fit, slim and trim. Besides, an uphill nature of walk would also benefit you. Actually, the devices that we adopt for balancing our weight play an incremental role in improving our level of efficiency because we find ourselves in a position to perform albeit for long time. Research suggests that people who engage in personality — appropriate activities and stick with the activities for a long time, enjoy their workout more and ultimately have a greater overall fitness experience. You should not forget that if you keep on practising these devices, even Life Time Fitness cannot be difficult for you.

The upcoming or budding generations who are found very much tempted to the corporate culture need to consider fitness as a revolution. They need to switch to their fitness journey which would considerably help them in getting a position in the corporate world. They need to look beauty in managing their bodies and the rock star personality they get would make them much more hireable and promotable. Managing our weight and fitness thus prove to be an important consideration which focuses on different types of exercises and the balanced diet.

The facts outlined above make it clear that if you keep on moving the practices of regularly walking and continue with the exercises of different types, the task of having a rock star personality would not remain difficult. Hence fitness of body remains to be the most important dimension of the management of body. Your figure significantly contributes to your personality. It is equally applicable for both the genders. All of us should accept the fact that in today's corporate world, it is also an important consideration for hiring or firing. The look culture is found more rampant and we also witness cases where an individual is fired because his belt buckle had shifted three notches too high. A landmark study from the Cornell University found that when a white female puts on an additional 64 pounds, her wages drop 9%. Conversely, we also hear cases when good-looking women manage a good position albeit over a more competent man. Walking and exercising help us in looking good.

Look smart and get hired. Believe it or not but in the today's world, your personality scores over any professional degree. Big bucks wait for people having a rock star personality.

◈ Sound Sleep for Sound Body

Day-by-day we are becoming much more susceptible to illness, depression and even injury. This problem is found not only in India but around the globe. If we start breaking the law of nature, we have to suffer. If we start flying without knowing the consequences, we are surely to be victimised. During the yester decades, a peculiar trend has developed. We are becoming sleep deficient. It has been found affecting our body and consequently, we have invited a number of health problems. Believe it or not, but the main reason for that is a disproportionate lifestyle considerably influenced by the material culture. Not getting enough sleep can cause all sorts of health and behavioural problems and it is against this background that we find a good number of youths irritated, agitated, tensed, stressed and depressed. Nurturing ambition is a good thing but violating the rule of nature is a dangerous thing. It is imperative that we sensitise the youths and the budding youth that if they keep on moving with this lifestyle; nobody will be potentially sound to protect them. It is midnight and you are working. You are on bed but with your laptop, cell-phone and again planning for the next morning. Too few zzz's can cause a myriad of problems which would harm us in different ways.

A recent study by the National Sleep Foundation in the US found that the average worker spends nine hours a day at the workplace, topped off by another several hours of work from home-decreasing total sleep time during the week. By 3 p.m., most workers hit an afternoon slump. Managing our time and changing our habits if delayed would invite serious health problems impacting body and mind. According to Dr. Mathew Edlund, author of "The Power of Rest", rest is as important as sleep and therefore people need to alternate physical activity with mental activity. Sometimes getting out of the office and working will restore you.

Our disrespect for sleep has been found developing and spreading around the globe. We can name it even a global epidemic because many of us have now forgotten the feelings of being rested and of course, they are aware of the fact that they are making preparations for the suicide of not only an individual but the entire generations. We find a number of factors responsible for the present condition but the most important reason is our increasing temptation to the new generation of information and communication technology which has made us sick. The researches reveal that 28% iPhone users check for Update Twitter before getting out of bed. Few Research found more than eight in 10 millennials sleep with a cell phone glowing by the bed, poised to despatch texts, phone call, e-mails and videos. We can easily realise its impact on our body and mind.

Because, we are not sincere to the lifestyles that we need; because, we find ourselves depending on fast and junk food and because, we do not sleep well for the duration of at least 8 hours in a day, it is likely to affect and even damage our digestive system followed by a number of health problems.

There is no doubt in it that quality of food and water, exercise and walking and aerobics sizably affect our body but failing the absence of a routined-sleeping and experiencing a stage of sleep deficit all our systems and sub-systems face a number of challenges and threats. We need consistency and continuity in the sleeping hours and time because the process of making up the sleep-deficit is found a time-taking process. The sleep disturbances of one night require so many nights for achieving a stage of normalcy.

Achieving a stage of soundness for body is urgently needed to increase the level of efficiency. Since a regular sleeping provides an opportunity to the different organs of the body to take rest, the process of rejuvenation gains a rapid momentum and we feel ourselves much more relaxed, fresh and energetic. We should be aware of the fact that sleeping is a state of rest in which the nervous system is inactive, the eyes are closed, the muscles are relaxed and the mind is unconscious. The relaxation of muscles and unconsciousness of mind act as a tonic for the body. Conversely, a disturbance of sleeping invites plethora of problems related to stress and disorders. We start feeling ourselves irritated, tensed and agitated which bring a drastic change in our attitudes and behaviour. The influences on body start influencing our mindset and outlook.

In the corporate world of today, it is imperative that we have a rock star personality and our different systems and sub-systems are properly charged and recharged to perform and deliver in a desired fashion. Sleeping is like a tonic which helps in injecting new life and strength to our body.

How to have a sound sleep, of course is a problem area. Because for sound sleep, it is pertinent that your mind is calm and cool and you are not stressed. You do not have any tension. But these things become difficult in this materialistic age where we have contracted avenues for sharing pains and sorrows due to the development of an abnormally structured micro family in which we find none to share. We generate ourselves and we have no option but to face the consequences. The intensity of problem is found reaching at a critical juncture due to the emergence of live-in relationships running into a live-in culture where you have a number of friends to share the happiness and benefits but none to share your personal pains and sorrows.

We are at a point of no return and therefore we have to find out the solutions. It is difficult for you to redesign your work schedule. It is not possible for you to keep yourself isolated. Willingly or unwillingly, you have to work hard to go with the wind. Hence, it is essential that you evince interest in spiritualism. As and when you get time, you should participate in the spiritual sessions. You should cultivate faculty of helping others. You have to make efforts to clean the stored or accumulated complexes. You have to regulate your behaviour of using the computer, lap-top, cell-phone, etc. These modifications would help you in keeping your mind calm and cool. Only then, it is possible for you to have a sound sleep.

In the face of facts outlined above, it is right to mention that not getting enough shut-eye can cause all sorts of health and behavioural problems and therefore particularly the corporate professionals who have been found ignoring the required duration of sleeping should be careful. You are not supposed to push your bed time back to fit in extra work because a time will come when you will find yourself helpless. When you promote a jump-start for the day, you also need to ensure that during night you get not less than eight hours of sleep. The main thing is combining your job requirements and your lifestyles. Your disrespect for sleep, emerging as a national epidemic may affect even the coming generations. You do not get time for your food. You do not get time for walk and exercise. You do not get time for laughter. You are interested in working more and earning more. You are tired at work. Your mind is exhausted. You are intelligent enough to diagnose the consequences. Inviting a stage of suicide cannot be considered to be your wisdom.

Gradually, you are found susceptible to illness, moodiness and depression. It can elevate your cortisol levels, which can put you a spare tyre around your waists, affect your skin and cause wrinkles. Not only this, a major problem to the appetite and the digestive system cannot be ruled out. Your muscles, different organs of body and more so your mind cannot deliver goods and you are sick. How to sleep better, it is your outlook. None to help you. A disciplined lifestyle is the only solution to bring things back on the rail.

- Regulate your behaviour.
- Mind your lifestyle.
- Eat a light dinner at least two hours before sleeping.
- Keep your laptop, smartphone and computer out of your bedroom.
- Cultivate the habit of laughtering.
- Try to release the stored complexes in your mind.
- Help others as much as you can.
- Go through meditation.
- Try to be submissive to your associates and friends.
- Avoid eating junk or fast food.
- Ensure eight hours of sleep.
- Participate in the spiritual sessions.
- Evince interests in developing family relationships.
- Drink plenty of quality water.
- Substitute your mental work with the physical work.
- Never invite a stage of sleep deficit.

- Entertain your mind.
- Get time for exercise and walk.
- Mind your to-do list.
- Strengthen this realisation that you cannot do everything.
- Pray almighty God before sleeping.
- Shut-eye and allow different organs of your body to take rest, the muscles to relax and mind to be unconscious.

◈ Top Priority for A Rock Star Personality

Change is a natural phenomenon. The cycle creates a condition in which we find ourselves helpless because we have no option but to adopt to practise and to make it possible. With the increasing domination of corporate sector, we find emergence of corporate culture with a new lifestyle and a new perception of life moving towards material culture. It is in this context that we find new cult of hiring czars, picking smart talent from college campuses at whopping salaries putting even products of leading B-Schools to shame. Getting more bucks even more than doctors and engineers is not possible if you have a rock star personality. You have a promising future and you can bag even a so-called C level post like a CEO.

A Rock Star Personality helps in getting more bucks

Who is high-flier in today's corporate world? Who are grabbing the plush jobs? Amazing, he/she is an average boy/girl next-door with a down-to-earth practical approach to life. This is an age of new generation with new theme, new philosophy and new perception. We do not find any logic behind commenting good or bad, right or wrong because if we start going against the wind or current, we throw ourselves in the world of uncertainties and risks.

Shrey Gupta, studying at Shri Ram College of Commerce (SRCC), New Delhi, coming from Varanasi, not a bookworm, President of the Students' Union, loving music and evincing keen interests in organising events has been hired at a starting salary of ₹ 39 lakh per annum with Deutche Bank.

◈ Not the only case

Two years ago, Adit Mathur, son of a former cricketer, Amrit Mathur, got a salary of ₹ 32 lakh, due to his expertise in the basics gave him an edge over others.

Each and everyday, we witness new cases of hiring people with a zippy attitude, leadership skill, communicative ability and humility. The corporate sector, of late, looks for creative leaders and they are very much optimistic that the kids they recruit are creative leaders. Of course, they start working at the bottom of pyramid but because they are dynamic with a rock star personality, they are usually doers and bear the efficacy of easy blending in a multi-cultural environment. The young talent has the confidence to work anywhere and therefore they get corporate appreciation. It is against his backdrop that we find big firms resulting only from the top universities. They cherry-pick or choose the best from available, with strings to their bows such as football captains and leaders of orchestras, entice them with offers of fancy dinners and expensive wine and educate and train them in tune with their requirements; they provide the best results. It is also found that they pick students from leading universities and colleges and then send them to do MBAs from premier institutes after two years. Bill Byham, considered as the father of modern hiring methodology opines, "The best way to select people who will thrive in your company is to identify the personal characteristics of people who are already thriving and hire people just like them. "The behavioural expert, Preiti Junneja opines, "We are looking out for people with positive attitudes and skills, not knowledge. We need young people who have tolerance for stress and behavioural flexibility to handle crisis.

Forbes magazine reports that companies are on a lookout for people "who can come up with new ways of communicating and collaborating that inspire and connect employees around the world. Companies need managers who can anticipate and thrive on change. "Actually, the corporate sector is found looking at the young talent expected to be the creative leaders of tomorrow. They need visionaries who can anticipate future change. They look for people with high intellectual handwidth and a daring attitude. They look for people having adaptability, agility and the potentials to think beyond today. It is due mainly to the fact that we find them looking for fresh talent in the leading colleges where they get people commensurate with their requirements.

The above mentioned facts make it clear that with new perception we need to develop our children. We are supposed to provide freedom to our kids to follow their dreams. It is better that your child tackle everyday problem with their own interests and efforts. Don't protect him/her from difficulties. Let them emerge as a problem-solver. They need to be adaptable and agile and interested in shaping their personality rather than getting lost in books during their school years. We cannot negate that freedom provides an opportunity to grow. It provides an opportunity to survive and even to thrive.

Earlier quoted Shrey's father Alok Gupta talks about the secrets of success of his son. He says, "I gave my son freedom to think and act. I never pressurised him to join an IIT or become a doctor. As a parent, I encouraged him to ask questions, develop an interest in music and even share jokes. That's been the greatest differentiator between him and other children. He honed his leadership skills, logic, intuition, thinking, communication and mannerism, as there was no pressure from us. Money was never the driver for success. Shrey himself says, I feel great about getting this fantastic offer. I was not the topper in my college. I grew up in Varanasi and this is a dream that comes true. I went through 10 rounds of interviews. I was frank about my ability and intelligence. If I did not know the answer to something, I admitted to it. I think they saw that I had leadership skills. I like taking charge and initiating things."

A change in the priority order becomes significant to be creative. If we find the corporate world changing their attitudes while recruiting people, it is due to the fact that they have found such people very productive. They like women who are active without being domineering. They like the poise and assertiveness of a young man who emerged as the leader. They feel that hiring is not like recruiting people with the right experience but with the right mindset. Since they have experiences that people with the right mindset have proved their excellence.

In view of the above, it is right to say that budding and upcoming youths of today need to make it sure that they have outstanding personal qualities. They have a vision. They are creative. They have leadership and capacity to establish in the larger interest of organisation where they work. They are supposed to cultivate skills not knowledge. They are supposed to show their leadership skills as and when the circumstances necessitate. They believe in the philosophy that dreams of young kids if fulfilled provide to them an additional strength to perform.

In the changing scenario, the educational institutions in general and the B-Schools in particular need to change their strategies for developing people for the corporate sector. Right from their enrolment to the completion of course, they have to make it sure that personal score of an individual get top priority. Synchronising personal scores with the professional degree is the emerging need of the hour. The communication excellence, leadership skills, in-depth knowledge of basics, etiquette and manners, intuition, logic, thinking, adaptability, zippy attitude, humility, agility and ability to think beyond today are some of the properties which would make them distinct to others. How and in what way, we inject these properties in the personality of our young kids requires to be our prime responsibility for making them hireable and promotable. A majority of us feel that rock star personality is enough for talent scouts to offer to them the big bucks. Even ordinary talents can get plush jobs in the corporate world, if they have a high degree of personal score. They can emerge as high flier, though they are down to earth but have a strong sense of personal approach to life.

SUMMARY

In this chapter, you have gone through different facets of management of body. Before starting next chapter, be sure that the following facts are well versed.

Basics About the Body: Human body is a complicated system consisting of millions of cells organised uniquely and functioning dynamically. It is a system working with the support of eight subsystems such as the Skeleton, Muscles, the Circulatory and Respiratory systems, the Urinary system the Glandular system, the Nervous System and the Skin.

Management of Diet: This is found concerned with the management of foods that we need to meet the requirements of cells. While eating foods, it is to be ensured that we are making available to our body the required ingredients such as Carbohydrates, Proteins, Fiber, Vitamins and Minerals. Sound management of diet makes the ways for sound management of body.

Know About the Energy Requirements: Depending on age, height and weight, we find variation in the energy requirements. The requirements of protein for different persons cannot be uniform.

A Balanced Diet Sheet: All of us need a balanced diet sheet. While preparing diet sheet, it is to be ensured that transferred nutrients are providing strength to the metabolic function. The nutrients regulate the accumulation of toxin within the body responsible for chronic diseases. The dieticians may help us in this task.

Food Making a Balanced diet: It is significant that different groups of foods are included while having a balanced diet. A fair combination of cereals, dairy products, non-veg items, fruits and vegetables is essential to balance the diet sheet.

The Key Indian Food Items: The cereals, pulses, vegetables, nuts, fruits and oil seeds, fish and sea foods, milk and milk products are normally found in the Indian food items.

Matters to think off about foods: We need to develop our awareness of the items like canned tuna, whole grains, plant oil, fresh vegetables and fruits, herbs and spices to adopt a healthy diet sheet. Some of the healthy foods are to be eaten everyday. We need to avoid junk or fast food. We need to prefer foods found healthy in omega fatty acid, vitamins and fiber.

Wise Regulation of Food: We need to care our cells and to regulate our thought patterns. We are not supposed to strive for nutrients which may increase our weight. We need to make it clear that we eat food not ingredients. We need to assign due weightage to vegetables, beans, brown rice, seasoning packages, adding good things in our diet. We need to make sure nutrition and cleansing. We should eat good food first.

Awareness of vaccination, immunisation and diseases: Each one of us need to be sensitive to the vaccination, immunisation, different types of diseases to promote the preventive measures.

Water for Body: We need plenty of water to activate the digestive system and avoid the problem of dehydration.

Top Priority for Rock Personality: In today's corporate world, we find personality of an individual getting top priority and therefore we need much more precaution while managing diet and our physique.

Walk an Exercise: Daily walk and exercise need due place in our lifestyles.

KEY TERMS

Vaccination	Diabetes
Immunisation	Anaemia
Personal Hygiene	Food Triangle
Fatigue	Vitamins
Skeleton System	Minerals
Muscles System	Fat
Circulatory System	Proteins
Respiratory System	Nutrients
Urinary System	Fiber
Glandular System	Potable Water
Liver	Sleep Deficit
Cells	Junk Food
Alkaline	Meditation
Acid	Rock tar Personality
Carbohydrates	Viral Disease
Cereals	Degenerative Disease
Calory	Alzheimer Disease

EXPECTED QUESTIONS

1. Focus on the basics about the human body which is found to be a very complicated system.
2. Throw light on the different dimensions concerned with the sound management of human body.
3. Do you find diet and its management an important consideration for having a sound health. Justify your arguments.
4. Explain the food items generating alkaline.
5. Discuss the food items generating acid.
6. State and explain the different nutrients found in the food stuff.
7. Throw light on the defined motives influencing the combination of the different food groups.
8. What do you mean by Body Mass Index? Explain the role of nutritious diet in ensuring healthy body. Also point out the debilitating diseases like cancer, diabetes and stroke which can be prevented with the help of a balanced diet sheet.
9. Focus on the food stuff making the balanced diet specially in the Indian perspective.
10. What do you mean by Food Triangle? Explain the mixes helping you in having a sound health.
11. Focus on the key Indian food items which can provide the required nutrients to our body.
12. Explain the different points to be considered while selecting the food items to be included in your diet sheet.
13. Discuss the precautions to be followed while adopting the food items throwing a positive impact on our body, mind and emotions.
14. What do you mean by Vaccination and Immunisation? Explain its role as a preventive measure.
15. Do you find activating the sensitisation process relevant for a number of infectious and communicable diseases? Defend your arguments.
16. How do you conceptualise the potable water which may be helpful in regulating and controlling the water-prone diseases? Justify your opinion.
17. Explain the role of walking and exercise in keeping us fit.
18. What do you mean by Rock Star Personality? Explain its role in making you hireable and promotable particularly in the present corporate world.
19. Who is high-flier in today's corporate world specially with the view point of getting high bucks? Do you justify its growing importance? Justify your answer.
20. Explain the impact of sleep deficit on your body.

APPLICATION EXERCISES

1. "Healthy body engineers a sound foundation for the development of a healthy mind vis-à-vis an attractive personality." Comment on this statement in the face of recent developments in the corporate sector specially while hiring and firing people.

2. We need to manage our body in such a fashion that it remains productive. In the capacity of a corporate professional, explain the important considerations helping you in having a sound physique.
3. "Food is for Cells." Do you agree with this viewpoint? Justify your answer.
4. "Adjust your diet, take simple, wholesome, easily digestible, give up hot, pungent curries and chillies." In the light of this statement, explain the diet sheet to be followed by the corporate professionals.
5. How and in what way you will be successful in making a balance of alkaline-forming foods and acid-forming foods helpful in maintaining a sound health? Focus on the food groups containing different levels of alkaline and acid.
6. "We do not find even a single food group which can nourish the body with all the vital ingredients required." Do you agree with this view? Justify your answer in the face of healthy nutrients for healthy body.
7. "A 2009 study by the National Diabetes, Obesity and Cholesterol foundation (N-DOC) found that around 35% of the children in the 14-18 age group,: mostly reading in private public schools of India and specially coming from the affluent segment are over-weight or obese." In the face of this observation, throw light on the diet-sheet which can resolve the problem of overweight and obesity.
8. Make a diet-chart considerably supplementing nutrients to our cells specially from the Key Indian Food items.
9. Can you justify the consumption of junk or fast foods by the corporate professionals? Defend your argument.
10. To have a healthier diet, it is pertinent that we eat foods found rich in omega fatty acid, vitamins and fiber. Do you agree with this view point? Justify your answer.
11. You have been working as a corporate executive. How and in what way, you plan to regulate your food habits which can help you in keeping fit? Explain with sufficient evidences.
12. The very sense in promoting immunisation programme is to minimise the intensity of problem due to some critical diseases. In the light of this statement, focus on the relevance of developing awareness.
13. By regulating diet and balancing our lifestyles, it is easier for us to keep our body sound. Comment on this statement.
14. Vaccination is a treatment with the help of a vaccine in which a substance is injected into the body to cause it to produce antibodies for providing immunity against a disease. In the light of this statement, focus on the organisation of sensitisation programme to develop mass awareness.
15. "A number of diseases are found either water-prone or food-prone." In the face of this statement, throw light on the relevance of quality water and healthy food for the sound development of our body.
16. "Water is a necessity for digestion and absorption of the foods taken by us. It is a vital constituent of diet. We find it a substance in which bodily chemical reactions take place." Comment on this statement.
17. "WTO data confirm that 21% of all communicable diseases in India are water-borne." In the face of this statement, throw light on the measures to be adopted to increase the supply of potable water.

18. What do you mean by Potable Water? Do you find the Indian masses getting adequate safe drinking water. Justify your arguments and explain the role of Potable water for the sound management of our body.
19. Exercise is probably the most important tip to stay fit and healthy. Comment on this statement.
20. "The upcoming and budding generations who are found interested in serving the corporate sector have no option but to consider fitness as a revolution. They need to switch on their fitness journey which would help them in having a sound physique. Do you agree with this opinion? Justify your answer.
21.. Who is high-flier in today's corporate world?

    Who are grabbing the plush jobs?

    Amazing he/she is an average boy/girl next-door with a down-to-earth practical approach to life. Surprisingly, he/she is not a bookworm, not a topper but President of Students' Union, Captain of a team, an excellent event manager. They have been getting whopping salaries putting even products of leading B-Schools to shame.

    In the face of these new developments in the corporate world, focus on the points which can make you more hireable and promotable.
22. Shrey Gupta, studying at Shri Ram College of Commerce (SRCC) New Delhi; coming from Varanasi, not a book worm, President of the Students' Union, loving music and evincing keen interests in organising events. The Deutche Bank hired him at a starting salary of ₹ 39 lakh per annum. Focus on the fact that motivates organisation for hiring people.
23. Sound sleep for sound body. Do you agree? Defend your arguments.

BACK-UP MATERIALS

1. www.hindu.com
   www.healthyeating world.com
   www.healthyforms.com.

   The Importance of Having a Healthy Body.
2. www.en.wikipedia.org.runway culture.net

   Take care of your inner beauty
   The meaning and purpose of yoga
   Human Beauty
3. www.indianetzone.com
   www.yogaforums.com
   www.indianexpres.com

   Diet and Meditation
   Personality in Yoga
4. www.nos.org
   www.webhealthcentre.com

   healthyindia.org
   Hygiene

5. www.webhealthcentre.com
   en.wikipedia.org
   www.statefundca.com

   Promoting Good Health

6. www.fronttierlaw.com
   www.the hindubusinesslive.com
   legalservicesindia.com
   Physical Appearance

7. www.spas.about.com

   Seeing the Beauty in Managing Our Bodies

8. Jha, S.M. Hospital Management
   HPH, Mumbai, 2011

9. Too busy to sleep!: The Hindustan Times,
   June 14, 2011

10. Contentment is spirituality: The Times of India,
    April 17, 2011

11. Jha, S.M. Potable Water for All-A Mission: The Hindustan Times 30, January 1999.

◆ ◆ ◆

3 MANAGEMENT OF PERSONAL HYGIENE

Good hygiene practices not only protect health of an individual but virtually health of all those having a direct contact. Hygiene plays an effective role in attaining physical and emotional soundness. Activating the sensitisation process is urgently needed to make society aware of the standard of hygiene.

CHAPTER DESIGN

Introduction – Personal Hygiene: The Concept – Dimensions of Personal Hygiene – Bathe Daily – Hand Washing – Trimming of Nails – Haircare – Clean Clothes – Oral Hygiene – Home Hygiene – Kitchen Hygiene – Bathroom and Toilet Hygiene – Water Hygiene – Laundry Hygiene – Food Hygiene – Medical Hygiene at Home – Workplace Hygiene – Excessive Personal Hygiene and its effects – Personal Hygiene Education and Training – Personal Hygiene influencing Emotion – Activating the Sensitisation Process – Personal Hygiene for Corporate Professionals – Summary – Key Terms – Expected Questions – Application Exercises – Back-up Materials.

CHAPTER OBJECTIVES

This chapter aims at studying the various dimensions of personal hygiene. Standard of hygiene is an important dimension of personal care management without which our physical and emotional soundness is difficult. The motive of this chapter is to make society aware of the problem of hygiene so that they protect themselves and prove to be a lesson for others. The bacterias and viruses are commonly spread amongst those people who are not careful to the hygienic conditions. By managing hygiene, we may keep ourselves physically and emotionally sound. People in general and the corporate people in particular need to realise the effectiveness of good personal hygiene.

MANAGEMENT OF PERSONAL HYGIENE

◈ Introduction

We cannot negate that physical health and mental health are found inter-related. If we feel good, we find ourselves healthy. Good personal hygiene has been found neglected in the Indian society where even literate segment appears disinterested to the standard of hygiene required for physical and emotional soundness then what to talk of the illiterate and backward segments. By managing hygiene, we not only protect ourselves but also make the conditions safe and risk-free even for others. Improving personal hygiene is thus found to be an important consideration in the present world where we find masses getting less time for managing hygiene.

Standard of hygiene is an important dimension of personal care management because our failures to keep up and maintain a standard hygiene result into a multi-pronged harmful effects. We are found ourselves infected and in addition also make the ways for a number of social, environmental and psychological problems. It is right to say that hygiene plays an incremental role in looking and feeling physically and emotionally sound. It is in this context that good hygiene practices not only protect individual health but practically health of all those having a direct contact. The bacteria and viruses commonly spread in an environment where the rate of insensitivity is high. Hence, it is of paramount importance that we assign due weightage to standard personal hygiene and make society aware of the positive and negative effects.

The management of personal hygiene includes in its purview a number of facets such as children personal hygiene, personal hygiene education and training, personal hygiene guidelines and a number of allied problems directly or indirectly influencing the process of infection. In a true sense, personal hygiene is a collection of practices which we habitually perform to maintain good health. It is not only related to the well-being of human beings but albeit to the surroundings, atmosphere and ecology responsible for providing to us a healthy living condition.

The various facets that we need to go through for maintaining personal hygiene are very much related to our habits which we cultivate during the learning process. Hence, the society and family are the pace setters. A highly conscious society and well-educated parents have a different perception of the standard of hygiene. It is also right to mention here that we are ourselves responsible for expanding the purview of personal hygiene. Since we find the problem of environmental pollution at its peak, the hygienic considerations are also changing.

In the Indian perspective, a majority of us are not habitual and sincere while washing our hands before eating and after using those articles which carry dust or dirty elements or after handling garbage, after coughing or sneezing, after handling pets or other items where we find possibilities of infection through bacteria and viruses. We never mind that most of the infections especially colds and gastroenteritis are caught when we put our unwashed hands which carry germs on them. This makes it essential that we are very particular to washing of our hands and wrists with clean soap and water and after washing, dry our hands with towels or tissue paper towels. This is an essential dimension for personal hygiene on which we focus in the present chapter.

We generally forget that nails are an important carrier of germs. This makes it essential that we regularly trim our nails and keep them in good shape. The nail beds need due care for preventing infection. We need to trim them weekly and brush them daily so that no dirt or residue remains beneath the nail. The best time to cut our nails is after bathing when they are soft. We also need to moisturise our nails and cuticle regularly.

The personal hygiene also focuses on practising good oral hygiene. We need to remember that mouth is more prone to collecting harmful bacteria and generating infections. It is pertinent to mention that most of us are not aware of the strong link between gum diseases and narrowing of the arteries which can lead to heart attack and stroke. Infection of gums is found through the bacteria which gradually enters the blood stream, activates the immune system and make the walls of artery inflamed and narrowed. The bacteria enter the blood and attack to the fatty deposits found present in our arteries and cause further narrowing. This necessitates minimising the accumulation of bacteria in our mouth and emphasise on regular brushing of our teeth at least twice a day. We need to wash the toothbrush and to replace them when the bristles become deshaped. Maintaining good oral hygiene also necessitates visiting our dentists at least every six months.

Particularly in the corporate culture, we find management of hair also drawing our due attention. Washing hair at least every other day is essential to keeping our hair and scalp healthy and in a good shape. The problem of lice and dandruff need necessary attention at the earliest. We need to cut our hair frequently and to shape them in tune with our profession.

In addition, we also need to wear clean clothes. It is not to be forgotten that dirty clothes are the source of contamination and cause serious skin disorders. Washing clothes and linen on a regular basis also need priority attention in the context of tips for personal hygiene. This is an important division of personal care management which a majority of us undermine. Good hygienic habits are easy to begin and maintain which protect ourselves and even others from the illness. We need to be very particular to the socks that we use. We should not forget to clean them regularly. Like this, the inners that we use need due attention. Personal hygiene thus requires to maintain the standard and this is possible when we develop a habit and spend a few minutes of our time in managing its different dimensions.

◈ Personal Hygiene: The Concept

Personal hygiene is the collection of practices a person habitually performs to maintain good health. Almost all the dimensions of personal hygiene can be managed personally even with minor care and precautions. Hygiene plays a significant role in looking physically and emotionally well. This cannot only protect individual health but the health of all people who come into contact. It is maintaining an appearance that conforms to societal expectations of what a well-groomed man or woman should look like. It is also meant a well-trimmed beared for men, shaved legs and professionally arched eyebrows for women. Maintaining total body cleanliness is important for good personal hygiene and therefore even small things play a big role in knowing about the details of personal hygiene.

Personal hygiene is important for all the age groups, but it is much more important for the kids because a clean kid is a healthier kid which makes it easier for us to have a stock of professionals who can develop a sound aesthetic sense for sensitising the budding generations. Personal hygiene includes in its purview social, psychological as well as emotional aspects and keeps us physically sound. It is a device for feeling ourselves good which is important for mental health. It brings a change in our appearance and helps us in looking clean outwardly as well as inwardly by promoting a healthier lifestyle.

Personal hygiene is a foundation on which we engineer a sound personality without which professionals in general and the corporate professionals in particular find it difficult to add additional attractions to the ambience efficacious of generating service culture and fragrance. Body and mind are found interrelated. If we do not maintain good hygiene, it is to affect our health and consequently we find its harmful side effects on our mind vis-à-vis on our emotion.

Hygiene is the practice of keeping oneself and one's surroundings clean in order to prevent illness or disease. Thus, it is also concerned with the cleanliness of surroundings where we live and work. With a change in our lifestyles, we find copious avenues for an invasion on hygienic condition where we work. The key boards of computers, lap tops, our cell phones are found much more sensitive to virus and bacteria and this necessitates a new definition for hygienic surroundings because a majority of us never mind them and invite numerous problems on that account. We cannot negate that to maintain standard hygiene, a high level of awareness is needed. This necessitates an intensive sensitisation process amongst all the segments, specially in the Indian perspective where general masses lack civic sense then what to talk of the aesthetic sense.

The conceptual exposition thus makes it clear that personal hygiene is synchronising the practices which a person habitually performs to maintain good health and healthy surroundings which may play a catalytic role in the development of personality and effective in keeping ourselves physically and emotionally well.

◈ Dimensions of Personal Hygiene

While designing a conceptual framework for the personal hygiene, we obviously feel that it is due mainly to our insensitivity that day-by-day the functional areas for personal hygiene are found expanding at a high pace. If we remain insensitive to the problems to be instrumental in generating an unhygienic condition, the process of expansion would continue even in future. Our focus here is on the dimensions which may help us in maintaining the norms and cultivating the habits. The motive is healthy living where perception of quality would depend on our habits. Healthy environment and surroundings, health policy of the government and health education are the important considerations for expansion or contraction in dimensions. The efforts made by government, corporate sector and social organisations for improving the quality of environment also influence the nature and size of dimensions. Since we have found all the concerned very much insensitive to the environmental problems, our efforts for studying the dimensions need innovations.

The dimensions for personal hygiene focus on taking bathe, washing hands, trimming nails and hair, cleaning clothes, practising good oral hygiene, necessitating due personal care and institutional support. We cannot negate that cultivation of habits and inculcation of knowledge are the important considerations. We go through all the dimensions, one by one and focus on the measures required to have good personal hygiene.

◈ Bathe Daily

Whether we feel grungy or not, it is pertinent that we cultivate a habit of daily shower preferably every morning which would keep us clean and fresh and would also be effective in keeping us odour-free. The rejuvenation of skin is essential which requires minutely cleaning of our body to prevent acne, blemishes and other skin eruptions. The scrubbing of our arms, legs and torso would slough off the dead and dry skin and would help us in keeping our skin healthy and refreshed.

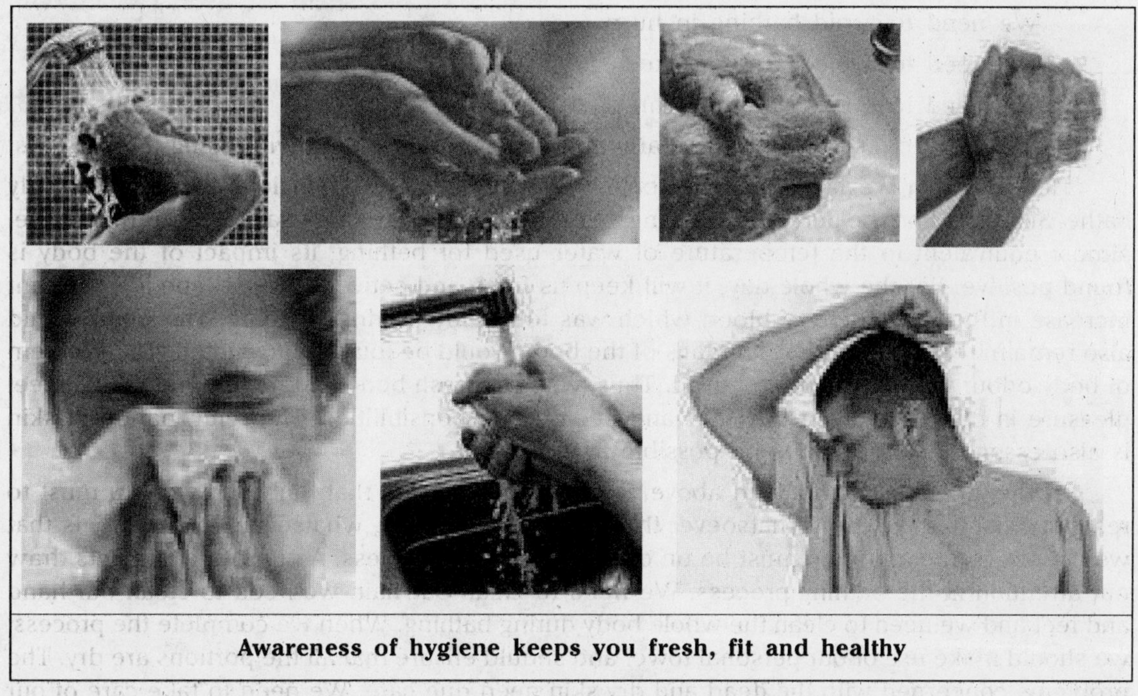

Awareness of hygiene keeps you fresh, fit and healthy

Since time immemorial, we find bathing getting due place in each and every society, culture and country. Some of the earliest descriptions of western bathing practices come from Greece. The Romans have been found emulating a number of Greek bathing practices and later on they surpassed the Greeks in the size and complexity of their baths. We find ruins of Roman bath in archaeological excavations in Europe, Africa and Middle East. The Romans have been found developing baths in their colonies. They have the credibility of elevating bathing to a fine art.

With the decline of the Roman Empire, the public baths played a big role earlier witnessed reversal because the European populace were found influenced by this belief that frequent bathing may promote diseases and sickness. This belief could get new strength because the Medieval Church authorities were found very much interested in closing down the public baths. They realised an increase in immorality and diseases due to public baths.

The Indian ancient literature specially concerned with bathcare should not be overlooked where we find focus on some of the important considerations which we generally do not mind. The following verses from Visnusmirti need due attention:

परनिपानेषु न स्नानम् आचरेत्।

न अजीर्षे । न च आतुर: ।

न नग्न : । न रात्रौ राहुद्दर्शनवर्जम्।

न सन्ध्ययो: ।

प्रात: स्नायी अरुणकिरण ग्रस्तां प्राचीम्

अवलोकक्य स्नायात् ।

We need to avoid bathing at public places or at other places.

We need to avoid bathing at the stage of indigestion.

We need to avoid bathing in hurry.

We need to avoid bathing naked.

We need to avoid bathing in night.

We need to take bathe in the early morning, facing east and witnessing the sun rays.

Hence, when we talk about personal hygiene, the first dimension is to have a daily bathe. Since we find the period of morning and more so early morning having low temperature, almost equivalent to the temperature of water used for bathing, its impact of the body is found positive. For the whole day, it will keep us fresh and active. There will be a significant increase in the circulation of blood which was found low during sleeping. The mind would also remain fresh and almost all organs of the body would be found rejuvenated. The problem of body odour would also be removed. Thus, with the fresh body and fresh mind we will feel pleasure in discharging our business and personal responsibilities. The rejuvenation of skin is also essential which would be possible after shower.

In the face of facts outlined above, it is right to mention that daily shower is a must to respect personal hygiene. Whatsoever the practices we adopt, whatsoever the products that we use the prime attention must be on cleanliness and freshness. A number of aspects draw our attention in the bathing process. We need to clean our hair, we need to clean our hand and feet and we need to clean the whole body during bathing. When we complete the process, we should make use of our personal towel and should ensure that all the portions are dry. The problems concerned with the dead and dry skin need due care. We need to take care of our legs and torso. We need to ensure healthy and fresh skin.

In this context, it is pertinent that you take care of the quality of water used for bathing. In no case, you should make use of the contaminated or polluted water. Hence, it is right to say that daily shower is a must. The time, place, duration, sources are the important considerations to take the pleasure and enjoy the benefits of bathing.

Gradually, we find development of bathing as an art and more so an effective source for maintaining personal hygiene. A number of bathing products are used in the process such as shower gels, soaps and sponges. In this context, it is to be made sure that water used in the bathing process is clean and fresh.

In the Indian perspective, we find bathing getting priority attention. A majority of us believe that a daily shower is a must but just a very few of them are aware of the precautions to be adopted in the process. The timing, duration and sources are some of the important aspects necessitating due attention of concerned person. We have linked bathing with religion and have identified certain places for bathing both from religious and medical viewpoints. Gradually, we find its development in different forms specially for rejuvenating skin. The hot springs are found not only in India but in different parts of the globe and we find people taking benefits of bathing there. Bathing or soaking in hot spring, hot tub, mud bath, peat pulp bath, sauna, steam bath are the different processes adopted for maximising the intensity of benefits. Of late, we also find bathing helping in the development of tourism industry. Ayurvedic spa, Cruise Ship spa, Day spa, Destination spa, Medical spa, Mineral springs spa, Resort/hotel spa, Mobile spa have been found attracting new generation of the society and making ways for the development of tourism industry. It is right to mention that directly or indirectly we find them closely associated with bathing in one or other forms.

The supply position of quality water has been found emerging as an important problem not only in the urban areas but even in the villages. Our changing lifestyles and the increasing requirements are found adding much more complexity to the deposits of water. The increasing insensitivity aggravates the magnitude of problem. The contamination and pollution of water need to be regulated and this necessitates not only a rigid governmental regulation indeed a strong sense of realisation to mend our habits. The rivers, ponds and sea water need due care. The water deposits need an optimal harnessing. The cultivation of habits requires a transcendental priority.

Bathing practices in the modern society may be developed as a fine art but we also need to make us fully aware of the fact that a fine gift of nature and an essential item to save and protect our life system should not be misused or polluted.

Scintillating freshness you need, rejuvenation you need, protection from germs you need and for that bathcare is essential that we cannot deny. Whatsoever the bathing bar you use or whatever shower gel you use or whatsoever the water you use must be helpful in keeping you refreshed for the day long. Of late, we find a number of products in the market and you may opt for a suitable product in tune with your requirements and affordability. The most important thing is to treat bathcare as an important dimension of healthcare and adopt all the practices possible for you. One thing is important in the very context that you should be particular to the time and duration.

◈ Hand Washing

Another dimension of good personal hygiene is concerned with washing our hands. It is amazing that a good number of people are not aware of the relevance of hand washing after using the rest room, before making or eating food, after handling pets, garbage, after coughing or sneezing. It is important for us to sensitise the masses that most infections, especially colds and gastroenteritis are caught when we put our unwashed hands, which carry germs on them, to our mouth. This makes it essential that we are careful while washing our hands and adopt the practices required to keep our hands free of germs.

How and when to wash our hands require due attention. We need to follow the right way to wash our hands. To keep our hands clean, it is significant that we use warm water which should not be cold or hot. We can use soaps considered to be antibacterial or even we can use general soaps. If we suspect that our hands have come into contact with someone who is infected, it is pertinent that we use an alcohol hand sanitizer. While washing, we need to rub our hands and to scrub the surfaces. Both sides of our hands, wrists, between our fingers and around our nails, a continuous rubbing for twenty seconds would provide us effective results. We need to rinse well under warm running water and to dry it with a clean towel, preferably paper towel. As and when we make use of the public restrooms, it is pertinent that while flushing and while touching handles, we take support of paper towel. Later on, we should use moisturising lotion.

In this context, we need to develop our awareness of alcohol rubs, gels/rinses found to be excellent hand antiseptics, provided they contain more than 60% alcohol. The alcohol-based hand rubs considerably reduce the number of germs on skin. We find the process very fast. Here we need some precautions such as we remove hand and arm jewellery, make it sure that our hands are visibly clean and rub hands until the product is dry.

When should we wash our hands is also an important question. We need to wash our hands before preparing or eating food, after going to the bathroom, after changing diapers or cleaning up a child who has come back from the bathroom, before and after tending to someone who is sick and after blowing our nose, coughing and sneezing. After handling an animal or animal waste and after handling garbage. In addition, it is also significant that we wash our hands before or after treating a cut or wound.

Here we need much more precautions and are required to make it sure that in no case we use a single damp cloth to wash the hands of a group of people. A common hand towel is not to be used and we should cultivate the habits of using disposable paper, towels. Germs rapidly thrive on the moist surfaces and therefore, it is significant that we do not use sponges or non-disposable cleaning clothes. We should also avoid using a standing basin for rinsing our hands. All of us need to remember that hand washing is an old but necessary ritual for living a good and healthy life, thorough and frequent hand washing is imperative. Let's make it sure that our kids cultivate a habit of washing their hands.

◈ Trimming of Nails

Not only with the viewpoint of good personal hygiene but also with the motto of beauty, we need to take care of our nails. This requires weekly trimming of nails and their proper brushing with soap so that no dirt or residue remains beneath the nail. Hanging of nails and development of infected nail beds require due care to provide strength to the management of good personal hygiene. While managing nails, it is pertinent that fringe nails are trimmed straight across and slightly rounded at the top whereas toenails should be trimmed straight across. Trimming nails after bathing would be convenient because after absorbing water we find them soft. The nails also need regular moisturing. A majority of us specially in the Indian society do not care proper and timely trimming of nails which invite numerous problems. This necessitates due sensitisation to develop mass awareness of the problems due to dirt and residue remaining beneath the nail. We find it an essential dimension of good personal hygiene requiring personal care. It is significant that we cultivate the habits of maintaining good hygiene specially amongst kids and teens. This is due mainly to the fact that cleanliness especially for young children is the basis of healthy living. Hence, it is the responsibility of parents to teach them and become good and adducible example to them.

◈ Taking Care of Our Hair

Proper management of hair is considered essential for personal hygiene and even for projecting our external outlook. This makes it essential that we are sincere to the washing of our hair at least every other day if not everyday. Keeping our hair and scalp healthy and in good shape would be helpful in minimising the problem of lice or dandruff. Healthy hair makes it essential that we are also sincere to the cutting of our hair frequently. It is right to mention that longer we wait to get our hair cut, we extend invitation to more frail and brittle. It is upon us to make use of hair washing products in tune with our choice and requirements. A number of lotion and shampoo are found available in the markets containing specific features. Making place for lice and dandruff cannot be considered hygienic and therefore we need proper care of our hair. Necessary action at the earliest cannot be negated. Since we find hair playing a significant role in improving our external outlook, it is pertinent that whatsoever the style we adopt is commensurate with our professional requirements.

◈ Wearing Clean Clothes

Cleanliness is the backbone of personal hygiene. Our clothes must be fresh and neat and clean. We need to change them as early as possible. We cannot deny that dirty clothes are a source of contamination and may cause numerous skin disorders. We need to wash them regularly. It is essential for us to wash clothing and linens on a regular basis. In some of the professions, we find our clothes and linens becoming vulnerable points for carrying viruses. Particularly in the hospitals, the people working or serving there need to be careful to their dresses, uniforms, linens and other items used there for maintaining good hygiene, it is significant that we cultivate a habit of wearing clean clothes. Here, we need to make it sure that our clothes are not washed from the contaminated water.

◈ Taking Care of Oral Hygiene

We consider mouth the most sensitive area of our body with the viewpoint of collecting harmful bacteria which is found very effective in generating infections and creating and aggravating numerous problems. The researches also reveal that there is a close relationship and a direct link between gum diseases and narrowing of our arteries resulting into heart attacks and stroke. This is due mainly to the fact that bacteria causing gum diseases infects gums and enter our bloodstream, activates the immune system and makes our artery walls inflamed and narrowed. It is also due to the fact that bacteria enter the blood and attach themselves directly to our fatty deposits found present in our arteries resulting into further narrowing. This makes a strong advocacy in favour of the fact that we should minimise the process of accumulation of bacteria in our mouth and for that brushing of teeth atleast twice a day and floss daily cannot be undermined. We also need to be particular to the tooth brush that we use and should change it at an interval of three to four months when we find bristles deshaped. It is also pertinent that we store our toothbrush at a place where it can easily dry. Good oral hygiene if neglected may invite plethora of problems and therefore it is essential that we sensitise masses regarding the harmful effects and make them aware of the processes to be followed for good or standard oral hygiene. Here, it is also imperative that we visit our dentists at least every six months so that early steps are taken to minimise the problem.

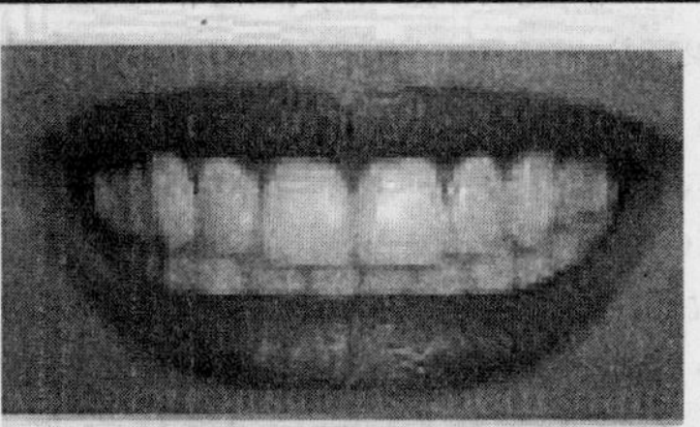

While maintaining good oral hygiene, it is also significant that we are sincere to the product that we use. It is essential that we go through the ingredients in the toothpaste that we use. There are a good number of brands in the markets, no doubt, but the herbal products have an edge over others. A cure and immediate cure is essential even the magnitude of problem is low. Breath odour can be a problem of general nature but may pave avenues for a number of serious problems, to be of critical nature if not detected at an early stage. Early detection may simplify clinical diagnosis and may be successful in curing.

Teaching good oral hygiene necessitates due attention of parents so that they succeed in cultivating habits amongst their kids. We need to assign a transcendental priority to our mouth which is very sensitive for collecting bacteria. It is not only significant that our teeth are odour free. It is equally important that we find them white and well shaped. We cannot negate that management of personal care remains incomplete if we are not sincere to our teeth. Ensuring good oral health is essential to general health which we should not undermine. Feeling and looking teeth healthy prevent offensive breath odour. All the dimensions of personal care or projecting our personality are found to be ineffective, if we find our mouth facing odour problem.

Particularly, the corporate people are supposed to be very sincere to their external outlook and this makes it essential that in addition to other dimensions, they are also honest to the management of oral hygiene.

◈ Managing Home Hygiene

Home hygiene focuses on practising the measures to be helpful in preventing or minimising the diseases or controlling the spreading of diseases in domestic home. This helps in preventing the spread of diseases and therefore it is imperative that we are aware of measures to keep our homes free from infections. It is concerned with the various domestic situations clubbing hand hygiene, resipiratory hygiene, food and water hygiene, general home hygiene, care of domestic animals and home health care. Preventing the spread of infectious diseases is our motto which helps us in breaking the chain of infection transmission. The International Scientific Forum on Home Hygiene has developed a risk-based approach which is based on the analysis of hazard where we focus on the critical control point. We also call it targeted hygiene which identifies the routes of spread of pathogens in the home and apply hygiene procedures at critical points on right time for breaking the chain of infection. We find pathogen a micro organism that can cause disease. All of us are the main source of infection either in the homes or at the public places. In addition, foods (mainly raw) and water and domestic animals are also the carrier. All the sources need due Care for time-honoured prevention. In the context of sources, the sites accumulating stagnant water such as sinks, toilets, waste pipes, cleaning tools, faceclothes considerably help the growth of microbial and may be instrumental in becoming a reservoir of infection. The germs come from these sources via mucous, faeces (food waste), vomit, skin scales, etc. The risk groups are found to be the worst victims either directly or via food or water and may be effective in developing infection. We cannot deny that the main carriers for spread of germs in the home are the hands which may be considered as the super highways for the spread of germs. In the process, we find food contact, surfaces and cleaning clothes and utensils also aggravating the magnitude of problem. The household linens or towels also become instrumental in spreading the germs. Utilities such as toilets and wash basins also play a big role in the infection process. Of course, we invented these items for dealing safely with human waste but due to mismanagement and our increased unawareness, we find them sizably effective in making the problem of

critical nature. Particularly when we find someone sick or suffering from diarrhoea, it is much more impact generating that we assign due weightage to the safely disposal of human waste but due to poor sanitation, specially in the Indian condition, it is of paramount importance that we sensitise masses of the harmful effects of our insensitivity or unawareness.

By good home hygiene, our focus is on targeting hygiene procedures specially at the critical points and more so at an appropriate time so that we succeed in making an attack on the chain of infection. Eliminating germs before they spread further is an important step which we should not forget. The hygienic cleaning procedures need our priority attention which may be helpful in controlling direct transfer of infection from surfaces via hands or food to the mouth, nasal mucosa or the eye. Removal of pathogens from critical surfaces thus cannot be undermined. The removal may be mechanical or through products effective in inactivating the pathogens.

◈ Managing Hygiene in Kitchen

It is significant that we are very careful to the problem of hygiene in kitchen which provides to us food. The contact sites are found very vulnerable if not managed properly and there we should ensure routine checking of hand, food and drinking water found as the contact sites and surfaces in the kitchen which would reduce the risk of spreading the germs. We need to make it sure that our hands are properly washed and whatsoever the food materials and utensils we use are clean. In addition, it is also pertinent that food materials and cooked food items are well covered. We need to administer insect killing devices very carefully.

◈ Hygiene in Bathroom and Toilet

The toilet seats and flush handles, door and tap handles, surfaces, bath and basin surfaces in the bathroom and toilets are considered the contact sites where we find possibilities of infection. Of course, the infection risk from the toilet itself may considerably be reduced if we are sincere to their proper maintenance. Particularly when we find someone in the family having diarrhoea, it is pertinent that we are careful to the flushing point where harmful effects of aerosol (spray) cannot be denied. Cleaning of toilets and hand wash facilities is found important for preventing odours. Water left stagnant in the pipes of showers may develop problem of contamination with germs which may become airborne when the shower is turned on. Irregular use of shower may also create problem. It is pertinent that we are sincere to proper cleaning of surfaces and walls for minimising the possibilities of fungal infections. It cannot be denied that primary sources of fungal growth are inanimate surfaces. It is imperative that we make our bathrooms and toilets safe and socially acceptable. This would encourage people to follow the norms for good home hygiene. In less developed countries like ours, it is also essential that we encourage people for using the toilets and washing their hands.

◈ Managing Drinking Water

We need to make it sure that drinking water is safe for consumption. This necessitates safe storage of water. In the Indian context availability of safe drinking water or potable water remains to be a critical problem. Access to safe drinking water is found at a critical stage not only in India but also in some of the developed countries of the globe. We need to make ourselves aware that water is contaminated during storage at home when we find infected hands touching it or the storage tank is not clean. This necessitates proper treatment of drinking water. We can make use of chlorine or iodine for chemical disinfection of drinking water. We may also prefer boiling or may go through filtration with the help of ceramic filters. Disinfection through solar is also found to be an effective method when we do not go through chemical disinfection. Today we find more sophisticated devices for water treatment. Here it is pertinent that whatsoever the devices we use for water treatment are safe and effective.

◆ Laundry Hygiene

The items coming in direct contact with the body such as underwear, nappies, towels, faceclothes are considered to be contaminated with pathogens during laundering, we find scope for transfer or micro organisms from contaminated to uncontaminated items of clothing and linen.

This increases our sensitivity to the maintenance of good hygiene standard for managing laundry. Skin-to-skin contact and indirect contact with contaminated objects such as towels, sheets and sports equipment to be instrumental in the transmission process need due care. Hygienic cleaning of clothing and linen makes it essential that we are very much conscious of the temperature which would minimise or would remove the possibilities of transmission from contaminated to the uncontaminated. Washing at 60°C or above or washing at 30-40°C with a bleach-based product result into decontamination of fabrics. However, we find some types of fungi and viruses which cannot be inactivated and removed. We should not forget that washing at a temperature of 40°C or below with a non-bleach product cannot be adequate for decontamination.

◆ Food Hygiene

Our increased insensitivity to the hygiene in kitchen maximises the possibilities of food poisoning at home. This draws our attention on the norms of WHO. The first consideration is preventing the contamination of food with pathogens spreading from people, pets and pests. Thus the three Ps can considerably protect us from the kitchen hazards. The people working there need to make it sure that cooked and raw foods are separately stored and preserved which would prevent the contamination of cooked foods. It is also imperative that we cook foods for an appropriate length of time and are sincere to the appropriate temperature required for cooking mainly to kill the pathogens. While storing food, we need to make it sure that place is safe and free from insects. The water and raw materials used for cooking must be safe. With minor precautions, we can regulate major dangers. Proper cooking and safe preserving need our priority attention which we often do not care. While managing food, or cooked or even uncooked materials, we fail in regulating the points of infection. We are not sincere while covering them and this makes ways for flies and other insects to come and destroy. We touch pets and forget to wash our hands. We nurture love for pets and animals but forget to keep them clean.

◆ Medical Hygiene at Home

The hygienic practices bearing the potentials of minimising the diseases and spreading of diseases in the process of administering medical care to those who are found infected or who are found at the risk point of infection in the home are in the category of medical hygiene. It is not possible or very difficult to make available to all the members in a family an in-depth knowledge of good hygiene. This makes it essential that in a family at least one member of the family should have an in-depth knowledge of members in the family. Particularly, patients coming from hospitals, found sick using catheter or requiring replacement of bandage are considered at higher risk of infection. A Career in a family needs to know that if hygiene practices are not correctly carried out, the risk of infection specially coming from the discharged patients would be of high magnitude. In the Indian society, we find people insensitive to these problems. Administration of medicine and medicare if not done properly may aggravate the intensity of infection.

◈ Workplace Hygiene

It is not only significant that we talk about home hygiene because failing the hygienic conditions at the workplace, the physical and emotional soundness of employees cannot be possible. In almost all the organisations, the professionals managing the environment at the workplace bear the responsibility of ensuring a hygienic condition where working people find and feel themselves safe and secured. It is amazing that in the Indian context we find a good number of employees not aware of the practices which they need to perform to maintain a good health. Any institution or organisation where we find assembling of people of different educational and family background, the possibilities for the spreading of bacteria and viruses are found at a large scale. On the one hand, we find employees insensitive to the practices while on the other hand, we also find absence of organisational culture resulting into a risk-prone organisational climate. This necessitates due focus on the problem of workplace hygiene.

There are a few selected categories of organisations where we find intensity of problem at its peak because people assembling or coming there for using the services lack civic sense. Making the conditions safe and risk-free is our prime responsibility which we need to take care on a priority basis. At almost all the public places, hospitals and healthcare centres, public transport services, educational institutions, etc., we find unhygienic conditions and insensitive or unaware people. Hence, if we are really interested in the problem of hygiene, the first and foremost task is to activate the sensitisation process.

The mismanagement of toilets, unawareness of cleaning hands after using computers, handle of the doors of toilets, mobile phones, problems related to coughing and sneezing, improper use of handkerchiefs and tissue paper, improper use of dustbin, unawareness of using air-conditioning machine and required temperature, lack of sun rays in a majority of the offices, handshaking without proper care of hands, etc., are some of the common problems making the workplace risk-prone. The corporate professionals need to ensure a hygienic working condition where employees feel themselves well protected. The inadequacy of safe drinking water and increasing insensitivity of professionals to these problems necessitate an action plan which may be instrumental in resolving the problem.

It is also significant to mention that almost all the problems related to hygiene at the workplace are due to unawareness and therefore the corporate professionals should feel themselves responsible and to activate the sensitisation process. In addition, it is also imperative that they ensure hygiene at the workplace. The dresses of employees, their shoes, hands are considered vulnerable with the point of bacterial infection. Imparting training facilities may be helpful in minimising the intensity of problem and therefore it is significant that they organise training programmes, workshops to make employees aware of the emerging hygiene problem.

◈ Excessive Personal Hygiene and its Effects

Of course, we need to be sincere to the various dimensions of personal hygiene so that we face the dismal health problem but here it is also important to mention that excessive personal hygiene is a peculiar condition which cannot be undermined. In 1989, Strachan observed that there was an inverse relationship between family size and development of atopic allergic disorders — the more children in a family, the less they develop these allergies. This makes it clear that lack of exposure to infection is in early childhood transmitted by contact with older siblings which may be a cause of the rapid rise in a topic disorders. Due to improved quality of household amenities and development of higher standards of personal cleanliness, we find people becoming much more sensitive and this is also an important reason for the same. On the one hand, we need to be sincere to the various dimensions of personal hygiene while on the other hand also need to be aware of the fact that our increased sensitivity to personal hygiene makes it essential that a fundamental change in lifestyle is made possible. We have substantial evidence to authenticate that some microbial exposures in the early childhood can protect against allergies. It is not meant that we neglect hygiene measures, indeed our focus is on the fact that we adopt hygiene measures and are regular and punctual in maintaining the life-styles we follow. The atopic diseases may be susceptible to the standard of personal hygiene we adopt. The hygiene behaviours need our due attention because we find them as the foundation of public health. The International Scientific Forum on Home Hygiene has developed a risk-based or targeted approach to home hygiene which makes it clear that hygiene measures need to be focused at the time and places found most critical for the transmission of infection. Sustaining normal levels of exposure to the microbial flora of our environment would be helpful in building a balanced immune system and therefore it is pertinent that we are sincere to the balancing of our immune system.

The above mentioned facts make it clear that we need to develop our awareness of the immune system and the measures and practices which may be helpful in the balancing process. We can make our homes hygiene-friendly but it is difficult for us to make the environment or the places where we work infection-free. It is not possible that we confine ourselves to our homes. The kids and children would go to schools and colleges and we are also supposed to be out for attending places where we work or even public places where we find much more scope for infection. If we make our systems much more hygiene-conscious, it is quite natural that we make our immune system much more susceptible to infection or reduce our immunity to infection. It is due mainly to the fact that most important thing in the management of personal hygiene is balancing the immune system. In the plain words, we can say that our lifestyles and life behaviours not only need to be careful to the personal hygiene measures but in addition, it is also pertinent that we leave scope for the development or resistance power.

◈ Personal Hygiene Education and Training

Unless we keep on moving the process of nurturing and developing kids in the face of incoming developments; our tasks of developing healthy and quality people would turn into a fiasco. Increasing heat of globalisation and the mounting domination of corporatisation make it essential that our budding and upcoming generations are well aware of almost all the dimensions of healthcare and personality developments so that they establish an edge over others and meet the requirements of corporate culture. No doubt, the awareness of good personal hygiene is significant to all of us, but we find its relevance to the kids and young children on which rest the future of a nation. Cleanliness especially for young children is the basis of healthy living. We cannot deny that poor living conditions, unhealthy environment and indecent behaviour affect all us but young children found of gullible nature are the worst victim. Untidy kids come out from the untidy parents. If children are clean and tidy, the coming generations are found well protected. This makes it clear that kids hygiene is the overall goal of cleanliness. Healthy bodies make ways for healthy living and healthy mind. Our awareness as a mother and father and more so our commitments to the budding generations determine the future of a nation. A clean child is a healthy child. Good hygiene for good health, this needs conceptualisation of all the segments found insensitive to the health problem. Particularly in the Indian society, we are found insensitive to the hygiene problem and therefore education and training programme require due focus.

We cannot deny that poor living conditions not only affect our health but we also find their influences on our mindset and emotion. If we start educating and training our kids, the task is considerably simplified because today's children are tomorrow's parents. A positive state of body and mind is considered significant which cannot be possible when children do not know the practices to be followed in the process. We need to act like a mirror for our kids. Children are copies of adults and our deeds and misdeeds, good or bad habits are copied by them. If children are clean and tidy, it is due mainly to the fact that we have imparted proper education and training facilities to them vis-à-vis conducive environment in which they find it easier to follow and learn. Hence, it is pertinent that we are sincere and honest while developing healthy environment for kids. We need to develop and spread good hygiene standards as benchmarks for high quality services which may strengthen children and youths and may provide new culture to the families and neigbbourhoods. If we present before kids and children an example by maintaining good hygiene, they in a very natural way start copying the same. The kids and children need our support. We cannot deny that family happens to be the best source for educating and training kids and children and the task may be on the shoulders of parents. They need supporting help from their parents. Daily personal hygiene practices need an intensive sensitisation process. We need to formulate and implement specific policies championing the issues related to kids's hygiene.

Learning starts at home and parents are the best trainer. All children need support of adults who can help and guide them in almost all the concerned areas. The most significant stage in the life cycle of an individual requires to be educated and trained and considerably managed by the parents which would simplify the task of educational institutions. Personal hygiene, no doubt, assumes a place of outstanding significance in the life and behaviour management of all of us but the children need its clear understanding on a priority basis specially in the Indian society where we find them neglected.

Developing awareness and sensitising masses of the relevance of personal hygiene also need institutionalised support. When the kids start attending schools, the first task before the teacher is to educate and train students in the field of personal hygiene. Inculcation and cultivation with the help of childhood educator to enable students to know basic health practices or caring for their bodies assume a place of outstanding significance to keep them fit for the life time. Of late, the schools can do it in a very effective way with the help of visual exposure or through playing of drama. Unwanted and unhealthy practices need to be prevented and this focuses on keeping students or nurturing kids in such an environment and ambience where they witness everything right. Proper daily hygiene practice is crucial specially for school-age children because a number of health problems crop up and spread in schools, day-care centres where noses, mouths and hands spread germs. Kids and germs may be on hands and therefore parents as well as the early childhood educators are supposed to play a meaningful role. It is amazing that in the Indian society, a majority of the parents lack awareness and even adults and educated people are found ignorant of personal hygiene. This necessitates multi-cornered steps and the early care health professionals are required to play here a meaningful role by promoting appraisal, screening, assessment as a referral processes. The Syllabi for kids and children need to assign due weightage to the management of hygiene which may play a decisive role in shaping his personality. Besides, the media also are required to play a meaningful role by promoting personal hygiene with the help of creative slogans and campaigns developed by world-class marketing professionals. Activation of the sensitisation process is the main thing which may be adopted by all the concerned segments. For the generation of awareness specially amongst aged people; the state and local-self governments may come forward. Since we find problem of emergence of a hygiene-less society in the Indian perspective at its peak, it is imperative that multi-pronged efforts and multi-cornered support inject new lease of life to the budding generations. Creation of climate and cultivation of habits are urgently needed.

Good hygienic practices need priority attention. Parents, teachers, care providers and or adults are supposed to be the role model. Our personalised efforts create a climate and our involvement in the process makes the weather. We should not forget that as a teacher and as parents we posses tremendous potentials to make a child's life miserable or joyous; tool of torture or an instrument of aspiration; hurt or heal or humiliate or activate their sense of humour.

◈ Personal Hygiene: Influencing Emotion

Our failures to keep up a standard of hygiene have many implications. A majority of us are found unaware of the multi-pronged harmful effects which make ways for plethora of problems. We find ourselves much more prone to infections and illness. We find and feel ourselves physically and emotionally well and all due to our awareness or sensitivity to the importance of personal hygiene in our life system. If we assign due weightage to the personal hygiene, the ways for epidemic or even epidemic outbreaks are sealed. In this connection, it is significant that we develop our awareness of the fact that personal hygiene is also related to social and psychological aspects. Poor living conditions affect all of us. We find influences on physical health vis-à-vis on the mental health. Sejal Gandhi, a great health educator considered health as not only the absence of physical disease or sickness of the mind but a positive state of both the body and mind as well. If we find everything right to our physical health, we find minimum possibilities of something wrong with our mental health. Actually, we need to understand both the body as well as the mind. In the Indian perspective, the magnitude of insensitivity is of high order and therefore magnitude of problem is also at its peak.

This focuses on physical and mental relationships which we variably fail to understand. How do we look has a close relationship with how do we feel. We start feeling good because we look good. This promotes self-esteem vis-à-vis the self-confidence. We can't negate that personal hygiene is important for each one of us adults as well as the children. The task of promoting good health actually turns into a fiasco, if we are unaware of the hygiene practices. The different dimensions of personal hygiene considerably influence our health. And if we are infected and diseased; our mind set is disturbed. We fail in having the confidence that we need. The social and psychological aspects thus are influenced. Our main focus is on children because children are most likely to suffer from such conditions than adults. We cannot deny that mother can significantly play the role of a successful health educator. This is due mainly to the fact that children are found closely related and associated with their mothers.

In this context, it is also right to mention that the physical and mental well-being of children sizably rest on the kind of relationships they have with the adults. If they find or witness that their parents are not sincere to the hygienic practices, the task of educating them is found much more difficult. Cleanliness requires a transcendental priority in the management of personal hygiene. In the Indian social system, a majority of the children do not have accessibility to high quality, safe and healthy environment both physically and mentally. This obstructs the process of developing hygienic conditions. Healthy habits and attitudes can not be possible if we fail in inculcating the habits of living clean.

◈ Activating the Sensitisation Process

We cannot refute that a majority of us are fully unaware of the relevance of personal hygiene in keeping them physically and mentally fit and therefore what to talk of the kids and teens when we find even educated and matured segments inviting ailment problems on that account. We live in an age where aesthetic sense is found getting due priority but what to talk of the aesthetic sense when we find a majority of us albeit unaware of the civic sense. Insensitivity makes the ways for the emergence of serious problems and it is against this backdrop that we raise a strong advocacy in favour of mass sensitisation. Kids and teens if nurtured in a right way engineer a sound foundation for the constitution of a family in which we find everything right. And this ultimately paves avenues for the development of a sound social system in which we find people physically sound and mentally disciplined. Not only in India but around the globe, we find qualitative system of education replaced by the quantitative system which has made informal education insignificant. The organisations vis-à-vis the society focus on the quantitative gains making people much more calculative. The parents, educational institutions and even media are found insensitive to these negative developments. It is against this backdrop that we find general masses becoming much more sensitive to the formal education but less receptive to the informal or non-informal education. This necessitates innovative promotion to develop mass awareness and inculcate habits of adopting healthy living conditions for healthy mind and healthy body.

The public health policies have been found neglected in a majority of the states and we find it an important reason for the increasing unawareness. Hygienic practices influence the quality of life and all of us e.g. children, youths, families and neighbourhood are benefited. In the process, we need to be creative, strategic and collaborative to get the desired results. Access to high quality, safe and healthy environment may simplify our task. The training, consultation, conference, publications, media, health clubs and other health membership services may prove to be much more effective process. We need professional touch and personalised services to make our efforts much more productive.

Sensitising masses for hygienic practices cannot be considered the lone responsibility of government. In a true sense, this task will remain unfulfilled unless, we find involvement of both the government as well as the private sector. In addition, the social organisations also bear the responsibility of activating mass awareness programme in the larger interest of the budding generations and upcoming youths. The conceptualisation of social advertising for the promotional hygiene would play an important role in the development of a hygienically conscious society where people are physically sound and mentally disciplined. Promoting good health focuses on promoting personal hygiene. This is due mainly to the fact that hygienic practices influence the quality of healthy living where cleanliness gets top priority. The villages need to be the thrust area where we need an intensive care.

A majority of the people living in villages lack sanitation services. The governmental measures to enrich the sanitation facilities have been found ineffective. What to talk of the villages when we find people living in the huts and cottages of towns and cities hygienically irresponsible. Hence, it is imperative that awareness programmes with the support and cooperation of professionals and media are activated both in the rural and urban areas. When we talk about institutional support in the sensitisation process; the multi-cornered support where central and state governments, local-self government, non-government organisations, public and private corporations need to come forward to inject new life and strength to the messages and themes of social advertising. Strengthening the sense of self-realisation must be the prime motto when our advertising professionals start designing the posters, composing the themes and slogans and identifying the vehicles for the travelling of themes and ideas.

Of course, we find multi-dimensional avenues for activating the sensitisation process but the most effective source is parental support. This is due mainly to the fact that children live with their parents and they copy each and everything as they witness. The process of learning starts at home and the parents, particularly the mothers have been found most effective in developing awareness. Thus, it is right to say that parents, teachers or early childhood educators should inspire and become the role models. Supply of handouts on health issues, publication and wider circulation of health magazines, sharing knowledge and experiences with the parents, teachers and or adults can make a difference in combating kids' health problems.

Giving a neat and tidy appearance is considered significant which is not to be possible unless we educate and train our kids for higher things. Individual looks are considered important to most of us and it is in this context that personal grooming is a very important practice in keeping a presentable appearance. In the developing corporate culture, it is not only important that we educate and train kids just with the motto of keeping them physically sound and mentally disciplined but it is also essential that we assign due weightage to the grooming aspect of hygiene which incorporates several acts such as hair washing, combing and cutting as needed, clipping and cleaning the fingernails and toenails as well. Looking good and attractive both for men and women, not restricted to a particular age group but for all who nurture a positive feeling make ways for optimism. We cannot negate that civic sense and aesthetic sense are interrelated and for which the first lesson is our awareness of personal hygiene. Unless we start the process from our kids, the task will remain unfulfilled. It is not proper that when we talk about personal hygiene, our focus remains confined to the corporate sector. Actually, we find its relevance for all of us irrespective of the fact that we serve public or private sector or belong to a particular age group or gender. Even regional considerations should not stand as a barrier because we find the rural areas and the rural people, specially in India very much insensitive to the hygiene. They may construct a beautiful building but we find them not so serious while planning for sanitation, managing for toilets and caring for their pets.

◆ Personal Hygiene for Corporate Professionals

We are aware of the fact that hygiene plays an incremental role in looking and feeling physically and emotionally sound. Actually, we find a close relation between physical and mental health because something wrong in the body is to affect our mental system. Good personal hygiene has been found neglected specially in the Indian context and therefore we also find increasing cases of body odour. Though we find its significance to all of us but particularly the corporate sector where we are supposed to make a microscopic anatomy of albeit small things; it is found to be much more important. Corporatisation is based on attractions and therefore it is the responsibility of corporate professionals that they are sincere and honest not only to the surroundings and ambience where they work but also to the various dimensions of personal hygiene to keep themselves fresh and healthy. Of course, it is an essential part of workplace etiquette. Daily shower or regular bath preferably every morning and making use of the product which add fragrance and remove odour need due attention of professionals. If we need quality skin, we need a regular shower. The scrubbing of our arms, legs and toes slough off dead, dry skin and help our skin stay healthy and fresh.

You are aware that handshake is an essential part of business etiquette. This makes it essential that your hands are neat and clean, nails are properly trimmed and you minimise possibilities of carrying dust and dirty elements particularly after sneezing and coughing. We need to be very particular to the washing of hands and wrists with clean soap and water and after washing, dry our hands with towels or paper towels. The nails are an important carrier of germ and therefore we have to trim them in a good shape. The best time to cut the nails is after bath when they are soft. Management of hand occupies a place of outstanding significance particularly for the corporate women because in the hand shaking etiquette we do not find any place for gender discrimination. In the corporate society, it is acceptable. So far as the trimming of nails are concerned, the women prefer a different style. For both, the corporate men or corporate women, it is imperative that they care their hands with the viewpoints of cleanliness and attractions.

Oral hygiene requires proper care. Good oral hygiene is essential for both the genders. We should be aware of the fact that mouth is found more prone to collecting harmful bacteria and generating infections. There is a close relationship between gum diseases and narrowing of the arteries which can lead to serious health problem. This necessitates minimising the accumulation of bacteria in our mouth and for that we need regular brushing of our teeth, at least twice a day. If we talk about problem of odour, it is also due to gum problem. Hence, proper brushing with proper products may be helpful in resolving the problem. It is pertinent that corporate professionals are sincere to the management of oral hygiene to have a proper smile in the business meeting or interacting with their associates or clients.

The corporate men or women need due attention on hair. It is significant that they are careful to the management of scalp and keep than healthy and in good shape. The problem of lice and dandruff need necessary treatment at the earliest. Proper washing of hair with quality product is, essential. If we talk about the facial appearance, the hair that we adopt play an important role. Healthy hair makes it essential that we take care of hair cutting frequently to avoid the problem of frail and brittle. While making use of hair washing products such as lotion and shampoo, we need care on the specific features that we need. While adopting hair style, the corporate professionals need to look over the style adopted by their successful associates. Both for men and women, the style would vary depending on their face structure. They can seek the cooperation of hair stylists for this purpose. Size and cleanliness of hair are the important considerations particularly for the corporate professionals. The corporate women need special care on their hair style which should not be disturbing. Whatsoever the hair style you follow must be in tune with the organisational culture.

The clothes that you wear also need a sound management. It is not only significant that you are careful to the style of attire. It is equally important that you are sincere to its proper cleaning. You need to remember that your dresses may also be a reason for body odour, mainly when we find use of polluted or contaminated water for cleaning of clothes. Well-laundered and hygienically-laundered clothes may help you in resolving the problem. We cannot negate that dirty clothes are the source of contamination and may cause numerous skin disorders. This necessitates proper washing of clothes and linens. In some of the professions, we find washing of clothes requiring special care. Particularly persons working in the hospital and healthcare centres need priority attention on the washing of their dresses or uniforms. We should prefer to wash our clothes, manually or in the washing machines but essentially in the homes which would keep us free from the possibilities of odour or bacterial or germ infection.

Of course, we need hygiene everywhere; either at workplace or at homes, due care is needed. The bathroom, toilets, kitchen are the most vulnerable areas where we need personal care. We have to regulate direct transfer of infection from surfaces via hands or food to the mouth, nasal, mucosa or the eye. Removal of pathogens from critical surfaces is significant which may be manual or mechanical. To keep kitchen infection-free, it is pertinent that we regularly check hands, foods and water considered to be important contact sites. Proper cleaning of utensils is essential. The surfaces of kitchen need due attention.

The toilet seats and flush handle, door and tap handles, surfaces, bath and basin surfaces are the contact sites where we find possibilities of infection. Water left stagnant in the pipes supplying water to kitchen and toilets may be an important source for contamination and infection. It is imperative that we make our bathrooms and toilets infection-free.

Purity of drinking water is also an important consideration which we need to ensure. Proper treatment of drinking water should not be overlooked, chemical disinfection of water is effective specially with the support of chlorine or iodine. Disinfection through solar is also found to be an effective method. Whatsoever the devices we adopt, the prime consideration is getting potable water in adequate quantity, particularly for the corporate women which would bring shining of skin in addition to the ordering of the digestive system.

The increasing cases of obesity make it essential that we avoid taking junk or fast food. The corporate men or women do not get time for cooking and therefore they prefer fast food. Hence, it is imperative that they develop their awareness of food hygiene. Proper cooking and safe preserving are found often neglected. In addition, it is also significant that they are aware of the art of cooking and the required temperature for cooking a particular item.

Awareness of medical hygiene cannot be ignored because this will help them in preventing the diseases and spreading of diseases. We are found in a position to minimise the possibilities of infection if we have a good knowledge of hygiene. This will also help us in preventing the side-effects of medicine.

The above mentioned basic facts related to personal hygiene need due attention of corporate professionals. They need more care because they work in a stressed environment. Making an invasion on the personal, social and psychological problems is pertinent and awareness of personal hygiene makes it easier. If we find ourselves sensitive to the hygiene, our children would get an opportunity to learn. They will inculcate habits of living neat and clean. Hence, it is imperative that corporate professionals in particular know about the standard of personal hygiene. They can learn from their associates or even they can educate and train their associates. The workplace etiquette is an important area of discussions specially for the corporate professionals and when we find them aware of the problem, they would be very much instrumental in promoting hygiene. Actually, it should be a part of organisational culture. Healthy physique and healthy surroundings cannot be possible unless we know about the personal hygiene. In a true sense, hygiene is a foundation on which we engineer a sound personality without which people in general and the corporate people in particular find it difficult to add additional attractions to the ambience efficacious of generating fragrance at the workplace environment and nurturing emotions for sound relations with the business associates. Physical and emotional soundness make our tasks much more easier.

Personal hygiene training is found essential in almost all the organisations because a majority of us even highly educated lack awareness of personal hygiene. The educational institutions in general and the Business Schools in particular need to adopt it as a part of their curriculum. At least, the growing finishing schools should not overlook it.

SUMMARY

In this chapter, you have gone through the different dimensions of personal hygiene. Before starting another chapter, be sure that the following facts are well versed:

Personal Hygiene: The Concept: Hygiene is the practice of keeping oneself and one's surroundings clean in order to prevent illness or diseases.

Dimensions of Personal Hygiene: There are various dimensions of personal hygiene such as taking bath, hand-washing, trimming of nails, haircare, dresscare, care of Oral Hygiene, Home Hygiene, Kitchen Hygiene, Bathroom and Toilet Hygiene, Drinking Water Hygiene, Laundry Hygiene, Food Hygiene, Medical Hygiene at Home and Workplace Hygiene.

Bathe: It is a process of shower helpful in keeping us clean and fresh. It is also active in rejuvenating skin and keeping us odour-free.

Hand-washing: It is a process of keeping our hands clean and keeping them free from germs. It is found helpful in preventing a number of food-prone diseases.

Nailcare: It is concerned with proper trimming of nails and their proper brushing so that no dirt or residue remains beneath the nail.

Haircare: This focuses on washing the hair to keep the scalp healthy and overcome the problem of lice and dandruff.

Clothes: This is found related to the proper cleaning of dresses which we wear which prevents infection and skin disorders.

Oral Hygiene: This is concerned with proper brushing of teeth. It keeps our teeth clean and germ free.

Home Hygiene: This throws light on practising the measures to be helpful in preventing or minimising the diseases or controlling the spreading of diseases in domestic home.

Kitchen Hygiene: It is concerned with the food items and utensils used in the kitchen so that their proper care regulate food-prone diseases.

Bathroom and Toilet Hygiene: Proper cleaning of bathroom and toilets is essential to minimise the possibilities of infection.

Drinking Water Hygiene: If we drink potable water, the water-prone diseases can be controlled.

Laundry Hygiene: This is cleaning of our dresses and linens so that possibilities of infection and contamination are minimised.

Food Hygiene: It is careful consumption of food so that food-prone diseases are controlled.

Medical Hygiene at Home: This is concerned with medicare so that harmful or side effects are minimised.

Workplace Hygiene: It is concerned with the workplace hygiene to make the environment at the workplace clean and healthy.

Excessive Personal Hygiene: It is an optimal point where we succeed in having a balanced immune system.

Personal Hygiene Education and Training: It is to make people aware of the effectiveness of personal hygiene.

Personal Hygiene and Emotion: It is to explain the relationship between hygiene and emotion.

Activating the Sensitisation process: It is to create mass awareness so that people come to know about personal hygiene.

Personal hygiene for corporate Professionals: This focuses on hygiene with the viewpoint of corporate professionals.

KEY TERMS

Hygiene	Excessive Hygiene
Oral Hygiene	Allergies
Trimming Nails	Immune System
Rejuvenation	Emotion
Odour	Epidemic
Torso	Infection
Soaking	Mass Sensitisation
Spa	Sanitation
Lice	Tidy Appearance
Dandruff	Sneezing and Coughing
Shampoo	Bacteria
Home hygiene	Gastroenteritis
Toilet Hygiene	Bristles
Laundry Hygiene	Arteries
Food Hygiene	Aerosol
Medical Hygiene	Solar
Workplace Hygiene	Pathogens

EXPECTED QUESTIONS

1. What do you mean by Personal Hygiene? Focus on the different dimensions of personal hygiene.
2. Explain your viewpoints regarding Oral Hygiene. Throw light on the measures helping you in having a good oral hygiene.

4. Focus on the effects of daily shower on your body. What precautions you have to follow when you face the problem of body odour?
5. Explain hand-washing as an important dimension of personal hygiene.
6. Throw light on the following helping you in having a good hygiene:
   (*a*) Nailcare
   (*b*) Haircare
   (*c*) Dresscare
7. What do you mean by Home Hygiene? Throw light on the following in the very context.
   (*a*) Kitchen Hygiene
   (*b*) Bathroom and Toilet Hygiene
   (*c*) Drinking Water Hygiene
8. What do you mean by Laundry Hygiene? Explain its relevance in having a good hygiene.
9. What do you mean by Food Hygiene? Focus on the role of food hygiene in having a sound body.
10. Write a reasoned note on Workplace Hygiene
11. Do you find excessive personal hygiene instrumental in making you allergic? Justify your statement.
12. Explain the relevance of personal hygiene education and training programme for making society aware of the role of personal hygiene in having a sound body.
13. Do you find personal hygiene instrumental in influencing our emotion? Defend your arguments.
14. Explain the relevance of developing awareness programme for good personal hygiene.
15. Do you find personal hygiene an important consideration specially for the corporate professionals of India who are generally found insensitive. Justify your statement.

APPLICATION EXERCISES

1. Whether we feel grungy or not, a daily shower is a must. Explain this statement with due focus on relevance of daily shower.
2. "Taking bath, washing hands, trimming nails and hair, cleaning clothes, practising good oral hygiene are some of the dimensions of personal hygiene necessitating personal care and institutional support." In the light of this statement, explain the various dimensions of personal hygiene.
3. "Good hygiene practices not only protect individual health but virtually health of all of us having a direct contact." Comment on this statement.
4. You suspect that your hands have been infected by coming into the contact of your friend who was infected. Explain the measures you will adopt to wash your hands.
5. "A majority of us specially in the Indian society do not care proper and timely trimming of nails which invite numerous health problems." In the light of this statement, explain the role of nailcare for good personal hygiene.
6. "Making place for lice and dandruff cannot be considered hygienic." In the face of this statement, focus on the measures you would adopt for haircare.
7. "The researches reveal that there is a close relationship between gum diseases and heart problem." Do you agree? Justify your arguments and focus on the measures helping you in having a good oral hygiene.

8. "The International Scientific Forum on Home Hygiene has developed a risk-based approach which is based on the analysis of hazard where we need focus on the critical control point." Since you are supposed to be aware of good personal hygiene, explain the critical control point.
9. The kitchen, bathroom and toilets are the sensitive points where you need due attention. Explain the measures to be adopted by you for keeping them risk-free.
10. "Any institution or organisation where we find assembly of people coming from different educational and family background, the possibilities for the spreading of bacteria and viruses are found wider." In the face of this statement, throw light on the measures you would practise to make the workplace risk-free.
11. "If we make our life systems much more hygiene-conscious, it is quite natural that we make our immune system much more susceptible to the infection or reduce our immunity to infection." Comment on this statement.
12. "We cannot deny that family happens to be the best source for educating and training kids and children and the task may be on the shoulders of parents. Untidy kids come out from the untidy parents. Unhygienic conditions not only affect our body but we also find their influences on our mindset and emotion."

    In light of the above statement, explain the role of personal hygiene education and training programme in the Indian perspective.
13. "We often fail to understand the physical and mental relationships. How do we look has a close relationship with how do we feel. We start feeling good because we look good. This promotes self-esteem vis-à-vis the self-confidence." Comment on this statement and explain the influences of personal hygiene on emotion.
14. "We live in an age where aesthetic sense is found getting due priority but what to talk of the aesthetic sense when we find a majority of us albeit unaware of the civic sense. Of course, insensitivity makes the ways for the emergence of serious problems. This necessitates a well-organised sensitisation programme.

    Do you agree with this statement? Explain your viewpoints in the capacity of a corporate professional.
15. "The workplace etiquette necessitates workplace hygiene without which the workplace discipline is found difficult. Actually, hygiene is a foundation on which we engineer a sound personality without which the corporate professionals would find it difficult to add additional attractions to the ambience efficacious of generating fragrance at the workplace environment."

    In the face of this statement, throw light on the relevance of personal hygiene to the corporate professionals.
16. "A majority of the population in India do not wash their hands before eating and after using those articles which carry dust or dirty elements or after handling garbage, after coughing or sneezing, after handling pets or other items where we find the possibilities of infection through bacteria and viruses. They find themselves infected and also affect others. The vicious cycle keeps on moving."

    Do you agree with the above statement? Defend your arguments.
17. "The keyboards of our computers and laptops, our cell phones are found much more sensitive to bacteria and virus which necessitates a new definition of hygienic workplace." Comment on this statement.

BACK-UP MATERIALS

1. www.citehr.com
   www.corporategurukul.com

   Hygiene and skin care

2. search 4 beauty blogspot.com

   What are the requirements for charm and beauty
   Healthy hair, skin care, nails, teeth and bones, rest and relaxation

3. www.hindu.com.blogs.one india.in

   Civic Sense

4. www.missattymaam.wardrobe.com
   www.essortmut.com
   www.citygirlstyle.com

   Grooming and Appearanc

5. www.nos.org
   www.webhealthcentre.com
   healthy india.org

   Hygiene, Medical hygiene, Home and everybody life hygiene, hand hygiene, respiratory hygiene, poor hygiene at home, hygiene in the kitchen, bathroom and toilet, laundry hygiene, medical hygiene at home.

6. www.mindtools.com
   www.sosuave.com
   www.askmen.com

   Nailing for personal hygiene

7. spas.about.com

   Managing our bodies

8. www.bplans.com
   www.ehow.com
   www.ibisworld.com

   Bathing, spa treatment

9. www.webhealthcentre.com
   enwikipedia.org
   www.statefundca.com

   Personal Hygiene Resources
   Personal Hygiene Tips for Good Health
   Maintaining Good Hygiene
   Kids Hygiene
   Daily Hygienic Practices

10. www.hindu.com
www.healthyeatingworld.com
www.healthyform.com
Importance of Having a Healthy Body

11. en.wikipedia.org
runwayculture.net
Take care of your inner beauty

◆ ◆ ◆

4 CIVIC AND AESTHETIC SENSE

Civic sense is nothing but social ethics. It is a school of thought.. It is a consideration by the people of a civilised and disciplined society. It is more than that.

CHAPTER DESIGN

Introduction – Civic Sense: the Concept and Percept – Dimensions of Civic Sense – Justification for developing Civic Sensibility – Cultivating Civic Sensibility – Educating Your Child about the Civic Sense – Civic Insensibility to Bio-medical Waste – Civic Sense of the Rural Folks – Civic Sense of the City Folks – Civic Sense and the Corporate World – Aesthetic Sense – Cultivating Aesthetic Sense – Aesthetic Sense and the Corporate World – Summary – Key Terms — Expected Questions – Application Exercises – Back-up Materials.

CHAPTER OBJECTIVES

This chapter aims at studying the civic and aesthetic sense specially in the Indian perspective where a majority of us lack civic sensibility then what to talk of the aesthetic sense. The motive is to sensitise the readers to the dimensions, justifications, conditions in the urban and village India and relevance of civic and aesthetic sense to the corporate world. With the motto of educating the upcoming generations and regulating the present generation; this chapter attempts to develop the society to be civilised and disciplined. The softness, tenderness and politeness are the personal score essential for the corporate people which would hardly be possible unless we have civic and aesthetic sensibility.

CIVIC AND AESTHETIC SENSE

◈ Introduction

You are driving a vehicle and find someone overtaking without considering left or right, you are crossing the roads and find someone gossiping there without considering that it is to obstruct the movement of traffics, you find someone throwing the wastage on the roads, you find someone urinating by side of the road, eating something and throwing the packaging on the roads and doing everything at the public places which are not expected from a citizen. Lack of civic sensibility finishes the dividing lines between humans and animals. Nobody to check us; nobody to guide us. We do whatsoever we like.

The stinking public latrines or urinals, scattered garbage of even domestic wastage on the roads, unawareness of traffic sense, insensitivity to personal hygiene, gross misuse of public water supply services and electricity services, etc., are a staunch testimony to this proposition that till now, we have not been successful in making our human resources civilised. In this scenario, how we can think about Gross Happiness Life Index to be high. It is really amazing that on the one hand, we have been promoting corporatisation while on the other hand lack even the civic sense which draws a line between the civilised and uncivilised society. Of course, the lack of civic sensibility is found of high order specially in the Indian social system where even so called educated people do not know about the civic sense then what to talk of others.

When institutions become insensitive, the individuals are bound to be unaware. Actually, our highly focused steps for promoting formal education kept the informal or nonformal education in the bottom line or in reverse gear and we started forgetting even the basics. The educational institutions, parents, social organisations and NGO started undermining informal education and resulting from which we have created a big force of uncivilised and indisciplined people. Of course, we have been successful in enriching our thematical competence but when we talk about the civic sensibility, we lag far-far behind. It is against this backdrop that we need to reprioritise our development agenda and change our perceptions and predilections.

In a true sense, the civic sense is not required to be developed on an organised basis because in a civilised and developed society, we find our kids learning everything just by witnessing the activities of their family members. In the Indian context, we find it essential because when parents are not aware of the civic sense; how we can expect civic sensibility from their children. Our personal score come to zero when we lack even some of the basics of a civilised society.

Civic Sense is nothing but social ethics. It is a consideration by the people of a civilised society which is found concerned with the social norms. Its area is found wider and therefore we may not confine it just to keeping the roads clean. It is more than that. It has to do with maintaining the legal considerations, respect for fellow men and women and maintaining decorum in the public places. We cannot deny that a number of countries have been found functioning in a smooth manner because of the strong civic sense found amongst its people. It is really amazing that we find educational institutions keeping mum on the issues related to civic sense with the exception of a couple of lessons in schools at the primary stage. The family members and educational institutions may play an incremental role in improving the quality of lives just by adding civic sensibility. Not only this, a majority of the problems related to personal hygiene may be resolved if we have civic sense. It is significant to mention that in the Indian society, the civic sense has dropped to an all-time low in recent years which is obvious from the current state of the society. We need to curb the downswing and in the very context, parents or a family can play a vital role.

The increasing cases of separatism, vandalism, intolerance, increasing road rage, etc., are all examples of lack of civic sense. Gradually, we find people becoming much more impatient and less-and-less tolerant of each other. Even developed cities and towns of the country have been facing multi-dimensional problems on that account because people lack considerations for fellow city-dwellers. The small towns and cities and even rural areas of the country are found in the same boat. This leads to a lot of problems. Disregard for the law is a primary cause for lacking civic sense. An individual having high civic values is not found of resorting to shortcuts and unethical tactics to get his/her work done. Like this, we find him/her very much instrumental in resolving the social and communal problems.

Somehow, most Indians do not care much for civic sense. And this attitude is prevalent across all sections of the society. Of late, we find people so much driven to their personal goals, that civic sense as an ethic has become a low priority. There are spit marks, urine, vulgar graffiti, random garbage and overflowing sewers at every nook and corner of India. It is unpleasant to comment that no city in this country has managed to fight this menace. It is not in good taste that we pin everything on the government and do not question our own unethical behaviour. Roads are dirty because nobody cleaned it, rather than due to the fact that somebody dirtied it. Such dirt and grime exist because everybody does it. If we find cases of epidemics, it is due to the absence of personal hygiene. However, we find none of us sensitive to the problem and a majority or almost all of us continuing to indulge in such behaviour in spite of knowing the harmful effects.

In the present scenario, we need to strengthen our realisation that civic sense is a school of thought in itself. It is belief in hygiene, respect for law, respect for other members of the society and respect for social ethics and human behaviour.

When we talk about the corporate world, our prime focus is found on the aesthetic sense which is not to be developed unless we find ourselves good in civic sensibility. It is in this context that we also go through the development of aesthetic sense. Actually, civic sense engineers a sound foundation for the development of aesthetic sense. Attraction considerably influences the process of corporatisation and aesthetic sense makes the ways for attraction. The three important considerations we find here are understanding the beauty of nature, receiving the beauty of art and enjoying the beauty of life. The ultimate focus, we find on our zest for life which is possible when we are creative and optimistic. In a true sense, we find attraction and optimism interrelated and impacting each other. The moment we start loving nature our temptation for beauty starts gaining a rapid momentum and resulting from which we start loving ourselves and promoting self. We take interest in managing our body and practise all the measures, to be instrumental in managing our looks. We adopt professionalised measures to help us in managing our dresses, hair, shoes, socks and accessories them in tune with the required conditions. This brings a radical change in our personality and makes place for nurturing the positive feelings. We evince interests in managing the ambience and are found sincere to the quality of environment. All these developments that we find become effective in the development of aesthetic sensibility.

Cultivating aesthetic sense thus occupies a place of outstanding significance. Of late, we find people becoming inhuman and lacking humane. They are found unaware of empathy and therefore we do not expect from them personal philanthropy. Because, we find people becoming insensitive to the aesthetic sense, it is quite natural that they start nurturing negative feelings. If we start caring for the civic sense, the ways for aesthetic sense are naturally paved.

If we turn our eyes on the ancient Indian civilisation, we witness there copious avenues for the development of aesthetic sense. Our ancient traditions, art, poetry, literature, dance, drama, paintings, music, customs and culture are so rich that we find enough opportunities for taste-refinement. Today, we find taste-perversion and an important reason for such a negative development is our detachment with art and culture.

For the development of aesthetic sense, it is imperative that we start loving nature, link our relationships with art and culture and inject new life and strength to our lives. If we have temptation for beauty, we have zest for life. Hence, the most important dimension for the development of aesthetic sense is protecting, preserving and promoting, nature. Ultimately, you succeed in having love for self.

In view of the facts outlined above, the civic and aesthetic sense thus prove to be the important traits for the development of personality in tune with the existent corporate requirements. Enriching personal score is a time-taking process which results into value-addition. This makes us productive. The corporate people cannot thrive unless they keep on moving the value-addition process. Let's hope that we receive the problem in a right fashion and make sincere efforts to make people sensible. Either we talk about civic sensibility or our focus is on aesthetic sensibility, the main focus is on making available to the corporate sector, people with high personal score to be instrumental in excelling competition. The very foundation of corporate world rests on aesthetic sensibility. The workplace requires an ambience generating fragrance and making it convenient to the employees to perform. The interiors require a pleasant expression for generating attraction. The working people need attractions to impress upon the clients, customers and associates. And, we find none who dislikes beauty, attractive appearance and coming fragrance from nature. This necessitates due focus on developing aesthetic sense amongst the working people.

The different properties of aesthetic sense benefit the working people and the corporate sector in many ways. The employees developing temptation for aesthetic sense are found of creative nature. They are found optimistic and nurture positive feelings. Since they have love for nature; they have zest for life. And if they have zest for life, they happen to be creative. The creative, positive and optimistic employees happen to be the assets for an organisation.

Around the world, we find corporatisation gaining a rapid momentum. This has been making ways for aesthete. A number of areas have been developed to champion the cause of workplace environment and the working people. The beauty industry has been found developing at a high pace. The fashion designing and the allied industries have significantly been contributing to the employment-generation and capital formation processes. Like this, we find aesthetic sense and aesthete becoming relevant to the corporate sector and corporate culture.

Amidst hustle and bustle, stress and tension; the life of common people is becoming too much complex and boring. They have made ways for high level of expectations which may or may not be fulfilled. The volatility in the business environment is likely to continue. This may develop pessimism. Career-addition is found mounting, specially amongst youths of the present generation. This makes it essential that their aesthetic experiences are made much more sensible to regulate taste-perversion. In this context, we expect too much from aesthetic refinement. The aesthetically sensible and refined people are generally found to be morally and ethically sound.

Aesthetically refined people develop love for music. If they start playing music or watching, the entertainment shows; we find them relaxed, energy rejuvenated and level of efficiency increased. If they develop love for natural scenes, mountains, hills, wild-life, there will be a reversal in the stress and complexes they have accumulated. Hence, we find all positive points in favour of developing aesthetic sense particularly amongst people who are serving the corporate sector or have a temptation for the corporate world.

The facts outlined above make it clear that we need corporate people with high personal score. How and in what way, we can be successful in developing civic and aesthetic sensibility; in addition to the other traits would determine the magnitude of our success. Making ourselves different or distinct has been proved to be an effective strategy to establish an edge over the competitors.

◈ Civic Sense: Concept and Percept

At the very outset, we need focus on the conceptual aspect of civic sensibility which is meant making citizens aware of the formalities they are supposed to practise in a civilised society. The civic sensibility necessitates awareness of day-to-day formalities dividing a line between civilised and uncivilised citizens such as awareness of personal hygiene, traffic sense, disposal of domestic wastage, awareness of using public utility services in different forms, awareness of environment, etc. A majority of the people specially in India are not aware of the civic sensibility, of course they may be educated.

The civic sensibility comes from the family and society where we live. The educational institutions and media also need to make society sensible so that the citizens are found to be civilised and disciplined. Spitting, sneezing, coughing, urinating at public places are not only a part of our nasty habits but we also find them unhygienic to be responsible for a number of health hazards. The parents bear the ultimate responsibility of making their children sensible so that they cultivate the habits and lead a civilised and disciplined life. Hence, we find family an important source for sensitising the kids and children from the very first stage of beginning the learning cycle.

Crux of the problem is that a good number of people even educated and living in towns and cities are found unaware of the civic sense. Since the parents lack awareness, the kids or children fail in developing the civic sense and we find a significant increase in the number of uncivilised and indisciplined people in the society. We cannot negate that civic sensibility makes the ways for positive developments and in due course, we find development of aesthetic sense. This is transfer from one generation to another generation. The kids watch our activities and start copying and adopting. But the task of developing civic sense is found much more difficult when kids and children witness everything adverse.

Civic sensibility, of course, is an essential trait specially in a cultured and civilised society where you are not supposed to act and behave in your own way. The family and society play the role of a pace setter and willingly or unwillingly, you have to follow. The concept and percept of right and wrong are developed by the society. Hence, it is a time-taking process, but the social activists and reformists need to audit the emerging trends so that the derailed systems are brought back on the rail. The educational institutions and media are required to play the role of an eye-opener responsible for sensitising, educating and making them aware of the required and desired improvements. The governmental regulations are supposed to activate the process.

If we do not follow the traffic rules or if we break them, it is due mainly to the fact that we have failed in cultivating a habit. If we do not throw the domestic wastage in the dustbin; the household rubbish may create health problems but we are helpless because we have cultivated the habits of throwing them as per our conveniences. If we misuse the centres for public utility services, it is meant that we are unaware. Insensitivity and unawareness make the ways for negative developments. We prove ourselves to be uncivilised because we keep ourselves unaware of the practices followed by the civilised society. Ultimately, it is society that defines the norms.

In the Indian society, the economic activities during the yester decades have been found at a low pace which sealed doors for multi-dimensional qualitative improvements. The illiteracy, backwardness continued for the long time and the social system and the cultural norms were found maintaining the day-long coming customs and traditions. The emergence of knowledge as a power was delayed and poverty and economic backwardness obstructed the development of character as a power. It was against this background that norms for the development of a civilised society could not be received by a majority of the population, specially in the Indian perspective. In this context, the development of civic sensibility was quite difficult and resulting from which we could not assign due weightage to civic formalities.

The amenities and facilities make the ways for the development of sensibility. Since the civic bodies delayed the process of developing and expanding the civic amenities and facilities and the educational institutions and media failed in sensitising the general masses; the civic sensibility could not emerge as a force and we remained unaware, uncivilised and indisciplined. Unaware, because we find lack of individual and institutional efforts to sense the society; uncivilised, because we do not know the essentials to be civilised and indisciplined, because we commit mistakes but do not confess. Against this background, we have remained insensible and allowed the coming generations to remain in the same boat.

The facts outlined above make it clear that the most essential considerations of a civilised society are found neglected even today. Of course, we have accelerated the pave of development by initiating qualitative improvements in the field of formal education but miserably failed in striking a balance between formal and informal. The consequences are very alarming because even highly educated segment of society lack civic sensibility and it is against this background that we find them insensitive even to the fulfilment of minor and basic civic formalities. Thus, the task becomes too much difficult because we find a significant increase in the number of educated but uncivilised and indisciplined youths having enough money in their pockets but lacking even the basics. Sensitising uneducated is easier but awaring educated is difficult because their growing inferiority complexes obstruct the process and stand as a barrier. It is an unvarnished fact that superiors may not have any complex and ego. Complexes develop only amongst the inferiors.

In the present scenario, we have limited options and we need to make use of our potentials in such a fashion that general masses come to know the relevance of civic sensibility and practise them in a right way. The process is to be initiated by the parents and for that it is essential that they are themselves sensible because only then the vicious circle of insensibility can be broken.

We need civic sensibility

In the face of facts outlined earlier, it is right to say that civic sense is, a school of thought which may benefit individuals, society and nation in a big way. Whatsoever perception, we have of the civic sense, ultimately we name them unspoken social norms making people civilised and disciplined. The animals and other living beings are not concerned with the norms which are found for us but at the same time it is also right to say that they also follow or are supposed to follow the norms of their community failing which they are boycotted from their own community. Thus, the following facts clarify the concept and percept of civic sense.

- Civic sense is a school of thought, accordingly a number of ideas are included to protect and promote social interests.
- Civic sense is nothing but social ethics. When we name it social ethics, our focus is on the ethical norms guiding and regulating the behaviour of people living in the society. Society cannot survive and thrive unless and until we find conceptualisation of social ethics.
- Civic sense is a consideration by the people for the unspoken norms of society. By this, we sensitise the people living in the society of the existent norms they have to follow. Our acts speak of our civic insensibility. These are the norms which divide a line between civilised and uncivilised, disciplined and indisciplined and human beings and other living beings.
- Civic sense is a believe in hygiene which regulates our behaviour in homes or at public places or at workplaces where unhygienic practices result into a number of health hazards.
- Civic sense is a respect for other members of the society either as our own family members or other members, Respect to others thus becomes a part and parcel of civic sense.
- Civic sense is also traffic sense which makes us aware of the different aspects essential for our safety and conveniences. It is to regulate the cases of road accidents and to minimise the number of road rages.

CIVIC SENSE: DIMENSIONS

1.	HOME HYGIENE	Management of Household rubbish, Toilets, Urinals, Pets, Premises, Kitchen, Childcare, etc. Awareness of personal hygiene,
2.	PUBLIC HYGIENE	Awareness of using public utility services at railway stations, bus stops, airports, hospitals, etc.
3.	TRAFFIC SENSE	Awareness of crossing roads, driving, over-taking traffic signals, change of lane, turning vehicles, volume and quality of horns and keeping roads clean.
4.	BEHAVIOURAL SENSE	Our behaviour with members of family, awareness of etiquette and manners, gestures, postures, body language, etc.
5.	RELATIONSHIP SENSE	Our behaviour with other members of the society, our sense of respect for elders and sense of affection for youngsters.
6.	ENVIRONMENTAL SENSE	Awareness of environmental pollution, water contamination, sound pollution, afforestation, use of water, etc.
7.	COMMUNAL & COMMUNITY CARE	Awareness of promoting communal harmony, caring members of the community for social harmony
8.	LEGAL SENSE	Awareness of civic laws.

UNSPOKEN SOCIAL NORMS

SOCIAL ETHICS

Fig. 4.1: Dimensions of Civic Sense

- Civic sense is also an environmental issue where city or village people need to develop their awareness of those practices which may contribute to the process of environment pollution, ecological imbalance, water contamination, planned afforestation, etc.
- Civic sense is also found to be an issue throwing light on the problems concerned with conflicts amongst religion, ethnic groups and different races. Communal harmony, social peace, inter-religion cooperation and cohesion make civic sense an important driving force for the entire community.
- Civic sense is also concerned with civic laws which make us disciplined and civilised.

It is imperative that all develop their awareness of the civic sense and practise them on the ground in the larger interest of the entire community.

❖ Dimensions of Civic Sense

Educating ourselves or educating others cannot be meaningful unless we keep ourselves fully aware of the different dimensions of civic sense. It is really amazing that the most important thing of personal care management which makes us sensible, civilised and disciplined have not received due weightage. In the Indian perspective, we find civic insensibility at its peak. We witness unhygienic conditions in our own homes then what to talk of the public utility centres. We feel ourselves strong by disrespecting, insulting and even assaulting our own family members then what to talk of our behaviour with other members of the society. We feel ourselves elevated by polluting the environment then what to talk of keeping them clean. Our parks or other public places speak of our civic insensibility. An in depth knowledge of civic sense would enrich our knowledge bank vis-à-vis would make the society civilised and disciplined.

To make present and coming generations aware of the different dimensions of civic sense, it is imperative that parents or other family members, educational institutions and media and non-government organisations act as a promoter.

All the dimensions of civic sense are considered as the different traits instrumental in value addition process of our personality which make us sensible, civilised and disciplined. How and in what way, we inculcate habits and add to our personal score and to what extent, we transfer these traits to the upcoming generations determine the contributions of social ethics to the transformation of human capital.

1. Home Hygiene:

A majority of us are found unaware of the different dimensions of personal hygiene and invite even critical health hazards. It is pertinent that we educate ourselves vis-à-vis educate and sense our children to learn and practice. Since we spend a major portion of the day in our homes, it is sizably to influence our civic sensibility. Disposal of household rubbish in the trashbins, use and maintenance of our toilets and urinals, management of our pets, cleaning and beautification of our campus and premises, cleaning of our kitchen from where we get our foods are some of the important aspects if not cared may prove to be dangerous. Educating our children in these areas play a very effective role in improving the quality of sensibility.

2. Public Hygiene:

In the Indian perspective, we find the public utility services becoming a major source for the transfer of diseases. It is due mainly to the fact that we do not know to make use of public toilets, urinals and how to keep the roads clean. Almost all the public services found at railways stations, bus stops, hospitals, parks or other places need our due attention. We do not know how to use them and therefore even the best efforts for keeping them clean are found ineffective. We lack civic sensibility and we do not find public authorities sincere to the punitive measures. We need to make ourselves aware that such conditions prevailed even in developed countries like USA and Germany till the beginning of 1970s but situations improved, as soon as the public authorities started imposing fines for flouting the civic rules.

3. Traffic Sense:

With the increasing pressure on roads, it is imperative that we consider traffic sense as an important component of civic sense so that cases of accidents, traffic disturbances and road rages are regulated. This throws light on our awareness of crossing the roads using the zebra crossing, the rules for driving and overtaking, change of lanes, turning vehicles on the roads, volume and quality of horns, that we use by our vehicles, the volume and quality of music system that we have in our vehicles. It is against civic sensibility and civic rules that we throw the rubbish of our household materials on the roads. Unless we practice the punitive measures, the habits are not to be regulated. It is significant that we educate ourselves and sense and sensitise our children and others regarding the traffic sensibility.

4. Behavioural Sense:

The behavioural profile of an individual in a family plays an important role in making him/her civilised or uncivilised, disciplined or indisciplined. How do we behave with other members play an important role in the development of our personality, respect to elders and affection to youngsters in a family make the atmosphere congenial. This also makes ways for the development of positive feelings and creativity.

5. Relationship Sense:

Expanding relationships in the society, contacting and interacting with other members of the society, nurturing positive feelings for others make the social environment friendly vis-à-vis bring a number of positive developments in your personality. Social harmony plays an important role for social peace. This, makes it essential that each and every member of the society make sincere and honest efforts to regulate social unrest. This paves avenues for making the environment at the workplace much more cohesive. Contracting sense of respect for elder members of the community appears to be a negative development of today harming us in many ways.

6. Environmental Sense:

It is amazing that when we talk about protecting and promoting the quality of environment, we find a majority of the people unaware of the problem of environmental pollution in different forms. We contaminate the water and drink the same and make ways for a number of water-prone diseases. We create noise, invite sound pollution. We cut forests and invite the problem of ecological imbalance. Almost all the rivers of the country or seas or ponds are found polluted and crux of the problem is that we are ourselves responsible for the same. This makes it essential that we educate and sense the society regarding the problem of pollution, its harmful effects on us and promote measures to regulate pollution.

7. Communal and Community Care:

We find society a composition of different living beings and when we talk about caring for the environment and plants, it is also pertinent that we focus on the problems harming the interests of community and generating communal feelings. People accepting different religions coming from different races and ethnic groups have an equal right. Awareness of promoting communal harmony, caring members of the community for social harmony and inter- and intra-religion cooperation need our due attention.

8. Legal Sense:

It is our responsibility that we make society aware of the civic rules and civic responsibility. The civic bodies and village panchayats can play a meaningful role in the very context. They should take support of professionals and NGOs for this purpose. If we make society aware, the ways for practising the punitive measures are clear. We need to make use of social advertisements, publicity and public relations for sensing and sensitising the community. Display of posters, organisation of exhibition are the measures helping us in activating the process.

The measures outlined above are the different dimensions of civic sense. We need to make society aware of the dimensions making them sensible, civilised and disciplined.

◈ Justifications for Developing Civic Sensibility

Civic sensibility helps the development of a civilised and disciplined society in which the possibilities of being hygienic are considerably maximised. It makes the ways for the development of aesthetic sense on which the corporate development activities vis-à-vis your hiring significantly depends. Because we find a majority of the Indian population unaware of the civic sense, it is imperative that our educational institutions and media initiate focused efforts to make them sensible because unless they have a high degree of civic sensibility, we cannot consider them a bonafide citizen. Besides, the parents also bear the responsibility of educating and sensing their children to the civic formalities because by making them sensible, the increasing misuses of civic amenities and facilities would also be regulated. It is quite natural that before making our children sensible, we make ourselves sensible. If we find our kids and children unaware of civic sensibility, it is sizably on account of our negative personal score. There are a number of reasons justifying the relevance of civic sensibility in the present corporate world explained in the following passages:

1. Civic Sensibility Makes the Ways for Aesthetic Sensibility: For climbing the corporate ladders, it is pertinent that we are aware of aesthetic sense which is not to be possible unless we have a high level of civic sensibility. The first stage of being civilised is civic sensibility because this makes us aware of a number of formalities which if not completed make our task of becoming an aesthete much more difficult. Corporate world assigns due weightage to physical appearance or an attractive facial appearance or people having better look. This is supported by the logic that better-looking people are found creative and optimistic. If we find citizens sensible to the civic formalities; they develop a zest for life and for that they start loving beauty and nature.

2. Civic, Sense Makes us Civilised and Disciplined: Drawing a line between civilised and uncivilised; disciplined and indisciplined appears to be essential to make the society sensible. Contrary to it, if we lack awareness of civic sense, it becomes difficult for us to follow and maintain the norms established by the society of sensible citizen. To complete our civic formalities, in the face of socio-cultural requirements, to make use of the civic amenities and facilities like a bonafide citizen of the country and to take care of basics of hygiene make us civilised and disciplined. Our sensibility to the defined norms make us civilised whereas our willingness to follow the norms make us disciplined. Awareness of civic sense is thus justified for each one of us.

3. Civic Sensibility improves the quality of Hygiene: It is amazing that even educated segment of the society is found unaware of the relevance of personal hygiene for keeping them physically sound. It is due mainly to their insensitivity to the civic sense that we find them facing the food-prone, water-prone and communicable diseases. Cleanliness is an important consideration for respecting personal hygiene and our civic sensibility makes the ways for keeping us clean. A majority of us specially in the Indian perspective lack awareness of personal hygiene. They do not know the relevance of washing hands, nails, and bathe. They do not know the role of contaminated water in promoting water-prone diseases. They are not aware of the harmful effects of environment pollution and noise or sound pollution. They pollute even safe drinking water by washing their clothes and even animals. It is all due to lack of civic sense.

4. Civic Sensibility Regulates the Misuses of Civic Amenities: On account of high demographic pressure, the scarcity of safe drinking water and electricity power is a critical problem in India. But people lacking civic sensibility have been found misusing them and aggravating the problem of non-optimal supply. The public utility services in general have been facing numerous problems on account of poor sensibility of users of services. They are not aware of the way of using the toilets. Besides, the public transportation services also create problems on that account. We find heavy pressure on roads and a majority of the people either driving cars or heavy vehicles or bicycles or walking on roads lack traffic sense. This results into problem of traffic jam and road accident and necessitates civic sensibility so that masses are aware of the right way of using the civic amenities.

5. It Simplifies the Process of Managing the Traffic: A significant increase in the number of vehicles and frequent movement of people from one place to another are found increasing the pressure on roads. The intensity of problem aggravates further when we find them lacking civic sense. They are not aware of the traffic rules and we find all of them becoming impatient. The problem of rash drive is the result of civic insensibility. When we drive without knowing the results; the possibilities of accidents are found of high order. The management of traffic control becomes difficult when we find sensibly deficient people on the roads.

6. Civic Sensibility Simplifies the Process of Building Character: We cannot deny that building of character is a difficult task. The extent of problem aggravates further when we find people unaware of the civic sense. For the building of character, it is imperative that people are civilised and disciplined. Because this helps strengthening self realisation, the people start understanding the differences between right and wrong, lawful and unlawful, decent and indecent. This simplifies the task of building character. But when we find people unaware of civic sensibility, the task of building character becomes difficult. Since they happen to be uncivilised and indisciplined, our efforts prove to be unproductive.

7. Civic Sensibility Paves Avenues for Practising Self Regulation or Social Regulation: It is due to civic sensibility that we find people understanding their defined role in the social system. They regulate their behavioural profile, evince interest in respecting the rules and regulations, do not venture to commit mistakes and therefore possibilities of practising self regulation are found wider. But when we find them uncivilised and indisciplined, they start violating the social and legal norms resulting into social unrest.

❖ Cultivating Civic Sensibility

A civilised society nurtures some expectations from the citizens of the country considered as members of society. Since the uncivilised and indisciplined members may disturb the social order, it is imperative that family and social institutions play an incremental role in activating the sensitisation process. It is against this background that we need to go through the various areas where we find possibilities of civic insensibility helpful in making the people even uncivilised. The various dimensions, presented below need an intensive care.

I. Ensuring the awareness of civic formalities: In a civilised society, we expect that members are fully aware of the day-to-day civic formalities. The process starts right from the early morning when we wakeup and start making preparations for the formal activities. We are supposed to wash our eyes, mouth, face and hand. Proper brushing of mouth for dental care and cleaning tongue need due attention. We need to make use of quality product for mouth washing. When you go to toilets, make it sure that it is used and cleaned in a right way. When you eat something as breakfast or lunch or dinner, washing of hands should not be forgotten. When you take bath, ensure that water used by you is of quality.

2. Ensure that you have a traffic sense: It is considered to be the most important dimension of civic sense. A majority of the people are found unaware of the traffic sense. For all of us, it is pertinent that traffic rules are given due importance. Either pedestrian or cyclist or people driving bike, cars and light and heavy vehicles, belonging to any group or segment need to be aware of traffic sense. You need to be aware of the fact that the parking of car on the roads or by side the road has been found to be a problem area. Hence we are not supposed to obstruct the process of smooth movement of traffic, we are not supposed to stand on or by side of the road because we find them against the traffic rules. While overtaking and crossing lanes, we need much more precaution. The increasing cases of road accidents are due to our unawareness of the traffic rules.

3. Ensure proper management of waste: The problem of waste management has been found to be a disaster area. A majority of the people specially in the Indian context are found unaware of the proper management of waste. You will find people throwing household rubbish materials on the roads. It is not only to question our civic sensibility but also to invite environmental problems. We need proper care while disposing of the waste, where our focus should preferably be on electronics waste or biomedical waste. With the increasing popularity of use-and-throw culture, we find waste management becoming a disaster area.

4. Ensure proper use of public utility services: In the Indian perspective, we find public utility services worst affected. The people do not know the way of using and cleaning the toilets. Of course, the parents fail in educating or training their children. Hence, it is pertinent that we sensitise them in a right way. The stinking public utility centres need our priority attention. The hospitals face numerous problem on that account. The educational institutions and the road and rail transport services are found in the same boat. It is due to lack of civic sense that we find a large scale misuse of civic amenities and facilities. We are not aware of using the essential services in a right way. We do not educate and sense our children for regulating misuse because we find ourselves insensitive to this problem. This makes it essential that the parents, educational institutions and media accept joint responsibility of sensitising, the public. Actually, by misusing the services we create a gap between, the demand and supply.

5. Ensuring awareness of personal hygiene: It is really amazing that even educated segment of the society is not aware of the problem of personal hygiene. They do not know the importance of washing hands, trimming and cleaning the nails, cleaning and disinfecting the clothes, personal care to the toilets, cleaning of hair and skin, cleaning of their homes, etc. This causes a number of health problems. We are unaware of food and water-prone diseases. We less know about the communicable diseases. We invite problems for ourselves and trap the whole society to suffer. To what extent, the flies and mosquitos harm us; we are unaware. A very few of us know about the relevance of vaccination and immunisation. This makes it essential that we activate the sensitisation process and make society aware of the dangers and motivate them to cultivate a habit of respecting hygiene.

6. Ensuring awareness of lifestyles: We invite a number of problems, due to our lifestyles. We do not have any timing for breakfast, lunch and dinner. We do not know what to eat, when to eat and how much to eat. We are not sincere to the sleeping hour. We do not care for exercise and walking. The way in which we live proves to be an important reason for myriad of health problems. You cannot move the life system to move in your own way. There are certain norms, which you have to follow. You need a lifestyle which can keep you healthy. You have to overcome the situational and professional barriers.

7. Ensuring awareness of nature: The high intensity of environmental problem is due to our wrong decisions. We become responsible for aggravating the magnitude of problem. We do not care for plantation. We do not care for the problem of water pollution. We face the problem of high intensity of noise or sound pollution but do not regulate the playing of loudspeakers at an unacceptable volume of sound. What to talk of the individuals when we find even institutions and organisations not assigning due weightage to nature and environment. On the one hand, we find high level of deforestation but nobody to care for plantation and afforestation. Cultivating the habits of promoting plantation is found to be an important problem.

Cultivating civic sensibility is our prime task and we have to intensify efforts for developing refined civic sensibility. Unless and until, the civic sense is strong, it will be difficult for us to think about civilised and disciplined society. How can we expect to be a bona fide citizen of the country when we lag far-far behind.

◈ Educating Your Child About the civic Sense

Before you start educating your child about the civic sense, you need to make it sure that you have been working with high civic sensibility and are well aware of the different dimensions of social ethics. If you develop a habit of throwing the household rubbish in the trashbins, it is quite natural that your kids will copy it. Conversely, if they witness that you have not been sincere to your civic sensibility, all the efforts to make them sensible would turn into a fiasco. In a true sense, we find civic sense at school of thought in itself. It is belief in hygiene, respect for other members of the society and projection of humane and humanised behaviour. It is respect for socially accepted norms which is not to create problems for others. It is concerned with your patience. It is nothing but social ethics. It is also concerned with traffic sense driving sense, crossing roads, and all our activities making scope for disturbing others. Hence the area is vast but all are concerned with our action and behaviour making ourselves sensible or insensible.

Educating present generation is nothing but an attempt for engineering a sound foundation for the development and growth of the coming generations. Educating others with our actions and behaviour has been found to be much more effective and it is against this backdrop that we need to educate and sense our children by proving ourselves sensible. We are morally bound to educate and sense the present generation. We need to teach them the importance of civic sense and to illustrate or exhibit before them that how and in what way the toilets, surroundings are kept neat and clean. But the task becomes too much difficult when children witness their parents or others spoiling the surroundings. Development of a subconscious habit and development of an automatic habit are the two different stages or steps. Keeping surroundings clean is a subconscious habit and when the practices are continuously followed for a few days or weeks, we find its transformation into an automatic habit. And if you form an automatic habit, your activities become an example for others.

The educational institutions can also play an important role in the entire process. This may be practised exclusively by those students who live in hostels. As a social service programme, if adults witness kids and children cleaning the marks of spitting on the walls, removing the garbage from the roads, collecting the poly bags from the roads and drains; they can shame them in a very effective way. Such activities of school-going small children would be a lesson for the insensible adults.

Thus, the main purpose is to sense and sensitise the society. Either it is done by parents or it is practised by children; the motive remains the same. When we find people becoming insensible; they prove to be uncivilised and indisciplined. Because we find today telecast media becoming very much popular, the concerned TV channels may prepare serials and small stories to be effective in the sensitisation process. If we find today civic insensibility at its peak, it is due mainly to the fact that people of almost all the age groups, almost all the religions and regions have started disrespecting civic sensibility.

◈ Civic Insensibility to Bio-medical Waste

We cannot gauge the intensity of harm to us due to the mismanagement of bio-medical waste and the prime reason for this is our civic insensibility. The private clinics and government hospitals both of them are found responsible for the same. The responsibility is found on the hospital manager who is considered responsible for the mismanagement of hazardous bio-medical waste. In a majority of the hospitals, we find use of plastic materials found non-biodegradable and aggravating the magnitude of problem. Since we find mismanagement of hospital waste, a number of informal organisations have been found making use of non-biodegradable like syringes, plastic bottles and glass items without their proper recycling. They either buy or collect these materials for no price and supply the same to the distribution outlets who for high rate of commission promote these products responsible for a number of diseases. The communicable diseases thus get a friendly carrier and the ultimate sufferers are the patients. It is a part of civic insensibility because any type of wastage cannot be thrown at the place which is to harm the population and environment.

Bio-medical waste is found of two types such as bio-degradable and bio-nondegradable. The bio-nondegradable waste is found in the form of syringes plastic bottles, etc. Many hospitals are found burning plastics. The entire plastic waste is being incinerated or reduced to ashes. Incinerator ash is being collected by workers without a protective gear and is being dumped with other wastage whereas it should be collected in black bags to be disposed of in landfills. We find that the incinerators are thrown even very close to the populated area albeit in big cities of the country. A large number of private hospitals or clinics make provision for a common waste facility because they lack a separate disposable facility for the hazardous bio-medical waste. There are a number of nursing homes and private clinics dumping their bio-medical waste without disinfecting or segregating into the dustbins of Municipal Corporations. The bio-degradable waste is found in the form of bandages, human body parts and blood. We mix them with general waste.

Hence, it is right to motion that due to the mismanagement of bio-medical waste, we invite a number of environmental and health problems. This is against civic sensibility and therefore the hospital management needs to make proper arrangements for their disposal. The hospital staff in general need due care for the proper disposal of bio-degradable and bio-nondegradable waste. They need to collect them in a scientific way and thereafter to dispose of them in such a manner which is not to create health and environmental problems. In hospitals, we find OTs a vulnerable centre where a number of bio-degradable and bio-nondegradable materials are used. The doctors do not take it seriously knowing well the fact that if those materials are used would be a fatal. The hospital other staff do not realise the consequences of mismanagement of bio-medical waste. Civic sensibility is also meant that our actions or decisions should not harm others. Moreover when we find bio-medical waste to be hazardous to the common people, it is against civic laws that we are not sincere to the management of those waste. The ultimate responsibility is found on the shoulders of those who are directly or indirectly involved in the process.

◈ Civic Sense of the Rural Folks

India is a country dominated by villages and therefore whatsoever the developments we find in the rural areas of the country throw a major impact on the urban areas. We cannot deny that general people living in villages are found fully unaware of civic sense. Since they lack civic sense, it is found considerably affecting the civic conditions of urban areas of the country because due to increasing heat of globalisation, we find people with rural base dominating and impacting the urban population and culture. It is right to mention that so far as the development of public utility services in the rural areas of the country is concerned, we find almost a dismal result. Answering to the natural calls in the open air is found very common in Indian villages. What to talk of the men when we find even women also adopting this so called regal style in absence of toilets in their houses. It is really amazing that people have developed their sensitivity to the cell-phone culture and they are also found spending on that head but their attitude to the development of toilets in their houses is found negative which has been forcing them to make use of the open air services. It is really shocking that even educational institutions lack the basic civic amenities facilities. We cannot negate that the most important reason for the development of such a negative attitude and trend is their insensitivity or unawareness of civic sensibility. Of late, we find increased migration of rural population to the big cities and towns of the country and this also proves to be a burden on the urban civic amenities and facilities and thus the magnitude of problem aggravates further particularly in the urban areas. This makes it essential that the sensitisation process is activated even in the rural areas and in addition, the government and NGOs accept the responsibility of developing toilets in villages. The educational institutions needs top priority because inculcation of civic sensibility amongst kids and children would pave avenues for the development of toilets in private houses. If this is not coming from the side of parents let it come from students' side.

The increasing cases of epidemics in different forms found in villages also affect the urban population because willingly or unwillingly, they are forced to go to towns for medicare. Personal hygiene needs a transcendental priority both in the rural and urban areas of the country. The rivers and ponds of villages are heavily misused and increase the problem of water contamination. The rural folks do not know the impact of unawareness on their health. The pet animals also add to the problem. The problems like spitting, sneezing and coughing are found uncared. Even parents are unaware of the civic sense then what to talk of the children. The dirty living conditions make their homes unhygienic found very friendly to different types of diseases. We do not find any provision for trash or dustbins. They throw the rubbish household garbage as per their conveniences. When we find urban folks not aware of the traffic sense then what to talk of their counterparts living in the rural areas. We cannot deny that the lack of civic sense amongst rural folks not only harm the villages but also the towns and cities because we find migration of rural population to the cities and towns at a high pace.

We find other side of the coin presenting a bright picture. The people with rural base are found intelligent and diligent. This helps them in achieving academic excellence. Since we find rural parents even witnessing an attitudinal transformation, they prefer to send their children to the towns and cities for getting education and this brings a radical change in their educational qualifications. On that basis, they are in a position to get opportunities in the job markets but negative traits of their personality harm them in different ways. They lack civic sense and therefore aggravate the magnitude of problem. They lack traffic sense and become a party to the increasing problem of road accidents and road rage. They do not know how to use the personal toilets and therefore make the public toilets or urinals much more dirty. If they are employed in an organisation, the problem aggravates there. Thus, lack of social ethics existent amongst rural people of the country also add to the problem of urban people and the institutions or organisations where they work. Particularly, the manual labour migrating to the urban areas for job purposes creates a big problem. They do not have their own toilets or urinals and therefore we find them answering to the natural calls in a regal style even on roads.

In view of the aforesaid facts, it is right to say that government and NGOs need to sensitise the rural folks preferable in the rural areas of the country so that parents find themselves efficacious of educating and training their children in the said perspective. The educational institutions working in the rural areas bear an outstanding responsibility of educating and sensing their children. Right from the primary level of education to the top level, the informal education needs priority attention. The civic bodies cannot be spared from the responsibility of keeping their homes neat and clean. The Village Panchayats need to accept the responsibility of sensitising and regulating the rural folks and their actions disrespecting the civic sensibility. To the extent, it is possible, these organisations need to get themselves involved in the process of educating and sensing the rural people. The NGOs need to organise night classes for women and adults not getting time during the day time. The government managed primary and high schools need to educate the children by enriching their informal education programme.

We cannot deny that the intensity of problem is at its peak and it is not be resolved unless and until curative as well as the preventive measures are taken. The Indians either living in the rural areas or in the urban areas by and large have the same habits. It is also an unvarnished fact that for regulating their bad habits; we need to take support of punishment or punitive measures. In any part of the globe, if there is civic sense, it is due to the fact that we find the concerned authorities very much tough to those who flout the civic rules. At the initial stage, it is to be regulated by punitive measures and then in due course, we find an increase in the inculcation of habits and thereafter its transfer to the budding generations. Simultaneously, we need to activate the sensitisation process. Poverty cannot be an excuse. When you have money to buy the cell-phone; you should have money even to construct a toilet. Moreover, you get the financial support from the government, you should not have any option but to regulate your behaviour.

◈ Civic Sense of the City Folks

Biggest problem confronting the city vis-à-vis the country as a whole is lack of civic sense. Former Indian President A.P.J. Abdul Kalam rightly says, "Why do we Indian as a whole score so poorly on civic sense? What intrigued me is that the same Indian who let his dog dirty the pavement in India would not throw as little as a bus ticket on the pavements of Singapore!" This speaks of the attitude of the Indians in India and abroad. The main reason for this attitudinal transformation is fear-psychosis. If we do in India, because nobody to check it. We regulate our behaviour and habits abroad, because rules are there strictly enforced and person irrespective of its status and position cannot venture to floute or violate.

Of late, in the big cities we find a peculiar as well as a dangerous trend promoted by upcoming youths or budding generations in particular. Flamboyant two-wheeler drivers, throwing caution to the winds and without an iota of concern or even extremely small amount of concern for fellow pedestrians, so called stunt masters of today drive with gay abandon on footpaths, whether on the ground level or on the flyover. The reckless and thoughtless two wheeler drivers have been found driving even on important roads of the cities even at ultra-furious pace. Traffic cops normally just swish away and complaint made in this regard. The rules are flouted with impunity and without fear, caring a damn for the country's image, inconveniences of fellow citizens and even their own lives. The high speed vehicles and smooth roads where we find rash drive very much effective in increasing the cases of accidents for which we find our civic insensibility responsible. A sense of fear becomes essential to regulate such cases.

Indians in general, irrespective of the fact that they live in big cities or small cities, and towns or in the rural areas, are by and large insensitive to the importance and value of civic sense. Throwing trash or waste material as and where we like, spitting without any concern for others and answering natural calls in every available vacant place and space are a staunch testimony to this proposition that the rate of insensitivity is found of high order. At many places, you will find construction materials on the roads even dumped in a crude manner or just outside the house or building underconstruction. It is not simply a matter of inconveniences but an important reason for serious health hazards and responsible for diseases like malaria, diarrhoea and many viral infections.

Malcolm Wolfe puts it across very well when he states, "Most people believe in personal hygiene and corporate filth or disgusting dirt. They believe that they have all the right to throw anything on the street, as long as it does not affect them personally. In other ways, their attitude is why to bother, if my waste thrown on the streets spoils the shirt of the other person, but does not spoil mine." This makes it essential that we sense and sensitise the entire community, specially in terms of civic sense.

In Malaysia, the roads are so clean that we may think to lay there. If you put any waste even your saliva from mouth will invite policemen's attention and you will be put on jail for a day. In India, certain areas are designated as urinals. The stench becomes over powering and the rest of the public are unable to use this area. Most men do not think twice before committing such an act. In the government hospitals in particular, the visiting hours are not adhered to. Visitors come in hoards, bring eatables and bring not only germs but also carry hospital germs home. There are a number of people who do not mind spitting out of a moving vehicle. It does not matter where the spittle or salvia flies. They may travel in expensive vehicles, also maintain it very well have the latest gadgets inside, employ drivers to drive and clean it regularly. But when the urges come on, the owners or passengers roll down the windows and spit.

People do not think while throwing garbage on the roads. Some of us even deface the historic monument. They write dirty messages and feel that it is the only way to express their love. Even in apartment complexes, there are people who throw hair, chocolate wrappers, fruits waste or so. Those who have pets do not care for other road users. They take their pets for the walks and to answer the call of nature. They allow their dogs to use the center of the road as the public animal toilet. It is most common to find plastic wrappers, papers, paper plates and broken bottles on the beach.

There are a number of countries where littering is an offence and people who are caught are fined. This has created a generation of clean people who do not litter at public places. When we visit those countries, we find even ourselves very obedient but when return, we come back to our old habits.

We cannot deny that a majority of the city folks lack civic sense. If you look at the roads, boundary walls, stairwalls, inside lifts, markets, inside public transport, hospitals, and other areas; this observation is found right. We should not forget that our wrong habits make the ways for critical problems. Even swine flu is caused by the absence of hygiene. Inspite of knowing the harmful effects, we find a majority of us promoting civic insensibility.

You are riding a vehicle on the road and waiting for the green signal at a junction in your city. Since there is a digital timer also, you turned your vehicle to neutral and soon the signal turned green. Unfortunately, you could not start the vehicle immediately. The commuters behind you, sound horn recklessly and harshly. We need to feel that provided we face the same problem at the signals, how and in what way we react. It is not proper that we only think about our own conveniences or inconveniences. It is, of course, barbarious to think in such a way.

Almost all the cities and towns of the country in India, by and large face the same problem. Parking vehicles on the roads is found a common problem which you have to overlook. The road-rage may obstruct you but have to bear, the overtakers may misguide you but you have to remain patient. The drivers known for rash driving may harm you but you have to face.

Bangalore resident Sujatha Bagal says "I have been abroad and seen at first hand as to how their citizens respect civic rules. I saw with my own eyes as to how a German mother taught her little boy back to carry the candy paper till the next trash bin." What to talk of others when I myself have witnessed a Cypriot kid in Nicosia Park, though not more than three years old coming to the trashbin for throwing the waste packaging.

Just reverse, we find a majority of the Indian ladies instantly dropping garbage on the roads just before their houses. Conversely, I have witnessed Cypriot ladies while cleaning their houses, also cleaning the roads before their houses. Peeing or urinating openly is a habit in India and one can witness a number of urines running down the walls in the Indian cities. It is not a matter of poverty or backwardness; more so, it is a matter of our shamelessness, unawareness, making us habituated. Sujatha Bagal again says, "I remember 3 years back when I used to deal in jewellery. I went to a 17-storey building in Mumbai where all the wholesalers, have their showrooms. Each and every of them a multi-multi millionaire and the offices were very small, functional by immaculately clean. When I dropped outside on the aside to walk to the next door. I could feel a stench mixed with disbelief coming up my nose. I walked further when I looked into the joint floor-toilet of these multi-multi millionaires it was disgusting as the train station toilets in Germany's small towns looked back in the 1970s. If these jewellery dealers were to invest jointly $ 2000 once and for maintenance another jointly $60 per month, it would have made this toilet look like a palace. But it is no, it doesn't happen now, and I don't believe it will happen in India even in the next 1000 years. Because, it requires a feeling of co-ownership, of a joint cause, eyes, call it civic sense. And that is certainly not one of India's strongest traits."

In almost all the big cities of the country, we find by and large the same problem. Now Hyderabad is globally known as a hi-tech city but there is not sufficient infrastructure to support or cater to the burgeoning population, a sizeable portion of which settles down in slums and sidewalks upon arriving into the city. They lack toilets and we find them respecting natural calls or peeing of roads. You will witness the same case in Delhi and New Delhi, when you think of enjoying the pleasure of morning walk on the roads.

The above mentioned facts make it clear that we Indian need civic sensibility failing which we cannot be called a sensible citizen of the country. In the short run, we need to take the regulatory support and in the long-run we need to educate the society. It is in bad taste that we do not assign due weightage to the development of civic sense. Ultimately, it is the responsibility of a family or particularly parents who need to sense and sensitise their kids or children. Answering to natural calls in a regal style wherever we find an empty space or a boundary wall, whether it is in the heart of the city or in the interiors will continue unless we educate ourselves. You will find a number of cases when people bring their pet dogs and dump their dirties in front of others' houses. We find public parks becoming dumping yards and centre for anti-social activities.

What to talk of other activities when we find even prostitution and drug-trafficking taking place in public parks. There are also areas where public parks are used as toilet zones specially by the hut dwellers. What to talk of the uneducated segment of the society when we find albeit educated and well-heeled people involved in the process. Actually, we least bother about, keeping the surroundings clean. With every passing day, we find cities becoming dirtier and it is due mainly to the lack of civic sense.

Day-by-day, we find the migration of people from the rural areas to the urban areas of the country gaining a rapid momentum and the intensity of problem reaching to its peak. To resolve the problem, Malcolm Wolfe suggests, "Two things are needed. Education and Enforcement. Also, the media need to get themselves involved in the process of educating the public in all languages. As on now, some areas are a huge health risk and the residents, don't even know about it. The general public need to be sensitised and encouraged to improve their civic sense. It's better to not wait for the people who matter, but rather it's better to mobilise the people's power and ensure a drastic change in civic consciousness. I also recommend the proper usage of 'Right to Information Act' to bring about the needed changes."

We cannot deny that sensitisation, is a long-term process but, we need an immediate solution which draws our attention on deterrent, punishment by implementing the "Rule of Law" uniformly and ruthlessly. The motive is to increase civic sensibility and it is not to be possible unless we take support of Rule of Law. In the developed countries like USA, Japan, Germany, Sweden and Singapore, etc., people not venture to flout civic rules. If they venture, they are punished.

American, expatriate Anthony Silcola, who works as a senior manager in a top-notch city-based, firm, affirms this and says, "The fines for throwing the garbage and litter are extremely high in the US, somewhere between ₹ 12,000/- to ₹ 40,000/- per infraction. The US was pretty bad about littering in the 1970s, but these fines helped to control the litter or rubbish left at a public place in the most cities of US. Spitting is as disgusting in the US as it is in India and it is often overlooked. Urinating is akin to public nudity and indecency in the US and the fines for those infractions are large as well. Indian authorities could add so much money in fines to the public coffers if the police would just enforce rules like these."

The facts outlined above make it clear that the general public or folks in almost all the cities of the country lack civic sense and at the same time, we also find civic laws becoming ineffective. We lack civic sense and transfer our habits to the coming generations. Hence, the Rule of Law is required to be implemented uniformly and ruthlessly. Let's hope that even this sensitive problem is not politicised and with the cooperation of all of us it makes possible for us to keep cities clean and free of debris or scattered pieces of rubbish by both daytime crew and special crews working during night when most businesses are shut down for the day. In a true sense, we need a special task force to resolve the problem.

◈ Civic Sense and the Corporate World

The corporate world makes place for the best and therefore corporate people are required to prove themselves to be the best. They are supposed to look even small things in detail. They need world-class thematical competence and intuitive sense of judgement. They need to prove themselves ethically and behaviourally sound. They need a rock star personality and an attractive facial appearance, an established leadership skill full of creativity, etiquette and manners, a professional approach and a personal touch, human-orientation and humanised leadership and what not. Amidst all traits, if we find them lacking civic sense; it may be a strong reason for their firing. It is against this background that our focus here is on ensuring civic sensibility.

The process of corporatisation considerably rests on perfection. It is not even imagined that corporate people lack sense of spitting, sneezing, coughing and gossiping at the important places of presentation, interaction, deliberation and discussions. Indeed, it is expected from them a high level of sensibility to address civic formalities. But in the Indian perspective, we find a number of employees lacking civic sensibility. The places where they need aesthetic sense, we find than unaware of even the civic sense. The Business Schools do not focus civic sense because even kids and children are supposed to be aware of the civic sensibility then what to talk of the Finishing Schools whose focused approaches are found concerned with the facial appearance and accent. At this juncture, we find ourselves at the cross-roads where none to guide us; none to support us. In a true sense, we need to be ashamed of our deficiencies and weaknesses for which we are not responsible.

May be that you have gone through some of the lessons related to civic sense at elementary stages of your education but the impact is, almost dismal. Actually, if we witness our parents and even family members doing something insensible, we witness even other members of the society not aware of civic sensibility, the education becomes meaningless. Even today, we find people both in the urban and rural areas not following the norms which they should follow specially while fulfilling the civic formalities. In villages, what to talk of the men when we find even women going outside for toilet purposes. The young child in a family even in the urban areas are not aware of using the toilet. All the public utility services are found mismanaged. The educational institutions lack toilets; the private houses in villages lack toilet facilities. And this scenario, we witness albeit in the 21st century.

Of course, we have also been successful in accelerating the pace of corporatisation and resulting from which we find corporate sector and corporate culture in a dominating position. But the personal score of an individual need more care and orientation specially by enriching the informal system of education which has remained neglected both in rural and urban areas of the country. The corporate professionals need an intensive care for ensuring the inculcation and cultivation of habits so that possibilities of committing a mistake are ruled out.

The people serving the corporate world need to go through self-evaluation of their personal score with the help of a check-list mainly concerned with the awareness of informal side of development. Based on that, they can make themselves sure about the deficiencies found in their personal profile.

- Are you very much particular while disposing of the household rubbish?
- Are you particular while educating and sensing your children about the right uses of toilets either personal or public?
- Are you careful while washing your hands before and after cook and before and after taking meal?
- Are you sincere while educating and sensing your children about washing of their hands?
- Do you follow the traffic rules?
- Are you aware of the rules for parking your vehicles?
- Do you educate and sense your children about crossing the roads and following the traffic rules ?
- Do you educate and sense your children about the disposal of packaging in the trashbins or dust bins either in home or in the institutions where they read?
- Do you educate and sense your children about cleaning of their noses with the help of handkerchiefs or tissue papers?
- Are you particular to resolve the problems of spitting, sneezing and coughing at workplaces?
- Do you educate your children about the etiquette and manners?
- Are you sure that in no case or even by mistake, you will not breach civic formalities?

Like this a number of questions, if honestly answered, would make you and your children aware of the civic sensibility which would benefit you in many ways. You will be in a position to identify the deficiencies and to recover them on time.

It is not only significant that you are sincere and particular at your workplace. Actually, you need to form a habit of showing civic sensibility everywhere otherwise you may not be sure that the mistakes you have committed at your homes would not be repeated at the workplace. The inculcation of such habits would be useful to the kids, or your children living with you. They will automatically copy each and everything and will start practising at homes or at the educational institutions or public places. The sensibility they have copied as a part of the learning process makes it sure that they never witness anything wrong. This is a process of shifting of sensibility from one generation to another. If you are sensible, your children are bound to be sensible. The moment we find an individual sincere and honest to the civic sense, we find engineering of a sound foundation for the development of aesthetic sense, a strong force for getting success in the corporate world.

◈ Aesthetic Sense

Corporatisation is found based on attraction because it provides to us an opportunity for establishing our distinction. If we have love for nature and beauty, we start appreciating the people who look us beautiful. If we have aesthetic sense, we show our temptation to the artistic taste, beautiful and natural surroundings and ambience. Appreciation is a result of our perception. Since we like, we notice and appreciate. Each one of us are found fascinated to beauty because human beings in general nurture interests for it due to a high degree of psychological instinct.

Creativity happens to be the lifeblood of corporate culture. An individual starts loving nature, if we find him/her perceiving something different. You have to look something different to others. Your surroundings and premises and ambience need an edge over others which is to be possible from an aesthete having appreciation for art and beauty. We cannot deny that an individual with such trait serves the corporate world in a right fashion.

The corporate culture believes in positive feelings and thoughts and this is to be possible when we have awareness of aesthetic sense. Strengthening clientele relationships, impressing upon the business associates and customers make it essential that organisations have better-looking people. This necessitates an intensive effort for getting people nurturing a zest for life, full of creativity and a positive attitude. The increasing love of an individual for nature makes life vibrant, colourful and happy. The quality of life is increased, the level of thinking is increased and simultaneously, the taste is developed and all due to our close association with nature. We cannot deny that nature provides to us the most frequent and varied kinds of aesthetic experiences such as softness, smoothness and tenderness. We start experiencing our properties in music, dance, literature, painting, carving, sculpture, etc. The aesthetic experiences are found expressed in form of ideas, emotions and values representing the cultural refinement of a society. Ultimately, we find people searching beauty in life by improving human relationships and enjoying happiness.

The cultivation of aesthetic sensibility is found essential for taking the pleasure of life. Amidst hustle and bustle, hurry and worry, stress and tension; the life is becoming too much boring. This may develop pessimism and make place for negative thoughts. Career-addiction is found mounting specially amongst youths of the present generation which has been making an invasion on their mental peace. Hence, it is significant that our aesthetic experiences are sensible so that scope for perversion of taste is regulated. Aesthetic refinement is therefore essential so that we succeed in improving the quality of our aesthetic experiences. Aesthetic sensibility and morality are found interrelated. The aesthetically refined people are found morally sound. It is in this context that in modern corporate culture we find relevance of aesthetic refinement.

◈ Cultivating Aesthetic Sense

Of late, we find people becoming inhuman and lacking humane. They are found unaware of empathy then how we can expect from them personal philanthropy. Becoming true and human makes ways for a number of positive developments in our behaviour. Because we find people becoming insensitive to the aesthetic sense, it is quite natural that they are dishonest and inhuman. Materialism has started dominating our behaviour. Hustle and bustle, tension and dissension, stress, and depression are the results of our failures in this materialistic world. Taste-perversion is due to our dissociation with aesthetic sense. If we turn our eyes to the classical Indian civilisation, we find much more refinement in our taste and behaviour. Our ancient tradition, art, poetry, literature, dance, drama, paintings, music, customs, culture are found rich and it is against this background that we had a refined taste which today has been perverted. The main reason for such a degeneration is increasing domination of material culture. This necessitates a new beginning.

Cultivation of aesthetic sense would pave avenues for qualitative improvements. Our love for nature and beauty and our zest for life would revive, if we show our temptation to aesthetic sense. Enjoying the gift of nature and harnessing the benefits of nature are the two opposite considerations. When first helps us in protecting nature, the second helps in exploiting nature. Corporatisation made ways for the development of material culture and this has started dominating our attitudes and behaviour.

A study of Harvard Business School makes it clear that it is all due to system of education that we have promoted during the yester decades. The quantitative system of education has started dominating the qualitative system. When the first promotes calculations, benefit, gains, profits, self; the second promotes values, morality, honesty and empathy. Starting from the America and the spreading to the different parts of the globe; the quantitative system of education, of course, accelerated the pace of economic transformation but slowed down the process of social transformation resulting into a big gap in the society. The streams of education to be instrumental in promoting our ethics and morality outlived their significance and the faculties making us materially sound gained popularity. All of us started tasting the fragrance of economic advancements, materialistic gains, opulent lifestyles and forgot the words like sympathy, empathy, philanthropy. The aesthetic sensibility, no doubt could get place but just for exposition and therefore internal feelings were found deshaped.

Addiction makes the ways for tension and dissension. The upcoming or budding generations have been experiencing the problem of career-addiction. Actually, it is money-addiction. If we get, we find ourselves satisfied and if not, we get stress, tension and everything negative in the form of thoughts and feelings which open doors for pains and sorrows. This necessitates sincere and honest efforts for cultivating aesthetic sense.

The gurgling brooks, the rustle of leaves, the chirping and singing of birds, the thunder of clouds, and the roar of oceans are the gifts of nature. All of us equally share the beauty for which we are not required to pay anything. If we find natural calamities harming us, it is due to the imbalance for which only we are responsible. The focus here is on understanding the beauty of nature and enjoying them in a right fashion to inject new energy to our mind. Linking our relationships with nature is significant to bring happiness.

◈ Receiving the Beauty of Art

Human beings are known for creativity and innovations. It is due to the mind provided to them by almighty God. If we link our relationships with the nature, we succeed in refreshing and purifying our mind which can write something, can create something or can innovate and discover something. We find creation of human beings in different forms such as music, dance, literature, painting, carving, sculpture, etc. This reflects the quality of people and their association with nature. This also expresses our aesthetic sensibility and cultural refinement. We cannot deny that art is the result of our emotional and artistic sensitivity and sensibility. Firstly, we find development of aesthetic sense, then we find creation of idea and after that we find translation of ideas into writing, painting, carving, dancing or into different forms of art helping purification and rejuvenation of our mind. It is not to be refuted that ultimately our aesthetic sense is found responsible for the positive contributions. The creation and expression of ideas cannot be possible it we do not have aesthetic sensibility.

◈ Enjoying the Beauty of Life

We are the best creation of almighty God. We need to enjoy the beautiful life. We need to create the zest for life. This makes it essential that we are optimistic, for that we need to be positive and again for that we need to be creative which is not be possible unless we develop and strengthen our relationships with the nature. Actually, we need to change the perception of life. The development of positive feelings, nurturing mindness for others, helping them to the extent it is possible make place for optimism. We start evincing interests in life and get an opportunity to enjoy. We cannot deny that all these are the positive properties which provide to us the positive results and in return, we get happiness, the ultimate motto of life.

The aesthetic sensibility paves avenues for the development of positive feelings. We find ourselves to be optimistic because we start loving ourselves. We develop temptation of leading a lavish lifestyle and for that we need to enrich our personal score or properties to prove our excellence. We cannot deny that our lifestyles speak of our quality of taste and motivate us to develop taste in apparel, attire, etiquette and manners, facial appearance or looks, household objects, etc., or say physical appearance. This again recycles our zest because we start loving beauty created by God and brushed up by ourselves.

The facts outlined above make it clear that there is nothing more appealing than a man with a sense of wit and fun and there is nothing more paying than an aesthete.

Energising emotional and human capabilities depend on our efforts for enriching aesthetic sensibility which in due course may also be effective in improving the professional excellence.

With the passage of time, the contours of development have undergone radical transformation and resulting from which we find our utilitarian efforts witnessing innovations. This has been possible due to the role played by aesthete in restructuring the value-addition process. It is in this context that we find aesthetic considerations becoming increasingly important in numerous practical areas such as engineering and industrial design, town planning, landscape designing, interior decoration in an innovative form. Aesthetic flavour in these areas have been successful in attracting customers and redefining the concept of ambience. The service environment is now found much more productive where the providers feel pleasure in performing and the customers as well as the visitors feel pleasure in evidencing and gaining new experiences. But again we find commercialisation of aesthetic sensibility. The aesthetes have now a big market.

Whatsoever the positive or negative developments, we find in the socio-economic systems and subsystems due to aesthetic sensibility and its commercialisation can be regulated in the larger interests of upcoming generations, if we respect or honour the limits. Aesthetic sensibility makes ways for the development of morality because ultimately, we have to love beauty and nature. The moment we start loving nature and beauty we find our zest for life increasing very fast and in the process, we have no option but to bid a goodbye to the multi-dimensional complexes.

◈ Understanding the Beauty of Nature

Aesthetic considerations make it essential that we perceive beauty in a right fashion. Looking pleasant and soothing to our eyes, throwing positive impact on our mind; it is the beauty of nature. It is concerned with feelings, expression or embodiment. What a scientist or a philosopher discovers; we consider it truth and what an aesthete projects, we call it beauty.

Increasing love for nature increases zest for life

Nature is beautiful. Nature has provided enough materials to make this world beautiful. Human beings make beautiful objects by their hands by making use of their intelligence, imagination and creative feelings. A beautiful face is a thing of joy forever which proves to be a source for happiness creation of poems and at times even for battles. In the history, the face of the Helen of Troy, Cleropatra and Noorjahan caused much turmoil in their respective lands. Thus, we find beauty showing both the positive as well as the negative influences.

Beauty is not only related to the human beings, but even to the nature. The plants, trees, animals, birds, rivers, seas are the gifts of nature and we find them playing a big role in making the environmental conditions beautiful. Thus we find beauty in life and all the living beings are found beautiful, the lofty mountains, the deep values, the shifting patterns of clouds in the sky, etc., are the gifts of nature and we find them beautiful.

◈ Aesthetic Sense and the Corporate World

Again and again, we make a strong advocacy in favour of attraction for momentising the process of corporatisation. It is due mainly to the fact that the very foundation of corporate world rests on perfection which may either be related to your professional excellence or may be associated with your personality. The corporate world looks for better-looking people because they are supposed to be very creative and optimistic. We cannot negate that the aesthetic sense brings a number of qualitative improvements in their inner and outer qualities. An aesthete assigns a transcendental priority to the facial appearance because it is considered to be the most vital force for creating a positive impression. Since first impression is considered to be the last impression, your looks prove to be productive in many ways. You succeed in impressing upon your superiors; because you respect the organisational culture, you succeed in influencing your associates, clients and customers; because you follow the dress code. The people having aesthetic sensibility have a high level of taste vis-à-vis the positive attitude and etiquette and manners. They take even small things in detail and associate themselves with the established corporate brand and image. They are always hireable and promotable and get big bucks for their sensible investment dressing.

It is against this background that aesthetic sense draws priority attention of all of us who evince keen interests in climbing the corporate ladders. The different dimensions of aesthetic sensibility such as your attire or apparel, your facial appearance, your shoes and socks, your ties, your wrist watch and pen, your briefcase or bag, your hair style, etc., play an incremental role in the development of your personality. All the associated and allied areas need your personal touch and professional approach. Actually, grooming is an essential part of looks which plays a significant role in the value-addition of your facial appearance. Of course, you need world-class professional excellence because you have an ambition to remain at the top of the hierarchy or at the peak of the corporate ladders but if you are not sincere to your looks, this may also cause firing.

It is in this context that we need to assign due weightage to the aesthetic sensibility because aesthetically — deficient people are found to be of negative attitude and the corporate world always looks for optimistic people having a high degree of sensibility and creativity. For getting success in life, it is essential that you have a zest and if you are an aesthete, it is possible. You get yourself ready for your office; you stand before the mirror and if you find everything in tune with the expectations of your organisation, there is a smile on your face and from here, we find beginning of a positive thinking in your behaviour which helps you vis-à-vis promotes the organisational interests.

The aesthetic sense thus keeps on moving your love for self and nature and beauty makes your life vibrant, colourful and happy. This also brings in you softness, tenderness and politeness. Since you have enriched your personal profile, your success in the corporate world is almost secured.

SUMMARY

In this chapter, you have gone through different aspects of civic and aesthetic sense. Before starting another chapter, be sure that the following facts are well versed.

Civic Sense: Civic sense is a school of thought. We also call it social ethics or unspoken social norms. It is a belief in hygiene. It is a respect for other members of the society. Civic sense also includes in its purview our awareness of the civic laws.

Dimensions of Civic Sense: There are a number of aspects to be included in the civic sense such as home hygiene, public hygiene, traffic sense, behavioural sense, awareness of relationship, environment, community care and legal sense.

Civic Sense of the Rural Folks: The rural folks of India lack civic sense which appears to be an important reason for the increasing cases of epidemics in the Indian villages. We do agree with this view that due mainly to increasing insensitivity, we find bodies like village panchayats and non-government organisations becoming defunct in the Indian villages.

Civic Sense of the City Folks: By and large, we find rural folks as well as the city folks in the same boat, specially in respect of civic insensibility. A number of problems crop up on that account. The increasing cases of breaking of civic laws and lack of authorities to regulate the same obstruct a trend of reversal. Almost all the centres providing public utility services present a dirty look and the magnitude of problem is found at its peak.

Justifications for Developing Civic Sense: There are a number of justifications for inculcating civic sense. The civic sense makes the ways for aesthetic sense, it makes us civilised and disciplined, improves the quality of hygiene, regulates the misuses of civic amenities, simplifies the process of managing the traffic, simplifies the process of building character and paves avenues for practising self regulation or social regulation.

Cultivating Civic Sense: In today's society, it is imperative that we make efforts to inculcate civic sense by ensuring the awareness of civic formalities, traffic sense, management of waste, proper use of public utility services, awareness of personal hygiene, awareness of life styles and awareness of nature and environment.

Civic Sense and the Corporate World: The corporate professionals need an intensive care for ensuring the inculcation of civic sense. Etiquette and manners cannot be possible unless we have civic sensibility.

Aesthetic Sense: Aesthetic sense is meant our temptation to beauty and nature. The cultivation of aesthetic sense is found essential for taking the pleasure of art and beauty.

Cultivating Aesthetic Sense: Our love for nature and beauty, our zest for life, our positive feelings and optimism depend on aesthetic sense. For that we need to receive the beauty of art, enjoy the beauty of life and understand the beauty of nature.

Aesthetic sense and the Corporate World: The aesthetic sense brings in you softness, tenderness and politeness. It keeps in moving your love for self, your love for nature and beauty and makes your life vibrant, colourful and happy and we find these things essential for the corporate world.

KEY TERMS

Civic Sense	Social Regulation
Aesthetic Sense	Biomedical Waste
City Folks	Rural Folks
Urban Folks	Stunt Masters
Social Ethics	Rash Drive
School of Thought	Littering
Vandalism	Cypriot
Separatism	Corporate World
Road Rage	Zest
Hygiene	Empathy
Home Hygiene	Optimistic
Public Hygiene	Creative
Traffic Sense	Creative
Behavioural Sense	Sculpture
Relationship Sense	Gross Happiness Life Index
Communal Sense	City Dwellers

EXPECTED QUESTIONS

1. What do you mean by Civic Sense? Explain its different dimensions,
2. Discuss that how and in what way the different dimensions of civic sense help an increase in civic sensibility.
3. Throw light on the civic sensibility that we find amongst the rural folks in the Indian perspective.
4. Focus on the civic sensibility that we find amongst the city folks in the Indian perspective.
5. Deliberate upon the measures to be helpful in regulating the increasing cases of civic insensibility found amongst both the rural and city folks.
6. How with the help of a check list, you will evaluate your personal score related to civic sense?
7. Explain the measures to be effective in inculcating civic sense amongst your children.
8. Focus on the justifications for developing civic sense in India.
9. Throw light on the areas where we find possibilities for flouting the civic rules.
10. What do you mean by bio-medical waste? Explain mismanagement of bio-medical waste as a part of civic insensibility.
11. Why do you justify civic sense an essential consideration for the people serving the corporate world
12. What do you mean by Aesthetic Sense? Explain its relevance to the corporate world.
13. Focus on the essentials for the development of aesthetic sense.
14. The beauty of art, beauty of life and beauty of nature need to be perceived in a right way for the development of aesthetic sense. Do you agree? Defend your arguments.
15. Write a reasoned note on civic sense in the Indian perspective.
16. Write a reasoned note on aesthetic sense with special reference to the corporate culture.
17. We find a number of cases when Indians though have a cell-phone in their hands but for answering natural calls, they do not have their own toilets. Comment on this statement.
18. Do we find poverty and unawareness the two important reasons for breaking the civic laws by the Indian? Justify your arguments.

APPLICATION EXERCISES

1. "The stinking public latrines or urinals, scattered garbage of even domestic wastage on the roads, unawareness of traffic sense, insensitivity to personal hygiene, gross misuse of public utility services are a staunch testimony to this proposition that we are uncivilised and need to inculcate civic sensibility."

   Comment on this statement and focus on the role of civic sense in the modern business world where people are also becoming indisciplined.
2. Do you favour that increasing cases of separatism, vandalism, intolerance, racism, road-rage are also due to an increase in the civic insensibility? Justify your viewpoints.
3. "Civic sense is a school of thought." Comment on this statement.
4. "Why do we Indians as a whole score so poorly on civic sense? What intrigued me is that the same Indian who let his dog dirty the pavement in India would not throw as little as

a bus ticket on the pavements of Singapore!" In the face of this statement of Former President of India A.P.J. Abdul Kalam; focus on the attitudinal differences that we find in the present case.

5. "In Malaysia, the roads are so neat that we will think to lay there! If you put any waste, even your salvia from mouth, will invite policemen's attention and you will be put on jail for a day!" Do you find it judicious to improve civic sensibility in the Indian perspective? Justify your viewpoints.
6. "You went to a shopping complex to buy some clothes. On return, you will find your bike is blocked by many more bikes behind. You could not even take your vehicle because behind your vehicle another big row is formed. It is common in almost all cities of India. Focus on the suggestive pleasure to resolve such problem.
7. "Most people believe in personal hygiene and corporate filth. They also believe that they have all the right to throw anything on the street as long as it does not affect them personally. In other ways, their attitude is, why to bother, if my waste thrown on the streets spoils the shirt of other person but does not spoil mine." Throw light on the above statement in the face of civic sensibility.
8. "A walk-in to places like NTR Marg footpath, Raj Bhavan Road footpath, Lifestyle Mall flyover, etc., will allow one to sample the sight of reckless and thoughtless two wheeler drivers driving on them at ultra-furious, pace. Traffic cops just swish away any complaint made in this regard."

   Throw light, on the measures to chisel them on the right path.
9. "German mothers teach their kids civic sense by carrying and throwing themselves the candy paper in the trashbin. On the other hand, in India garbage is dropped instantly when it occurs anywhere, anytime, they clean their homes but throw the household rubbish on the roads, the Cypriot old ladies clean their homes and simultaneously clean the roads before their homes." Comment on this statement.
10. "A number of people assume that civic sense is just about keeping the roads clean. Actually, it is more than that. It has also to do with law-abiding, respect for fellow men and maintaining decorum at the public places."

    In the face of above statement, focus on the different dimensions of civic sense.
11. "Answering to the call of nature in the open air is found very common in the Indian villages. What to talk of the men when we find even women adopting this so called regal style. May be that they have cell-phone but they do not have toilets."

    In the face of above statement, throw light on the civic sensibility amongst the rural folks in India.
12. "A majority of the city folks lack civic sense. If you look at the roads, boundary walls, stairwalls, inside of the lifts, markets, inside public transport, hospitals, park and other areas by and large you find lack of civic sensibility everywhere. Parking vehicles on the roads is found a common problem which you have to overlook. The road-rage may obstruct you but you have to bear. The overtakers may misguide you and even may complicate your driving but you have to face."

    Comment on the statement in the face of civic sense amongst the city folks in India.
13. Focus on the relevance of education to take your children much more sensible. Also explain the role of educational institutions in promoting the informal education for generating civic sensibility.

14. There are a number of reasons justifying the relevance of civic sensibility in the present society. Focus on the reasons justifying sensibility for the development of personal score in tune with the requirements of corporate world.
15. "Since the uncivilised and indisciplined social members may disturb the set order, it is imperative that family and social institutions play an incremental role in activating the sensitisation process."

    In the light of this statement, explain the dimensions you will take care for cultivating civic sense.
16. "Creativity happens to be the lifeblood of the corporate culture. An individual starts loving nature provided she/he has aesthetic sense if we have aesthetic sense, we show our temptation to the beautiful and natural surroundings and ambience." Comment on this statement in the face of aesthetic sense found to be essential in the corporate world.
17. "Our ancient culture, art, poetry, literature, dance, drama, paintings, music, customs and traditions are found rich and therefore we have refined taste and creative minds.

    Do you agree with this statement? Defend your arguments.
18. "Linking our relationships with nature, receiving the beauty of art, enjoying the beauty of life and understanding the beauty of nature are essential for the development of aesthetic sense." Comment.

BACK-UP MATERIALS

1. www.citehr.com
   www.corporategurukul.com

   First Impression
   Corporate grooming, Hygiene and Skin care
   Hands and feet, Make-up, Accessories, Hair
2. search 4 beauty.blogspot.com

   Requirements for charm and beauty
   Healthy hair, Skin care, Nails, Teeth and Bones, Rest and relaxation
3. www.hindu.com.blogs.oneindia.in

   Civic Sensep
   Poor Civic Sense of City Folks
   Poor Civic Sense of Rural Folks
   Teach your child about the civic sense
4. www.minoritycareernet.com
   www.mindingmanners.com

   Minding Your Corporate Manners
5. spas.about.com

   Business of Beauty
   Beauty Salon
   Beauty Treatments
   Beauty Salon Products

6. www.webhealthcentre.com
   en.wikipedia.org
   www.statefundca.com

   Bathing Products
   Grooming Products
   Hygiene Practices

7. www.frontierlaw.com
   www.thehindubusinessline.com

   Physical Appearance
   Environment and Nature

8. en.wikipedia.org.runwayculture.net

   Human Beauty
   Ugliness
   Take care of your inner beauty

9. www.indianetzone.com
   www.indianexpress.com

   Human Personality

◆ ◆ ◆

5 MANAGEMENT OF MIND

Healthy mind paves avenues for the development of a healthy body. In the world of hurry, curry and worry and amidst hustle and bustle, it is difficult for us to have a healthy mind. This necessitates scientific management of mind so that the purification process gains a rapid momentum.

CHAPTER DESIGN

Introduction – Healthy Mind – Meditation and Mind Purification – Yoga: A Conceptual Exposition – Yogic View on Human Personality – Yoga and Ethics – Karma Yoga: Understand the Perception – Yoga in Combating Stress – Yoga Postures – The Sun Salutation – Lotus Posture – Shoulder Stand Posture – Head Stand Posture Fish Posture – Plough Posture – Accomplished Posture – Corpse Posture – Wind Release Posture – Cultural and Spiritual Forces Combating Stress – Participation in Spiritual Sessions for Combating Stress – Working Holiday for Combating Stress – Sleep Better for Combating Stress – Gardening for Combating Stress – Entertainment for Combating Stress – Pet-Therapy for Combating Stress – Retail Therapy for Combating Stress – Healthy Mind for Healthy Body – Summary – Key Terms – Expected Questions – Application Exercises – Back-up Materials.

CHAPTER OBJECTIVES

This chapter aims at studying the different dimensions helping a scientific management of mind. The stockpile of multi-faceted complexes create problems after accumulation. This necessitates a well managed clearing process. Cheerfulness and warmth bring happiness. Mind and mood affect the workplace environment. Spiritualism at the workplace paves avenues for mind purification. The motive of this chapter is to sensitise the readers to the various dimensions of busting stress so that the employees feel themselves relaxed. We should not forget that nothing like a sound mind, nothing like happiness and nothing like a good laugh making ways for laughter.

MANAGEMENT OF MIND

◈ Introduction

Material culture considerably influenced by the corporate culture makes the ways for the development of the levels of expectations which enrich the stockpile of multi-faceted complexes and resulting from which we are tensed, stressed and depressed. We find much more sensitivity in our mind and the stored complexes disturb the entire process of thinking and creating something innovative. Agitated mind cannot be healthy. It is quite natural that we cannot be successful in fulfilling our needs, requirements and expectations and which if remain unfulfilled paves copious avenues for nurturing agitations. The likes and dislikes crop-up as the by-product of development processes and a continuous accumulation of such likes and dislikes make place for stress which agitates our mind and makes it indisciplined and unhealthy. It is an unvarnished fact that stress-free mind is found to be healthy, creative and productive because we find it calm and cool. This makes it essential that sincere and honest efforts are initiated to clear the stored complexes. The non-reactive observation of oneself mitigates the strength of these complexes which can be cleared by sensitising the masses. The professionals managing the affairs need to receive it that if we start serving the interests of humanity by fulfilling the humanitarian commitments; the stockpile of complexes disturbing our mind, accumulated in different forms start a reversal. Developing awareness of people serving the organisation that intellectual-self and path of devotion help clearing the stored complexes requires due attention of professionals.

Healthy mind paves avenues for the development of a healthy body and vice versa. Accumulated complexes obstruct the process of developing mind and body. In the changing scenario, it is not possible that people regulate their spending behaviour. This may open doors for the development of stress. The most important thing in the very context is to organise education and training programme related to Yoga which would make it easier to reverse the process. It is significant that yoga is not promoted as a cult and as a fashion rather than as a way of life.

Yoga is a science. It is a set of technique to protect and promote the interests of human beings. It is a systematic, methodical and practical discipline and more so, an experimental science of self study. It has no relation with any religion and therefore anybody coming from any religion can practise yoga. We cannot negate that Indian sages and saints previously used Yoga to experience the deepest self. It is a tradition, indeed a living tradition dating back for centuries which was codified by "Patanjali" in the Yoga Sutras written about the second century BC. Such an old tradition needs due attention of corporate world as an effective prescription to counter the side-effects of material culture.

The scientific management of mind makes the ways for cheerfulness and we cannot negate that cheerfulness and warmth spread like viruses. The rise and fall is the very property of corporate sector. If we find the economy booming, we should keep ourselves mentally and potentially ready to counter the recession and depression. If we witness a pay hike; we should also keep ourselves ready for a pay cut. If we witness creation of new job opportunities; we should also keep ourselves ready for retrenchment. But the crux of the problem is that we never make preparations to counter an odd situation rather become much more addicted to the positive side and make the ways for stress and depression. We cannot deny that a happy employee is a productive one. A study by the Yale School of Management makes it clear that mind and mood affect the work environment. Actually, emotions spread like viruses. Cheerfulness and warmth spread most smoothly whereas irritability is found less contagious and depression spreads hardly at all. Keeping the employees happy is an important functional responsibility before a corporate professional. It is due to the fact that when we find ourselves happy, laughter is found easier and natural. We laugh and make others to laugh. The neurologists opine that laughter involves highly complex neural systems. It represents the shortest distance between two people because it instantly inter-lock limbic systems. Keeping employees cheerful and happy thus is the most productive process of increasing the operational efficiency and productivity. The working group must be emotionally high to have a true work culture.

Of late, we find emotional challenges complicating our tasks. We hardly find even a single day when we do not experience some sort of emotional challenges. This necessitates laughing and sharing laughter. But the task of sharing is found very much difficult. It is an art of managing mind through scientific Yoga, devotion and meditation which makes our tasks much more easier. It is against this background that we find management of mind emerging as the most effective dimension of personal care management. The professionals in the today's context bear the responsibility of creating joyful experiences for their subordinates. They may form a group of like minded people and provide to them an opportunity to go out to find something to laugh. They may organise even a laughter show and albeit spiritual sessions in addition to the formal Yoga training. These devices would keep the employees fresh where there would be lesser possibilities for irritation and agitation.

Nothing like a sound mind. Nothing like happiness. Nothing like a good laugh. The entire focus is on the management of mind which makes it essential that all possible efforts are initiated to keep employees happy. We may practise meditation or other devices so that people serving our organisations inculcate habits of nurturing positive feelings. Spirituality at the workplace paves the avenues for humanised leadership where we may expect place for ethically and morally sound employees who may rekindle new hopes and aspirations to work smoothly where we find new definitions, new perceptions and new priorities of lifestyles engineering a sound foundation for multi-dimensional odds and challenges.

Purification of mind is considered essential and this focuses on the substitution process which makes it significant that we replace negative feelings by the positive feelings. The positive virtuous thoughts of mercy, love, purity, forgiveness, integrity, generosity, humility, etc., help the destruction of evil thoughts like hatred, lust, anger, greed, pride, etc. When we start attacking directly on the vicious thoughts, the task is found much more difficult. Self-realisation makes it essential that we have a pure mind. Attaining the stage of supreme peace makes it essential that we find our mind free from desires, cravings, worries, delusion, pride, lust, attachment and likes and dislikes. The concentration and meditation make our tasks of entering the domain of supreme peace easier. The most important thing in the purification process is to make place for good thoughts in our mind because we pollute the world with our bad thoughts and help the world by our good thoughts. How and in what way, the professionals make the ways for accommodating good thoughts in the mind of people serving their organisations is an important issue which requires an effective solution.

The different paths of removing the accumulated complexes help us in purifying our minds for concentration and meditation. The people serving the corporate sector in particular nourish a number of complexes in their minds. This is due mainly to the fact that they welcome the imaginations which cannot be fulfilled. Actually, we need to learn the art of enriching our potentials which automatically make ways for the fulfilment of our desires. Earning more cannot be unfair but here we are not supposed to make an invasion on our culture, norms and traditions which may throw us in the reverse gear.

Of late, we find people showing a craze for the modern westernised culture; they are found hankering after the materialistic gains; they do not have any schedule and any lifestyle; they are agitated, irritated, stressed and depressed to such an extent that we do not find them sleeping without taking sleeping pills and laughing without visiting the laughter shows or clubs. If we find no place for emotions in our mind and heart, it becomes difficult for us to establish the difference between human and animal behaviour. Addiction to material culture cannot be considered to be a positive sign of development. Ultimately, it is going to affect the quality of our mind and sooner or later, we find everything becoming unproductive.

While measuring human quality, we also need to assign due weightage to the human and ethical dimensions of personality. Of course, the level of performance is an important indicator but the public or private sector organisations cannot survive or thrive if we find them facing the crisis of morally and ethically sound people. The vicious circle of value erosion and ethical degeneration can be reversed; if we find organisations encouraging, motivating and luring quality people. The thirst for materialistic gains requires to be regulated. The craze for earning more and spending more is required to be minimised. The ways through which we are moving forward cannot be instrumental in the mind-purification process. The budding generations are to be the worst sufferers; if we delay the process of purifying the mind. The stockpile of complexes accumulated in our mind are required to be cleared.

◆ Healthy Mind

Mind is a regulator and if we find something wrong with it, the task of having a healthy mind is difficult. This necessitates focus on some of the requirements helping us in having a healthy mind. We cannot even imagine about a healthy body if we lack a healthy mind. Agitations make our mind unhealthy and therefore it is imperative that we are particular to the factors agitating our mind. If we do not get what we desire and if we get what one dislikes and further if we nurture uncontrolled emotions, the doors are opened for agitations. Actually, accumulation of likes and dislikes makes the ways for stressed-mind and this one agitates the mind which makes our mind unhealthy. This also speaks of the fact that stress-free mind is a healthy mind. Cool and calm mind keep us healthy. This necessitates due attention on keeping our mind stress-free. Since in the present world, we find a number of sources for the development of stress, it is pertinent that our focus is on distressing the mind.

The environment in which we live; the workplace where we work, the peers and subordinates and superiors with whom we interact and deal with are the sources for accumulation of day-to-day complexes. We find generation of complexes an ongoing process and therefore accumulation is but natural. The stockpile of stored complexes considerably stress our mind. Hence, the most important task before us is to clear the accumulated complexes. How and in what we clear the complexes determine the health of our mind.

We cannot deny that environment in which we live has been making our task much more critical. With the emergence of corporate culture and with the increasing heat of globalisation, we find the fuelling process for the creation and generation of stress becoming more smooth. The material culture is found at the stage of maturity. The new definition and perceptions of family has been aggravating the intensity of problem. The contraction in the size of family and the emergence of live in relationship pave avenues for aggravating the stress. Thus corporate professionals find it difficult to clear the stockpile of complexes. We find each and everyone instrumental in generating tension but none of them helpful in the diffusion process. Our non-reactive observations mitigate the life and strength of these complexes. But only mitigation cannot be a resolution and therefore we need continuity for clearing the accumulated complexes.

There are a number of prescriptions for removal of accumulated complexes and we have to diagnose the effectiveness of each one of the prescription for a successful resolution. The path of service, path of intellectual analysis and the path of devotion are considered effective measures. It is in this context that we make a strong advocacy in favour of path of meditation or devotion where we find emphasis on Yoga. Concentration helps in keeping our mind calm and cool. The self realisation comes through meditation where we start realising the difference between right and wrong, deeds and misdeeds and good and bad.

We cannot deny that a strong mental capacity is vital for the people who live and work in an environment generating tension and stress. The professionals need to perceive it that ability of mind to concentrate and adopt to pressures from the environment makes them much more effective and productive because we find people staying calm and focused despite different forms of adversity. The people specially working in hospitals and particularly in the emergency ward are supposed to remain effective even if the working conditions generate tension and stress. Increasing the level of wisdom of employees serving your organisation make them intellectually sound which paves the ways for the development of blissful self where they succeed in improving their human personality. Preserving happiness, avoiding negative thoughts or emotions from getting in their way enable an individual to overcome physical, emotional and psychological struggles. In the process, you are supposed to be aware of Yoga, Pranayam and Meditation. It is significant to mention that deep meditation provides us an opportunity to experience the peace of inner self.

Healthy mind of working people helps professionals in different ways. The task of making employees sincere, honest, value-based and personally committed is considerably simplified, if we provide to them an opportunity to develop their temptation to Yoga and the path of meditation. As soon as they start keeping them attached with the path of devotion, we find them tempted to the spiritual sessions. Gradually, the minds become insensitive to the complexes and sensitive to happiness. They start learning the art of preserving happiness and are found less agitated and stressed. They start setting examples for others.

Managing healthy mind thus is an important dimension of personal care management. Managing self is, of course, the most effective prescription for managing mind. We cannot negate that success in the present knowledge economy comes to those who know themselves, their strengths, their values and how they best perform. May be that your organisation has been making arrangements for diffusion of tension by organising Yoga and spiritual sessions. But it is pertinent that we develop our awareness of the existing environment at the workplace at our own and equip ourselves with the measures which help us in becoming much more resistant. How and in what way we regulate our behaviour of becoming agitant and tensed determine the magnitude of our success. If you are sensitive to the odds, you find them everywhere. Hence, the most important aspect is to be insensitive to the factors responsible for agitating you. And, this is possible when we are tempted to the path of devotion and meditation.

We should not forget that the most important function of mind is wisdom "Buddhi". Often, we find this faculty of mind clouded over by the habitual inner noise of attractions and aversions. Hence, we need to assign due weightage to the clarity of "Buddhi" wisdom which may guide us what is useful and what is not useful. Our inner Buddhi or wisdom have good perspective. This necessitates a continuous cultivation of Buddhi, of course, gradually, lovingly, thoroughly but persistently and intently learning the art to listen and act with the support of inner wisdom. It is an unvarnished fact that the path of devotion helps us even in this endeavour.

◈ Meditation and Mind Purification

Meditation follows concentration through which wordly thoughts are shut out from the mind and divine thoughts get a place. The different postures of Yoga make the mind firm, pranayam makes the body light and steady. For meditation and concentration, we find Padmasana or Siddhasana suitable. We cannot deny that world is full of miseries and sufferings. Particularly in the corporate culture where we find material culture dominating us; there are a number of avenues for pains and afflictions. Meditation leads to the knowledge of the self which brings about the eternal peace, supreme bliss and prepare us for the integral experiences or direct intuitive knowledge. This makes meditation a powerful tonic; more so a mental tonic and even nervine tonic. This provides to us holy vibrations which penetrate all the cells of the body and cure the diseases of the body. Since we find corporate people of today witnessing a number of odds and challenges; it is imperative that they meditate at least for half-an-hour which would increase their spiritual strength in the battle of life at least for one week. Half-an-hour of true meditation provides to you one week to struggle.

There are different kinds of meditation and which one is suitable for you depends on your type of mind. Meditation varies in tune with your taste, temperament, capacity and type of mind. You may consult a teacher or perceptor to know the nature of your mind and the correct method of meditation for you. If you meditate; you succeed in purifying your mind. You need to practise meditation in a solitary room and then to close your eyes. The posture should be "Padmasana." You may meditate on the effulgence in the sun, splendour in the moon, glory in the stars, beauty in the sky. This is a right way of meditation particularly for the beginners.

While meditating, it is essential that you are aware of the obstacles such as laziness and fickleness of mind. This focuses on your diet and practice of pranayam. Hidden subtle desires, sleepiness, excessive tossing of mind from one object to another, excessive monkey nature of mind are also the obstacles which you have to regulate. You also need to avoid wrestling with the mind. You should not use any violent efforts in concentration and are required to relax all your muscles and nerves. Essentially, you have to relax the brain. If evil thoughts enter the mind do not make use of your will force in regulating them because this will fatigue yourself. It is right to mention that the greater the efforts we make to regulate the evil thoughts, the more evil thoughts return with redoubled force. If you are indifferent to the evil thoughts, this will pass off soon. Or, you may also substitute evil thoughts with the good thoughts. The cheerful thoughts, a brisk walk, singing, prayer, pranayam, laughter would help you in removing depression and preparing yourself for meditation.

The present corporate culture has engineered a sound foundation for the development of material culture which activates the process of nourishing evil thoughts because we find mind always materially focused. Of course, we do not find anything wrong in earning and spending in a right fashion and direction but the very bad thing with the materialistic gains and pleasure is its transformation into a craze and thirst which make ways for addiction and deviation. We find ourselves helpless and do not take rest unless everything is destroyed. We cannot get pleasure in a laughter club or show because laughter is but natural, no doubt, a result of our cheerfulness and happiness. Hence our focus should also be on searching avenues for serving humanity which would open new vistas for getting happiness; truly speaking, nothing like happiness.

Meditation needs concentration of mind and this makes it essential that we select a suitable place such as a solitary place and spiritually vibratory conditions because cool place is considered indispensble for the concentration of mind. Silence is essential for meditation because without which we cannot think about concentration. Try to imagine a place like "Mussoorie" and "Himalayas" in your own house. When we talk about the appropriate time for meditation, it is 4 A.M. in the morning which we call "Brahammuhurta" found conducive for spiritual contemplation. Try to make it sure that part of the day or night which is less disturbed for you or when your mind is free is preferred for meditation. The most important thing is peace because without mental peace, it is difficult to meditate. You should also keep in your mind that when you live on milk and fruits or when you fast, the meditation is found very much effective. When we talk about concentration, it is to be made sure that you concentrate on the lotus of the heart or at the space between the two eyebrows and close your eyes. We can also concentrate on heart or crown of the head. We cannot deny that different postures of yoga make the mind firm and pranayam (techniques of breathing) makes the body light. "Padamasan" or "Siddhasan" would be suitable posture for meditation whereas other postures such as Sirshasan, Sarvangasana, Matsayasana, Paschimottanasana are good for general health.

Keeping in view the outstanding benefits of meditation, it is right to opine that meditation activates the process of mind purification. In the present materialistic world where we find a number of avenues for agitation and irritation, stress and depression; it is pertinent that we have a clean mind. How and in what way we promote the purification process would determine the rate of our success. The most effective way is contracting scope for the accumulation of complexes and expanding ways for substitution of positive feelings. For getting a success in the present world, you need a sound health or sound body and again healthy body needs a healthy mind. If you adopt the path of service, the path of intellectual analysis and continue to evince interest in devotional and spiritual sessions; the task of distressing the non-reactive self observation is found easier. The path of service opens doors for the development of your inner strength. You start experiencing everything positive. This paves avenues for attitudinal transformation. Agitation opens new vistas for the development of stress and this complicates our task of mind purification. If you keep on moving the process of purifying your mind, it is easier for you to develop a holistic personality because in the process you get success in building your character and establishing distinction. Hence, meditation makes it easier for you to disallow the entry of evil thoughts in your mind.

◈ Yoga: A Conceptual Exposition

A Science clubbing set of techniques to protect and promote the interests of human beings to unite ourselves with the highest nature is "Yoga". It is a systematic, methodical and practical discipline and more so, an experimental science of self study. It is a way of life not a cult which cannot be reduced to the status of just an exercise programme as presently commercialised in a videotape. Yogic Asanas or postures and Pranayams are the two wings of Yoga. Yoga does not contradict or interfere with any religion and may be practised by everyone either agnostics or members of a particular faith or religion. We consider yoga as powerful techniques for creating a sense of inner peace, harmony and clarity of mind. In a true sense, it is an essential tool for our survival as well as for expanding the creativity and joy of our lives. The root of Yoga is "Yuj" which is meant unity or yoke. Despite of a number of arguments and debates, we discover its root in the East which dates back for centuries, codified by a scholar and teacher named "Patanjali" in The Yoga Sutras, written about the second century B.C.

Of course, there is much confusion about the concept of Yoga because we find a number of approaches but all described by the name Yoga. It is right to mention that a mountaineer may adopt a number of ways but the target is to reach at the top of the mountain. If we see at peak from the plains, we find the paths different but if we reach at the top of the mountain and view from the peak the plains, the view is by and large the same. Like this, the yogic paths may have diversity but the different paths are not conflicting, indeed effective in accommodating the various inclinations, personalities and temperaments of people adopting the yogic paths with the same goal. The various paths of Yoga are Hatha Yoga, Karma Yoga, Jnana Yoga, Bhakti Yoga, Kundalini Yoga, Mantra Yoga and Raj Yoga which is also called "Ashtanga Yoga" or "the eight-fold path" such as Yama, Niyama, Asana, Pranayam, Pratyahara, Dharna, Dhyana and Samadhi.

It is a science strengthening our realisation that disease affecting any specific part of our body is not really a disease confined only to that part but in a true sense, it is a manifestation of some disharmony in the body-mind complex of the whole personality. Yoga is found to be an effective way of dealing with mind which also helps in resolving the psychosomatic diseases, disorders like heart and cardiovascular diseases. Thus emerging as a technique of balancing emotion and mind, yoga proves to be a device to manage stress, regulate agitations, build character and develop a personality which is found adducible to others. It brings and preserves happiness and makes us potentially sound to achieve the target. It also proves to be a path for having a sound body. In the modern age of hurry, curry and worry and hustle and bustle, the yoga is considered an effective device to manage tension and becoming much more resistant to the multi-dimensional odds cropping up each and everyday as a by-product of material culture.

◈ Yogic View on Human Personality

Of course, we find personality something that is innate is an individual and nourished and enriched by using various methods. However, the yogic view on personality is found distinct to others. The yogic view divides personality into five layers which helps in developing a unique personality. Beauty lies in uniqueness. Attraction is found in uniqueness. The five dimensions of personality, they go through are physical self, energy self, mental self, intellectual self and blissful self. Each of these five dimensions serve as five layers to the human personality, the absence of which prevents one from attaining balance and a holistic personality is found missing. We may also call them different stages.

The physical self represents the senses and therefore here we find focus on the physical faculties of body. The Yama and Niyama of Yoga make a strong advocacy in favour of diet management and the lifestyles. Physical soundness of an individual considerably depends on the diet and lifestyles. While going through the management of body, we have gone through the problem in detail. A number of diseases and health problems crop up due to the diet schedule and lifestyles which we undermine. It is right to mention that yoga postures or exercises focus on the management of diet without which we find them becoming ineffective. In the present world, we need to keep ourselves ready to struggle and our capacity to fight would depend on our mental balance and physical soundness. We need to develop our consciousness of the quality of food that we take, water that we drink and personal hygiene that we follow. A majority of the people specially in the Indian perspective are found unaware of the sensitivity of these small things which bring to us big results, of course, negative.

The energy self is the second layer or stage which is sizably influenced by the first layer. Here we find our focus on the energy or strength that determines our capacity to perform. Our vitality and intensity to deliver goods to the organisation where we work or serve influence the magnitude of our success. In the present materialistic world and particularly in the present corporate culture; we find performance an important index to measure our contribution. The yogic view focuses on the role of Prana or energy in the body and their assimilation towards various parts of the body. How and in what way, we can get a success in gaining, maintaining and retaining our energy would make our task of getting a success much more easier. The three stages need continuity. We have to cultivate the habits of gaining energy by taking quality food, drinking potable water following the norms for personal hygiene. The lifestyles for the total life would provide continuity. The proper uses of energy would help us in the retention process.

The mental self focuses on a strongest mental capacity for an individual. Of late, we find the environmental conditions not friendly and therefore a number of problems crop up. We find ourselves irritated, agitated, stressed and depressed even due to small problems. Stress-friendly society, stress-friendly economy showing much more volatility, stress-friendly environment at the workplace and stress-friendly environment at places where we reside make it essential that we enrich our strengths to counter and it is to be possible when we have a strong mental self. Staying calm and focused despite adversity is not an easy task. Ability of our mind to concentrate and adapt to pressures from the environment inculcate new faculties of developments and we succeed in having a strong mental self. The yoga helps us in concentrating and staying calm. We find ourselves effective in activating the substitution process in which we find a qualitative change in our conduct.

The intellectual self is also an important stage where we find focus on wisdom. Of course, we cannot deny the instrumentality of our thematical excellence in showing and establishing distinction but our discriminatory power and knowledge remain incomplete, if we are insensitive to the informal studies. It is not only significant that we have enriched our formal studies; it is equally or even more important that our efforts are of concerted nature when we go through the informal studies. A majority of us in the existing social system lack informal knowledge. It is against this background that we find them insensitive to civic sense, aesthetic sense, etiquette management, personal touch and interests in meeting the humanitarian commitments. We do not go through the literature which may be helpful in enriching our knowledge bank. We show less interest in going through the contributions and achievements of leading personality in our society then how we can adduce examples. For becoming intellectually sound, it is also imperative that we go through the literatures and books of noble men.

The blissful self is found to be the ultimate goal which focuses on having a holistic personality where we have enriched our potentials of preserving happiness, cheerfulness by activating the substitution process. Countering emotional, physical and psychological struggles is a difficult task which makes it essential that we have developed competence or have cleared the stockpile of complexes which are found accumulated in different forms and infect our mind and heart in a big way. The path of meditation and devotion may be successful in cultivating the faculties while discharging the accumulated complex and yoga can make it possible. We need to involve ourselves in serving the society, helping the disadvantaged group and becoming human while behaving. If we involve ourselves in the spiritual sessions; if we adopt and promote yoga as a way of life; if we promote the substitution process; if we make place for positive feelings to our mind, the avenues would be paved for bidding a goodbye to the negative feelings. The moment we get a success in eliminating the negative feelings, our task of developing a holistic personality is found complete.

In the days of hurry and worry, and hustle and bustle, it is pertinent that corporate culture makes place for ethical dimensions and start motivating people found morally and ethically sound. On the one hand, they need people having thematical excellence of world class while on the other hand, they also need people found committed to the value system.

◈ Yoga and Ethics

Material culture makes a direct attack on the ethical dimensions resulting from which we find people in general lacking morality and becoming unproductive to the organisation as well as to the society. This makes a strong advocacy in favour of Yoga which bears the efficacy of developing a holistic personality found to be behaviourally decent and ethically sound. It is an unvarnished fact that ethics is a means to yoga. The people having right conduct have ideals, principles and motives. They strictly follow them, remove the weaknesses and defects and develop good conduct. It is not to be forgotten that meditation comes by themselves when we nourish the ethical perfection. Just to practise meditation is not to bring the positive results because we find people meditating for long period but nourishing the same jealousy, hatred, idea of superiority, pride egoism, etc. Ethical discipline is essential for success in yoga which is the result of right conduct in life. We cannot deny that mind becomes pure by cultivating habits of friendliness, compassion, complacency and indifference towards happiness, misery, virtue and vice. If we show friendliness, the dirt of envy bids a goodby. When we show empathy and keep ourselves involved in removing the miseries of others, the dirt of the desire to harm others is automatically removed. Thus people attaining ethical perfection by practising right conduct get a success in developing a magnetic personality. The practice of Yama (rules of social behaviour) which is abstinence from injury and killing is the very foundation of Yoga without which, we cannot build the superstructure of yoga. Niyam (rules of individual behaviour) is the observance of some of the essential traits. Thus Yama and Niyam are the two moral backbones of Yoga. We find them effective in purifying the mind.

In view of the above, it is right to mention that if we attain ethical perfection by practising yoga, it becomes easier for us to develop a holistic personality having the potentials to influence millions. Character gives us strong personality. We find morally and ethically sound people commanding respect everywhere. Our right conduct such as honesty, sincerity, truthfulness, kindness, liberal heart always command respect and influence on the people.

We are mortal so may die but character remains. It is character that provides to us the real force and power. Knowledge as a power fails in showing the result in absence of character. Without character, the attainment of knowledge is impossible. Noble traits and good character help in developing a tremendous personality. We need to be polite, civil and courteous. Good manners and soft words are our properties. Humility brings respect by itself because it is a virtue that subdues the hearts of others.

In the corporate world, we lack holistic personality. We find people, of course having world-class thematical excellence but not having holistic personality because often we do not find them tempted to good conduct. It is in this context that policy decision makers need to focus on luring people to yoga which would make it easier to increase the number of people found to be ethically and morally sound. We find image of people, closely linked with the image of organisation. Increasing the number of quality people in an organisation is also meant increasing the number of value-based people.

◈ Karma Yoga: Understand the Perception

Achieving a state of spiritual blessedness is possible when we succeed in adopting the path of blissful action. We cannot undermine happiness and it is not to be possible unless we perceive Karma Yoga in a right fashion. Karma cannot provide to us happiness unless we are aware of the right meaning of Karma as explained by Lord Krishna in Bhagavad Gita. Karma cannot be considered as Yoga unless we perform in the defined way. In this context, it is imperative to understand the six components of Karma Yoga.

The first component makes it essential that whatever activity we do is not against the socially and ethically accepted code of conduct. If we deceive people, if we harm others; and very importantly, if we do which we do not expect from others; such as if we do not expect from others telling lies or deceiving us then it is quite natural that we also follow the same path. If we expect from our superiors that they are decent in behaving; we also need to be respectful to them. If we expect from our life partners to be loyal, he/she should also be loyal. This is considered to be the basic and the minimum step towards Karma Yoga.

The second component of Karma Yoga focuses on the fact that whatever role we have chosen to play in life, we perform ourselves carefully and diligently. We leave no scope for laxity and negligence. Wasting time and energy disturbs the process and therefore we are supposed to discharge the defined responsibilities meticulously. We need to be honest while performing.

The third component throws light on performing without expecting any fruit. It is not meant that our actions would not bring any result. If we perform in a right fashion, it is quite natural that we get the desired results. If we are not getting, it is to be realised that we have committed mistakes while performing. We need to view and audit our actions and to identify that where we have failed in having concentration. It is significant to mention that when we start thinking about the results or fruits, it becomes difficult to concentrate and in absence of concentration, the quality of work is spoiled. For getting the best, we need to be sincere and honest to quality which cannot be maintained in absence of concentration.

The fourth component of Karma Yoga emphasises on accepting the results that we have got for our actions considering as the blessings of almighty God without making an evaluation that it is more or less; sufficient or insufficient. In this context, it is also pertinent to understand· that our results also depend on our past Karmas and cooperation that we get from others while performing. The justice system of almighty God is to be accepted and it is also to be remembered that God cannot be unfair. Our deeds are rewarded and our misdeeds are punished. We need to learn lessons from our misdeeds and to perform in a right way. We need to learn lessons from failures to witness triumphs. Improving the quality of our performance is the real motto of God for the unsatisfactory results that we get.

The fifth component of Karma Yoga focuses on absence of a sense of becoming a doer or performer. If we get extraordinary results, we need to be submissive. We are not supposed be an egoist. We should accept that when we have got an extraordinary success, it is due to the cooperation of a number of people who have directly or indirectly helped us. The parents, teachers, family members, superiors and subordinates and society have extended us cooperation and a conducive environment to perform and therefore we have got the desired results. Finally, we cannot forget almighty God for all our achievements.

The sixth component emphasises on sharing the results of our actions. If we have received a success in our life, it is due to the cooperation of a number of people and therefore it is to be made sure that all of them share the results; be it money, knowledge or credit. We should not forget that our achievements or credibility is enriched when we start sharing others. We should prefer to spend a portion of our income on charity.

In view of the above, it is right to mention that Karma Yoga requires to be conceptualised on a priority basis. The path of blissful action or achieving a state of spiritual blessedness cannot be possible unless we perceive Karma Yoga in a right fashion. It is also to be emphasised that the most important thing either to survive or to thrive; either for an individual or for an organisation or institution is to achieve the state of happiness. If we perform honestly, as a result we achieve great happiness and nothing like happiness which provides to us an opportunity to laugh found very much instrumental in rejuvenating and multiplying our potentials.

Of late, we live in an age where corporate culture has been dominating the socio-cultural and economic environmental conditions. Since we find material culture prevailing, it becomes difficult for us to achieve happiness. We do not get an opportunity to laugh and even for that we need to visit laughter clubs and shows. This keeps us agitated, stressed and depressed. It is in this context that, we find Karma Yoga becoming much more relevant. On the one hand, the corporate professionals need to practise Karma Yoga while on the other hand, they also need to promote it so that their subordinates conceptualise the right perception of Karma Yoga. We cannot deny that right conceptualisation of Karma Yoga by different echelons of people serving an organisation would strike a balance between social, national, organisational and individual interests. Karma Yoga makes our life happy and contented. This bestows on us purity of mind which cultivates faculties of qualitative improvements. All of us agree that contentment is the real thing which may keep us happy. And happiness is the only thing which may provide to us an opportunity to laugh. Hence nothing like happiness and nothing like laughter. The professionals need to create a condition where people working with them in different capacities achieve the stage of contentment. This would make possible spirituality at the workplace where people would feel pleasure in performing. In a true sense, work culture cannot be possible if we find people influenced by psychophobia. If they start realising their defined responsibilities, the process of getting the desired results is switched on.

◈ Yoga for Combating Stress

The society where we are nourished, the environment in which we work; the cultural patterns which we adopt; the genetic properties that we inherit and the expectations that we nurture make place for stress which makes an invasion our body and mind to such an extent that we find ourselves physically and mentally ill. Stress is a condition in which we do not find ourselves normal. It is the state of an organism where we find a threat to our well-being. Actually nobody knows what is stress. A number of measures are adopted to make an assault on stress however the instrumentality of Yoga in combating stress has an edge over others.

Yoga, in a true sense, is a way of life. The eight-fold path of yoga if practised in a right way may be helpful in creating a condition in which we develop our resistance power to counter the odds and seal the doors for the entry of stress. The Yama (Rules of Social Behaviour), Niyam (Rules of individual behaviour), Asana (Postures), Pranayam (Techniques of breathing), Pratyahar (Non-attachment), Dharana (Concentration), Dhyana (Meditation), Samadhi (Ultimate goal) are the different sub-systems of yoga and if we follow the total system of yoga in the right consequences such as observing rules, practising body exercises and yoga postures, we find them impacting not only in feeling ourselves relaxed but also in disciplining the entire system where body and mind start coordinating each other. The postures of Yoga like Sukhasana, Padmasana, Vajrasana, Siddhasana, Yogamudra, Sarvangasana and Shavasana help in preventing stress if we find them followed by pranayam and meditation.

Yoga is a culture which prevents disharmony, stress and disease. No medicine is needed to cure the mind which is considered as a regulator of the whole body. Yoga develops immunity to several disorders and ensures coordination of mind and body by providing a unique rhythm to the system. Meditation results into coolness of mind because we find it followed by concentration. The stress can be managed and prevented in a right way, if we follow the norms for yogic postures and assign due weightage to pranayam. Yoga is not limited only to body but also touches the psyche aspect or the soul.

Stress is disharmony or imbalance which is not only physical but more so psychological. We cannot deny that the ego problem, frustration, conflict, mismatch between expectations and dissension and tension are due mainly to the false notions. All of them adversely affect the body and mind. The eight-fold paths of yoga work in different ways and become instrumental in combating stress. The Yama or rules of social behaviour focus on Ahimsa, Satya, Asthey, Brahamcharya and Aparigraha making an adverse condition for false egos, attachments, disharmony due to variations in discipline and expectations. If we respect social behaviour, our mind is found to be disciplined. The Niyam or rules of individual behaviour such as Shoucha, Tapa, Santosha, Swadhyana, Iswarapranidhana make available to us linear path of life where we witness positive strokes without inviting a stress-prone situation. Working in a stress-friendly environment paves avenues for the development of a number of problems which ultimately affect our mind as well as the body, a condition in which our actions and behaviour are found abnormal.

The pranayam which we call techniques of breathing provide tranquillity to mind and remove anxiety and stress from the mind. The non-attachment known as pratyahar is a message given to the mankind which always keep us free from stress where we do not give undue importance to minor things or do not take any notice of the small or pretty things. The concentration or Dharana helps us in balancing our thoughts and provide to us an inbuilt power to strengthen mind and reduce the failure, frustration, anxiety and stress. The Meditation known as Dhyana provides to us a powerful anti-stress weapon provided the thought process is equilibrated. We consider thought a silent healer found more effective when we face the problem of psychomatic disorder. The ultimate goal or Samadhi is considered as the ultimate state of mind found corresponding to the stage of self-actualisation of the need as envisaged by Maslow.

The above mentioned facts make it clear that all the paths of yoga are instrumental in combating stress and anxiety. The paths provide myths to our mind and body and thus are found effective in removing the stress-friendly problems. We find these measures helpful in improving self image, better perspective about self and others, better understanding of feelings of others and helping us in fixing the level of contentment. And when we attain the stage of contentment, it is quite natural that we are in a position to bid a goodbye to all the allied problems.

The postures of yoga in general and Shavasana in particular has been found effective in combating stress and anxiety. Presently, we find people in general and the corporate people in particular heavily stressed. This creates numerous problems and ultimately affects the level of operational efficiency of an individual. The different postures of yoga such as Talasan, Parvatasana, Utkatasan, Vikshasana, Ardhvakrasan, Trinokasan, Sukhasan, Padmasana, Vajrasana, Yogmudra, Simahasan, Pavanmuktasan, Bhujangasan, Shalabhasan, Makrasana, Sarvangasana, Shavasan are found helpful in combating stress. In the process, it is pertinent that we have a good teacher to educate us about the different postures and their relative merits.

While deliberating upon yoga, we cannot undermine the role of Salutation to Sun or Surya namaskar. There are different stages of salutation to sun and we need to go through stage-by-stage.

◈ Yoga Postures or Exercises

The different postures or exercises of Yoga are found effective in managing both body as well as the mind. We find them instrumental in removing a number of diseases and further helpful in increasing our resistance power. It is essential that we move forward step by step to get the best results. While practising different postures, we need to follow the guidelines. In the present zero figure-conscious and health-conscious society; the postures of yoga or the different exercises of yoga can be successful in purifying mind and body to nourish positive feelings.

◈ Surya Namaskar — The Sun Salutation

This posture focuses on saluting sun. There are different steps of Surya Namaskar. We find variation in different postures shown in different steps.

Step One: In this step, we stand facing the direction of sun and in the processes, it is essential that our both feet touch, hands are brought together, palm-to-palm at the heart. This can be practised very easily.

Step Two: In the second step, we raise the arms upward, bend them backward slowly and stretch the arms above the ahead.

1

2

Step Three: In the third step, we exhale slowly bend forward, touch the earth with respect until the hands are in line with the feet and head touch knees.

Step Four: In the fourth step, we inhale and move the right leg back away from the body in a wide backward step, keep the hands and feet firmly on the ground, with the left foot between the hands and raise the head.

Step Five: While exhaling, we need to bring the left foot together with the right, keep our arms straight, raise the hip and align the head with the arms to form an upward arch.

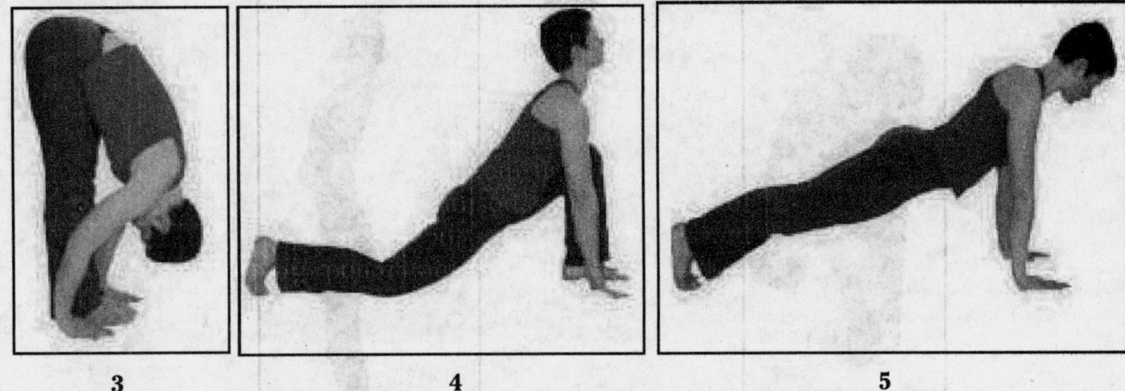

3 4 5

Step Six: We exhale and lower the body to the floor until the feet, knees, hands, chest and forehead touch the ground.

Step Seven: We inhale and slowly raise the head and bend backward as much as it is possible, bend the spine to the maximum.

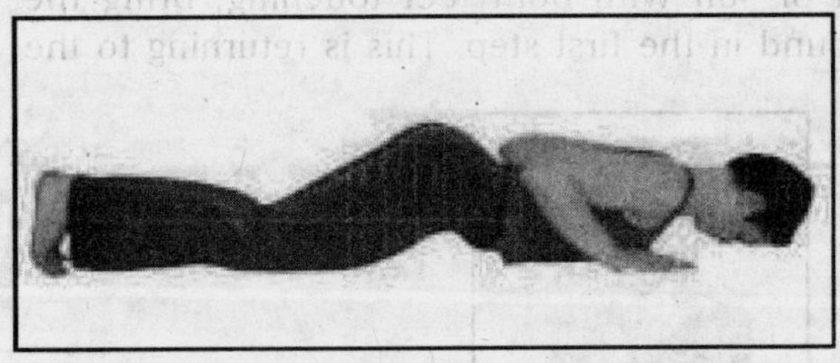

6

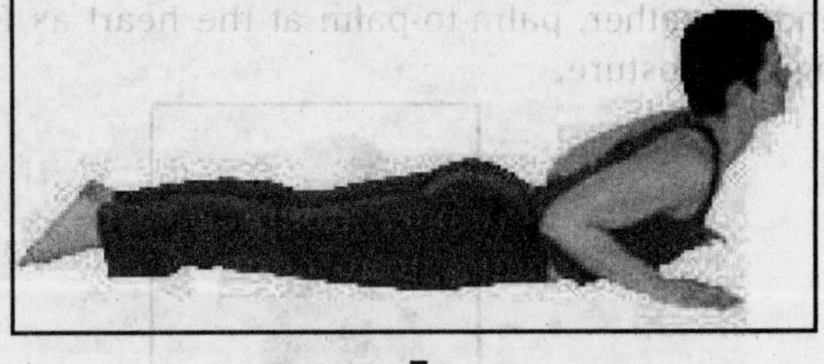

7

Step Eight: While exhaling, we bring the left foot together with the right, keep our arms straight, raise the hip, align the head with the arms and form an upward arch.

Step Nine: We inhale and move our right leg back away from the body in a wide backward step, keep the hands and feet firmly on the ground with the left foot between the hands and raise the head.

8

9

Step Ten: Exhale slowly bending forward, touch the earth with respect until the hands are in line with the feet and head touching knees.

Step Eleven: Inhale and raise the arms upward slowly bend backward, stretching arms above the head.

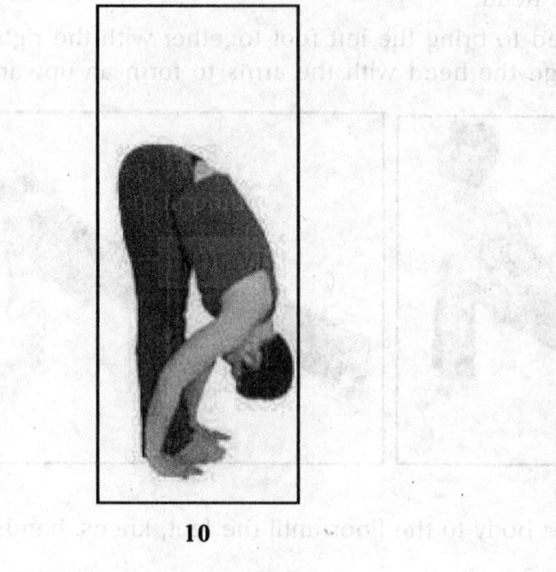

10

11

Step Twelve: Stand facing the direction of sun with both feet touching, bring the hands together, palm-to-palm at the heart as found in the first step. This is returning to the original posture.

12

12

TWELVE POSTURES FOR THE SUN SALUTATION

All the twelve postures for salutation to sun have been presented in the above mentioned figure. The Sanskrit word Surya means Sun. Namaskar is the Hindi word for Namaste, from the root name to bow. Namaskar means salutation, salute, greeting or praise. In the original Sanskrit, the pronunciation is soor-yee-ah-namaskar.

In the Hindu religion, we find special respect for sun which is considered to be the lifeline. This provides energy and life to almost all the living beings existent on this planet Earth. With the help of twelve postures, we worship Sun.

YOGIC EXERCISES

◈ Padmasana (Lotus Posture):

At the outset, we need to spread a blanket on the ground and then to sit facing North or East. After that, we spread the legs forward and take hold of our right foot and keep it on the left thigh, place the left foot over the right thigh, place the hands on the knees, make a finger-lock and keep the hands over the left ankle. It is to be ensured that we sit erect, keep the back, neck and head in one straight line, close our eyes and begin meditation. It is to be made clear that more steady we are, the more we concentrate and make our mind one pointed. If we are steady in our posture even for one hour, it is possible for us to acquire one-pointed mind which help us in feeling infinite peace. We find this posture more effective for meditative purposes. We cannot deny that this helps us in recharging our mind. Meditation leads to the knowledge of the self which brings about the eternal peace, supreme bliss and prepare us for direct intuitive knowledge. We find it a mysterious ladder which reaches from earth to heaven, from darkness to light, from pain to bliss, from restlessness to abiding peace and from mortality to immortality. Knowledge of the self is essential but it cannot be attained without meditation. Padmasana makes the ways for meditation. In a true sense, meditation is a powerful tonic and specially nervine tonic through which all the cells of body are penetrated and the diseases of the body are cured. If you find difficulty or pain in the padmasana, you can try ardhapadmasana. In that case, instead of placing both feet on the thighs, only one foot is placed on the top of the opposite thigh and the other is placed under the opposite thigh.

LOTUS POSTURE

◈ Sarvangasana (Shoulder Stand Posture):

In Sarvangasana, you need to spread a blanket on the floor and lie on the back quite flat, raise the legs, hip and trunk slowly and have to support the back with the two hands and rest the elbows on the ground. Here, you have further to press the chin against the chest and have to remain in this posture initially for five seconds which in the gradual practice can be increased to twenty minutes. This posture makes your spine elastic and therefore keep us young for the long time. To get maximum benefits of this posture, after performing this posture, you should do matsyasana.

SHOULDER STAND POSTURE

This asana makes your spine elastic as well as promote alertness. Besides, the upper and lower back pain is removed.

◈ Sirshasana (Head Stand Posture):

For an all-round development of body, the posture Sirshasan is considered as king of all postures. Spread a blanket, sit on two knees, make a finger lock by interweaving the fingers, place them on the ground, keep the top of your head on the ground between the finger-lock and raise your legs slowly till they are vertical in the process, the jerks are to be avoided. It

HEAD STAND POSTURE

is safer to learn this posture by the side of a wall and take help of your friend to have a balance. The headstand posture helps in having an equilibrium throughout the body and mind. At the outset the duration of this posture should be limited to 15-30 seconds and gradually you may increase it. This posture should not be practised when you are suffering from high or low blood pressure and women should not practise it during the period of menstruation. This posture is a powerful blood purifier and a nervine tonic.

◈ Matsyasan (Fish Posture):

Like padmasana, you need to form the foot-lock and then lie flat on the back, stretch the head back so that the top of your head rests on the ground firmly on one side and the buttocks on the other, make a bridge or an arch of the trunk, place the hands on the thighs

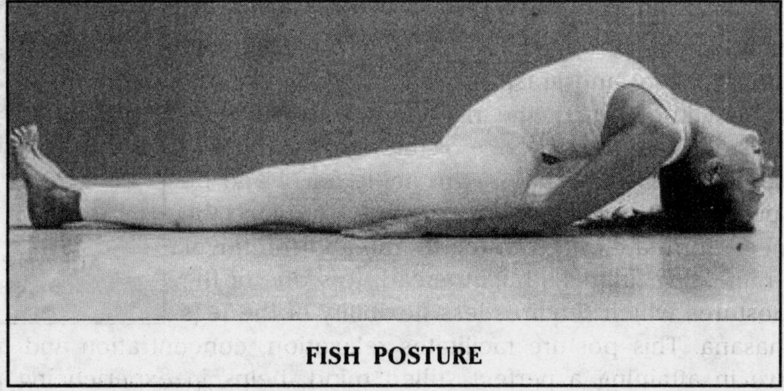

FISH POSTURE

or catch hold of the toes. You have to remain in this posture for three seconds or half the period you devote to sarvangasana. This posture is done immediately after performing Sarvangasana. This posture is found removing a number of diseases and constipation. This posture creates a great expansion and stretching of the chest which helps relieving upper respiratory congestion and benefits the heart. Besides, the sinus are drained and opened from the inversion of the head. The thyroid and parathyroid glands are stimulated as well.

◈ Halasana (Plough Posture):

In this posture, you have to lie flat on your back, keep the hands at the sides on the ground with the palm facing the ground, join both your legs, lift the legs slowly up as found

PLOUGH POSTURE

in the Sarvangasana but have not to bend the legs and raise the hands. After this, you have to lower the legs until the toes touch the ground above the head and keep the knee close. You should remain in this posture initially for five seconds which in the gradual practice can be increased to five minutes. To back to the original position, you have to raise the legs slowly. With this posture, all the muscles and ligaments in the calves and thighs are stretched resulting into greater leg flexibility. It is useful for people suffering from leg cramps. This posture should be accompanied by the Sarvangasana. It is an excellent morning posture.

◈ Siddhasana (Accomplished Posture)

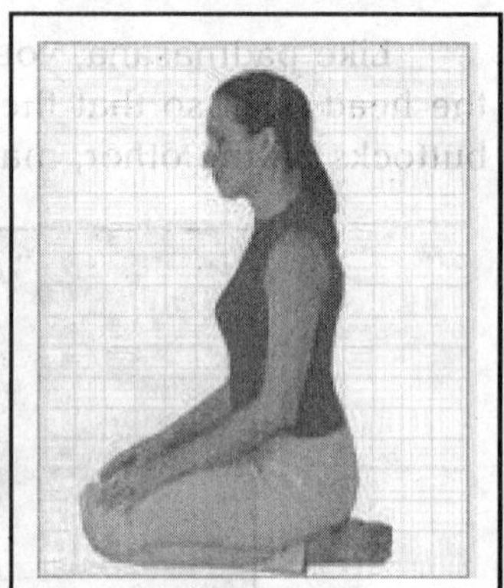

ACCOMPLISHED POSTURE

It is known as Adept pose and in this posture we begin in a seated position, bend the left knee and grasp the left foot with both hands and place the heel against the perineum and the sole of the foot against the inside of the right thigh. Exhale and reach down and loop the forefinger of the right hand around the big toe of the right foot and grasp the left foot with the left hand. Bend the right knee, grasp the right foot with the right hand around and place the outside edge of the right foot where the calf and thigh of the left leg meet, right ankle navel and be as close to the pubic area as possible. With palms up, place the hands on the knees, form a circle with the thumb and forefinger and extend the remaining fingers straight ahead. It is one of the simpler sitting postures which requires less flexibility of the legs than the Padamasana. This posture facilitates relaxation, concentration and meditation. It is found effective in attaining a perfect stilled mind, helps in experiencing peace which results from meditation. It is effective for meditation and therefore when we talk about managing our mind, this posture should be preferred. The duration for this posture should be for a minimum of one minute and may be extended to ten minutes.

◈ Shavasana (Corpse Posture)

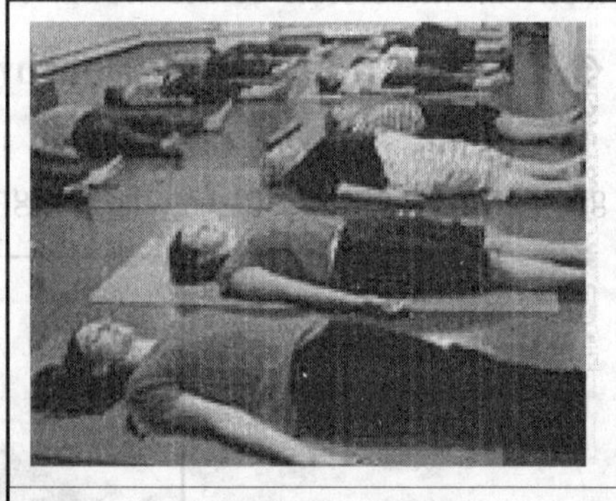

CORPSE POSTURE

We also call it the Corpse Pose. In this posture, lie flat on your back with your legs together but not touching, arms close to the body with the palms facing up, keep your eyes gently closed with the facial muscles relaxed, breath deeply and slowly through the nostrils from head to the feet bring your attention to each part of the body, consciously relax it before proceeding on to the next. Remain in this posture for between 3-5 minutes or longer. This posture keeps your body and mind completely relaxed. Not only the body should be motionless but even the mind should, also be quiet. This posture prepares you for meditation. Generally, we should begin our yogasana with Shavasana. The rejuvenation of body and mind is possible with this posture.

◈ Pavanmuktasana (Wind-Release Posture)

It is wind-releasing posture. In this posture, inhale and the right knee and pull it close to the torso with both hands while interlocking the fingers just below the knee. Keep the left leg flat on the floor, hold the inhaled breath for a few seconds then exhale slowly through the nostrils and lift the back, shoulders and head off the floor and touch the knee with the forehead. Hold the inhaled breath for a few seconds then exhale slowly and return the back, shoulders and head to the floor and remain holding the knee. Hold the inhaled breath for a few seconds then exhale while bringing the right leg to the floor. Lie flat on the back in the Shavasana for a few seconds then repeat beginning with the left leg.

This posture will help you in releasing gastro-intestinal gas. It also helps in removing constipation.

WIND-RELEASING POSTURE

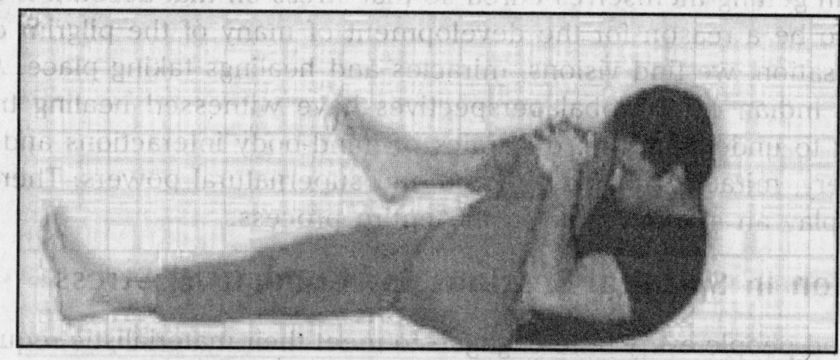

◈ Cultural and Spiritual forces Combating Stress

The prime consideration is making an attack on stress and in the process we find even cultural and spiritual forces effective. A deep religious experiences are found effective in curing the sick. The father of hypnosis, Abbe Faria advocates that a patient's receptive attitude plays a decisive role in the healing process. Everyday all of us witness miracle or dramatic cases of cures. Even the leading medical experts admit that patients set their own regenerative process in motion. The religious rituals also show positive effects. We may debate over the issue but the cases are found each and everyday and we name them miracles. This way or that way, if we reach to the receptive stage, the effects turn to be positive.

Of course, we find a number of scientific advances developing a sound educational background; however the traditional beliefs about illness/stress and misfortune are yet to be replaced. The beliefs guide the health seeking behaviour of patients. The spiritual forces have been found impacting the mental illness and we find people getting helps from the faith-healers. In the process of healing, we find beliefs an influencing force.

The management of mental disorders and stress is also possible through cultural factors. The cross-cultural psychiatric research has polarised into two school of thoughts such as the ethic approach and emic approach; the former advocating the universality of mental illness whereas the later arguing generation of mental illness from within cultures. Almost in all the societies, we find professional psychics who enter a state of dissociation and exhibit their gifts. It is argued that they come under the influence of God, ancestral spirit, deceased person or extra-terrestrial being. The witch, witchcrafts and witch doctors are found everywhere. The beliefs of patient also help them in getting a success. We also argue that illiteracy, backwardness, poverty and superstition help in the development of such practices. One thing that we cannot negate that mental and spiritual forces cannot be separated. Actually, we find a close relationship between mental health, culture and religion.

Meditation provides you energy and refresh your mind

In many places, we find faith healers getting a success in providing effective healthcare services. In Goa, the faithhealers from the Catholic Church are found an important source of healthcare. In India, the effectiveness of traditional medicine has a long history. If we find people facing health problem, they are found interested in getting themselves cured so that stress on that account is removed. The afflictions prove to be a reason for the development of many of the pilgrim centres. Since the dawn of civilisation, we find visions, miracles and healings taking place. Almost all the cultures either in Indian or in global perspectives have witnessed healing traditions. It is of course difficult to understand the dynamics of mind-body interactions and therefore we name them mystery, miracle, healings, sacred and supernatural powers. There is no doubt in it that beliefs play an effective role in the entire process.

◈ Participation in Spiritual Sessions for Combating Stress

Today, we find people every time engaged to meet their materialistic requirements. The corporate culture, no doubt, has aggravated the magnitude of problem. How to achieve the target of your organisation keeps you mentally and physically engaged. In a true sense, we find people heavily stressed and depressed on that account. Right from morning to the late night when they go to bed for spending the restless night; we find them planning and thinking about their career. The more they achieve, the more they target. It is in this context that we realise the relevance of our participation in the spiritual sessions. The saints, prophets, dharmgurus, religious trusts organise spiritual sessions in which they focus on the spiritual canons with reference to Gita, Ramayana, the Bhagavata, Vishnu-Sahasranama, Latika-Sahasranama, Aditya Hridya, the Upanishads or the Yoga Vasishtha, the Bible, the Zend Avesta, the Koran, the Tripitakas, the Granth Sahib, etc. Presently, we find a number of TV channels based on religion. If you attend these sessions or study these holy books from half an hour to one hour daily, the process of thought purification would be initiated which would keep you happy. If the process keeps on moving for the long time, you will feel a change in your attitudes, behaviour and the resistance power.

The spiritual sadhanas help you in following the Niyam or the rules of individual behaviour. We cannot negate that our spiritual attachment, make us efficacious of spiritualising the professions we adopt. Today, we find a number of problems cropping up due to job related stress. The youths in particular maintain a hectic lifestyle, a competitive workplace environment or stress-prone environment which has been found changing the value system of the workplace. We find youths becoming overambitious and thus much more susceptible to stress related disorders. The Multinational Corporations dominating the economy believe in the principle of squeezing the most from their employees. The fast track jobs of software, advertising, private banking, insurance and other financial services have been working like blood sucker. People working there have no option but to work and work till they invite big problems for themselves. Corporate people work like the migrated birds. From one state capital to another state capital, from one country to another country, they keep people all the time engaged in travelling and it is found to be a strong factor in the stress related problems. We cannot deny that when we stress the body everyday without any rest, the risk of breakdown grows faster.

Despite of multi-dimensional odds, the corporate culture has been found attracting the upcoming youths. Of course, it is new definition of lifestyles which has been tempting them. At least for a few decades, this culture would gain popularity and therefore the youths in general and the budding youths in particular need to develop their fascination with spiritualism failing which they would make the task much more difficult for themselves vis-à-vis for the coming generations. It is an unvarnished fact that the new definition of happiness that we have written today would continue to invite myriad of problems which would circle us in such a fashion that we would find it difficult to come out.

❖ Working Holiday for Combating Stress

Persistently harassed people are found much more friendly to stress because we find them agitated and irritated. In the corporate culture, we find a significant increase in the number of people feeling themselves harassed or actually harassed. It is in this context that we make a strong advocacy in favour of sending the corporate executives out for a spot of calm for business and pleasure. The adventure holidays, eating off an aircraft wing, picking fruits in an orchard neighbouring a jungle or packing fishing rod along for some fun and all in a day's work may look amazing but of late, we find executives choosing to go far from the maddening crowd for some peace as they huddle for their meetings under thatched roofs. Trips to luxury resorts, trekking adventures, eco-lodges actually work as incentives for the harried worker. This offers to them a breathing space from the humdrum office routine for a spot of rejuvenation and a sense of adventure. They get an opportunity to refresh and feel themselves much more energetic to perform and deliver. It is against this background that we find eco-cottages gaining much more popularly specially amongst the corporate executives. Since we find them close to the nature, they find themselves refreshed. A retreat for corporate managers ready to do without their mobile phones and wi-fi is a new experience with a productive result to combat stress. A place close to the river banks, forest or jungle is found eco-savvy and suitable for conducting meetings under open thatched roofs, alongside overnight stays at the national park and fishing trips where the silence is broken by the call of birds. The plans can be discussed without any interruption. It is pertinent to mention that meeting outside a stiff corporate environment also helps co-workers bond.

The cosmopolitan towns and cities are becoming much more disturbed. The quality decisions, rest on productive deliberations and discussions and in a stiff corporate environment the possibilities for an interruption cannot be ruled out. In addition, we find corporate executives over-pressed. This makes it essential that we prefer and identify Valley where executives can take a breath with nature, walk amidst large lush green orchards, pick apples, peaches and apricots plant/trees because we find there a tranquil space which may be productive for corporate training sessions. An intellectual stimulus along with a dose of culture has been found much more productive.

The prime theme is to identify environmental conditions found friendly to nature and peace. Purification of mind cannot be possible in a condition where we find the working conditions keeping you far off the nature. Mixing business with pleasure is an innovative strategy to rejuvenate corporate people found often stressed, agitated and irritated. It is imperative that we mitigate the problem at the initial stage of its development. Continuous pressure of work cannot be considered a sound strategy for accelerating the rate of productivity. Career-oriented corporate people, target-based action plan are some of the recent developments which have been found aggravating the magnitude of problem. We need to combat and promote the mixing up process.

◈ Sleep Better for Fresh Mind

Fresh mind enables you to make productive decision. Being a corporate professional, you need to make use of your mind which if not fresh may affect the quality of your decision. Accumulated complexes obstruct the process of having a fresh mind. The increasing pressure of work, amounting stress on account of environment at the work-place and the high level of expectations keep employees physically and mentally engaged. Mind is a regulator and it we find something wrong with it, the task of having a fresh mind is found much more difficult. Though you are yawning but your working hour is increasing and for that even you push your bed time back to fit in extra pressure. Almost all the corporate men or women are found in the same boat. We find them facing the problem of sleep deficit. It is against this background that we need much more strength to our advocacy that sleep better for fresh mind.

The behavioural aspects are found closely associated with our mind. If we are agitated, tensed and stressed; our mindset and outlook, attitudes and behaviour cannot be normal. We cannot expect etiquette and manners from the working people found to be heavily stressed. It is not possible for the employees to regulate their working hours because they are over-ambitious. Hence, the only solution left before them is to disrespect the bed time and reduce the sleeping hours. This aggravates the intensity of problem and we find employees much more agitated. Rest and relaxation followed by a sound sleep keep our mind fresh.

The scientific management of mind makes the ways for cheerfulness. And cheerfulness and warmth become instrumental in keeping our mid fresh. A study by the Yale School of Management makes it clear that mind and mood affect the workplace environment. We cannot expect normal behaviour from the stressed employees. The main reason for stress is keep deficit. Hence it is imperative that in the changing scenario, the employees bring a change in their work-schedule as well the sleep-schedule. This will work as a tonic and the employees will find themselves fresh and rejuvenated.

Combating on stress is a prime consideration in the present corporate culture and the most effective prescription for this is to follow a schedule of eight-hours sleep. It is not only the concern of employees but also of management that a condition pro to sleep-deficit is to be regulated. If not, this will tell upon the performance level vis-à-vis the health and mind of employees. Such a stage is to be avoided.

A survey of leading hospitals specially in the cosmopolitan towns of the country reveals that a majority of the corporate youths face the problem of stress. They are inviting a stage of depression and it is a negative development in the Indian context which would trap even the budding and upcoming youths of the country. In the present scenario, it is imperative that we refresh employees and provide to them the required time for rest, relaxation and sleep.

◈ Gardening for Combating stress

Your temptation for nature is an important consideration for providing to you a stress-free lifestyle in which you nurture zest for your life. It would be utopian to think that there would be a stress free environment in the corporate world because it is known for uncertainties, it is known for volatility and it is well known for ups and downs. It is not possible for you to bid a goodbye to the corporate world which provides to you a lavish lifestyle. Hence, the only thing that you need to make possible is minimising the intensity of stress generated by the corporate culture. It is against this background that we talk about your interests in gardening and plantation which would show wonderful results.

For each one of us, it is imperative because we find the process helping us in different ways. Of course you work in the cosmopolitan towns and cities and therefore you may have space constraint. But you may take help of different pots for gardening and plantation at the available vacant places on the roofs or in the balcony, inside the house and outside the house, if possible. The ornamental shadow plants inside the house would provide you a soothing feeling. There are a number of plants which can be grown even in pots. You need to develop awareness and evince interests in nature.

Nature and Pet bust stress

Since you also face the problem of time constraint, you will be required to bring some minor modifications in your to-do list. Even half-an-hour of time would keep you maintained and make you fresh. This device of combating stress is also based on the theme that if you have a love for your plants, you will be required to care. This will divert your attention and for diffusion it appears to be the most effective dimension. Because you are addicted to your career and are nurturing a high degree of ambition, it is imperative that your attention is diverted. While taking care of our plants, the process of diffusing tension is on because as and when you view your plants, they start calling you and it becomes difficult for you to ignore them.

In the process of nurturing high degree of ambition, you have made enough rooms for the accumulation of complexes and this happens to be the main reason for stress. Since you start loving nature, the cleaning of stored complexes also gains a momentum. You start feeling yourself relaxed. Your mind gets a fresh energy. You feel yourself stress-free. The rejuvenation process provides an additional energy to your mind. Gradually, you inculcate a habit and we find a basic change in your outlook and behaviour.

Your love for nature is, of course, the most effective prescription for combating stress. This helps in bringing positive developments in your personality. Besides, you also contribute to the value addition process by improving the quality of environment.

This may also be promoted at the workplace by the concerned organisation in the name of improving the quality of ambience at the workplace.

◈ Entertainment for Combating Stress

The increased volatility in the business environment becomes instrumental in increasing the intensity of stress before the corporate people. Besides, the unfriendly environment at the workplace aggravates the magnitude of stress and we find employees facing a number of health and behavioural problems. The employees as well as the organisation need to adopt devices which may be effective in diffusing the tension and minimising the stress. It is in this context that we focus on entertainment as a tool for combating stress.

We are well aware of the fact that in the face of day-to-day problems we find high-level accumulation of complexes in the minds of corporate people. They have a high level of expectations, high degree of ambition, dream of leading a lavish lifestyle and everything amidst a high intensity of competition. They want to earn more and for that they have to work more. The rest, relaxation and sleeping are undermined. A majority of the employees serving the corporate sector face the problem of sleep-deficit. In addition, we also find them nurturing negative thoughts and feelings. Hence, we find functioning of mind not in a normal condition which may invite serious health and psychological problems.

This draws our attention of entertainment to refresh mind and diffuse tension. The corporate employees should prefer outing and should also cultivate the habits of viewing the entertainment programmes. They may opt for movies, drama shows, music and dance programme, circus, etc. This would be instrumental in refreshing their mind and rejuvenating their energy.

The organisation may also consider frequent organisation of entertainment programmes. Particularly in the evening of Friday, such type of programme may be witnessed by a majority of the employees. While selecting programme, they should prefer those programmes which may provide opportunities for laughing and laughter. Or, they may also organise cultural shows, joke programme, music programme to entertain the employees. Development of a club or association would make the organisation process much more convenient. You are not supposed to motivate the employees because when they find the programme entertaining a majority of them visit.

The corporate people are found engaged in mental activities and if we make use of our minds for a lone time, its capacity to receive, perceive and deliver would adversely be affected. The quality of intuition is sizably influenced by the quality of mind and when the employees are found over-pressed with the defined responsibilities, its adverse impact is found on our sense of judgement. We feel ourselves indecisive and find ourselves inactive. Actually, it tells upon the level of our performance. They may also go for rest and may provide to us an opportunity to the mind to relax. Rest and relaxation would also be helpful in minimising stress. You should publicise the contributions of your organisation and only then you may expect positive results.

If we do not find such an event, sponsored by the organisation, we may also think of organising such events in association with clubs which may show wonderful results.

◈ Pet-therapy for Combating Stress

Companions help you in getting pleasure. Developing friendship with animals or birds has been found effective in diffusing the tension. Stress is the result of centralisation of negative thoughts which all the time keep your mind engaged. Amidst uncertainties and fluctuations, its intensity is found high. By nature, we find human beings thinking on a particular issue and making use of their mental force to know the reasons and find out the solutions. The people serving the corporate sector are found in the same boat. They are over-ambitious and have a low level of tolerance. Once they are stressed, we find them in a vicious circle and the task of coming out from the trap of stress is found complicated. It is against this background that we look for a solution and in this context, we find pet-therapy to be helpful.

The dogs, horses and cows are considered best companions for us and if we start evincing interest in making them pet, the diversion of mind is found possible. We find diversion, the first stage for diffusing stress because it is due to concentration or centralisation of our mind on a particular issue and the moment we find diversion, the diffusion gains a rapid momentum and may be that it is just for a moment but we are free from the stress The negative effects of stress are found minimised with a break which may be even for a small duration. This makes it essential that we cultivate the habits of loving the animals and birds and make them pet. In this context, it is also pertinent that ultimately it is the result of love. Based on the same philosophy, if we start loving kids and children and spend even a few minutes of our valuable time with them, the diversion gains momentum and again we find diffusion from tension in action. Hence, it is love for others, may be animals or birds or kids and children, which helps combating stress.

If you find it difficult to opt for pet animals or birds you may prefer to visit zoos, bird sanctuaries where there will be a diversion and you will find yourself stress-free. We cannot deny that stress is a result of mental disorder which requires proper treatment intended to relieve or heal. If we talk about pet-therapy, it is the same way of treatment. If you find dogs as pet, they force you to love. Because we find them very much loyal, a condition is created when you are forced to reciprocate and such a reciprocating behaviour injects life to the diffusion process. The moment you start loving them, you start sparing time for them and you even start thinking for them and the duration of diffusion thus gains a rapid momentum. Consistency in the process may even make you stress-free.

In view of the above facts, it is right to say that pet-therapy may be an effective device to make us and keep us stress-free. The animals, dogs and horses have been found very responsive to the human beings and therefore we find nothing wrong in developing a habit of making those animals pet and taking the benefits. Like this, cows have also been found responsive. But out of all, we find dogs to be the best friend of human beings who well know the art of pleasing you and forcing you to reciprocate.

◈ Retail Therapy for Combating Stress

The emergence of shopping as a fashion is found to be a recent development in the modern corporate world. A good number of modern retail outlets have been developed in different towns and cities making available to the corporate people a suitable place for diffusing tension and gaining pleasure. They earn more and in the process make the conditions much more friendly to stress. The retail outlets provide to them an opportunity for shopping and enjoying.

The British psychologists, based on a recent survey, observe that retail therapy has been proved to be an effective device for combating stress. In the corporate culture, we find emergence of new retail formats such as shopping malls, shopping plaza and kiosks where the visiting people find a number of opportunities for shopping and entertainment. Since people serving the corporate sector have enough money in their pockets, it is possible for them to make use of shopping a device to get pleasure. A number of articles of their choice are found in the shopping malls and by buying those articles, they enjoy and get pleasure.

Survey conducted by the British psychologists is based on the interviews conducted in different outlets. The shopping outlets and the customers visiting there were interviewed. This survey helped researchers in gauging the impact of shopping on the moods of customers. They called it a retail therapy. The survey observed that a good number of people visit shopping malls or other modern outlets just for diffusing tension and combating stress. It was found that 62% of the visitors preferred shopping for gaining pleasure and 28% visitors spent money for enjoying or celebrating their successes and achievements. It was observed that retail therapy considerably affects the mood of those who visit the outlets. Because they come for shopping to diffuse tension and combat stress, they do not mind the money spent for shopping. It was also found that in the process, the main thing is fulfilment of your desire followed by diversion from the stress-generating reasons. It is not essential that you buy only expensive items because even cheap items also provide to them an opportunity for gaining pleasure.

The report of research published in the Journal of Psychology and Marketing reveals that only 1% visitors were found repenting after shopping. Celebrities visit modern outlets in a very good number. Because they have enough money, they feel pleasure in buying the articles of their choice. Since they get pleasure in shopping, it is quite natural that there is a positive impact on their behaviour. Hollywood stars spend huge money while shopping because shopping provides to them a pleasure. They visit retail outlets for refreshing their mood, mind and attitudes.

The above mentioned facts make it clear that shopping has been emerging as a device for getting pleasure. Diffusion of tension is the result of happiness that we get after shopping. In the shopping malls, we also find the entertainment centres and therefore we find shopping helpful even in refreshing, relaxing and rejuvenating.

Laughter the Biggest Stress-buster

◈ Laughter for Combating Stress

Nothing like happiness, nothing like laughter. The sound of laughing coming from your heart impacts your mind and due to chemical reactions switch on diffusion of tension and keeps us stress-free. It is in this context that we find laughter found to be the most effective prescription for combating stress. The corporate people are found heavily stressed. It is due mainly to their high level of expectations which each and everyday take a new shape and make an additional addition to its intensity. Of course, we find opening of laughter club to help those who do not get an opportunity to laugh but here it is not to be forgotten that natural is natural and artificial is artificial.

Nurturing high level of expectations cannot be wrong but soon or later, we have no option but to think in favour of self-regulation failing which an endless story of inviting complications may trap us so closely that we may never come out and ultimately make ways for a number of complications. It is against this background that the most important lesson for the people serving the corporate sector is to ensure a command over the expectations. Happiness is considered to be an effective device for reenergising the zeal or zest. The most important and the very strong force obstructing the ways of happiness appears to be the negative feelings and thoughts. Positive thoughts and feelings, serving others, helping those who need make ways for the discharge of negative thoughts from your mind and simultaneously, we find big rooms for the entry of positive thoughts. Negative thoughts and feelings never come out unless you allow the positive thoughts to enter. Hence, we are ourselves responsible for positive or negative pleasure or displeasure, happiness or unhappiness. We are less-stressed by ourselves and more stressed by the happiness of others.

What to talk of laughter, when we are not in a position to laugh. We reject the moment for laughing and seal the doors for laughter. This makes it essential that people in general and the corporate people in particular manage their lifestyles in such a fashion that they get time for everything. Even scientific rules reject an imbalance in work profile and concentrate on a sense of proportion making it easier to maintain a balance. If we respect balance, the avenues are paved for happiness and pleasure.

The facts outlined above make it clear that to the extent it is possible we need to activate efforts for capitalising on the opportunities. It is not possible or it is almost utopian to think that the environment at the workplace would ever be stress free. Actually, when we create opportunities for stress; how we can think that it is not to come. Hence, it is pertinent that we start cultivating the habits of helping others and getting pleasure by witnessing the happiness of others which would bring happiness for ourselves.

Laughter is thus found to be an effective device to combat stress. Opportunities are existent but we have to keep our eyes open so that the process of identification and capitalisation is not delayed.

We call laughter a healing agent. We need to identify the situation where we find a sense of humour. The transformation of stress into humour cannot be denied. Sometimes, an effective way to heal a situation is to step away from it. In this context, we need to try reading a funny book or watching a comedy film/show. We can get together with friends and share silly jokes. A good laugh relaxes you and provides to you a space where creative solutions to any problems come easily. Don't forget your right to relax and be cheerful.

We should not forget that happiness is not dependant on particular circumstances. We can be as happy while working on a project in our office as we are while listening to beautiful music or playing with our child. The most important thing is sharing an equal opportunity for happiness. Happy individuals move on to create happier families and institutions. Laughter is a gift to be cherished. All of us should not forget that being happy is as essential as making progress in your career. Laughter is found more contagious than a yarn or a sneeze or cough or anything else. As soon as we start laughing, other people begin to laugh. We also need to remember that in addition to the domino effect of joy and amusement, laughter also triggers healthy physical transformation in the body. Humour and laughter strengthen our immune system, boost our energy, diminish pain and protect us from the harmful effects of stress. We cannot deny that laughter is a priceless medicine which can easily be administered. Humour is a powerful antidote to stress. Nothing works faster or more dependably to bring our mind and body back into balance than a good laugh. Humour lightens our burdens, inspires hopes, connects us to others and keep us grounded, focused and alert. Laughter relaxes the whole body. It makes an invasion on physical tension and stress. It boosts our immune system and decreases stress harmones and increases immune cells. It triggers the release of endorphins and chemical reactions bring a positive change. It protects the heart and improves the function of blood. We cannot deny that shared laughter is one of the most effective tools for keeping relationships fresh and exciting. Laughter indeed is the best medicine.

Every laughing person is an ambassador of happiness. It is a great stress management tool. Because laughter distracts us from any problem or worries we may have, it has the healing power or at least diminish every pain. It is in this context that we call laughter the biggest stress-buster. Laughter gives us instant happiness. Within moments, we forget our distress and burst into a big laugh. This makes it essential that people in general and corporate people in particular do not forget the importance of laughter on combating stress. The corporate professionals need to make it a point to make the environment at the workplace much more conducive for themselves and for people working with them.

Organising laughter show by the organisation cannot be denied to improve the working conditions and make possible work culture. How and in what way to develop the sense of humour amongst the working people happens to be an important functional responsibility before the corporate professionals. We need to stress the need for clean jokes and humour in our life for a better and healthier life. Combating on stress is essential which necessitates laughter.

◈ Healthy Mind for Healthy Body

Healthy mind paves avenues for the development of a healthy body. In the world of hurry, curry and worry, it becomes difficult for us to provide peace to our mind. This is due mainly to the increasing domination of material culture on our lifestyles. We frequently fail in arresting our temptation for a lavish lifestyle which brings a significant increase in our materialistic requirements. We have to spend more and therefore we need to earn more. This makes us irritated, agitated, tensed, stressed and depressed. The stockpile of multi-faceted complexes cannot be cleared unless we regulate our spending behaviour and start evincing our keen interest in serving the interests of humanity. This focuses our attention on the scientific management of mind.

Cheerfulness and warmth bring happiness to employees. A happy employee is found to be much more productive. Mind and mood affect the workplace environment. When we find ourselves happy, laughter is found coming from our heart in a natural way and resulting from which we laugh ourselves and create a condition for others to laugh. It is due to the fact that neurologists find laughter involving highly complex natural system because it instantly interlocks the limbic system. This makes it essential that professionals create a condition where their associates feel pleasure in remaining happy and laughing.

The corporate professionals need to perceive that nothing like a sound mind. Hence, the focus must be on the scientific management of mind. Spiritualism at the workplace paves avenues for the humanised leadership. Purification of mind is considered essential and for that we need to practise the substitution process in which the negative feelings are replaced by the positive feelings. The virtuous thoughts like mercy, humanity, love, purity forgiveness, integrity, generosity, etc., help the destruction of evil thoughts like lust, hatred, anger, greed, pride, etc. Unless we have a pure mind, it is difficult for us to have self realisation. The concentration and meditation help our mind to be pure.

There are a number of ways to have a pure mind but in the process we find Yoga and Meditation to be very effective in discharging the accumulated complexes. Hence, the corporate professionals need to promote those devices for purifying the mind of their associates. Combating stress requires priority attention of corporate professionals because it appears to be the root-and-branch of all problems. Make your employees stress-free. The cultural and spiritual forces also help in combating stress and therefore the professionals need to organise the spiritual sessions. In addition, the provisions like working holiday has also been found instrumental in combating stress. However, we find Yoga the most effective prescription for combating stress and therefore the corporate professionals need to ensure the organisation of exclusive session for Yoga for almost all categories of their employees. This would show a wonderful result.

Managing healthy mind is thus an important condition which would benefit the organisation in many ways. If you keep your employees stress-free, they are found sincere, honest, committed and value-based. You will witness a significant increase in his/her level of efficiency vis-à-vis decency in their behavioural profile. If you find employees making place for the negative feelings, it is not only to affect their mind but we find its harmful effects even on their body. Agitated, tensed, stressed and depressed employees face the problem of accumulated complexes which affect their aptitude vis-à-vis the digestive system and resulting from which a number of diseases crop up. Hence, it is imperative that as a corporate professional, you initiate sincere efforts to keep the employees happy.

Meditation throws a major cascade impact on your body. It is a powerful tonic; more so a mental tonic and even nervine tonic providing to you holy vibrations and penetrating all the cells of the body and curing diseases of the body. The cheerful thoughts, a brisk walk, singing, prayer, pranayam, laughter help you in removing depression and preparing you for meditation. The posture Padmasana is recommended for meditation. You may meditate on the effulgence in the sun, splendour in the moon, glory in the stars and beauty in the sky.

Often, we talk about happiness but achieving happiness particularly in the material culture is found difficult. This focuses our attention on "Karma Yoga". We need to receive Karma Yoga in a right perspective. Accordingly, the employees are expected to follow the socially and ethically accepted code of conduct, to be honest while performing and this one without expecting any fruit. They are not supposed to be the egoist. We cannot deny that right conceptualisation of Karma Yoga by different echelons of people in an organisation would strike a balance between social, national, organisational and individual interests. This bestows on us purity of mind which cultivates faculties of qualitative improvements. Contentment is the real thing to keep us happy. This would make place for spirituality at the workplace where people would feel pleasure in performing.

Mental and spiritual forces cannot be separated. In many places, we find faith healers getting a success in proving effective healthcare services. A deep religious experiences are also found effective in curing the sick. It is due to the fact that a patient's receptive attitude plays a decisive role in curing the sick. The medical experts also admit that patients set their own regenerative process in motion. The religious rituals also play a positive role. The topic may be debatable but one thing is clear that our beliefs play a catalytic role in the curing process. The mental problem is also found from within the cultures. It is, of course, very-very difficult to understand the dynamics of mind-body interactions and therefore we name them mystery, miracle, healings, sacred and supernatural powers. In the centre of everything, we find beliefs playing an effective role in the entire process.

The facts outlined above speak of the direct relationships between body and mind or vice versa.

SUMMARY

In this chapter, you have gone through different dimensions of ensuring healthy mind. Before starting another chapter, make it sure that the following facts are well versed.

Healthy Mind: Stress-free mind is a healthy mind. Cool and calm mind keep us healthy. Healthy mind makes place for healthy thoughts and positive feelings.

Meditation and Mind Purification: Meditation follows concentration through which wordly thoughts are shut out from the mind and divine thoughts get a place. The different postures of Yoga make the mind firm and stress-free. Half an hour of true meditation in a day provides to you one week to struggle.

Yoga: A Conceptual Exposition: It is a science, a technique to protect and promote the interests of human beings to unite them with the highest nature. It is a systematic, methodical and practical discipline and more so, an experimental science of self study.

Yogic View of Personality: The five layers of yogic personal make us distinct to others. The five dimensions of personality we go through are physical self, energy self, mental self, intellectual self and blissful self.

Yoga and Ethics: Yoga helps in attaining a balanced mind and ethical perfection. Ethics, in a true sense, is a means to yoga.

Karma Yoga: The Perception: We need to understand Karma yoga in a right fashion. The five components of yoga need to be perceived in the very context. The first component focuses on our activities to be socially and ethically acceptable. The second component throws light on the fact that whatever role we have chosen, we perform. The third component emphasises on performing without expecting any fruit. The fourth component hammers on accepting the results that we get for our actions. And the fifth component focuses on absence of a sense of becoming a doer or performer by providing credit to others for the extraordinary results you have got.

Yoga for Combating Stress: Yoga helps us in combating stress. The eight-fold path of yoga may be helpful in creating a condition for developing the resistance power to counter the odds and seal the doors for combating stress.

Yoga Postures: The different postures of yoga need to be practised such as Surya Namaskar, Padmasan, Sarvangasan, Sirshasanam, Matyasan, Halasan, Siddhasan, Shavasan, Pavanmuktasan.

Cultural and Spiritual forces for Combating Stress: Participation in cultural and spiritual sessions helps us in achieving a balance which helps combating stress.

Working Holiday for Combating Stress: Mixing business with pleasure is an innovative strategy for combating stress and it is in this context that we find corporate sector making provision for working holidays or paid holidays for outing. A place close to the river banks, forest or jungle is found eco-savvy and suitable for making business decisions. A retreat for corporate managers ready to do without their mobile phones and wi-fi is a new experience with a productive result to combat stress.

Sleep far Combating Stress: The corporate people are found heavily stressed. They are found career-addicted and always nurture dreams for tomorrow which obstruct sound-sleeping and invite stress. This focuses on sleep of night hours in a day. This makes our mind fresh and injects new energy.

Gardening for Combating Stress: Temptation to nature is an important consideration for combating stress and it is in this context that we focus on gardening which would help you in loving nature. The diversion of mind would be instrumental in combating stress. Your love for nature is, of course, the most effective prescription for combating stress.

Entertainment for Combating Stress: If you make use of your mind for a long time its capacity to receive is minimised. This throws light on rest and relaxation. If we start witnessing the entertainment programmes, we find diversion which helps in combating stress. The cultural shows, joke programmes, music programmes, drama shows, dance programme, etc., may be organised even by the companies.

Pet-therapy for Combating Stress: Pet-therapy is found to be an effective device to make us and keep us stress-free. The animals in general and pet dogs, cows and horses in particular have been found instrumental in combating stress. It is also based on the principle of diversion of mind. Since we find stress a result of mental disorder, the pet-therapy is a process of relieving or healing.

Retail-therapy for Combating Stress: Shopping, of late, has been emerging as a device for getting pleasure. Diffusion of tension is the result of happiness that we get after shopping. The British psychologists observe that retail therapy is an effective device for combating stress. A number of retail outlets particularly malls provide to you an opportunity and a place for diffusing tension and combating stress.

Laughter for Combating Stress: You should not forget nothing like happiness and nothing like laughter. Your lifestyles make the ways for stress and therefore try your best to keep yourself happy and nurture positive feelings for others. If laughter is not natural, visit laughter club. This will help you in diffusing tension and combating stress.

Healthy Mind for Healthy Body: Healthy body for healthy mind or healthy mind for healthy body; we find both the conditions interrelated. In the world of hurry, curry and worry, tension and dissension, it is quite natural that we make place for stress. Nothing like a sound mind. The virtuous thoughts like mercy, humanity, love, purity, forgiveness, integrity, generosity, etc., help the destruction of evil thoughts like lust, hatred, anger, greed, pride, etc., responsible for the illness of mind. Hence, it is imperative that all of us serving the corporate sector or other organisations or institutions pave avenues for happiness which would make the mind fresh and healthy.

KEY TERMS

Yoga	Cultural Forces
Stress	Spiritual Forces
Posture	Work Holiday
Meditation	Eco-lodges
Pranayam	Pet Therapy
Human Personality	Retail Therapy
Physical Self	Laughter
Mental Self	Hypnosis
Ethics	Psychics
Individual Behaviour	Ancestral Spirit
Social Behaviour	Witch
Karma Yoga	Witchcrafts
Lotus Posture	Faithhealers
Shoulder Stand Posture	Miracles
Head Stand Posture	Hath Yoga
Fish Posture	Karma Yoga
Halasana	Bhakti Yoga
Plough Posture	Kundalini Yoga
Accomplished Posture	Raj Yoga
Corpse Posture	Yoke
Wind Release Posture	Hustle and Bustle

EXPECTED QUESTIONS

1. What do you mean by a healthy mind? Focus on the role of meditation for mind purification.
2. Define Yoga. Throw light on the yogic view of personality.
3. Explain the role of different postures of yoga in keeping your mind stress-free.
4. What do you mean by Personality? Explain the five layers of yogic personality.
5. Focus on the role of yoga in protecting and promoting ethics.
6. What do you mean by Karma Yoga? Explain the five components of Karma Yoga to be helpful to the corporate people.
7. Throw light on the instrumentality of yoga in diffusing tension and combating stress.
8. In the changing corporate world, we find corporate people heavily stressed and how and in what way the different postures of yoga can be helpful to them in combating stress?
9. Do you find cultural and spiritual forces to be effective in combating stress? Justify your statement.
10. Of late, the corporate sector has been found making provisions for working holiday to improve the level of efficiency of the employees. Do you find this provision to be effective in combating stress? Present your view points.
11. Explain the role of sleep-deficiency for aggravating the problem of stress and focus on the fact that sound sleep may be helpful in combating stress.
12. Explain the effectiveness of gardening or your temptation to nature for combating stress.
13. Do you justify the instrumentality of retail-therapy for combating stress? Defend your arguments.
14. Explain the instrumentality of pet-therapy for keeping you stress-free.
15. Do you find happiness and laughter to be effective in combating stress? Justify your arguments
16. The destruction of evil thoughts is essential to keep your mind fresh and stress-free. Do you agree with this viewpoint? Defend your arguments.
17. Explain the inter-relationship with body and mind affecting the potentials of each other.
18. Discuss the practices to be adopted for managing the mind of corporate people.

APPLICATION EXERCISES

1. "Healthy mind paves avenues for the development of a healthy body. This necessitates scientific management of mind so that the purification process gains a rapid momentum." Comment on this statement in the context of emerging corporate culture.
2. "Yoga is a science. It is a set of technique to protect and promote the interests of human beings. It is a systematic, methodical and practical discipline and more so an experimental science."
3. "While meditating, it is essential that you are aware of the obstacles such as laziness and fickleness of mind. This focuses on your diet and practices of pranayam". Comment on this statement with suitable examples.
4. "In the present materialistic world where we find a number of avenues for agitation and irritation, stress and distress; it is pertinent that we have a clean mind." Do you find yoga helping you in having a pure and fresh mind? Defend Your arguments.

5. "The five dimensions of personality are physical self, mental self, intellectual self, energy self and blissful self." Explain their role the development of personality.
6. "In the today's corporate world, we lack holistic personality. We find people, of course, having world-class professional excellence but not having a holistic personality because we often find them disrespecting social conduct." In the face of this statement, explain the role of yoga in promoting ethics.
7. "We cannot defy that right conceptualisation of karma yoga by different echelons of people serving the organisation would strike a balance between social, national, organisational and individual interests." Focus on this statement in the context of corporate people.
8. "The eight-fold path of yoga if practised in a right way would increase the resistance capacity of the corporate people who are found heavily stressed." Do you agree with this statement? Defend your arguments.
9. "The yoga postures help in combating stress." Comment on this statement.
10. "The father of hypnosis, Abbe Faria advocates that a patient's receptive attitude plays a decisive role in the healing process. Each and everyday, we witness miracle or a dramatic case of cure. Even the leading medical experts admit that patients set their own regenerative process in motion." Do you agree? Justify your viewpoints.
11. "The spiritual sadhanas help you in following the rules of individual behaviour. "In the light of this statement, focus on the role of participants in spiritual sessions in combating stress.
12. "Of late, we find eco-cottages, adventure holidays, eating off an aircraft wing, picking fruits in an orchard neighbouring a jungle or packing fishing rod along for some full and all in a day's work preferred by corporate executives for making decisions in a peaceful and eco-friendly environment."In the face of this statement, explain the role of working holiday for combating stress.
13. "A majority of the corporate people today face the problem of sleep-deficiency due to heavy pressure of work and career-addiction." Do you justify sound sleeping essential for combating stress? Defend your arguments.
14. "The moment you start loving nature, the cleaning of stored complexes starts gaining a rapid momentum." Discuss this statement and focus on the role of nature for combating stress.
15. "The entertainment programmes are found effective in combating stress." Comment on this statement and throw light on the role of entertainment programmes for combating stress.
16. "The dogs and cows are considered the best companions for us and if you start evincing your interests in making them pet, the diversion of mind starts switching on the diffusion of stress." In the light of this statement, explain the role of pet-therapy for combating stress.
17. "A survey conducted by British psychologists reveals that a large number of people visit shopping malls or other modern retail outlets just for diffusing tension and combating stress." Do you agree with this viewpoint? Justify your arguments.
18. "Cheerfulness and warmth bring happiness to employees. A happy employee is found to be much more productive. Mind and mood affect the workplace environment. When we find ourselves happy, natural laughing is found coming from our heart which creates a condition for laughing by others The neurologists find laughter involving his complex natural system because it instantly interlocks the limbic system."

Throw light on the statement outlined above and explain the role of healthy mind on health body and vice versa.

BACK-UP MATERIALS

1. www.yogacards.com
   www.yogajournal.com
   www.yogawiz.com
   Yoga Postures Step By Step
2. www.mentalhealth.about.com
   www.selfimprovement success.com

   Negative and Positive Thoughts
   Feel good about yourself
   Emotions affect your health
3. www.indianetzone.com
   www.yogaforums.com
   www.indianexpress.com

   Human Personality
   How to Meditate, Yoga, Meditation
   Experience the peace of the inner self
4. Swami Sivananda; Easy Steps to Yoga
   A divine Life Society Publication, Tehri-Garhwal, 1194
5. Cindy Krischer Goodman, CEO of BalanceGal LLC,
   a provider of news and advice on how to balance work and life.
   Too busy to Sleep? The Hindustan Times, June 14, 2011.
6. search4beauty.blogspot.com
   Rest and Relaxation
   Holistic Health
7. www.nos.org
   www.webhealthcentre.com
   healthyindia.org
   Get enough sleep everyday
8. www.frontierlaw.com
   www.the hindubusinessline.com

   How to be mart and cool?
9. www.hindu.com
   www.healthyeatingworld.com
   www.healthyforms.com

   Mental health
10. I believe in finding peace, The Times of India,
    August 7, 2011
    timeslife@timesgroup.com

11. Sorrows don't last: The Times of India
December 12, 2010
timeslife@timesgroup.com

12. Too busy to sleep?: The Hindustan Times,
June 14, 2011
Cindy Krischer Goodman, CEO, BalanceGal LLC

13. Contentment is Spirituality: The Times of India,
April 17, 2011
timeslife@timesgroup.com

◆ ◆ ◆

6 ETIQUETTE AND MANNER

In the emerging cross-cultural society, the employees are considered an extension of the corporate brand and therefore social graces and polish need a transcendental priority. Our outward behaviour, etiquette and manners, soft-skills need due attention to establish distinction and get the competitive advantages in the modern corporate world.

CHAPTER DESIGN

Introduction – Business etiquette and Business Ethics – Corporate Society vs. Etiquette – Social Graces and Polish – Etiquette for Facing Interview – Etiquette for Introducing and Paying Compliments – Workplace Etiquette – Dress Etiquette – Dining Etiquette – Disastrous Ravines – Etiquette for Corporate Success – Summary – Key Terms – Expected Questions – Application Exercises – Back-up Materials.

CHAPTER OBJECTIVES

This chapter aims at studying and understanding the different dimensions of business etiquette. It is high time that we sensitise upcoming youths and enrich their personal score. Socially acceptable behaviour, if breached; code or polite behaviour, if not followed; etiquette and manner, if undermined make our task at climbing the corporate ladders much more difficult. The etiquette and grooming experts feel that whole package of attitude such as body language, behaviour, communication and etiquettes govern our professional growth. Business etiquette can make or break our business. Guru of graces feel that continuing lack of social graces cannot give to us the competitive advantage. Enriching the personal score of an individual is an area of top priority which we generally undermine while setting the order.

ETIQUETTE AND MANNER

◈ Introduction

Emergence of a disciplined and civilised society makes our task much more difficult in which we are supposed to respect and honour the social code. It is but natural that human beings and animals can't behave in the same fashion. Looking distinct is found to be an outstanding property of the human beings which tempts the society to regulate the personal style of an individual, so that they do not break the social regulations. Gradually, when we start nurturing the culture, the limitations and boundaries increase further. The social regulations start defining what to do and what not to do. The conventional laws of courtesy start impacting our behaviour. We are supposed to be much more courteous. The increasing level of education brings a significant increase in the formation of attitude and influences our outward behaviour.

During the yester decades, the contours of development have undergone radical transformation. The centuries and centuries of the emergence of social constitution have made ways for innovative developments in almost all the areas. Each and everyday, we find something new to be conceptualised by us. With the passage of time, the buzzwords change, the concept and percept change and more so, the expectations of society vis-à-vis the organisations change. If we keep ourselves unaware of the incoming changes, we suffer. Conversely, if we keep ourselves updated; our efforts are suitably priced and rewarded.

Organisational culture can't remain static. We find much more dynamism in the face of multi-dimensional developments in the society. The organisational culture in the public sector is found sizably different to the culture that we find in the private sector. Like this, the organisational culture of domestic organisations considerably vary from the Multi National Corporations. With the increasing heat of globalisation, we find the domination of MNCs reaching to its peak. And, it is against this backdrop that we find corporate culture expecting a lot from their employees. They consider employees as an extension of the corporate brand and therefore they expect that corporate brand is expressed uniformly throughout the world. They advocate that global uniformity helps them in developing the team spirit and nurturing the team culture. In a true sense, we find emergence or a corporate society in which etiquette and manners of employees serving the organisation need priority attention.

When we talk about etiquette, it is concerned with the conventional laws of courtesy. It is decorum in which we find place for polite and socially acceptable behaviour observed between the members of same profession. It is the code of polite behaviour in a society. In the process, the employees are required to be courteous and their speech or action must be polite.

When we talk about manners, our focus is on the outward behaviour or attitude towards others. It is also personal style of acting or bearing or a way in which something is done. In every educated and civilised society the etiquette and manners become a part and parcel of relationships. It is against this background that we find corporate society of today assigning due weightage to etiquette and manners.

The corporate trainer, of late, has been found in big demand. Sabira Merchant is a busy woman. She happens to be first corporate trainer of India who has barely a free day left on her calendar. Of course, she is not a CEO but she teaches CEOs a thing or two about conducting their business which invariably they lack. The India Inc., has now realised the instrumentality of corporate etiquettes in an increasingly global competitive environment and it is in this context that we find guru of graces like Merchant in big demand. She rightly opines, "We have just woken up to the tact that soft skills are as important as hard skills to get an edge in the current competitive environment." It is right to say that during yester decades, there has been mushrooming of Business Schools albeit in small towns and cities of India but a majority of the students coming from these schools lack awareness of corporate etiquette and manners. There is no doubt in it that finishing schools have been found addressing everything from voice and accents to dining etiquette to dressing up basics but a, majority of us have not been successful in strengthening their realisation that their products cannot do anything without knowing etiquette and manners.

Pria Warrick, Executive Director of the Pria Warrick Finishing Schools rightly realises that we Indian have a predilection towards education, caring little for manners. She points out, "It's, always been a case of study hard, get good grades and everything else will be taken care of." She finds lack of social graces even among some of the highest placed Indian executives. Lack of social polish and communication skills prove to be a major factor for our failures in the corporate world. It is in this context that we find even Infosys thinking over it on a priority basis and they have built a Global Education Centre in Mysore teaching more than 50,000 students leadership and corporate manners.

Pria Warrick has expertise in the field of etiquette and grooming and she feels that there has been a significant increase in the kind of soft skills which the companies of today need. She says that whole package of attitude, body language, behaviour, communication and etiquettes account for your professional growth, because technical skills account for 15% and the business and social graces account for 85%. We cannot deny that Indians lack basic international workplace etiquette, from dressing properly to punctuality to making inoffensive small talk especially to women executives. May be that the corporate world of today undermine it but what we can do when we lag behind in addressing body language, posture, handshake and the body odour. If we have to be hireable and promotable, these negative traits need a departure.

In view of the above, it is right to mention that professional excellence cannot be possible in absence of professional growth and if we undermine corporate etiquette and manners, the professional growth remain incomplete.

The Business Schools of today bear the responsibility of educating and training students even in the field of corporate etiquette and manner. The Finishing Schools are mushrooming because the Business Schools, specially in the Indian condition, do not concern themselves with the additional attributes and traits as a part and parcel of social behaviour. How to inculcate and cultivate social graces amongst the up coming or budding youths, is an important functional responsibility before the Business Schools of modern corporate world.

Of course, we are not supposed to bid a goodbye to the world-class thematical competence by enriching the subjective knowledge of our students but here it is also significant to mention that of late, the corporate sector has been found spotting the best fish in the pond because they pick the best graduates, educate and train them in tune with their requirements and offer them more bucks, the whopping salaries which may put even doctors, engineers and MBAs to shame. Hiring czars from college campuses has been gaining a rapid momentum because the Business Schools have not been following the norms while supplying finished products to them. Believe it or not, but the emerging trends in the corporate sector of India indicate that the new high-flier is the average boy-next-door with a down-to-earth practical approach to life; not the extraordinary who are grabbing the plush jobs. In the today's corporate world, a college degree and a rock star personality is considered enough even for big bucks. Hence, it is high time that we assign top priority to the basics which would give us an edge over others. The example of Shrey Gupta, a student of Shri Ram College of Commerce (SRCC), New Delhi is adduced because he has been hired at a starting salary or ₹ 39 lakh per annum with Deutche Bank. He was not a bookworm. He loves music and evinces interest in organising events. He himself says, I was not the topper in my college. I grew up in Varanasi and this was a dream which came true. I went through 10 rounds of interviews. I was frank about my intelligence. If I did not know the answer to the questions they asked, I admitted to it. I think they saw that I had leadership skills, like taking charge and initiating things. We cannot deny that strength of Shrey is in his humility. He was distinct to others. He had interest in asking questions, developing interest in music and even sharing jokes. He honed his leadership skills, logic, intuition, thinking, communication and mannerism. The hiring experts of today say that the ultimate candidate should have a zippy attitude. By zippy attitude, the focus is on bright, fresh or lively. They are found interested in getting the creative leaders. They look for dynamic and a rock star personality. They feel that it is easier for them to survive and thrive albeit in a multi-cultural environment.

In the corporate world of today, we find people with personal characteristics in a big demand. They prefer young people having a high level of tolerance for stress and efficacious of behavioural flexibility to resolve the crisis. They pick people with positive attitudes and skills not knowledge. They have examples that people with these traits are thriving today and even in future their polite behaviour, flexibility and creativity would be found productive not only to them but albeit to the organisation and nation.

◈ Business Etiquette and Business Ethics

At the outset, it is significant that we understand the difference between business etiquette and business ethics. We consider business etiquette a conduct prescribed by convention or by authority to be used while interacting with business associates. If we talk about business ethics, it is the principles of right or good conduct governing business people and organisations. Whatsoever the differences that we find between the two are almost clear. Etiquette is a conduct with business associates supported by conventions whereas the ethics is a conduct governing business in a fair way. Suppose, we have two executives. The first executive has been educated in the business schools of international standard, well aware of where to shop, always feeling comfortable while communicating and dining even in the five-star hotels and feeling ease in all the situations. He/she has a knack for remembering people by names, a natural, salesman/woman, a networker who is driven in success. He/she knows how to attract people serving his/her organisation for buying shares. Due to his/her polite behaviour, the success is found very easy for him/her.

Another executive who is not well polished, not so much interested in the cocktail party of the company, not interested in developing his career in the office. But his goals are customer and employee satisfaction. He is honest and bears the efficacy of making quality decisions. He feels himself bold and is in a position to look at himself in the mirror without any guilt. He has made a little improvement in the business etiquette.

The two executives have an attitudinal difference and the prime reason for such a difference is their business ethics.

When we talk about the business etiquette, the focus we find is on our behaviour which should essentially be polite or polished. Our appearance, conduct in the business environment are the determining factors. Thus, we find etiquette an action or actions we take when we are with others. Unethical acts are performed in secrecy and therefore it is only you who is aware of your mistakes, misdeeds; unless and until you are caught. It is easier to be highly polished but it is extremely difficult to be a highly ethical one. And it is very-very difficult to balance the two in your personal score. An individual knowing the qualities of striking a balance between etiquette and ethics defines and redefines success and finds it easier to be at peak.

The above mentioned facts clarify the difference between etiquette and ethics. We cannot be wrong in our observation that etiquette can be dramatised but ethics cannot be dramatised. To be polished and polite can be acted but to be fair and honest cannot be acted. In a true sense, we find both of them essential traits for personal score. Assigning due weightage to mannerism, politeness, soft skills cannot be underestimated in the business world where we find our foundation resting on the rapport we develop and the relationships we establish where body language and voice significantly contribute to the process and the words you use are found at the bottom.

We consider business ethics the principles of right or good conduct governing business, people and organisations. The values and ethics are central to any organisation. Values are defined as those things, which are important to or are valued by someone; may be an individual or an institution, or organisation. Values are the embodiment of what an organisation stands for and consider as a base for the behaviour of its members. Values are what we as a profession judge to be right. Values determine what is right and what is wrong and doing what is right or wrong is what we mean by ethics. Thus to behave ethically is to behave in a manner consistent with what is right or moral. We cannot negate that the concept and percept of right and wrong is the gift of society. Virtually, every society makes some determination of morally correct behaviour. We also find organisations defining what is right and what is wrong for members of the organisation. Ethical codes are there to govern our behaviour. Thus the codes governing the behaviour of members of business organisation that you can do it and you cannot do it are the business ethics that we often talk about. The members of business organisation are made it clear that doing this is right and doing that is wrong.

Building an ethical climate becomes essential for the organisation which we call here corporate ethics. The business organisations evincing interests in the creation of ethical climate take help of ethical codes. Here we find ethical institutional practices or ethics conceptualised by corporations. Making explicit ethics policies and activating the sensitisation process for practising ethical codes imparting training on how to deal with the situations with an ethical dimension are some of the efforts helpful in conceptualising ethics by an organisation. Socially responsible behaviour of organisations now have been practised by a good number of organisations around the globe and therefore, we do not find corporate ethics a regional phenomenon rather than a global phenomenon.

An executive educated in the best schools, knowing well where to shop, well trained in the finishing schools, achieving perfection in soft skills, assigning due weightage to facial appearance, behaving politely with business associates and found well-polished establishes reputation in the field of etiquette and manners. It is not essential that he/she is ethically sound. Whatsoever the personal score that we have talked about can be developed in an individual by educating and training them in an effective way. But when we talk about ethics, this is principles of right or good conduct governing business people and organisation and it is difficult to make an individual honest who can look at himself/herself in the mirror without guilt just by educating and training. The etiquette experts can judge that how polished we are by our behaviour but the ethical experts find it difficult to judge an individual that he/she is ethical because unethical acts are performed in secrecy. It is only you who can answer that you are ethical or unethical.

◈ Corporate Society vs. Etiquette

Though we find etiquette playing an important role almost in all the areas but if we talk about the corporate society, the etiquette and manners play a catalytic role. Your soft words have the efficacy of transforming albeit negative into positive. Your polite behaviour considerably rewards you but conversely, your aggressive and rough behaviour throw you in the reverse gear. There are different occasions for introduction, presentation and compliments and salutation where you need to show the excellence of your skill. We cannot deny that corporate society is much more sensitive. Facing interviews, initiating presentation, managing events, dealing with the clients, exposition of image, initiation of dialogues are some of the critical areas or problem areas where we feel ourselves potentially unsound. It is against this background that our youths though thematically sound fail in transforming the opportunities into possibilities and further possibilities into realities.

In the corporate society, we find different persons with different positions working together. The superiors to subordinates and vice versa, the business associates working in different capacities need to interact with different motives. They need to interact with their clients and visitors. They need to present during conventions. They are also supposed to attend to be hireable and promotable. It is pertinent that on the basis of their polite behaviour, they are successful in projecting their positive image. Lack of social graces, social polish and communication skills are our negative score which obstruct the process of development. Leadership and manners are our basic requirements determining the magnitude of our success. The corporate society assigns a transcendental priority to etiquette which makes us socially graceful, organisationally productive and individually witnessing a win-win situation.

Corporate society promotes the emergence of a cross-cultural or multi-cultural society in which the levels of expectations of people coming from different countries of the globe cannot be identical. The business associates belonging to different social systems and cultural patterns receive and perceive politeness and conduct in different ways. Since the developed countries of west are found rich in etiquette and manners, due to strong corporatisation strengthening the base of national economy since long, it is quite natural that expectations of top management from the employees remain the same. We consider employees an extension of corporate brand and therefore it is not wisdom that each one of us start thinking and acting in different ways. Willingly or unwillingly, we have to maintain similarities in body language, paralanguage, use of words and other aspects to make scope for nurturing mannerism.

Softness or politeness is liked by all. Social graces and polish give you adequate return in different ways. The concept and percept of domestic and global workplace environment cannot have uniformity.

To be aware of etiquette and mannerism, it is imperative that employees are well aware of the culture of workplace environment. Workplace etiquette considerably rests on the organisational culture. Educational background, family background and regional background also play a significant role in defining and redefining the concept of corporate manner, dining culture, shopping behaviour, eye contact, gestures and postures, tone, temperament, voice and what not. The level of tolerance of all the people working in an organisation cannot be equal. It is also equally right that generation of stress-prone environment by different categories of organisations cannot be on an equal footing. Hence, the corporate society based on corporate culture can not define corporate etiquette and manner in different ways. It is in our larger interest that we know about etiquette and mannerism and conceptualise them without making any comment or bringing any modification.

In every educated and civilised society, the etiquette and manners became a part and parcel of relationships. When we talk about manners our focus is on the outward behaviour and personal style of acting or bearing. It is in this context that corporate society of today assigns due weightage to etiquette and manners. In the changing scenario, it is significant that we perceive etiquette and grooming in the global perspective. The whole package of attitude, body language, behaviour, communication and etiquettes account for our professional growth and in these areas a majority of the Indian lag behind. We need to improve ourselves in addressing body language, posture, handshake and the body odour. The corporate trainers need to mind even small things to make a difference. Of course, we find nothing wrong in enriching our predilection towards education but at the same time we cannot allow ourselves to remain poor in the field of etiquette and manners. From voice and accents to dining etiquette and shopping style; we need to be much more particular to educate and train our existing and budding generations. We cannot deny that specially in the Indian context, we need special care because we lag far-far behind.

You are supposed to handle a number of situations specially in the corporate setting. We need to realise that corporate etiquette is a business skill complementing core competencies. We, specially in the Indian setting, do not follow the manners and courtesy in our daily lives. Our incivility and rudeness need due care. The violent anger arising from the conflict with the driver of another motor vehicle even on road itself has made entry for terms like "Road Rage". The roadways have been facing the crisis and even our career may suffer if we accommodate behaviour of this nature. Caution and awareness may be helpful to us in preventing side tracking of our career. We expect the emergence of social potholes during the most common corporate encounters. If we are careful, the possibilities of plugging the potholes are possible. American corporate society, European Corporate Society and Indian Corporate Society cannot have different manners because in the corporate world, we have one society, one culture and therefore identical etiquette and manners.

◈ Social Graces and Polish

Of course, we find nothing wrong in having a predilection towards education, studying hard and getting good grades but if we lack social graces and polish; our tasks of getting a success in the volatile corporate world is found much more difficult. We cannot deny that India has some of the world's best educated engineers, business tycoons and albeit technology wizards but when we talk about social polish and communication skills, we put ourselves behind the competitors. It is against this background that we find opening of a number of finishing schools and what to talk of others when we find companies like Infosys opening a Global Education Centre is Mysore teaching more than 50,000 graduates leadership and corporate manners. Organisational culture is a part and parcel of social culture. With the increasing heat of globalisation, we find an expansion in the organisational boundary. Emergence of a multi-cultural society is the result of recent developments in which we find graces, manners necessitating a new perception specially in the Indian perspective where people still say that looks culture is nothing but bunkum or nonsense. Adman Piyush Pandey, Executive Chairman and Creative Director, Ogilvy & Mathers, South Asia says, "My work should do the talking for me, not my shirt." We cannot deny that our contributions rank first but when we rank first both in outfits and performance; our position at the top of the corporate ladder is found secured.

Guru of graces around the world make a strong advocacy in favour of social graces and polish. Sabira Merchant, Pria Warrick, Shiv Agrawal and many others feel that soft skills are as important as hard skills. Etiquette and grooming experts also believe that an in depth knowledge of the changing international workplace etiquette is essential to make our products socially and globally productive. Elegance cannot be overlooked in the corporate world where a majority of us fail in climbing the corporate ladders. It is in this context that we find them looking for visionaries having high intellectual bandwidth and a daring attitude. They look for people with adaptability, agility and ability to think beyond today. They are on a lookout, for people who can come up with new ways of communicating, collaborating and connecting employees around the world. Unless they have social graces, the task of having a competitive edge would remain difficult. A distinctive personal gesture or way of speaking, behaving in a way that is acceptable to the society, enriching the personal score in the face of global standards need due attention of institutions involved in the process of educating and training people for the modern society.

In the changing scenario, we cannot deny that social etiquette can make or break our business. Whether, it is a client luncheon, networking event, job interview or sales call; we cannot move forward in absence of social graces. Today, business encounters are filled with opportunities to display polish and poise. Good manners help others see value in their self worth and feel at ease in the process of doing business. This helps to establish client relationships evolving into loyal, core customer relationships helping sustain corporate success. It is difficult for us to undermine corporate or business etiquette or social graces and polish, specially in the global market place where we find high intensity of challenges. The professional excellence of corporate people or other experts may be helpful in resolving the crises. We cannot deny that the multinational market place is found to be more challenging and chaotic when comes to protocol. International etiquette requires due attention in the very context. Formal dining and the social graces may help you and your staff shine even in the critical situations. Our occasional missteps and bad manners need to be avoided at different stages.

Making an invasion on etiquette errors is significant which would make you socially graceful. There are some tips which you need to note.

- You are working as a manager and you have received an invitation from the director of another department in the company. This invitation is for attending an important product launch. It was requested that you have to call a specific individual to confirm your attendance but you forget. Two weeks later, the inviting host extends to you a personal invitation for interacting socially with key customers at the launch. You give an enthusiastic "Yes".

- You had received an invitation for a breakfast seminar at a local hotel 10 weeks ago. You were not careful to the information related to attire. Because you work at a software company where dress code is business casual and when you enter the meeting hall, you find everyone else in business attire. Here it is significant that you should seek information prior to the event. If there is a communication gap, you need to be overdressed for the circumstances.
- You had been invited to attend a product launch meeting. The time far arrival is 9 A.M. and for opening remarks, it is 9.30 A.M. You are late by twenty minutes. There is a breakfast buffet for guests during this time. Actually, you did not notice the two internal e-mails related to the summarised agenda asking you to arrive between 9 and 9.15 A.M. It is your responsibility to be on time.
- You failed to review the guest list that was sent to you in advance. You had only 10 minutes before the presentation begins. Now grab a plate of food and bottle of water. With both hands engaged you have no option but to say hello to clients. Because your hands are not in a proper condition, nobody is interested in shaking hands with you, shake hands after you have properly eaten and washed your hands.
- You sit down on a table just three minutes before the meet begins. Of course everyone at the table knows you but only three of eight people know each other. You start speaking with the familiar people and overlook others. It is essential that you introduce everyone in the group.

The above mentioned mistakes are against social graces which would harm you in different ways. Hence, you need to be careful to the tips mentioned above because etiquette errors complicate your task of becoming socially graceful which is possible when you know about good manners.

We cannot deny an invasion on good manners and etiquette, if we are not disciplined in managing our words and behaviour. Social graces cannot be possible if our words injure or harm others because such a negative trait of our personality makes us indisciplined and uncivilised. Social polish makes it essential that we make softness an integral part of our personality and nurse and nurture it to regulate our behaviour, body language and facial expression. Becoming soft to our superiors is not the only thing that we need to showcase in the present context because it happens to be our compulsion. We cannot negate that an acid test of personality trait is found when we interact or converse with our subordinates. Being a corporate global citizen, you cannot survive or thrive without social graces and polish.

Let's go through some of the verses of Kabir and try to practise them for the development of social graces.

Madhur vachan hai sukhadi
Katuk vachan hai teer
Sravan dwar hai sanchare
Sale sakal sareer. *Kabir Chaura Path, Sakhi 301, P. 461*

Shabad ju aisa voliye
Tan ka apa khoeya
Auran ko sital kare
Apan ko sukh hoai *Kabir Sakhi Granth, Sakhi 58, P. 298*

Social graces rest on softness, sweetness and politeness and therefore we need to make use of soft words while communicating, conversing, ordering and instructing. If we find our words rough or bitter, we find it painful even for ourselves then what to talk about others. A number of problems crop up in our life system which we may not feel in the short run but of course in the long run but by that time, it is too late and we considerably harm our life system. It is right to mention that our words matter and therefore we need to be more careful while making use of words for verbal or written communication. We need to make use of those words which keep others cool and make ourselves cooler.

The corporate trainers make a strong advocacy in favour of social graces and social polish for the professional growth of an individual because they have evidences to testify its sizable contribution to the development of professional excellence. Lack of social graces even among some of the highest placed Indian executives prove to be a major factor for their failures in the corporate world. If we evince interests in climbing the corporate ladders, our priority attention must be on social graces and polish.

◈ Etiquette for Facing Interview

If you are looking for a job, a planned outfit is considered to be important. You do not know when the job opportunity is available and therefore it is pertinent that you have one well fitting and the coordinate "interview outfit". At the very outset, it is significant that you develop your awareness of the dress code of the organisation where you have to face the interview. There is nothing wrong in contacting the concerned organisation for knowing the appropriate dress for this interview. After getting information, you need to make preparations. It is to be remembered that looking good is not to cost a fortune. Right place would make the arrangements affordable.

◈ Grooming Checklist:

You need to make preparations for the interview day in the face of grooming checklist given below:

- ❐ You have to bathe or shower in the morning.
- ❐ Brush and wash your teeth and use mouth wash.
- ❐ Whatsoever the outfit you need must be clean and well pressed.
- ❐ Keep your undergarments and other accessories ready.
- ❐ Your shoes must be polished. Make it sure that heels are not run-over.
- ❐ Your nail and hands must be neat and clean.
- ❐ Wear cologne or scented toilet water, but very lightly.
- ❐ Wash your hand and make it neat, carry a comb.
- ❐ Women should apply make up lightly and should carry powder and or lipstick to freshen up before the interview.
- ❐ Men need to be freshly shaven.
- ❐ A wristwatch to keep track of the time.

◈ Mind First Impression

First impression is the last impression, you need not to forget it. The moment you walk into the room, just within 15 seconds, a person will size you up. You should not forget that what you wear speaks a lot about you, such as what you are, whether you like it or not. The first impression that you make is visual. It is important that you pay attention to even small things in detail from head to toe. Appearance makes the difference. This may be a cause for your selection or even for rejection. This provides to you a competitive advantage and therefore take it seriously. Make it sure that the first impression about you is a positive one. The persons in the board size you up in the face of your performance. You loose or you carry. If you carry, the chance is positive. In a true sense, on the basis of your performance and appearance, you strengthen the perception of experts that you are careful about your looks and you are serious about finding a job. In the corporate sector, your body language and appearance score 55%, your verbal tone 38% and your verbal context 7%. Hence, your outfits prove to be an important consideration for your selection or elimination. How and in what way, you manage your looks and present yourself would determine your result. Actually, you have to see everything in detail.

Believe it or not, a majority of rejections that we find today in the corporate world are due to appearance. Both for hiring and firing, we find your facial appearance playing a decisive role. A survey conducted by the New York University comes to this conclusion that No.1 reason why people are not hired because of how they present themselves at the interview. It is not wisdom that you keep yourself away from first impressions which is so important for your success. You never-never get a second chance to make a good first impression and therefore capitalise on the opportunity. What a prospective organisation wears and what are their dress codes? Know it and present yourself for the interview you want to be wearing the same “uniform” that organisation wears. This will act in your favour because they would start considering you as a part of their group. You need to make it sure that when you are called for an interview, the organisation already knows that you can do the job. Now it is upon you to okay their perception by projecting your image as a confident candidate with a professional look that mirrors their dress code. The only thing you need to know that what image they expect from a candidate and you make it possible.

◈ Your Shoes a Problem Area

May be that you do not take it seriously but your shoes may also be responsible for your selection or elimination. Mr. A was one of the two finalists for a high salary position. He had already been interviewed twice and was on the third round of interview for speaking with the CEO. He was escorted to the office of CEO by a Human Resource Manager. After the interview was over, Mr. A felt that he would be chosen for the job because he had the right contacts and the potentials to make that organisation more profitable.

When he received the call a few days later, it was shocking for him to know that other candidate had been selected. He asked the HRM, why he was not chosen. The HRM replied, “Do” you remember when we were walking up to the CEO’s office? Mr. A replied Yes. HRM said, well I looked down and noticed your shoes were scuffed up. While offering a job, the organisation has to see that who is in a position to distinguish his/her personal score. It was possible for you to control your shoes but you did nothing about it. It is assumed that you do not pay attention to details.

This makes it clear that you mind each and everything sincerely and professionally, pay attention to details and with your facial appearance, ensure the organisation that you control everything that you can.

◈ Show Respect to the Organisation

A company encouraged by its past success was to hire three to four new project managers. Mr. A was well aware of the concept Dress for Success which hinted him that suit must be for interview. His one close friend also decided to be interviewed. He was not aware of the tips for getting success in interview and therefore he decided to wear his navy blue blazer, blue button down shirt, khaki coloured pants and slip-on shoes, to be put on and taken off quickly shoes. The man who was aware of the tip for interview was offered $ 28,000 more than high end of the initial offering and reason was that he respected the person interviewing him.

◈ Exposing Thematical Competence

Particularly for the new job seekers, it is essential that they have gone through the subjects, at least the concerned basics. Have a look at your CV which has been sent by you earlier and be prepared to justify the qualifications you have mentioned there. Besides you need to update yourself in the context of current events, emerging problems inside and outside the country, the newspapers and current reporting. You should also enrich your knowledge bank regarding the interviewing company with the help of its Annual Report. The social issues, economic issues, political issues, environmental and cultural issues also need your due attention.

◈ Making Psychological Preparation

It is imperative that students or candidates seeking interview make themselves mentally prepared to face the questions to be asked by the experts in the interview board. The questions, may also be embarrassing and therefore how and in what way you have to respond need due priority. This is found very much related to the personality and mindset of the candidates. There must be honesty in answering questions. When you cannot answer admit your inability. You will yourself invite a number of problems when you start answering those questions which you do not know. It is significant that as a candidate you have a clear perception of your prospects in the concerned organisation where you face the interview. Know your strengths and weaknesses and make preparations accordingly. Self-confidence is essential for getting a success.

◈ Time Management

It is essential that you reach to the place of interview on time at least, 20-30 minutes earlier to get yourself relaxed and get a feel of the organisation. You need to manage your activities right from the very morning. In no case, you are supposed to be late.

◈ Self Management

Your entry, answering questions, asking questions and leaving the place of interview are some of the important areas where you need due attention. You should have the ability to adjust yourself within the environment. Manner of opening and closing the door, walking, greeting and taking the chair are significant. All your activities prove to be a testimony of your etiquette. Entry is the stage where you get an opportunity to make first impression. You should not forget that a natural pleasant expression with a smiling face makes a better impression. Gloomy, grim or serious expression, stressed and depressed facial appearance are negative parts of your personality. While answering questions, feel yourself comfortable because the interviewers are supposed to know your plus points. The questions are asked with the motto of knowing your competence, personal qualities or score, character, attitude to work and life, career goals. The candidates are also given the opportunity to ask questions. If not, you may seek permission to ask. While asking questions, you need to be polite. While leaving, make it sure that the interview is over. You have to thank, collect and pack your papers, get up gracefully without scrapping the chair and wish them a Good Day. The time you arrive and the time you depart are considered highly sensitive especially with the view point of etiquette and manners.

◈ Presentation

In some of the cases, we find presentation also organised with the motto of selecting candidate. Normally, it is with the motto of informing, explaining and persuading the audience or even with the motive of expressing the view point. It is delivered to a small, knowledgeable audience at a conference, seminar or a business meeting. For giving a good presentation, it is pertinent that you have some knowledge of the formal aspects. You need to know about the environment where you have to give presentation. It is your responsibility to ensure that all the supporting infrastructural facilities are available at the venue for presentation. The position and projection of equipment are to be checked to avoid complications. You need to know about the time allowed for giving presentation. It is also essential that you know about other speakers. The quality of audience determines the quality of your presentation. If you come to follow about the perception of audience about you, the task of fulfilling their expectations would be found easier.

Know presentation etiquette

Creation of first impression is found significant even for an effective presentation. You have 10-15 seconds of time for positive impression which would help you in different ways. While starting your presentation, state your name even though you have been introduced. Because, it reinforces your presence. While delivering, follow a style which would be convenient to you. You may start with Good Morning, ladies and gentleman. Introduce yourself precisely and then start your presentation. The introductory remarks must build rapport and should create a condition where audience get time to adjust with your personality.

Of late, you may use visual aid for making your presentation effective. With the viewpoint of both the audience as well as the speaker, the visual and is found effective. The data, diagram, graph, etc., can be presented in a very effective way if you make use of power point presentation. Here, it is essential that you keep the slide simple and avoid too much movement or too much colour. Avoid using sound to accompany the slides. Prepare visuals carefully so that we find them matching with the speech. Finally, give a short summary of the main points explained by you. When you complete your presentation, it is proper that you invite questions from the audience. To make your presentation lively, it is pertinent that you introduce the question session well so that people are encouraged to ask questions.

At last, you are supposed to thank the audience for giving you the time and attention.

Today, we find presentation emerging as an important device for testing the communicative ability of an individual. The audience are found in a position to rate your quality. But preparation of presentation is found to be an important dimension and therefore, it is essential that you have used your excellence in getting it prepared.

◈ Etiquette for Introducing and Paying Compliments

Both while introducing and complementing, you need an in depth knowledge of etiquette and manners. We consider it a primary requirement for people in general and the corporate people in particular. The most important thing is cultivating a pleasant and friendly way of speaking which a majority of us lack. Our volume should be low and gestures should be regulated. It is essential that we make eye contact with the other person(s). We have to respond by nodding our hand and maintaining an upright posture. If appropriate make use of occasional filler such "I See" or "that's interesting" or "Really" as the situations necessitate. There must be variance in voice to avoid monotony. You should also have a command over paralanguage.

◈ Introducing Yourself

Making first impressions is significant in the corporate world and while introducing yourself you get a time of 20-30 seconds for that. The corporate professionals need to mind the following:

- You need to remember that business introductions are based on hierarchy. To make it clear, a person of greater authority is introduced to a person of greater authority. You should not forget that in business etiquette, there is no place for gender discrimination like ladies first.
- It is not to be forgotten that a client always comes before anyone in the organisation.
- The selected officials come before a non-official. You need to introduce a non-official person to an elected official. Whenever you introduce someone from the Press or Media, include this information in your introduction in order to warn the person, particularly a public official that the conversation may be on record.
- Introduce a junior executive to a senior executive.

While introducing people, you are supposed to help the newly acquainted persons to start and carry on a smooth and friendly conversation. Here, it is significant that you comment briefly on the background of each.

If no body is to introduce you, just introduce yourself to the other guests. Extend your hand, smile and say, I am........, from........ mention the name of your organisation. Always use both, your name and surname while introducing yourself. Speak in an engaging tone which must be interesting and memorable vis-à-vis professional, but not take more than 15 seconds to deliver. You need to consider that what information would be interesting to others. When you attend a business function, it is appropriate to say where you work and in what capacity you serve the organisation, but when it is not business function, avoid furnishing job information. Mind it that self introduction is a gifted opportunity to you where you have an opportunity to expose yourself.

◈ Paying Compliments

In a true sense, we find paying compliments an art. You need to learn it. When we talk about compliments, it is actually expression of appreciation. Expressing everything gracefully makes it essential that we have right information about the concerned people. While complementing, you can include his outstanding contributions such as a well-conducted meeting, a well-argued case competent collection of data, excellent presentation or conduction, etc.

The following facts need your due attention while paying compliments:

- Compliments must be moderate and genuine. You are not supposed to flatter.
- You should not forget that exaggerated expression lacks strength in your sounds. You have to express it in a positive, sincere and friendly manner. Maintaining eye contact is essential with the person to whom you are paying compliments. There must be smile on your face while complementing.
- Compliments should not have ulterior motive. Never give a compliment to get a return. Compliments for compliments should not be your motive.
- While complementing, never speak of your own achievements or contributions.
- Use positive adjectives to compliment well.

◈ Responding to Compliments

Responding to compliments that you have received is also significant. You are supposed to acknowledge compliments and thank the person paying to you the compliments. It is not in good taste that you feel yourself embarrassing and reject the compliments. While acknowledging and thanking, you have to be graceful. There must be a smile on your face.

The corporate etiquette makes it essential that you have a friendly way of speaking. Actually, you need to cultivate a habit of speaking well. Good manners and etiquette carry some meaning and we find them impacting your personality. Politeness in behaviour is found easier when we succeed in inculcating politeness in our communications. This is an art which you can develop. Enriching our personal score is considered the most important thing in the present business world. Your polite behaviour is considered important at all. Actually, you need etiquette and good manners at each and every stage where even a minor mistake may cause to you a major damage. Of course, damage control takes too much time and your additional energy. Hence, it is imperative that you are very much professional while making your behaviour polite. Your words, language, body language, paralanguage help you in many ways.

◈ Workplace Etiquette

With the increasing heat of globalisation, we find environmental conditions at the workplace becoming much more vulnerable. Both at domestic and global levels, we need an in depth knowledge of the changing scenario so that our efforts are productive to establish excellence as a courteous professional. There are a number of problem areas or disaster areas making our task much more complicated. It is our prime responsibility to identify them on time. The involuntary bodily functions, unawareness of the rank and position of staff, unawareness of the dress code and lack of corporate party manners are found some of the important problem areas where we need to enrich our knowledge bank. Welcoming newcomers, showing courtesy to our colleagues making ourselves likeable and pleasant to work with, business meeting etiquette and awareness of the physical fitness of people serving the organisation cannot be underrated in the very context. We cannot deny that environment at the work place depends on the organisational culture. Workplace etiquette makes it essential that we have an indepth idea of the workplace environment.

Acknowledgement of rank and status of staff: The workplace etiquette concerned with acknowledging an individual depends on the organisational culture. When a senior executive or a woman of any status enters a room, we stand. In the corporate circles, it is pertinent that we follow the protocol. Unless a newcomer executive offers his/her hand, we have to wait. While shaking hands, we need a firm grip but squeezing is not expected. We are supposed to look at the professionals directly in their eyes while greeting them. While exchanging business cards, we need to be polite to look at the card and make some sort of comment even if it is just a confirmation. While meeting people of celebrity status, we are not required to offer our hands first. While travelling with other professionals, it is to be remembered that the principle of first-in and first-out is followed. At professional meeting and cocktail parties, we need to present ourselves on time. You are not supposed to leave until the senior executive has left the party. Our awareness of the protocol is essential to avoid the complications.

Preparations for Involuntary Functions: It is essential for corporate professionals to keep themselves ready for the unwanted circumstances which may disrupt a business meeting. It becomes difficult to control sneezing and if it is herculean, a number of problems are to crop up. It is in tune with etiquette that you are ready for that involuntary function like sneezing and you have an easy access to a Kleenex or a paper tissue or a handkerchief so that you resolve the problem at the earliest possible. Another peculiar situation is created by wind pass. If the gas is passed silently, it is problematic; and if it is with a sound; you are a laughing stock. Hence, it is proper that you do not keep yourself in an embarrassing situation and control it till the meeting is over or regulate your diet to avoid such problem.

Awareness of Dress Code: If you are attending a party, it is essential that you come to know about the dress code. If you find a communication gap, you need to overdress for circumstances. Proper business attire in tune with the circumstances needs your due attention. By ignoring dress code, you make an invasion on the required etiquette. If you attend the private club invitations, you need to be aware of the dress codes for club. If you are indecisive, you may call the club to have an idea.

Handshake Etiquette: If at the workplace, you are required to handshake, it is to be made sure that you extend your right hand, grasp the hand of the person you are meeting so that the thumbs interlock. Grip firmly, pump twice and release. Because we find handshake a cornerstone of doing business, the gender cannot be a factor.

Etiquette for welcoming newcomers: It is your prime responsibility to welcome the newcomers. The seniors perform this job. The concerned newcomer should be briefed about their jobs. The staff at any level should be introduced to any newcomers they encounter.

Extension of courtesy is essential to everyone you meet either a receptionist or the CEO. Here, it is pertinent that you avoid asking personal questions from the newcomers such as qualifications, percentage, marital status, age, income, etc. Since we find name an important symbol of our identity, you need to be careful while pronouncing, spelling or mixing-up the name. If you are superior, the first name is used. Even you are equal or friends, this practice is adopted. If you are not aware of the status and position of the newcomers firstly you should use the surname, preceded by Mr, Mrs or Ms.

Courtesy Etiquette: At the workplace, you need to greet everyone cheerfully, with a smile on your way into the office. The two words e.g., Please and Thank you would help you in many ways. There must be a smile on your face while appreciating since we find friendliness an important consideration for the workplace etiquette it is significant that you make it clear that all of you are the part of the same team. You need to be polite while hiring help from your peons, drivers, delivery boys, etc. When you talk on phone it is to be made sure that you do not talk loudly. The voice should be clear and the words should be soft. While instructing or even while getting instructions, you need to be graceful. There may be occasions like birthdays, wedding days, the staff concerned receiving a personal gift, good dishes and words of appreciation from the bosses and colleagues should not forget the words of compliments. Make it sure that while leaving, you are particular to switch off the concerned points so that the last person to leave the office is not required to switch off all the lights, computers, air-conditioners. As and when you ask for a cup of tea, coffee or a cold beverage, the co-workers are also to be offered.

Professional etiquette at the workplace thus is found concerned with a number of areas where organisational culture proves to be a pace setter. With the increasing domination of MNCs, specially after globalisation, we find western culture defining and redefining the corporate etiquette and manners. Since we find a different scenario at the global workplace environment, it is quite natural that corporate professionals keep themselves aware of the etiquette and manners at the workplace in global perspective.

Make yourself Likeable: At the workplace environment, the corporate professionals need to make themselves likeable so that their associates feel pleasure in working with them. Negative thoughts are to be removed from your mind. Never use words like I can't, I am busy, it is not my concern. Try to avoid criticising your associates and when you are criticised, behave like a professional. Don't make it personal. Never try to look through people's computers, e-mails or letters, handbags or wallets. Never borrow any item from your associates and when abnormal conditions necessitate, be punctual in returning. Don't misuse property of your office. Keep your workplace in perfect order. Be friendly with your colleagues, men or women but don't forget the limits. Don't indulge yourself in the office gossip and avoid deliberating upon critical and vulnerable topics like religion, politics, money and sex. The standards of personal hygiene must be maintained. Let your desktop remain a desktop, don't convert it into a place for worship because you are supposed to work with your associates who may belong to different religions and faiths. Make it sure that you are not creating unnecessary sounds distracting your associates. Punctuality is an important consideration and therefore be punctual, know the art of managing your activities. Don't forget to switch of your mobile phone. Before attending a meeting, do your homework. If there is an established seating pattern, accept it. With a brief recognition of the chair and other participants, you need to acknowledge the opening remarks. When the discussions are going on, allow senior persons to speak first. Even if you do not agree with the deliberations, don't interrupt. With the permission of chair, express your viewpoints. While speaking, try to be precised. Never divulge the discussions of meeting with the third party. It is a breach of business etiquette. At last, thank the person who organised the meeting.

Ensure Healthy Competition: It is to be ensured that competition within the organisation is healthy. Your behaviour should mirror the group norms. Communication gap makes place for a number of problems and therefore you need to identify the cause of the mess-up and to resolve the problem. You are supposed to regulate your annoyance and temper. Never strive to pull a colleague down. It is not in good taste or a poor taste that you are involved in back-stabbing. Envy and jealous among associates ruins the workplace environment for everyone. When you are efficient, you should not grudge for the success of others.

The above mentioned facts make it clear that workplace environment is a matter of serious concern where we find a majority of us involved in breaching of the business etiquette. Acceptable business attire and polite behaviour help you in many ways. Study the workplace environment, understand it in a right fashion and make it sure that with the help of mannerism, you succeed in having a sound resolution of even the critical problems. With the increasing domination of MNCs, we find emergence of a distinct organisational culture considerably influencing the workplace etiquette.

◈ Dress Etiquette

We cannot deny that corporate clothing is the most important thing for building a positive corporate image. This makes it essential that corporate professionals are well aware of the attire they need to wear on a particular occasion. The goals for the day, the persons to be interacted, the venue of meeting, the wearabouts of clients with whom you have to interact, the wearabouts of superiors and the wearabouts of co-workers are some of the facts you need to be aware of for avoiding mistakes in selecting the attire. You should also be aware of the fact that appearance can make the difference in getting or not getting a job. This is helpful in hiring and may be responsible even for your firing. The corporate world is a place

Aware of Dress Etiquette

where you are supposed to know, how to dress. In any organisation, we find a culture and when we work for that organisation, it is quite natural that we happen to be a part of that culture. When we are a member of that culture, we reflect the values of that organisation. This makes it essential that we fit with the culture of that organisation and in this context our appearance is found to be an important determinant. If we look different to others, it is meant that we are not respecting the culture of that organisation. In a true sense, we find dresses magnifying our behaviour and silently conveying a number of things about our attitudes. If we wear wrinkled clothes, the people think that we do not care. If we do not care the occasions for which we wear, people doubt about our professionalism. If we do not care the mixing of colour, we transmit wrong messages about our behaviour. Hence, it is imperative that we are sincere to the dress code and wear the dresses in the face of organisational culture and situational requirements.

The clothing styles vary in tune with situations. For formal business, a clean pressed suit is the best way to go. If this is not available, a suit jacket with coordinated slacks to match is the next choice. Tie with white, blue or light brown colour or light coloured shirt complimenting the suit may be preferred. The shoes may be of black or brown colour and the socks dark. For informal business, a sport coat with coordinating slacks is the first choice. If this is not available slacks with shirt and tie are the next choice. For casual wear, clean and pressed khakis are recommended.

The Business Casual has three levels such as basic business casual, standard business casual and executive business casual.

Basic Business Casual: This is for those days of the business office when you have to work without client contact. It is also appropriate for some informal off-site training sessions, retreats or company-sponsored sporting events. Such type of dressing is considered relaxed level of dressing found suitable for less traditional industries. Here we find only two pieces — a top and a bottom. No jacket is necessary. Men or women can choose casual pants and may add a short or long-sleeve shirt, high quality T-shirt, Knit top or sweater. Women also have the option of choosing casual skirt and top, a casual dress or a jumper.

Standard Business Casual: We find standard business casual for casual meeting and workshops. The standard business casual visualises the middle level of standard business casual consisting of a top and a bottom, teamed with a third piece. The type of dress is worn on a daily basis, specially for less formal industries and appropriate for meetings within the company. We find the dresses more tailored than basic casual in fabrics such as wools, wool-blended, silk-blended, microfiber, and twills. The additional layer in the form of a casual are unstructured jacket, cardigan or pullover sweater, the scarf or vest which may add a professional touch to the tailored pants or skirts teamed with a casual shirt, knit top or fine-gauge sweater. Particularly for men, we include a collar in these ensembles.

Executive Business Casual: We find it the most formal mode of business casual dress which is found close to the traditional business dress. The features are luxurious fabrics such as wools, cashmere, silks and linens, expert tailoring and a contemporary flair effective in conveying influence. While meeting with the business clients, making a presentation or leading a meeting, the executive business casual dresses are used. This mode makes a call in favour of a structured jacket at all times but not necessarily a tie. Men may opt for sport coat or blazers, pants in wool, silk, linen or blended, solid or patterned shirts or fine-gauge knit, cashmere or silk sweaters. While women may select matched or unmatched pant suits in wool, linen, silk or blended.

The corporate professionals while following the dress code or while focusing on dress etiquette need to make it sure that they never commit the mistake of dressing too casually for any business situation. Dressing down too far can cost customers, jobs, promotions and opportunities. It is better that they exceed expectations and prefer to "dress for where they are going not for where they are at."

The corporate people need to dress appropriately, consistently, dress with special attention to colour, dress for your body type, dress the best quality you can afford dress with fineness, dress into the present and dress for the part or role you have to play. If you dress according to where you want others to see you heading, you may find more doors opening. It is right to say that professionals need to dress for where they want to be not where they are.

The corporate apparel must generate delusion to make body emerge stylish and graceful. The style, the fit and the colour are important considerations which you need to remember. The aesthetic appearance makes ways for the components which affect the visual sight of the dress. An elegant look is essential for the corporate people and this makes it essential that mixing and matching are given due weightage. The more careful you are, the more professional look you have. Adapting to corporate life makes a strong call in favour of proper business attire and for that you need proper dresscare. You live in an age of investment dressing, it is to be stored in your memory.

◈ Dining Etiquette

Particularly in the Indian context, we find a majority of us not aware of the dining etiquette. Testing job candidates with a meal as an integral part of the job interview is also practised in the corporate sector. Breaches of professional etiquette during dining must be checked to be hireable or promotable. With the passage of time, we find significant changes in the rules of etiquette. This is due mainly to the fact that time cycle creates a distinct condition. During 1840s, the etiquette experts advised "Ladies may wipe their lips on the tablecloth, but not blow their noses on it." But today, we cannot allow it. A famous but true story about a gallant or brave gentleman may be quoted. That gallant gentleman noticed a bug or small insect in his salad and said nothing about it to the (hostess) woman responsible to welcome and entertain customers at a nightclub or war and ate the insect to avoid public embarrassment of that hostess. It is significant to mention that hostess also noticed it at the same time but she also said nothing about to that gentleman. After a long gap, the hostess rewarded that gentleman for his chivalry or say polite behaviour of a man towards woman. This is the extent of politeness that we need at different stages and in different situations.

While attending a dinner or lunch meeting, you are supposed to follow the time schedule. It is quite natural that you have to wait for the host or manager extending to you the invitation. Unless we find place cards, it is impossible for you to know the exact place where is your assigned seat. The most important thing you have to know is that in what capacity you are attending the meeting. Unless you are the guest of honour or the highest corporate-level person, it is not expected from you that you take the seat to the immediate right of the person conducting the meeting. It is also to be ensured that you in no case switch seats with someone else. It is proper that you wait for the person in charge who would signal you. With the start of meeting, you should not hold a personal side meeting of your own. You need to wait for the indication of in charge that the meeting is over and with this indication, the business discussions are to be concluded. Before the dinner or lunch is to be started, it is essential that you are aware of the dining basics. You have to wait until everyone is served; spoon your soup away from you and sip it from the side of the spoon. It is to be ensured that there is no slurping or drinking with a loud sucking sound; butter your bread one piece at a time; fold sweetener packets and then put them under the edge of a plate. It is important that you are courteous and considerate while talking with the restaurant staff.

There are some dining tips for the corporate professionals which you should not forget. When you visit a standard restaurant, the tableware may bewilder or confuse you. The bewildering array or beautiful clothing of the dining table is with the motto of creating a positive impression, utensils are placed before you and you have to understand the proper function of each utensil, the finger bowl placed before you is for rinsing the fingers at a meal, not for dipping the tea bag.

Just in a lighter vein, we can remind here the ancient episode of "I Love Lucy" where she asked for a tea-bag to go with her fingerbowl. If you witness an unusual dining device, it is proper that you leave the table and ask the server and always use utensils before you. For artistic presentation, there may be some of the utensils and you have to understand it. Never-never, leave a spoon in a bowl or a glass. No doubt, it is borish or to act like a bad mannered person when you touch the edge of the utensils. You are not required to gesture with a knife or fork. It is hoped that you are aware that a gesture is a movement of part of the body to express an idea or meaning or an action performed to show one's feelings or intentions.

◈ Wine Manners

In the corporate culture, we find acceptability of wine and therefore being a corporate professional, it is imperative that you are aware of the wine rituals specially at the dinner time. A majority of us are found unaware of the wine manners. Wine protocol tips aware you of the basics.

Know Wine Rituals

If you opt for the dinner table, it is essential that you make sure to reach-out for the wine list which word signal to the waiter that you are the person interested in drinking wine. At the end of the meal, this will ease your problem. When you are dining with the superiors or clients always make sure that you feign ignorance or pretend to feel ignorance about wine. You may speak like this, "I have horrible taste in wines. Can you help me? and then hand them the wine list. Unless you understand the wine ritual, your task is found to be much more difficult. There are a number of people specially in the Indian context found fully unaware of the wine rituals.

At the very outset, the waiter shows you the bottle. Here, you are supposed to have a quick glance and it is to be ensured that the wine before you is the wine that you ordered. Quickly, go through the name and vintage and nod. It is not expected that you examine the bottle. Don't choose a wine just because it has a high-tech name. The presentation of cork is found to be the most important aspect in the wine ritual. The waiter hands you the cork just for examining not for sniffing. You also need to make it sure that the bottle has been properly placed because improperly stored wines, *i.e.,* vertical placing would increase the possibilities of allowing the cork to dry-out which may cause air-breach and the wine will be like vinegar (sour tasting). If you sniff, it is to be quick and hand it back. We find almost dismal possibility of getting a bad bottle. Sniffing the cork would serve your purpose.

Tasting the wine is a second stage where the waiter would place a tasting amount of wine which you have to swirl or say, follow the spirally pattern. Take a very small sip, swish or move with a hissing sound. If you are satisfied, nod your approval to the waiter. Normally, you need not to think about sending the bottle back because you are not world-class "oenophile" or a "connoisseur" of wine or having world-class knowledge of wine. The wine manners never permit to serve a bottle of wine in which we find something wrong. Sommelier or wine waiter has an in-depth knowledge of wine and your position may be at stake and therefore don't think of returning the bottle.

The above mentioned facts make you aware of the wine rituals at dinner time which would be helpful to you in many ways. In the western culture, we find respect for wine. Since we find corporate culture considerably influenced by the western culture, it is quite natural that even in the Indian context, it gains social acceptability. What to talk of the newcomers, when we find even a good number of CEOs lacking wine manners. Embarrassing themselves by not understanding the simple wine ritual is not a wisdom. We should understand, at least, the basics. You should not forget that good manners form an integral part of every business encounter whether it is a client luncheon, networking event, job interview or sales call, social etiquette can make or break the rate of your success. It is quite natural that none of you would like to break.

The occasions may vary, the venue may change, the form may be different; either lunch or dinner, but the dining manners cannot be overlooked. You may attend the business meetings, attend the informal functions, visit the social functions, wedding functions, wedding anniversary, birthday party, etc., and everywhere you need etiquette. The awareness helps you in the projection or your image whereas ignorance tarnishes the image of both, the employees as well as the organisation. Believe it or not, it may also be instrumental in delaying your promotion and making a strong case even for your firing. You are expected to shine in any situation and if you do not know about the manners, your task is complicated.

It is not essential that business decisions are made only in the corporate offices. Actually, we find a number of corporate decisions made on golf courses and tennis courts and even on the dining table. The business meeting lunch has a specific purpose. The focus is on the fact that occasions determine your attire because you are not supposed to break the dress code. You also need to develop your awareness that club dress codes need to be followed when you are in a club. There is nothing wrong in calling the club and inquiring about dress codes. The club persons are supposed to provide this information routinely. Ignorance cannot be the execuse, specially in the corporate culture.

The dining etiquette thus makes it essential that you are aware of everything which may be required at the table or venue where you have to attend. Business of manners offer training in international etiquette, formal dining and the social graces to help you and your people to shine in any situation. In the corporate world, the client luncheon or a formal luncheon is frequently organised and therefore it is imperative that you keep yourself aware of the dining manners and the allied things. Caution and awareness help prevent or promote your career. The emerging new trends may sidetrack you in case of ignorance.

Good corporate manners cannot minus good dining etiquette. In the corporate world, we find dining table a frequently used place for the making of business decisions and developing business relationships. Hence, it is imperative that corporate professionals develop their awareness of etiquette and manners which would benefit them in many ways.

◈ Disastrous Ravines

Being a professional, it is your prime responsibility that you are very much professional while dealing with the common situations which prove to be the problem or disaster area, if you delay handling them in an appropriate fashion. Corporate culture requires professional excellence because we find much more vulnerability when even minor situations prove to be critical. Hence, the following common situations need your priority attention:

Handshake: In the corporate culture, we find handshake very common without any gender discrimination. But you have to make it sure that it is used as a tool for the projection of your personality and is administered as a cornerstone for doing business. There should not be any sign of weakness and therefore while handshaking, extend your right hand, grasp the hand of the person you are meeting or greeting and it is to be made sure that the thumbs interlock. Grip firmly, pump twice and then release your hands. You should not wait for other person to initiate a handshake. Limp-noodle handshakes must be avoided. A majority of the persons, specially in the Indian context are found breaching the handshake etiquette and thus transforming a positive factor into a negative one.

Greetings: While greeting, you should use a courtesy title with your manager and others above your manager unless they prefer to be addressed with the first name. The peers may be addressed by their first names. But in this context, it is pertinent that you do not make use of those words which may touch the sentiment of the concerned person. Greetings for pleasing not for irritating.

Gifts: In the corporate culture, we find offering of gifts on various occasions. The offering of gifts should be on the basis of divisions, sections, departments and teams. You need to make it sure that the gifts are consistent and equitable so that the employees do not feel themselves discriminated. Evoking positive emotions should be our motive while giving gifts and therefore we need to minimise the possibilities of ill will. Girls must be appropriate for recipients and therefore we need to consider the rank and profile of the persons to be gifted. For recipients, it is significant that they accept them graciously. In this context, it is imperative that you are well aware of the organisational culture for accepting gifts. If it is not in tune with the policy of your company, you should return the gift with thanks.

Thank you Notes: While giving Thank-you notes, it is to be made sure that it should be handwritten. If you make use of the printed cards, it should also carry a handwritten message. Just a signature is not to serve the purpose.

Formal and Semi-formal Events: The white tie event is the formal event in which globally, we find long gowns for the women. For men, the formal tailcoat with black trousers, while pique vest, white tie, white shirt with wing collar and black patent shoes. The black tie event is known as semi-formal event which is organised with the motto of information gathering.

The attire for black tie events depend on the regional customs and weather patterns. The basics for men, include a black tuxedo with a white, ruffle-free tuxedo shirt and a black tie. The basics for women include cocktail dresses or cocktail suits. It is pertinent that while participating in the events, you keep into consideration the attire.

Dinner-Lunch Meetings: In the corporate culture, we find frequent organisation of dinner and lunch for various purposes. As a professional, it is significant that you are punctual and arrive on time. You should also develop your awareness of the purpose of meeting so that the possibilities of committing mistakes are ruled out. Your awareness of attire and dining culture would help you in maintaining the organisational culture. There are a number of moments when we find a majority of the professionals specially in the Indian context breaking the etiquette. It is also imperative that you are aware of the wine rituals so that mannerism related to wine is not invaded. The corporate professionals should not keep themselves in an embarrassing situation by not understanding the simple wine rituals. Grabbing the cork, as if the waiter is handling to you a jar of warm spit is the result of our awareness. A majority of the professionals particularly in India lack wine etiquette and the main reason for the same is lack of socio-cultural acceptability of liquor. If we promote corporate culture, we have no option but to follow the corporate etiquette. The leading MNCs feel that corporate culture cannot, be viewed in domestic conditions rather than in the global perspective because employees serving an organisation are just an extension of the corporate brand.

Cell Phones: Of course, we find information technology playing and incremental role in defining and redefining the concept and percept of efficiency but we also find situations when they obstruct the process. We lack awareness of phone culture. There are times when it is found inappropriate to use but we lack a sense of proportion and therefore corporate etiquette makes it essential that you turn cell phones off, specially when you are in meetings, attending seminars, banquets or planned ceremonies. Do not stamp your personality a glaring neon sign for lack of etiquette.

Smoking: It is significant that you are aware of the workplaces where smoking is not allowed. If you work in a smoking environment and you also smoke, make it sure that etiquette is not breached. The rank of people present behind you or in your presence cannot be overlooked while smoking. Do not undermine the instructions regarding smoking.

Drinking: Of course, we find corporate culture allowing consumption of alcohol specially on defined occasions but each one of us need to respect the limits. We should never have more drinks than our host. If you prefer not to drink, a simple "No thank you" is adequate. You do not need to explain the reasons entailed behind.

The above mentioned disastrous ravines save us if we are aware of the devices. We find them emerging in a condition and making it essential that you have a ready made solution. Our awareness of corporate etiquette and manners keep us in an advantageous position. Hence, it is pertinent that corporate professionals keep on moving the practices of enriching their knowledge bank specially in the field of etiquette.

◈ Etiquette for Corporate Success

Getting success in the corporate world makes it essential that we assign priority attention to some of the important aspects which have remained neglected specially amongst a number of corporate executives coming from India. Confession makes the ways for transformation. Conventional laws of courtesy, decorum, social graces, polite behaviour and mannerism make our tasks much more easier. Mounting the corporate ladders makes it essential that we are very much professional to our approaches, sincere to our efforts and soft to our communication skills. Sky-rocketing popularity of corporate trainer, increasing number of finishing schools and increasing relevance of etiquette and manners make it clear that in the days and years to come the mannerism would be suitably rewarded. Guru of graces like Sabira Merchant, Pria Warrick and many others bear the responsibility of sensitising the upcoming youths of modern India that personal score of a majority of the potential corporate professionals are not of global standard which would make their tasks of mounting the corporate ladders much more difficult. In the emerging cross-cultural society, we need to view and review our concept and percept. The employees are extension of the corporate brand and therefore social graces, and polish cannot be relieved and perceived in isolation. Of course, the predilection of budding generations to the world-class thematical competence cannot be reprioritised but at the same time, it is also right to accept that we cannot undermine our outward behaviour, etiquette and manners and soft skills. We need to strengthen our realisation that soft skills are as important as hard skills to secure an edge over the competitors. Keeping pace with the growing demand of the corporate sector requires to be the best part of our strategy and against this backdrop, the educational institutions in general and the business and finishing schools in particular need to review their action plan. Developing students in the face of emerging corporate requirements and organisational culture happen to be the prime responsibility of ours which we cannot undermine.

It is a general observation of almost all the corporate trainers that we care little for manners and find lack of social graces in a majority of our students. The social polish and communication skills put us behind the competitors. In a true sense, we need focus on the development of whole package of attitude, body language, behaviour, communication and etiquettes. We also need to address body language, posture, handshake and the body odour. Amidst plethora of deficiencies that we find in their personal score, it becomes too much difficult for upcoming generations to climb the corporate ladders. On the one hand, we make a strong advocacy in favour of establishing our edge over the competitors by enriching our personal score while on the other hand, we find out students (products) lagging far behind. Hence, etiquette and manners need due attention without which our students may suffer. Success of an organisation and success of employees working there are found interrelated.

When we talk about etiquette, our prime focus is on polite behaviour. The mannerism which helps us in the projection of a positive image is found very much related to etiquette. For climbing the corporate ladders, it is imperative that on account of our behaviour, we have been influencing our associates vis-à-vis the clients. Besides, we have also acquired a high level of efficiency. Powerful looking clothing has been found impacting our attitudes and behaviour. The professional business attire, a suit and clothing that is found appropriate for our profession bring a radical change in our mindset and resulting from which we find a shift from the relaxed-mode to the professional-mode. This impacts our body language and behaviour followed by better posture, firmer handshake, maintaining eye-contact, striking to business, etc., and providing to us a greater visual power. Jackson Lewis, a law firm that specialises in personal issues, polled more than 1000 human resource executives who had implemented a dress-down policy. They reported a 30% increase in fictitious behaviour contributing to an increase in the sexual harassment lawsuits. Hence, we find a close relationship between attire, etiquette and behaviour. The business etiquette experts can determine how polished we are by our behaviour and how we conduct ourselves when we are in the business environment.

We need good manners at each and every stage. We participate, conduct or head the business meetings, we attend business functions, we are involved in presentation, we interact with the business associates and clients and no where we find possibilities of an edge unless we find politeness in our behaviour. Not only while communicating but even while conveying something with the support of our attire, the etiquette is found playing a meaningful role. We cannot negate that politeness proves to be a paramount force which may result in hiring or even firing. Good manners have a high influencing power bearing the potentials of hypnotising the associates as well as the clients. This makes it essential that while enriching personal score of people serving our organisation, we assign due weightage to etiquette or mannerism.

The increasing heat of globalisation and the mounting pressure of economic recession have been found influencing the behavioural profile of people in an adverse way. As and when we find our thoughts influenced by pressure, its analogous impact is found on our mindset. We start irritating, agitating, reacting, speaking and behaving in a different style which is, of course, unbecoming like a corporate professional. All invasion on politeness starts taking a shape, and we find aggressiveness in our behaviour. This makes it essential that corporate people make sincere and professionalised efforts to bid a goodbye to the environmental pressure generated at the workplace.

In this context, we also talk about social graces. Traditions and conventions may bring a change in the socially acceptable behaviour. This is due mainly to the fact that perception of society about a particular thing cannot remain static. During the yester decades, we have witnessed significant developments in the field of social regulations. Yesterday, it was not acceptable but today it is socially acceptable. The boundary of acceptability in the corporate society is fixed in the face of organisational culture. The corporate professionals need to know about the social graces and to practise them.

A strong mental capacity is vital for individuals who are living in stress-field environments. The ability of mind to concentrate and adapt to pressures from the environment makes them more effective. It enables us to stay calm and focused despite any form of adversity. Building self-esteem is an effective prescription to help corporate professionals in keeping cool and behaving politely. This makes it essential that corporate professionals feel good about themselves. They need to bring a radical change in their lifestyles. On the one hand, they need to manage diet while on the other hand, it is also significant that they assign due weightage to exercise. They may run, ride a bicycle, play a sport, climb up and down the stairs several times to keep their body fit. They may also take time to do this they enjoy. They can spend time with the people who make them feel good, who treat them well. With all these, they will be successful in building self-esteem.

Guru of graces feel that continuing lack of graces even among some of the highest-placed Indian executives cannot give to us the competitive advantage. The corporate world makes a strong advocacy in favour of an extra edge. Hence, we need to ensure that almost on all the fronts, we are number one. Adding attractive qualities to our personal score, showing a distinctive personal gesture or way of speaking and behaving in a way that is acceptable to the society are some of the important considerations determining the magnitude of our success. Socialising our behaviour, of course, would provide to us an extra mileage. Since we find global workplace environment nurturing a high level of expectations from the corporate professionals, it is imperative that they make sincere efforts to mould themselves in that culture. Corporate brand cannot permit employees to act and behave in the national or regional perspectives because global image necessitates global culture.

It is high time that we realise the importance of corporate etiquette in an increasingly competitive global environment, educate and train corporate people and the upcoming youths to enable them to climb the corporate ladders. It is significant to mention that overseas MBA Schools have special classes that even tell you that what colour of ties to wear with what suits, but in the Indian scenario, we find ourselves taking these things very casually. In the global perspective, we find an attitudinal transformation. People have assigned due weightage to soft skills but here we confine ourselves to the hard skills and till now are regulated by the predilection towards getting high grade and caring little for manners. This trend needs a departure. When we live in an age of globalisation, it is quite natural that we turn our eyes to the global organisational culture. Willingly or unwillingly, we have to move with the wind and follow the social graces in the international perspective.

SUMMARY

In this chapter, you have gone through various aspects of etiquette and manners in the context of corporate culture. Before starting another chapter, make it sure that the following facts are well versed.

Business Etiquette and Business Ethics: Business etiquette is a conduct prescribed by convention or by authority to be used while interacting with the business associates or clients whereas the business ethics is the principle of right or good conduct governing business people and organisations.

Corporate Society vs. Etiquette: American corporate society, European Corporate Society and the Indian Corporate Society cannot have different etiquette and manners because we have one society and one culture; therefore identical etiquette and manners.

Social Graces and Polish: Societal etiquette can make or break our business. Whether it is a client luncheon net, working event, job interview or sales call; we cannot move forward in absence of social graces. Of late, the business encounters are filled with opportunities to display polish and poise. Making an attack on etiquette errors is significant to make possible social graces.

Etiquette for facing Interview: The candidates looking for job have to face interview. They need to go through a grooming checklist. They have to be very careful to the first impressions because they never get a second opportunity to create first impression. They have to view things in detail, show respect to the organisation where they have to appear for interview, knowing the skill of exposing the thematical competence, make psychological preparations, managing activities to be punctual, managing self and if needed making preparations for an effective and attractive presentation.

Etiquette for Introducing and Paying Compliments: Introducing yourself and introducing others need etiquette. While introducing others, you are supposed to help the newly acquainted persons to start and carry on a smooth and friendly conversation. While paying compliments, it is pertinent that your compliments are moderate and genuine. The exaggerated expression lacks strength in our sounds. Compliments should not have ulterior motive and we need to use positive adjectives to compliment well. Here you should avoid speaking of your own achievements. Finally, you are also supposed to respond to compliments. Acknowledge compliments and thank the concerned person(s).

Workplace Etiquette: It is significant that corporate professionals are well aware of domestic as well as the global workplace environment so that possibilities of committing mistakes are ruled out. It is quite natural that international workplace is found very challenging and vulnerable. You need to understand the environment in a right perspective. A number of considerations need due attention of professionals to develop their awareness of the salient features. For avoiding etiquette errors, it is pertinent that they are aware of rank and status of staff, ready for involuntary functions, aware of dress code, handshake etiquette, welcome etiquette and courtesy etiquette.

The professionals are required to make themselves liable. This helps them in pleasing the business associates. If you are positive with them, they will have pleasure in working with you. In this context, you are also required to ensure healthy competitions. In a true sense, your behaviour should mirror the group norms. It is wisdom that you regulate your annoyance and temper. Your success is considerably influenced by your efforts for controlling etiquette-errors in managing the workplace environment.

Dress Etiquette: The corporate apparel must generate delusion to make body emerge stylish and graceful. The style, the fit and the colour need your due attention. An elegant look is essential for the corporate people and this makes it essential that mixing and matching have been given due weightage. Adapting to corporate life makes a strong call in favour of proper business attire and for that professionals need proper dresscare. The clothing styles vary in tune with situations. If we don't care the occasions for which we wear, people doubt about our professionalism. The goals for the day, the persons to be interacted, the venue of meeting, the types of meeting, the wearabouts of clients are some of the aspects necessitating your due attention. You should not forget that appearance may be an important reason for getting or not getting the job. In a true sense, we find our outfits magnifying our behaviour and silently conveying a number of things about our attitudes. Developing our awareness of the dress code of the concerned organisation is found to be the most important thing.

Dining Etiquette: Testing job candidates with a meal is an integral part of the job interview which is also practised in the corporate sector. There are a number of occasions when we have to take lunch and dinner and if we are not aware of the dining etiquette, it will question our image and personal score. There are some dining tips which need due care. Breaches of professional etiquette during dining must be checked to be hireable and promotable. The wine rituals and manners also need due attention of professionals. The wine rituals specially at dinner time are found important which a majority of us do not know. In the corporate culture, it is pertinent that you are aware of the wine manners and do not embarrass yourself as and when the situations necessitate. The dining etiquette makes it essential that you know everything which may be required at the dining table or venue where you have to attend.

Disastrous Ravines: Etiquette errors are found very common, specially in the Indian context. There are some of the areas where we commit mistakes such as handshake, greetings, offering gifts, giving thanks, white-tie and black-tie events, dinner and lunch meetings, cell-phones, ornaments, smoking and drinking. It is only our awareness which would provide to us an effective prescription.

Etiquette for corporate Success: Guru of graces feel that for climbing the corporate ladders, it is significant to know about etiquette. Adding additional qualities to our personal score make available to us the competitive advantages. We need to enrich ourselves in soft skills where we lag behind. Corporate brand cannot permit us to act and behave in a different way.

KEY TERMS

Etiquette	Social Polish	Courtesy Etiquette
Manners	Wine Rituals	Basic Business Casual
Guru of Graces	Wine Manners	Standard Business Casual
Grooming Experts	First Impression	Executive Business Casual
Business Ethics	Disastrous Ravines	White-tie Event
Soft Skill	Handshake Etiquette	Black-tie Event
Corporate Society	dining Etiquette	Hostess
Social Graces	Dress Code	Oenophile
Chivalry	Vinegar	Connoisseur

EXPECTED QUESTIONS

1. What do you mean by Business Etiquette? Is it different to Business Ethics. Justify your statement.
2. Do you find etiquette essential for the modern corporate society? Defend your arguments.
3. Social etiquette can make or break our business. In the light of this statement, explain the instrumentality of social graces and polish in having good manners.
4. Explain the etiquette for facing interview in the corporate sector.
5. Focus on the preparations needed for giving a presentation.
6. How and in what way, an interview seeker would be successful in creating positive first impression?
7. Explain the etiquette required for introducing and paying compliments helpful in creating first impression.
8. Focus on the workplace etiquette and throw light on the points where preparations are needed.
9. Do you find workplace etiquette essential for developing rapport with the business associates? Justify your opinion.
10. What do you mean by dress etiquette? Explain it in the context of corporate workplace.
11. Do you find dining etiquette essential for testing your personal score as a corporate professional? Defend your arguments.
12. What do you mean by wine rituals? Explain it in the context of corporate business.
13. Identify the disastrous ravines instrumental in breaching the corporate manners and throw light on the measures helping you in bridging the ravines.
14. Write a reasoned note on the role of business etiquette for climbing the corporate ladders.
15. Explain the complexities found in the international workplace environment increasing the possibilities: of breaching the etiquette and manners.
16. Explain the role of finishing schools in the development of soft skills.

APPLICATION EXERCISES

1. "Etiquette can be dramatised but ethics cannot be dramatised." In the capacity of a corporate professional, throw light on the above statement and divide a line between etiquette and ethics.
2. "Corporate etiquette is a business skill complementing core competencies. The corporate society based on etiquette makes us socially graceful, organisationally productive and individually offering a win-win situation." Do you agree with this view? Justify your arguments as a corporate professional.
3. "Social etiquette can make or break our business. Whether it is a client luncheon, networking event, job interview or sales call; we cannot move forward in absence of social graces. Today, business encounters are filled with opportunities to display polish and poise." Comment on this statement in the capacity of a corporate professional.
4. You have been given call to face interview for an appointment in the corporate sector as a fresher. Throw light on the grooming checklist you will need to go through before attending the interview.

5. Entry is the first stage where you get an opportunity to make first impression. You should not forget that a natural pleasant expression with a smiling face makes a better impression. Gloomy, grim or serious expression, stressed and depressed facial appearance are negative parts of your personality. Comment on this statement.
6. "Both while introducing and complimenting, you need an in depth knowledge of business etiquette and manners. We consider it a primary requirement for people in general and the corporate people in particular."

   In the light of above statement, throw light on the important considerations required for introducing and complimenting.
7. "Unawareness of the workplace environment makes ways for breaching the etiquette. We cannot deny that environment at the workplace depends on organisational culture. Workplace etiquette makes it essential that we have an in depth knowledge of the environment where we have to work with the business associates." Do you agree with the above statement? Justify your stand.
8. "Workplace environment is a matter of serious concern where a majority of us breach the business etiquette. Study the workplace environment, understand it in a right fashion and make it sure that with the help of mannerism, you succeed in having a sound resolution." Comment on the above statement in the capacity of a corporate professional.
9. In the capacity of a corporate professional, focus on the business attire needed for basic business casual, standard business casual and executive business casual.
10. "The more careful you are, the more professional looks you have. Adapting to corporate life makes a strong call in favour of your business attire and for that you need dress etiquette. If we do not care the occasions for which we wear, people doubt about our professionalism."

    In the face of above statement, focus on the role of business attire in making us hireable and promotable.
11. Testing job candidates with a meal has emerged as an integral part of the job interview because this helps interviewers in identifying the breaches of dining etiquette by the interview seekers.

    In the capacity of a corporate professional, justify the role of dining etiquette.
12. "A famous and true story about a gallant or brave gentleman is quoted. On the dining table, he witnessed a bug in his salad but said nothing about it to the hostess at a nightclub and ate the insect to avoid public embarrassment to that lady. It is significant to mention that even hostess also noticed the bug in his salad palate. But she also said nothing about it to that gallant. After a long gap, the hostess rewarded that person for his chivalry."

    In view of the above cases, throw light on your viewpoints regarding chivalry or behaviour of a man towards woman as an essential part of dining etiquette.
13. "There are a number of people specially in the Indian context not aware of the wine rituals and manners. Good corporate manners cannot minus good dining etiquette. This necessitates our awareness of the wine rituals. In a true sense, we find it a part and parcel of the corporate etiquette. In the face of above statement, throw light on the wine manners as a part of business etiquette.
14. "Breaching of etiquette may not only damage your career but in addition may also tarnish the image of your organisation where you serve. The disastrous ravines if not bridged properly may deprive you of getting the competitive advantages in the corporate world."

Do you agree with this statement? Justify your arguments in the capacity of a corporate professional.

15. "Etiquette and grooming experts feel that in the Indian context we care little for manners and find lack of social graces in a majority of our students. The social polish and communication skills put us behind the competitors."

    In the light of this statement, suggest measures to make the upcoming and budding generations potentially sound to climb the corporate ladders.

BACK-UP MATERIALS

1. www.scu.eduethics
   www.business.ethics.com

   Ethical Behaviour
   Building an ethical climate
   The Line Between Business Ethics and Business Etiquette

2. www.minoritycareernet.com
   www.mindingmanners.com

   Minding Your Corporate Manners
   Professional Etiquette in the Workplace
   Corporate Manners
   Professional Etiquette when Dining
   Understanding the Wine rituals

3. www.hindu.com.blogs.oneindia.in

   Civic Sense

4. Swami Sivananda: Easy Steps to Yoga
   Ethical Discipline
   Control of the Sense

5. What's age got to do with it? The Times of India;
   July 24, 2011.

◆ ◆ ◆

7 MANAGING ETHICS AND BUILDING CHARACTER

Philanthropy comes from the heart of the people which makes place for desire. The focal point is not that you give back to the society rather than it is humility and your attachment with humanity that transforms your attitudes. Managing ethics is, of course, managing yourself.

CHAPTER DESIGN

Introduction – Ethics: The Concept — Business Ethics: The Concept – Why Business Ethics? Area for Unethical Practices – Factors Influencing Business Ethics – Unethical Practices in Business – Ethical Codes – Ethics Training Programme – Corporate Ethics vs. Corporate Image – Ethical Dilemma – Managing Ethics in Business – Building Character – Summary – Key Terms – Expected Questions – Application Exercises – Back-up Materials.

CHAPTER OBJECTIVES

This chapter aims at studying the various aspects influencing the management of ethics in business. The Indian business tycoons need an attitudinal transformation which may help them in developing personal philanthropy, the most important thing for respecting ethics and building character. The motive of the present chapter is to sensitise corporate people to strengthen self realisation without which practising ethics would remain just a formality. The moment we start motivating people having good conduct, the people having bad conduct would naturally be demotivated. Managing Ethics and Building Character need top priority.

MANAGING ETHICS AND BUILDING CHARACTER

◈ Introduction

The task of developing holistic personality remains incomplete, if we fail in managing ethics and building character. Employees serving an organisation are considered an extension of the corporate brand and as and when we find cases of unfair and unlawful practices promoted by them, it is to tarnish the established image of an organisation. Any organisation should not encourage short-term gains for the long-term pains; because in a majority of the cases such type of result is due to unethical, unlawful and unfair practices. It is in this context, focus is on the ethical dimension of personality development which simplifies our task of building character. We cannot negate the instrumentality of managerial proficiency of an individual and even cannot overlook the contribution of facial appearance and rock star personality to the persuasion process but if we start undermining morality; our tasks become much more difficult, if not in short-run, of course in the long-run.

In an age of societal globalisation, we find ethics and etiquette emerging as major determinants personal or organisational success. There is no doubt in the fact that corporations have been found making sincere and honest efforts for developing etiquette and manners of their employees but so far as the ethics are concerned, the emerging scenario cannot be claimed to be impressive. Ethics matter because it makes good business sense to do the right thing. Good corporate ethics result in attracting better talent, retaining customers, retaining employees, attracting new customers, positively impacting return on investment and projection of a fair corporate image. Hence, it is significant that we assign due weightage to ethical dimensions.

Ethical behaviour means getting the right kind of behaviour from people. It is an activity that results into the right things being done. When we talk about the right things, the organisational culture and employees happen to be the determining force. The conceptual aspect of business ethics finds it as the principles of right or good conduct governing business people and organisations. The concept and percept of "right" or "wrong" cannot be changed. But today, we find it a gray area. We rationalise everything from taking the new magazines; from the doctor's waiting area, to the sharing of our latest software to borrowing ink cartridges from the office by simply saying, "everyone does it." The small acts, of course, have small consequences in short run but in the long run, we find their transformation into the bigger acts with bigger consequences. Since the unethical acts are performed in secrecy, and nobody comes forward for confession; the task of identification is found much more difficult. Unless you are identified and caught, you happen to be ethical.

It is only an individual who knows about his/her ethical or unethical practices. In a true sense, the ethical check may help us in sorting out the dilemmas. Kenneth Blanchard, author of the "The Power of Ethical Management" suggests that when you are faced with an ethical problem, the ethical check may help you. Do you consider yourself legal? Are you violating either civil law or common policy? Are your activities balanced? Do you find your activities fair to all concerned in the short-run as well as in the long-run? Will it promote win-win relationships? Actually, it is possible for us to avoid ethical dilemmas at work by being fair and doing only what is right, being honest and dealing justly, being accountable and keeping our words.

Ethical behaviour is found to be the bedrock of mutual trust. To behave ethically is to behave in a manner that is consistent with what is generally considered to be right or moral. Only society can answer to the question, what is right? or what is wrong? It is right to mention that every society makes some determination of morally correct behaviour. Societies not only regulate the behaviour of their members but also define their societal core values. Thus, morally correct behaviour cannot be incidental in different societies. In the Islamic countries, the religious stricture define what is right and what is wrong. In the United States, the right or wrong is based on Judeo-Christian heritage.

In the corporate society, the organisation defines what is right or what is wrong. It is upon the strategic leaders of an organisation to build an ethical climate. There are different steps for fostering corporate ethics. The actions of the strategic leadership, the way they deal with ethical issues and the pattern of top leaders' behaviour determines organisational values. The second step focuses on making explicit ethical policies and the third one is concerned with increasing awareness for practising ethical codes. Knowing what actually is going wrong in the organisation is essential for understanding the ethical principles. The information system may be helpful in identifying the ethical breaches or the potential ethical breaches. The task of identification is, of course, much more difficult.

Ethics make or break the business. Unethical practices cannot continue for the long time. Long-term profits is the real thing that determines stability in your success and growth. For a business to achieve long-term profits, it is imperative that customers nurture a positive impression about the organisation. This makes it essential that you have been successful in gaining the confidence of your customers and clients. Your trustworthiness is found responsible for the positive or negative results. Practising ethics make the business whereas breaching ethics break the business.

Business ethics have a long-lasting impact on the customers and a positive impression on their minds builds trust resulting into fetching a business by getting more and more customers while retaining the older ones. The business ethics simplify your task of gaining the confidence of customers. Hence, you need to be much more sincere to customer care and the way of dealing with customers to keep them satisfied to retain them. In the process of creating and retaining customers, the business ethics play a catalytic role because this speaks of the image of your organisation and ultimately your trustworthiness is rewarded.

Ethics is a far-reaching concept and goes beyond the idea of making money legally. Ethical values are away ahead of earning money. In a true sense, we find ethics more about earning long-lasting relationships in business and the relationships that you succeed to maintain and retain turn into the business because we find a significant increase in the number of customers and expansion of markets. A good number of organisations are found concerned with making money without considering the business relationships and more so, these organisations seldom bother to base their business on ethics.

Ethics is an integral part of running a business and hence ethical values accompany business by default. It is true that without following certain ideals in business, any organisation cannot be successful. We do not find any wisdom in getting short-lived success and as and when your success is attained without a strong foundation of ethics, the life-span of success cannot be long-lived. A business cannot prosper without an ethical base. Here we talk about the persistent success which is the result of strong foundation of ethics.

The use of company resources for personal benefits cannot be ethical. In addition, taking undue advantages of business resources is also bound to be unethical. Using the wealth of the business for personal reasons is not ethical. Using company funds for personal reasons is unethical. Indeed, a thoughtful and a careful utilisation of resources of company is a part of the business ethics. Accepting bribes, pleasing the so called important clients, favouring a part of the customers while becoming unfair towards the others is against business ethics. Almost all the organisations need to nurture and strengthen their realisation that the primary aim of business is not just to maximise profits. Actually, working just for profit is unethical. They need to cater to the needs of the society and work towards benefiting the masses and only then, we find them ethical.

Founding business on ethical values and following them or conceptualising them in a true sense need priority attention in today's business world where in common practices, the ethics are not found even at the bottom of their agenda. The management professionals need to adhere to ethics and should accept it as a part of business. This necessitates that corporate professionals have an indepth knowledge of business ethics so that they succeed in regulating the unethical practices. What to talk of the non-profit organisations albeit the profit making organisations are required to perceive the fact that they are not just for profits. Such an attitudinal transformation would make the ways for business ethics.

When we find corporate people conceptualising business ethics, this makes it clear that they have remained successful in adding new dimensions in their personal score. Because they are ethical, we find their conduct good and character different from others. This proves to be his/her strength and originality.

We cannot negate that ethics is the science of morals and that branch of philosophy which is concerned with human character and conduct. Character focuses our attention on strength and originality in the nature of a person and conduct throws light on the way of our behaving with others. Conduct is behaviour. Deportment, carriage, demeanor, conduct and behaviour are synonymous terms. The conduct is the root of prosperity which increases fame and makes an invasion on all the evils. It is superior to all the branches of knowledge. Good conduct brings in fame, longevity, wealth and happiness either for an individual or for an organisation or institution. Therefore when we find an organisation morally and behaviourally sound they defeat people and the ways for prosperity for that organisation are opened. People having a right conduct succeed in having a magnetic personality.

Hence in the today's context, the corporations have no option but to assign a transcendental priority to the building of character. Character gives to us a strong personality having the potentials to influence people because people respect a man who has good character. He/she found to be honest, sincere, truthful, and liberal-hearted always commands respect and influences on the people. Hence, the character-building is found of paramount importance. We can die but our character and thoughts remain alive. It is the character that gives a real force and power to us. Character is power. Of course, in today's context, we find knowledge emerging as a power but without character, the attainment of knowledge is impossible. This makes it clear that we cannot protect our existence, if we fail in building our character. Because the community starts ignoring and disrespecting them and ultimately, we find beginning of self-realisation but by that time, it is too late and we have no option but to suffer. Unblemished or spotless character considerably helps us. If we remember people, it is due to their wonderful character. Of course, it is a mighty soul-force and like sweet flower that wafts its fragrance far and wide. A man of noble traits and good character possesses a magnetic personality. Personality is nothing but character. You may have thematical competence of world class, you may have the managerial proficiency to make the process of generating wealth much more effective, you may also have etiquette and manners but if you have no character, it is difficult for you to have a real position in the society because your words and eyes are found powerless and consequently, you find it difficult to command and govern.

It is against this background that we need to go through the problems, related to ethics and spotless character of people serving the organisation. Of course, the task is difficult but not impossible. Since we go through the problems of business ethics, it is quite natural that our focussed approaches remain confined to the business or corporate world. Managing ethics and building character are the two key areas of study. We need a prescription which may be effective in making an assault on the negative thoughts of upcoming and budding generations who have started nurturing a dream of overnight trading and an easy walkover.

◈ Ethics: the Concept

In Latin language, we call it Ethicus and in Greek, it is Ethicos which has originated from ethos and is meant character or manners. It is the source of morals or we may call it the recognised rules of conduct. Thus ethics is the study of morals which throws light on standards, rules and codes of conduct governing the behaviour of individuals and groups.

◈ Business Ethics: the Concept

The business ethics are moral principles defining right and wrong behaviour in the business world. The society is to determine the concept and percept of right and wrong. It is also considered as the evaluation of business activities and behaviour as right or wrong. We may consider it a systematic study of moral or ethical matters pertaining to business, industry or related activities. It is more so the handling of values in the business world. In the plain words, we may consider business ethics as the application of ethics in business. Thus the conceptual aspect of business ethics finds it as the principles of right or good conduct governing business people and organisation. The organisational culture and the employees happen to be the determining force for defining right or wrong. Building an ethical climate happens to be the responsibility of strategic leaders in an organisation. In the corporate society, the organisation bears the responsibility of defining right and wrong.

◈ Why Business Ethics?

As and when we start crossing the limits; the avenues are paved for regulating our behaviour. The business organisations have been provided a legitimate right of making profits but they have started adopting unfair and unethical practices to achieve the target. The focussed approaches for making profits albeit started searching ways for profiteering. The policy decision makers were found involved in the process. Ultimately, the business organisations started facing the ethical problem which considerably invaded on their image. For short-term gains, they started inviting long-term pains. The customers and clients strengthened their realisation that they are being exploited. The trustworthiness of business organisations was found questioned. Both in quantitative and qualitative terms, the business organisations suffered a lot. This made it essential that ethical behaviour of business goes through an audit. Are policy and decision-makers fair? Are they ethical? Are the employees working there fair and ethical?

Are they honest to the shareholders and government? Are they discharging their social obligations in a right fashion? Are they following the ethical codes in a right perspective?

Business ethics make and break the success of business. Practising ethics and breaching ethics are the two different conditions. When we are ethical, customers trust and when we breach ethics, customers distrust. Any business organisation cannot survive if the customers start distrusting on their conduct and behaviour.

The following facts justify the application of ethics in the business:

1. Business is a subset of the Society: We cannot deny that business is a part of the society which operates in the society and is nurtured by the society. The customers come from the society and we cannot even imagine the existence of an organisation failing the proper responses from the customers. Hence, it is judicious that social sanction on which the business stands must be repaid in the form of social welfare. Earning social sanctions makes it essential that an organisation significantly contributes to the process of social transformation so that the emergence of a prosperous society keeps on moving the process of creating customers and expanding markets. Both the aspects are found interrelated. Gaining the trust of customers makes it essential that you have a fair image. Trustworthiness proves to be an important dimension for surviving or thriving in the society. Your positive image writes about you a fair story. The moment you start involving yourself in the unethical, lawful and unfair practices; we find a direct invasion on your image and the customers start distrusting you. An attack or invasion turns into an attack on your existence. It is against this backdrop that business organisations need to be ethical.

2. Playing Role as a Corporate Citizen: We find business organisations an essential organ of the society found very much instrumental in the process of creating wealth. They need to define their role as, a responsible corporate citizen. It is not expected from a citizen that he/she is involved in the unethical or unlawful practices and like this, it is also expected from the business organisations that they prove themselves to be a responsible corporate citizen.

3. Using Social Assets: All the business organisations stand on social assets, created from the public money or the tax money. The supporting infrastructural facilities such as roads, power, communication, etc., play the role of a pace setter. Because you make use of the social assets, it is imperative that you are ethical to the society. Not only this, it is also expected from you that you make a significant contribution to the national exchequer by paying your tax contributions.

4. Increasing Financial Irregularities: In a good number of oganisations, we find small and large cases of financial irregularities. The persons responsible for managing the accounts are found involved in the process. The financial statements are not presented and displayed in a legal way. The cost-computation is found breaching the social and ethical considerations. The profit-margin is becoming abnormal. The manipulations have become a common feature. The policy decision makers appear deliberate in promoting the unlawful and unethical practices. These aspects also make it essential that organisations assign due weightage to the ethical consideration.

5. Unethically managed human resources: The increasing heat of globalisation has been found paving avenues for the exploitation of human resources. In a majority of the organisations, the hiring and firing are not on lawful grounds. The motivational plan is found irrational. The pay structure or packages have become abysmally disproportionate. A big gap exists between top and bottom levels. The selected a few persons have been getting the advantages at the cost of those who have significantly contributed to the process of profit maximisation. Hence, this is also a strong reason for the application of ethics in the modern business world.

6. The Quality consideration is neglected: We cannot deny the fact that quantitative improvements have not been making an edge over the qualitative considerations. Either we talk about the goods manufacturing organisations or our focus is on the service generating organisations, a quality-gap is existent. The organisations fail in fulfilling their promises. Often, the customers complain a big gap between the quality-promised and quality-delivered. Globalisation, no doubt, has nurtured a high level or expectations but generally we are not professional while fulfilling our commitments. This is partially due to managerial deficiency and partially on account of human faults. The employees serving the organisations fail in maintaining the quality. The intensity of competition is high and resulting from which the task of marketers proves to be much more complicated. The designed strategy fails in achieving the desired targets. Hence, the ethical dimensions need due care.

7. A Threat to the Organisational Culture: In the corporate world of today, even the MNCs working in India fail in maintaining the organisational culture. Though, they claim a lot but the ground realities are not the same. We cannot deny the fact that the task of policy decision makers is found to be much more complicated when they find their employees non receiving things in totality. A majority of the organisations in almost all the areas face the problem of organisational threat in different forms. A threat to the work culture, a threat to the etiquette and manners, a threat to the corporate personality and facial appearance, a threat to the civic and aesthetic considerations and a threat to the ethical dimensions make it imperative that corporate policy makers assign due weightage to the management of workplace environment.

The above mentioned facts make it clear that practising ethics is an urgent need, specially in the corporate world where unethical and unlawful decisions are found galloping. Where laws and regulations fail, the ethics get a success. Where stringent measures fail and rough words fail, the polite behaviour gets a success. Social graces command even the critical problems. World class thematically sound managers also need to go through the fact that conduct and behaviour of their employees sizably determine the magnitude of success. We cannot rationalise each and everything in the business world. If we do not have a right and ethically sound business sense, our task would be much more complicated. In an age of societal globalisation, we need a microscopic audit of even the macro problems. Ethics make or break the success. Use of company resources for personal status or benefits cannot be ethical. Ethics is an integral part of running the business. Unless we make place for an attitudinal transformation, our efforts cannot be result-oriented. Unless we are insensitive to the small problems, we cannot have a command over the big problems.

◈ Areas for Unethical Practices

At almost all the levels of business activity, we find unethical-practices gaining a rapid momentum such as at stakeholders-level, personal policy-level, societal-level and internal policy-level. This necessitates an indepth study.

Stakeholders' Level: The stakeholders of the company are employees, customers, shareholders, banks and other leading financial institutions and government. The employees complain about the problem of job insecurity, substandard and unhygienic environment at the workplace, inadequacy of welfare facilities, disproportionate or unbalanced structure of pay, lack of participative management.

The customers as stakeholders complain about quality of product, irrational pricing policy, discriminatory pricing, false claims about the product in the advertisements.

The shareholders expect capital appreciation and steady and regular dividends and witness lack of information, threat to the minority shareholders, window dressing balance sheets and problem of insecurity at the time of mergers, amalgamation and takeovers.

The banks and other financial institutions want safety of borrowed funds and prompt repayment of loans.

The government wants time honoured compliance of rules and regulations, timely payment of taxes and other dues and role of company as a partner in the development of national economy.

Personal Policy Level: There are cases of misuse of office care, stationery and other items and facilities for personal use. We also find cases of misuse of powers by the business houses and their involvement in political activities.

Societal Level: The corporations, have not been found assigning due weightage to the process of social transformation. The poor and downtrodden are found neglected. There are also cases of discrimination against a particular section or group and further non-optimal contribution to the better quality of living conditions.

Internal Policy Level: The unethical considerations are related to the unfair practices relating to compensation, layoffs, perks and promotion. Lack of communication at all the levels is not satisfactory and absence of transformational leadership aims at better and higher things in life.

The above mentioned areas for unethical and unlawful practices make it essential that corporate policy makers and the top-level managers seriously think about the problem of ethics so that all the concerned areas and levels are successful in fulfilling their expectations. They need to strengthen their realisation that unless and until they get the cooperation of all, the business houses would witness myriad of challenges and threats. In this context, it is also right to say that only regulatory provisions would not serve the purpose. Ultimately, we find ourselves responsible for the unethical practices and only we can resolve them.

◈ Factors Influencing Business Ethics

Business ethics are influenced by the different factors such as corporate or organisational culture, leadership, the characteristics of individual in the business, environment and strategy but the ultimate factor that we find is the quality of people serving the organisation responsible for practising or breaching ethics.

1. Corporate Culture: Culture of an organisation considerably influences ethics. The organisations believing in promoting ethics make sincere efforts to involve ethically sound people. Internal culture of an organisation determines the attitudes of people working there. The policy decision makers are found honest in formulating and implementing the codes of conduct. Conversely, an organisation whose image is tarnished due to unethical behaviour of people working there find it difficult to practise ethics.

2. Leadership: Of course, we find leadership an influencing factor but even leaders are influenced by the organisational culture. We cannot deny that character is the most crucial and dominating element of leadership and it we find them promoting unethical practices, the avenues for unethical practices are broadened. This makes it essential that we are very particular while selecting leaders because it also speaks of the organisational attitudes.

3. Environment: The environment at the workplace is also responsible for breach of promoting business ethics. If at a particular place, we find other organisations facing the problem of ethical degeneration it becomes difficult for a particular one to promote ethics. Unethical practices are found infectious. Hence, the environment of the place where an organisation is located also influences ethics.

4. Quality of People in the organisation: An organisation dominated by the quality people finds it difficult to practise unethical practices and conversely, if we find bad people in a large number, the promotion of ethical practices are found difficult. Thus, ethical or unethical practices considerably depend the quality of people serving the organisation.

5. Strategy: The strategic decisions of an organisation also influence ethical or unethical behaviour of people. The strategy focuses an a number of factors such as how and in what way, the organisation would excel competition, how the different functional areas would contribute to the success of the organisation and how the resources would be allocated. Thus, strategy makes it easier or difficult to practise or breach ethics.

The above mentioned facts make it clear that the most dominating factor is the quality of people dominating an organisation. Hence, character happens to be most effective dimension responsible for ethical and unethical practices in an organisation. At almost all the levels, we find people fully aware of the fact that what happens to be the image of an organisation which is the result of our ethical or unethical decisions.

◈ Unethical Practices in Business

Of course, the organisations have now started realising the importance of ethics in business; however a large number of unethical, unlawful and unfair practices, are found very much instrumental in tarnishing the corporate image. In the business world, the unethical practices are found in different forms in almost all areas of the strategy formulation and implementation and a large number of people from the business are found involved in the process.

In the field of HRM: The decisions related to the financial and non-financial incentives, cases of sexual harassment, discrimination with the different categories of employees, invasion on privacy, inhuman behaviour of superiors with the subordinates, exploitation in different forms, etc., are unethical necessitating due attention.

In the field of Production: The safety and security considerations inside the factory, environmental considerations, post-accident treatment, health hazards in different forms, compromise with the quality of product, etc., cannot be considered ethical.

In the field of Finance: Wrong computation of costs, disproportionate profit and pricing, unfair transactions with the stock markets and banking or other financial institutions, false financial statements, wrong reporting, tax evasion, cheating shareholders, etc., are found unethical.

In the field of Marketing: Unethical and unsocial advertisements, false and misleading presentation of facts, deliberate omitting of the required information, trade puffing, creation of ambiguities in the minds of customers, plagiarism, transmission of wrong facts to the customers, deceptive pricing, price firing, inflamated pricing, packaging, eco-friendly packaging, bait and switch pricing, inadequate warranties, manufacture of flammable stuffed animals, shoddy goods, manufacture of non-biodegradable plastic products, etc., cannot be ethical.

In the field of Society: Black Marketing and hoarding, cheating the investor, shop lifting, air pollution, water pollution, land pollution, discrimination on the basis of gender, caste or race, child labour, sexual harassment, corruption and bribery, corporate crime, emotional exploitation, etc., cannot be considered ethical.

In the field of Information: Security threats, attack on computer system, computer crime, internet crime and abuse of computer, unethical hacking, health risks due to IT, etc., cannot be considered ethical.

Day-by-day, we find a significant increase in the unethical practices in business and the codes and regulations are found becoming ineffective. This is due mainly to the fact that we find lack of ethics in the people involved in the process of managing the business. Hence, the most vital aspect for managing ethics is a sound management of people. Unless we ensure supply of quality people, the unethical practices will keep on moving even with high intensity. This necessitates a sound strategy for managing ethics in business.

◈ Ethical Codes

The ethical codes are statements of the norms and beliefs of an organisation distributed to all its members after proper discussions, deliberations and conceptualisation by the middle and top level of the management magnifying the ways in which the senior people serving the organisation make it sure that other people follow the norms and act and behave in the defined fashion. The corporate code of ethics help employees to know what is expected in ethical terms when they encounter a particular situation. The codes impact the behaviour of employees depending upon the norms mentioned there. It is quite natural that we find variation in the codes of ethics in the different categories of companies. The ethical code describes the general value system, the ethical principles and the specific ethical rules that a company attempts to practise.

The codes of ethics focus on making organisation a dependable citizen, demonstrating honesty and fairness in relationships with the stakeholders, comply with the regulations related with safety, health and security, the dress code and reliability in attendance and punctuality. The organisations are supposed to be honest and ethical to the customer by making available to them the products commensurate with the promises made by them and conveying true claims for products.

While drafting a code of conduct, it is significant that we identify the key behaviours to adhere to ethical values proclaimed the code of ethics. It should indicate wording, ensuring that employees conform to behaviours specified in the code of conduct. It is also required to obtain review from the key members of the organisation so that the provisions are in accordance with the laws and regulations. All the areas need to be covered while developing a code of conduct. The guidelines for following the instructions of superiors, maintaining confidentiality, not accepting costly gifts from the stakeholders, complying with laws and regulations and not making use of the property of company tor personal use.

Developing ethical codes in a business is not a new phenomenon. During the yester decades, we have witnessed drafting of ethical codes by a number of organisations in India or abroad. However, the unethical practices have been found gaining a rapid momentum. Hence, the business organisations need to perceive that only designing or drafting of codes cannot serve their purpose. Are they really interested in following the norms to be ethical to their stakeholders? Are they judicious while fixing the proportion of profits? Are they honest while computing the costs? Are they ready to accept that business world is full of vulnerability and volatility and therefore ups and down in the profits, rise and fall in the development graphs which would not make the ways for unethical and unfair practices? Are they making rooms for the conceptualisation of the principle "Not just for Profit"? If organisations appear interested in becoming ethical, they cannot remain unethical.

◈ Ethics Training Programme

We also find cases where unawareness or insensitivity results into the unethical practices. A number of employees are found unaware of the codes and regulatory provisions. This necessitates an intensive training programme so that employees come to know about the dividing lines between ethical and unethical. The accounting methods, sales and marketing procedures of purchase and safety, technical system service conditions of employees are some of the areas where we find copious avenues for unethical practices. The training programme organised for different levels of staff would make them aware of the policy of the company on the ethical issues. It is also significant that workshop is organised to let them know the cases and possibilities. Such an organisation of training programme with much more frequency would help employees in the identification process.

The training programme, if effective would be helpful in minimising the unethical practices. In this context, it is pertinent that top management has been extending to the programme the best possible cooperation. There should be open discussion on the realistic issues and dilemmas. The cases of ethical violations are to be identified and the possibilities are to be explored. It is also pertinent that a mechanism is developed for reporting. The deliberations should also be on the motivational factors that how and in what way the employees promoting ethics in the business are to be motivated. All the literature concerned with code of ethics and laws enforcing ethical conduct are to be circulated to the concerned persons to minimise the possibilities of a communication gap.

Building commitment to ethics is considered essential in the very context. The commitment of top management to ensure the availability of adequate resources and moral support involving the chairman of the company for supporting the training programme and if needed formation of an ethics committee may be considered. Some senior level managers are to be made responsible for coordination for time honoured implementation. There should be frequent dialogues with the concerned persons while preparing codes, policies and procedures.

The ethical standard of the company is to be clarified. The mission of company, purpose and beliefs need to be taken into consideration. The penalties for violation or obligations should also be clarified. It is also pertinent that systems are built to support ethical behaviour. The most important task before the management specially in the today's context is to build the organisational climate and to inform all the concerned regarding the organisational culture, perception of organisation regarding social responsibility and making available advisory services if needed in case of doubts and confusions.

Sensitisation is a process to hammer and to make employees conscious of the role they are supposed to play. The trainers need to keep into consideration that a gap in the transmission and reception process is immediately bridged. Finally, it is to be made sure that all the concerned know about the codes, laws and regulations and their various provisions.

◈ Corporate Ethics vs. Corporate Image

Ethics matter because it makes good business. Ethics can make or break the business. When good corporate ethics become instrumental in developing your business, the breaches of ethics endanger the success of your business. Good business sense is found significant to the success of business and the good corporate ethics help in the process. If you do the right thing, you succeed in attracting the better talent to your organisation, retaining the quality employees, retaining the loyal customers, attracting new customers, getting positive effect on return on the investment and making possible positive effect on corporate reputation. This makes it essential that ethical dimensions get due place in business. The following facts justify the instrumentality of corporate ethics in the projection of a positive corporate image.

1. Attracting better Talent: By better talent, our focus is on the quality of people serving the organisation. Talent in an individual focuses on the different traits found in the personality of people found interested in serving your organisation. The thematical competence of world class, working with a sense of personal commitment, believing in humanised leadership and nurturing the faculty of personal philanthropy and above all evincing interest in promoting social interests, are some of the properties for considering an individual of better talent. Good people prefer to serve organisations having a global reputation and an established brand image.

2. Retaining Employees: Of late, an important problem before the corporate world is the dropping of retention rate specially related to the quality people. It is difficult to get people having better talent but it is much more difficult to retain them. This is due to the fact that people with more traits get a number of opportunities. They have options and they are interested in making use of their options. It is a general observation that high retention rate is found in those organisations where people get a high level of respect. The organisations practising ethics make sincere and honest efforts to get them satisfied. Satisfaction makes the ways for retention.

3. Retention of Customers: The customers in general believe in quality. They expect that the goods or services made available to them are also affordable and therefore when their expectations are fulfilled, it is quite natural that they prefer to continue. Trustworthiness of those organisations is found of high intensity. The customers are confident that even if there is something wrong with the products they have bought, the recovery process would be taken care. The promises related to the after-sale-services would be honoured and in no case they are to be cheated. Such a strong perception engineers a sound foundation for the retention of customers. Creation, satisfaction and retention are found interrelated. If customers are satisfied with the quality and are confident of the ethical practices, they prefer to continue. It is due to trustworthiness that you have an established image and again it is due to your image that you have been successful in injecting new life and strength to the perception of customers about you and your relationships. Customer and clientele relationships are considered to be the backbone of business success.

4. Attracting new Customers: Retention makes the ways for creation. It is due mainly to the fact that your well established image vis-à-vis the word-of-mouth promotion are found active in the sensitisation process. It becomes easier to sensitise and persuade new customers because quality-wise and price-wise, you have an edge over the competitors. In the face of your significant contribution to the process of social transformation; you have many things to strengthen their realisation that in no case they are to be cheated. Since you have been honest to the interests of your stakeholders in general, your promotional campaigns are found creative in nature and distinct to others. Good corporate ethics thus make it easier for you to attract even the new customers.

5. A positive effect on Return on Investment: More business, more profits, it is a general business principle. Earlier discussions have made it clear that due to good corporate ethics, you have been successful in earning a good name. The process of creating and retaining customers gains a rapid momentum and resulting from which we find a significant increase in the scale of business. In the age of globalisation you have am opportunity to promote global business. Since you practise ethics, it is possible that you are honest while computing the costs and setting the price. Of course, the rate of profit due to a large-scale business would move upward. This will result into a high rate of return on investment.

6. A positive effect of Corporate Image: We cannot negate that image is the result of our contributions. If we make positive contributions and keep on moving the process, we have a positive image. If we talk about an organisation honestly practising ethics, almost all the constituents of stakeholders are found satisfied. Because we promote social cause, our recognition in the society; our identity in the society; our image amongst the customers, provide to us a distinct name. The name that we earn turns into our identity. The process keeps on moving and we get an established corporate image.

The facts outlined above are a staunch testimony to this proposition that good corporate ethics provide to us a good return. If we have been successful in thriving, it is due to ethics. If we have been successful in establishing a distinct image, it is also due to ethics. In an era of societal globalisation, we prove ourselves to be a leader and it is also due to good corporate ethics. Thus, it is an unvarnished fact that corporate ethics has emerged as an important determinant of corporate success. Once again, we repeat. Ethics matter because it makes good business sense to do something right. Ethics make the business and prove to be a strong force for having a win-win situation. Ethics provide to us a distinct identity. Hence, the organisations need to promote ethics so that the emergence of a prosperous society keeps on moving the cycle of development. Because with the prosperity of society, we find copious avenues for the expansion of markets.

◈ Ethical Dilemma

In a true sense, dilemma is a situation necessitating a choice between equally arguments. It is a situation in which we are supposed to make a choice between the alternatives found equally undesirable. Since we have to make a choice between alternatives having equally undesirable, the task is difficult and therefore we name it a dilemma. It is a stage where we have to consider about the equally strong conflicting positions making us indecisive. What to do and what not to do. What is right and what is wrong. There are a number of conditions when we find ourselves in a conflicting situation. As and when we find the problem concerned with ethics, it is an ethical dilemma. The stage keeps us indecisive and we find it difficult to assess that doing this would be ethical or unethical.

Kenneth Blanchard author of "The Power of Ethical Management" suggests that when you are faced with an ethical question; it is pertinent that you give yourself an ethics – check for sorting out dilemmas by examining an issue at different levels. You are supposed to ask yourself: Is it legal? Will you be violating either civil law or company policy? Is it balanced? Is it fair to all concerned in the short term as well as in the long-term? Does it promote win-win relationships? How will it make you feel about yourself? Will it make you proud? Would you feel good if others knew? You are faced with dilemmas and find it difficult to answer or resolve.

The prescription is to help us to get out from the ethical dilemmas which is very simple provided you are fair because by doing fair you do only what is right. If you are honest and judicious, the task is found easier. Right is right and wrong is wrong. Fair is fair and unfair is unfair. Actually, we are not faced with the dilemmas that it is fair or unfair or ethical or unethical rather that with the dilemmas that doing this will have these implications and what would be their impact. A professional is supposed to come out from the dilemmas at work by being fair and doing only what is right being honest and dealing justly; being accountable and keeping his/her word; being responsible so that others know they can count on you; commenting to your tasks and to your people; being loyal and standing by those you are committed to. Any executive can be a highly polished one. It takes an extraordinary executive to be a highly ethical one.

For getting a victory or an easy walk over in commanding the ethical problems, it is imperative that you do not trap yourself in the dilemmas rather than avoid ethical dilemmas at work and the most important thing that you find here is to be fair. It is your conduct that makes your task easier or complicated. Once again, it is resolved that we do not find any substitution of fairness. Ultimately, it is our conduct that is to help us in promoting ethics. A stage of indecisiveness should not persist in the business and the moment you are unfair, you find yourself weak. Hence, the corporate world requires to make it a point that they do their best to increase the number of fair and honest people in their organisation.

◈ Managing Ethics in Business

Gone are the days when we believed that business is not meant for ethics. During the yester decades, there has been an attitudinal transformation and it is against this background that we find a number of examples of promoting ethics by the business houses. Of course, we also find cases of breaching ethics but it is also not to be forgotten that sooner or later, it becomes instrumental in the tarnishing of corporate image and consequently, the organisations involved in the process suffer a lot. The most important thing in practising ethics is related to realisation that how and in what way you perceive the ethical and unethical considerations. It is ultimately the society that draws a line between the two. You may consider it fair and ethical but the society may reject your perception. If you make use of the corporate resources for personal benefits, pleasure and status, it is absolutely unethical.

Billionaire business tycoon, Mukesh Ambani's 27-storey residence Antilla has come in for much flak and censure. Even Tata Group Chairman, Ratan Tata says that the Ambani's residence is an example of rich Indian's lack of empathy for poor. Making a towering statement of wealth specially in a country like India where millions of under-privileged fail to get albeit the minimum basics cannot be a fair step and we may call this step unethical. Blatant and unbashed displays are nothing but for magnifying the status which may be considered not only immoral but even inhuman. May be that Ambani's steps, are lawful based on financial norms and the accounting procedures but it is also to be remembered that it is society which is to draw a line between ethical and unethical practices and keeping in view the living conditions of a majority of the Indian society, the steps taken by Ambani cannot be ethical.

Stable and prosperous society engineers a sound foundation for the development of an organisation. If you make society prosperous, there will be a significant increase in the number of customers which would recycle the process of development. It is an age of societal globalisation in which countless eyes watch your activities and punish or reward you in tune with your contributions. May be that you do not experience it in the short-run but in the long-run, you will realise it and by that time, it will be too late. Personal choice is not meant crossing the limits for displaying your status and more so in the Indian society. It is all a matter of taste. And doing everything as you like just to have the opulent lifestyles may not be your good taste specially in the midst of poverty. Enjoying your wealth which you have created though your so called hard work and entrepreneurial excellence is not only the result of your hard work but also of thousands and thousands of those employees who have worked hard for you and millions and millions of those customers who have paid exorbitant prices for the goods or services they have consumed or used. Sun draws moisture from the earth to return thousand fold more in the shape of rains which recycle the process and like this, if you make a prosperous society, you get the advantages. Hence, the main thing is your perception of ethical and unethical practices without which you just complete the formalities. The business tycoons of India should turn their eyes on Bill Gates who made a significant contribution to the society.

Managing ethics is not meant that you have coneptualised code of conduct, your accounting procedures are lawful, your financial statements are intelligently drafted, you are very much particular to the payment of dividends and discharge of tax liabilities and your financial institutions are also satisfied with your transactions. In a true sense, it is something more. As a top management of the organisation, you are satisfied that customers are not paying the exorbitant prices and you are not earning abnormal profits. You have to make it sure that even the employees at the bottom level of the hierarchy are paid compensation or incentives to meet their requirements. You have to ensure that underprivileged and disadvantaged segments of the society are getting adequate assistance from you in the name of social welfare. You have earned from the society and you have to give back to the society. Unless you work with this attitude, the ethical considerations would remain unfulfilled. Social commentator "Pritish Nandy" while conceding that it's no body's case that the rich shouldn't live luxuriously, believes they should curb their urge to be ostentations or temptation to showy display which is intended to impress. Echoing the same thought Anu Aga says, "I don't feel comfortable with opulent lifestyles because in the midst of poverty it's not in good taste." I think both of them are correct in their feelings because the main thing is the social system and structure where we do anything.

Though we also find cases of making significant contributions to society but when it comes to personal philanthropy, we find crisis of person like Azim Premji in our corporate world. It is high time that business tycoons of India take lessons from Warren Buffetts, Bill Gates, Paul Allens and Azim Premji and come forward to help the society which would manifest their positive thoughts regarding business ethics. The main thing is a change in the mindset or an attitudinal transformation without which all our plans and strategies for practising ethics in the business would turn into a fiasco. Hence when we talk about managing ethics, our prime focus should be on philanthropy and let's hope that Indian business tycoons evince their personal interests in talking about their personal philanthropy. In this context, we cannot overlook "Tata" emerging as a shining example of personal philanthropy.

As and when we find a change in the outlook or mind set of a corporate leader, the avenues are broadened for practising ethics. If you nurture an attitude like a king, you should also make place for the feelings that the king has a subject too. If you do not care for your subject your kingship and your kingdom would remain in danger. Of course, an individual has the right to create wealth, he/she is also free to live like a king. We can't but tut-tut in agreement. Actually, corporate philanthropy and personal philanthropy if well nurtured in the minds of business tycoons would bring an attitudinal change and this will be a real condition for practising business ethics.

Today, we live in an age of new generation of information and communication technology and therefore a well organised techno-driven information system may be helpful in making available to us the cases of ethical breach. The reporting system would determine the magnitude of our success because on that basis we would, be in a position to take a decision related to the motivational and demotivational measures. Before we recruit staff, it is imperative that we have details regarding their conduct and behaviour and character and family background. From the very beginning, we have to make them aware of the organisational culture and the code of conduct. Sensitisation plays a very significant role in enriching the personal score of employees. The established ethical standard of an organisation, the mission, purpose and beliefs are found instrumental in building the organisational climate. In a true sense, it is the established corporate image that simplifies practising ethical measures.

The strategic decisions also need our focussed efforts for almost all the functional areas, we need an action plan. The quality and pricing where we find scope for breaching ethics need priority attention. The management of waste, particularly when we find it of hazardous nature requires a transcendental priority. The collection and recycling of packaging and environmental considerations need your due attention. It is really amazing that an organisation makes profit but the management of product wastage and packaging fail in getting their attention. Promoting condition for the pollution of environment cannot be ethical. We find a number of cases when the industries throw polluted water into rivers and seas without making any treatment. Can we consider it ethical?

Profiteering cannot be ethical and we find several cases when artificial scarcity of product and hoarding become instrumental in exploiting the customers. The governmental regulation are found ineffective and the ethical considerations are found breached. The ultimate sufferers are the customers. We can gauge the levels of their exploitation at different stages and levels. Can we consider it ethical? Unless we find organisation considering these issues with a personal touch and emotional feelings, the resolution of problem is difficult.

Making personal use of the assets and property of company where we work cannot be ethical. If we find office or staff car, it is not for our personal use. People working at any level of the organisation need to make it sure that personal is personal and the institutional is institutional. Even you are not supposed to borrow the small items: from your associates because it is not in tune with the organisational culture.

To be more specific in the Indian perspective, we find advertisements of almost all the organisations false and misleading. A big gap between the claims and realities of the product cannot be ethical. Using high words of appreciation for the product in the messages and themes of advertisements cannot be ethical particularly when there is no any relation between the literature and actuals. We find regulations becoming ineffective and therefore, it is only ethical considerations which my protect the customers from the false and misleading advertisements. The safety and security considerations are found neglected and due to it the employees suffer a lot. The post-accident treatment is not upto mark. The losses of lives in case of accident need due care. The preventive measures and the disaster management need priority attention.

The facts outlined above make it clear that for a sound management of ethics, it is imperative that at all the levels, there is a need of personal and human touch. If we talk about ethical considerations in business, we cannot confine it to the top management because personal philanthropy cannot be successful in delivering goods to the stakeholders at large unless employees in general work with a mission that all doors for breaching of ethical considerations have been sealed. It is high time that we consider it as a part of the corporate brand which would help us in projecting the corporate image.

The ethical considerations vary in tune with the regional and cultural considerations. The American society the Islamic society and the Indian society cannot have the identical considerations. The governing forces vary and consequently, the ethical considerations change. We have witnessed hunger, illiteracy, power and water shortage and therefore are not certain that our stomachs would remain full for a few generations. Warren Buffette and Bill Gates come from a land of plenty and therefore they perceive things in a bit different way. Gradually, we will also witness a change in our personal philanthropy and then the conceptualisation of ethics would be found easier. An individual living in scarcity for long time finds it difficult to be ethical but we also find cases when poor people have proved to be more ethical than the rich people. Hence the ultimate thing is character of an individual which makes him/her ethical or unethical.

Philanthropy comes from the heart of the people which makes place for desire. The focal point is not that you give back to the society rather than your humility and an attachment with humanity that transforms your attitudes. Your policy decisions then are found in the larger interests of your stakeholders and only then you are ethical. If you, while charing the board, make a microscopic, audit of your policy decisions and you feel yourself satisfied that interests of all the constituents of stakeholders have been taken care; you prove yourself to be ethical. This is due to the fact that you are sincere and honest to your mission. Believe it or not, it will bring a radical change in the attitudes of your team because positive or negative thoughts always start from the top.

Managing ethics, of course, is managing yourself. Your employees became dishonest and immoral when they witness that at their cost a leader is leading a ostentatious lifestyle and this one when they find it difficult to meet albeit the basics. Designing a code of conduct is upon you and that you can. But, it is much more impact generating that your employees make place for self realisation; otherwise the cases of breaching would be common.

Managing self is thus found to be important of all. Things should come from your core heart. You think for your subject and the subject would think for you, even if you consider yourself a king.

◈ Character or Personality?

Building ammunitionless guns cannot solve our purpose. Character building cannot be undertaken just by reading books. Depending much more on personality and becoming insensitive to character may complicate our task. Professional psychologists as well as the spiritual psychologists need to develop a prescription which is to make an attack on the increasing unethical practices. It is amazing that almost all the sections or segments have been found initiating focussed efforts for the development of personality but so far as the building of character is concerned, we find none of them showing additional interests. Personality means that we are trying to appear as something we are not. The modern connotation, "He has a nice personality," is a suspect word. When you say to a man that he has a good personality, it means that "I say the fellow looks to be something which he is not!" He appears good, may be he is bad! This makes it clear that personality is something we put on outside, which we are not inside. You have a personality at the office; you have a personality at home; you have a personality with your children; you have a personality at the club... Depending much more on personality cannot be advisable because it is your intuitive ability to make a judgement that plays a decisive role. Making use of personality and our intuitive ability may provide to us the desired result. Gun without bullet cannot serve our purpose and like this, personality without character carries no meaning. Development of personality is easier but so far as the building of character is concerned, we find it much more difficult and even a time-taking process.

Character building is a brick-by-brick process, just like the building of house. It is also important to mention that we do not build a personality. When a man of character stands before us, we do not need to say, "He is a man of personality." Because in a true sense, often they have no personality whatsoever. If they slip out of this place, we may not even recognise him. Your wearabouts and outfits play a very dramatic role in the development of your personality. You change the outfits and your personality is changed. Even recognition of an individual is found difficult due to a change in the wearabouts or the outfits. It is due mainly to the fact that personality is external which can be changed. When we talk about character, it is not like this, because there we find significance of internal property. We find reflection of character in our activities and words. We do not find their imprints on our face. We do not find its relationships with the quality of our dresses. Because character is like the sunlight and the sun is not aware that it is shining. A man of character has not even the awareness that he is a man of character. Because, we find its shine on everything that they do. It is due mainly to the fact that we find such people influencing and attracting the masses. You cannot accuse candle for attracting the insect. Hence building of character is a difficult task. If we have a mix of the two-personality and character; we get the best result.

◈ Building Character

Character and knowledge, if both the powers work together; a new story of development is written. During the yesteryears we find emergence of knowledge as a power but so far as the character as a power is concerned, it is yet to get a social recognition and corporate acceptability. Of course, it is unfortunate but a true observation. Though character gives a strong personality and we also respect a man who has a good character but there are many places where we find unfair commanding fair, dishonest governing honest and unethical practices having an edge over the ethical. If the process of reversal is accelerated, there will be a significant increase in the number of honest, sincere, truthful, kind and liberal-hearted people found efficacious of throwing a positive influence It is against this background that we need focus on building character.

Character-building is of paramount importance, if we talk about the development of a holistic personality. A man may die but his character remains, thoughts remain, deeds and even misdeeds remain. Character in a true sense is our identity. Emergence of knowledge as a power is not to continue if we obstruct the emergence of character as a dominating power. A man of noble traits and good character possesses a magnetic personality. It is high time that society starts recognising the relevance of character. If society starts boycotting the honest persons, there will be a significant increase in the number of honest and morally sound people.

We talk about ethics. We talk about morality. But we less talk about the organisational or institutional or social responsibility to the moralists. Not only this, very surprisingly we start projecting dishonest people and demoralising the moralists. It is high time that we reverse the trend and start respecting people having an unblemished and spotless character. With such an attitude, we can expect something positive. A significant fall in the number of people having a good moral character is also due to the fact that we have stopped motivating and promoting them.

A man of noble traits and good character possesses a magnetic and charismatic personality. Personality is character in a true sense. A man may be thematically of world-class and may also have international recognition, but if he has no character, he has no real position in the society. This is the concept and percept of character which has outlived its identity in the present materialistic world. How and in what way we get back the real position of character in the corporate society of today is an important problem before the corporate professionals.

The policy decision makers have to make the ways for people having a good character. When we start talking about ideologies without considering the peculiarities of the materialistic world, our efforts cannot be proactive. Actually, we need to view things in detail. Why do you find your employees promoting unfair and unlawful practices? Why do you find them insensitive to the etiquette? Why do you find them nurturing greed even for small things? Of course, the answer is not so plain.

We cannot audit anything in isolation. The mounting scarcity of honest people, behaviourally-decent and value-based people in the society and organisations is due to the fact that they not get even the due. The moment we start motivating people having a good conduct, the people having a bad conduct would naturally be demotivated. What to talk of their social identity of moralists when we find even their own family members not supporting them or even demoralising them because they lag far behind the dishonest people specially in terms of meeting the materialistic requirements. Hence, the task of character-building cannot be fulfilled unless the individuals or institutions start respecting and motivating the people having a good moral character.

Our focus here is on the fact that organisations are required to play here a meaningful role. Because the identification process particularly at the organisational level is found difficult, the employees in general appear to be value-based unless and until they are caught. Confession is but utopian. No body is to accept that he/she is dishonest. Hence, it is much more rational for the corporate professionals that they practise spiritualism at the workplace. The organisation of spiritual sessions may be helpful in the transformation process. The willing employees may take part in the process and the unwilling persons are not to be pressurised. Besides, the regulatory practices also require due attention to activate the identification process.

It is also significant to mention that spiritualism at the workplace becomes difficult when we find high-level people in the organisation found involved in the unfair, unlawful and unethical practices. When a king becomes dishonest, it becomes difficult to make its subject honest. Hence, the top management of an organisation should do fair and look fair. They need empathy to create a favourable condition at the workplace. They need to show their temptation to personal philanthropy so that people working their adduce examples and make themselves fair. How and in what way, they are making use of the assets and wealth of the organisation also play an incremental role in the character-building process. If Bill Gates shows his personal philanthropy, he has sufficient grounds to regulate the unethical behaviour of the people serving his company. When Azim Premji and Tata show personal philanthropy, they have moral strength to punish people having bad conduct.

In making people dishonest, a number of factors are found instrumental such as personal, social and institutional. Besides, the circumstantial factors also make people dishonest. An individual is honest but he/she is so much pressurised due to critical personal problems that we find his/her strengths likely to be shakened. If we find society disrespecting the dishonest, the moral strength of honest people is found strengthened. If we find in an organisation, a majority of the people dishonest, the honests in minority are found at a critical point.

The facts outlined above make it clear that character-building is a difficult task. However, we need to create a condition where honests remain honest and dishonests are motivated to be honest. Since we find materialistic considerations dominating our behaviour, it is pertinent that we are sincere and honest to the interests of people serving us. We need to ensure that they are getting in tune with their contributions. We have to make it sure that whatsoever the incentives we pay to them are sufficient to meet their requirements. In addition, we also need to take care of the corporate brand and image because we consider employees an extension of the corporate brand. We should not forget that our image is tarnished by paying to them a low wage structure. Our empathy may turn them to be fair.

Character is that property of an individual which makes him/her different from others. This is strength and originality in the nature of an individual. It is also concerned with the reputation and image of an individual. In a true sense, it is the most dominating score of our personality. The corporation found successful, in managing ethics get a success in building the character of people working there. The ethical considerations of an organisation play a significant role in building the character. In today's context, we find it an outdated subject. Of course, the genesis to this unpleasant developments happens to be the system of education. The qualitative as well as the quantitative system of education are found instrumental in the process. Earlier, the qualitative system of education had an edge over the quantitative system of education but today, we find an adverse condition. It is, of course, due to the increasing domination of material culture where everything is quantified in terms of materialistic gains. A majority of us are found to be very calculative. The organisations are calculative and the employees working there are also calculative and ethical practices have become here meaningless. You are productive to the organisation because your contributions have helped them in maximising profits. They are least concerned with the fact that what business culture unethical practices you have adopted to maximise their profits. Such a calculative attitude has business culture made the organisational climate pro to the targeted results but anti to the ethical norms. Earlier, the qualitative system of education talked about ethics, values, morality but presently we find a changed scenario where we only talk about profits in terms of organisation and pay and position in terms of people working for them.

In view of the above, it is right to say that managing ethics and building character are becoming complicated issues. This requires concerted efforts and enormous cooperation of almost all the segments. It is an exercise necessitating an overhauling in the socio-economic and cultural systems. It is an effort well-supported by the cultural norms. We cannot develop a prescription overnight. At the outset, we need to create a climate and only then can talk about an action plan. The motive is to make the organisational culture befitting to the Indian society and Indian culture where business tycoons are found interested in developing personal philanthropy.

A brick-by-brick process consumes more time but shows the desired results. Building an ethical climate in the organisation is the main thing which requires involvement of all. Let's hope that the most dominating property of our personality proves to be the most vital force of corporate image where the interests of stakeholders remain protected and prosperity of an organisation is found fully secured.

SUMMARY

In this chapter, you have gone through different dimensions of ethics and building character. Before starting another chapter, be sure that the following facts are well versed.

Ethics: the Concept: Ethics is the study of morals which throws light on standards, rules and codes of conduct governing the behaviour of individual and groups. It is the recognised rules of conduct.

Business Ethics: the Concept: The business ethics are moral principles defining right and wrong behaviour in the business world. It is a systematic study of moral. The society defines right and wrong.

Why Business Ethics: There are a number of justifications for the conceptualisation of ethics in the business. The business is a subset of the society. The social sanctions make it essential that the corporations contribute to the social transformation process. Besides, we also need to practice business ethics because the organisational culture is formed in danger. The social graces can be possible and the misuse of social assets would be minimised by practising ethics. To regulate the financial irregularities, regulate exploitation of human resources and establish organisational culture, the ethical considerations are found significant.

Areas of Unethical Practices: The areas for unethical practices are at stakeholders level, personal policy level, societal level and internal policy level.

Factors influencing business ethics: The different factors influencing business ethics are corporate culture, leadership environment, domination of immoral people and the strategic decisions.

Unethical Practices in Business: The unethical practices in business are in the field of employees, finance, marketing, society and information management.

Ethical Codes: Ethical codes are statements of the norms and beliefs of an organisation distributed to all the members after proper discussions, deliberations and conceptualisation by the middle and top level of management.

Ethics Training Programme: This is a step to make employees aware of the possibilities for unethical and immoral practices in the expected areas. The employees come to know about the dividing lines between the ethical and unethical practices.

Corporate Ethics vs. Corporate Image: The corporate ethics is found instrumental in projecting a positive corporate image through attractive better people in the organisation, retaining quality employees, retaining old customers, creating new customers, throwing positive impact on the rate of return of investment and corporate image.

Ethical Dilemma: It is a situation necessitating a choice between identical arguments. It is a situation in which we are opposed to make a choice between the alternatives found equally undesirable.

Managing Ethics in Business: Managing ethics in business throw light on managing yourself and managing everything which we find wrong.

Character vs. Personality: Character building is a brick-by-brick process just like the building of a house. Man of personality and man of character, both are found different.

KEY TERMS

Philanthropy	Business Tycoons
Societal Globalisation	Character
Dilemmas	Personality
Ethical Behaviour	Persona
Judeo-Christian Heritage	Professional Psychologists
Ethical climate	Spiritual Psychologists
Corporate Citizen	Brick-by-Brick
Tax Evasion	Material Culture
Plagiarism	Connotation
Trade Puffing	Wearabouts
Ambiguities	Outfits
Price Firing	Intuitive
Billionaire	Corporate Image
Demeanor	Synonymous
Organisational Culture	Transformational Leadership
Amalgamation	Mergers

EXPECTED QUESTIONS

1. What do you mean by Ethics and Business Ethics? Justify application of ethics in business.
2. Focus on the key areas found sensitive to the unethical practices in the business.
3. State and explain the important factors influencing the application of unethical practices in business.
4. Discuss in brief the different forms and areas where unethical measures are practised in the business.
5. Do you feel that ethical codes would be effective in regulating the unethical practices in business? Defend your arguments.
6. Explain the suitability of ethical training programme in making the employees aware of the dangers of unfair and unethical practices in business
7. Justify the instrumentality of corporate ethics in projecting or tarnishing the corporate image.

8. Write a reasoned note on Dilemma in corporate ethics.
9. Throw light on the practices you will like to follow for conceptualising ethics in business.
10. Do you find character-building essential for the application of ethics in business? Justify your arguments.
11. Explain the two different conditions for practising and breaching corporate ethics specially in the Indian perspective.
12. Discuss the different levels where unethical practices have been found gaining a rapid momentum.
13. Throw light on the difficulties while practising ethics in business.
14. Explain the factors you will like to consider while drafting the business code for regulating the unethical practices in the business.
15. Do you find character emerging as a power in the corporate sector where we find a significant increase in the number of unethical practices? Defend your arguments

APPLICATION EXERCISES

1. Ethical behaviour is found to be the bedrock of mutual trust. To behave ethically is to behave in a manner that is consistent with what is generally considered to be right or moral."

   Comment on the above statement in the capacity of a corporate professional.
2. The use of company resources for personal benefits cannot be ethical. Do you agree with this statement? Justify your arguments.
3. "Business ethics make and break the success of business. Practising ethics and breaching ethics are the two different conditions. When we are ethical, the customers trust and when we breach ethics, the customers distrust. Any business organisation cannot survive if the customers start distrusting on their construct and behaviour."

   In the capacity of a corporate professional, throw light on the above statement,
4. "Do you find breaching of corporate ethics instrumental in tarnishing the corporate image? Defend your arguments.
5. "Billionaire business tycoon, Mukesh Ambani's 27-storey residence Antilla has come in for much flak and censure. Even Tata Group Chairman, Ratan Tata says that the Ambani residence is an example of rich Indian's lack of empathy for poor." Do you agree? Justify your view points.
6. "Doing everything as you like just to have the opulent lifestyles may not be your good taste, specially in the midst of poverty. Enjoying your wealth which you have created through your hard work and entrepreneurial excellence is not only the result of your hard work but considerably of thousands and thousands of those employees who have worked hard for you and millions and millions of those customers who have paid exhorbitant prices for the goods or services they have consumed or used."

   Comment on this statement in the capacity of a corporate professional.
7. "If you nurture an attitude like a king, you should also make place for the feelings that the king has his subject too. If you do not care for your subject, your kingship and your kingdom would remain in danger. "In the light of statement outlined above, focus on the role of personal philanthropy for practising ethics in business.

8. "To be more specific in the Indian society, we find advertisements creating a big gap between the claims and realities about the products advertised."

   Do you find such practices of unethical nature? Justify.

9. "Character and knowledge, if both the powers work together, a new story of transformation is written."

   Throw light on the above statement.

10. "The codes of ethics focus on .making organisation a dependable citizen, demonstrating honesty and fairness in relationships with the stakeholders, complying with the regulations related with safety, health and security, the dress code and reliability in attendance and punctuality."

    In the face of above statement, focus on the role of ethical codes for practising ethics in business.

11. Do you feel that a well organised ethical training programme would be effective in developing awareness and maintaining ethical standard in a company?

    Defend your arguments.

12. When you are faced with an ethical question, it is pertinent that you give yourself an ethics check for sorting out dilemmas. Explain that how and in what way, you ask yourself.

13. Of course, we find cases of making significant contributions to society by a number of organisations in the Indian context but when we come to personal philanthropy, we face crisis of persons.

    Do you agree? Justify your statement.

14. "Spiritualism at the workplace becomes difficult when we find even high-level people involved in the unfair and unethical practices. When a king becomes dishonest, it becomes to make the subject honest. "Comment on this statement in the face of changing attitudes of Indian business tycoons.

15. "Nothing replaces honesty".

    In the face of above statement, throw light on the power of character for respecting business ethics.

16. For respecting ethical considerations, you need to be careful at different levels. Explain the different levels necessitating your due attention.

17. Should business tycoons feel happy with the opulent lifestyles specially in the Indian perspective where we find millions and millions of people not getting even the basics? Defend your arguments.

18. "Warren Buffetts, Bill Gates, Paul Allens and Azim Premji have been found promoting personal philanthropy."

    Do you find personal philanthropy making ways for practising ethics in business? Justify your answer.

19. "Good conduct brings in fame, longevity, wealth and happiness either for an individual or for an organisation."

    Examine this statement in the Indian context.

BACK-UP MATERIALS

1. www.scu.eduethics
   www.businessethics.com
   Ethical Behaviour
   Corporate Ethics
   Values and Ethics
   The Character of Values and Ethics
   Ethical Responses

2. www.mentalhealth.about.com
   www.self-improvement-success.com
   Emotions affect health
   Spirituality and Health

3. Swami Sivananda: A Divine Life Society Publication
   Ethical Discipline
   Purification of Mind
   Conquest of Mind

4. search 4 beauty.blogspot.com
   Relearning Attitudes
   Path of Meditation
   Paths for removal of accumulated complexes

5. What's age got to do with it?: The Times of India,
   July 24, 2011

6. Contentment is Spirituality: The Times of India
   April 17, 2011

7. Say true to your work: The Times of India,
   July 3, 2011

8. Loving begins with you: The Times of India, June 5, 2011.

◆ ◆ ◆

8 MANAGEMENT OF LOOKS

What is pleasant to our eyes is found acceptable to our mind. Better-looking people are found more productive because we find them creative and optimistic. The success story of the corporate sector is found based on optimism. There is nothing more appealing than a man with a sense of wit and fun. There is nothing more paying than an aesthete. Shifting from the relaxed mode to the professional mode makes a strong advocacy in favour of corporate looks. Better wardrobe, big bucks.

CHAPTER DESIGN

Introduction – Looks: the Concept and Percept – Globalisation and the Corporate Looks – Corporate Culture: Local and Global – The Dimensions of Looks – The Management of Wardrobe for Corporate Men – The Management of Wardrobe for Corporate Women – Select the Right Professional Business Suit – Tips for Corporate Women Professional – Investment Dressing – Saree as Corporate Wear – Grooming – Accessorising – Leveraging Colour – Manage Your Hair — Manage Your Shoes – Your Make-up – Your Wristwatch Tie as a Sense of Pride – Spectacle Frame for Your Face and Personality – A great Looking Briefcase – The Pen Reflecting Your Personality and Taste – Regulate the Body Odour – Promotional Corporate Apparel – Organisational Responsibility – The Wardrobe for Academics – Emerging Trends in the World of Corporate Looks – Summary — Key Terms – Expected Questions – Application Exercises – Back-up Materials

CHAPTER OBJECTIVES

Corporate world makes the difference between today and tomorrow. The corporate culture buzzwords of yesterday have become ineffective today and we are not sure that what buzz-words we have conceptualised today will remain effective even tomorrow. The motive of this chapter is to develop awareness of the different dimensions helping in managing the looks in the face of changing organisational culture. The corporate brands cannot be expressed regionally, rather than expressed uniformly; either locally or globally. Powerful looking clothes impact our mindset and attitudes. We start believing in professional mode. We are found creative and optimistic and play a big role in building and projecting the corporate image. Awaring people of the relevance of looks who are interested in serving the corporate world is our motive.

MANAGEMENT OF LOOKS

◈ Introduction

Creativity transgresses the limits of physical boundaries. Matching of nature's creation with our creative actions injects to our looks a new life and an additional attraction. An affluent desires something more than a poor. The beauty needs more than a beauty care. To look good, attractive and impressive, it is essential that we take proper care of our health such as we keep ourselves neat and clean, sense and sensitise ourselves to the wearabouts of the organisation where we work or plan to work, take care of personal hygiene and make our facial appearance much more promotable and hireable. Of course, you would not like to be fired just due to the fact that your belt buckle has shifted two or three notches too high. Each and everyday, we witness cases when good-looking people manage a good and distinct position albeit over a more competitive man. Believe it or not but a college degree along with a rock star personality is enough for talent scouts to offer you big bucks. We cannot negate that appearance factors make a place right from the time, we make preparations for entering the corporate world. Your looks can either boost or hinder your professional growth, regardless of your qualifications. This makes it significant that you make your wardrobes an important factor for rising up the corporate ladder. Your large or shabbily dresses or scruffy or old or worn clothes project your negative image. You need to be a differentiator. Our appearance should project a positive feeling and an optimistic facial expression which may provide to us a competitive advantage. When our competitors or counterparts do not match with our thematical competence we get much more and even they match, we get something more. It is against this backdrop that we find much more strength in the fact that better wardrobe, more success.

Corporate culture is considerably influenced by the look culture. This is also due to the fact that if we are well-dressed, neat and clean and look smart our elegant appearance help us in the development of optimism vis-à-vis in the creation of a positive feeling. What you, have inside, people know later but what you have outside people know first. In a true sense, in the corporate world of today our wearabouts prove to be an important factor in the development of our career. Making ourselves much more hireable is significant and for that we need to enrich our awareness of the organisational expectation vis-à-vis the organisational culture specially related to the attire.

Better looking people are found to be more positive and productive because we find them creative and optimistic. The success of corporate sector is found based on optimism. They look for creative leaders. What is pleasant to our eyes is found acceptable to our mind. Better dresses mean development of a sense of confidence which is found to be a determining force in the decision making process. Thematical competence, professional excellence, no doubt, have an edge over others but we do not find anything wrong in synchronising both so that we succeed in getting the competitive advantage. We need to be hireable and promotable which cannot be denied, if we make place for excellent performance and decent appearance. A majority of us believe in this proposition that wardrobe is an important factor in our rise up, specially in the present corporate world.

Corporate manners cannot be underrated in the present business world and therefore we need to link it with our personality development programme. It is in this context that we find etiquette emerging as an important force which a good number of finishing schools have been found promoting. The Business Schools need to play a dual role where they educate and develop people in the face of emerging corporate requirements. It is right to mention that a majority of the Indians are, no doubt, very much tempted to thematical competence but very less receptive to the etiquette and manners, dresses and wearabouts. The Business Schools abroad organise special classes and inculcate all the faculties required for developing personality in totality. On the one hand, they are very much professional in developing thematical competence while on the other hand, we also find them instrumental in shaping their looks. It is significant to mention that overseas MBA Schools have special classes that even tell you what colour ties to wear with what suits. Walking upright and with confidence, wearing a well-tailored suit and talking clearly without fillers 'like' or 'you know' makes you stand out or to be easily noticeable.

Giving an extra edge to your personality is a crying need of the hour which corporate executives need to realise. We cannot deny that wardrobes of average Indian corporate executives require a crying help. The major disaster areas are pens and shoes. We find colour combination in the same boat. It is best to play by the rules. In an age of globalisation, we cannot keep ourselves isolated. Look culture is taking a competitive shape and therefore we need to establish an edge. What to talk of men when we find albeit women executives not so much professional to their appearance. The colour combination, maximum use of ornaments, inadequate knowledge of wearabouts are the problem area.

Etiquette and grooming experts feel that actually we need a transformation in the whole package of attitude, body language, behaviour, communication and etiquettes. They also feel that 15% technical skill and 85% business and social graces account for our professional growth. We need to confess that a majority of the Indians lack the international workplace etiquette, right from dressing properly to punctuality while making inoffensive small talk, especially to women executives. The body language, posture, handshake and body-odour need due attention especially amongst corporate executives without which they cannot think of giving an extra edge to their looks. Developing awareness of look culture is significant and in this context, it is pertinent that in addition to the wearabouts, we also learn some corporate manners. We appreciate our predilection towards education for enriching our thematical competence but at the same time also confess that we are very much insincere or insensitive to corporate manners. We cannot deny that such an insensitivity would confine our boundaries and would deprive us of getting the global benefits and the competitive advantages.

The above mentioned facts make it clear that in the present corporate world, we need a microscopic evaluation of our appearance. The dresses that we wear, the shoes and socks that we use, the ties that we select, the colour combination that we adopt and the hair style that we follow play an important role in the determination of our success rate. At the outset, we need to understand the requirements of international workplace environment and thereafter the Business Schools or the Finishing Schools have to develop corporate people. Keeping ourselves at the first ladder should not be our motto and if we are interested in climbing up the corporate ladder; we have no option but to perceive that look culture is more rampant today and its intensity would increase even in future. If we receive these developments in a right fashion; our appearance would differentiate us.

We cannot deny that human beings by nature are impressionable. We also agree that each one of us feel pleasure in witnessing attractions in ambience and fragrance in appearance. Client-interface is becoming much more significant for excelling competition and as and when we have an interface with our clients or customers; we find our looks having a domination.

Without having a gender discrimination, we need to inject strength to the fact that all of us take pleasure in looking good things. Good looks help in securing a better pay and position. A research by Daniel Hamermesh, a Professor of Economics at the University of Texas at Austin observes that the best looking women, the top one-third at any workplace, make about 10% more annually than those in the bottom sixth of the genetic pool. The facts are there, of course, we may find a variation in degree or percentage.

The corporate sector is looking for and picking better-looking people over others. A number of psychological reasons are entailed behind but one thing is very much clear that a majority of the better-looking people are found productive because whatsoever we find pleasant to our eyes appeal us. A better dress sense means more confidence. Dr. Samir Parikh, Chief of the Department of Mental Health, Max Healthcare calls judgements on better-looking people by citing a US study of the jurors who were shown pictures of criminals and the slightly better-looking criminals were awarded lesser punishments! The survey makes it clear that 79% (82% in MNCs) feel a better dress sense means a more confident you. Even 69% feel that a shabby appearance does lead to negative stereotypes about the person as snoppy, lazy or slow.

Thus, we find management of our looks assuming a place of outstanding significance specially in the present corporate world and in the emerging corporate culture, we find wisdom in promoting look culture. Our upcoming and budding youths need to be much more sensitive to the corporate etiquette and manners. Our Business Schools need to educate and train them in the required fashion. By developing them in a right fashion, we can make the coming generations much more optimistic, positive and productive.

◈ Looks: The Concept and Percept

By Looks, our focus is on the facial appearance of an individual. This throws light on the dimensions helping us in making our facial appearance much more attractive and impressive. Face is considered to be an index of our mind and whatsoever attractions that we make possible speak of our taste and temperament. Civilisation and culture vis-à-vis the professional requirements define "Looks" which may vary from time to time. Looks cannot be dissociated with our attitudes. It is due to the fact that we find people with positive attitude evincing interest in looking well and conversely, people with a negative attitude prefer to continue with an ordinary look. What do we find pleasant to our eyes are pleasant even to our mind, responsible for the formation of attitudes. We cannot negate that a shabby appearance leads to a negative attitude and vice versa. If we are well-dressed before the mirror and feel ourselves satisfied with the dresses and make-up that we wear, this makes place for optimism. Contrary to it, if we stand before the mirror with shabbily dresses or scruffy or old or worn clothes; this speaks of our pessimism and negative attitudes. A number of instances testify that better-looking people are found much more productive because we find them creative and productive. Better dresses mean a sense of confidence and a strong sense of determination to live with pleasure and joy. Our wearabouts thus are found to be an incremental force in the projection of actually what we are.

Looks thus are the individual or institutional efforts through which we find a transformation in our facial appearance. It is concerned with better-living and decent-looking. It is an effort to make our appearance elegant. It is a device to boost the professional growth in an individual to make him/her much more hireable and promotable. We may also consider it a device to make an individual a differentiator to get the competitive advantages. It is also an effort to get more pay package. In precise, we find looks playing as an instrument to promote culture and civilisation.

The concept and percept of looks cannot remain static because civilisation and culture are sizably influenced by socio-economic transformation. Globalisation transformed the economy, changed the society and considerably influenced cultural patterns and civilisation. It started dominating everything and emerged as a culture which we named as corporate culture. Looks thus were found redefined in which attraction in the appearance was found essential. In this face, even Looks emerged as a culture and the dominating corporate culture started influencing the look culture. The motive was to differentiate and to establish an edge. With the increasing impact of corporate culture on the look culture, a number of dimensions were found included for projecting the facial appearance and promoting the corporate etiquette and manners. Without having genetic, racial and gender considerations; our sensitivity to the look culture gained a rapid momentum and proved to be a part of personality development.

◈ Globalisation and the Corporate Looks

Globalisation injected new life and strength to the process of corporatisation which made ways for attraction. We defined and redefined workplace environment; started realising the significance of ambience and hired and fired even on the basis of facial appearance. Such an attitudinal transformation engineered a sound foundation for the development of look culture. Corporate people realised the significance of facial appearance and this paved copious avenues for adding additional attractions to their physique. The urban legends, corporate legends evinced keen interests in defining corporate looks. Emergence of corporate culture specially in the cosmopolitan towns and cities and increased migration of people from the rural areas to the urban areas, made the recent developments acceptable albeit to other segments. Looks and presentation, proved to be a productive base making people much more hireable and promotable. It was against this backdrop that even in the Indian context, we started witnessing new developments, new lifestyle, new concept of facial appearance, increased sensitivity to wearabouts, hair style and footwear virtually made folklores of our culture and civilisation ineffective. Changing the perception of predilection emerged as a fashion and we also witnessed people accepting it as a passion.

Mounting corporate ladders bear the efficacy of defining and redefining the socio-cultural patterns and systems. It was against this background that Globalisation of economy started making ways for the globalisation of fashion, culture and civilisation. Good-looking and well-dressed people were found getting a lucrative pay-packet. Of late, we find a strong sense of realisation specially amongst the upcoming and budding youths that they can get everything in the corporate sector and therefore temptation or fascination to the high corporate positions are found at its peak. Of course, they have perceived facts and realities in a right way. Gone are the days when we believed that none to care your wearabouts. In a true sense, we find today a different scenario.

The corporate sector would continue to pick better-looking people even in the coming days. They advocate and we find them even right in their proposition that better-looking people, well-dressed people, fashion-loving people, good-looking people nurture a positive attitude and therefore a majority of them are found optimistic. Corporatisation rests on positive people, optimistic people, and productive people. If we have a lust for attraction, the doors for the development of negative thoughts are sealed. The most important thing in the development process is to make the upcoming generations positive.

We can not negate that human beings by nature are found fascinated or tempted to witness attractions pleasant to their eyes. With the increasing heat of globalisation and further with the mounting levels or income, a large number of people even in the Indian context are potentially sound to make place for adopting and promoting look culture. Of course, it is not a gender issue and therefore we find both the men and women considerably influenced by globalisation which has been impacting our lifestyle, behaviour, attitudes and even culture and civilisation.

◈ Physical Appearance Portrays Personality

In the corporate world of today, we find some of the words gaining much more significance such as Person, Personality, Career, Outfits, Apparel, Attire, Looks and Physical Appearance. We cannot negate that corporatisation is found based on attraction. The professionals are supposed to make sincere and honest efforts to bring a radical change in your looks so that your outfits start speaking of the corporate brand image. May be that a person is not recognised by its outfits but his/her career can definitely grow or fall depending on his/her clothes. In the modern business world, the corporate attire is not just preferred but it is expected and an impeccable or faultless style of dress is a must for everyone and more so for people interested in climbing the corporate ladders. Corporate outfits portrays personality and position of a person. Both for hiring and firing, we find physical appearance of an individual emerging as an impacting power. Clothes you wear reflect how smart you are and how classic your choice is. If a person is well dressed he/she is able to earn respect from other people and this makes it essential that you also respect the organisational culture and perceive the concept of investment dressing in a right fashion. The dressing sense of a person speaks of his/her success and shows how much confident a person is. Corporate clothes help uplift the business and prove to be a vital force both for your hiring and firing. It is very much related to your physical appearance, your outlooks, your facial appearance and ultimately your success. Top class corporate image is found associated with the top class corporate attire because we find top class corporate outfits very much instrumental in bringing elegance and making you proficient. It is against this backdrop that people evincing interests in joining the corporate world need to assign due weightage to the different dimensions which may be helpful in enriching their looks.

The new cult of hiring czars makes a strong advocacy in favour of hiring people having a rock star personality which is found enough for talent scouts. On the basis of your physical appearance, you are in a position to get the big bucks. May be that you consider it amazing but we find even your average boy next door becoming a high-flier, of course, they have a down-to-earth practical approach to life, and they are dynamic with a rock star personality. What impresses recruiters are youngsters with leadership skills, creativity and high intellectual bandwidth and a daring attitude. They look for people with adaptability, agility and the ability to think beyond today. They look for people with positive attitudes and skills. They look for people nurturing optimism and having the temptation to be a high-flier. In a true sense, we live in the corporate world where personality scores over any professional degree. And physical appearance portrays personality.

Enriching the physical appearance thus proves to be an important consideration for your successes or failures. It is an age of grooming and therefore we find etiquette and grooming experts in big demand. The corporate culture is considerably influenced by the look culture. It is why we find, Sabira Merchant an internationally acclaimed corporate trainer in big demand because she has hardly a free day left on her calendar.

Of course, she is not a CEO but we find her teaching CEOs some important thing about conducting the business. She says that we have just woken up to the fact that soft skills are as important as hard skills to get an edge in the corporate competitive environment. Like this, Pria Warrick, Executive Director, Pria Warrick Finishing School says that it's always been a case of study hard, getting good score and grades and everything else are taken care of probably that according to her we find lack of social graces even among some of the highest placed Indian executives. We cannot negate that we have globally competent engineers, business majors and technology wizards but often it is our lack of social polish and communication skills that puts us behind competitors. It is against this background that we find companies like Infosys have woken up to it and have built a Global Education Centre in Mysore. We need to educate our youths leadership and manners because these traits would make them globally sound.

In today's context, the companies need to address body language, posture, handshake, etiquette and manners because our youths lack these traits responsible for their lagging behind. We cannot deny that the average Indian executives' corporate wardrobe is almost a cry of help. There are a number of disaster or problem areas where they need proper training. Honing certain behaviours like walking upright and with confidence, wearing a well-tailored suit and talking clearly without the fillers "like" or "you know" need due attention for excelling competition.

Actually you need to develop your awareness that if you are not professional in your outfits, this may be a reason even for your firing. We find a number of cases when employees are fired because their belt buckle had shifted three notches too high. Or, we also witness cases where good-looking woman could manage a good position. In the changing scenario, it is not a taboo or social restrictions because we find looks pegging over merit. The whispered voices in the society are not to regulate the corporate culture. It has its own way, its own wave and its own direction. If we follow, we are rewarded. And if not, we find others to snatch because it all boils due to looks and presentation, especially when we have two people with the same competency.

It is an age where you are supposed to take even minor things in detail. May be that in your eyes, these things are minor or small but in the corporate culture, we find them having a high rank and position and therefore you need to enrich your knowledge bank. Appearance factors have an edge right from the time you send your CV. Of course, there are a number of psychological factors influencing the corporate social polish. The better looking people prove themselves to be more productive. Any one of us can not deny that when we stand before a mirror with an attractive look, its provides to us the optimism; the desire and willingness to stand and the temptation and fascination to enjoy the pleasure of life provided to us by the almighty God. Hence the perception of corporate world regarding the physical appearance and looks can not be wrong because they want optimistic people nurturing interests of enjoying. They look for people interested in smelling the fragrance of the corporate world and advocating with confidence, *"Hum Janam Bita Ke Jayenge, Tum Janam Ganva Ke Jaoge."*

Anybody on this planet Earth cannot have disrespect for beauty and disregard for attractions. It is more so the law of nature that we are impressed by viewing good things. People like something distinct and it is our physical appearance that makes us a differentiator. Make it sure that your looks can help or hinder your professional growth. A landmark study from Cornell University found that when a white female puts on an additional 64 pounds, her wages drop 9%. Why we should prefer to be shabbily dressed when we find it a reason for developing pessimism. Why we should think about economy in dressing when we are paid for that. Enriching our personal characterists is the most important thing that we need to consider on a priority basis because we live in an age of investment dressing. If you allow such a condition and assign due weightage to your physical appearance, you succeed in getting the big bucks. Now it is upon you to enjoy life or to reject and develop pessimism.

If we focus on the physical appearance, it is not meant that we bid a goodbye to the predilection of developing world-class thematical competence; indeed it throws light on the fact that we need not to disrespect the position of physical appearance in the corporate culture because ultimately we have to live in this culture. Why we should not prefer to be high-flier when we have the opportunities and we have the qualities. The only thing that we need is to educate and train the upcoming youths and the budding generations in tune with the changing corporate requirements. The Business Schools and the Finishing Schools while developing their curriculum or while developing their product should not remain unaware of the changing corporate requirements.

In view of the facts outlined above, it is right to say that physical appearance requires priority attention in today's context. A survey conducted by the Sunday ET and Synovate with the motto of gauging whether appearance plays a part the professional growth proves that not everything is stuff of water cooler chats, as a whopping 71% of the corporate executives agreed that what you wear is a big factor in your climb up the corporate ladder. In another survey, Organisational learning and Marketing, Manpower India, it is found that 79% MNCs as opposed to 65% of domestic firms reckon that your clothes can make your career. These facts and figures are a staunch testimony to this proposition that we cannot undermine the importance of wardrobe in rising up the corporate ladders. We have to agree that appearance makes us more hireable and promotable.

It is against this background that we find management of physical appearance clubbing a number of dimensions. Actually, we need personality in totality and here physical appearance assumes a place of outstanding significance. Manage your wardrobes and manage your wearabouts; look attractive and impressive, develop a personality magnifying elegance, develop a zippy attitude and be optimistic, the corporate world is looking for you. Opportunities are here and it is upon you to capitalise.

◈ Wardrobe Management for Your Hiring and Firing

It is very difficult to believe the wonders of corporate world, where the quality of wardrobe is considered a decisive factor for hiring and firing. Anybody serving the corporate sector or nurturing a temptation for serving the corporate world cannot keep themselves unaware of the management of their wardrobes for getting big bucks in the business world of today. The growing popularity of the corporate trainers is a stauch testimony to this proposition that your complete outfit consists of a number of considerations. This is an age of investment dressing where organisational culture plays a meaningful role. Style and status, distinctness and elegance of your looks significantly contribute to the process of personality development. The dress policy of an organisation is a dominating factor where your looks translate into better pay and better appraisals. Your sloppy appearance may lead to negative stereotype perception about the person as lazy or as slow even though he/she is good at work.

Appearance is found to be an important factor to make you promotable. Employees are found superseded on the basis of his/ her appearance. In the adjoining figure, Chennai, Mumbai and Delhi display highest instances of individuals bypassed as they did not dress for success.

Source: The Economic Times, Oct. 24, 2010

Do you know of anyone who has superseded on the basis of his or her appearance?

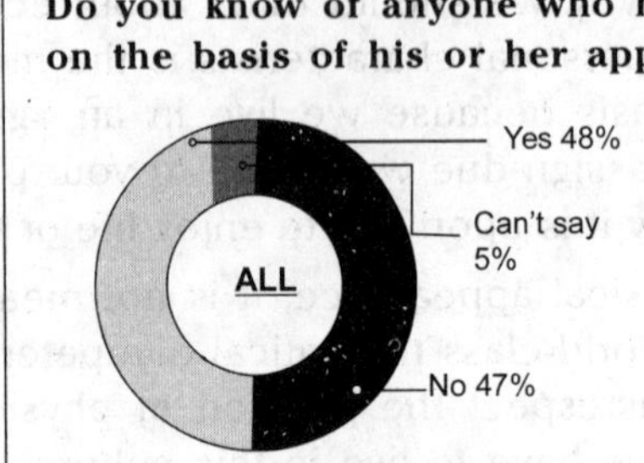

Overall, polarised views. Chennai, Mumbai and Delhi display highest instances of individuals bypassed as they did not dress for success.

It is also found that obese people get a raw deal at their workplace. 72% of the people as respondents agree that in Mumbai, obese people are not treated right at their place of work. The adjoining figure clarifies it.

Do obese people get a raw deal at their workplace?

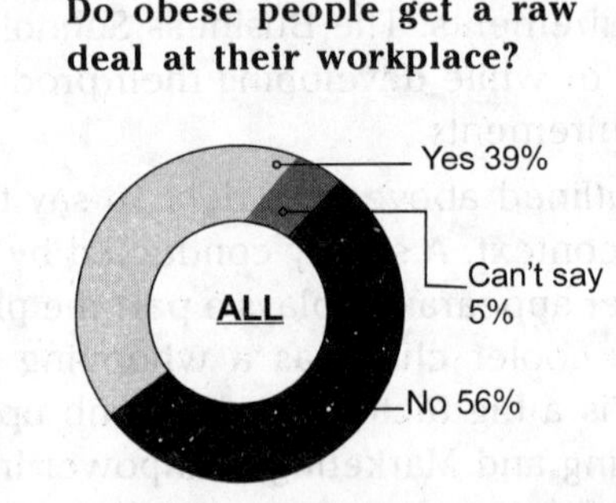

More number of respondents polled disagree. 72% of respondents in Mumbai (the highest) agree that obese people are not treated right at their place of work.

Age is also found to be a hindrance to promotion. A whopping 87% in Chennai and 81% in Mumbai feel that age is hindrance to promotion. This is clear from the adjoining figure.

Does age become a hindrance to promotion?

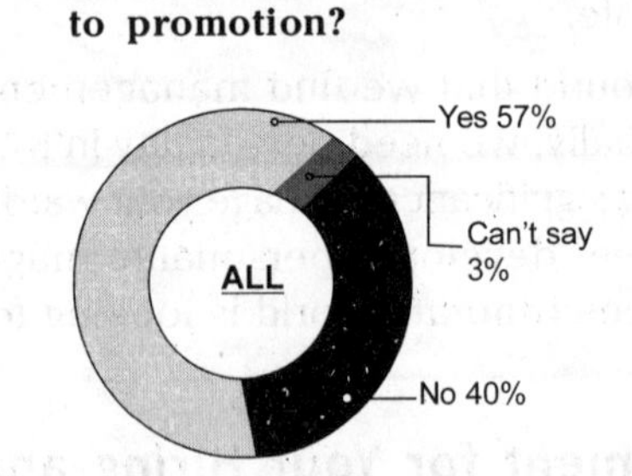

A whopping 87% in Chennai and 81% in Mumbai feel age is a hindrance to promotion. Otherwise it's near polarised views. Across demographics more say age hinders promotion.

Source: The Economic Times, Oct. 24, 2010

Looks become responsible for discrimination particularly at the time of recruitment. In Chennai and Bengaluru, you need more care while getting recruited. In Mumbai too, the corporate executives and managers claim that discrimination on the basis of looks is common.

Do employers discriminate on the basis of looks at the time of recruitment?

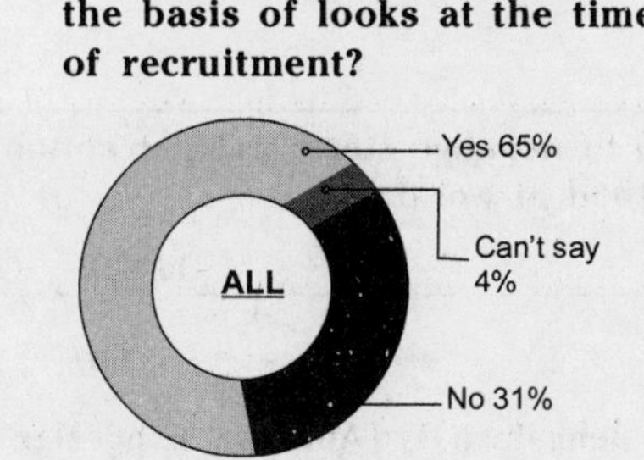

In Chennai and Bengaluru, be aware of how you dress if you want to land up that job. In Mumbai too corporate executives and managers claim that discrimination on looks is commonplace.

Youthful appearance plays an important role in getting the job or even getting promotion or in keeping or retaining clients. Barring Delhi, in all other cities, a majority feel that a youthful appearance does help in getting a job.

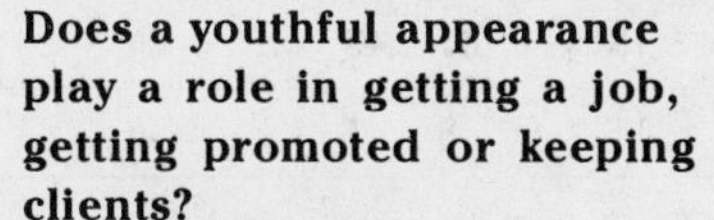

Does a youthful appearance play a role in getting a job, getting promoted or keeping clients?

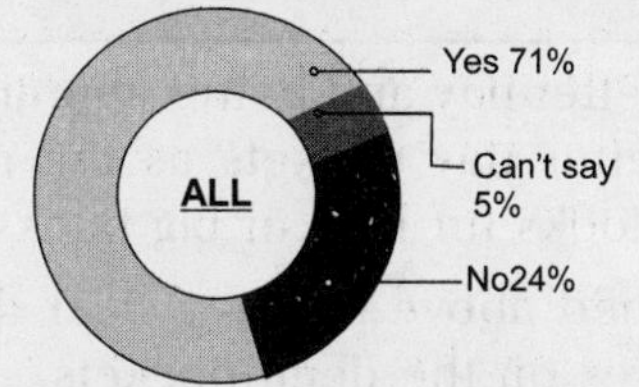

Barring Delhi, that saw a split view, across all the other cities and demographics, majority feel a youthful appearance does help in getting a job and improved client relations.

Change your appearance to get a better deal at work. A number of Delhities are found willing to alter their appearance if it is to help them in getting the job. But the Bengaluru, Chennai and Mumbai have an opposite view.

Would you change your appearance to get a better deal at work?

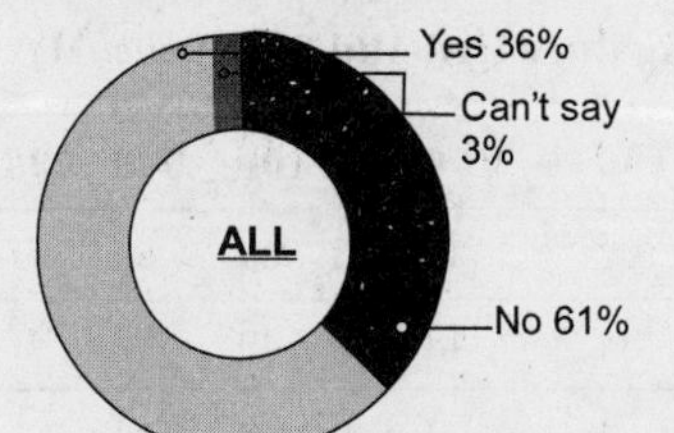

More Delhiites would be willing to alter their appearance if it helps them professionally. In contrast, Bangaluru, Chennai and Mumbai have an opposite view.

Appearance matters a lot in Mumbai, Chennai, Kolkata and Bengaluru. Actually sloppy appearance leads to a negative image and therefore we consider it an important factor for first impression. The figures given below clarify it.

FIRST IMPRESSION

Does sloppy appearance lead to negative sterotypes/perception about the person as lazy or slow, even though he/she may be good at work?

	CITY									LEVEL		GENDER		AGE				
	All	Del	Mum	Kol	Chen	Bengaluru	Hyd	Ahd	Pun	Line Exec	Mgr	Male	Fem	20-30 Yrs	31-40 Yrs	41-50 Yrs	MNC	Indian
All	**802**	**100**	**100**	**100**	**100**	**100**	**100**	**100**	**100**	**509**	**293**	**525**	**277**	**405**	**261**	**136**	**339**	**463**
Yes	69	49	91	86	89	71	51	56	61	69	69	70	68	71	69	66	75	65
No	26	35	8	13	11	18	41	43	37	26	26	26	26	24	28	26	22	29
CS*	5	16	1	1	0	11	8	1	2	5	5	4	6	5	3	8	3	6

* Can't say Figures in %

Good looks translate into better pay and better appraisals. This makes it clear that looks do matter and can land you better pay packets as the respondents of Chennai feel. This requires focus on having better looks for high or big bucks. The figure given below clarify it.

The facts and figures outlined above make it clear that wearabouts play a meaningful role. The following figures focuses on the deep pockets.

Do good looks translate into better pay and better appraisals?

	CITY									LEVEL		GENDER		AGE				
	All	Del	Mum	Kol	Chen	Bengaluru	Hyd	Ahd	Pun	Line Exec	Mgr	Male	Fem	20-30 Yrs	31-40 Yrs	41-50 Yrs	MNC	Indian
All	**802**	**100**	**100**	**100**	**100**	**100**	**100**	**100**	**100**	**509**	**293**	**525**	**277**	**405**	**261**	**136**	**339**	**463**
Yes	54	68	67	23	86	62	43	43	43	59	47	55	53	55	58	46	56	53
No	41	26	26	75	14	34	48	57	49	37	47	39	44	40	37	50	38	43
CS*	5	6	7	2	0	4	9	0	8	4	6	6	3	5	5	4	6	4

* Can't say Figures in %

All the dimensions narrated earlier make it clear that looks do matter and this may also help you in getting the better pay packets. The social graces and accent help you in enriching your personal score. Since we find soft skills even establishing an edge over the hard skills, it is imperative that our priority attention is on making society aware of the priorities which may help people in getting a respectable position in the business world. Actually, we have a predilection towards education, caring little or even nothing for manners which has been damaging the career prospects of the budding generations.

It is amazing that in the Indian context, even top executives lack the basics and face the problem of wardrobe crisis. We care nothing for etiquette, civic and aesthetic sense. Hard study, good grades and getting top position are our goals. We never mind body language, gesture, posture, handshake, accents and many small things having a major impact. Honing certain behaviours and traits cannot be undermined specially in the present corporate culture such as walking upright and with confidence, wearing a well-tailored suit and talking clearly without using the fillers 'like' or 'you know' but a majority of us do not mind. Addressing everything from voice and accents to the dining etiquette to dressing up basic are now found very common in the educational institutions of the developed countries.

In the changing business world, we cannot undermine the instrumentality of wardrobe in getting big bucks. What to talk of the people of low position when we find average Indian executives' wardrobe almost in a deplorable condition. A majority of our students lack awareness of international workplace environment or etiquette. In an increasingly global competitive environment, the guru of graces may resolve your problems. Overseas MBA Schools have special classes which educate and sense students even what colour of tie to wear with what suit. Not only the educational institutions but even the parents from the very beginning are found sensing and sensitising their children the basics which help them in due course. We Indian need to mind these things on a priority basis.

The corporate world is full of wonders with much more volatility. We find people fired even due to shifting of belt buckle. We find people getting big bucks for appearance. These are not the whispered voices in the aisles or streets of the town but the realities of the present world experienced by each one of us; each and everyday. Willingly or unwillingly, we have to accept the realities of the present business world where what you wear is an important factor for climbing the ladders of the business world. We cannot deny that our looks can help or hinder our professional growth regardless of our qualifications and specialisation. The world where you are punished even for putting extra weight on your body, the world where your appearance surfaces or even proves to be a key differentiator at the workplace; you need much more care failing which even small things may be responsible for your firing. Appearance impacts and it will continue to impact. We like better-looking people over others. It is quite logical and significantly psychological.

Educating, sensing and sensitising the present generation cannot be overlooked in almost all the areas where they need special assistance. What to talk of the leading business and finishing schools when we find urgency of conceptualising the dress etiquette and manners even by the general educational institutions and this one even at the primary and secondary stages of their education. This will inculcate faculty of personality development specially amongst the upcoming or budding youths who urgently need due attention. Because they nurture the temptation to plush jobs, a constant care is essential.

The hiring experts believe that the ultimate candidate should have a "zippy" attitude, or fresh or lively attitude in which we find scope for injecting the required properties or attributes. How and in what way they develop the leadership skill, a rock star personality, prove to be doers and blend easily into a multi-cultural environment; the corporate trainers have to make sure. Besides, it is also to be ensured that they keep themselves engaged in enriching intuition, coiling creativity, evincing interest in music, developing a high level of communicative ability and mannerism.

A positive development that we find in today's business world is high priority to the youngsters. It is a good sign and therefore the youths have to capitalise on the opportunities. Of late, the companies prefer to recruit young people with positive skills, not knowledge but they should also have the tolerance for stress and behavioural flexibility to resolve the crisis. Keeping in view the increasing demand of visionaries, it is pertinent that we provide to them an opportunity to learn. Adaptability, agility and the ability to think beyond today would make them potentially sound for the modern business world. They will be efficacious of anticipating the emerging changes and challenges in the existing business environment.

Since we find our focus here on the corporate people, it is imperative that we intensify efforts to enrich the entire process of development and make them hireable and promotable. Appearance factors thus appear to be much more significant to make people hireable and promotable. Putting on additional weight on your body is found to be a negative factor in the present corporate world. The look culture is becoming rampant in today's condition. It is also to be ensured that corporate people do not undermine the quality of their wardrobe. The dress down policy cannot be acceptable in the present corporate culture because it is found strengthening the relaxed mode. It is also argued that large or shabbily dressed people develop a negative attitude. In a true sense, the appearance becomes very much instrumental in the differentiation process.

Wardrobe management is found sizably influenced by the organisational culture. The local corporate culture cannot be differentiated with the global corporate culture. Though we find employees becoming much more liberal to the dress code policy when they are transferred to the regional branches or suburbs which cannot be considered right because employees are considered an extension of their corporate brand. This makes it essential that employees should not invite a problem like a dress-culture-shock. The corporate brand must be expressed uniformly. This simplifies the process of developing team-spirit vis-à-vis the team-culture. Maintaining a consistent image is significant which projects the company's standards and culture to its clients. We cannot deny that bridging the gap between employee-image and corporate-image is imperative not just locally but globally too.

The facts outlined above make it clear that you need to receive dress policy of an organisation and make sincere and honest efforts to practise it. You live in an age of investment dressing and if you invest on your dresses and looks. This is to help you in getting a handsome return on your investment. Accessorising is an important dimension of wardrobe management; you need to remember it.

Making a mix of different accessories commensurate with your professional requirements and situational compulsions is an important consideration without which your outfit remains incomplete. Your attire, shoes, socks, ties, watch, briefcase play a meaningful role in projecting your personality.

Not only the men but even women are found joining the corporate world in a good number. Each and every woman planning for joining the corporate sector should watch the American movie, "Working Women" which would help them in shaping her corporate looks. You are in office, you may be in a business meeting, you may also attend the business parties or formal or informal functions and at different occasions, your looks need due attention and proper care. There are number of cases where due to better-looking facial appearance, the corporate women have been successful in getting the big bucks. On the other hand, there are also cases when just due to the fact that a few kilograms of additional weight were added and this one resulted into firing. The figures presented earlier also authenticate that women are subjected to more image scrutiny than men. In Mumbai and Chennai, 78% and 74% respectively support that women are more at the receiving end of the look culture. Good looks help in securing a better pay. A research by Daniel Hamermesh, a professor of economics at the University of Texas at Austin observes that the best looking women, the top one-third at any workplace, make about 10% more annually than those in the bottom of six of the genetic pool. Willingly or unwillingly, we have to accept the fact that good-looking women manage a good position in a company even over a more competent man.

In a true sense, the corporate culture is found based on attraction which is equally applicable for both the genders. However, it is also right that women are formed in an advantageous position. Whatsoever the reasons are entailed behind the gender consideration, one thing is almost clear that men or women serving the corporate sector need to assign due weightage to look culture. It is against this background that we find focus on managing the wardrobe for making you more hireable and promotable.

In view of the emerging corporate culture, it is right to say that appearance plays an incremental role in making an individual a successful corporate executive. The available cases testify that it is also responsible even for firing. The corporate policy makers argue that the people assigning due weightage to their outfits are found of positive nature because they nurture optimism. Since they respect the organisational culture; they are benefited. Conversely, the people not sincere to the organisational dress code work in a relaxed mood and develop negative traits in their behaviour which is found influenced by pessimism. The organisations do not prefer to continue them which may also result into their firing. Hence, the corporate people need to assign due weightage to the wearabouts. They may promote it on an individual basis or may also seek institutional support with the help of concerned personal care organisation.

◈ Corporate Culture: Local and Global

With the increasing heat of globalisation, we find a large scale expansion of markets from country to country, state to state and even town to town. This becomes an important reason for a significant change in the attitudes of employees specially regarding the organisational culture vis-à-vis the dress code. The dress code policy of an organisation no doubt remains the same but just on paper. The employees transferred from one country to another country, from cosmopolitan towns to small towns and even from general towns to the industrial towns face dress culture shock because they witness a big gap. This is due mainly to a change in the perception. We often forget that employees are an extension of their corporate brand and therefore its conceptualisation and expression uniformly irrespective of cultural and regional variations need due attention. The offices may be set up at different places but organisational culture remains the same. Unless it is made possible, the team spirit and team culture cannot be possible. The dress code of an organisation is found closely linked with corporate culture which projects corporate image. Consistency in image necessitates consistency in perception. The expression of standards and culture of a particular corporation to its clients becomes difficult when we find a variation. Hence, it is of paramount importance that the existent gap between employee image and corporate image is bridged both in local and global perspectives. Brand-image-projection takes time but brand-image-erosion is found very fast. Actually, we find a correlation between the corporate culture and corporate image. The dress code plays a very positive role in the process of strengthening their relationships. The corporate professionals bear the responsibility of bridging the existent gap.

You serve an organisation and you are naturally influenced by the culture nurtured by that organisation. If not, you suffer. Place carries no meaning. You are an extension of the corporate brand and this makes it essential that you honour the code irrespective of the fact that you work at the headquarters or are transferred to a remote branch. "Melanie Griffth", a character in the movie "Working Girl" injected life to her realisation that unless she brings a change in her New Jersey image, she cannot be accepted as a Manhattan professional. Accordingly, she made possible some minor adjustments in her outer image, changed her wardrobe, hairstyle and even her voice and due to these modifications, she could be successful in revealing her inner qualities. We have no exceptions but to accept that the task of exposing inner qualities is found easier, if we have been successful, in reshaping our outer image.

Local corporate culture and global corporate culture cannot move forward in the different directions. The direction is one and it is the corporate culture, not just locally but globally too. For maintaining corporate culture, it is imperative that corporate brand is expressed uniformly. A situation like "dress culture shock" is found when we start believing that dress culture is meant only for the corporate offices found located at the headquarters.

Powerful looking clothes virtually change our mindset and we start switching from relaxed mode to the professional mode. The impact of that positive change in our attitude is found in our body language and behaviour and we find better posture, firm handshake, eye contact and sticking to business, everything positive and productive. Jackson Lewis, a legal consultant specialising people in the field of personnel issues polled more than 1000 human resource executives who had practised a dress down policy. They reported a 30 per cent increase in the fictitious behaviour resulting into an increase in the sexual harassment lawsuits. This speaks of the fact that dress-down-policy makes an invasion on attitudes of people serving our organisation and they start receiving even serious things in an ordinary fashion which makes the ways for the development of a plethora of problems.

Thus we find strong justifications in favour of uniformity and no relaxation or compromise with the dress code policy. If we are liberal, the implications are well known. How you carry yourself make the ways for how you are perceived. Actually, you do not dress for the position you have. You need to dress for the position you want. The corporate sector is found serious to the culture accepted by them. It is due mainly to the fact that they have sufficient grounds to authenticate that as and when they were liberal to their dress code policy, a number of negative developments took place. We cannot negate that clothing and behaviour are found interrelated. Corporate culture has no place for relaxed mode. They are based on professional excellence and only professional mode can protect and promote their interests. And professional mode becomes difficult when we do not look like a professional.

In view of the above, it is right to observe that people evincing interests in serving the corporate sector need to nurture and strengthen their feelings that projection of personal image must be on the foundation of corporate image. The moment we start bridging the gap between personal image and corporate image, we start witnessing a positive impact on business relationships. Not only this, we also succeed in enriching our potentials to build the rapport and fit with team. Further, we start making significant contributions to the development of team spirit and team culture. We find organisation thriving and our career prospering. The consistency in image cannot be denied in the narrated situations.

The cycle of development keeps on moving. Since we have maintained consistency in the development of our image, the clients or customers start realising our standards. We get positive responses from them not only from a particular region or country but from the entire globe which simplifies our task of having a global image. We exist and thrive in cosmopolitan towns and cities and we are well known albeit in remotest parts of the globe. Since we show respect to the corporate culture; in return we get rewards. Actually when we are honest and sincere to our own developments, how any one can perceive that we would not be governed by the same attitude. Commitments to self, engineer a sound foundation for showing commitments to others.

◈ The Dimensions of Corporate Looks

At the outset, it is imperative that we develop our awareness of the emerging dimensions for the development of corporate looks so that we find ourselves competent enough to capitalise on the opportunities.

Wearabouts constitute the various facets related to the dresses that we wear. Clothing must be suitable for a particular purpose. It requires to be matched with our professional requirements. This focuses our attention on the management of wardrobes where we find emphasis on the entire collection of our clothes. The colour mix, style and design may vary in the face of gender. Since we go through the problems related to corporate looks, it is quite natural that our prime attention is on the dresses to be suitable for the corporate executives. The climatic condition, suitability of fibre and texture and colour requirements for a particular event need due attention to have an innovative appearance.

In the context of developing corporate looks, we cannot undermine the hairstyle. Elegance is considered to be the most vital aspect for the development of corporate looks. The size of the hair neither be small nor be long. This throws light on the hair cutting after a regular interval. It is significant that both the genders are sincere and particular to the quality of hair and for that they need due treatment of scalp.

The shoes and socks cannot be underrated for the projection of corporate looks. We need a match between the colour of shoes and socks. It is imperative that we are sincere while maintaining our shoes and keep our socks neat and clean.

The wrist watches and pens are also the problem areas where a majority of us are not sincere. It is not significant that we have expensive wrist watches and pens. It is much more impact generating that we make place for them in tune with our requirements.

The jewelleries and ornaments are also the problem area particularly for women executives where we find a majority of the women insensitive.

Both for men and women, we find ties and their colour occupying a place of outstanding significance in the corporate looks. There should be a fair match between the shirts and ties selected for different working days of the corporate executives.

The dimensions which we include in the corporate looks play an incremental role in differentiating our looks for which we are suitably paid. How and in what way, we project our facial appearance require an in-depth knowledge of the corporate requirements and manners. The Business Schools also need to play the role of Finishing Schools so that awareness is developed amongst the potential executives. A smooth finish is our motto. He/she should must be good at work but in addition, sloppy appearance projecting careless and disorganised appearance, loose fitting of a garment cannot be helpful in getting the desired results.

◈ Clothing and Your Behaviour

Powerful looking clothing such as professional business attire, a suit, darker colours, etc., commensurate with your profession bring a change in your mindset. A shifting from relaxed mode to the professional mode is found existent with the powerful dressing. Such a positive change in attitude brings an analogous change in the body language and behaviour. Resulting from which, we find better posture, firmer handshake, maintaining eye contact, sticking to business, enhancing your visual power.

Powerful Looking Clothing

Jackson Lewis, a law firm, specialising in personnel issues on the basis of a research revealed that dress down policy of an organisation makes the ways for negative developments. Hence, it is imperative that we are sincere to our wearabouts so that people do not get the liberty of inferring negative remarks. Clothing is also found to be an inner cue affecting our image. Feeling good about how do we look make us feel good about ourselves. This helps in developing the presence of personal. Thus "feel good" is also a factor instrumentalising our self image. Successful clothing is found influencing our emotion when we find our colleagues complimenting with supportive attitudes. This, ultimately brings an increase our level of efficiency.

Karen Dixon, 42, supervisor, The Mercadien Group, Princeton, NJ, indicates "Dressing in a professional yet stylish manner can give you a tremendous feeling of confidence that is exhibited to others through your attitude and actions." But when we feel that our wearabouts are not in tune with our profession, there is a negative impact on our level of efficiency. This causes a drain to our self image. Bridging the gap between personal image and corporate image is found significant. Throwing a positive impact on the clients is significant which is not to be possible unless we dress for the position that we hold. Emily Oswald, 22, Account Manager. TrailGraphix, DC quotes the observation of his mother, "My mother always said you don't dress for the position you have. You dress for the position you want. He further says that after three months with my company, I was promoted. Out of 300 people in my company, and out of 35 other account managers, I am the youngest one. When I meet with clients, who are typically fifty-year-old attorneys, I always dress more professionally. There is nothing comfortable about wearing a suit and heels but it does affect how you carry yourself and how you are perceived. Dressing professionally has definitely helped me move up quickly in my company, Dixon observes.

Of course, we find wearabouts impact generating for both the genders but a survey reveals that 75 per cent of the respondents believed that appearance at work affects how women are perceived by others more so than their male counterparts. Nearly 8 per cent of the respondents said that clothes, hairstyle and make-up make a significant difference in their perceptions and confidence that a woman has the skills and knowledge to perform her job.

It is in this context that we find management of wardrobe becoming much more significant to the corporate women. If you "feel good", it is quite natural that development of a sense of confidence is found existent in your behaviour which influences your level of efficiency vis-à-vis the perception of others about your behaviour. This makes it clear that appearance and performance are interrelated which makes the ways for the creation of image which may be positive or negative. Standing before the mirror and making a self evaluation help us in becoming positive and this paves avenues for the development of 'halo effect' which focuses on the fact that if we know certain positive things about an individual, we tend to have a general impression that he/she is positive; though contrary results are also expected. If you are nicely dressed and look well; you have greater confidence or abilities and this high level of confidence brings a significant increase in your performance level.

How do we perceive ourselves also plays an important role in the formation of attitudes of others. Successful clothing or wearabouts effective in adding additional attractions to our personality is also to influence our emotion because "looking good" throws a cascade impact on "feeling good" which provides a bigger boost to our energy level. Karen Dixon's observation appears to be right. The clothing further is also to influence our behaviour. Ultimately, you are paid for the investments you have made in your dresses. You should also remember that an indifferent professional image focuses on your indifferent attitudes and your clients may not respond in a positive way. If you are consistent in projecting your professional image which is well-defined in the face of organisational culture, it is to bring a radical change in your professional excellence because you are in a position to influence your clients.

In an age of globalisation, we cannot welcome variations in the market conditions. Of course, we find a change in the local conditions but a situation like dress culture shock is to be regulated. We need to strengthen our realisation that employees are an extension of the corporate brand and therefore even if we witness a change the corporate brand is to be expressed uniformly. Universal representation with the same brand and image is significant irrespective of the fact that we find a change from country-to-country or from state-to-state or even from town-to-town.

The aforesaid deliberations make it clear that clothing is closely associated with our behaviour. Powerful-looking employees have a high level of efficiency. Hence, the corporate men and women cannot undermine the dress code and dress culture. First impression based on non-verbal communication have positive as well as the negative effect. It is upon you to be serious and sincere to our wearabouts and manage your wardrobes in such a fashion that your clients perceive everything positive about your behaviour. Let the inner qualities come out. Let the apparels speak something positive abut you. Let the accessories and make-up change or transform your facial appearance. Let the grooming inject new attractions to your personality.

◈ The Management of Wardrobe for Professionals

Of course, we cannot negate that merit is still the king but at the same time it is also right to say that the very foundation of corporate sector rests on attractions in ambience and creativity in appearance. All of us want to be hireable and promotable and in the corporate world, the task appears to be difficult when we become insensitive to our wearabouts. Your looks can boost up or hinder your professional growth. We find appearance a differentiator equally effective for both the genders. Human beings by nature prefer to view beauty. By adding additional attractions to our facial appearance, we bring perfection in nature's creation. This makes it essential that we assign due weightage to the management of our wardrobes failing which the task of climbing the corporate ladder would be much more difficult. Be smart, get hired and in keeping you smart, the wardrobe plays a very effective role.

A majority of the corporate leaders feel that what we wear is a big factor in our professional growth. Better wardrobe, more success. Our insensitivity to wearabouts may deprive us of getting the desired position. This makes it essential that we develop our awareness of the crying requirements of corporate world and make place for attractive and quality business or office clothes in our wardrobes. The stock of wearing apparel to be placed in our wardrobes must be in tune with the changing corporate preferences. The design, style, colour, fibre and texture need due attention for the projection of a decent look. We need to play by the rules and to honour the elegance. To make an invasion on the disaster areas, we need right identification for both the genders.

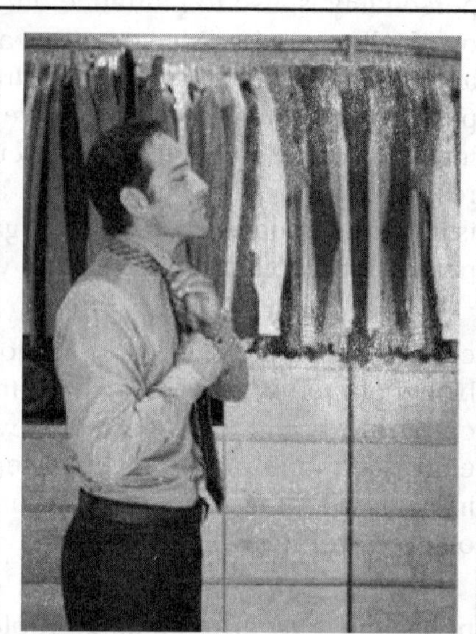

Better wardrobe more success

An elegant wardrobe adds additional attractions to your personality. Too, matchy-matchy cannot be helpful in having a win-win situation. Workwear requires to be redefined and refashioned in the face of changing corporate culture. Climbing the corporate ladder is our motto and in the process wearabouts cannot be underrated. While managing looks, it is imperative that we look presentable, clean and well groomed at our workplace. Our workwear should have a match with our personality because we dress for success. In a true sense, we need attitudinal transformation in an age of globalisation and to bid a goodbye to this perception that thematical competence is the only parameter to rate the scale of our success. Looks must be appropriate for the workplace and we need to wear the dresses in tune with the professional requirements. Gone are the days when we perceived that many colours cannot be worn to office. Today, we feel that our working clothes can be colourful but not too loud for the office. We find flat shoes to complement our professional appearance. Jeans, T-shirts, a soft-soled shoes cannot be included in the list of workwear. Know about your business apparel and mind your profession, designation, seniority and corporate culture. Don or put on appropriate workwear and do not look folly. Wearing wrinkled shirt and suit at the workplace in particular would draw unwanted attention of people and you are not supposed to be insincere and careless while maintaining and arranging them in your wardrobes. You need to make it sure that your business apparel help you in looking well groomed and crisp. Of course, the dress code of your office determines the workwear to be placed in your wardrobes. You must remember it that your office attire speaks a lot on your behalf. We are not supposed to commit any mistake while managing our wardrobes because whether you want to impress your boss or to have an interview or to conduct a big meeting at work; your workwear is one of the keys to get success in the business world.

The management of wardrobe makes it clear that requirements of office need top priority. We consider shirts as the staple of the wardrobe. White coloured shirts or light coloured shirts are the best option. Pinstripe shirts are also good option. We can also include a few sports shirts in our wardrobe for casual events. Even if wearing of suit is not mandatory in your office; make place for a few of them so that you need to keep yourself ready for any special event. Classic single breasted two button styles are the best options. Blazers are the perfect outfits to get place in your wardrobe. When you do not feel like wearing suits, the blazers may be preferred. You need to keep a stock of dark coloured pants and khakis. While managing for winter, sweater vests and pullover need to be stocked in the wardrobe. In this context, it is also to be ensured that your workwear should not be flamboyant and loud because the office decorums do not allow a condition which makes an invasion on your looks.

If you are invited to a corporate party, your preferences of wearabouts need due attention. In some of the cases, you are supposed to wear a tuxedo which is a man's dinner jacket. The first choice of colour in this context for men is black and white but here it is essential that it is tailored to give you a perfect fit. Besides, the charcoal grey and black may also be the colour palettes to be tested. You should not undermine the role of tie in projecting a positive image to be considered perfect for your personality.

With the increasing participation of women in the corporate sector, it is pertinent that we also focus on the wearabouts exclusively for them. A black coloured blouse and a black pencil skirt can make women trendy but, of course, appropriate for office. Like men, it is also essential for women that they mind their designation, position and profession. Projection of a professional image is essential. If they go to the corporate party, they need to stick to the black-coloured dress. Women need more precautions while making use of accessories. Of course, it is a problem not getting an easy resolution that how much jewellery is really too much in the face of your professional image. However, try silver or platinum accessories with your black dress or you may also wear a nice belt.

Dressing up for the party is found problematic both for men and women. Particularly corporate or office parties need your priority attention. Selection of appropriate attire for formal parties would not make an invasion on your professional look. You have to prefer a suit, if you have to attend the office. If you are going to interact with your clients and more so are representing your organisation as a senior level, your looks cannot be casual.

The most important thing that we need to care is the dress culture of an organisation which you are supposed to adopt. At each and every stage, you are required to receive them in the right perspective. This will help you in getting hired and protect you while getting fired.

"Working Girl" movie tells the story of how a girl from the "wrong side of the tracks" succeeds in this over-pressed business world. The movie teaches us about the power of first impressions. Melanie Griffith, an important character knows that she must remake her New Jersey image for her acceptance as a Manhattan professional. She practises and brings a change in her wardrobe, hairstyle and even her voice. By giving a new look just by making some simple adjustments in her outer image, she was given an opportunity to reveal her inner qualities. She was instantly welcomed into the high stakes world of merger and acquisitions. She was convinced that the first task before her is to look the part. We cannot negate the instrumentality of packaging whether we are considering a house, a product or a person. In the present world, we find cover of a book, the looks of an individual and the architectural flavour of a house playing an important role in the formation of impression. We think that what looks attractive or reliable from the outside must surely be on the inside. It is the first impression that determines our success. We find face value an important consideration while hiring people and it is in this context that we raise a strong advocacy in favour of managing our face value. Your wardrobe, hairstyle, smile and posture are found important. Working girls or working boys; both are found in the same boat. Of course, your economic and educational levels, your social position, your level of sophistication and success, your aesthetic sense are found based on your packaged face value. The other considerations such as trustworthiness, compassion, reliability, intelligence, capability, humility, friendliness and confidence provide to you an opportunity to communicate and therefore now is the term of your voice for presentation. The success of "Griffith" as a Manhattan professional was due mainly to the face value. "Manhattan" an island near the mouth of the "Hudson River" forms a borough of the city of New York. An administrative division of the New York city has a different culture and for Griffith it was significant that she provides to her face value a special touch in tune with the culture inherited by the organisation. She practised and got a success.

The old proverb we need to practise even in the modern business world; "first impression is the last impression." In a majority of the cases, we find our perceptions regarding first impressions correct. The repetition of sub-conscious judgements make place for trusting and believing in our instincts. It is also due to the fact that we do not like to admit that we had committed mistakes in the identification process and therefore we cling to our opinions in lieu of making a modification. Thus in the present corporate world, we have no option but to package our facial appearance in such a fashion that subconscious remarks are in our favour. When you succeed there, your task at the later stage is made easier.

We live in an age of Investment dressing

We cannot negate that by packaging our face value in the required fashion, we respect those persons who are interviewing or those organisations where we are working. And it is quite natural that we get reward for the same. Appearance is considered to be the first reason or even number one reason for our rejection or not getting hired. It is due to the fact that we need to have a command over it. We can make it in tune with our requirements and if we are not doing it, this shows our insincerity to the details. Actually, we find some others making it possible and creating an opportunity for hiring, successful in differentiating and responsible for our rejection.

New York University surveyed 152 companies and asked them to question "What are some of the reasons you do not hire people?" They came up with 48 reasons. The No. 1 reason why people are not hired is because of how they present themselves at the interview. A majority of us or at least a good number of corporate executives feel that clothing is also an inner cue affecting our self-image. Feeling good about our facial appearance injects new strength and life to our personal presence. Emotional high of a successful clothing is a real fact that we cannot deny because we find a significant increase in our energy level which boosts up our confidence level. Dressing up in a professional stylish manner can give us a tremendous feeling of confidence that is exhibited to others through our attitudes and actions. In this context, we also need to view other side of the coin. The persons interviewing us or organisations for whom we are working develop a feeling that when his/her sincerity is not to his/her own personal appearance; how we can expect their involvement in the organisational activities. Willingly or unwillingly, all of us accept that even without a single exception we are tempted to look beautiful things. Here it is also right to say that developing disinterests in our facial appearance is a sign of pessimism and a vital reason for the development of negative attitude and behaviour which an organisation cannot like.

We cannot deny the relationships between clothing and behaviour. Jackson Lewis, a law firm that specialises in personal issues, polled more than 1000 human resource, executives who had implemented a dress-down policy. They reported a 30 per cent increase in flirtatious behaviour, contributing to an increase in sexual harassment lawsuits. When we wear more powerful looking clothing such as professional business attire, a suit, darker colours and clothing that is appropriate for our professional requirements, we find a direct impact on our mindset which switches us from "relaxed mode" to "professional mode". This impacts our body language and behaviour e.g., better posture, firmer handshake, maintaining eye contact, sticking to business, etc., and providing us a greater visual power. In a true sense, we find responses of people in the face of dresses that we wear. This is due to the fact that people viewing us take a liberty of interpreting what we are communicating through our dresses. We need to dress for the position that we want. Dressing professionally, no doubt, helps us in climbing the corporate ladders. Both the genders need to strengthen their submission that by underrating facial appearance, they will suffer. Since they need to develop their facial appearance in the face of professional requirements, they have no option but to be sincere to almost all the dimensions which would make them hireable and promotable.

The most important thing in the very context we need to go through is to develop our awareness of organisational culture related to the wearabouts. The local corporate culture and the global corporate culture, of course, may have variations but one thing is not to be forgotten that global cutting-edge organisations perceive all too well that employees are an extension of their corporate brand and therefore irrespective of the fact that branches are located at a small place and town, the corporate brand is to be expressed uniformly throughout the world. This would promote team spirit and make ways for team culture and much more consistency would be found in the corporate image to be instrumental in the projection of corporate standards and culture to its clients. The crux of the problem is that we need to develop our potentials of bridging the gap between employee-image and corporate-image which is found imperative not only locally but albeit globally. There are some of the precautions which need our priority attention while managing our wearabouts.

- **Identify the levels of expectations:** You need to dress appropriately commensurate with the levels of expectations of your organisations where you propose to go or where you work. Dressing alluringly or attractive or temptive must fit to your profession and situation. Corporate culture and team culture are the considerations which you need to perceive in a right fashion. Whatsoever your organisations expects from you, it is to be fulfilled. You are not supposed to look provocative and at the same time you need to look creative.
- **There must be consistency:** You need to be consistent while managing your wearabouts. When you prefer appropriateness, it is pertinent that it is maintained. You are not supposed to transmit mixed messages regarding your wearabouts. The way you silently present yourself must be consistent with the professionals goals as well as the expectations of audience.

- **You need to dress up with special attention to Colour:** It is an authenticated fact that colour is a powerful communicator which has emotional as well as psychological effects on both the wearer and observer. The colour magnifies our behaviour, perception and responses. Hence, we need to make us of colour to project and promote our interests.
- **Mind your body type:** You need to be selective and in this context, it is to be made sure that your body shape is given due weightage. This makes it essential that you are aware of your body type and make a fit for your shape. Look should not be disheveled and this makes it essential that we do not wear too long or too small dresses.
- **Select the affordable quality:** You need to make your wardrobe of quality not of quantity. Itchy fabric and poor fit need to be removed from your wardrobe. The quality outfits have a longer life and this works out cheaper in the long run.
- **Dress with Finesse:** Impeccable grooming habits need to be cultivated. We should not forget that little is more off-putting than body and food odours, greasy hair, over make-up torn socks, etc. We need to care all the components which help us in making the big picture and developing a packaged look or facial appearance.
- **Make your appearance professional:** You should not forget to make your facial appearance professional. You are supposed to play a client-oriented role. It is quite natural that your clients prefer to look in your appearance a professional touch.
- **Move with time:** Time cycle necessitates a change. Do not forget that you live in the 21st century. Do not forget that you live in an age where corporate culture is dominating. Looking old-fashioned cannot help you. Up-to-date wardrobe is a crying need of the hour. Loud points need a departure from your wardrobe. Live in present which would benefit you in many ways.
- **Your dress for the Role that you play:** Where you are and where you want to go. David Watson, 39 Vice-President, Train Right Solutions opines, 'I live by this motto when it comes to professional dress. You dress for where you want to be, not where you are. If you want to be a corporate executive, it is quite natural that you dress like an executive. By developing your facial appearance, you feel a part of the organisation where you have to go and this provides an additional strength to your personality and you are successful in playing the defined role.
- **Attitudinal Transformation is essential:** Bid a goodbye to the past and adopt the present. The wardrobe which you had during your early period of education cannot be continued. Since you prefer to join the corporate world, it is imperative that you change your attitudes and provide to your wardrobe a corporate look. You need a training in this context which would provide to you a new strength and a new level of energy. Because you are sincere and serious, others expect to receive you in the same fashion.

The above mentioned facts may be productive to enrich your facial appearance. Once again, you need to inject additional strength to this proposition that first impression is the last impression. Dress for Success; Dress for increasing the confidence level; Dress for developing optimism; Dress for getting the benefits; Dress for becoming the differentiator are some of the considerations necessitating your attention. If you show respect to your facial appearance; others cannot discourage you. It is not only significant that you are amongst the finalists. It is much more impact generating that you have finally been selected. Transforming potentials into actuals requires a microscopic audit. You may not mind that your rejection was due to the fact that your shoes were scuffed up. You are not serious to the marking of scuffs on your shoes. Your competitor was very much sincere to even small aspects and therefore, he was selected. They feel that when you do not have a control on your shoes; how can you ensure attention to details.

Dress for Success

A majority of us believe that corporate outfits portray personality and position of a person. The clothes that we wear reflect our smartness vis-à-vis the quality of our choice. If we are well dressed, we respect the organisations where we work or serve. Corporate outfits also speak of our dressing sense and success story. This also helps us in attracting our clients and customers. Quality clothes give to the employees a sense of pride and belonging. Hence, it is pertinent that we view everything in detail and practise them with a professional touch to have a professional look. Business attire is not meant the boring attire. We need to make them result-oriented. We get respect for our clothes and do not find even a single case when in a civilised society, the naked people get respect.

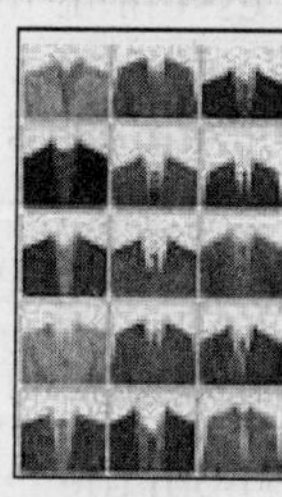

The management of wardrobe thus requires an in-depth study of different aspects. Define the benefit areas and adopt them. Identify the disaster areas and remove them. We need to make a mix of styles for formal business informal business and casual wear. If we talk about the formal business attire, a clean pressed suit is the best way to go. Tie with white, blue, a light brown colour (beige) or other light coloured shirt that compliments the suit. Wear black or brown shoes and dark socks. When you have to take a decision regarding the informal business attire, a spot coat with coordinated slacks is the first choice and slacks with shirt and tie are the next choice. In respect of casual wear, the clean pressed khakis are recommended. Avoid wearing jeans. A shirt with a collar, complimentary shoes are recommended. Avoid wearing sports shoes.

You need following guidelines for clothing, accessories and corporate grooming. Mind, what to do and what not to do.

Clothing: Don clean and ironed clothes. Keep your pockets empty. Do not keep in your pockets bulging keys and tinkling change. Do not wear loud, bright colours such as greens, reds or purples. Do not wear jeans or shirts. Do not wear sports clothes. Do wear buttoned shirts. Do wear a tie if possible but make it sure that it is knotted firmly. Prefer fabrics found to be skin-friendly. A clean and well pressed suit, white tie or blue coloured tie is the best way to go.

Accessories: Wear clean and polished shoes. Do not wear baseball caps or sunglasses. Do not wear chains or unpolished shoes. Do not caps or sunglasses. Do not wear athletic or sleep shoes. Do not wear chains or necklaces. Do not wear sandals.

Corporate Grooming: Keep your hair clean and neatly styled. Use deodorant. Make it sure that your fingernails are clean and properly trimmed. Do not smoke, chew gum or tobacco. Shave your facial hair. If you are beard, it should be neatly trimmed. Moustaches should also be properly trimmed. Maintain good oral hygiene such as brush twice a day and rinse mouth well. Change your socks everyday. Use powder on the feet to avoid smell. Keep your hands neat and clean.

A majority of us believe that corporate outfits portray personality and position of a person. This makes it essential that we are sincere to our wearabouts or the business attire. The clothes that we wear reflect our smartness vis-à-vis the quality of our choice. If a person is well-dressed he/she earns respect from other people. Corporate outfits also speak of our dressing sense and success story. This also helps us in attracting the clients or customers. Corporate clothes help uplift the business to earn fame in the market. Quality clothes give to the employees a sense of pride and belonging. Make your looks more proficient and elegant. It is pertinent that we view everything in detail and practise them with a professional touch. It is to be perceived in a right fashion that the business attire is not meant boring attire. This makes it essential that we build our wardrobes with a little black dress, a look that we can easily take from day-to-evening and a black or a navy blue blazer with a matching shirt and pants. With this basic wardrobe, we can mix and match our tops and bottoms and further accessorise with jewellery and shoes. We get respect for our clothes and never find even a single case when naked people get respect.

The management of wardrobe thus requires an in depth study of different aspects. Define the benefit areas and adopt them. Identify the disaster areas and remove them. Accessories belong to both the groups. When accessories are blended with your professional requirements and organisational culture; you are considerably benefited. Conversely, when accessories prove to be the problem or disaster areas, you are punished for that. The shoes, pens, jewelleries or ornaments, socks if not managed and cared properly prove to be the disaster areas. A pair of shoes can either complement our look or may also kill it.

Particularly the management of wardrobe and personal care for men draw our attention on the following:

- Wear clean and ironed clothes.
- Wear clean, conservative and polished shoes.
- Wear clean and nicely styled hair.
- Wear buttoned shirts, not show your chest.

- Avoid wearing loud, bright colour such as green, red and purples.
- Do not wear ripped Jeans and T-shirts.
- Do not wear sport clothes and clothing with large designer labels.
- Wear a tie and make it sure that it is firmly knotted.
- Do not wear sandals.
- Do not wear chains or necklaces.
- Do use deodorant.
- Make it sure that your finger nails are clean and properly trimmed.
- Shave your facial hair and if you wear a beard and moustaches, trim them properly.
- Maintain good oral hygiene and avoid smoking.
- Use little powder on the feet to avoid smells.
- Change your socks everyday.
- Do not wear sunglass or baseball caps.
- Avoid keeping bulging keys and tinkling change in your pockets.
- Wear traditional fabrics and ensure skin-friendly fiber.

◈ The Wardrobe for Working Women

With the increasing heat of globalisation, we find a significant increase in the number of working women in almost all the areas. This makes it essential that we exclusively focus on the management of wardrobe for them. Gone are the days when they half-heartedly perceived the role of facial appearance. Today, they have no option but to be sincere and serious while managing their wearabouts. Actually, we cannot think of ignoring attractiveness in a culture that pays a premium on appearance. For women at work, appearance is concerned with issues about looking appropriate, looking the part. Dressing for evening is found to be a fun activity whereas dressing for work is a chore. But in the present business world, the working women are not supposed to take it as a boring task.

During the yesteryears, we find women emerging as a successful executive and evincing much more interest in the corporate culture. The work culture has become increasingly fluid and informal and this has made it essential that women prefer softer dressing. In many workplaces, cardigans stand in place of jackets, T-shirts or sweaters in place of shirts. Dressing provocatively is now not preferred. A woman wearing a sober coloured suit is categorised immediately as career-oriented, serious and ambitious.

The wearabouts for working women, of course, become a critical issue and therefore once again, we need to perceive the organisational culture. Like men, the women are also required to show respect to the dress code and corporate culture. An in depth knowledge of business wear or office wear is considered significant. It is to be made sure that workwear is not flamboyant and loud which is considered against the decorum of the office wear. If you are invited to a formal corporate, you may stick to the black dress. If you have a great figure, you can afford to wear the little black dress in your wardrobe but here it is also significant that you mind your necklines as well as hemlines. Messing with the professional image cannot be allowed even in the office party.

A majority of the women commit mistakes while making choice regarding the accessories. How much jewellery is really too much is a subjective concept. Silver or platinum accessories may be preferred with black dress or you can also wear a nice belt. It is pertinent that you are also aware of the disaster areas and in many cases we find jewelleries and shadis becoming a problem area. Dressing up for the corporate or office party is significant both for men and women. A perfectly worn business suit can make you appear trendy and fashionable. Of late, we find corporate women doing experiments with the business suit to make themselves trendy in a different way. Looking up-do-date and very fashionable cannot be promoted unless it is a part of the organisational culture. Creating a good impression is the motto. Experimenting with business suit does not mean that you only focus on the suits and ignore your skirts, trousers, shoes, make-ups and accessories.

Your business apparel must be well pressed, neat and clean. Creation of a good impression is your motto but in this context, it is also pertinent that you have awareness of the possibilities of sexual harassment at the workplace which has gained a rapid momentum in the present corporate world. We cannot negate that provocative dresses mount to sexual harassment, complaints vis-à-vis erosion of corporate image. Inviting costly lawsuits cannot be encouraged due mainly to the increasing cases of sexual harassment. Since we find a significant increase in the number of working women, it is imperative that sexual harassment policies and training need due attention of corporate policy makers. The working employees are required to be given knowledge of inappropriate behaviour and dresses to be preferred.

Do more with less will make your wardrobe economic but proactive. Wardrobe refashioning in the face of organisational and professional requirements is essential for the making of an elegant wardrobe. Mixing and matching of clothes need your due attention in the very context. A careful selection of clothes is essential. The selection of clothes of solid colours may be preferred because you get the outfit combinations. The best basic colours are black, white, ivory, beige, champagne and navy. The repetition of solid colours is much better than the patterned colours. In the process of mixing or matching, you have to avoid matchy-matchy. It is not significant that how many dresses you have in the wardrobe. It is much more relevant that you have made a sound mix to bring elegance in your personality.

Particularly working women need to consider certain pairs of things to go very elegantly together. Match your umbrella to your trench coat. Have a full set of matching luggage and matching toiletry bags. Match your luggage to your outfit and wear complete lingerie sets. Match your outfit to the occasion. Mind the difference between formal and informal. Make use of your sense that your wearabouts for office and event and party cannot be identical. Do not look provocative. Do not wear provocative. Wear dresses found instrumental in bringing elegance. Wear dresses effective in projecting positive image of your organisation. Wear dresses bringing optimism in your facial appearance. Mixing and matching elegantly help you in this direction. In any case, your look should not be casual.

Creating a style statement of your own is significant. All you need to be is presentable, clean and well groomed at your workplace. You need to dress for success. You need to ensure that your wearabouts match your personality. You carry the image of your company. By making possible minor adjustments in your outer image, it becomes easier for you to reveal your inner qualities. The psychologists, communication experts and image consultants make a strong advocacy in favour of the fact that first impressions become the last impressions. Professional achievements, family background and educational credentials and thematical competence of an individual, no doubt, count but his/her facial appearance significantly dominates.

The leaders play a positive role in the image building process. The corporate professionals may act both as a motivational and demotivational force. When professionals set examples, the followers are motivated and move forward in the right direction. Conversely, if they do something wrong, the followers become not only angry but in addition also repeat the mistakes committed by their leaders. It is to be ensured that in no case, the employees have been tarnishing the corporate image. The managers bear the responsibility of setting the direction.

- **Strengthen Global Training Programme:** With the increasing heat of globalisation, we find emergence of a cross-cultural society. The MNCs have been found defining and redefining the cultural and behavioural patterns. This makes it essential that upcoming or budding generations evincing interests in corporate culture develop their awareness of the basics. The customers and clients have a number of expectations from the employees. In terms of expected behaviour and corporate image; we do not find any boundary. Hence, it is imperative that organisations schedule a training programme for the employees in the face of recent global developments. The threshold barriers that we find existent in a large number of people are, of course, rich in inner qualities but very poor in terms of facial appearance may be removed only through an advance global training programme.
- **Special instructions for business meeting:** The business meeting of an organisation requires due focus on its culture. If organisations remain silent and do not provide any instruction to the different categories of employees; we find possibilities of deviation and violation of codes. Hence, what specific dress would be allowed for business, meeting by the different categories of employees responsible for event management, presentation need clarification well supported by written instructions.

Developing awareness requires priority attention of organisations particularly in the Indian condition where we find people insensitive to the emerging corporate culture. The Business Schools need to sense and sensitise their students so that they evince their interests in developing facial appearance and enriching professional excellence. In a true sense, the corporate culture is found sizably influenced by aesthetic sense, etiquette and manners. The organisations, of late, are found sincere to the outfits. The role played by the finishing schools requires to be promoted by the Business Schools. The expectations of organisations from the employees would increase further. They want that their employees perceive and practise even minor things with high level of seriousness. If they are not sincere to their own outfits; it is but natural that they cultivate the habits of viewing even big things very casually. Hence, the organisations, specially in the Indian perspective need to sense and sensitise their employees in the face of expectations they nurture from them. The philosophy entailed behind exposing outfits is to inculcate habits of taking things in totality.

The domination is well supported by the fact that they are efficacious of differentiating themselves. They are in a position to create an impression by the corporate apparel they wear. Check on what your senior female colleagues wear if you are confused about the right dress code. You can also check websites for help. You may discuss with your friend regarding the recently introduced dress code. The focus is on updating your knowledge about the corporate apparels.

It is not essential that your wardrobe is expensive. It is much more impact generating that it has a fair mix; such as mix of designer pieces and stellar pieces. A nice classy white blouse with a tailor made black pant may do wonders but do not wear them regularly.

Some feminine dresses like sweater dress or a classic business suit and a formal skirt may also be a choice. You should prefer to go for the tested dresses. While making use of accessories, you may go for formal boots, leather belts but to the extent it is possible you should avoid junk jewelleries.

You cannot underrate the significance of shoes as corporate outfits. High heels are really great but you need to make it sure that your shoes are comfortable for the whole working day. In this context, it is also imperative to consider that if you are not used to high heels, this may complicate your task if you fall from the stairs. In a true sense, you need the aura of corporate person, and therefore choose the foot-wear commensurate with your corporate apparel. Shoes must be safe, practical and stylish.

◈ Saree as Corporate Wear

Corporate culture is considerably influenced by the western culture and therefore it is quite natural that corporate wardrobe or corporate wear less think about the dresses of east specially as business or office wear. It is against this backdrop that we find saree considered as disaster area and corporate culture is yet to make place for it. Actually, we should not be critical to the dresses magnifying the cultural identity of a country or region. The corporate boardrooms specially in the Indian perspective need to accommodate the dresses which have potentials to show elegance. It is in this context, we advocate in favour of saree as corporate wear. Both for office and party wear, the corporate women should not be deprived of wearing saree which has a distinct look. If we make use of the Indian markets and are well supported by the Indian customers; the development of bias to the Indian dresses cannot be pragmatic. The corporate boardrooms while formulating policies regarding the dress code need to make ways for those dresses which are not found to be provocative and saree has the potential to look cultured, cool and sincere. Hence not only as casual wear but even as business or office wear, saree may show wonders. There are a number of cases to authenticate the instrumentality of saree because some of the successful women entrepreneurs wearing saree have made it clear that corporate boardrooms need to review their dress code.

The inspirational women of business overcoming great odds and thriving as a beacon are examples to be quoted and followed while making deliberations regarding the suitable business apparels in tune with the national and cultural requirements in the Indian perspective. We have younger western wears and the matured Indian options. Of course, the corporate culture finds it, difficult to make a compromise with the organisational culture which cannot be different in the different national and cultural perspectives; however we need to identify the outstanding properties of a particular culture and further to explore the possibilities of their options to get a positive result. We have a number of examples of Indian women prospering as CEOs and at the same time wearing Sarees which considerably help them in the exposition and projection of their profile as an internationally acclaimed corporate professional. It is quite natural that we find diversity in their viewpoints but here it is also true that sarees have been found their number one option which make their personality distinct to others. Shifting from one image to another or morphing cannot be respected specially to get the competitive benefits. Globally known corporate beacon, dazzling like a fire, lit on the top of the corporate mountain such as Naina Lal Kidwai, Chanda Kochhar, Meera Sanyal, Madhabi Puri Buch and Shikha Sharma feel that the traditional pinstripe bankers' suit may have morphed into silk sarees in India but we also find other favouring more diverse dressing style. The seniors among them like Assocham Chief Swati Piramal, Director of Piramal Healthcare are found resplendent or bright and colourful in an impressive way whereas the brigade of juniors feel that they are more comfy or comfortable in western wear during the business hours at least. Hence, before coming to a conclusion, it is pertinent that we go through the lifestyles and opinions of some of the corporate tycoons.

CHANDA KOCHHAR,

42, Executive Director
ICICI Bank

Kochhar has the credibility of building a strong 8,000 team of dedicated people and she has enabled ICICI Bank to become a large player in the market. The secret of her versatility is the right mix of strategy formulation and implementation. An Executive Director of ICICI Bank since 2001 has extended that fine sense of balance to her personal life. She has managed to find enough time for her children. Actually, what she has been doing in Bank has been conceptualising even in her family that is a good support system.

Her feelings, about the silk sarees are found positive where she favours shifting from traditional pinstripe bankers' suit to the Silk sarees image. Really, she has proved to be an ambassador for Indian culture because she prefers to wear a heritage saree to the public seminars.

NAINA LAL KIDWAI

46. Vice-chairman & Managing Director,
HSBC
Securities & Capital Markets

NAINA LAL KIDWAI
46, Vice-chairman & Managing Director, HSBC Securities & Capital Markets

She happens to be the first Indian lady to have graduated from the Harvard Business School in 1982. Repeatedly featuring in Fortune's listing of powerful women amongst a handful of Indian professional managers. Kidwai is considered an iron lady. No doubt, the world of investment banking has sizably been dominated by male but we never find Kidwai fazed by the men around her. She has been at the forefront of a number of high profile deals. India's most high profile professional Investment Banker, Kidwai has been a team player and she also nurtures interests in Indian classical music and wildlife tours. A hard worker iron lady, Kidwai believes in defining professional excellence.

Fortunately, Kidwai also prefers to wear Saree.

SHIKHA SHARMA

**44, Managing Director & CEO,
ICICI Prudential Life Insurance**

Shikha Sharma stands out as a start-up specialist. When ICICI was looking for someone to head its insurance joint venture, Sharma was singled out for the job. The IIM Ahmedabad alum, has always been found honing her entrepreneurial excellence at ICICI Securities and ICICI Personal Financial Services. She has start-up hunger and based on her entrepreneurial excellence we find Shikha Sharma very successful in boosting a 33% share of the private insurance market. She believes in defining vision and works towards it.

**SHIKHA SHARMA
44, Managing Director & CEO, ICICI Prudential Life Insurance**

Shikha Sharma has also been found tempted to wearing sarees. Her preference to elegant sarees, acting as brand ambassador for Indian attire, fascination for Indian culture make a strong case for promoting sarees in the list of corporate attire.

VIDYA CHHABRIA

**54, Chairperson,
Jumbo Group**

Comprising 28 companies, 20,000 employees spread over 25 countries and businessing consumer electronics, liquor and machinery, Vidya Chhabria is the chairperson of $2-billion enterprise. Circumstantially, a corporate wife started working as a chairperson and proved her excellence by defining policy and empowering her managers for implementation. After passing away Manu Chhabria, she had no option but to involve herself in the hot seat of the group which has $600-million worth of assets in India including companies like Shaw Wallace and Mather & P & Platt. Working out of Dubai, she presides over the Jumbo Group Corporate Management Board which is responsible for outlining group strategy and vision. Human resources happen to be her top priority and therefore we also call Mercer, the world's largest HR consulting house to chart out an HR roadmap for group flagship Shaw Wallace.

**VIDYA CHHABRIA
54, Chairperson, Jumbo Group**

Recollecting memories of her housewife days, she feels pleasure is spending time with her daughters when we find her in free time.

It is worth mentioning that Vidya Chhabria also promotes Indian attire.

ARNAVAZ 'ANU' AGA

61, Chairperson,
Thermax

ARNAVAZ 'ANU' AGA
61, Chairperson,
Thermax

Anu Aga as a Chairperson of the Pune-based Thermax has the credibility of visualising her profile as Ms. Conscience. She has been found promoting humanity and serving society and promoting personal philanthropy. She has the capability of making hard-nosed business decision. Anu Aga remarks that professionally the most difficult thing I have had to do is to ask people to leave. This magnifies her humanised leadership quality which considerably helped her in resolving even the major problems.

Anu Aga also has been an ambassador of Indian attire.

RANJANA KUMAR

57, Chairman and Managing Director,
Indian Bank

RANJANA KUMAR
57, Chairman and Managing Director,
Indian Bank

A career banker, Ranjana Kumar was educated all over the country because her father was in the Airforce. Like all good leaders, we find Ranjana Kumar making it all sound to simple. Kumar believes that the large workforce of public sector banks is an additional advantage and therefore if we make a productive use of this workforce, the private sector would be left way behind. We consider Kumar a super banker bearing the potentials of transforming the negative into positive.

Ranjana Kumar has also been an ambassador of Indian attire.

LALITA GUPTE

55, Joint Managing Director,
ICICI Bank

LALITA GUPTE
55, Joint Managing Director, ICICI Bank

Powerful women have shown their powers in the ICICI Bank. The credibility for this goes to the Chairman N. Vaghul who desires to create an equal opportunity workplace. ICICI have always been great places to work for women. Lalita Gupte is considered as a poster-girl of this revolution. She joined ICICI in 1971 straight from Jamna Lal Bajaj Institute of Management Studies. Twenty-three years later, she became the first lady to sit on its board. In 1999, she was made Joint Managing Director and COO. Today Gupte heads the international business group. For her ability of creating leaders, Gupte is found respected within the bank.

Gupte has also love for Indian attire.

SHOBHANA BHARATIA

46, Vice-chairperson & Editorial Director, The Hindustan Times Ltd.

SHOBHANA BHARTIA 46, Vice-chairperson & Editorial Director, The Hindustan Times Ltd.

We consider Bharatia as a headline maker. Bharatia is daughter of Chairman K.K. Birla and of course this helped her in getting her first break but she has proved her excellence in transforming Hindustan Times. Bharatia believes in delegating responsibility to professional editors and managers but prefers to oversee everything. All due to her efforts that it is more than work, it is a passion. She has love for the Indian attire.

We have gone through the profile of some of the leading Women of India who served the corporate sector and promoted corporate culture but at the same time also nurtured positive feelings about the Indian attire. The banking brigade's preferences for elegant "sarees" have made them ambassadors for Indian attire. From ICICI Bank MD & CEO Chanda Kochar and HSBC India CEO, Naini Lal Kidwai to ICICI Prudential Life Insurance MD & CEO, Shikha Sharma, we find them working as brand ambassadors for India attire. That sentiment is also shared by the Svelte Vandana Luthra, founder and mentor of the VLCC Group as she opines that I like to wear Indian outfits for conferences abroad as I am presenting my country to the entire world. I am very fond of the rich variety of textiles and colour in traditional wear. Manisha Girotra, MD and Chairperson of the Swiss Bank UBS is also often seen wearing a saree to all formal occasions. Rita Soni, country head, responsible banking, Yes Bank who was born in the USA says Sarees' elegant colour makes it her preferred choice for formal gatherings.

In view of the aforesaid facts, it is right to mention that sarees cannot and should not be rejected as corporate attire. The prime focus must be on the organisational culture regarding the outfits. The dress code policy of an organisation remains to be the most effective base for decision-making. Projection of a personal image must be on the foundation of organisational image or corporate image. The boardrooms need to make an anatomy of the dress code policy. Of course, we need to follow the best of east and west. For accelerating the pace of development, we need professional mode and the policy makers need to ensure that outfits do not prove to be a barrier. Sulaja Firodia Motwani, Joint MD of Kinetic Engineering opines, "Sarees and Salwar Kameez are graceful but wearing trousers and skirts help her stay in reasonably good shape." She further remarks that as you grow in your position, simpler cuts and more understated colours and subtle jewellery looks much more graceful.

The deliberations cannot be identical because different entrepreneurs with different attitudes perceive positive as well as negative. The prime focus is on the fact that corporate culture while formulating dress policy should not undermine national culture and the attire promoting national image. What to talk of the domestic companies even the Multi National Corporations can market their products in an effective way when they assign due weightage to the regional conditions and respect the sentiments and emotions of people living there. Showing respect to the Indian attire will mean showing respect to the Indian culture which in turn would mean getting respect for the products that we market. The responses of customers are considerably influenced by the relationships developed by an organisation and in the process we find clothings and outfit acting as a link. If we find Sarees well-known for elegance and if we find them much more graceful, the corporate boardrooms should be much more liberal to the dress policy making place for Indian attire.

◈ Tips for Corporate Women Professionals

Wardrobe and oufits for Women need attention on the following:

- You should have enough shirts, blouse, or other tops to get you through the week.
- You can wear cotton or silk blouses and fine-gauge wool, silk or cotton tops.
- A coat dress or sheath that matches a suit jacket provides you a nice change of pace.
- Bathe or shower daily and rinse your face at least two times a day.
- Drink plenty of water to keep your insides clean.
- Wear very little or even no perfume.
- Hands should be clean and smooth.
- Keep your nails clean and properly trimmed.
- Remove underarm and leg hair regularly.
- Nail colour should match clothes or neutral.
- Wear comfortable well-fitting shoes.
- Dry, feet thoroughly and use talcum powder.
- Make possible match of footwear with the handbag.
- Wear closed shoes or sandals or slippers of quality.
- Blend into neck area so that there is no visible link.
- Eye make-up to the natural brow line.
- Avoid shiny and elaborate *bindi*s.
- Wear lipstick to compliment the colour of your outfit.
- Earrings, bangles, rings should be well harmonised with the clothes.
- Avoid very large earrings, and bangles.
- Avoid wearing glass bangles and *bindi*s with western formals.
- Wear a conservative hair style.
- Wash your hair once a week with mild soaps or shampoo.
- If your hair is long tie-up in plait to avoid coming in the way.
- No flowers at any time during working hours.
- Use very little hair oil.
- No-no to perfumed oil.
- You need an individualistic look by accessorising it with classy things.
- Adorn yourself with a black, coffee or chocolate coloured suit with pear earrings and necklace.

- Adorn simple diamond jewellery such a pendant, a ring or a diamond studded watch.
- Scarf is essential to add zing to almost every outfit.
- Black pumps with about 1½ to 3 inches heel prove to be the ideal footwear for your business suit.
- Carry a handbag, a briefcase or a purse of quality.
- Wearing a business suit is almost mandatory and therefore develop your awareness of the ladies' business suits.

◈ Corporate Women Professionals Need/Proper Accessorising

Of late, we find a significant increase in the number of corporate women professionals which has been creating a big market for women business suit. A classy business suit will not only make you feel good but will also reflect your persona. Actually, you need an individualistic look so that you look different from others. This requires proper accessorising. Here, we find some tips specially for corporate women related to hygiene and skin care, hands and feet and make-up. Go through the following minutely and practise them sincerely.

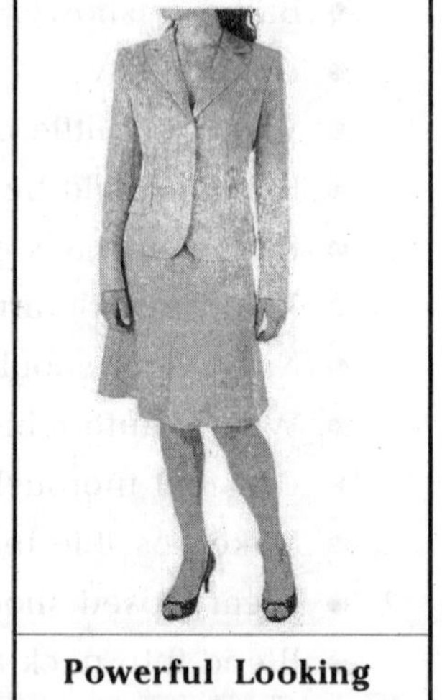

Powerful Looking Clothing

Personal Hygiene and Skin Care: Bathe or shower daily and rinse your face at least two times a day. Brush and gloss daily. Drink plenty of water to keep your insides clean and to keep your skin fresh on the outside. Remove underarm and leg hair regularly. Wear very little or no perfume to have a natural look.

Hands and Feet: Your hands should be clean and smooth. Keep a small bottle of lotion to keep your hands moisturised. Keep your nails clean and trim them properly. Wear comfortable well-fitting shoes. Use talcum powder to prevent dry smells. Match your footwear with the colour of your handbag or with salwar, chudidar or trousers. Wear closed shoes or sandals of quality.

Make-up: Cosmetics help you in highlighting your best features. Match foundation to skin tone for a natural look. You can also use face powder with foundation or alone. Eye make-up applied to the natural brow line is the most attractive. If you do wear eye make-up, match or blend it with your natural colour. Light *kajal* and eyeliner is okay. Avoid elaborate make-up and dark rouge. Avoid shiny and elaborate *bindi*s. Wear lipstick to compliment the colour of your outfit. Use natural shade like light brown or light maroon. Avoid dark or bright colours.

Accessories: Harmonise eye rings, bangles, rings, etc., with the clothes. Avoid very large earrings and bangles making a lot of noise. Avoid wearing glass bangles and *bindi*s with western formals. A pearl necklace is beautiful and of course, all in one. Adorn simple diamond jewellery. We find scarf adding zing to almost every outfit in the wardrobe of women. A brown-black marble stone with a cream suit or a pink or a white suit gives you a classy and confident look to your persona. We also find scope for junk jewellery. If you have some nice, big beads junk neckpiece, do not hesitate to wear it along with your suit in the same colour. Black pumps with about 1½ to 3 inches heel is found to be the ideal footwear for your business suit. Blouses are more prominent than other accessories and so wear right kind of blouses with your suit. You can carry a handbag, or a briefcase or a purse but of quality.

Care your wardrobe

The professional women thus serving the corporate world or interested in serving there need due attention on above mentioned facts which would help them in many ways. Wear ladies' skirt suits or women's trousers and jackets, accessorise them in tune with the requirements of corporate culture. Wear business suits to look distinct, display extra proficiency and have a more matured and elegant look. Women executives need to look different to others.

◈ Select the Right Professional Business Suit

The business suits, of course, have been found gaining popularity and we find sufficient reasons for the same. If of right choice, the business suits display an extra proficiency and an intellectual and elegant look. But here it is significant that you have taken into consideration the following:

- The decisions related to fabrics are significant while ordering for the business suits for women. The fabrics used are gabardine, light weight wool, wool crepe, silk, linen and rayon blend. All seasonal fabrics are used and your choice should be well supported by the seasonal requirements and organisational expectations.
- You need to make it sure that shoulders do not have excessive padding.
- For better show, you may also look for trims and styling lines on the business suits.
- Be sure of the wrinkle factor of the suit material. You can test it by grabbing a part of the suit with one hand and crunching it all up with your fist. In the process, when fabric falls out of your hand, the material is wrinkle prone.
- Jacket should have adequate space for a blouse, vest or a cardigan.
- Make it sure that there are no puckers.
- Check out the lining so that it is not to poke out lower than hemline at the edge of the sleeves or at the bottom suit jacket.
- Ladies' skirt suits and women's trousers and jackets are the options.
- Look for suit jackets found fully lined and pants which are lined to the knee.
- The colour options are black, navy blue and charcoal gray.

The Corporate World Looks for You

◈ Grooming

Your neat and tidy facial appearance carry some meaning in the present corporate world where value addition through attractions needs priority attention. When we talk about grooming, our focus is on ensuring proper preparations through value addition which make people commensurate with the organisational culture. We find grooming one of the distinguishing factors of the successful and a well-kept secret of investment dressers. Investment dressing is a process through which we are educated to pay attention to detail concerned with our facial appearance. A regular look and a flawless look cannot be identical. Grooming encompasses attention to hair, nail, skin and bodycare.

Before leaving the house, we need to stand before the mirror to make it sure that there is nothing wrong with our facial appearance. Look for and remove any stray threads at the hems of trousers, skirts, blouses, etc. It is to be made sure that lingeries or your underwear fit properly and it is not to be so tight that develops a cut mark into your body under clothing. You also need to ensure that your clothes skim the body rather than clinging it. When you wear jackets, ensure that the hem covers your bum. The ill-fitting jackets make look sloppy and uncomfortable. Trousers should be hemmed to fall at the perfect length. Shoes should be cleaned, buffed and polished at both tips and heels. Hair should be neatly cuffed. Do not forget that your hands are the first impression people have of you. Make sure that it is a good one. Nails should be kept clean and well-manicured and pedicured. Avoid use of excess accessories. If you prefer bold jewellery pieces, choose one that makes a statement and prove to be a focal point. Since this is a time for a final touch, you need a minute observation.

Get ready and make sure that your preparations are in the face of today's fashion mantra of business tycoon mavens. We cannot negate that the manner in which we dress speak and carry ourselves are tools which we use to communicate with the outside world. Dr. Albert Mehrabian an internationally acclaimed psychologist significantly contributes to the non-verbal communication. He observes that non-verbal communication has a strong edge over the verbal communication. He remarks that words only count for 7% of all communication and while a whopping 93% is non-verbal. Our ability to put it together through our hair, clothes and grooming habits is an excellent tool of non-verbal communication. A tool which is generally overlooked requires our priority attention if we really groom for success. In a true sense, what we wear speak of our status, taste, lifestyle, personality, attitude and credibility. Our dresses speak volumes about us even we do not utter a single word. This is our investment in dressing for which we are suitably rewarded. Investment dressing is thus meaningful and productive. Invest to have a look of authority, confidence, capability and elegance. How others perceive about your appearance is the real thing for which you have to enrich your knowledge bank.

◈ Investment Dressing

With the increasing domination of fashion mantra in the business world of today, it is but natural that concept and percept of wardrobe management have a new boundary and a new height. We cannot negate that corporate culture injected new life and strength to the non-verbal communication and we were found successful in communicating through our hair, clothes and grooming habits. What we wear in our work environment speaks a lot about our status, taste and lifestyle. Accessorising proves to be an important dimension to make the non-verbal communication much more effective. Perfectly tailored black dress efficacious of skimming your body, accessorised with pearls or a silk scarf and classic leather pumps or light shoes are found significantly changing the perception of corporate looks. It is against this background that we find investment dressing occupying a place of outstanding significance in the corporate world of today. We find a majority of people nurturing a high level of expectations in the concerned areas. They want to create a better impression when they go for job interview; they want to attract the attention of that special someone; they want to excel competition; they want promotion and in all the areas; they are found getting a productive result of investment dressing.

The way in which we dress speak volumes about us without uttering even a single word. We need a look of authority and we find our dresses in a position to project.

Investment dressing is all about learning how to dress well. This injects new life to our facial appearance and we also get a look of confidence, capability and attitude. We cannot perceive it like burning plastic on a shopping spree. In a true sense, it is an investment in ourselves. We are well aware of the cliches about first impression. People believe what they witness. The clients not only receive what you transmit during presentation but in addition, they also minutely observe your appearance, dresses and therefore even your excellent presentation is not found productive unless you ensure grooming through proper accessorising. It is due mainly to the fact that your look is detracting from the brilliance that is coming from your mouth and obstructing the process of reception because you are not taken seriously. The same set of presentation but with a difference in which we find black dress perfectly tailored to skim your body, not cling to it, associated with pearls or a silk scarf and a classic leather pumps or say professionally accessorised and you find your presentation much more productive because each one of us forms impressions sizably based on appearance, if not for all the time at least initially.

The above mentioned facts make it clear that investment dressing has been gaining popularity in the corporate world and in the coming days its speed will increase further because if we invest with the particular motive, make use of the services of experts and our efforts are focussed, we do not find any reason for not getting the desired result. If we expect excellent both in inner and outer qualities. The process seals doors of detraction and excellent presentation with excellent looks get a positive response.

◈ Accessorising

Proper Accessorising is need of the hour

Corporate culture has made ways for women professionals and it is in this context that we find a significant increase in the demand for women business suits. Nobody can doubt and question the impression generating potentials existent in the business suits because a classy business suit will not only make us feel good but in addition will also exhibit a confident reflection of our persona. Acceleration in the value addition process becomes essential to get the maximum benefits and therefore we find business world of today making a strong advocacy in favour of momentising the accessorizing process so that we have an individualistic look magnifying our sense of creativity. Of course, we need to identify the classy things in tune with the organisational culture. We find the following accessories adding much more productive value to the business suits.

- **Pearls:** In this world, we find pearls most appealing and subtle jewels in which we find all in one. It is beautiful, simple and classy making our facial appearance much more attractive. Hence, the corporate women while going for business meeting or while making an important presentation need to adorn a black, coffee or chocolate coloured suit with pearl earrings and necklace. Now you have a professional as well as a feminine look.
- **Diamond:** The corporate world makes a special position for the key word "Class". When you wear business suit while accessorising make it sure that you have adorned simple diamond jewellery such as a small diamond pendant or a diamond ring or a diamond studded wristwatch which would provide to your facial appearance an elegant look.
- **Scarf:** In the wardrobe for women, we find scarf considered as a chic accessory adding zing to their outfit. A classy and confident look is possible when we mix a brown or black marble stole with a cream suit or a pink stole with a white suit.
- **Junk Jewellery:** Of late, we find junk in new stones gaining much more popularity and therefore we find scope for junk jewellery. You can wear big beads junk necklace along with your suit in the same colour. Hence you need to have a nice collection.
- **Black Pumps:** You need an ideal footwear for your business suit and the black pumps may serve your purpose. Make it sure that your option is in favour of a comfortable and class black pumps. It should not cause inconveniences to you while working.
- **Blouses:** Wearing the right kind of blouses with your suit is an essential condition which you cannot undermine. Make place for some glossy and chick blouses in your wardrobe.
- **Handbags:** You need to select which suits your persona and therefore you can make use of a big leather bag, or a briefcase or a purse.

While accessorising, we cannot undermine our professional image. We take care of a number of accessories ranging from our jewellery to our perfume to our notebook or briefcase.

◈ Leveraging Colour

We consider colour a powerful communicative tool which affects us physiologically, psychologically and emotionally. Colour is the first thing that people notice about an outfit

Leverage colour, a powerful communitive tool

because by wearing colours we look and feel fabulous. For leveraging colour, it is not only significant that we know about our preferences but it is much more impact generating that we adopt the colours and shades which match with our personality and profession. In this context, we may seek the cooperation of colour consultant, accredited image consultant or even tailor, dressmakers and stylist. You should not forget that the most important thing in managing colour is monochromatic dressing or say dressing in one colour which produces a strong unbroken line helping you in elongating the body and looking slim. To have a monochromatic look, you may invest in pieces with different textures such as silk, charmeuse adds a hint of feminity and velvet adds a dash of romanticism. It is preferable to add colour to the inside of an outfit where ties, scarves, tops and jewellery, etc., can be used. It is also significant to mention that a bright colour close to the face draws the eye upward and adds interest to an ensemble. The most slimming colour are dark neutrals, black, dark brown, chocolate, espresso, charcoal grey, navy blue. These colours make your looks thinnest. It is a well considered fact that cool colours like blues are calming whereas the warm colours like reds are stimulating. The colour red evokes characteristics such as passionate, impulsive, dynamic while blue is associated with attributes such as traditional, stable and refined.

How do we leverage colour in investment dressing is an important decision-making area. This focuses our attention on incorporating colour into our wardrobe to ensure a positive result.

The corporate professionals are required to attend offices, business meeting as well as formal and informal parties. Here the leveraging of colour is significant to momentise the value-addition process. This draws our attention on essential colours. If you have a limited number of new items of clothing in your wardrobe for the whole year, pick clothes of solid colours which can be repeated much better than the patterned materials. The best basic colours are black, white, ivory, beige, champagne and navy blue. Besides, you can also consider adding a few pastel coloured pieces suitable for daytime wear. Your preferences for solid colours simplify the accessorising process. With minor efforts, you can transform a day-time outfit into evening wear by removing a scarf and adding a long strand or pearls. While mixing and matching, you are supposed to seal doors for too matchy-matchy.

◈ Manage Your Hair for Every Occasion

In the management of looks, we also need due attention on hair. We are supposed to make it sure that our hairstyle fit the dress code of the organisation where we work. It is significant that we opt for a conservative hairstyle which should not draw attention away from our face. In this context, we also need to ensure that our hair is clean and nicely combed. We should avoid applying a lot of gel which may have wet hair look. A comb is to be in your pocket or bag and you may get time in the restroom or toilets for checking your hair. The management of hair is not only concerned with women but albeit with the men.

Keeping your hair clean by administering quality products is significant which may not only help you in looking attractive but may also be helpful in protecting your hair. Occasionally, we may use the services of beauty salon, hair salon, beauty parlour and spas. We should not forget that healthy and glossy hair depend on a wholesome and nutritious diet. Hair is made of protein and therefore our preferences should be diet containing rich protein which would make our hair strong and healthy. For lustrous hair, the minerals are also effective. Vitamin A and B containing rich foods need to be included in our list such as eggs, mango, liver, dark green leafy vegetables, carrots, dried apricots, whole grain cereals, peas which would ensure healthy hair. Zinc and essential fatty acids guard against dandruffs and dry scalp. Foods such as shellfish, pumpkin seeds, nuts and vegetable oils, sardines, mackerel and salmon are good sources of zinc and essential fatty acids. Alfala juice in combination with spinach or coriander if taken daily will help the hair to grow fast. Healthy hair is not only long lasting but in addition, we also find it charming due to shine and therefore haircare with the support of protein is preferable.

Proper management of hair thus makes it essential that both the genders men or women establish a match of their hair with face and organisational culture related to hairstyle. When we talk about the corporate executives, it is significant that they are very particular while giving a stylish but elegant look of their hair. Use of olive oil is also found useful for sparkling hair because it contains essential fatty acids.

Grooming is an important dimension for the right projection of our facial appearance and therefore, it is significant that corporate men or women are particular to the management and maintenance of their hair. They need to keep them neat and clean and to make possible a frequent use of deodorant. Hairstyle should, of course be conservative but attractive. Use of soaps or shampoo to wash hair and to void smells to dry hair cannot be undermined. Particularly for women, it is pertinent that if hair is long, there should be proper tying in plait or pony-tail while working specially to avoid knotting and coming in the way. They should also avoid using flowers at any time during working hours. In addition, they need to use very little hair oil and bid a goodbye to the perfumed oil.

◈ Hair Style for Your Lifestyle

Manage your Hair for Every Occasion

In the corporate world, we find hairstyle occupying a place of outstanding significance just as the corporate wearabouts. For corporate professionals, a medium or shorter length is recommended because this minimises the problem of maintenance. Professional image is found significant for making decisions related to colour, highlights and hair accessories. A flattering colour, layers and cut that is found versatile goes a long way while deciding on the hairstyle commensurate with the expectations of the corporate world. Working women generally prefer the style which requires minimum time for proper maintenance. Long hair which can be tied-up neatly and help up the nape is found good because it provides a neater look. Accessorising of hair no doubt is found significant but you should stay away from wild and vivid hues and flashy hair accessories.

If we talk about our personality, the hairstyles speak of the personality we have. The right hairstyle projects our best qualities. Choosing a hairstyle depends on a number of factors but important of all is the facial structure such as the oval-shaped face, the round face, square-shaped face, diamond-shaped face, inverted triangle-shaped face and the triangle-shaped face. The variation in hair style is also influenced by the professional and situational requirements. Of late, we also find provisions or options like hair extensions, wigs, colour and haircuts to project our personality. The athletes, corporate professionals, free spirited are the different categories for the different types of personalities. Thus personality, career, life activities, facial structure, age and budget are the factors to influence an individual for a particular hair style.

An in depth study of the facial structure is considered significant to pick a particular style.

The Oval-shaped Face: It is considered the most ideal shape of face found naturally balanced and noticeably longer. This structure takes place for a number of hair styles. Maintaining the lateral balance of the face needs due attention. Besides, the middle parts are to be avoided because this may elongate the face too much. In all the conditions, we may not allow elongation.

The Round Face: This face structure has curved facial lines and cheekbones found clearly wider than the brow brone and the jawline. In this face structure, we find elongation important where any length of hair may work. The dead centre parts, low side parts, heavy bangs, severe designs, flat styles, very fully styles need to be avoided in the round face structure.

The Square-shaped Face: In this face structure, low aide parts, fullness at the jaw line, heavy bangs are to be avoided. The square-shaped face, the browline, cheekbone and jaw line have approximately the same width. The carves may be used in this face structure to soften the squareness of the face. Here we should prefer the styles that fall along the jaw or longer.

The Diamond-shaped Face: This face structure has the cheekbones found clearly wider than the browbone and the jawline. Here the goal is to lengthen the face to balance the width at the cheeks and also to soften the angularity of the face. In this face structure, we need to avoid the hair pulled back on the sides, revealing the hair line. Here we can elongate the face with long style and can keep fullness around the jawline.

The Inverted Triangle-shaped Face: This face structure has a browbone which is found larger than the jawline. Here the goal is to balance the upper and lower portions in the face and also to soften the prominent V-shaped chin. Adding fullness at the jawline is found helpful. The length of hair should be up to shoulder but in no case it should be shorter than the chin. The curved bangs, straight bangs or side bangs may be used to hide the wide forehead. The exposure of hairline on the forehead is acceptable but it should be steered away from low side parts.

The Triangle-shaped Face: This face structure has a jawline which is found considerably wider than the browbone, cheeckbone and greater than the browbone but less than the jawbone. Here the motive is to balance the face by adding width at the cheeks and brow and at the same time minimising the jawline. Short hair works best with this face structure. Adding width to the top of the hair helps balancing the shape of face.

For having an attractive hairstyle in tune with the face structure and corporate culture, it is pertinent that we seek the cooperation of hairstylist. Achieving the hair goals is the most important thing. You should be aware of the differences that we find between that alone and stylist The hairstylists would help you in fulfilling your expectations because we find them having expertise in the concerned area. They are in a position to perceive your requirements in a right fashion. Since the hairstyle that you adopt have a correlation with the corporate expectations and your face structure, it adds additional attractions to your personality and projects the outstanding qualities you have.

The way in which you dress-up and the way in which you style your hair assumes a place of outstanding significance in the corporate world. While working, travelling or socialising, your job demands something different. Actually, you need a hairstyle for every occasion. Soft, smooth and shining hair adds additional attractions to your personality. Just like you, your hair is different and different hair needs different solutions. Fulfil the requirements of your job and honour the situational demands.

◈ Style Your Hair

Soft, smooth and shiny hair; either for women or for men.

And this one for every occasion.

Working, travelling or Socialising,

Your job demands a style.

Your hair is different, because you are different.

Make your hair different because you are different

Avoid excess ironing and exposure to chemical,
Make it sure that it is neither dry nor rough,
it is for a particular occasion;
Because you need a hair style for every occasion,
Working, travelling or socialising,
You job demand it all.
A Clean Scalp ensures healthy and shiny hair
Take care of the ends of your hair for healthy shine.
Routine haircare controls common hair problems.
Shampoo is for your scalp,
Conditioner is for your hair shaft and ends.

◈ Regulate the Body Odour

Our food habits are found responsible for the development of body odour which needs to be regulated. If we are not sincere to the management of oral hygiene, our teeth may have dragon breath. This makes it essential that we seal doors responsible for body odour. We are required to make it sure that in the very morning and even after dinner, we brush our teeth. If we take some breath mints or mouth spray with us, the problem may be resolved. It is not to be forgotten that it is difficult for us to identify the odour to our breath and detection is by others. Bad breath is considered to be a turn off in many ways. Cardamom can be used for great breath. Chew few seeds of cardamom to overcome bad breath and relieve flatulence.

Avoid wearing perfume or cologne. If the person interviewing you or interacting with you is allergic to something you are wearing, they in a very natural way would not be happy with you because they would be sneezing the whole time as long as you are with them. Here, it is also pertinent to mention that when you wear the same perfume or cologne over a long period of time, you are found numb to that scent and you become accumulated to your own body odour. In this context, you may add fragrances in shampoos, deodorants and body soaps then you smell fresh but without cologne or perfume. Make it sure that your perfume, body lotion and body soap have the same scent.

We need to sense and sensitise employees that our bodies produce two kinds of sweat such as "Eccrine" and "Apocrine." The body-odour culprit is apocrine which is found in groin and undream areas. The sweaty smell occurs when apocrine reacts with the bacteria on our skin. Some of us are cursed with bigger and more active apocrine glands whereas some of us are not as successful as others in getting rid of the bacteria on our skin. They should be given different tips. Bathe at least once daily with an antibacterial soap. Use a deodorant with aluminium or zinc. The odour-friendly bacteria need to be killed. Wash clothes at home using an odour-fighting detergent. Freshen up in the bathroom with a towel. Avoid the regular consumption of spicy or sharp-smelling foods. Make your body odour-free.

Whatsoever the measures we adopt, the motive is to keep ourselves free from the bad breath. By showing our sincerity to the oral hygiene, it is easier for us to get rid of the problem of odour coming from our mouth. We need to identify the reasons for odour and to make it sure that mouth, clothes and body; the concerned sources for odour are regulated in a right way. All the measures adopted by us to project our facial appearance turn into a fiasco, if we do not remove the odour problem. You need to develop awareness of the products available in the market which can keep you odour-free. How do you look, of course, is significant that we cannot undermine that How do you small have an edge because the tolerance level of smell is found very low. Ultimately, it is our responsibility to detect and regulate. No doubt, we can take support of our family members because self-detection of odour is not to be possible. Both preventive as well as the curative measures are to be adopted to regulate the problem of body odour. We need not to be hesitant while confessing that Indian are not sincere to their body odour. This proves to be a problem or disaster area and if we do not remove it, all our efforts for managing the wearabouts prove to be meaningless due to the body odour.

Since we find it a problem associated with hygiene, it is imperative that all of us practise the preventive measures which need due attention on managing mouth and managing body. Our food habits also account for the problem of body odour and therefore we need to avoid sharp-smelling food items. The odour comes through the pores, which is the opening of the sweat-gland. We also find cases when our neglected feet create odour problem specially due to socks. If hands tend to sweat, we should inculcate habits of keeping hanky or tissue handy specially while shaking hands. If you have limited number of shoes and socks, the odour problem would be in different forms and therefore you should have a good number for a frequent change. In summer, you should dry your feet thoroughly specially between toes and use talcum powder to prevent dry smells. A cosmetic treatment or manicure may be preferred to look hand fresh without any odour for a pleasant handshake. Personal hygiene practices such as seeing a doctor, seeing a dentist, regular washing and bathing and healthy eating may also be helpful to prevent the problem of odour. The frequent uses of body hygiene products including soap, hair shampoo, toothbrushes, tooth paste, cotton swabs, antiperspirant, facial tissue, mouthwash, handwash, footwash would minimise the odour problem.

Eating spicy and smoke-generating food items may aggravate the odour problem and therefore you should avoid eating these items. Smoking and sweating also play an incremental role in aggravating the problem of body odour and therefore, we should regulate them. It is also significant to mention that excessive body hygiene to regulate the problem of body odour may affect our skin, because excessive application of soaps, creams and ointments can adversely affect the natural processes of the skin or can deplete the skin of natural protective oils and fat solubles content and therefore we need to be particular while making use of the hygiene products. Washing clothes in dirty and polluted or contaminated water make the ways for odour and skin problem. This makes it essential that we are very much particular to the washing clothes at home and using an odour-fighting detergent. It is also pertinent that we adopt devices for killing odour-causing bacteria. We find some of us heavy sweaters and they should prefer to use antiperspirant/deodorant containing aluminium chloride. We should also think of using a prescription soap.

In view of the above, it is right to say that problem of body odour may complicate our task in different ways and therefore each one of us should remain careful while regulating the problem of body odour.

◆ Your Make-Up

Accessorising is found instrumental in enriching your outfits in tune with the corporate culture where you succeed in adding additional attractions to your personality. It is significant that you look attractive and for this, you need due attention on your make-up. Both the genders need to be careful while using the devices which may provide to them an attractive look. Highlighting your best features by making your look prettier is an important reason for using cosmetics.

In this context, it is to be made sure that you have a natural look which necessitates matching foundation to skin. This requires blending into neck area to remove the visible link. The application of foundation should be light. You may use face powder with foundation or may wear it alone. The motive of administering foundation is to make the skin smooth and eliminate the facial shine. Your focus should also be on the eye make-up and you can apply it to the natural brow line to add attraction. Efforts should also be taken to match or blend the eye make-up with your natural colour. Use of light *kajal* and eyeliner may be preferred. You need to avoid elaborate make-up and dark rouge. In addition, shiny and elaborate *bindi*s are also to be avoided. If you use *kumkum*, ensure that it is not to spread. If you wear lipstick to compliment the colour of your outfit, prefer neutral shades like light brown or light maroon. Extremely dark or bright colours or bright reds and fluorescent colours are to be avoided.

The prime motive of the corporate men and women is to look natural and attractive. Actually, we live in a world that strives for perfection. In a world where we find possibilities of modifying everything for the sake of perfection, it is to be ensured that whatsoever the practices we follow to look attractive do not make the ways for losing naturality.

You need to know the difference between beauty clinics and the beauty parlours because you are supposed to make use of their services. The image consultants may also be helpful to you. You need institutional supper if not regularly, at least casually. Though all of us are born with beautiful skin but as the years roll by, the skin needs the beauty which can be maintained. The vagaries of pollution, seasonal fluctuation, climatic change as well as internal and external stress affect the quality of our skin. Protecting the intrinsic beauty of our skin is significant which is possible with institutional support. The beauty clinics help you in resolving your skin problem. Acne and pimples need services of skin specialist not of beauty parlours. We cannot deny that your beauty lies in the hands of those who have a specialised knowledge of the subject.

Because you earn more, you are in a position to spend more. You need to develop your awareness that yours expenses term to be an investment. If you look attractive, you get an opportunity to continue. Personal grooming is found essential both for men and women. When we talk about your make-up, the prime focus is on your look and appearance in the face of your profession.

The increasing heat of globalisation has related a condition like economic boom which has made possible a significant increase in the level of income vis-à-vis a change in the spending power and behaviour of people. Of late, we find people beauty conscious and against this background, we find a fillip in the development of beauty industry which has evidenced more than 60% growth in the cosmetic industry. The Tier 1, Tier 2 and Tier 3 cities are the customers of the product. In a true sense, the concept of beauty care has changed tremendously over the years and so the requirements of clients vis-à-vis their expectations are also changing. New people look for specialists exclusively for speciality services in tune with their professional requirements. The beauty clinics are found fulfilling their expectations. Adapting to corporate life is essential for climbing the corporate ladders and therefore the corporate professionals cannot undermine make-up. Appearance makes the difference and make-up brings a radical change.

The beauty clinics bear the responsibility of providing a matching foundation to our skin for a natural look that we need. The facial shine is required to be eliminated which is found active in making our look unnatural. The dark rouge and elaborate make-up cannot be acceptable. Both the genders men and women need make-up to provide to their facial appearance an attractive look. What products in what quantity they need to use depend on nature and type of skin of an individual. As a preventive measure, it is significant that we are very much particular to the food items and the quality of water that we drink. Particularly women need plenty of water to keep their insides clean and keep their skin fresh on the outside. The men are required to shave their facial hair and if they wear a beard, it should be neatly trimmed. Besides, the moustaches should also be trimmed. You should not forget that make-up is closely associated with your facial appearance which can make the difference in getting or not getting the job; in hiring or firing; in getting promotion or in delaying it. It is due mainly to the fact that correct appearance proves to be your competitive advantage.

The above mentioned facts make it clear that corporate men or women either interested in getting promotion or even for holding the status and position they have should assign due weightage to make-up. The upcoming and budding youths nurturing interest in serving the corporate sector also need to be sincere to their make-up. May be that you need institutional support or you may be yourself competent of wearing the make-up you need. The most important thing is perceiving organisational culture in totality and further to strengthen the realisation of your employers that you are sincere and honest to the details. Highlighting your best features is significant and this makes it essential that you look prettier. It is right make-up which is to meet your requirements. You have money in your pocket and therefore you are in a position to spend. You want money in your pocket and even for that you have to spend. Actually, it is not an expenditure; indeed an investment for which we get return. Now, you have to take a decision but you have no option.

◈ Manage your Hands

In the corporate culture, you will be required to shake hands and therefore it is pertinent that you are serious while keeping your hands and nails clean. Paying attention to details is significant in the corporate world and the task remains incomplete unless we develop our awareness of nailing. You need to know that nails are formed mainly from keratin which is a kind of protein. While managing our diet, it is imperative that our daily food includes all the essential amino acids to supply adequate nutrients to our nails. Healthy nails are found strong, smooth and pink. Besides, we need to develop our awareness of hand hygiene. This focuses on proper washing of our hands with soap and water or using waterless hand sanitizer such as an alcohol hand gel which can be used specially when we are at public places. Today, we find people in general and corporate executives in particular making a frequent use of computer, laptop and cell-phone whose keyboards are an important source for carrying infection and making it essential for us that we are very particular to hand hygiene. We need to sensitise people that hands are a very common carrier of various types of germs. Hands and wrists need to be washed to prevent the spread of bacteria and viruses.

In this context, it is also significant that we keep our nails frequently trimmed and in good shape which would prevent the problem of hang nails in which a loose strip of dead skin hangs from the edge of fingernail and infect nail beds. Weekly trimming and daily brushing with soap would keep our nails clean. The fingernails should be trimmed straight across and slightly rounded at the top whereas toenails should be trimmed straight across. The best time to cut our nails is after bathing when they are found soft.

Clean hands, an important consideration for personal hygiene has been found neglected even in the educated society. This makes it essential that we activate the sensitisation process. Particularly the working women should develop their awareness of manicure and pedicure. The manicure refers to a treatment for the hands, incorporating the fingernails and cuticles and application of nail polish. The pedicure refers to a treatment for the feet, incorporating the toenails and softening or removal of calluses. We find nail salons where manicures and pedicures take place.

The healthy nails need healthy foods containing Zinc. All of us need awareness of the required nutrients for healthy nails. It is pertinent which we call that we have foods successful in removing the deficiencies of zinc which we can by consuming green leafy vegetables, fish, poultry, meat, liver, dried dates, raisins, bajra and jaggery. Zinc containing food items are excellent for brittle nails. Olive oil is good for sparkling nails and hair. The motive is to keep our hands clean which would make us comfortable while shaking hands in the formal or informal meetings. Particularly hygienic considerations make it essential that nails are healthy and for that we need to be careful.

You should not forget that your hands are the first impression people have of you and therefore make sure that it is a good one. Keep your nails and feet clean and well manicured and pedicured. It is important for both the genders.

◈ Your Wristwatch

Since long, we find both the genders very much fascinated to wearing wristwatches partially for managing time and partially with the motto of adding additional attractions to their physical appearance. Gradually, it also emerged as a status symbol and wearing expensive watches specially amongst the corporate men and women was found to be a fashion. Because we find accessorising an important dimension for the projection of our personality, it is imperative that we go through the problem in today's perspective so that it is not to harm us as a problem or disaster area. During the yesteryears, we find a basic change in the style of wrist watches and due to its increasing demand specially by the corporate men and women professionals, we find much more expensive wristwatches available in the markets. Expensive and sophisticated wardrobes and accessories adding value to our status and personality speak of the fact that we are much sincere and professional to the rank and position we hold or are willing to hold. Such an optimism makes us much more recreative and productive. It is in this context that while deliberating on accessories we assign due weightage to the wristwatches that we wear. But here our focus must be on the expensive and stylish wristwatches in tune with our body structure and personality. We cannot deny that accessories create an accent and elegance to our monotonous office outfit. It is upon us that how and in what way we transform our facial appearance and make it attractive and elegant.

In a majority of the conditions, we find wristwatch proving a disaster or problem area because we undermine the quality of watches that we wear. Hence, it is imperative that you are sincere to its quality and style with its internationally acclaimed brand name. You should not forget that a branded watch can be the ultimate accessory with your business suit. Since the corporate world is found very sincere while managing time, it is significant that you are also sincere while keeping track of the time. Adapting to corporate life is meant observing everything minutely in the face of organisational culture. Of late, we find a number of international brands in the field of wristwatch and while exercising your options you have to think over the corporate image. This is applicable to both the genders.

◈ Best Watch Brands

- A. Lange & Sohne
- Rolex
- Jaeger-LeCoultre
- Baume & Mercier
- Tissot
- Breitling
- IWC
- Cartier
- Swatch
- Harry Winston
- Panerai
- Phillipe Phatek
- TAG Heuer
- Piaget
- Omega
- Mavado
- Chopard
- Zenith
- Toy Watch
- Vacheron Constantin
- Rado

Wristwatch adds additional attractions

Accessory not, just for aesthetic value. For corporate men or women wearing a classy looking watch is very important as it gives him or her a refined and sophisticated look. The price that you pay for buying the watch is not just for its craftsmanship, design and style because you pay for brand and also pay for your status. Global recognition increases its value and therefore you have to pay. The best watch brands for men are Tag Huer, Breguet and Breitling. The best watch brands for women are Cartier, Movado and Van Cleef & Arples. Generally, women prefer design watches. Actually whatever we wear on our bodies reflects our personality and project our mood for the day. Normally, we find men crazy for sophisticated mechanical and classic watches. Classic watches match with formal clothing and sophisticated watches are best for businessmen who have to attend the business gathering. Women as we are aware that they love jewellery and so the first choice is always fashionable jewellery watches. Business women choose unisex watches, with large dials as their thinking level is totally different and high. They want to stand shoulder to shoulder with men and therefore we find them very selective while choosing watches.

The corporate men and women thus need to be selective while wearing watches. They need to be choosy and they are required to make it sure that their options are in favour of internationally acclaimed brands. Of course, we find question of affordability because expensive and luxury watches cannot be purchased by general corporate employees and therefore you also need to select the quality that you can afford because almost all the brands have a range found to be affordable.

Of late, we find wristwatch mobile phone. We generally forget our mobile phones and for them we find W100 watch with mobile phone. This watch has multimedia features. It has a touch screen 65k TFT with 1.3 megapixel camera and FM Radio. It has 1GB of storage memory.

If you wear watch, please make it sure that it is not to be a problem area. The position that you dream to hold or at least the position that you hold would determine your choice. Since accessorising is also related to your status, it is imperative that while making choice for the wrist watch, you are sincere to elegance and sophistication.

◈ Managing Your Shoes

Particularly when we talk about wearabouts in the corporate culture, it is quite natural that we focus on everything in the changing perspective. A microscopic review of each and everything concerned with our looks are found essential. It is in this context that we talk about the management and maintenance of our shoes and socks. It is not significant that you have quality shoes. It is equally important that you are very particular to its proper maintenance and spit and polish them for proper shining. High level sensitivity to your looks is considered essential.

Mr. A was one of the two finalists for a high salary position. He had been interviewed twice and was one of the third interview that involved face to face with the CEO for the final round of interview. He was escorted to the office of CEO by the Human Resource Manager. When they had finished the interview, Mr. A was very confident that he would be chosen for the job. He was convinced that he had the right contacts and would be successful in making this company more profitable to excel competition. When he received the call a few days later, it was to inform him that the other candidate had been chosen. Of course, he asked why he was not chosen and the Human Resource Manager said, "Do you remember when we were walking up to the CEO's office? He said Yes. Well I looked down and noticed your shoes were scuffed up. Now you would argue that what did your shoes have to do with it. You are aware that only one person is going to get the job. The organisation has to use whatever it can to differentiate you from other candidates. You had a control over your shoes but you did nothing about it. So the assumption is that you did not pay attention to the details. When you are insincere to your own looks how and in what way you would mind the details of the organisation where you have to work.

We cannot deny that it is an age of packaging and therefore you are also supposed to package your personality in such a fashion that even a minor thing is sincerely cared. So far as the colour of your shoe is concerned, the black colour is the first choice. In this context, you also need to care your socks which should be neat and clean and of right colour to go with your shoes.

Both the genders need to manage their shoes in the face of organisational culture. In addition to business suits, you need focus on your skirts, trousers, shoes, make-ups and accessories. The colour of the shoes preferably be black. To look trendy, the shoes must be of latest design but at the same time acceptable to the culture of your organisation where you work. While attending informal meetings; you have an option. Be particular that you are very careful to the maintenance of your shoes and spare time for proper spitting, polishing and shining. Make it sure that your shoes do not create any noise while moving from one place to another. While selecting shoes, you also need to care about your socks. The colour of socks should not be laud instead soothing and having a match with the trouser. Make place for more shoes in your wardrobe and use in tune with the business and party requirements.

Accessorising is an important decision-making area of projection. If we focus on shoes, it is due mainly to the fact that a pair of shoes can either complement your look or may kill it. If we continue to be cheap with our feet, the task of exposure or projection found much more difficult. You are supposed to buy quality shoes and keep them buffed and shined. A mix of expensive and inexpensive shoes makes your wardrobe affordable and economic. You should prefer to wear inexpensive shoes during your commute to and from work and change into your good shoes after you reach the office. Such an arrangement would also increase the life of your expensive shoes. The most important issue in the corporate world is our outfit because wrong outfits convey the wrong message and we are deprived of climbing the corporate ladders.

Keep on wearing clean, conservative and polished shoes of quality and do not wear athletic or slip on shoes. For both the genders, it is imperative that they have adequate number of shoes so that airing can be done to remove smells. Particularly in the summer, it is essential that we ensure use of talcum powder to prevent dry smells. In the corporate world in particular, we cannot deny that our shoes occupy a place of outstanding significance which should be of world-class, comfortable and well-fitted. We need to ensure with western formals, our priority especially for women should be closed shoes. Footwear requires to be matched with the colour of handbag or with salwar, chudidar or trousers. While managing shoes, our socks also need due care. All of us are aware of the fact that socks and shoes smell and smell very bad and therefore our maximum precaution would regulate the problem area. We need to keep sufficient number of socks so that our socks are changed everyday.

With the corporate culture becoming stronger and stronger, we find shoes getting a dominating position in the projection of our persona and development of our personality. It is against this background that we find a galloping increase in the footwear industry where the shoes are becoming much more expensive and attractive. We need to mind the occasions and situations and to select the shoes commensurate with the changing requirements. Harmonising appears to be a consideration and therefore the corporate professionals need to match their shapes with their suits, trousers or pants.

Look the part perfectly when you stride into any corporate setting. Sharp, decisive and commanding. Walk the corridors of power exuding a cool confidence. Identity the surest way to get to the top. Make it a point for hiring, not firing.

Shoes portray your personality

Your shoes portray your personality. Don't take it lightly. Investment dressing would benefit you in many ways. Wear for the position that you want to hold.

◈ Tie as a Sense of Pride

Accessorising is an important dimension of enhancing personality, specially when we talk about the corporate world. There are a number of aspects which we consider in the very context but so far as the role of tie is concerned, we find it very effective in the enhancement process. We consider it as a sense of pride and a feeling of belonging to a specific team or organisation. Particularly the upcoming generations evincing more interest in joining the corporate sector or serving the corporate world have been found more conscious about how they look and how people perceive them. Actually, transmission and reception both the processes are found interrelated. By accessorising, we transmit and if the right process has been adopted it is received in a right fashion. Of late, we find people becoming more conscious about their appearance. This is, of course, in tune with the organisational culture promoted by the corporate sector.

The tie is used to make people feel proud and much more confident about themselves. We also wear tie as a mark of statement of authority. There are many occasions when we wear a tie but here our focus is on the corporate ties. Ties are also found popular in schools and colleges and worn by many students across the country. But we discuss the problem in the face of corporate requirements. Casual business attire or we may also call it business casually played a big role in revolutionising the environment of American offices during the decade 1990s. The Society for Human Resource Management makes it clear that 95% of US companies adopted the casual day policy in the year 1999 as compared to 24%

in 1992. In the same context, casual clothing manufacturer Levi Strauss claims that 75% of the American workers dressed casually everyday in 1999, as compared to 7% in 1992. Thus, it is clear that during 1990s, we find a significant change in the shape of casual business attire.

The high-tech companies of California Silicon Valley has the credibility of initiating a shift in which a number of young and Internet entrepreneurs refused to wear business suits and were often found in denim jeans and cotton T-shirts. Gradually, we find its imprints across the country and resulting from which most companies moved toward casual attire and finally the business casual could get a place in the office at all times. The organisations were adopting it also to encourage the talented employees in a shinking labour pool. A good number of American workers started viewing casual office attire as a perk because in their eyes this creates a less stratified work environment in which more focus is on employees' contribution rather than their wardrobes.

Some of the experts believe that casual attire creates a number of problems for companies. They virtually dismissed the emerging trend towards the business casual and opined that image is one of the most important characteristics of any business and it would make sense that the way a company's employees dress would say much more about the company's image.

In an article, Wearables Business, Brian Anderson writes, "While the goals of corporate casual dress code includes improving employee moral, enhancing productivity, lowering status barriers and fitting in with the corporate climate of customers, the wrong code can undermine a company's credibility." He further says, "A clear definitive explanation of a corporate casual dress code is rare. What is acceptable at one mortgage broker's office may be completely unacceptable at another — even if they are different branch offices of the same company. "We cannot negate that dress code is an important part of organisational culture and such a flexible trend would play a role in tarnishing the corporate image. It is also expected that employees; may tend to work less seriously when they are dressed casually. The unclear dress code policies may also contribute to the problems with employees taking advantage of situation by wearing sloppy rather than casual attire to the office. One thing is very clear that we find much more scope for abuses in wearings by the employees in case of casual attire to the office and therefore it is in the larger interest of an organisation that dress code policy is strictly followed.

In view of the facts outlined above, it is right to say that formal office attire is found very much instrumental in projecting a positive corporate image. The most important thing is organisational culture and the dress code policy accepted and adopted. You need to understand the dress code of your company and to follow it in the best possible way. Showing respect to the organisation where you work is an important aspect which is possible when you understand and practise them in the desired way. You need to wear for success; you need to wear for the established brand image of your company. May be that the casual dress code policy helps you in competing with your women counterparts who never stuck to a corporate uniform and have also a wider selection when it comes to choosing attire.

Whatsoever the reasons we find entailed behind, about the dress code policy of an organisation, it is right to say that casual is casual and business formal is business formal. The organisations promoting casual dress policy finds it difficult to establish a culture when cases of abuse witness a significant increase. Dress down policy cannot be useful to an organisation. It may increase absenteeism and tardiness and establish a culture different to the corporate culture where you will find your employees wearing albeit halter tops, stretch pants, jeans, shorts, sandals and shirts without collars.

The most important thing you need to consider is to conform to or comply to your company culture and respect the attire they permit. If we find suit-wearing companies like financial organisations, sales organisations, accountants and consultants; you need attention of ties. For understanding dress code of organisation, it is better that you turn your eyes on the CEO. If your CEO does not wear a suit then this will be a good indicator for you to leave your suit at home.

Since, we consider tie a status symbol, the corporate people should not make it a disaster area. This focuses on quality of tie and its colour. In this context, you should follow some guidelines. Your silk ties are a status symbol. In the selection process, we have scope for adding a personal style. The so called red stripped ties are considered popular for business. While choosing, look at corporate culture. At any stage of accessorising, you are not supposed to forget the elegance you need for enhancement of your personality. Since we find corporate culture, image and brand very much related with the employees who are considered an extension of the brand, it is imperative that while selecting tie, you are sincere to its mix with the suit you have selected as a business attire. You are not supposed to make fashion a statement but to conform to your company culture and this necessitates the most popular suit colour for business, known as dark gray and navy blue. Even though pin-stripes are occasionally worn, the most conservative colour for the shirt is pure white followed by blue. After making a choice for suit and shirt; you need to make a choice for neckties. The stripped neckties are found most popular. But here, you should avoid novelty neckties because it carries a tacky or poor reputation to business. Don't forget that it may be even a problem or disaster area for you.

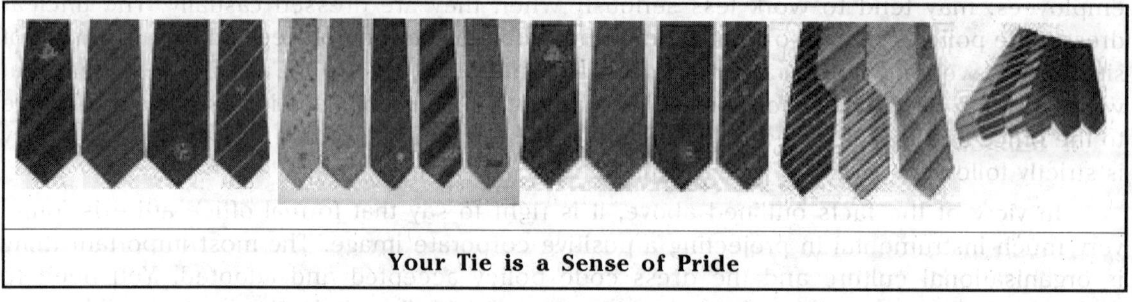

Your Tie is a Sense of Pride

A decision maker is not supposed to commit a mistake while making choice for his/her own accessories. It is already mentioned earlier that corporate image, corporate culture, corporate brand are the important considerations you have to remember even while selecting ties. The more conservative your company, the better off you will be wearing conservative colours and designs on your ties. Dark navy blue neckties and burgundy silk ties are considered as excellent business neckties. The choice may vary from occasion-to-occasion and season-to-season. Unless your company is very conservative, the neckties of light colours such as light blue or even pink and orange ties are quite popular specially in the spring and summer. In wardrobe, you need to arrange your ties in a right order so that you find different colours and shades ready for you in tune with your requirements.

The facts outlined above make it clear that in the annals of neckties, we find so many turning points. They have changed slight joy over the years, no doubt, but the main purpose has remain unchanged. In past, we worn it as a status symbol and even today we wear it as a status symbol. We also wear it as a mark or statement of authority. In today's society, we wear tie in all the important business and personal events such as wedding, important meeting, working, at a funeral, to a business function or job interview for transmitting something about the status and personality in business and private functions. Hence, its management is considered important so that we do not find a gap between transmission and reception. Either we talk about sense of pride, or feeling of belonging to a specific team; neckties are important across the globe.

◈ Spectacle Frames for Your Face and Personality

Complementing our face and personality cannot be wrong specially when we believe in the value addition process. The very base of corporate sector is found based on exposition without which process of corporatisation remains incomplete. Accessorising with professional touch is considered significant for adding additional attractions to our face and personality. It is in this context that here we talk about the spectacle frames. Of course, for many people, the spectacle frames may be nothing more than a necessity to help them see but we also find some of us evincing interests in creating an opportunity to develop individuality and possibility of making a fashion statement. One thing is sure that spectacle frames may be helpful in projecting your personality provided you are very much selective. Today, we find a number of brands making available to us the spectacle frames found light and stylish, crafted in the most slender titanium to rock solid for the roughest handlers. With the help of optical dispensers, you may be successful in getting the frames to be effective in enhancing your personality. The leading brands have frames to suit every face, shape and prescription. Because corporate employees are considered an extension of the corporate brand, it is imperative that they respect branded products, such as Porsche, Rodenstock, Hugo Boss, Pro Design, Silhouette, Anne et Valentin, Jonathan Sceats, Convertibles, Gucci, C4 Yourself. While selecting, the optical dispensers are to help you to select the style and shape for your face and personality.

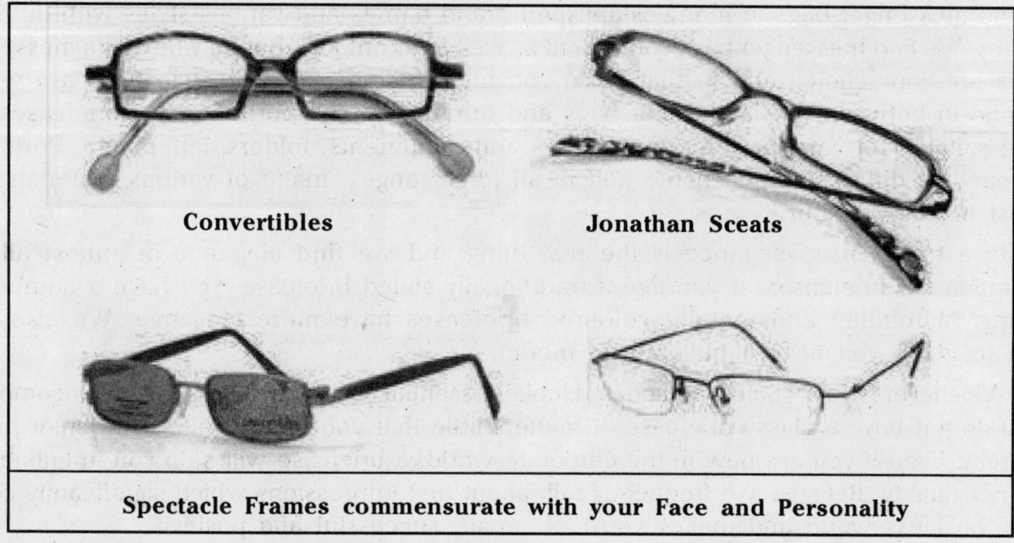

Spectacle Frames commensurate with your Face and Personality

Today, so many different types of frames are available in the markets and from rimless to the more bold colourful shell frames can suit you depending on your personality, attitude and sense of style. We cannot negate that the shape of face plays a very meaningful role in the selection process. Of late, we find companies making larger ranges of frames from light weight materials such as titanium and Genium which provides comfort as well as strength to the frames.

An important factor determining the overall weight of the frame is the lenses which should be lighter and thinner to maximise comfort of your glasses, and to the best suit your prescriptions. A mix of the lighter weight materials in both the frame and lenses considerably reduces the pressure on your nose. Hence with the development of lense technology, the wearers have now more options.

◈ A Great Looking Briefcase

Enriching your business style is considered significant and in this context, a great looking briefcase is found an essential part of your wardrobe. Projection and exposition cannot or should not be overlooked even if we find ourselves number one in presentation. You are taking your business seriously, of course it is significant but you also need to show them that you are respecting the organisational culture and promoting the corporate image. In the corporate world, the briefcase and its quality also plays an effective role in improving your business style. It is against this background that we focus here all the briefcase exclusively for the corporate people.

Bid a goodbye to the traditional box-like briefcase because the foundation of corporate world is found based on exposition. Over the years, we have witnessed significant changes in the styles commensurate with our changing taste. You need to make it sure that briefcase in your hand is classy and is reflecting a sense of sophistication and style to your clients and colleagues. The businessmen of today need to assign due weightage to the quality and style of briefcases.

Of late, we find, a messenger bag a great choice. It looks great and works great. Earlier, we also called it backpacks often seen on the back of bicycle couriers and school kids. Today, we find messenger bags in many established brand names and various styles with different features. We find messenger bags convenient as well as affordable. But may be that a messenger bag is not your choice and in that case, you may prefer a portfolio-style briefcase which is found in between the messenger bags and briefcases. The portfolio-style briefcases are found suitable for carrying important papers and documents, folders, letters, etc. Portfolios are found in different brand name and in all price ranges, made of various materials and almost in many colour.

In a true sense, elegance is the real thing and we find elegance in almost all the generations of briefcases. If you like a traditionally styled briefcase, you have a number of options. Aluminium and metallic-coloured briefcases have more elegance. We also find them tough, if you have a bullet-proof model.

Whichever is your choice, an updated look is essential. Corporate looks, remain incomplete, if you do not have a classy briefcase. It matters little that you are a senior or a junior in the hierarchy. Even if you are new in the corporate world, a briefcase will help you in enhancing your personality. Because we frequently talk about first impressions which significantly count in the business world and makes you look smart, successful and positive.

Since you are supposed to be careful to your personality and looks, it is pertinent that you are sincere to the material and quality of briefcase. We cannot negate that leather briefcases are always in fashion. We find them durable. It is one-time investment and available in various styles. They have different compartments to cater to the multi-dimensional requirements of an individual. There are compartments for business card slots, key pockets, pen lops, mobile pockets, etc.

We can easily carry our files, documents, papers to and from the office. Laptop cases are available in the leather briefcase which can protect your expensive items. Both men and women can choose from top-loading and front-loading whichever style they find comfortable.

◈ For Corporate Men

When we talk about briefcases for men, we find them helpful in enhancing your personality. We find them available in different styles such as flip-flap, detachable wheeled catalogue case with or without removable sleeves. You should not forget that leather briefcases have the same impression as we find of the formal wear. It provides to you the formal office look.

Briefcases enhance your personality

It is helpful in creating a desired impression. It is instrumental in enhancing your personality. It is to provide safety to your belongings. It helps you in having a formal office look. Enrich your business style by having leather briefcases.

◈ For Corporate Women

Gone are the days when leather briefcases were exclusively owned by the men. Today, we have witnessed a significant change and we find even women having a respectable position in the corporate world. The modern leather briefcases are found effective in

enhancing their personality. Style statement cannot be overlooked in the business world and we cannot deny that quality leather briefcases have a style statement. We find these briefcases available in different colours such as orange, red and yellow in addition to the traditional colours like black and brown.

We cannot deny that briefcases have become now a stylish accessory particularly for the corporate people. They need to assign due weightage to the briefcases they carry which make their appearance professional. They also need to think over the safety of their documents and for that safe and steady look need due attention. You also need to make it sure that your briefcase remains cool in hot weather and warm in winter. Your briefcases should also have different compartments in tune with your requirements. It is wiser to buy an expensive briefcase so that it looks stylist and lasts long. Expensive accessories not only enhance your personality but also give you a smart and elegant look.

◈ Tan Leather Briefcase: A Corporate Choice

Looking stylish and professional is an important personal score of corporate people and in this context, you should prefer to buy your briefcases in tan leather. Since today, we find laptop computers are also carried in briefcases; you should not forget this feature of your briefcase. It is an unvarnished fact that when we talk about materials of briefcase, the best choice is leather, preferably tan leather. In many of the stores, you do not get briefcases of your choice and therefore the best place to look would probably be online.

In this context, you also need to remember that online stores are found to be cheaper. Of course, the Departmental Stores would charge a premium for leather briefcases mainly due to low demand. The main thing while making a choice is your requirements. If you need a briefcase just to hold a small amount of papers then you should prefer a much smaller simplified briefcase. And if you need to hold papers documents as well as your laptop then you will need more space.

In the tan leather bags, there are different types such as tan leather Satchel, Leather Clutch Handbags, White Leather Hobo Bag, Brown Leather Hobo Bag, Camel Leather Bag, Leather Barrel Bag, etc. The tan leather Satchel is a type of bag which normally has a strap that is worn over the chest. The leather Clutch Handbags are found of medium and small sized and often have a short handle or strap. The White Leather Hobo Bag is a very popular style of handbag often carried by hottest stars. The white leather tote is found to be the best type of bag. The brown leather hobo bag has a crescent shape. We find these bags for different other purposes but not for business purposes. The camel leather bag is found to be one of the best options which has unique advantages and disadvantages. The leather barrel bag is found useful for travel when it is in large size.

Both the corporate men and women need to remember that even they always carry a briefcase, there will be times when they will be required to go to a luncheon and their briefcase will stay behind. The purses and briefcases are found important for both of them interested in having an updated look, an elegant look. A great looking briefcase is an essential part of your wardrobe. The first impressions remained the last impression even yesterday; we find the same thing of course today and are sure that albeit in future, there will be no change in the importance of briefcase in reflecting a sense of sophistication and style, status and position for modern businessmen and women evincing interests in the corporate world. A briefcase will make you look stylist, successful, sincere and professional.

◆ The Pen-Reflecting Your Personality and Taste

We consider pen the most practical and utilitarian inventions ever created. This helps you in communicating in a personal way. It is a very personal accessory reflecting your personality and taste. Complementing an outfit is considered significant and with pen we find the process of making an outfit complete. Though new generation of information and communication technology has been found minimising its importance but nobody can deny that pen is an essential part of an overall look and a lifestyle. Whether you are writing a thank you note, a letter on a card; the ink source has no substitute and it is pen. We find everywhere pen very much instrumental in making a statement; whether it is on your desk or in briefcase, or when you attend a meeting, a great suit, a great portfolio and a great pen just fit together. Of course, with the acceptance of corporate casual attire, the luxury writing sector was considerably affected because people were not required to wear formal attire everyday.

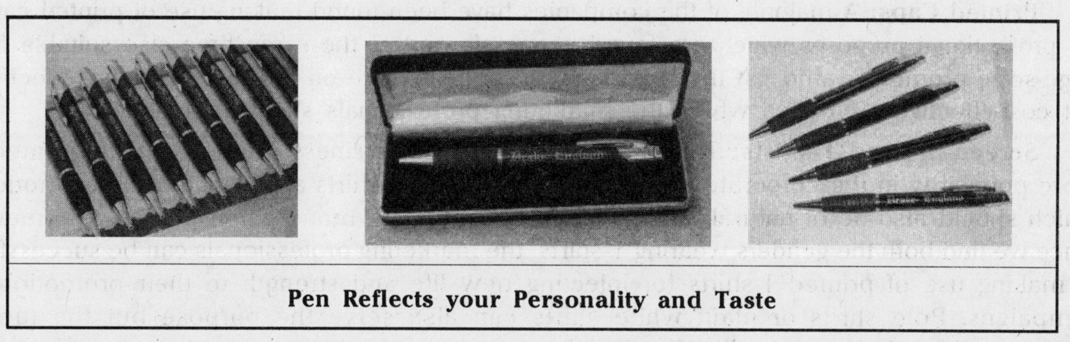

Pen Reflects your Personality and Taste

It is right to mention that a pen represents not just practicality but also personal style. The right pen can add a bit of colour and flair to the monochrome business suit and fit in perfectly. The elegance in personality remains incomplete unless you have a branded pen matching with your business suit. We can view pen also as a fashion accessory and can serve as a personal style statement as much as anything else we might put on. No doubt, every individual has different personal taste but if we talk about the corporate people, the pen in your pocket, or in your briefcase must be of quality. It is an unvarnished fact that good quality of pen cannot only work better but also adds to your personality and even lasts longer.

The leading brands in the field of pen are Cross, Lamy, Parker, Luxor, Submarine, Waterman, Sheaffer, Mont Blanc, Zebra. The corporate people should prefer branded pens. The outfit of corporate people is found complete with good quality branded pen because communicating in a personal way is found impressive with a high quality branded pen. Accessorising is an investment process specially for the corporate people. An overall look and a lifestyle; a personal accessory reflecting your personality and taste; the high quality pen adds to your personality that corporate people should not forget.

◆ Promotional Corporate Apparel

When we talk about corporate apparel, it is but natural that our focus is on almost all the dimensions which may help us in business promotion. How and in what way, we make use of clothing as a device from promotion needs due attention of corporate boardrooms when they start formulating policies for the dress code and organisational culture. Promotional clothing focuses our attention on the dresses bearing the potentials of attracting the people and providing comforts to the people who wear. The marketing people wear those dresses for promotional purposes. The T-shirts and sweatshirts are found to be the dresses gaining much more popularity in the business world. The fabrics for the dresses that we select for promotional purposes preferably be cotton. Of course, nothing can replace the natural fiber. So far as the colour is concerned, white or dyed provide an excellent setting for company brand, logo and tagline. While initiating and activating the promotional campaigns, the marketing people may promote the brand of their company with the help of apparel they select. The printed caps, screen-printed T-shirts. Company jackets are the different options which the marketing professionals can choose as promotion apparel.

Corporate apparel helps promotion

Printed Caps: A majority of the companies have been found making use of printed caps for promotional purposes which are found economic and at the same time also suitable for large-scale promotion amongst the masses. The company logo on the top rim helps effective but cost-effective promotion which the marketing professionals should not undermine.

Screen-printed T-shirts: This is also an option for business promotion gaining much more popularity in the corporate world. The fashionable T-shirts are selected for promotion which should also be of natural fabrics. These T-shirts with brand name attract customers. Since we find both the genders wearing T-shirts, the marketing professionals can be successful in making use of printed T-shirts for injecting new life and strength to their promotional campaigns. Polo shirts or plain white shirts can also serve the purpose but the most important thing is brand positioning which cannot be ignored.

Company Jackets: We also find company jackets an option for promotion through corporate apparel. Of course, we find this option much more expensive than others; yet your employees and customers would like it. In all the conditions, we find jacket a necessary item used by almost all the segments either as travel-wear or as daily use. The brand position must be identified with the motto of exposure of high level so that promotional campaigns are found effective.

A mix of different options is to be preferred by the marketing people found to be proactive but cost-effective. To be more specific in the Indian context, promotion through corporate apparel has been found much more effective in developing awareness and activating the sensitisation process.

◈ The Wardrobe for Academics

Academics need a distinct look. Facing a critical audience and delivering lectures or making presentation by the academics make it essential that their dresses are comfortable. The academics need to opt for a dark gray or navy blue instead of black clothing which makes people look awful or unpleasant. The day-to-day attire and the occasional attire of academics can not be identical. Going tieless in the day-to-day attire is, of course, appropriate but when you have to speak on a particular occasion at a formal presentation, a plain, solid colour dress shirt and a tie that goes well with your suit is the right choice. The blow tie has a stronger tradition and you should not look like a clown; therefore avoid it at all costs. Alternatively, a simple woven tie in one colour is found less distracting for the viewers and can be viewed even from the back of a large hall and, of course, with good remark. Ordinarily, the harried academics who believe in attacking others are found undermining their looks and therefore by adding a few to his/her ensemble, there is a chance of surpassing the appearance of most of the persons present in the hall. Personal touch in your formal presentation outfit cannot be ignored but overdoing the accent should be regulated. Academics in general are found eccentric and therefore if you are something more than the others, it will provide to you an additional benefit. In the competitive world of academia, we do not find anything wrong in looking distinct. Carry a handkerchief inside your pocket and be sure to whip it out as and when the situations call for it.

The looks of academics and the looks of corporate executives cannot be identical. While managing their wardrobes, they need to give a stylish touch. With the increasing domination of corporate culture, we find a change even in the looks of academics because they are also supposed to address them. Keeping in view the climatic conditions some minor modifications in the wardrobes of academics cannot be negated. Generally, we find academics tempted to the casual culture but here it is also imperative that they are not habitually casual to their looks. During yester decades, we find a significant change in the fundamentals of the well-dressed casual impacting the wearabouts of almost all the segments. Hence, we do not find anything wrong in the refashioning of the wardrobes for the academics. If we talk about the daily wear for the academics, a majority of them get rare opportunities to play the dandy. In the corporate world, we find temptation of people to the stylish and fashionable appearance increasing fast corporatisation and promoting westernisation of fashion, culture and civilisation. The people are found much more fascinated to the informal wearabouts where we find enough scope for looking dandy. Sport coats, worn open and without a tie or a bow tie, or a pin collar to add a metallic flash to our style; whatsoever the options we use, the academics have been found developing a craze for relaxed fashion. Nothing right and nothing wrong in the world of academics specially when we talk about their wearabouts because for everything they have their own predilections, perceptions and interpretations.

◈ Organisational Responsibility:

The potential employees and actual employees, no doubt, bear the responsibility of making themselves aware of the expectations of organisations regarding wearabouts and business attire but at the same time, it is also pertinent that organisations also consider and convey to them some of the basics so that a gap between the expectations and realities is bridged. It is in this context that we focus on the following:

- **Casual Dress or Formal Dress:** The organisations should make it clear that they Can allow casual or relaxed dress or would be rigid to the formal dress as their office or business attire. Of late, we find a few of the organisations allowing casual or relaxed dresses with the motto of encouraging creativity but the consulting psychologists feel that continually relaxed dress leads to relaxed manners, relaxed morals and relaxed productivity which may increase the number of complaints. Hence, the organisations should not invite such a situation which may pave ways for the negative developments at the workplace. An informed decision is significant to respect the organisational culture and the business goals.
- **Issue of Dress Guidelines:** There is nothing wrong in issuing guidelines regarding the dress expectations of organisations at the workplace. A stage of confusion is

to be removed which necessitates formulation of a policy regarding dress. The dress code for different echelons of management would minimise scope for confusion and misunderstanding amongst the employees.

- **Training for Professional Appearance and Etiquette:** You may also think in favour of organising a seminar for professional image of employees. A majority of them lack corporate manners. They do not assign due weightage to the corporate looks or distinct corporate image. Of late, we find the finishing schools educating and training potential corporate executives for inculcating and cultivating corporate etiquette, culture and manners but if we find organisations instrumental in initiating and activating the process of enriching the personality profile of employees; the results would be more positive.
- **Imparting Sexual Harassment Training:** With the increasing number of working women, we find an analogous increase in the cases of sexual harassment in different ways. Of course, provocative dress is an important reason for such a situation resulting into flirtatious behaviour. If we delay the process of regulating the behaviour, there will be a significant increase in the costly lawsuits and in addition, we will also find loss in morality, decline in productivity and an invasion on corporate social or public image. This necessitates due focus on the formulation and implementation of sexual harassment policies. Sensitising employees through training programme would minimise the possibilities of sexual harassment at the workplace.
- **Corporate leaders need to present an example:** An invasion on corporate image makes the ways for numerous negative developments.

◈ Emerging Trends in the World of Corporate Clothing

During the yesteryears, we find emergence of new trends even in the context of corporate clothing. The general fashion stores have been paving the ways to more cool and comfortable formal wear. The Business Casual is found to be a new perception in the corporate world of clothing where you can wear a suit even without a tie. A number of corporate houses of today have been found accommodating such clothing in their business protocol. Besides, we also find them allowing chequered half-sleeved shirts as office wear. Of late, we find natural fiber getting priority attention. The cotton fiber, no doubt, continues to be our first priority but recently we find bamboo fabric and tencel clothing also gaining popularity. Both of them are found eco-friendly with a number of additional advantages. Nowadays, the bamboo clothing is making place because it is smooth, luxuriously soft and drapes gently. The cultivation process of bamboo is eco-friendly and most of it is organic bamboo. The manufacturing processes that involves transforming bamboo the plant into bamboo the fabric is eco-friendly. The designers as well as the customers adore or respectfully love the excellent properties of chemically manufactured bamboo rayon but here it is pertinent that use of heavy chemicals in the manufacturing process is regulated. The increasing popularity of bamboo fabric for corporate apparel is well supported by a number of additional benefits which we do not find in other fabrics. The bamboo fabric has natural softness like silk. It is more durable and less expensive than silk. It can be laundered along with normal clothes in the washer and dryer. It is non-irritating and good albeit for the sensitive skin. Bamboo is found to be anti-fungal and anti-bacterial because of the bacteriostatis agent found in the bamboo plants. It prevents odour-producing bacteria from multiplying and spreading in the cloth due to the presence of bamboo kun and thus we have sufficient ground to consider bamboo apparel much more hygienic. We find bamboo a good absorbent which absorbs water from the body faster even than cotton and therefore, specially during the warm and sweaty months, it is preferred.

Like this, we find tencel clothing also becoming popular. There are a number of reasons for its popularity such as it is a natural fiber and offers a flattering drape. Amongst the environmentally sustainable textiles, we find tencel clothing one of the best choices. Here it is significant to clarify that tencel is a brand name which is owned by Lenzing Fiber of Germany. It is a recently improved fabric made from a fiber that is generically called Lyocell. The increasing popularity of brand name has virtually made Lyocell as Tencel. The feelings in tencel are almost like rayon. It is light weight, breathable, soft and comfortable. The corporate people planning for buy new work-wear may opt for tencel. The material lasts for a long time and are also shrink-restant. The maintenance-free clothes may be the best option in the present business world where you do not bother for wrinkling, easy packing and quick dry. The fiber is biodegradable and economic and thus a good choice for eco-friendly apparel. In the tencel fabrics, we find a variety of colours which is highly absorbent. It is made from the cellulose found in natural wood pulp.

The choices related to fiber are Cotton, Bamboo, Tencel, Silk and some of the organisations have also been found readjusting their business protocol by promoting business casual. From branded to the generic, we find stylish clothing ranges. The suits are found available in different styles and materials. We also find offices where jeans, T-shirts are allowed as office wear. The organisational culture in some of the corporate houses has been found changing where they believe that your work should speak for yourself not your clothes. However, it is significant that we develop our awareness of the organisational culture and make sincere efforts to make sure that whatever we wear go with our personality. Thus it is a clear cut observation that we should dress in clothes that conform to the dress code of the workplace. The fashionable and colourful dresses are meant just for informal meetings and functions. Cool and casual look are emerging as features of not only the wedding gowns but even of corporate apparel. The earlier style of junk clothes and jewelry is almost going into oblivion. Light embroidered clothing is found getting a new place. Of course, we find a significant change in fashion but so far as the business apparel is concerned, we hardly find major change or innovation. Thus if we talk about the recent developments or the emerging trends, we find a significant change in the texture of business suits and shirts. Earlier, these shirts were found formal but these days certain casual appeals have been found getting place in the formal official look. In the business parties, we witness this striking change which necessitates a minute observation of the corporate attitudes and expectations regarding business apparel.

In view of the emerging trends in corporate apparel, it is significant to mention that the increasing heat of globalisation has considerably influenced the fashion, culture and civilisation but so far as its impact on corporate wear is concerned, we find it of low intensity. The business world is yet to make sufficient place for the modern fashion except a very few of the business houses where we find it a matter of professional and situational requirements. We observe the influences of modern fashion in our informal functions and in business parties, no doubt, but the corporate wardrobe happens to be the matter of corporate culture. For building a positive corporate image, it is imperative that you do not commit mistakes by opting for cheap clothing which may significantly influence your corporate image. It is not wrong to buy a cost-effective item but there we find possibilities of being cheated. The focus must be on minimising scope for a mismatch between office wear and the office environment.

Corporate world is full of wonders, identify and capitalise

Both the genders, men and women, need to develop their awareness of the attitudes of organisation vis-à-vis the dress code and require to have a wardrobe commensurate with organisational requirements and professional compulsions. Unless corporate preferences establish an edge over the personal preferences; the task of mounting the corporate ladders would continue to be difficult. Compromises with personal make the ways for getting the institutional or organisational rewards. Unless you sacrifice, your task is difficult.

Corporate world makes the difference between today and tomorrow. The corporate culture buzzwords of yesterday are found outdated for today and we cannot be sure that what buzzwords we have coined today would continue to remain effective albeit for tomorrow. The people interested in serving the corporate world have no option but to be fully aware of the developments taking place each and everyday. Climbing the corporate ladders and touching the peak make it essential that we are much more sensitive and do not delay the process of adopting and incorporating. Accessorising is a process that provides to us an opportunity to differentiate. On the one hand, we need world-class thematical competence while on the other hand also realise the instrumentality of looking distinct. Brilliance comes not only from our mind and mouth but also from our facial appearance. If we find something wrong with our looks, the possibilities of detraction can not be ruled out. The clients do not receive things seriously and resulting from which even our excellent presentation may turn into a fiasco. Hence, it is imperative that we respect the organisational culture and adopt them at the earliest. We do not get excuses for the mistakes that we commit. We do not get even second time for making a choice.

Of late, we live in the world of investment dressing where our wardrobes need to be much more sophisticated. What do we spend for our wearabouts are our personal investment or investment for grooming and personality development. If we consider dressing an investment, it is quite natural that we get due return for our investments. If we consider dressing a compulsion, we respect corporate culture. The increasing heat of globalisation has globalised fashion, culture and civilisation and it is against this backdrop that local corporate culture and global corporate culture cannot move forward in the different directions. A situation like dress culture shock is to be avoided. In a true sense, the corporate brand cannot be expressed regionally because this may promote discrimination. We need to ensure that the corporate brand is expressed uniformly either locally or globally.

We cannot get success with the relaxed mode. Actually, we need professional mode for excelling competition. Our posture, handshake, eye contact, body language and behaviour and facial appearance having distinction need priority attention. We have a dress code and it is to be followed because culture and code cannot move in the different directions. Clothing and behaviour are interrelated and further behaviour and culture are also interwoven. Professional mode is a crying need of the hour and we find it difficult to act as a professional if we do not look professional. We need a global image and this necessitates a global look.

Powerful looking clothes such as professional business attire, business suit proper accessorising found appropriate for business directly impact our mindset and we find a significant change in our attitudes. Shift from negative to positive is found existent and this is due mainly to the fact that we have developed personal image on the foundation of corporate image.

Forbes magazine reports that companies are on a lookout for people "who can come up with new ways of communicating and collaborating that inspire and connect employees around the world. Companies need managers who can anticipate and thrive on change." In a true sense, they need visionaries who can anticipate future changes. They look for people with high adaptability, agility and the ability to think beyond today. They identify the personal characteristics of people who are already thriving and hire people just like them. They look out for people with positive attitudes and skills not knowledge. They do not compromise with the business apparels in tune with the existent organisational culture. And ultimately, your personality score over other traits. They defend that a compromise with the facial appearance prompts people for developing a relaxed mode where we do not expect any place for the professional mode.

The tidal wave of corporate culture has been growing and in the coming years, the upward trend will continue. The domination of MNCs will keep on moving and the global corporate culture would become stronger and stronger. The dress culture shock makes an invasion on the attitudes of people serving the organisation. Willingly or unwillingly, a majority of us are found strengthening their realisation that people working there are just an extension of their corporate brand which should essentially be expressed uniformly throughout the globe to promote team spirit and nurture team culture. Consistency in corporate image is significant, because it speaks of the standards of companies. And we cannot albeit imagine of compromising with our image. You should not forget that your sincerity to the business attire would bridge the gap between employee-image and corporate-image. Hence, the organisation has no option but to bid a good-bye to the dress-down policy.

The way in which we groom ourselves and the way in which we dress carry important meaning for the expected facial appearance. We need to make it sure that our outfits have a match with the corporate image. We are expected to reflect the value of organisation where we work. During yesteryears, we have witnessed a significant increase in the strength of nonverbal communication and the trend is to continue further. We need to understand the appearance psychology which may pave avenues for getting success both at personal and organisational levels. We have to accept the fact that clothes make the man. Naked people have little or no influence on the society. Grooming and clothing with a sense thus need priority attention in today's corporate world.

Actually, it is an age of investment dressing where you invest on your dresses and succeed in getting the big bucks. It is an age of accessorising where you are supposed to take care of even minor things of your facial appearance. Viewing everything in detail is your prime responsibility because due to your decisions related to attire you either sufferer or gainer. We also find cases when good-looking woman manages to get a position in a company over a more competitive man. Or, you are fired because the dress etiquette was breached. Or, because your belt buckle has shifted three notches too high, you are fired. It is right or wrong. We are not supposed to deliberate upon the issue but to watch the recent developments and to make them possible. Better wardrobe, more success; it is happening and we do not find any sign that in near future there will be a change in the emerging scenario. In a true sense, it has become a part and parcel of the corporate culture. For picking better-looking people, they argue that there are psychological reasons entailed behind. Better-looking people are thought to be more productive. On the basis of mental stereotyping, they feel that what is pleasant to eyes appeal us.

In view of the above, it is right to mention that the very foundation of corporatisation rests on attractions. By making our facial appearance much more attractive, we influence our associates and clients. Because we are sincere to our looks, it is inferred that with the same seriousness, we manage the business. We are better-looking and it is not meant that we are only better-looking. Indeed, we are No.1 in thematical competence and again No.1 in facial appearance. We are optimistic, creative and what not and therefore we have the potentials to remain No.1 in the corporate world. We spend and earn and keep on moving the cycle. We get the competitive advantages because our competitors lag behind. We respect etiquette and you breach and therefore we have an edge.

Of late, we find the business of smart hiring. Pick one smart talent from college campuses, train them properly, make them productive, reward them suitably and earn from them as much as you can. If you have an art of spotting the best fish in the pond, of course you have an opportunity to capitalise. If you have a zippy attitude and potentials to mix-up in a multi-cultural environment; the modern corporate world makes a hunt for you.

Polly Courtney author of the book, Golden Handcuffs: The Lovely Life of a High Flier based on her experiences opines, "Don't let the money blind you. The big city firms recruit only from the top universities they cherry-pick students with strings to their bows-football captains and leaders of orchestras and entice them with offers of fancy dinners and expensive wine. But the life is tough. Don't ignore the other side." Actually, they look for people with high intellectual bandwidth and a daring attitude. They look for people with adaptability, agility and ability to think beyond today. Hence, the emerging trends indicate that for climbing the corporate ladders, you are required to be No.1 in almost all the areas. If you keep on moving the process of enriching your personal scores, you prove to be No. 1.

DRESS FOR SUCCESS

***Source:* The Economic Times, October 24, 2010**

Shaping of personality is a crying need of the hour and for that it is imperative that you are adaptable and agile, a problem-solver, nurture tolerance for stress, behavioural flexibility to handle crisis, physical fitness and attractions and more so you are optimistic, creative and assertive. The international business environment is complex today and would be much more critical tomorrow. It is an age of your acid test where you cannot expect an easy walkover.

Actually, it is an age of investment dressing where we count dress for success. The wardrobe has emerged as an important factor for getting a respectable position in the corporate world. You can go to the peak of the corporate ladder, if you perceive dress culture in a right fashion. The MNCs in particular have been found assigning due weightage to wardrobe as 71% of the respondents feel. In respect of other Indian companies, we find this 65%. The most important thing is your professionalism in managing the wardrobe. It is quite natural because today we find corporate world going through an attitudinal transformation and assigning a transcendental priority to the non-verbal communication. You are supposed to receive everything in detail and even a minor mistake may be a reason for your firing. Accessorising is an important dimension for the classic management of wardrobe which you need to store in your memory.

Of late, we find management of looks becoming significant specially in the corporate world and the employees undermining it albeit suffer on that account. The corporate world has been found discriminating employees over looks. We find this significant for both the genders. Such discrimination is found 27% in the case of men and 55% in the case of women. Almost 54% of the respondents feel that discriminatory attitude is existent over looks of the corporate employees. Thus for both the conditions to be hireable or promotable, you need to be particular to the management of wardrobe. And while managing your looks even small things are given big importance. If we talk about the Indian companies, it is found 53% in case of women and 21% in case of men. Thus both the MNCs and domestic companies are found discriminating employees over looks. This is a big change in the attitude that we should not undetermine.

Good looks have always been a paying proposition because based on psychological considerations we find people preferring attractions. The good looking people are found successful in getting better pay and ensuring positive appraisal. In the case of MNCs, the 56% of the respondents agree with the role of good looks in getting better pay and ensuring better appraisal. Even in the Indian companies, it is 53%. Hence the people working in the MNCs or domestic companies cannot overlook the management of their looks.

It is quite natural that all the employees either working in the MNCs or in the domestic companies are interested in getting a lucrative pay or package or promotion or a positive evaluation of their looks. Hence, it is significant that you assign due weightage to your facial appearance. A galloping increase in the development of beautycare industry is a staunch testimony to this proposition that the demand position for the beauty products would sizably increase in the coming days.

Better turnout also plays an important role in the modern corporate world. We find 79% of the respondents assenting that a better turnout makes the ways for the development of confidence level in the working employees. In the context of Indian companies, this percentage is found to be 78% when in respect of MNCs it is 82%.

The facts and figures outlined above make it clear that your thematical competence is not the only thing specially in the corporate world. If you are not sincere and professional while managing your wardrobe, its multi-dimensional implications would harm you in different ways. All the aspects narrated earlier go through the dimensions for the projection of your personality. The wearabouts if not managed properly would prove to be an important reason for your firing. Getting job, ensuring promotion, creating good impression and establishing image are the important considerations which we need to care while managing our looks. Right from the entry to the last point, we find looks playing an important role.

The facts and figures may have some minor variations but around the globe we find almost the same trend specially in the corporate world. It is not to be forgotten that corporate culture is not influenced by the national or regional considerations because they consider employees just an extension of brand and even minor variations may influence the corporate or brand image. Since we find MNCs dominating the global economy, it is quite natural that even the domestic companies are influenced by the cultural patterns set by them. Better looking people are found optimistic. This is the main theme that we find honestly conceptualised by the corporate world. And we do not find it wrong because based on psychological considerations each one of us nurture weaknesses for attractions. May be that it is more for women and less for men as the survey reveals but we find it relevant today and it will remain relevant even tomorrow. Looking for optimistic people, creative people cannot be wrong because if you have zest for your life, you want to make it sure that all the doors for negative developments are sealed.

In view of the above, it is right to mention that during the yesteryears, we have witnessed an attitudinal transformation which is in favour of attractive and impressive facial appearance. Since we appear to be crazy for the opulent lifestyles, we have no option but to trap ourselves for better looking which would make us much more submissive to the organisational culture.

SUMMARY

In this chapter, you have gone through the key areas found essential for managing your looks specially in the face of changing corporate culture. After going through, make it sure that the following facts are well versed:

Looks: the Concept: By looks, our focus is on the facial appearance of an individual in tune with the changing corporate requirements.

Globalisation vs. looks: Globalisation of economy made ways for the globalisation of fashion, culture and civilisation. Such a change in the socio-economic set up, engineered a sound foundation for the development of look culture which received wider acceptability in the corporatisation process.

Local and Global Corporate Culture: The emerging corporate culture started influencing the globe. Employees are considered to be an extension of the corporate brand without any geographical, social and cultural limitations. Consistency in image necessitates consistency in the conceptualisation process.

Dimensions of Corporate Looks: Wearabouts constitute various facets related to the dresses that we wear the hair style that we adopt, the shoes and socks that we wear, the wristwatch and pen that we use, the jewelleries and ornaments that we wear, shirts and ties that we wear and in addition some of the basics concerned with personal hygiene such as management of nails, hands and feet.

Management of Wardrobe for Corporate Men: An elegant wardrobe adds additional attractions to your personality. Too matchy-matchy cannot be helpful in having a win-win situation. Looks must be appropriate for the workplace. We need to be presentable, clean and well groomed. Our business wear should have a match with our personality because we dress for success. We need to develop our awareness of business apparel. Since we find a close relation between organisational culture and organisational dress code, it is pertinent that we keep on moving the process of value addition. Enriching your wardrobe is thus of prime importance where you have to take a decision regarding colour mix for formal and informal meetings and functions.

Management of Wardrobe for Corporate Women: With the increasing number of women in the corporate sector, it is significant that we categorically think over their wearabouts. A classy business suit makes women feel good and in addition also reflect their persona. Proper accessorising is found significant to add value to their facial appearance. You need to take care of your hands and feet. Cosmetics help you in highlighting your best features. Accessorising need due care. You need to harmonise and customise accessories in the face of your professional requirements. Your hairstyle and shoes need due attention. You need to look distinct.

Grooming: Here our focus is on ensuring proper preparations through value addition which make people commensurate with the organisational culture. Grooming is one of the distinguishing factors of the successful and a well-kept secret of investment dressers.

Investment Dressing: Investment on dressing with a particular motive, making use of the services of experts for focused grooming, communicating through non-verbal communication, accessorising in a scientific fashion and making investments in facial appearance with the motto of developing a professional image for getting the desired position is known as investment dressing.

Accessorising: It is a process of value addition where we take a decision regarding pearls, diamond, scarf, junk jewellery, black pumps, blouses and handbags in the case of corporate women. In a true sense, it is a device to have an individualistic look where both men and women need due care.

Leveraging Colour: It is concerned with our knowledge of mixing colour in tune with our formal and nonformal uses. This helps us in increasing the power of colour.

Managing Hair: It is an important dimension of grooming for both the genders. The style of our hair speaks of our personality. The right hairstyle projects our best qualities. Face structure is an important consideration for adopting a particular style.

Managing Hands: This is found concerned with personal hygiene. You need to wash your hands and to make it sure that nails are timely and properly trimmed. We need to develop our awareness of manicure and pedicure.

Managing Shoes: It is significant that you wear quality shoes and socks and are very particular to its proper maintenance and regularly spit and polish them for proper shining. Black and brown colours are the best option.

Regulate Body Odour: We need to remove the body odour. This necessitates twice brushing of our teeth and also to take some breath mints or make use of mouth spray. We need to avoid wearing perfume or cologne. The motive is to keep ourselves free from the bad breath and the body odour.

Promotional Corporate Apparel: This is making use of clothing as a device for business promotion. Here, our focus is on the dresses bearing the potentials of attracting the people. Printed Caps, Screen-printed T-shirts, Company Jackets are used in this context.

Organisational Responsibility: The organisations need to issue guidelines and instructions related to casual dress, or formal dress, expectations of organisations regarding the wearabouts, imparting training for professional appearance and etiquette, imparting sexual harassment training so that employees are sensitised.

Emerging Trends: Of late, we find investment dressing getting priority attention and this necessitates a sophisticated wardrobe. Both the genders need to develop their awareness of the organisational expectations regarding attire. Relaxed mood is now not to serve their purpose. They need professional mode which requires an in-depth knowledge of corporate apparel. The corporate culture requires creative and optimistic people which is not to be possible unless we find corporate men and women nurturing keen interests in enriching their facial appearance.

KEY TERMS

Attire	Grooming
Apparel	Accessorising
Looks	Business Suit
Corporate Wear	Investment Dressing
Wardrobe	Scarf
Body Odour	Black Pumps
Aesthete	Hairstyle
Wit	Beauty Parlour
Fun	Beauty salon
Bucks	Wristwatch
Buzzwords	Manicure
Finishing Schools	Pedicure
Business Schools	Footwear
Non-verbal Communication	Oral Hygiene
Soft Skills	Deodorant
Hard Skills	Dress Code
Leveraging	Dandrufs
Manicure	Spectacle
Persona	Promotional Apparel
Personality	Sexual Harassment
Corporate Trainer	Business Casual
Hiring	Business Protocol
Firing	Tencel
Obese	Texture
Corporate Culture	Golden Handcuffs
Professional Mode	High Flier
Relaxed Mode	Lense
Shabbily Dresses	Czars
Scruffy Dresses	Zippy Attitude
Pinstripe Shirts	Sleeping Shoes
Wrinkled Shirt	Impeccable Grooming

EXPECTED QUESTIONS

1. Focus on the concept and percept of looks in the present corporate world. Do you find looks closely associated with the profession and organisational culture? Justify your arguments.
2. Do you find corporate employees an extension of corporate brand? How and in what way the local corporate culture and the global corporate culture cannot move in the different directions? Defend your arguments.

3. Throw light on the various dimensions of corporate looks in the face of increasing domination of MNCs.
4. Explain the essential requirements for the management of wardrobe for corporate men.
5. State and examine the management of wardrobe for corporate women.
6. Throw light on the tips to be productive to the corporate men for the projection of a sound physical or facial appearance.
7. What tips would be useful to the corporate women for enriching their facial appearance commensurate with the emerging corporate culture? Explain.
8. What do you mean by Investment Dressing? Do you find investment dressing essential for getting the big business bucks? Justify your answer.
9. What do you mean by accessorising in the context of business attire? Do you find it significant to the corporate employees? Defend your arguments.
10. State and explain the important areas for managing the outfits of corporate people.
11. What do you mean by Grooming? Explain its relevance in the projection of facial appearance.
12. Focus on the aspects responsible for body odour and suggest the measures which can help regulating it.
12. Do you find leveraging of colour helpful in increasing the impact of wardrobe of your personality? Defend your arguments.
13. Throw light on the responsibility of organisation to the employees specially while making them aware of the dress code to be followed.
14. Enumerate the role of hairstyle, shoes, hands and body odour in the management of facial appearance.
15. Focus on the role of Finishing Schools in the development of corporate people.
16. Do you find corporate apparel to play an important role in the management of looks for the corporate people? Justify your viewpoints.
17. Explain the emerging trends in the corporate attire.

APPLICATION EXERCISES

1. Our upcoming and budding youths need to be much more sensitive to the management of wardrobe which would considerably help them in getting big bucks. Comment on this statement in the face of emerging and dominating corporate culture.
2. The corporate sector would continue to pick better-looking people in the coming days. Do you agree with this view in the capacity of a corporate professional? Justify your arguments.
3. Melanie Griffth, a character in the American movie "Working Girl" injected life to her realisation that unless she brings a change in her New Jersey image, she cannot be accepted as a Manhattan professional. Was she right in her observation? Comment.
4. Do you find corporate employees just an extension of the corporate brand and a follower of the corporate culture, not just locally but globally too? Defend your arguments as a corporate professional.
5. Wearabouts constitute the various facets related to the dresses and accessories. In the capacity of a corporate professional, throw light on these facets.

6. An elegant wardrobe adds additional attractions to the facial appearance of corporate men and women. But here, too matchy-matchy cannot be helpful in having a win-win situation. Do you agree? Justify your opinion.
7. New York University surveyed 152 companies and asked them to question. "What are some of the reasons you do not hire people?" They came up with 48 reasons. The No.1 reason why people are not hired is because of how they present themselves in the interview. In the light of this observation, throw light on the fact that how and in what way clothing is also an inner cue affecting our self image.
8. Sabira Merchant, a business woman considered as India's first corporate trainer is not a CEO but she can teach CEOs a thing or two about conducting their business. In the light of this statement, focus on the traits to be developed by the potential corporate managers interested in joining the corporate sector.
9. Mr. A was one of two finalists for a high salary position in the corporate world. He had been interviewed twice and was one of the interview that involved face-to-face with the CEO for the final round. He was very confident of getting the job. But unfortunately, the decision was in favour of Mr. B. He asked the Human Resource Manager why he was not chosen and the HRM said, Do you remember when we were walking up to the CEO's office, it was noticed that your shoes were scuffed up.

   In view of the above, throw light on the attention to the details for getting the best.
10. Pria Warrick, Executive Director of the Pria Warrick Finishing School, says, "Companies need to address body language, posture, handshake and the age-old Indian pitfall, body odour." Do you agree with her views? Defend your opinion.
11. Shrey Gupta who's studying at (SRCC) Shri Ram College of Commerce and is the President of the Students' Union has been hired at a starting salary of ₹ 39 1akh per annum with Deutsche Bank. Shrey's father Alok Gupta says, "I gave my son freedom to think and act and never pressurised him to join IIT or become a doctor. As a parent, I encouraged him to ask questions, develop an interest in music and even share jokes." Of course, it is the secret of Shrey's success. Do you agree? Do you find basics the most important thing for hiring by the corporate sector? Justify your viewpoints.
12. Jackson Lewis, a law firm that specialises in personal issues polled more than 1000 human resource executives who had implemented a dress down policy. They reported a 30% increase in the firtatious behaviour contributing to an increase in the sexual harassment lawsuits. In the face of this result throw light on the dress policy to be adopted by the corporations.
13. Do you advocate Saree as a corporate attire in the Indian perspective?
14. In the capacity of a corporate professional, throw light of the accessories to helpful in enriching your outfits in tune with corporate requirements.
15. "The Sunday ET and Synovate survey to gauge whether appearances play a part in professional growth proves that not everything is stuff of water cooler chats. As a whopping 71% of the corporate executive polled agreed that what you wear is a big factor in your climb up the corporate ladder." Do you agree? How and in what way your appearance makes you more hireable and promotable? Defend your arguments.
16. Your down-to-earth practical approach to life, your knowledge bank related to basics, your zippy attitude, your facial appearance and your awareness of wearabouts make you much more hirable and promotable in the present business world. Do you agree? Justify your arguments.

17. In the corporate world of today, your hair style occupies a place of outstanding significance just as the corporate wearabouts. The hairstyles speak of your personality. The right hairstyle projects your best qualities." Comment on this statement and suggest the hairstyles to be adopted by the corporate men and women in different situations.

BACK-UP MATERIALS

1 www.frontierlaw.com
www.the hindustainessline.com
www.legalservicesindia.com

Corporate Personality
Physical appearance Affects Personality

2. www.bplans.com
www.ehow.com
www.ibisworld.com

Beauty Salon Industry
History of Bathing
Spa

3. spas.about.com

Beautyworld India 2010
Business of Beauty
Beauty Salon
Beauty Treatments
Beauty Salon Products

4. www.korencheng.com
www.pierss.com
artofmanliness.com

Building a Wardrobe
Dress for Success No Myth
The Well-groomed Woman
Developing Sartorial Skills
The Well-groomed Man
Your never get a second chance to make a first impression

5. www.mindtools.com
www.sosuave.com
www.askmen.com

First impressions are important
First Impressions Power
The Relationship between Appearance and Interview Success
The Relationship between Clothing and Behaviour
The Relationship between How Your Dress and your Professional Goals
The Relationship between Local Corporate Culture and Global Corporate Culture
Daily Wear for Academic, formal Academic Dress
Personal Accents
Sample Wardrobe
Wardrobe Essentials

6. www.beautybehaviours.com
   www.articlesbase.com
   www.infobih.com
   Hair Styles personality
   How Your Hairstyle Makes Public Your personality
   Choosing a Hairstyle for your Lifestyle

7. www.economictimes.com
   en.wikipedia.org
   www.narree.com

   Saree is way to go for Indian Women CEOs

8. www.nos.org
   www.webhealthcentre.com
   healthy-india.org

   hygiene, Medical hygiene

9. www.watch-wiki.net ask metafilter.com
   www.brandedwatchsonline.com
   Best Watch Brands

10. www.fibre2hashion.com
    www.articleshmarticle.com
    www.abacus-caree.com

    Traits Associated with Individual Appearances
    Investment Dressing
    Corporate Wear
    Tencel Clothing
    Clothing with Bamboo fabric

11. www.missattymaam.wardrobe.com
    www.essortmus.com
    www.citygirlstyle.com

    Wardrobe Essentials
    Workplace Dresscode
    Grooming and Appearance
    The Three Levels of business Casuals

12. www.tradeindia.com
    www.suits4menonline.com
    www.theguidetomenssuits.com

    Wardrobe Essentials
    Match Making
    Matching Your Clothes Elegantly
    Pick Solid Colours

13. www.leathertree.com
    Tan Leather Briefcase

14. www.citenr.com
www.corporategurukul.com
Adapting to Corporate Life
First Impression
Corporate Groming Do's and Dont's

15. www.ties.scasues.co.in
www.indiamart.com
Corporate Ties
Dress for Success
Learning and Understanding Your corporate Dress Code

16. Wearabouts: The Economic Times
October 24, 2010
A smooth Finish

17. Hired Young: The Times of India,
February 13, 2011

18. Real Women, Real Experiences,
The Times of India,
June 26, 2011

19. Buy me Beauty, The Times of India,
July 10, 2011

20. Jha, S.M.: Services Marketing; Himalaya Publishing House Pvt. Ltd., Mumbai, 2011.
Chapter 15: Personal Care Marketing. pp. 470-91.

21. What's age got to do with it? The Times of India, July 24, 2011.

◆ ◆ ◆

9 LEADERSHIP SKILL

Honing leadership skill is found significant to counter the mounting volatility in the business world. We need strong management with strong leadership because strong leadership with weak management may be worse than the reverse.

CHAPTER DESIGN

Introduction – Leadership: the Concept – Managers vs. Leaders – Leadership: the Typology Theories of Leadership – Learning Leadership – Leadership Skills – Emerging Challenges in Developing Leadership Skills – Responsibility before the Business and Finishing Schools – Summary – Key Terms – Expected Questions – Application Exercises – Back-up Materials.

CHAPTER OBJECTIVES

This chapter aims at studying some of the important dimensions of leadership skills. The motive is to sensitise the readers to the relevance of leadership skills for countering the challenges in the business world. The Business and Finishing Schools bear the responsibility of honing leadership skills so that supply position is in tune with the demand position. The readers come to know the changing requirements of the present corporate world.

LEADERSHIP SKILL

◈ Introduction

Mounting volatility in the business environment makes it essential that an organisation assigns due weightage to the leadership skill of a manager. This is due to the fact that leadership successfully copes with the change. You need to make it sure that your organisation is overmanaged and in addition, you have also to ascertain that it is not underled. Thus, ensuring strong leadership with strong management may be helpful in excelling competition. You also need to remember that strong leadership with weak management is not to serve your purpose because sometimes we find it worse than the reverse. There is no doubt in it that leadership complements management but it is not to replace management. In a true sense, the changing scenario or corporate world makes it essential that leadership and management complement each other.

Management controls people by pushing them in the right direction whereas leadership motivates them by satisfying their basic needs. We cannot undermine the instrumentality or motivational forces in improving the performance level of people. The risk bearing capacity of leaders is found of high order and as and when we start countering the multi-dimensional changes in the business world, it is quite natural that in the process, we find high intensity of risks. Surviving and thriving in an adverse condition is a real thing that determines the magnitude of our success. When we plan to get the desired results or when we propose to march forward on the paths of risks and uncertainties; we will have to keep ourselves ready for both the conditions, triumphs, or failures. Actually, we learn from both but mostly from our failures. The youths have a high risk bearing potential; they know the skill of countering the challenges. This makes it essential that we create wider opportunities for the young employees. The upcoming youths are found believing the realities that climbing the corporate ladders, specially in an adverse condition, sizably rest on the shoulders of youths.

In view of the above, it is right to say that leadership trait of an individual is an important dimension of our personality and while hiring and firing, we have to understand the leadership potential of an individual. It is against this background that we find, of late, the business world looking for people having the leadership quality. Around the globe, we find emergence of a new trend. The big city firms recruit only from the top universities, they cherry-pick students, with strings to their bows-football captains and leaders of orchestras. What impress recruiters today are the youngsters with leadership skills.

The father of modern hiring technology, Bill Byham says, "The best way to select people who will thrive in your company is to identify the personal characteristics of people who are already thriving and hire people just like them. "If we turn our eyes on the successful corporate people of today, we find a majority of them sound in leadership skill. Actually, they like the poise and assertiveness of a young man who can emerge as a leader. They look for creative leaders who are found dynamic with a rock star personality. Usually they happen to be doers and blend easily into a multi-cultural environment. The companies look for people with positive attitudes and skills, not knowledge. They need young people who have tolerance for stress and behavioural flexibility to handle crisis. In this changed scenario, it is imperative that people evincing keen interests in climbing the corporate ladders develop leadership quality and bring in their attitudes the behavioural flexibility. In an age of multi-cultural workplace environment, it is imperative.

An outstanding plus point that we find in the people having leadership potentials is their risk bearing capacity. They try to lead, take a risk and learn from both the triumphs and failures, and such a learning process helps development of honing leadership. It is in this context that we find corporate world seeking out people with leadership potentials and exposing them to career experiences designed to develop that trait. The people having leadership skill like taking charge, accepting challenges, countering the threats, initiating and penetrating things and ultimately getting a success in excelling competition. Having leadership skill is thus found of paramount importance.

We cannot undermine the potentials or an individual in coping with the change. We cannot underrate the risk bearing capacity of an individual. We cannot underweight the relevance of behavioural flexibility and creativity. And then, we cannot deny the outstanding contributions of people having leadership potentials. If we keep ourselves satisfied with survival, we cannot thrive. The leadership quality of an individual paves avenues for initiating risks, accepting challenges, adjusting with the situations and excelling competition.

It is not meant that we find management irrelevant. Because it is about coping with the complexity. Its practices and procedures are significantly a response to one of the most significant developments of the 20th century which could made possible emergence of large organisations. Good management brings a degree of order and consistency to key dimensions like quality and profitability.

Thus, the two important facets of modern corporate world Leadership and Management are the two distinctive and complementary systems of action which has its own function and characteristic activities and we find both of them essential for success in today's business world. Either we talk about coping with complexity or our focus is on coping with change; the target is success which is not to be achieved unless both of them complement each other.

In this chapter, we focus on leadership skill and therefore go through the aspects which may be helpful in honing leadership skill but it is not meant that we promote leadership at the cost of managerial proficiency.

Indeed, it is meant striking a balance between the two. Strong leadership and strong management may increase the efficacy of an organisation to excel competition. It is against this background that we find much more focus on leadership potentials of people so that by educating and training them in a right fashion, they develop both the traits.

Creating a culture of leadership is found significant in today's context and this requires creation of challenging opportunities for young employees. This may be in the form of new products or services. Institutionalising a leadership-centred culture may be helpful in the creation of corporate culture where people would value strong leadership and further would strive to create it.

Developing leadership is considered significant. We cannot negate that development of an individual begins with his/her family. All of us experience the traumas associated with separating from his or her parents but this makes ways for the development of leadership. The two different courses of development are possible; first is development through socialisation which prepares individuals to guide institutions for maintaining the existing balance of relations and the second is development through personal mastery which impels an individual to struggle for psychological and social change. The first line of development produces managerial talent whereas the second line of development produces leaders. For the development of society, both of them play a meaningful role.

When we talk about leadership, in the context of business or corporate world, our focus is on identifying the leadership potentials in an individual and by educating and training, honing the process of development and making them productive. Of course, they develop leader-managers, because they do not feel that people cannot manage and lead. During the yesteryears, we have witnessed business world making a search for people having leadership potentials. It is also found that business houses have developed Business Schools and Finishing Schools to inculcate and cultivate the leadership and managerial traits. It is in this context that we find Infosys have built a Global Education Centre in Mysore, teaching more than 50,000 graduates leadership and corporate manners.

Whatsoever the new developments that we find during the yesteryears are in the face of emerging corporate sector and increasing intensity of competition. With the increasing heat of globalisation, we find MNCs dominating the national economy which has made ways for a number of new developments paving avenues for myriad of challenges and threats. The corporate world has become much more competitive and volatile. The process of technological sophistication has gained a rapid momentum which has engineered a sound foundation for the emergence of techniculture. The deregulation of markets and increasing heat of globalisation has made place for strong international competition. In addition, overcapacity in capital-intensive industries, an unstable oil cartel, raiders with junk bonds and changing demographics of the workforce are important factors responsible for a shift in the corporate world. Amidst new developments, the corporate world realises the importance of business leaders who have the potentials to face the challenges and threats to excel competition.

◈ Leadership: The Concept

At the outset, it is essential that we go through the conceptual aspect of leadership. Distinct to management, the leadership is not mystical and mysterious. It has nothing to do with "Charisma" or other exotic personality traits. We may not consider it a province of a chosen few. In the recent years, the term leadership has emerged and got a special position in the business world. The multi-dimensional developments in the business world, taking place around the globe, are responsible for a large-scale use of the term business leadership. Leadership is about coping with change. More change, much more demand for leadership.

We consider leadership a parental concern for anyone who needs to motivate, guide and inspire people. Since we find leadership helpful in motivating people by satisfying basic human needs, its impact on people is found of high order. We may also consider it a device helpful in attracting strange feelings of identity and difference or of love and hate. It is found as a regulator just like the analogy of pressure cooker. Of course, for cooking, a particular degree of pressure is essential but if this balance is not maintained, we find it not only affecting the quality of food but also instrumental in inviting dangers. We may also consider leadership a process of translating their personal values into calculated action.

Leadership also makes possible creation of a holding environment found at the initial stage in which condition is created for diverse groups to talk to another group about the challenges. Based on interactions, deliberations and discussions, a leader clarifies the assumptions behind competition perspective. It is to ensure a sense of belonging, recognition, self-esteem, feeling of control over one's life and the ability to live up to one's ideals touching us deeply and eliciting a powerful response. It is also a device of maintaining the sequence and pace the direction and speed of work.

Leadership makes us responsible for directing, protecting, orienting, managing conflict and shaping norms. A leader is supposed to provide cover to the employees. It is in this context that we find leadership very much instrumental in gaining the popularity of employees.

When we consider leadership as a device to be helpful in many ways, it is to cope with change. Because change is found to be everywhere, the leadership appears to be an effective prescription. Sequencing and pacing are the two important considerations to establish leadership. It is an effective prescription to counter the challenges, mainly caused by volatility and high intensity of competition in the business world.

While perceiving leadership in a right fashion, we need to make it clear that leadership complements management; it does not replace it. The act of leadership is coiled in the essence of institutionalising a leadership-centred culture. Leadership is a quality, it is a property, it is a trait.

It is the capacity to translate the vision into reality. More so, it is the process of encouraging and helping others to work enthusiastically towards objectives. It is the behaviour of an individual to influence others. It is a group phenomenon which involves interaction between two or more people. It is the set of qualities or characteristics attributed to those who are perceived to employ such influence. It is an interaction between persons with the motto of influencing.

Thus, we receive the concept and percept of leadership in different ways but one thing is almost clear that it is a big source for projection both at personal and institutional or organisational levels. Due to leadership traits, an individual becomes successful in projecting his/her image and based on the same traits he/she succeeds in projecting the image of organisation. It is the increasing significance of leadership that the word "leadership" has been widely used in different streams. The political, social and business are the areas where we find leadership gaining much more popularity. We may consider it the ability or potentials: of an individual or we may also consider it a trait or quality but one thing is clear that it is an art to influence or impress upon an individual or a group.

Vision is an important dimension of leadership through which we find a leader making use or his/her emotional appeal to transform the attitudes of members of his/her team. When we talk about leadership as a process, this is very much related to the influencing process but when our focus is on leadership as a property, it is concerned with the qualities, attributes or traits which simplify the influencing process. It is also considered as a group phenomenon where we emphasise on the interaction between two or more people.

The facts outlined above make it clear that in today's business world, the leadership has gained an outstanding significance and it is against this background that we find corporate world making a search for leaders. If they look for a captain of a football or cricket team or if they look for team leader of an orchestra party or if they prefer to employ the leaders of students' union; the main theme is that they have a leadership quality based on that they can influence the employees working with them and the set target can be achieved. When our focus is on the transformational leadership, it is concerned with transformation of attitudes and behaviour of the employees by the leaders with the help of emotional intelligence and appeal.

The corporate world of today is found much more volatile. Frequency in change is gaining a rapid momentum. The corporate world requires strong leaders and strong managers failing which it will be difficult for them to excel competition. Of late, if you have to thrive, you need creative leaders found well-versed in handling the situations for shaping the holding environment by interacting and deliberating upon the issues related to challenges and threats, clarifying the assumptions behind competition and achieving the target.

◈ Managers vs. Leaders

The managers and leaders cannot be successful with identical properties. Both of them need to realise their functional responsibilities and based on that the required properties or traits are to be developed to be the goals of managers arise out of necessities rather than desires. Leaders, on the other hand, adopt personal, active attitudes towards goals. The business world cannot survive unless both of them with the required properties or traits continue to serve the business world. It is significant that the business world finds ways to train good managers and develop leaders at the same time. This necessitates an in depth knowledge of the required properties and the existent organisational culture. We cannot not deny that business leaders have much more in common with artists, scientists and other creative thinkers than they do with managers. The thought experiments thus become an important aspect for the development of leadership and the logics of strategy and imposing the constraints of computer exercises are found to be of secondary importance.

Leadership is different from management. We find them the two distinctive and complementary systems of action. Each has its own function and characteristic activities. Both of them are found significant to the success in an increasingly complex and volatile business environment. It is against this background that we find successful corporations not waiting for leaders to come along rather than seeking out people with leadership potentials and exposing them to career experiences for the development of that potential. It is also an unvarnished fact that everyone cannot have potentials to act as successful leaders as well as the successful managers. Some people have the capacity to become excellent managers but not strong leaders and some others have great leadership potential but they have difficulties in becoming strong managers.

Management is about coping with complexity and therefore complex organisations cannot survive if they do not have quality managers. We find good managers having the potentials of maintaining a degree of order and consistency to key dimensions like the quality of product and the profitability. By contrast, leadership is about coping with change. Since we find the business world becoming much more volatile and competitive, it is imperative that people with leadership quality serve the organisation. If we have to survive and thrive, it is pertinent that we develop our awareness of incoming changes, challenges and threats and based on the emerging problems develop prescription to be much more effective. The increased frequency in change always makes a call for creative leadership.

Management controls people by pushing things in the right direction whereas leadership motivates them by satisfying their basic human needs. Managerial processes must be as close as possible to feel safe and risk-free whereas the leaders evince interests in facing risks and accepting challenges.

Planning and budgeting play an effective role in the management process which is followed by setting targets or goals for the future, establishing detailed steps for achieving those targets and allocating resources to accomplish those plans. But when we talk about leadership, it starts with setting a direction, developing a vision of the future along with strategies for producing the changes required to achieve that vision.

The management is concerned with developing the capacity to achieve by organising and staffing and for that creating an organisational structure, staffing, and managing the jobs with qualified people delegating responsibility for carrying out the plan and identifying systems to monitor implementation. But when we talk about leadership, it is primarily concerned with aligning people where we find emphasis and communication channelising new directions to those who understand the vision and are found committed to its achievement.

Management ensures plan accomplishment and for which the managers take help of controlling and problem-solving. Both the formal and informal processes are adopted by a manager to monitor the results. But when our focus is on leadership, it is concerned with achieving a vision by motivating and inspiring people. Of course, we find multi-dimensional changes and challenges in the business world but the leadership skills successfully resolve them. The human needs, values and emotions are tapped by appealing and influencing the people found responsible for that.

However, we accept the fact that leadership and management are the two distinctive but complementary systems of action. Both of them are found essential for getting success in the modern business world. Either we talk about coping with complexity or our focus is on coping with change; both the streams play a meaningful role in the existence and prosperity of an organisation.

The volatility in the business environment has gained a rapid momentum specially in the 21st century which necessitates creative leaders and it against this background that organisations have already started making a search for successful leaders. It is found that a number of corporations due mainly to recession are undermanaged and at the same time, we also find them underled. Strong leadership with weak management cannot serve our purpose. It is a challenging task that how and in what way, a balance is made possible so that strong management and strong leadership are combined. This makes it essential that corporations, of course, on a priority basis look for people having leadership potentials and expose them to career experiences designed to develop that potential. Against this background, we find corporations around the world hiring and promoting the creative leaders.

The facts outlined above make it clear that leadership complements management, it does not replace it. The challenges are much more frequent, the intensity of competition is found high and in this emerging scenario; we need visionaries having the efficacy of anticipating the future and the most effective prescription for that is availability of a successful leader.

◈ Leadership: The Typology

The two different types of leadership coexist in almost all the work situations. It is significant that at the outset, we make ourselves aware of the formal and informal leadership.

Making use of a formal authority by a manager makes place for the formal leadership in which duties are assigned to the employees holding different positions. It is use of official position of a manager in which he/she may work as a manager as well as a leader. A manager gets an opportunity and responsibility to exercise formal leadership in relation to the subordinates who may act as a follower. We find a few of the managers having better understanding of the authority and formal relationships with subordinates and by making use of his/her influence, he/she succeeds in impacting on them which results into the increased level of productivity. Such type of organisation is found overmanaged an overled. We call such managers successful leaders. Since we find a manager making use of his/her managerial as well as the leadership skill for which he/she has formal authority, we call it a formal leadership.

In case of informal leadership, we find a person making use of his/her excellence in influencing the behaviour of others for which he/she does not have a formal authority. Of course, he/she is not formally appointed but we find him/her acting as a leader due to his/her actions and personal attractions due to non-verbal communication, handsome personality and high communicative ability.

It is also important to mention that a manager may act in both the conditions as a formal as well as an informal leader in some of the selected situations. In some of the cases, we find a manager acting as a formal leader and the same manager in another case also acts as an informal leader. When we find him/her acting as a formal leader, the manager follows the chain of command and exerts influence whose movement is downward or we may call it from leader to the follower or from a manager to the subordinates. Just reverse, when we find manager making use of his/her professional excellence and leadership skills for influencing employees outside the formal organisational chain of command, it is called an informal leadership. Since we do not find the managers having a formal authority, it is imperative that they show "charisma" or are competent enough to exercise their influence.

The facts outlined above, establish formal as well as the informal leadership. We cannot deny the fact both of them are found impact generating to make an organisation strongly-managed and strongly-led. In the modern corporate world, where we find multi-dimensional changes making the business environment much more volatile, it is pertinent that both types of leadership vis-à-vis high degree of managerial proficiency are available. We raise strong voices in favour creative leadership because adjusting with the changing situations and establishing in the multi-cultural or cross-cultural environment cannot be an easy task unless we have creative leaders with innovative vision to counter the challenges generated by strong competitors.

◈ Theories of Leadership

The two important facets draw our attention when we talk about leadership theories. Trait and Behaviour are found significant in the very context. We call the first trait theory of leadership and like this, the second behavioural theory of leadership.

Trait Theory: In this theory, we find focus on the traits required for a successful leader. Here, our focus is on the individual characteristics or property for the successful leaders. A number of experts have focused on the leadership traits. The most important thing is related to a strong desire for accomplishment. Because unless we have a strong desire, we cannot think about its accomplishment. The next is pursuit of goals and after that we find creativity and intelligence for solving the problem. The personality is also considered to be a trait because we find it effective in activating the influencing process. It is also significant that successful leaders have a low level of susceptibility to interpersonal stress and willingness to accept the behavioural consequences. We cannot undermine here the level of tolerance of a leader vis-à-vis the ability to influence people. The social interactions also draw our attention in the very context.

Behavioural Theory: This theory focuses on behavioural profile of leader found helpful in influencing others. While interacting, deliberating and discussing, this trait is found very much effective. How a leader should behave is the main theme that we find in the behavioural theory of leadership. The successful leaders on the basis of his/her behavioural profile succeed in getting the cooperation of subordinates which simplifies the task of increasing the level of performance. The level of satisfaction is also an important consideration when we talk about the behavioural theory.

An important study related to behavioural theory of leadership is from Ohio State University. This study talks about two important leadership dimensions. The initiative structure where we find focus on leader behaviour defining and organising the group tasks, assigning the tasks to employees and supervising their activities. The next refers to leader behaviour which is characterised by friendliness, respect, supportiveness, openness, trust and concern for the welfare of the employees.

Another study was made by the University of Michigan in which the two dimensions of leadership discussed are production-centered and employee-centred. The production-centered leaders set rigid work standards, organise tasks down to the last detail, prescribe the work methods to be followed and supervise the performance of subordinates. The employee-centered leaders encourage employee participation in goal-setting and in other work related decisions and help ensure high level of performance by inspiring respect and trust.

Both the theories are found suitable and while developing leadership quality, it is imperative that we do not undermine any one.

◈ LMX Theory

LMX or Leader-member Exchange or dyad theory focuses on the people found close to the leader. This theory is based on this assumption that the behaviour of leader depends on the nature and quality of subordinates working with him/her. It is also clarified in this theory that leaders form two groups of followers which may be known as in-groups and out-groups. It is found that in-group members are found more satisfied and they have high organisational commitment. Contrary to it, the out-group members are managed by formal rules and policies and receive less attention. This theory throws light on social exchange found between leaders and followers. The in-group members are found more close to the boss. We cannot deny that in this theory, the task of categorising the subordinates into in-group and out-group is found difficult.

◈ Contingency Theory

The Contingency theory of leadership is derived from the basic proposition that the most effective behaviour for leaders to engage in is contingent upon characteristics of the situation in which the leaders find themselves. This model is also known as Fieldler contingency model and in addition to this theory of leadership, we find the situational leadership theory and path-goal theory of leadership in this contingency category of leadership theory. According to the Fieldler theory, the effectiveness of a successful leader depends upon his motivational style and favourableness of the situation. The motivational factors are inter-personal relations or task goal accomplishment. The situational support is the extent to which the leaders can exercise control over the situation. The path-goal theory of leadership makes it clear that the leader's job is to use structure, support and rewards to create a work environment helping employees in achieving the organisational goals. According to this theory, the leaders bear the responsibility of clarifying the goals.

Earlier, we have talked about trait and behavioural theory. Thus, we find all the theories discussed here are important for the development of leadership. The prevailing conditions determine the intensity of impact of a particular theory. In the context of contingency theory, we also find the situational leadership theory. This theory requires focus on giving guidance and direction and offering socio-emotional support. This theory throws light on the maturity of followers as a contingency variable. Thus, we find here task-behaviour an important aspect found closely associated with the relationship behaviour. By task-behaviour, our focus is on the guidance and direction whereas by relationship behaviour, our emphasis is on socio-emotional support. This theory of leadership is found flexible in nature and therefore in today's context, we find situational leadership occupying a place of outstanding significance.

In view of the leadership theories outlined above, it is right to say that the most important task before a manager is to assess the situations and on that basis taking a decision regarding suitability that which theory would be effective and which style of leadership would be proactive.

Of late, we find much more volatility in the business environment and therefore, the situational leadership may be much more appropriate to counter the challenges that we find before a leader.

◈ Learning Leadership

The corporate world is looking for creative leaders. They offer big bucks and recruit even ordinary people having leadership potentials. They are recruiting captain of a football or cricket team; team leader of orchestra party and president of a students' union. They are visiting leading colleges and picking students having leadership potentials. In a true sense, we find ordinary candidates establishing an edge over the extraordinary. Change is a natural phenomenon. We can neither change the process; nor can turn the direction. If we have to thrive, we have to exercise the best option which may help us in excelling competition. We find the demand-side of the job markets moving towards a new direction; now it is upon us to cash or to suffer. The upcoming youths or the budding generations, the parents and the Business Schools vis-à-vis the Finishing Schools need to identify the direction of wind and to develop the traits, properties, attributes which may be pro to the development of leadership faculty. Parents need an attitudinal transformation. They need to provide to their children freedom to think and act. They need to encourage them to ask questions, develop an interest in music and even share jokes. These properties would make them a differentiator. They need to make it sure that their children hone their leadership skills, logic, intuition, thinking, communication and manners. The Business Schools and Finishing Schools need to cultivate skills not knowledge so that they are well aware of etiquette and manners. They need to cultivate confidence. Even Child Counsellors feel that in the changing scenario let your children tackle everyday problems, don't protect them from difficulties. Let them be a problem solver, adaptable and agile and try to shape their personality rather than getting them lost in books during their school years. Of course, you need an attitudinal transformation.

Learning is an ongoing process or a continuous process. Each and everyday, we have something to learn. Leadership has to take place everyday. The style has to be changed in tune with the changing situations and conditions. In the corporate or business world, we find adaptive challenges all the time. This necessitates a learning strategy. Leadership is a perennial concern for anyone who needs to motivate, guide and inspire.

The concerned individuals or institutions need to make it sure that how and in what way their products prove to be doers and develop the potentials on people to adjust easily into a multi-cultural environment. They need to be dynamic with a rock star personality. They have to come up with new ways of communication and collaboration that inspire and connect employees around the world. The corporate world needs people who can anticipate and thrive to change. They need creative leaders of tomorrow. They need visionaries who can anticipate future change. It is our responsibility that we educate and train them in such a fashion that they prove to be productive to the corporate world. Let them face the problems to be a problem-solver. Let them play with the difficulties to find out an appropriate solution.

The prospects interested in becoming corporate leaders need to develop their awareness of the traits and further with self and institutional support have to cultivate and inculcate the properties so that the business world considering their potentials hire them for a position. It is not essential that you are an extraordinary student. It is not essential that you happen to be a topper. Indeed, it is most important that you have a personality in totality. You have high communicative ability and potentials to influence the people. You are aware of etiquette and manners and have made place for aesthetic sense. You have a high degree of skill to accept the challenges and get the cooperation of your associates in countering the same. You take even minor things in detail. You are visionary and have the potentials to anticipate the changes to take place in the future. You believe in identifying the problems and take interests in getting them solved. You have skill to design strategy in both the conditions; either as an offender or as a defender. You have human touch and you believe in promoting humanised leadership. You evince interest in game, music, joke and doing something different to others.

Creating challenging opportunities for your associates or team members is an important functional responsibility before you as a corporate leader. The young employees working there need to face the challenges. You have to be clear that challenges, are not only for the top-level employees but, even for the lower-level employees. The new products and the new customers throw before you new challenges and it is an acid test of your leadership skills. Preparing people for small and medium-sized leadership jobs is also significant which would simplify the functional responsibility of top-level leaders.

We do not find any boundary for the development of leadership skills because we do not find any boundary for challenges and threats. We do not find any boundary for risks because we do not find any boundary for volatility. The most important thing, rather vulnerable thing in the corporate world is flexibility. And successful leaders develop the skill of transforming the vulnerabilities into opportunities. How and in what way, you can make it possible; it is upon you to decide.

In the present business world, we need more people to provide leadership because multi-dimensional complexities are there. Hence, it is to be accepted as an ongoing process when you succeed in establishing a leadership-centred culture. Actually, we need to realise the importance of leadership in the changing scenario. Your ability to nurture leadership would only not make your organisation overled but would also provide to you opportunities for future promotions. In a true sense, the process is to be institutionalised which cannot be possible unless, you have a big team of leaders at all the levels.

The changing business world makes it essential that upcoming youths or budding generations realise gravity of the situation. The parents need to realise the order of the day. The educational institutions need to realise the changing demand-position. The policy makers need to simplify the tasks of all concerned.

◈ The Skills Leaders Need

The conceptual aspect of leadership makes it clear that coping with change is the most important aspect that a leader requires at different stages of discharging his/her functional responsibilities. The managers and leaders act in a different way. A closer examination of each of the activities will clarify the skills required by leaders in the changing scenario.

1. Setting a Direction: It is found different to planning. When we find planning as a management process found deductive in nature; the setting of direction is found of inductive nature. Explaining things in a convincing way is significant and the leaders collect a broad range of information and look for patterns, relationships and linkage which make their task easier. Creation of vision and strategies is suitably and efficiently done by the leaders which make it clear that in the long run what type of business, technology and organisational culture would be effective for achieving the desired goals. People articulating such visions are broad-based strategic thinkers interested in taking risks. The most important aspect in the creation of vision in its effectiveness in serving the interests of customers, stockholders and employees. The vision ignoring the legitimate needs of stakeholders cannot be considered good. The overmanaged and underled companies frequently commit mistakes by concentrating on long-term planning and it proves to be a time-consuming device which cannot be productive in a dynamic business environment. Actually, the planning process without direction cannot be effective even it is concerned with the short-term plan. We cannot negate that a competent planning process serves as a useful reality check on direction activities but a competent direction-setting process provides a focus in which planning can realistically be carried out.

2. Aligning People: Aligning involves talking to so many persons. The target population can involve not only the subordinates, but in addition also bosses peers and staff in other parts of the organisation. Besides, the suppliers, government officials or even customers may be involved. The most important thing is that available one is efficacious of implementing the vision and strategies. Credibility happens to be a big challenge in leadership efforts which makes the messages much more responsive. The track record of the person delivering the messages, the content of the message, the reputation of communicators and consistency between words and deeds significantly contribute to credibility. Alignment makes it essential that in an organisation, there are sufficient number of people who have experiences and power which make them strong. Alignment of people is found successful in overcoming this problem by empowering people.

3. Motivating People: Coping with the barriers to change is significant. When we talk about leadership, it is considered to cope with the change. In this context, we find highly energised behaviour significant. The successful motivation ensures that we have enough energy to overcome the obstacles. Satisfaction of basic human needs proves to be a motivational force. When we motivate people and inspire them in a right way, we find an occasional burst of energy and the influencing process in satisfaction of basic human needs. A sense of belonging, recognition, self-esteem, a feeling of control over one's life and the ability to live up to one's ideals become instrumental in eliciting a powerful response. It is upon the leaders that how and in what way, the motivational processes are initiated and motivational force is, activated. Articulating vision of organisation in such a fashion that stresses the value of the audience they are addressing assign due weight to the concerned people and they evince interest in achieving the vision. This provides to the people a sense of control. Besides, extending the best possible support to the employees in understanding the vision in a right way cannot be undermined. They may provide coaching, feed-back support and role modelling which may be helpful as an effective motivational technique. The successful leaders are found recognising and rewarding success which not only gives to the employees a sense of accomplishment but also make them feel involved in the process of organisational development..

4. Creating a leadership culture: Creation of a leadership culture is considered significant to keep on moving the process of making good leaders. We recruit people having leadership potentials and in due course educate and train them in the required condition. Managing career patterns of people working with us is found helpful in activating the process. Developing a wide range of leadership skill is significant in today's perspectives. The people in 20s and 30s of their life cycle find it easier to make use of their leadership skill because at this stage and age, they have high potentials of bearing risks. They are competent enough to learn both from triumphs and failures. They are in a position to develop a wide range of leadership skills. This helps in developing a leadership culture. The task is to develop people for important leadership positions at the level of senior executives. To make it possible, it is significant that we make a search for people having leadership potentials. Who has considerable leadership potential and what skills they need to develop executives are to be identified and then with the help of time-planning, the leadership skills are to be developed. In that context, we may think in favour of two measures; first with the help of a succession planning which may be formal and second through high potential development process which may be informal. This necessitates an intelligent assessment of feasible development opportunities required essential for each candidate. If we keep on moving the process, it helps in developing corporate culture where people assign due weightage to strong leadership and make sincere efforts to create it. We need people having strong leadership potentials and we also need people who can make them strong leaders. This draws our attention on institutionalising a leadership-centered culture considered to be the ultimate act of leadership. Of late, we find corporate world making efforts in this direction and it is in this context that we find a big search continuing for people having strong leadership traits.

Currently, we find the business of smart hiring gaining a rapid momentum in the corporate world. The new cult of hiring czars or spotting the best fish in the pond is a new shift which is found moving towards leadership. It is amazing that people grabbing the plush jobs are not extraordinary. The new high flier is our average boy — next door, with a down-to-earth practical approach to life. The two examples are quoted here. Shrey Gupta who's studying at Shri Ram College of Commerce is also the President of the Students' Union. He's been hired at a starting salary of A 39 lakh per annum with Deutche Bank. Two years ago, Amit Mathur, son of former cricketer Amit Mathur, got a salary offer by the same bank for A 32 lakh, because his expertise in the basics gave him an edge over others. Both of them had leadership potentials. Shrey Gupta says, I think they identified my leadership skills. I like taking charge and initiating things.

The facts outlined above make it clear that corporate world is looking for people who have leadership potentials. When we talk about Shrey Gupta, he honed his leadership skills, logic, intuition, thinking, communication and mannerism and all these qualities are essential for the development of strong leadership. This emerging new trends indicate that corporate world has been looking for people having a zippy attitude. They like the poise and assertiveness of a young man who emerged as the leader. Hiring is no longer about finding people with the right experience but those with the right mindset. Gita Dang, founder Director of Talent Advisory

Service says, We are looking for creative leaders. Those kids will work at the bottom of the pyramid. They are dynamic with a rock star personality. They are usually doers and blend easily into a multicultural environment.

We are well aware of the fact that corporate world, of late, has been facing myriad of challenges and threats. And it is against this background that they need people having the potentials to adjust in a flexible environment. They feel that young talents have more confidence to work anywhere and therefore we find them getting the appreciation of corporate world. Polly Courtney wrote in her book, Golden Handcuffs: The Lovely Life of a High Flier. They cherry-pick students with strings to their bows, football captains and leaders of orchestras and entice them with offers of fancy dinners and expensive wine. Actually, they look for people who are trainable. These are great takeoffs but they may not end with path breaking super careers. Most of these firms recruit young talents from Ivy League Colleges globally and then send them to do MBAs from premier institutes after two years.

What impresses recruiters are youngsters with leadership skills. The corporate world has been found cultivating leaders who can tackle this new age of global competition. They look for people who can anticipate and thrive on change. Sangeeta Lal, partner at Transearch doing executive and CEO-level hiring says, We are looking at young talent that will make creative leaders of tomorrow. We need visionaries who can anticipate future changes. We look for people with adaptability, agility and ability to think beyond today. Thus, it is an age for creative leaders.

5. Identifying the Adaptive Challenges: The increasing frequency of change in the business environment of today has been making place for multidimensional challenges and threats. How and in what way, we accept and counter them determine the magnitude of our success. The creative leaders are considered to be potentially sound to identify them. The leaders are supposed to identify struggles, overvalues and power, recognise patterns of work avoidance and watch for the many other functional and dysfunctional reactions to change. Leaders see a context for change or create one. They give employees an idea of the market forces and point out precautions for shaping the future. Learning quickly to adapt to new challenges we are likely to face is significant to get the desired level of success. When a leopard threatens a band of chimpanzees, the leopard rarely succeeds in picking off a stray because the chimpanzees are aware of the way of responding to this kind of threat. Since they are aware of the way, they succeed in countering the threats and saving their lives. It is against this background that we need to make ourselves aware of the new challenges likely to come. Creating trust is considered significant to win the heart of employees responsible for your success or failures. For a successful strategy formulation, it is imperative that the leaders understand themselves, their people and the potential sources of conflict. When you know yourself, when you are aware of the strengths of your competitors or opponents and when you are aware of the environmental conditions; the possibilities of getting a success are found wider. May be that in the process, the leaders would know that whose values, beliefs, attitudes or behaviours are to be changed what shifts is priorities, resources and power are necessary and what sacrifices would be required to be made and by whom. And if you counter with precautions after making necessary preparations; the success is yours.

If we find corporate world looking for captains or orchestra leader; it is due mainly to the fact that they have properties to be adapted to challenges; they have skill to identity the situations; they have patience to educate and sense their team players; they have patience to receive the feedback and make necessary preparations and excellence of identifying the moment of offending or defending. During the yesteryears, the corporate world witnessed much more volatility and even in the coming years, we expect a number of changes. The leaders succeed because they do not plan for survival rather than they plan to establish leadership and from the very beginning make themselves aware of the challenges and threats likely to emerge. This engineers for them a sound foundation for excelling competition and getting a success.

In view of the facts outlined above, it is right to say that the business leaders need to know the skill of accepting the challenges and countering them like a fighter equipped with all the sources and resources for planning and getting a success. This makes it significant that we identify leadership property of the budding and upcoming generations and tap them, educate and train them, guide them, cooperate them to excel. If we are managerially proficient, we have also to make ourselves overled.

6. Regulating Distress: By distress, our focus is on extreme anxiety, pain or exhaustion for which we find sufficient reasons in the corporate world. We find adaptive work very instrumental in generating distress. When we start working on challenges, it is imperative that people working with us are distressed because they are unaware of the solution required for countering the challenges. Hence, it is the responsibility of a leader to make them aware of the new ways of learning so that distress accumulated on that account is regulated. The leaders in the very context are also required to strike a balance between having people feel the need to change and having them feel overwhelmed by change. Maintaining a productive level of tension is necessitated which makes it essential that a leader takes help of three fundamental tasks which would be effective in motivating people. The first task is related to the creation of a holding environment where a leader is supposed to regulate the pressure based on the analogy of a pressure cooker. The holding environment is a temporary place in which a leader creates the conditions for diverse groups to enable them interact, discuss and deliberate which may be helpful in clarifying the assumptions behind competitive perspectives and values. The second task is concerned with directing, protecting, orienting, managing conflict and shaping norms. In this context, a leader provides direction by identifying the adaptive challenges and framing the key questions and issues. Besides, a leader protects people by managing the rate of change and orients people to new roles and responsibilities by clarifying the business realities. Further, a leader helps exposing conflict and finally a leader helps in maintaining the norms. The third task is concerned with presence and poise and regulating distress which is considered to be the most difficult.

A leader requires emotional capacity to tolerate uncertainty, frustration and pain. The leadership demands a deep understanding of the pain of change and the fears and sacrifices associated with the same. The verbal and nonverbal cues of a leader would be instrumental in projecting the potential of a leader. Here, we find confidence of leader occupying place of outstanding significance and therefore, it is significant that a leader is in a position to communicate confidence because if we find employees, colleagues and customers realising some weaknesses in the confidence level of a leader, its negative impact on all of them cannot be ruled out.

Changes taking place in the business world provide to us an opportunity but in addition, we also find them active in creating an adverse condition. It is upon a leader to identify the nature and gauge the implications so that adjust its processes are not to create complexities. By its very nature, the adaptive work is found to be distress friendly but it is not meant that we seal doors for the creation of risks. Unless we develop our temptation to business risks, it is difficult for us to get the desired success. The distress would come, we cannot seal doors for its entry. What we can do in the very context is to increase our capacity to counter and resist.

In view of the above, it is right to say that a leader requires the ability to regulate distress coming due mainly to the challenges due to change.

7. Developing Humanised Leadership: Leaders or managers find it difficult to accomplish the organisational goals; unless in both the capacities we find them protecting and promoting the interests of humanity by meeting and fulfilling the humanitarian commitments and by showing and nurturing sympathy and empathy. If you show human touch in your behaviour; the employees working with you; the followers commanded by you extend their best cooperation even in a rough weather. The task of countering the challenges is found to be easier if the followers start respecting your command. The empathy shown by you makes the environment at the workplace much more congenial. Hence, it is imperative that while scanning the traits required to be developed by the leaders in a business; we also focus on the humanity and empathy which may make even our difficult tasks easier. We cannot negative that lack of personal philanthropy has been found common in the today's business world which requires a reversal.

During the yesteryears, we have witnessed much more frequency in change. The increasing heat of volatility in the global business environment is not to be slowed down. The challenges are to be multidimensional. Personal interests have an edge over the social and community interests. Lack of personal philanthropy is to aggravate further. In the face of all these negative developments in the business world there will be an acid test of your leadership. This necessitates development of leadership culture in an organisation which is not to be possible unless we find environment at the workplace becoming much more cohesive.

Diagnosing the problem is not the only motto of a successful leader. Indeed, he/she requires a prescription which is to be effective and even this is not to be possible if you lack humanity. In almost all the areas and for almost all the purposes, your human face determines the magnitude or your success. It is a trait which benefits you in many ways. Your words; your commands start impacting your groups, teams and followers, if their sense of realisation is positive. If they feel that as a leader, you have not committed any mistake while fulfilling the humanitarian commitments, the process of getting cooperation gains a rapid momentum.

It is against this backdrop that business leaders of today need much more focus on empathy and personal philanthropy. If we start believing that our success rate is the result of our leadership quality; if we start strengthening our perception that by making use of institutional and organisational assets and wealth for personal interests, benefits and gains; the interests, of humanity would remain unprotected.

We cannot deny that during the yesteryears, Indian business tycoons have marched forward to the path of progress but at the same time, we also find crisis of person like Azim Premji in the corporate world. The Indian business tycoons should take lessons from Warren Buffetts, Bill Gates, Paul Allens and Azim Premji. Such an attitudinal transformation would develop personal philanthropy amongst the business leaders which would be a service to the humanity vis-à-vis to the Indian society. In this context, we cannot overlook Tata emerging as a shining example of personal philanthropy.

◈ Emerging Challenges in Developing Leadership Quality

It is an unvarnished fact that overmanaged but underled companies cannot be strategically sound to excel competition. Crisis of leadership, if not removed on a priority basis would obstruct the flow of development. Changes are taking place and changes will take place because change is a natural phenomenon. Adjusting to the flexibility commensurate with the changing requirements of the business world is a matter of concern which requires due attention of business leaders. In the process of developing leadership, a number of problems crop up. How and in what way, we response would determine the magnitude of our success. Here, we focus on some of the challenges before the business world which require due priority. The contemporary issues like transformational leadership, encouraging women as a business leader, problems of women employment, charismatic leadership, etc., need due focus. The continuing crisis of personal philanthropy in the business world, specially in the Indian perspective, is also an emerging problem. Besides, we also find a majority of the Indians very much sincere to the enrichment of thematical competence but least interested in developing leadership potentials. It is against this background that an anatomy of some of the emerging challenges is found significant.

Transformational Leadership: This implies a process where we find ourselves interested in elevating our consciousness so that a shift is made possible which may be from one style to, another, or one culture to another. This ultimately focuses on raising the level of human conduct and the ethical aspects of both, the leader and the led. The business leaders of today deny conceptualising transformational leadership and therefore, we find crisis of personal philanthropy and empathy. If Tata group of companies are found distinct to others in terms profitability, professional excellence and social responsiveness, it is due mainly to the fact that we find on them the imprints of transformational leadership. If Tata talks about personal philanthropy and empathy, it is an attitudinal transformation which may protect and promote the interests of humanity. Such transformational leaders assign due weightage to the national and social interests. Maintaining our identity and sustaining our ethos if remain uncared may be helpful in transforming the economy but the process of social transformation would not gain a momentum.

Thus, in the changing scenario, we need more transformational leaders. Of course, the Indian business tycoons may not welcome such change but here they should not forget that if prosperity of subject remains neglected the prosperity of companies are found in danger. In a true sense, they need to contribute to the economy, society and humanity. Prosperity of a kingdom depends on the prosperity of its subject. We may strongly advocate in favour of corporatisation but here it is also imperative that we are sincere and honest to the interests of millions and millions of people who nurture high hopes and aspirations from the business tycoons.

◈ Women as Business Leaders: Break the Glass Ceiling

Of course, we find participation of women in the business world gaining a momentum but even till now, we find it very disproportionate. Though we find women very much successful in establishing leadership in the business world; however we find them confined to the lower paid jobs which has been obstructing the process of increasing the number of women as business leaders. We cannot deny that socio-cultural barriers have also been responsible for the present position and this requires an attitudinal transformation. The motive is to encourage women so that they are motivated to get the high-paid posts. We cannot negate that women have all the traits required for the development of leadership provided we make available to them an opportunity and make use of their potentials. The cultural patterns prove to be a barrier where we find women leading their lives in a bit different way, with a different lifestyle and a different mindset. It is against this background that they could not be successful in increasing their number. At the same time, it is also right to say that with the increasing heat of globalisation, we find an attitudinal transformation and resulting from which we find a significant increase in their enrolment in the business schools.

Women have all the traits to be a successful business leader and therefore we need to motivate them to business education. But in this context, it is also imperative that we remove the barriers complicating our task in different ways. We name those "glass ceiling" referring to the barriers keeping women away from reaching at the highest level of management in an organisation. They have limited opportunities to learn or advancement for expatriation and fewer opportunities to work in projects which may enhance their visibility exclusion from networks and dyads alike. The socio-cultural barriers also aggravate the magnitude of problem. We cannot deny the beginning but unless we find glass ceiling cracking into different pieces, the barriers would continue to obstruct the process of education, empowerment and top positions either in the business world or in other areas of their interest.

We have a number of examples when women reached to the pick of the business world; however they have taken most care of their family or children. Chanda Kochhar, Naina Lal Kidwai, Shikha Sharma, Anu Aga, Lalita Gupte, etc., are a few names though at the top of the business but have successfully optimised their family responsibilities. They have defined vision and have honed leadership skill. This speaks of the fact that women are potentially sound to discharge multi-functional responsibilities which cannot be done by their male counterparts. Hence, we need to promote women as business leaders and to break the glass ceiling. Particularly, the cultural barriers restricting women in different ways need a fresh look.

Not only at bottom level, but even at the top level, we need to be liberal to the women so that the process keeps on moving. At the same time, it is also pertinent that women do not forget their responsibilities to their family members and respect the socio-cultural norms. In the changing scenario, the opportunities would be available in a large number and policy decisions vis-à-vis attitudinal transformation would help them in capitalising on the opportunities.

◈ Charismatic Leaders: We Need Today

The increasing volatility in the business environment makes it essential, that we have leaders having the potentials to bear risks of high intensity. When we talk about a charismatic leader, our focus is on dynamic risk-takers considered to be an important trait for the development of business leaders who can show their expertise and self-confidence, express high level of performance and expectations and use symbols and language to inspire others. They have the potentials to motivate their followers or employees working with them. The employees, working with a charismatic leader feel satisfied. We cannot negate that such leaders throw major influence on the followers and hypnotise them in such a fashion that they can show a high level of performance. We can also know them as mentors who treat employees individually and guide them to take action. Since we find them a high risk-taker, it is imperative that in countries like ours such charismatic leaders are given due weightage. Influenced by idealised vision, we find such leaders never believing in status quo, or always striving for a change.

Since we find them innovative, they always make use of unconventional methods to transcend the existent order. In a true sense, we find the counter normative. They have strong articulation of future vision and are motivated to lead. They have high intensity of environmental sensitivity to cope with change. It is in this context that in the changing business world of today, we need charismatic leaders in a good number.

We are well aware of the fact that present business environment is found highly volatile where leaders with high sensibility and flexibility have been found getting the desired success. The leaders not striving for a change cannot be a high risk-taker and therefore the success rate of such leaders cannot be extraordinarily high. For getting an extraordinary result, it is imperative that we have elitists in a very large number; we have risk-taker in a good number and we have the required number of innovative leaders in the role of a transformer.

Of course, we find charismatic leaders very much effective in an abnormal condition when we find a crisis like situation but as and when the crisis is over, we find them becoming a liability. When in social, practical, cultural, spiritual and business areas, we find something wrong making an invasion on their existence, the charismatic leaders prove their excellence. But at the same time, it is also right to say that charisma brings a radical change in his/her personality and attitudes which may harm the interests of concerned organisations or institutions. It is in this context that Peter F. Drucker has been found much more critical to the charismatic leaders like Stalin, Hitler and Mao. To some extent, we find his observation logical because high rate of success transforms our attitudes and behaviour and we find emergence of negative trends.

In view of the facts outlined above, it is right to mention that because currently we find the business world facing an abnormal crisis where even our survival is in danger, it is a need of the hour that we have charismatic business leaders who can manage the crisis and bring the economy back on the rail but side-by-side, it is also imperative that we find development of personal philanthropy and empathy in their behavioural profile so that the expected negative thoughts are sealed.

Leaders need Emotional Intelligence: Emotions nurture emotions; emotions protect and promote emotions. If you have emotions; you have self realisation, empathy, adaptability and even personal philanthropy which keep you satisfied and keep others convinced. Business leaders getting success in the business world should not keep themselves detached with emotions. The moment they start sharing the credits of their success with their stakeholders; the ladders for development are made clear and you get an opportunity to gain and retain your position. This makes it essential for the business leaders to get success in the modern business world. We need to develop their awareness of the hallmarks of emotional intelligence and get them practised, sincerely and honestly. You also need to know that everything is found based on your intelligence for which you need to enrich yourself. Your excellence of studying and understanding yourself provides to you the excellence of reading and understanding the feelings of both which we know as emotional atonement where we find scope for mending our behaviour and changing our attitudes in a positive direction. The most important thing is self-realisation and the moment you start confessing; its direct impact is found on your outlook and mental conditions. For emotional intelligence, it is also imperative that you manage your emotions in a right way and do not overwhelm yourself for the successes in your credit. You need to be self-driven and strengthen your realisation that you are not the only person found making outstanding contributions to the success. You virtually need to deny gratification and exhibit patience for rewards because the moment you start craving for immediate gains; it is to damage you and to tarnish your image in the business world.

Crux of the problem is that business leaders or even social leaders have not been realising the role of emotions for establishing relationships and getting a success. If Tata in India could be successful in projecting his image as a philanthropist, it is due mainly to his emotional intelligence. We find the same case with Bill Gates or Azim Premji. Of course, we find a number of business leaders though getting a success in the business world but we find them at the bottom when we talk about emotions and therefore they lag far-far behind in respect of empathy and personal philanthropy. It is against this background that we find a crisis of business leaders having empathy. It is expected from the successful business leaders that they possess emotional intelligence.

In view of the above, it is right to say that for the development of leadership in the business world of today, the corporate people need not to bid a goodbye to emotions. How and in what way, they make place for emotions is an important problem. In this context, it is imperative that corporate people are involved in the social activities and organisations provide to them an opportunity to take part in the spiritual sessions. Though we find material culture making the task much more complicated because this closes doors for the entry of emotions as a personal trait. If present generation lacks emotional intelligence, there will be an analogous negative impact on the outlook of those persons which would obstruct the process of developing empathy and personal philanthropy.

◈ Responsibility before Business and Finishing Schools

The corporate sector is, of late, looking for people having leadership potentials. It is based on their assumptions that because leaders have vision, they are found in a position to anticipate the incoming changes and challenges; the task of accomplishing the organisational goals would considerably be simplified. Keeping in view the shift that we find the business world, it is pertinent that B-Schools and Finishing Schools accept it as a challenging task and ensure the inculcation of leadership, skills amongst their potential managers. It is quite natural that unless and until the organisations are over managed and underlined the emerging challenges cannot be translated into opportunities. Strong leadership and strong management would be the most important prescription to counter the multi-dimensional problems experienced by the business world.

Mushrooming of B-Schools cannot resolve the problem rather their contributions to the process of developing leadership skills would determine the magnitude of success. Right now, the B-Schools in general have been found concentrating on the development of managerial proficiency and undermining the relevance of leadership skills which of course can make them a successful manager but not a successful leader and resulting from which we find their products becoming absolutely unproductive in today's context. Of course, we find the opening of Finishing Schools gaining a rapid momentum but even then the Business Schools have not been discharging their functional responsibilities in the desired way. This has been affecting the supply side and we find a significant increase in the number of underled companies. This in a very natural way makes a call in favour of a close coordination between the Business and Finishing Schools.

Educating and sensing the prospects to cater to the changing corporate requirements happens to be the most important issue that we often forget. The opening of Finishing Schools gained a momentum due mainly to the fact that the existing B-Schools could not play the role they were required to play. If we do not witness the challenges; we cannot learn the skill of countering and encountering. We cannot formulate a strategy and cannot make preparations for time honoured implementation. Unless and until, we find our students lacking communication excellence, leadership skill, vision, creativity, adaptability and corporate looks; the task will remain difficult. They even lack etiquette and manners; they are not aware of civic and aesthetic sense; they lack personality, intuition and thinking. Anticipating and thriving on change is significantly needed but we find them potentially deficient. They do not involve themselves in the extracurricular activities. With limited personal score, they prove to be unproductive to the corporate world and therefore face the hiring problem. It is against this background that we find Infosys building Global Education Centre and even other companies thinking and acting in this direction.

To increase the supply position, it is imperative that we come to know the demand position. We need to know the changing requirements of corporate world and to educate and develop the potential managers in tune with their requirements so that they cater to the changing requirements of the corporate world.

The B-Schoo1s of today need the services of corporate trainer. We need to strengthen our realisation that soft skills are as important as the hard skills. We also need to perceive that absence of social graces from the present generations is to make their task much more complicated. Keeping pace with the growing demand is to be an effective strategy to balance the demand and supply position. Willingly or unwillingly, we have to accept the fact that India has some of the world's best educated engineers, business majors and technology wizards but often our executives lack social polish and communication skills that puts them behind competitors. The Business and Finishing Schools have to try their best to make available to the corporate world finished product.

We need Guru of graces who inculcate and cultivate the traits required by the corporate world. Honing certain behaviours like walking upright and with confidence, wearing a well-tailored suit and talking clearly without the fillers "like" or "you know" will make our upcoming generations stand out or to be easily acceptable. It is amazing that the average Indian executive's corporate wardrobe is almost a cry of help. It cannot be refuted that we are in the middle of the game and only quality corporate trainers and guru of graces can enrich our personal score to excel in the global environment.

We need to address much more to the potential managers from voice and accents to dining etiquette to dressing up basics. We find Pria Warrick, Executive Director of the Pria Finishing School right in her observation that we Indian have a predilection towards education and caring little for manners. She points out that it's always been a case of study hard, getting good scores and grades and everything else are taken care of but lack of social graces even among some of the highest-placed executives is a matter of serious concern that we need to ensure.

According to hiring experts, the ultimate candidate should have a zippy attitude. They like women who are active without being domineering. They like the poise and assertiveness of youngsters who can emerge as a leader. Of late, hiring is no longer about finding people with the right experience but those with the right mindset. It is our responsibility that how and in what way, we can make their mindset right. We need to make them adaptable and agile rather than getting lost in books specially during the school years.

The B-Schools and the Finishing Schools need to read the writing on the walls and to develop their products in the required fashion. They need to cultivate skills not knowledge. They need to increase their confidence for developing and displaying the leadership skills. Overseas the MBA schools have special classes that even tell you what colour of ties to wear with what suits. Hence, they need to renew their education, training and development programmes in the face of developments taking place around the globe and only then their tasks would be found complete. Striking a balance between soft and hard skills is a crying need of the hour; they need to store it in their memory box.

SUMMARY

In this chapter, you study the different dimensions of Leadership skill. Before starting another chapter, be sure that the following facts are well-versed.

Leadership: the Concept: Leadership is a perennial concern for anyone who needs to motivate, guide and inspire people. Leadership complements management; it does not replace it.

Managers vs. Leaders: Leadership is different from management. We find them two distinctive and complementary systems of action. Each has its own function and characteristic activities.

Leadership: The Typology: The leadership is found of two types such as formal and informal. Making use of a formal authority by a manager is formal leadership whereas in the informal leadership, an individual makes use of his/her excellence for influencing the behaviour of others without any formal authority.

Theories of Leadership: The different theories of leadership are trait theory, behavioural theory, LMX theory and the Contingency theory.

Learning Leadership: Learning is an ongoing process. Leadership has to take place everyday. This necessitates a learning strategy so that we come to know the latest developments and changing requirements of the corporate world.

Leadership Skills: The business leaders in particular need to develop the skill of direction setting process, aligning people, motivating people, creating a leadership culture, identifying the adaptive challenges, regulating distress and developing humanised leadership.

Emerging Challenges in Developing Leadership Skills: Mounting volatility in the business world makes place for the emergence of a number of challenges in the development of leadership. Of late, we need transformational leaders in which we find an attitudinal transformation. We need to motivate women for leadership and in this context to break the "glass ceiling" obstructing the process. We need charismatic leaders to be efficacious of managing the crisis. The leaders also need to develop emotional intelligence so that they develop social graces and get themselves involved in the social activities. They need to be visionary to anticipate the challenges.

Responsibility before the Business and Finishing Schools: In the face of emerging changes and challenges before the business world, it is significant that Business and Finishing Schools come to know about the corporate requirements and inculcate and cultivate the required properties to be a successful leader. They need to cultivate skills not knowledge. They need to review their education, training and development programmes in the face of corporate requirements. They need the cooperation and expertise of corporate trainers and guru of graces.

KEY TERMS

Leadership Skill	Philanthropy
Volatility	Transformational Leadership
Visionary	Glass Ceiling
Vision	Charismatic Leaders
Typology	Emotional Intelligence
Trait Theory	Hiring Experts
Behavioural Theory	Overled
LMX Theory	Overmanaged
Contingency Theory	Rock Star Personality
Path-goal Theory	Creativity
Leadership Culture	Cartel
Leopard	Raiders
Orchestra	Junk Bonds
Distress	Demographics
Humanised Leadership	Myriad
Etiquette	Formal Leader
Manners	Informal Leader
Empathy	Golden Handcuffs
Social Polish	Spiritual
Predilection	

EXPECTED QUESTIONS

1. What do you mean by leadership? Distinguish between managers and leaders.
2. Focus on the typology of leadership.
3. Explain the different theories of leadership and throw light on the suitability of situational theory in the present context when the business environment has become more volatile.
4. Explain the relevance of learning leadership in the present business world where we find high intensity of volatility.
5. Focus on the leadership skills to be effective in the modern business world.
6. Setting a direction, aligning people, motivating people, creating a leadership culture, identifying the adaptive challenges, regulating distress and developing humanised leadership are some of the skills determining the rate of success of the business leaders. Explain your viewpoints on the different dimensions of effective leadership skills.
7. Do you feel that overmanaged and underled companies cannot be strategically and tactically sound to excel competition? Justify your arguments and also throw light on the measures helping you in making your companies overmanaged and overled.
8. With the increasing intensity of volatility in the modern business world, we find emergence of some of the critical problems complicating the task of business leaders. In the capacity of a corporate professional, explain the challenges found to be critical in your eyes.
9. Throw light on the measures to be adopted to break the glass ceiling complicating the task of corporate women while performing and excelling.

10. Who are charismatic leaders? Do you find them effective in an abnormal condition in the business world? Defend your arguments as a corporate professional.
11. Explain the relevance of emotional intelligence in the development of leadership skills.
12. What do you mean by distress? Explain the measures to be effective in regulating distress found before the corporate people.
13. Identify the adaptive challenges before the modern corporate world where we always look for creative and innovative people having a vision.
14. How and in what way, you will be successful in creating a leadership culture in the modern corporate world where we find lack of institutionalised leadership-centred culture? Explain your viewpoints.
15. Throw light on the role of B-Schools and Finishing Schools in the development of leadership skills.

APPLICATION EXERCISES

1. "Effective leadership successfully copes with the change."

   In the face of increasing volatility in the business environment, throw light on the above statement.
2. The father of modern hiring technology, Bill Byham says, "the best way to select people who will thrive in your company is to identify the personal characteristics of people who are already thriving and hire people just like them." Do you agree with his statement? Defend your arguments.
3. "Creating a culture of leadership is found significant in today's context and this requires creation of challenging opportunities for young employees, specially related to new products or services."

   Comment on this statement in the face of mounting volatility in the business world of today.
4. "Around the world, we find emergence of a new trend in the business environment. The big city firms recruit only from the top universities. They cherry-pick students with strings to their bows — football captains and leaders of orchestras. What impress recruiters today are the youngsters with leadership skills."

   Do you justify this new trend. Defend your arguments.
5. "The act of leadership is coiled in the essence of instituionalising a leadership centred culture. Leadership is a quality, it is a property, it is a trait." Comment.
6. "Of late, the organisations are overmanaged but underled." In the face of this statement focus on the development of leadership skills amongst the corporate people.
7. "Learning is an ongoing process. Each and everyday, we have something to learn. Leadership has to take place everyday. The upcoming youths, the parents, the B-Schools vis-à-vis the Finishing Schools of today have to read the writing on the walls."

   In the light of above statement, throw light on the skills to be developed for successful leaders of the business world.
8. "The overmanaged and underled companies frequently commit mistakes by concentrating on long-term planning which proves to be unproductive in a dynamic business environment of today.

In the face of above statement, explain the measures you would prefer to adopt to make the companies over managed and overled.

9. "Coping with change is the most important aspect a leader requires at different stages of discharging his/her functional responsibilities."
   In the face of above statement, focus on the leadership quality requires in the changing business world of today.

10. "The people in the 20s and 30s of their life cycle find it easier to make use of their leadership skill because at this stage and age, they have high potentials of bearing risks. They are competent enough to learn from their triumphs and failures. Comment on this statement and focus on the traits required for the development of leadership skills.

11. "Currently, we find business of smart hiring gaining a rapid momentum particularly in the corporate world. The new cult of hiring czars or spotting the best fish in the pond is a new shift which is found moving towards leadership. It is amazing that people grabbing the plush job are not extraordinary. The new high flier is our average by next door."
    Do you find such shift in the business world to be helpful in increasing the competitive strength of an organisation? Defend your arguments.

12. "A leader requires emotional capacity to tolerate uncertainty, frustration and pains. The leadership demands a deep understanding of the pains of change and the fears and sacrifices associated with the same. The verbal and non-verbal cues of a leader would be instrumental in projecting the potential of a business leader."
    In the face of above statement, explain the leadership skills to be developed.

13. "Business leaders of today need much more focus on empathy and personal philanthropy."
    Do you find the corporate people of today practising it? Justify your arguments.

14. "Overmanaged and underled companies cannot be strategically sound to excel competition. Crisis of leadership if not removed would obstruct the process of development."
    In the light of above statement throw light on the emerging challenges before the corporate world.

15. "The charismatic leaders are found innovative. Influenced by ideal vision, we find such leaders never believing in status quo. They are dynamic risk-taker and feel pleasure in countering the challenges."
    Comment on the above statement.

16. "Management controls people by pushing them in the right direction whereas leadership motivates them by satisfying their basic human needs."
    Throw light on the above statement.

17. "The B-Schools and Finishing Schools need to read the writing on the walls and to develop their products in the required fashion. Striking a balance between soft skills and hard skills is a crying need of the hour."
    Comment on this statement.

BACK-UP MATERIALS

1. Harvard Business Review on Leadership, Harvard Business School Press, 1998
2. John P. Kotler: What Leaders Really Do; HBR, pp. 37-60.
3. Abraham Zaleznik: Managers and Leaders: Are they different? HBR, pp. 61-88.
4. Joseh L. Badaracco, Jr.: The Discipline of Building Character, HBR, pp. 89-113.
5. Ronald A. Heifetz & Donald L. Laurie: The Work of Leadership: HBR, pp. 171-197.
6. Charles M. Farkas & Suzy Wetlaufer: The Ways Chief Executive Officers Lead, HBR, pp. 115-146.
7, Dwight D. Eisenhower, At Ease: Stories I Tell to Friends: New York: Doubleday, p. 136.
8. Hired Young! The Times of India; February 13, 2011.
9. Thomas Teal: The Human Side of Management: HBR, pp. 147-170.

◆ ◆ ◆

10 MARKETING PERSONAL CARE SERVICES

A journey of million miles begins with a single step. The personal care services, day-by-day are becoming much more specialised and the users are becoming much more conscious and sophisticated. Actually, we find transformation of aprototype business into a big sector dominated by a large number of small and big players necessitating conceptualisation of modern marketing principles with the help and cooperation of world-class professionals.

CHAPTER DESIGN

Introduction – Marketing Personal Care Services: A Conceptual Framework – Organisational or Institutional Support for the Personal Care Business – Market Segmentation for Personal Care Organisations – Marketing Information System for Personal Care Services – Behavioural Profile of Corporate Users – Synchronising the Mixes of Marketing – The Product Profile – Promoting the Services – Channelising the Services – Pricing the Personal Care Services – Processing of Services – Physical Evidence – People-Marketing Personal Care Services in the Indian Context – Summary – Key Terms – Expected Questions – Application Exercises – Back-up Materials.

CHAPTER OBJECTIVES

This chapter of the study aims at clarifying the conceptualisation of modern marketing principles by the personal care organisations. The marketers making use of their world, class professional excellence may be successful in creating, satisfying and retaining customers. The study focuses on the formulation of a sound marketing mix. Since the development of a holistic personality requires enrichment of varied personal score, the users require an institutional support to develop their personality to face life in totality. The personal care organisations marketing successfully may get new opportunities to prosper and excel competition.

MARKETING PERSONAL CARE SERVICES

❖ Introduction

Enrichment of personal score is an ongoing process. We live in an age where organisational culture determines the quality and diversity of our personal score. The emerging corporate culture necessitates attachment of employees with the corporate brand because they are considered an extension of the established brand image of the company. If they respect the organisational culture, they have no options but to follow the norms and meet the expectations of their employers. They have to look and appear in tune with their expectations. This makes it essential that they develop the traits and properties which make them efficacious of catering to the corporate requirement. They need to have a rock star personality which is possible when they are physically sound. They need to be fully aware of the civic and aesthetic sense which make them civilised and disciplined and keep them polite. They need to be aware of the considerations for personal hygiene. They cannot prosper unless they have a sound mind which makes it essential that they have successfully cleared all the accumulated complexes and nurture stress-free attitude. They need to be aware of etiquette and manners and for that they require a high level of communicative ability to act and behave in a polite manner. They need to be ethically and morally sound and this is possible when they perceive character as a power. They have a temptation for looking attractive and are aware of the dress code of the company where they serve. They love nature and love themselves which may bring optimism in their attitude and further may also be helpful in making then creative and strengthening their zest for life. Besides, it is also essential that they possesses leadership quality to anticipate the incoming changes in the face of their imagination and wisdom. An optimal orchestration of all the traits and properties would make them individually, socially, organisationally and nationally productive.

Since we find a big list of personal traits, it is difficult for an individual to inculcate all the attributes of the personality unless he/she gets an institutional support. It is against this backdrop that we focus on the role of personal care organisations in simplifying the personality development process. During the yester decades, we have witnessed a significant development in the field of beautycare. The concept and percept of healthcare has also been found taking a new shape. The people in general are found becoming health and beauty conscious to get a respectable position in the business world. This has engineered a sound foundation for the emergence of world class, organisations in the field of personal care.

The thematical competence of an individual, no doubt, is a matter of prime consideration but at the same time, it is also important that in the present scenario, we inject in our personality the multi-dimensional attributes to cater to the modern corporate world. Just the academic excellence is not to serve our purpose and therefore we have to conceptualise, personality in totality. On the one hand, we need to be thematically of world class while on the other hand, we also need to have a number of additional traits and properties in tune with the emerging organisational culture.

We cannot negate that corporatisation is considerably based on attraction and it is not to be possible unless we have a corporate look. Exposition is considered to be an important dimension and projection for exposition is not to be possible unless we find ourselves well equipped. Around the globe, we find corporate sector initiating and activating professionalised efforts for strengthening the value-addition process without which our competitive strength cannot be increased. The personal care organisations working in India need to study the behavioural profile of business tycoons which would let them know the emerging organisational culture. In this context, they also need to know the behavioural patterns of potential users of services.

There are a number of services which can be managed individually even without having the institutional support but some of the selected services require help from the experts. We also find some of the services where supporting infrastructural facilities play an incremental role in the product development process. When we talk about managing the wardrobe, accessorising, investment dressing, managing the hairstyle, grooming, caring for our skin, managing the diet, managing stress, promoting Yoga, managing shoes, ties, briefcases and bags, oral hygiene and dental care, etc., the best results are possible only when we make use of the services of the concerned experts working with the leading personal care organisations of national and international repute. Of course, we find some of the finishing schools involved in the process of educating and training people with the help of reputed corporate trainers but the trainees find their task difficult unless and until they have a personal contact with the providers. Simply awareness is not to serve their purpose unless the services are personally used. Availability and accessibility are essential to have a direct contact with them.

With the growing impact of personal care in social as well as the business sectors, we find development of a good number of personal care organisations in almost all the areas providing single or packaged services. The future of personal carc business is found prosperous because the corporate culture has started influencing our lifestyles. Capitalising on the opportunities in a right fashion requires professional excellence. During the yester decades, we have witnessed qualitative improvements in the personal care business and the trend will continue even in the future. To be more specific in the Indian environment, where the problem of unemployment is found at its peak, the systematic and organised development of personal care organisations would create opportunities for wealth generation vis-à-vis job-creation and business expansion. The most outstanding benefit of personal care organisations is motivating people for developing and nurturing aesthetic sense which is found instrumental in developing optimism in our behaviour. If we start loving ourselves, we start loving nature and this energises our zest for life. Creativity takes a shape and we find ourselves much more productive. The corporate world looks for optimistic people having the potentials to adjust even in a flexible condition.

In the changing business world, the personal care organisations need a new vision because the business world looks for visionaries. They prefer people having aesthetic sense, optimism, imagination and wisdom. They look for people having etiquette and manners. The Indian social environment presents a very gloomy picture where we find a majority of us even not aware of the civic sense. Hence, the personal care organisations need to sensitise people in the face of emerging trends in the business environment. In the Indian markets, we find tremendous opportunities for the development of personal care services and the personal care organisations need to capitalise on the same. With the development of personal care services, there will be a significant increase in the number of potentially sound, civilised and disciplined people.

In the modern business world, we find aesthetic management getting an important place. The personal care services may also be effective in generating the civic sense and nurturing the aesthetic sense. A nicely dressed men or women attract us. A fairly managed physique keeps us smart. An individual with a high aesthetic sense makes the environment at the workplace much more attractive as well as hygienic. We cannot negate that faculties of development rest on the development of our personality. Creativity transgresses the limits of physical boundaries. To look good, attractive and impressive; it is imperative that we keep ourselves net and clean, well-dressed, decently groomed and in the process make it sure that we respect the organisational culture. An affluent desires something more than a poor. The beauty needs more than a beauty care. In almost all the countries of the globe, we find domination of corporate sector resulting into the emergence of corporate culture. It is an unvarnished fact that corporate culture substantially influences our lifestyles. It is against this background that we find western lifestyles influenced by western culture gaining popularity around the world.

Nothing is possible unless we have money in our pockets. With the increasing impact of globalisation, the economic scenario started taking a new shape. This made possible a significant increase in the disposable and discretionary incomes which paved avenues for a change in our life-styles. The credibility for these developments may be given to the corporate sector. Actually, globalisation of economy started globalising the fashion, culture and civilisation which impacted our attitudes and the behavioural profile. Such an attitudinal transformation was not only amongst the people serving the corporate sector but also amongst the general masses, of course with a minor difference in its degree.

Development in one area makes ways for development in other areas. Sophistication in one area brings sophistication in other areas. The attitudinal transformation found in the people serving the corporate world also influenced others and it is against this background that we find the lifestyles of even common people moving towards a shift. Resulting from which, we find a galloping increase in the demand side. This is found to be a positive development particularly for the personal care organisations.

It is not right that we are critical to the fact that beauty lies in the eyes of beholders but at the same time, it is also right that beauty also lies in the hands of those who have made it their business to make others look attractive, pleasing and more importantly impressive. With the increasing awareness of society, we find people becoming much more conscious to healthcare and beauty care. Of late, we find personal grooming becoming popular both in men and women. This has engineered a sound foundation for the development of a multi-billion dollar industry taking a strong shape in almost all countries of the globe. The upcoming or budding generations and youngsters in particular have developed a craze for looking attractive and impressive. According to the Indian Retail Survey 2010, the current size of the beauty care industry is about ₹ 10,000, crores and is rowing steadily at a robust 25% each year. Of course, the global economic recession affected it but it has regained its momentum with a bright future.

Year-after-year, we find a galloping increase in the demand of trained professionals. Currently, we find corporate trainers sensitising the potential customers and this has been injecting new life and strength to the demand side. Dr. G.S. Kochar, Director, VLCC Institute says, "The sudden wellness boom in society is giving a fillip to the trade. The growth is more in Tier 2 and Tier 3 cities compared to smaller cities but incredibly there has been a tremendous growth down the southern part of the country, specially in Chennai which was never so beauty conscious. There has been a 60% growth in the cosmetic industry in Chennai."

The facts outlined above make it clear that not only the beauty care sector but almost all the sectors concerned with the personal care have been found booming and therefore the personal care organisations find the emerging trends much more positive. Some of the areas are found for those who are medically qualified whereas some other areas are even for those who have knowledge of business and entrepreneurial excellence. The cosmetic surgery and body carving are found for those who are medically qualified. The beauty clinic, spas and health clubs, beauty consultants, product analysts, therapist, lab assistants, beauty advisors pedicurists, manicurists, nail technicians, skin and haircare, other technical and managerial staff have a bright future. People now prefer the specialists for the best results. The chemical engineers and people with management degrees also have a place as generalists. Besides, we find Hair colour or Perms specialists, Cosmetology Instructors, Image Consultants, Photo or Movie specialists getting an opportunity to work and travel with celebrities. Like this, a number of areas are found emerging for the concerned specialists and in almost all the areas, we find scope for business. Gradually, we find prospects looking for specialised services and the quality beauty products. What to talk of the beauty parlours, when we find beauty clinics in big demand.

A journey of million miles begins with a single step. The services day-by-day are becoming much more specialised and customers are becoming much more conscious and sophisticated. We find transformation of a prototype business into a big player. This is due to a significant increase in the demand position. This trend is to continue even in the coming years and therefore we find tremendous opportunities for those who are interested in the personal care business. It is in this context that we make a strong advocacy in favour of conceptualising modern marketing principles so that customers are created, their expectations are fulfilled and for the years and years to come they are retained. Professional excellence of world class would considerably simplify the process.

An outstanding task before the personal care organisations is to make an in-depth study of the changing organisational culture so that the services produced by them are found commensurate with the corporate world. The leading personal care organisations may also develop a sound marketing information system to get themselves aware of the developments taking place around the world. An organisation like Kaya Skin Clinics started with a prototype in Bandra in December 2002, has grown at an unprecedented pace as today we find Kaya having more than 100 clinics around the world, specially in the Middle East, in India across 26 cities and the main reason for such a galloping development of the companies is its professionalism which made possible customised and personalised services. Of course, the wellness boom in the society is giving a fillip to the trade and it is to continue even in the years to come. Almost all the concerned organisations need to prefer customisation in tune with the changing level of expectations of customers. Today, we find a number of beauty brands available in the market and therefore professional excellence of organisations to satisfy the customers would remain the only solution to excel competition. A fair match of product with the expectations of customers and requirements of business world would help them in the process. Since we find both the genders men and women showing their temptation to the business world, the personal care organisations would have to prefer personalised services. With creative promotional measures, they can reach to the customers around the world because we find them less price conscious but more quality conscious. They have domestic as well as the foreign customers and therefore a big scope is existent for modernisation and expansion. The electronic channel is also to help them in the process. The Indian personal care organisations are well aware of the Indian environment and therefore it is easier for them to make available the product without any adverse impact on their skin or hair or body. The processing of services need support of quality people and sophisticated technology. The service ambience of personal care organisations must be in tune with the changing levels of expectations of customers. Since a majority of the users belong to the corporate world, it is imperative that they focus on the exteriors having more visibility and the interiors having more elegance and flexibility. The customers look interested in having specialised services and therefore the personal care organisations also need to focus on the quality of technical, managerial and general staff.

Thus, the conceptualisation of marketing principles by the personal care organisations would be found helpful in ensuring to the customers world class services. The marketing practices having a personal touch and professional excellence would be found effective in creating, satisfying and retaining customers both at domestic and international levels. The survey results of Euro monitor dot hint a significant increase in the market for beauty products in the second decade of 21st century.

◈ Marketing Personal Care Services: a Conceptual Framework

At the outset, it is essential that we develop our awareness of the conceptual aspect of marketing personal care services which have a big list. Personal Care Marketing is considered to be a managerial device to market the services in such a way that customised services are made available to the users in the face of changing corporate requirements. It is an organised effort to formulate the different mixes of marketing in an optimal fashion helping users in having a high level of satisfaction. It is a process of developing marketing inputs to have a sound marketing output or it is a process of tailoring marketing resources. Managing marketing activities is an important functional responsibility before the marketing professionals which simplifies the process of making sound marketing decisions. The services are both in organised and unorganised forms but the personal care services for the corporate world are found in an organised way by small as well as the big players at domestic and international levels.

Personal care marketing focuses on the implementation of marketing principles generated by the personal care organisations in the face of changing levels of expectations of customers or users. The services may be packaged or even single. The marketing management throws light on the formulation of marketing mix such as product, promotion, price, place, process, physical evidence and attractions and people. The personal care organisations make use of the services of technical and managerial staff and develop the product in the face of expectations of customers and requirements of corporations. The services may be core as well as the peripheral. The professionals need to be much more innovative while developing peripheral services which make them distinct to others. It is a process of promoting the services with the motto of sensing, sensitising, persuading and transforming the potential users into actual and habitual users. The different components of promotion help professionals in the process. The services are required to be made remunerative or moderate and competitive but at the same time status and quality elements are not to be undermined. The channelisation of services found manually or techno-driven need to be proactive and cost-effective. The processing either with the support of technical and managerial staff or with the help of sophisticated technology must be on time and without any distortion or creating a quality gap. The service ambience should be effective in influencing the users. The technical and managerial or general staff need to be professionally sound.

Thus, the following facts are observed:

- Personal care marketing is a managerial process.
- It is a process well supported by the professionals.
- It is conceptualisation of marketing principles.
- It is an organised and systematic effort.
- It is managing the marketing activities with the motto of satisfying customers or users.
- It is considerably influenced by the customisation process.

◈ Organisational or Institutional Support for Personal Care

The corporate world believes in getting the best results from the efforts we make. It is quite natural that an individual due to some limitations may find the task difficult and therefore we find emergence of a number of personal care organisations for delivering services of world class. Because, it is an age of investment dressing where potential businessmen or women are found interested in making huge investments for the development of their personality. We witness opening of a good number of finishing schools in different parts of the country. In the developed countries of the globe, we find even Business Schools educating and training people in the same direction. The emergence of beauty care and health care sectors is the result of sudden wellness boom in the society which has resulted into the development of even world-class personal care organisations.

ORGANISATIONAL SUPPORT FOR PERSONAL CARE SERVICES

Score	Personal Care Organisations
Sound Physique	Taking support of dieticians, health care experts, Gym, jogging centres, Yoga Centres and psychologists.
Sense of Hygiene	Taking support of healthcare experts and experts in the civic bodies and NGOs. The dentists and other experts helping you in the process.
Civic and Aesthetic Sense	Taking support of educational institutions and beauticians and environmentalists. Getting support from family and society. Getting support from the experts in the concerned area.
Sound Mind	Taking support from the Yoga centres, Psychologists, medical experts. Developing temptation for spiritualism, meditation. Attending laughter club and making efforts for discharging the accumulated complexes.
Politeness in Behaviour	Taking support from educational institutions specially Business and Finishing Schools and psychologists.
Morality	Getting support of educational institutions and organisations promoting spiritualism and philanthropists.
Attractive Appearance	Getting support from beauty clinics, pedicurists, manicurists, nail technicians, perms specialists, therapists, spas and health clubs, beauty advisors, image consultants, etc.
Leadership	Taking support from the Business and Finishing Schools and the concerned experts and consultants.

The concerned personal care organisations need to focus on quality. They need to make their services nationally and internationally competitive.

◈ Market Segmentation for Personal Care Organisations

The personal care services are found productive to almost all the segments. Here, we focus on the corporate segment in which we find a combination of corporate people holding different positions and belonging to both the genders. In the different sub-segments, the needs and requirements of users cannot be identical. The providers of services need an in-depth study of the organisational requirements of users. It is significant to mention that business attire is considerably influenced by the organisational culture. What to wear and what not to wear, cannot be uniform in all the organisations for all the professionals. Formal business, informal business and casual wear are the different styles in which the needs and preferences of corporate professionals are found unidentical. Again, the age factor is also to influence the preferences because the young professionals and matured professionals cannot have identical requirements. We also find some of the organisations becoming liberal to the dress code whereas some others are found very conservative. Keeping in view the different types of policies adapted by the organisations where employees work, the marketing professionals serving the personal care organisations need to be particular to the organisational culture, specially regarding the attire.

A majority of the users specially in the Indian perspective lack etiquette and manners and civic sense and aesthetic sense considered essential for the employees in general and the corporate employees in particular. The concerned providers need to inculcate these traits to make them sensible, civilised and disciplined. Irrespective of the fact that they come from the rural areas or belong to the big cities and towns; almost all the potential or even actual employees lack awareness of lifestyles they need to have a sound health. They do not know how to diffuse the tension or combat the stress. The personal care organisations by making a segment to segment study can provide to them a group of packaged services. It is not to be forgotten that expectations of organisations establish an edge over the expectations of employees because a mismatch with the organisational culture cannot meet the requirements of both the beneficiaries.

Of late, we find women also serving the corporate sector in a good number and their needs and requirements vary with their men counterparts. The business attire, nailcare, healthcare, beautycare, haircare, handcare, footcare are some of the areas where the personal car providers have to be very particular to the women. This makes the employees more hireable and promotable. They also need to know about their positions and purposes because for business office or business meeting or business parties; the requirements cannot be identical.

The division of markets for personal care services into different segments or subsegments simplifies the identification process. The organisations come to know about the customers or users; their needs and requirements, taste preferences and very importantly, the culture of organisation where they work or serve. In the changing scenario, it is much more significant that by making a microscopic analysis, they make possible identification of emerging trends and formulate a strategy to suit the changing conditions.

Marketing Information System for Personal Care Services

Since the beginning of 1990, we find a significant change in the business environment. Of course, a number of factors are responsible for that but the most important reason for the high intensity volatility in the increased level of sophistication in the generation of information and communication technology. It is an unvarnished fact that quality of information considerably influences the quality of decision. With the increasing heat of globalisation, the demand for personal care services increased and gained a rapid momentum specially during the first decade of the 21st century. The corporatisation resulted into the emergence of corporate culture and started impacting the organisational culture. A number of personal care services were found institutionalised and developed in an organised form. The market started becoming much more competitive Thus the personal care organisations were required to manage information for improving the quality of decision to excel competition.

The demand position of personal care organisations considerably rests on the development of corporate culture which sizably influences the lifestyles of not only the corporate people but of all the segments and all the regions. It is in this context that we find high level of demand for personal care services and the concerned organisations need to improve the supply position. An in depth study of the organisational culture, multi-dimensional changes in the behavioural profile of users, high intensity of competition both at national and international levels make it essential that personal care organisations realise the importance of information for managing their decision.

The organisational or institutional compulsions vis-à-vis the personal preferences throw a major impact on the demand and supply position. With the development of corporate culture, a significant change was witnessed in the lifestyles of not only the corporate people but even others, because there was an increase in the disposable and discretionary incomes of general masses. We cannot negate that globalisation of economy has paved avenues for the globalisation of fashion, culture and civilisation. It is against this background that we find imprints of western culture on the lifestyles and behaviour of almost all the sections. The institutional as well as the individual requirements are found impacted by western culture because we consider globalisation another edition of westernisation.

The techno-driven information system may help personal care organisations in studying and understanding the organisational culture vis-à-vis the users' behaviour. The quantitative or qualitative transformation in the process can be gauged and the policy decisions can be made much more customised if we make use of the new generation of information and communication technology. In many of the areas of personal care services, we find even big players involved in the process and they can make the ways convenient even for the small players. The creation of opportunity proves to be meaningless if we fail in tapping them in tune with the available potentials or strengths. The information system simplifies the process of identifying the opportunities and capitalising them in a productive fashion.

◈ Behavioural Profile of Corporate Users

Your task of creating satisfying and retaining customers is considerably simplified when you find yourself fully aware of their changing levels of expectations. The businessmen and women found as users of the personal care services have no options but to shape the levels of their expectations in the face of changing organisational culture. In a majority of the conditions, we find organisations not compromising with the dress-down policy because this injects strength to the relaxed-mode and consequently results into low level of efficiency. Hence, the employees need to know in detail about the dress policy of the organisation and to ensure its implementation without any relaxation. The personal care organisations also bear the responsibility of intensifying the research activities to study and understand the corporate policy vis-à-vis the behavioural profile of corporate employees. This will help them in restructuring their business plans.

Change is a natural phenomenon. We cannot regulate it. Albeit, we cannot change its direction. This makes it essential that we keep ourselves aware of the incoming changes in the organisational culture both in national and international perspectives. With globalisation, we have witnessed the contours of development undergoing multi-dimensional transformation. In a true sense, the globalisation of economy been found globalising fashion, culture and civilisation and practically, we find it impacting our lifestyles. The personal care organisations cannot confine themselves to a particular segment. Of course, they have to make a microscopic analysis of all the concerned segments for whom they produce or generate the services. The corporate employees, cine stars, foreign tourists, front-line staff of the business organisations air hostess, participants of beauty contests, TV and theatre artistes, bride and bridegrooms, school and college-going boys and girls, business tycoons, political leaders, etc., are the segments found to be potentially sound to use the services of personal care organisations. This makes it essential that the qualitative and quantitative transformation in the core and peripheral services of the personal care organisations are not delayed.

Here, our focus is on the corporate users and therefore we keep ourselves confined to the behavioural studies of corporate users of both the genders. Of late, we find business sector attracting not only men but even women because they feel that by serving this sector, they would find it easier to have a sophisticated lifestyle. We cannot negate that this trend is to continue even in the coming years because once we are trapped in the fray of amenities and facilities; the comforts and conveniences and the pleasure and attractions that we develop and nurture for them our tasks of coming out from the trap prove to be much more difficult. At both, the domestic as well as global levels, the personal care organisations have a prosperous future. The task is to have an in depth study of the behavioural profile to gauge the levels of expectations. This makes it essential that the personal care organisations undertake research activities. Since the taste preferences of foreign companies in general and the MNCs in particular are considerably influenced by the western culture, it is quite natural that we find its imprints on the eastern culture. When wearing branded clothes and carrying high-end accessories become reflective of the high social status of young men and women, we can easily gauge the reflections of western culture on the upcoming and budding youths. When provocative dresses start becoming the symbol of modern and high status society, the degeneration in the social orders and cultural patterns cannot be regulated. Of course, our focus is on business because we talk about the marketing of personal care services but in today's business world, the business organisations should not overlook the impact of their decisions on the socio-cultural norms. There is no any place for perversion when we want to promote elegance.

The emerging trends indicate that almost all the segments happen to be the users of personal care services and therefore concerned organisations need to promote the strategy in tune with their changing taste preferences. The users in general are found interested in looking smart and trendy. We find a majority of them developing a high level of dress consciousness. Hence, the personal care organisations bear the responsibility of identifying their needs and requirements, lifestyles, attitudes and behavioural patterns. This is to be possible when they undertake an intensive research.

The income index is considered to be an important dimension influencing the behavioural profile of users. We cannot deny that during the yesteryears, there has been a significant increase in the discretionary income of common people which throws a major impact on our lifestyles. The increasing flow of information has played an important role on the expansion of corporate culture even in the suburbs and small towns and cities. The increasing spending power has been found fuelling the process of managing looks. Not only the women but albeit the men have developed temptation for visiting beauty clinics. The potential users belong to almost all the sections and segments.

The emergence of mall culture is the gift of corporate culture. The trend is to continue further. The general masses also use the services of personal care organisations, specially on different occasions. Decorating the brides and bridegrooms during wedding and festive season is now becoming common. This significantly generates business for the personal care organisations. What to talk of the matured people when we find even youths nurturing a temptation for Yoga, Gym and Jogging. The expansion of market and an increase in the number of potential users of services are found strengthening the base for the development of personal care organisations.

The increasing importance of etiquette and manners in the corporate world of today also make a call for the development of personal care organisations. The finishing schools are found educating and training people for today's world. What to wear and what not to wear, our accent or communication skill, etiquette for dining, the colour of shoes and ties, accessorising for grooming, our civic and aesthetic sense are found gaining prominence in the corporate world of today and therefore personal care organisations may expect big business in diversified areas.

The existent organisational culture of an organisation happens to be the main thing in the entire process. Willingly or unwillingly, the people serving the organisation have to respect the dress policy and therefore the personal care organisations have no option but to keep themselves aware of the changes and modifications. It is in the larger interests of personal care organisations that they do not remain confined to the corporate segment because even other organisations working at small and domestic levels are also influenced by the culture generated by the MNCs.

The developments taking place during 1990s and more so in the first decade of the 21st century have started showing their imprints on various segments. We cannot deny that fashion, culture and civilisation move with the emerging trends in the economy. A significant increase in the level of income of general masses and its imprints on civilisation, specially during the yester decades is a staunch testimony to this proposition that economy is a pivot around which all the allied forces cluster. The social leaders and the cultural forces find it difficult to regulate the changing order. Indeed, we also find them respecting the affluents and honouring the business leaders. If today we find a craze for western lifestyles, fashion, culture and civilisation; it is nothing but the impact of multinationals on the social and cultural forces. The wave of information has been found injecting new life and strength to the process of attitudinal transformation.

The personal care organisations while formulating their development strategies cannot undermine the recent transformation process because this is to govern their product profile. We do not find any sign of reversal in the trend and therefore the corporate culture would continue to dominate the socio-cultural and economic forces. This is considered to be a positive development specially for the personal care organisations because the task of diversification would be found more easier and the process of profit maximisation would gain a high level of frequency. The customs, traditions, culture and civilisation cannot remain uninfected. In due course, we find emergence of one culture known as material culture which impacts everything.

Capitalising on the opportunities is the most important thing in the business world. The personal care organisations have tremendous opportunities for almost all the sectors and segments. Psychologically, the human beings are considerably influenced by those forces which provide to them status, pleasure and satisfaction.

If we find material culture influencing our behaviour, it is but natural that the stylish and trendy lifestyles provide to us much more pleasure and satisfaction. In the today's society, we find financial status of an individual much more instrumental in shaping his/her social status. The modern living conditions considerably influenced by the western culture are found to be a status symbol. The material culture becomes responsible for both the opposite considerations such as upgradation or degradation, generation or degeneration, satisfaction or dissension because in a majority of the conditions, it becomes difficult to get practically what we do expect. However, it is difficult to check the temptation for material culture. It has emerged. It has started dominating. And we find its transformation as an ongoing process.

◈ Synchronising the Mixes of Marketing

It we have a delicious dish, it is the result of the excellence of a chef. If we take the pleasure of listening good music, it is the excellence of a musician who synthesises. And if we find the marketing decision much more proactive, it is the credibility of a marketing professional who has optimally synchronised the different mixes of marketing. In a true sense, excellent result depends on our perfection of mixing which becomes instrumental in developing professionalism.

The term Marketing Mix was first coined by Professor Neil H. Borden of the Harvard Business School. Both the term and concept have since been adopted throughout the world. Our focus is not here on going through the conceptual aspect of marketing mix, indeed it is related with the professional excellence of marketers required for having the quality marketing decisions.

With the increasing heat of competition, the relevance of professionalism started gaining a rapid momentum. With the increasing domination of globalisation, the relevance of quality innovation and promotion was found of high order. We cannot negate that the present global economy is based on perfection. An individual or an institution cannot survive in absence of perfection. Professional excellence is found based on perfection.

The personal care services started attracting the attention of corporate people and this made ways for the formal and organised development of services which resulted into the development of a number of personal care organisations clubbing varied services to the users coming from different streams of personal care organisations. The people in general were food becoming much more conscious to their health and looks. The domination of corporate sector was found at its peak which started instrumentalising the process of corporatisation. A large number of small and big players both at national and international levels were found involved in the process. The conceptualisation of modern marketing principle necessitated formulation of a sound marketing mix such as product, promotion, place, pricing, process, physical evidence and attraction and people. The success result is found based on the art of mixing.

◈ The Product Profile

Sooner or later, today or tomorrow; we are suitably rewarded for our positive contributions and albeit heavily punished for the negative one. Both for an individual or an institution, we find it true. The personal care organisations are responsible for the generation and delivery of services to the ultimate users. The services packaged or even single are provided on the demand of a particular user. Since we find various types of services, it is quite natural that any

Spa an Emerging Business

organisation cannot provide all the services in the group of personal care. In the personal care sector, we find involvement of small as well as the big players. The market is becoming much more competitive both at national and international levels. Hence, it is only product uniqueness and distinction which would be effective in excelling competition. The marketing professionals bearing the responsibility of designing a sound product profile need to have an in depth study of organisational culture and corporate image and brand. They also need to gauge the changing level of expectations of users vis-à-vis the emerging trends in their discretionary income which is considerably to influence the demand position. They have to explore the possibilities of developing a package commensurate with the organisational requirements.

The multi-dimensional product profile of personal care organisations help in enriching the personal score of an individual. The demand side presents a bright future due mainly to the growing popularity of corporate culture. The users considerably depend on the organisational culture. The dress-code-policy and the dress-down-policy of an organisation requires due care of personal care organisations to study the demand side and balance the supply position. Some of the organisations are found liberal to the dress-code-policy whereas we also find organisations very much conservative and they do not allow dress-down-policy.

With the increasing domination of MNCs, we find look culture gaining much more popularity. The personal care organisations need to be quality conscious because the users happen to be stylish and trendy and prefer to use the services as a status symbol. The established corporate brand and image need due care while designing the services. While developing a package, the personal care organisations need to practise it as a motivational

Hair and Face provide you Business

tool. Since we find corporate people holding different ranks and positions, it is required to be made sure that packaged services are meant for all the segments.

The most important product is concerned with health. It is imperative that the concerned personal care organisations with the help of experts make available the desired services. For keeping sound health, it is pertinent that we have awareness of diet management. The services of dieticians and healthcare centres may be availed for this purpose. All the groups such as grains and cereals, farm produces, dairy products, animal products need to be balanced in the face of individual requirements. The quality of water is also an important consideration. In addition, the exercise, gym, jogging, aerobics also need due attention. While managing diet, it is to be ensured that we take food for cells. With this perception of food, we are very much influenced by the quality and timing and in the process, the lifestyles of an individual is found impact generating.

The next in the list is the management of personal, hygiene which is found very much influenced by personal and environmental considerations. The handcare, nailcare, haircare, skincare, sanitation and kitchen hygiene are found important in the very context.

PRODUCT PROFILE

Sound Health	Management of Diet, Exercise, Gym, Jogging, Aerobics. Management of water.
Personal Hygiene	Handcare, Nailcare, Haircare, Skincare, Sanitation, Kitchen hygiene. Sensitisation.
Civic and Aesthetic Sense	Increasing civic and aesthetic sensibility by sensing and sensitising to make people disciplined and civilised. Facecare and Skincare. Dimensions of Civic and Aesthetic sense.
Healthy Mind	Yoga, Pranayam, Meditation, Combating stress. Awareness of sleeping and laughing. Discharge of accumulated complexes.
Etiquette and Manners	Politeness in Behaviour and developing mannerism in different areas.
Morality	Providing knowledge of ethics, spiritualism, empathy and personal philanthropy.
Leadership	Training and developing people to inculcate and develop leadership skill.
Looks	Knowledge of business attire and accessories to make the facial appearance attractive and impressive.

The chart given above speaks of the fact that personal care services are found of varied nature and therefore we find involvement of a number of organisations based on their expertise and speciality. The different dimensions of personality are to be taken care to enrich the personal score. The beautycare and healthcare organisations are also the provider depending upon the requirements of users. The quality of product is an important consideration which cannot be undermined. The packaging of services may be helpful in increasing the affordability.

The services promoting civic and aesthetic sense are found of outstanding significance, specially in the Indian context where we find a majority of the people lacking civic and aesthetic sensibility. The educational institutions and media play an important role specially while making masses aware of the relevance of civic and aesthetic sense in ranking people civilised and disciplined. The NGOs may also be helpful in activating the sensitisation process.

The healthy mind, stress-free mind make it essential that we are continuously discharging the accumulated complexes. We keep ourselves stress-tree and nurture in our heart and mind the positive feelings for others. This focuses on practising yoga, pranayam and meditation on a regular basis. Besides, it is also imperative that we have a regular lifestyle and practise the measures for combating stress. The participation in the spiritual session and the feelings of helping others may also be instrumental in diffusing tension. The service of centres for yoga may be used for this purpose. The soundness of mind makes it essential that we make place for the positive thoughts.

Lack of etiquette and manners is a common disaster area in the Indian perspective. If we lack politeness in our behaviour, we make place for tension and distress. The corporate trainers bear the responsibility of educating and training people so that behavioural profile and mannerism get due care. The Finishing Schools, Business Schools and other educational institutions need to assign due weightage to the development of traits to be effective in improving the behavioural profile of people evincing interests is joining the business world.

Value erosion is found to be a negative development of our personality which makes ways for ethical disorder. The character building is significantly required because it is to emerge as power. We cannot think about empathy and personal philanthropy unless we find people evincing interests in ethics. It is an essential trait for the development of personality which also rests on our temptation to spiritualism.

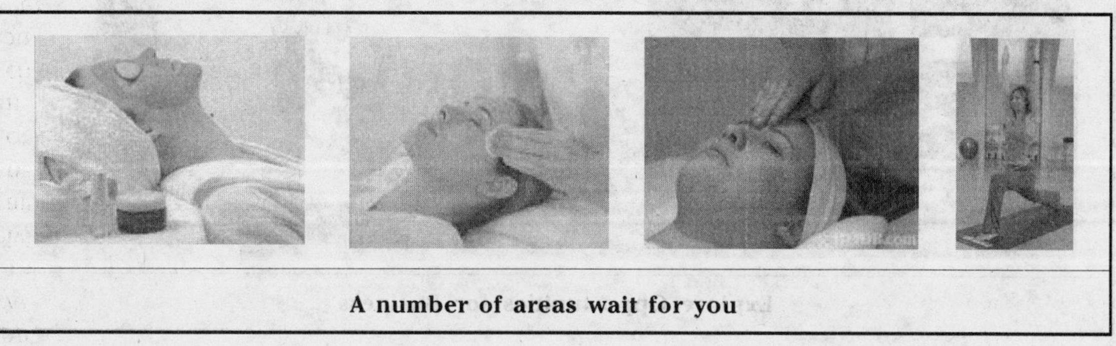

A number of areas wait for you

The corporate world, today, looks for people having leadership quality. The mounting volatility in the business environment makes it essential that corporate people have the potentials of anticipating the future. The business leaders are supposed to be creative and visionary who can simplify this task. The development of communicative ability is an essential task before the corporate trainers.

The management of looks or facial appearance includes in its purview a number of dimensions. It is significant that we have awareness of business attire. It is also essential that we are aware of the various dimensions to be found effective in the accessorising process. The management of wardrobe is an essential area for managing the wearabouts. It is not confined to a particular gender because businessmen or businesswomen cannot be successful in getting the high bucks unless they respect the dress code. The corporate trainers or management experts need to sensitise corporate executives to be sincere to the dress code.

A fair synchronisation of multi-dimensional personal score would be helpful in the development of personality in totality. To be hireable and promotable, the corporate looks need due care.

The marketing professionals bear the responsibility of formulating a sound product mix which can be helpful in establishing an edge over the competitive brands and firms. Though quality plays an outstanding role in almost all the organisations but specially when our focus is on the personal care organisations, we find quality a decisive factor. It is expected from the personal care organisations that they keep on moving the process of defining and redefining quality by intensifying the research and development activities. The healthcare and beautycare sector are the backbones of corporate culture and therefore the quality leaders find it easier to establish an edge. The brand and image of the concerned organisation cannot be undermined in the very context. The business attire, accessories, sound health and rock star personality, sound mind with much more creativity, high level of civic and aesthetic sensibility, etiquette and mannerism, ethics and morality, character and personality, leadership quality are some of the outstanding traits of our personality without whim the corporate culture cannot survive and thrive. The personal care organisations while developing product need to synchronise the competitive personal score in such a fashion that brand leadership is established.

Explore Opportunities for Business

Corporate brand and image rest on the organisational efforts for conceptualising quality as an ongoing process. Since we find MNCs dominating the global economy, it is quite natural that whatsoever the perception they have developed regarding quality in the base country is not infected or diluted in other countries where they market or produce their products. Expansion of market magnifies expansion and extension of brand image. Loss of image is considered to be the most damaging result when we talk about brand image. Of course, we find other aspects also instrumental in the projection of image, specially the promotional measures; but the impact of quality of product is found at the top. Promotion without product and quality innovation cannot last for the long time. This makes it essential that the personal care organisation assign a transcendental priority to product innovation and quality promotion.

Product uniqueness and distinctness are considered significant for establishing an identity and making the decisions highly effective and proactive. Making an individual distinct to others makes the ways for making an organisation best of all. Either we talk about the beauty products or our focus is on other products; ultimately it is uniqueness which can secure our present and future. It is against this backdrop that we make a strong advocacy in favour of world-class product.

The focus is on the personal score helping an individual developing holistic personality. A number of traits, properties or attributes are required to be inculcated or developed so that the enrichment process is found of high order. How can we expect an individual to be productive when he/she lacks civic and aesthetic sense, etiquette and manners, leadership and character, sound physique and productive mind, ethics and morality, sensitivity to the facial appearance or looks lack of creativity or so. In the existent corporate culture, it is imperative that the personal care organisations acting as a provider focus on quality whereas the corporate people acting as users of the services are ensured that even their high level of expectations would be taken care.

◈ Promoting the Services

Creativity makes the ways for sensitivity which paves copious avenues for acceptability making the promotional measures much more proactive. Of course, the personal care organisations need to define and redefine the quality but at the same time, it is also imperative that they promote the services in a creative fashion. It is an unvarnished fact that a majority of the people specially in the Indian context are found unaware of the personal score helping them in getting the high position and the big bucks, an essential consideration for the material culture. It is insensitivity that makes them scorewise deficient. The demand position for the personal care services can sizably be increased if the personal care organisations initiate and activate the creative promotional measures. It is against this backdrop that we strongly advocate in favour of creative and proactive but cost-effective promotion.

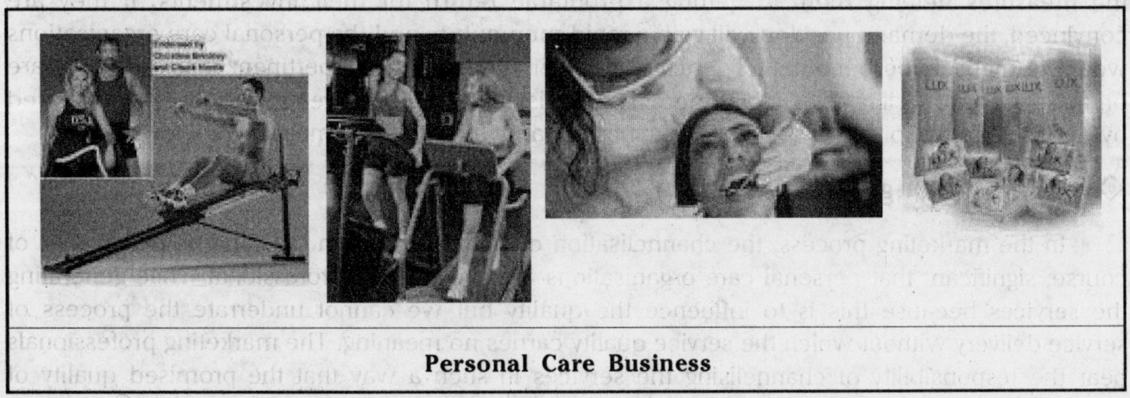

Personal Care Business

There are a number of components of promotion with varied impact on the users. The components like advertisement, publicity, sales promotion, personal selling, direct marketing, telemarketing, cause-related and sponsorship marketing and word-of-mouth promotion need to be blended in such a manner that users and potential users of the services come to know about the products and their effectiveness in getting a respectable position in the business world. They need to convince the users that it is an age of investment dressing where investments in personality development are always productive. Since we find technology playing an important role in almost all the areas, the promotional measures also need support of new generation of information and communication technology. The publicity measures can be much more effective and therefore the personal care organisations are required to develop their rapport with the media people, academics, celebrities, corporate trainers, business and finishing schools so that they convince the users and potential users regarding the relevance of personal care products for getting big bucks and high respect. The people engaged in channelising the services also need to be motivated to convince the users. The personal sellers with a high communicative ability need to be approached for sensitising the users. The telemarketers can also play a positive role in the sensitisation process. But we should not forget that word of mouth communication or promotion would be very much effective in the persuasion and transformation processes. The users act as a hidden promoter, if we find them satisfied with the quality of services delivered. The negative impact of word-of-mouth promotion is found of high order and therefore the personal care organisation should not leave scope for quality degradation or deterioration.

Promote your Business

The motive is to make users aware of the role of personality development in getting a respectable position in the corporate world. It cannot be refuted that today we find an attitudinal transformation where users and potential users cannot be hesitant or reluctant to the measures helping them in getting a profitable return for their investments. If they are convinced, the demand position will gain a rapid momentum and the personal care organisations would immensely be benefited. To increase the effectiveness, it is pertinent that personal care organisations are well aware of the emerging organisational culture. Creative promotion supported by service innovation lead to users' persuasion and their transformation into loyal users.

◈ Channelising the Services

In the marketing process, the channelisation of services have an outstanding place. It is, of course, significant that personal care organisations are sincere and professional while generating the services because this is to influence the quality but we cannot underrate the process of service delivery without which the service quality carries no meaning. The marketing professionals bear the responsibility of channelising the services in such a way that the promised quality of services reach to the concerned users on time and without any distortion. Particularly the gap between services-promised and services-delivered is required to be bridged to maximise the retention rate of customers. The concept of zero-level distribution or distribution through electronic channel has been found much more effective in the context of personal care services. With the development of information and communication technology, the concept of distribution has been found gaining popularity in an innovative form and the different categories of personal care organisations need to bring momentum in the conceptualisation process.

Service delivery through manual support or even we can do it with the help of electronics channels, the most important thing is quality and the marketing professionals are required to manage things in such a way that scope for service distortion is minimised. The users attending the beauty clinics; getting support for developing the leadership skill or information about the business attire and dress code policy, awareness of civic and aesthetic sensibility, management of diet, management of body, management of looks, management of mind, development of sense concerned with personal hygiene and etiquette and manners and building character are found quality-sensitive. Since the services are very much related with the enrichment of personal score; the time and quality elements need due care in the service delivery process.

The Points of Location (PoL) are considered significant, specially when we talk about the personal care services. The location of service generation and delivery points is an important consideration to maximise accessibility and magnify visibility. The professionals need to be sincere while identifying the location points. With the development of mall culture, we find it an important point for the location of personal care organisations. Assembly of people in a good number would be helpful in developing the awareness of people regarding the quality and punctuality. There are some of the centres for which availability of adequate space is found essential. When we talk about Gym, Jogging, Pranayam, Meditation, Yoga, Exercise, the adequacy of space proves to be an important consideration. It is also significant that the required supporting infrastructural facilities are available at the point of service generation and distribution.

The concept of developing personal care complexes where customers assemble in a good number cannot be underrated. Of late, we find much more frequency in the demand and supply position. It is imperative that the personal care organisations succeed in bridging the gap and for that the uses of technology need due care.

◈ Pricing the Personal Care Services

Commercial viability of an organisation depends on the remunerative price structure. This makes it essential that like other organisations, the personal care organisations also become calculative while formulating the pricing strategy. The emerging trends in competition, increasing level of discretionary income, galloping flow of information and changing lifestyles considerably influenced by the western culture are signalling a positive development in the field of job market which in future would sizably increase the demand position. In the different tiers of towns and cities, we find a big demand for the services of personal care organisations vis-à-vis for product of beautycare and healthcare. What to talk of the towns and cities when we find a significant change in the lifestyles of even the rural population. The increasing level of spending-propensity appears to be a dominating factor influencing the demand position. Since we find pricing decisions influenced by a number of factors, it is pertinent that marketing professionals make an in depth study of the market conditions for formulating a sound pricing strategy.

The existence and prosperity of an organisation considerably depend on profitability which is sizably influenced by pricing. A number of users of the personal care services come from the corporate sector and therefore it is pertinent that strategic decisions regarding pricing are made in tune with the propensity to spend. Corporate grooming requires special attention. How and in what way the concerned organisations make the pricing decisions nationally and globally competitive is an important consideration which would influence the demands position. The categories of towns and cities, the location point, the rank and position of corporate people as user of the services, the perception of users regarding the organisational culture and dress code, the perception of users regarding the investment dressing, etc., are some of the considerations influencing the pricing decisions of personal care organisations. The national or international character of the organisation where the employees work also influence the decision. With the development of corporate culture, we find MNCs dominating the economy of almost all countries of the globe. Since we find emergence of a multi-cultural or a cross-cultural society, it is quite natural that the nature of demand of the users would also be affected.

The personal care services are used with diverse motives. But of late, a majority of the users have been found using the services to visualise and project their style, status, attitudes, behaviour, respect to the organisational culture, getting high position and big bucks. This leaves minimum scope for users to be price-sensitive. Usually, we find them quality-sensitive. This makes it clear that personal care organisations assign due weightage to quality. Either the users plan to look attractive or they want to look smart and physically sound or their focus is on developing leadership skill or having civic and aesthetic sensibility; the personal care services help in fulfilling their expectations. The pricing decisions are also governed by the level of expectations of users. The increasing temptation of people to look smart, beautiful and impressive and the existing attitude of organisations regarding the outfits are also the important considerations governing the pricing decisions of personal care organisations.

With the increasing heat of globalisation, we find a significant increase in the demand position because a good number of people are found using the services. The pricing decisions are found chaotic, critical as well as challenging because we find world-class organisations evincing keen interest in the Indian markets. The incoming trends make it clear that the personal care organisations have a bright future for qualitative or quantitative transformation. How and in what way, the marketing professionals fulfil their assigned responsibilities would impact the competitiveness of the personal care organisations. There are some of the selected services where the personal care organisations have a bright future. Of late, we find people nurturing interest in a healthy lifestyles, modern lifestyles and westernised lifestyles which would also be helpful in creating new opportunities for the personal care organisations. Hence, the most important task before the marketing professionals is to be innovative and cost-effective so that the price structure is found commensurate with the paying capacity of the users. It is in this context that we make a strong advocacy in favour of a competitive pricing strategy.

Using pricing as a tactical strategy makes it essential that the personal care organisations increase the scale of operation and make or develop the services in the face of segment-to-segment study because the paying capacity of all the segments cannot be uniform. Even in the corporate sector, we find people working in different capacities and holding different positions. Hence, the marketing professionals are supposed to make it sure that there is no big gap between services-needed and the prices-charged. The professional excellence of marketers vis-à-vis the emerging trends in the corporate sector considerably influence the pricing strategy to be adopted by the personal care organisations.

The facts outlined above make it clear that the personal care organisations need much more precautions while making the pricing decisions. We cannot deny that global economic crisis has affected the personal care organisation but it is a temporary phase which has provided the personal care organisations an opportunity to be much more calculative while rationalising or setting the price structure. We have gone through various considerations of the pricing decisions related to the personal care organisations and feel that setting of price requires professional excellence. Satisfying and retaining the quality-sensitive users is, of course, a difficult task. How and in what way the professionals succeed in optimising the price and quality would determine the magnitude of demand-stimulation. Market-penetration is an important functional responsibility and the professionals serving the personal care organisations need to make it possible. Packaging the services may be an effective prescription to activate the stimulation and penetration processes. An acid test of marketing professionals is coiled in the essence of adopting pricing as a motivational tool.

◈ Processing of Services

In an age of the technology, the processing of services considerably influences the service quality vis-à-vis cost effectiveness. The quality tech-savvy providers; with the help of electronic channel define and redefine quality. It is against this background that we find the concept of service quality changing fast. The personal care organisations also make use of technology for processing. The beauty clinics, beauty parlours, hair dressing centres, Gym and Jogging centre, healthcare centres for promoting exercises, steam bath centre, nailcare centres, etc., are found technology-based. By and large, we find use of technology in almost all the personal care organisations. With the increasing uses of technology, we find a significant increase in the service quality and the quality gap. This focuses our attention on processing of services in tune with the changing requirements and level of expectations of users. To minimise the quality gap, it is pertinent that tech-savvy or tech-friendly people are employed and the required technology of new generation is promoted. The services promised must reach to the service users without any delay or distortion.

When we talk about the service-quality and service-delivery in the context of personal care organisations, it is imperative that the concerned organisations are sincere to the level of promises so that the gap between services-promised and services-delivered is either bridged or minimised to the accepted level. The two important considerations sizably influencing the processing are the environment in which the technology has been installed and the people by whom the technology is operated, diversified and maintained. The satisfaction to users is the prime consideration. Here, we should not forget that with the use of technology, we find a significant increase in the level of expectations and therefore both the processes such as service-generation and service-delivery need due attention.

The service quality model makes it significant that service providers do not undermine the possibilities of a quality gap which is caused by a number of factors. In some of the cases, the technology in itself creates problem whereas in some other cases, we find the operating people responsible for the problem. We also find cases where the high level of expectations of users is found responsible for the gap. The interrupted supply of supporting infrastructural facilities also become instrumental in creating the quality problem. Hence, it is pertinent that while processing of services, the professionals keep into consideration even the small things in detail.

The motive is to make available to the users time-honoured, quality-based and cost-effective services in tune with the level of expectations of users. Increasing the operational flow, customisation of services, maintaining the standard, involving the customers are the multi-dimensional objectives of processing for which the professionals have to ensure tech-savvy provider, new generation of technology and proper environment for excellent performance. The customisation is found much more significant to the personal care services which may increase the level of customer satisfaction.

◈ Physical Evidence

Tangibility makes the ways for the creation of impression. If we see, we feel; and our feelings result into expression. A majority of the services due to intangibility makes our task of persuasion much more complicated. The feelings of customers or users before using the services if positive pave avenues for the creation of positive impression. It is in this context that we focus on this mix of marketing which is found concerned with the servicescapes or service ambience or service environment. Like other organisations, even the personal care organisations need to develop an ambience which is found instrumental in generating the service culture. Since visibility plays an important role in creating a positive impression, it is significant that marketing professionals assign due weightage to the development of service ambience which would let potential users create and develop an impression. Since we find it very much related to the ambience, the providers of services feel pleasure in the service processing and delivery which brings a significant increase in the level of efficiency of people vis-à-vis the technology. On the one hand, the potential users, visitors infer ideas regarding the quality of services to be delivered while on the other hand, the employees working there get an ambience in which service quality can be improved.

The important dimensions in the very context are designing, facilities, signposts, equipment interiors, exteriors, displays, lighting, furnishing, ventilation, drinking water, sanitation, waiting lounge, scent, music, reports, brochures, parking, dresses and uniforms or wearabouts. If you enter a beauty clinic and the service ambience is in tune with the standards and specifications of services; you feel everything positive regarding the services to be delivered. Besides, a number of people work as back-line and front-line staff manually or with the help of technology which provide to them the comforts and convenience while performing which may be instrumental in increasing the level of efficiency of employees working there. Since we find a mix of varied services generated by the service organisations meant for personal care, it is quite natural that the various dimensions of servicescapes vary from organisation to organisation.

Professional excellence of marketers may be helpful in developing a mix keeping in view the nature of services, and the class or segment of users. We are aware of the different types of personal care services and the types of users visiting the personal care organisations. Both the genders are found concerned with the services attending the different centres with the prime motto of looking attractive. Besides, we also find users visiting the centres for managing their diet, physique, etiquette and manners, civic and aesthetic sense, etc., for the development of personality in totality. Because we concentrate here on the corporate users, it is quite natural that providers keep into consideration the organisational culture and the level of expectations of users. Keeping in view the lifestyles of corporate users, it is imperative that the personal care organisations focus on quality. The service ambience must be rich and effective in establishing distinction.

◈ People

We cannot deny the role of hybrid technology in accelerating the pace of development but at the same time, it is also right to say that ultimately it is quality of people that proves to be the most dominating force in the constructive or destructive ideas responsible for a rise or fall of individual or an institution. Like other organisations, the personal care organisations also depend on people for marketing the services. They need people having excellent personal score so that they prove to be competitive and productive and help organisations in excelling competition. Of course, the thematical competence has an outstanding contribution on to the development of people but in the today's business world, we need a number of traits and properties considered essential to survive and thrive. While recruiting, training and developing, it is to be ensured that people serving their organisations have the potentials to create satisfy and retain customers or users. Since we find a number of services generated with the support of technology, it is imperative that people working there are tech-savvy and have the efficacy of customising the services in tune with the changing requirements of customers.

In the changing scenario, it is pertinent that employees serving the personal care organisations are visionary bearing the potentials of anticipating the changes and challenges in the corporate world. The organisational requirements vis-à-vis the users' expectations need to be matched in such a way that personal care organisations come to know about the services to be delivered. This is possible when we find employees having a leadership quality. They need the potentials of identifying the requirements of different segments and to customise them to fit the organisational requirements. The users coming for haircare, nailcare, facecare, skincare, healthcare, awareness of wearabouts, personal hygiene, etiquette and manners, diffusion of stress and distress and laughter need to be received in a right way. In this context, it is also significant that employees working there have the capability of studying and understanding the organisational culture because a mismatch between users expectations and organisational requirements would be found meaningless.

Particularly the Business Schools and Finishing Schools bearing the responsibility of enriching the personal score of potential corporate managers need to develop them in a different way. It is not only significant that they make them thematically sound but at the same time it is also meaningful that they do their best to develop personality in totality. Product Uniqueness cannot be overlooked. Only then, we may find them commensurate with the organisational requirements. Unawareness of non-verbal communication makes them deficient. They should not forget that today non-verbal communication has an edge over the verbal communication. Crux of the problem is that particularly in the Indian context, we find even number of CEOs, not realising the relevance of non-verbal communication. The people as a submix of marketing need to strengthen their realisation that the enrichment of personal score should be adopted as an ongoing process. At the first stage, the concerned institutions and at the later stages, the organisation has to ensure the properties or traits without which they are found incomplete and they will remain incomplete.

◈ Marketing Personal Care Services in the Indian Context

The increasing business education, emergence of corporate culture due to galloping corporatisation and westernisation of fashion, culture and civilisation are same of the recent developments in the Indian context which signal a significant increase in the demand position for the products of personal care organisations. During yester decades, the MNCs have been successful in initiating and activating the process of attitudinal transformation. The people in general are now found becoming health and status-conscious, dress and beauty-conscious. A number of small and big players; domestic and foreign organisations are now found capitalising on the opportunities. The market is expanding and the customers or users are becoming much more ambitious. We cannot negate that globalisation is another edition of westernisation in which material culture has a domination and for anyone, it becomes difficult to bid a goodbye to the opulent lifestyles, which cage us for ever. Hence, the domination of material culture is to continue and for which we have no option but to inject new life strength and continuity to the corporate culture. Opportunities carry no meaning unless we capitalise. And capitalisation considerably rests on the professional excellence of marketers.

The personal care services have now been corporatised. A number of domestic and foreign players are now in the business. Since the demand is gaining a rapid momentum, the supply position is required to be improved. The personal care organisations in the changing context need to focus on professional excellence. The most important task before them has to study and understand the emerging trends in the business both at national and international levels. The providers as well as the users have been witnessing new developments. Strategical and tactical areas need to be studied in the changing perspective.

With the increasing domination of MNCs, we need a change in the organisational culture. Since the employees serving an organisation are considered an extension of the corporate brand, it is imperative that imprints of brand are found locally as well as globally. The business tycoons, national and global players have to focus on enriching the personal score of users in the face of changing corporate requirements. This will help creation, satisfaction and retention of users of services.

Conceptualisation of marketing principles and customisation of products would help personal care organisations in many ways. Since the potential users come from the different segments, it is quite natural that their requirements vis-à-vis the level of expectations cannot be identical. The handicaps and constraints in the development process are but natural. In a true sense, the acid test of professionals is found in an adverse condition. Developing personality in tune with the existent corporate culture would be a productive step. Unless, we inject new life and strength to this perception, the task of striking a balance in the demand and supply position would remain to be much more difficult.

The personal care organisations need to be innovative in their efforts so that they succeed in developing a package which helps their finished products in having a personality found to be potentially sound to face life in totality. Besides, it is also pertinent that they keep on moving the process of undertaking researches in the concerned areas specially for product uniqueness. We cannot negate that emerging trends in the national and global scenario would also influence the demand position and therefore service providing organisations cannot keep themselves indifferent to the latest developments.

Sensitisation is an important task of promotion and in this context the personal care organisations are required to make society much more conscious and aware. The demand for personal care services may gain a rapid momentum if we find society becoming much more health and beauty conscious. Consciousness through sensitisation and sensitisation through creative promotion needs priority attention of service providing organisations which may stimulate demand penetration. In the process, the healthcare organisations, non-government organisations, educational institutions and others concerned have to take part.

Affordability is an important consideration specially in the Indian context which cannot be overlooked because there are a large number of users who need the services but are not in a position to afford due to high price structure. Even we talk about the corporate users, the affordability of different echelons of management cannot be identical. Of course, a few of them do not mind the price but a majority of them find it difficult to pay. Hence, the service providing organisations have to explore avenues for cost-effectiveness. Striking a balance between price and quality is an important dimension.

Accessibility simplifies the task of attracting the users to the service providing organisations. How and in what way the users and potential users develop a temptation to avail the services by making use of the electronic channels is an important consideration to simplify channelisation. The service providing organisations need to identify the location points of potential and actual users and to improve accessibility by opening small service centres close to their workplaces and residential areas.

A number of services are now found technologically supported. It is quite natural that people serving the corporate sector have time constraint and therefore it is pertinent that the operational flow is considerably increased by making use of technology. In this context, it is imperative that the service providing organisations assign due weightage to the promises standards, specifications and time. The motive is to bridge the gap between service quality promised and the service quality delivered. On the one hand, they need to care the level of expectations of users while on the other hand, they also need to ensure that services are commensurate with the organisational culture, corporate brand and image.

The service ambience cannot be underrated and therefore the service providing organisations have to assign due weightage to interiors and exteriors. Creation of a positive impression is considered significant. This necessitates due attention on the servicescapes. The users visiting the centres are found in a position to have a positive impression about the service providers if they witness a sound ambience. The exteriors become significant with the viewpoint of, having a high intensity of visibility where the posters, banners lighting and location are found significant. This helps in simplifying in accessibility. When we talk about interiors our focus is on the internal arrangements to be instrumental in the formation of opinion before using the services and therefore tangibility occupies here a place of outstanding significance. The management of lighting, furnishing, ventilation, signposts, display of painting, music, ornamental shadow plants, display of technology to be used in the process the positioning of back-line and front-line staff and all other facilities which make the stay of users comfortable may be helpful in the formation of a positive impression or users about the service providing organisations. The management of service ambience is considered significant also with the view point of improving the level of performance of backline and the frontline staff. The service culture depends on service ambience and for which the service providing organisations need to make use of the services of experts for the development of service ambience.

Since we find a number of users coming from the corporate segment, it is imperative that the people serving the personal care organisations are behaviourally sound and tech-savvy. If they satisfy the users availing their services and keep on moving the process of satisfying them there will be a significant increase in the rate of retention. Particularly when we find service becoming much more competitive, it is imperative that the process of retention keeps on moving.

Professional excellence of marketers would determine the magnitude of success. Making the personal care services much more remunerative depends on making the services much more competitive which makes strong advocacy in favour of defining and redefining quality. The marketing professionals by developing quality marketing inputs can be successful in developing quality marketing outputs. The synchronisation of different mixes of marketing depends on the professional excellence of marketers.

The personal care organisations thus need to capitalise on the opportunities existent in the job markets. The increasing pace of corporatisation is found to be a positive signal which would bring a significant increase in the demand position. Since we find diverse nature of services provided by them, the demand position for almost all the personal care services would increase. Not only the small players but even the big players find a prosperous future. This makes it essential that all the concerned organisations assign a transcendental priority to the creation of services.

Of late, we find an attitudinal transformation and it is against this background that in the future, there will be a significant increase in the demand of personal care products. This will directly or indirectly involve a large number of organisations. The supply position of personal care products depends on the demand position. Since we expect a big increase in the demand position mainly due to globalisation of economy, fashion, culture and civilisation influenced by westernisation, the future of personal care business is found prosperous.

SUMMARY

In this chapter, you have gone through the conceptualisation of marketing principles by the personal care organisations. Before starting another chapter, make sure that the following facts are well versed.

Personal Care Marketing: A Conceptual Framework: Personal care marketing is a managerial process which is well supported by the professionals. It is an organised and systematic effort for managing the marketing activities for creating, satisfying and retaining the users.

Organisational or Institutional Support for Personal Care Services: There are a number of personal care services for enriching the personal score of people particularly serving the corporate sector such as sound physique, sense of personal hygiene, civic and aesthetic sense, sound mind, politeness in behaviour or etiquette, morality, attractive looks and leadership which require institutional support for better results.

Market Segmentation for Personal Care Organisations: We find personal care services used by different segments of society but here the focus is on the corporate users. Before conceptualising marketing, an indepth study of their behavioural profile is essential for studying and understanding them in a right fashion.

Marketing Information System for the Personal Care: The marketing professionals need to take support of information system so that the information concerned with users and markets are collected for developing a sound marketing mix.

Behavioural Profile of Corporate Users: Here we study the level of expectations, needs and requirements of users to get them satisfied and retained.

Synchronisation of Marketing Mix: For a sound marketing decision, it is essential that different submixes of marketing are blended in a right way by the professionals.

Product Mix: The services of personal care organisations, packaging and branding are studied here to develop a profile in tune with users' requirements. Product uniqueness helps increasing the number of users.

Promotion: The different components of promotion are studied here to promote the services of personal care organisations. The motive is to inform, sense, sensitise, persuade and transform.

Place: The channelisation of personal care services may be with the help of different levels or direct, manual or techno-driven.

Pricing: Affordability is an important consideration for pricing the personal care services but here it is, not to be forgotten that users are found to be quality-sensitive.

Processing: Increasing the operational flow is considered essential to bring momentum in the processing so that services are delivered to the users on time and without any distortion.

Physical Evidence: This focuses on the development of a sound ambience in which both the providers and users feel pleasure in processing, delivering and using.

People: The personal care organisations need quality people to develop quality product.

KEY TERMS

Personal Care
Beauty Products
Personal Score
Etiquette
Manners
Hygienic
Corporate Culture
Civic Sense
Aesthetic Sense
Morality
Psychologists
Dentists
Meditation
Spiritualism
Beautician
Personal Care Organisations
Dress-sown Policy
Dress-up Policy
Gym
Jogging
Yoga
Beauty Parlours
Product Uniqueness
MNCs
Aerobics
Stress
Empathy
Philanthropy
Attire
Nailcare
Haircare
Product Profile
Promotion
Channels
Electronic Channel
Discretionary Income
Disposable Income
Grooming
Physical Evidence
Servicescapes
Wearabouts
Distress
Posters
Banners

EXPECTED QUESTIONS

1. What do you meant by personal care services? Conceptualise modern marketing principles in the personal care organisations to make the services much more competitive.
2. Explain justifications for institutional or organisational support for availing the personal care services particularly by the corporate people.

3. Focus on the personal score required for a successful corporate employees specially serving the MNCs.
4. Explain the relevance of market segmentation for personal care organisations.
5. Focus on the instrumentality of information system for marketing the personal care services.
6. Throw light on the significance of studying the behavioural profile of the corporate users making demand for the personal care services.
7. What do you meant by Marketing Mix? Explain it in the context of personal care services.
8. What do you mean by Product Mix? Explain the important decision making areas for the formulation of a sound product mix for the personal care services.
9. Throw light on the role of promotional measures for informing, sensing, sensitising, persuading and transforming the potential users into actual and habitual users.
10. Explain the instrumentality of distribution channels for making available promised quality of personal care services to the users of business world.
11. Focus on the relevance of pricing decisions for the personal care services in the Indian perspective.
12. Explain the three additional mixes of marketing in the context of personal care services.
13. What do you mean by Physical Evidence as a submix of the marketing mix? Explain the role of service ambience for maintaining service culture by the personal care organisations.
14. Focus on the significance of developing quality people for making the personal care services nationally and globally competitive.
15. Explain the role or technology for time-honoured and cost-effective processing of personal care services.
16. Write a reasoned note on the marketing of personal care services in the Indian perspective.

APPLICATION EXERCISES

1. "We live in an age where organisational culture determines the quality and diversity of personal score required for getting a respectable position in the corporate world." Comment on this statement in the context of developments taking place in the business world of 21st century.
2. "In the changing business world, the personal care organisations need a new vision. They look for people having aesthetic sense, optimism, imagination and wisdom. They look for people having etiquette and manners. They prefer people having a rock star personality. They offer big bucks to those who have a special temptation for looks." Throw light on the above statement in the face of developments taking place in the corporate world.
3. "Personal Care Marketing is considered to be a managerial device to market the services in such a way that customised services are made available to the users in the face of changing corporate requirements." Comment on the above statement and justify the conceptualisation of modern marketing principles by the personal care organisations in the Indian perspective.
4. "The emergence of beautycare and healthcare sectors is the result of a sudden boom in the society which has resulted into the development of world-class personal care organisations in some of the selected areas." In the face of this statement, explain the different areas where we find tremendous opportunities to capitalise on.

5. "The techno-driven information system may help personal care organisations in studying and understanding the organisational culture vis-à-vis the users' behaviour." In the light of this statement, focus on the instrumentality of a sound information system for the personal care organisations.
6. "If we find material culture influencing our behaviour, it is but natural that the stylish and trendy lifestyles provide to us much more pleasure and satisfaction. The material culture becomes responsible for both the opposite considerations such as upgradation and degradation, satisfaction and dissension, generation and degeneration; because in a majority of the conditions, it becomes difficult for us to get what we do expect." In the face of this statement, throw light on the significance of behavioural studies in understanding the users of personal care services.
7. "If we have a delicious dish, it is the result of the excellence of a chef who has expertise in identifying and mixing the recipes. If we take the pleasure of listening good music, it is the excellence of a musician who has the art of synchronising. And if we have quality marketing decisions, it is due to the professionally sound marketers." Comment on this statement in the context of personal care services.
8. "The multi-dimensional product profile of personal care organisations help in enriching the personal score of an individual. The dress-code policy and the dress-down policy of an organisation requires due care of personal care organisations to balance the demand and supply position. In the light of this statement, focus on the product profile helping corporate people in becoming much more hireable and promotable.
9. "It is an unvarnished fact that particularly in the Indian perspective, a majority of us are unaware of the personal score helping in getting a respectable position in the business world. "Comment on this statement and throw light on the instrumentality on creative promotional measures in sensitising and persuading the potential users.
10. "The personal care organisations while delivering the services need to ensure punctuality, cost, economy and satisfaction; either manually or with the help of technology. In the light of this statement focus on the channelisation of services by the personal care organisations.
11. "The existence and prosperity of an organisation considerably depends on profitability which is sizably influenced by pricing decisions. The strategic decisions regarding pricing must be in tune with the propensity to spend. Comment on this statement and throw light on the affordability and quality considerations while formulating pricing strategy by the personal care organisations.
12. "The two important considerations sizably influencing the processing of personal care services are the environment in which the technology has been installed and the quality of people by whom the technology is operated." Discuss this statement in the face of processing as a submix of marketing.
13. "Tangibility makes the ways for the creation of impression. If we see; we feel; and our feelings result into expression which may be either positive or negative." Comment on this statement in the face of physical evidence as a mix of marketing.
14. "In the changing scenario, it is pertinent that employees serving the personal care organisations are visionary; bearing the potentials of anticipating the changes and challenges in the corporate world." Examine this statement in the face of people as an important submix of marketing.
15. "With the increasing domination of MNCs, we need a change in the organisational culture. Since the employees are an extension of the corporate brand, it is imperative that

imprints of brand are found regionally, nationally and even globally." Comment on this statement in the Indian perspective where personal care organisations have a prosperous future.

BACK-UP MATERIALS

1. www.bplans.com.
   www.ehow.com.
   www.ibisworld.com.

   Beauty Salon Industry Analysis:
   Critical Success factors of Beauty Industry.

2. spas.about.com.
   Business of Beauty.

3. www.Korencheng.com
   www.pierss.com.

   artofmanliness.com.
   Building a Wardrobe.

4. www.mindtools.com.
   www.sosuave.com
   www.askmen.com.

   First Impression Power.

5. www..beautybehaviours.com
   www.articlesbase.com.
   www.infobih.com.
   Hair Styles Personality.
   How Your Hairstyle Makes Public Your Personality Choosing a Hairstyle for Your Lifestyle.

6. www.watch=wiki.net ask.metafilter.com
   www.brandedwatchesonline.com.

   Best Watch Brands.

7. www.fibre2fashion.com.
   www.articleshmarticle.com.
   www.abacus.caree.com.

   Investment Dressing.
   Corporate Clothing Tencel Clothing.

8. www.missattymaam.wardrobe.com.
   www.essortmut.com.
   www.citygirlstyle.com.

   Wardrobe for the Young Professionals Grooming and Appearance.

9. www.tradeindia.com.
   www.suits4menonline.com.
   www.theguidetomensuite.com.
   Wardrobe Essentials, How to do more with less Match-making.

10. www.wikihow.com.
www.carryfitness.com
Business of Beauty Parlour
Value to Your Clinic

11. www.leathertree.com.
Tan Leather Briefcase

12. Wearabouts: The Economic Times, 24 October, 2010.

13. Jha, S.M.: Marketing of Personal Care Services;
Planning Selling, Annual Volume, 1989, New Delhi.

14. Jha, S.M. & Singh, L.P.: Marketing Management in Indian Perspective; HPH Pvt. Ltd., 1988 Chap. 34 pp. 1083-1126.

15. Jha, S.M.: Services Marketing, HPH Pvt. Ltd., Mumbai, New Revised and Enlarged Edition, 2011, Chapter 15, pp. 470-91.

◆ ◆ ◆

11 THE FUTURE OF PERSONAL CARE BUSINESS

The most important thing in the business world is creating a condition for addiction where customers or users become helpless and the stimulating forces prove to be effective in penetrating the impulse buying of users. Material culture brings a favourable condition for the opulent lifestyles which traps us and injects new life and strength to the personal care sector.

CHAPTER DESIGN

Introduction – Emerging Positive Trends in the Personal Care Business – Improving the Supply Position – Personal Care Business. The strategic Areas – The Tactical Decisions for Personal Care Services – The Future of Personal Care Business is Prosperous – Summary – Key Terms – Expected Questions – Application. Exercises – Back-up Material.

CHAPTER OBJECTIVES

This Chapter aims at studying the future of personal care business. With the increasing heat of globalisation and the increasing domination of material culture, the future of personal care business appears to be prosperous. The emerging positive trends are to be identified and professional excellence is to be used to capitalise on the opportunities which may keep on moving the process of market expansion. A significant increase in the discretionary income and an analogous rise in the spending capacity will increase the demand positions vis-à-vis will make the personal care busines prosperous.

THE FUTURE OF PERSONAL CARE BUSINESS

◈ Introduction

Rise and fall, up and down, boom and recession move in a cyclic order. If we are tasting the pleasure of a high economic order, we should also keep ourselves ready to taste the bitterness of recession and depression. If we enjoy the pleasure of a high position, we should also keep ourselves ready to face the disrespect on account of shifting or firing. Whatsoever the development patterns that we witness each and everyday; whatsoever the changes that we frequently face make it clear that an acid test of our professional excellence and managerial proficiency is found in a rough weather and it is also true that weather cannot remain static and if today it is fair; tomorrow or a day after tomorrow, it is sure to be unfair because weather also moves in a cyclic order.

The beginning of 21st century signalled a number of positive developments in the national as well as the global perspectives. Since the economic order was sizably impacted, the social order, cultural patterns and civilisation could not remain untouched. In a true sense, globalisation of economy made ways and opened new vistas for the globalisation of fashion culture and civilisation. The tidal wave of material culture started dominating everything and we just remained to be a silent expectator. Credibility for these developments, positive or negative, goes to corporatisation resulting into the emergence of corporate culture. Material culture, often traps us and willingly or unwillingly all of us become helpless and start taking the pleasure of materialistic gains.

The most important thing in the business world is creating a favourable condition for addiction where we find ourselves helpless and start hankering after the materialistic gains because it is pleasant to come out from poverty to solvency but very unpleasant to allow poverty or insolvency to get a reentry. The process of addiction has gained a rapid momentum during the yesteryears and therefore our lifestyles which changed during the boom would remain unaffected, albeit we find recession continuing for long. Besides, the corporate culture considered to be another edition of western culture has made sufficient addition to the attributes or traits required for people serving there. On the one hand, the organisational requirements have been advocating for enriched personal score while on the other hand, we also find general people tempted to the western lifestyles. This engineers a sound foundation for the development of personal care business.

The emerging trends in the consumer spending patterns indicate that personal care business has a prosperous future. We find Hong Kong, China, Singapore, Brazil and India witnessing a rapid increase in the spending patterns. The mounting domestic demand and increasing domestic investment financing are the positive developments in the Indian economy which has been helping India in turning into the second fastest growing economy in the world, just next to China.

We cannot negate that even in the coming years, the positive trends would remain existent. Hence, the growth of economy would continue to be a dominating factor because income level and spending patterns are found interrelated.

The MNCs have option but to depend on the Indian customers and the Indian markets. The adequacy of national resources, proficiency of human resources and the upward spending patterns would continue to inject new life and strength to the national economy of India.

Unless and until, the money is in our pockets, the lifestyles and the living standard would move towards solvency and affluency. This will continue to pump more financial resources for the development of economy. The continuing global recession is not to damage the Indian economy, at least in the near future. But here it is pertinent that investment patterns do not undermine the industries supplying products to the personal care sector in different ways and in different forms.

The Beauty world India 2010 reflects healthy market. The organisers of Beauty world India, based on a survey, are confident that not only the beautycare industry, but almost all the areas of personal care would have a profitable market because the demand position is to gain a rapid momentum due mainly to the strength generated by the corporate world. The Indian Cosmetic and Beauty Industry has witnessed a rapid growth in the last couple of years varying around 15 to 20% and the emerging trends indicate an upward movement in the trend. We cannot deny that whatsoever the past trends that we find in the development of beauty care industry set future-trends for attractive business in the subcontinent and therefore, the small as well as the big players have to explore avenues that how and in what way the existent and niche markets are to be optimally tapped. There are a number of new areas where we find developments and in this context, we need to showcase some of them such as cosmetics, skincare, haircare, beauty and hygiene products and accessories, professional care for salons, spa and wellness, fitness equipment, dental care, manicure and pedicure interior design and furniture for beauty parlours, fashion accessories as well as training centres for the development of required skilled people for different areas.

The requirements are expanding and the markets are day-by-day emerging. In this context, it is pertinent that professionals witness the developments identify the opportunities and capitalise on the same in an effective way. The creation of wealth, generation of employment opportunities, increase in the cost and standard of living are some of the positive developments to take place in future which would make the beauty care business an emerging sector of the national economy of India.

Since we find it an age of investment dressing, a majority of us evince interest in grooming themselves not just with regular haircuts and facials but something more such as aroma therapy, soothing massages, easy yoga, fat-reduction techniques, gym, jogging, aerobics, holistic treatment of mind, body and soul and everything possible which can help them in becoming much more hireable and promotable. In all the areas, we find potentials for the development of business. The personal care organisations involved in the process need to capitalise on the opportunities.

Of late, in the business world, we strive for perfection and it is the responsibility of personal can organisations that they assign due weightage to the people and technology who can deliver the best. There are a number of avenues but everywhere the process of defining and redefining the quality requires top most priority. The users, today, are found quality conscious. They tan their skin by using artificial light, starve to lose weight to look more attractive and everything from toes to noses now go through cosmetic surgery. A majority of us particularly tempted to the corporate world are found interested in having a charismatic personality. Willingly or unwillingly, they have to respect the organisational culture and the dress code policy of the concerned organisation where they work. Our awareness of business attire is considered significant. Actually, we need an in depth idea of wardrobe management and the Business Schools and Finishing Schools of today have to accept the responsibility of educating, training and developing people in tune with the changing corporate requirements.

There are a number of beauty products in which we find tremendous opportunities. In a true sense, we find beauty industry emerging as the most profitable business of the 21st century. It is imperative that we realise the significant potentials of this industry and promote them to make a sizable contribution to the process of national economic transformation. The demand side is gaining a rapid momentum and it is pertinent that prospering beauty industry improves the supply position. The concept of Modern Beauty requires due attention of the emerging personal care sector in general and the beauty care industry in particular.

We are well aware of the multi-dimensional areas of personal care and keeping in view the emerging trends, we have to develop them in such a fashion that employment opportunities are created and the required personal score are matched in tune with the corporate requirements. The small as well as the big players; domestic as well as the global players need to take part in the process and in return the national economy is to be benefited.

Business of beauty, business of personal care services are emerging areas and keeping in view the changes that we witness in the corporate world, it cannot be refuted that the demand position will gains a rapid momentum. This necessitates an increase in the supply position both in qualitative and quantitative terms. The personal care organisations need an in depth study of organisational culture, etiquette and manners, civic and aesthetic sense, development of a rock star personality, management of wardrobe development of leadership skills, awareness of personal hygiene, stress-bearing capacity of people serving the organisation and all the properties making them potentially sound to face and encounter albeit the rough weather. There are a number of products where we need to re-define the service quality and the personal care organisations need them while processing and delivering the services. They also need technology and tech-savvy people to make the services cost-effective and competitive.

The past trends provide to us a clear picture that in the first decade of 21st century the demand for beauty products has doubled. Euromonitor dot has made a nationwide survey which indicates that as compared to 2010, there has been a 17% increase in demand for beauty products in 2011 and this provides to us a clear signal that in the second decade of 21st century a boom like situation is to emerge which will write a new story for the personal care business.

◈ Emerging Positive Trends in Personal Care Business

Corporatisation makes the ways for qualitative transformation. We cannot deny that with the emergence of corporate culture a number of new developments took place; some of them were positive and some of them were also negative. The increasing domination of MNCs on the global economy considerably affected the development patterns in the national economy of India. In a true sense, the emergence of corporate culture made possible a big change in our lifestyles, behavioural patterns and levels of expectations. The youths in particular evinced keen interests in serving the corporate world because the public sector was not in a position to meet their high-level expectations. This made it essential that people desirous of serving the corporate sector or already serving the corporate sector develop their awareness of the potentials and traits which can simplify their task of climbing the corporate ladders. The expanding areas of personal score started making their tasks of becoming hireable and promotable much more complicated. It was against this background that during the yester years, the personal care organisations started taking a new shape.

It becomes very difficult to believe the wonders of the corporate world. The growing popularity of corporate trainers, particularly in the second decade of the 21st century is a staunch testimony to this proposition that style and status, distinctiveness and elegance of our personality and looks significantly contribute to the personal score. Of late, appearance is found to be an important factor to make us hireable and promotable. If we do not dress for success; we suffer. Actually, it is an age of investment dressing. The metropolitan cities like Chennai, Mumbai and Delhi display highest instances of individuals bypassed as they did not dress for success. It is also found that obese people get a raw deal at their workplace. We also find cases where age is also found to be a hindrance to promotion. A majority of us believe that looks become responsible for discrimination at the time of recruitment. Youthful appearance plays an important role in getting the job or even for getting promotion. These facts make it clear that in the present business world appearance matters a lot.

The developments outlisted above make it clear that in the present world of wonders, it is not only significant that you are thematically of world class. In addition, you need to add a number of score in your personality. The business tycoons feel that people developing a high-level temptation for appearance are found positive and optimistic and we need only those people who have a zest for life. We look for people having leadership quality civic and aesthetic sensibility, creativity, rock star personality having the potentials to be adjustable and nurturing a vision to climb the corporate ladders. We cannot deny that emerging new trends have made ways for a number of positive developments. It is not possible for an individual to add all the personal score required for getting a respectable position in the business world. This engineered a sound foundation for the development of institutionalised services which resulted into the development of a good number of personal care organisations.

With the increasing heat of globalisation, we find the Indian economy thriving. A large number of brands are found making the business environment much more competitive. In the years to come, the beauty care industry would witness multi-pronged qualitative and quantitative transformation and tremendous job opportunities are also to be created specially for the upcoming youths in the different areas of personal care such as beauty consultants, product analysts, lab assistants, beauty advisors, technical and managerial staff, pedicurists, manicurist, nail technicians, chemical engineers, photo or movie stylists, hair care and perm specialists, cosmetology instructors, image consultants, product distributors, *et. al*. A number of users changing from corporate or other sectors will improve the demand position. These developments will inject new life and strength to the national economy of India.

Beauty World India 2010 has cited the promising markets based on a survey which reveals, that in the Indian markets, we find return of confidence. The national economy is prospering and its impact on the personal care sector cannot be refuted. It is against this background that we find the beauty industry developing at a rate around 15 to 20% which may go even upto 25%. The beauty care sector has been found making a significant contribution to the economy and the positive trends would continue even in future. It is right to mention that revival of economy is likely to give a fillip to the trade.

The continuing positive trends signal a significant increase in the job markets and we find now upcoming youths interested in adopting it as a career. We cannot negate that demand for smart, well-informed, trained and tech-savvy professionals have increased more than three folds. If in the economy, we find creation of wider job opportunities, it is quite natural that the development processes keep on moving.

There are a number of areas where we find personal care services processed, created and delivered on an organised basis. Besides, we also find unorganised sector and small players engaged in the process. The people in general are now found health conscious. We find a considerable increase is the demand of personal care products, equipments, instruments etc. which is also a positive side of development. The users in general are to be tapped by the professionals serving the personal care sector. Continuing just to the corporate segment cannot be a remunerative proposition.

With the expanding purview of personal care, we find positive developments in almost all the concerned areas. The health care, civic and aesthetic sensibility, etiquette and manner, ethics and values building or character are now becoming essential for the people serving the corporate sector and we find revenues for business in almost all the areas which can be tapped professionally in the days to come. The personal care organisations are expected to develop personality in totality which makes people potentially sound to counter and encounter the adverse conditions to face and enjoy life in totality. They advocate for a place for spirituality in our educational system. This may empower the upcoming youths to face life in totality. The Euro monitor dot signals a prosperous future for the personal care products. The small as well as the big players need to be innovative.

◈ Improving the supply Position

The demand position for the personal care services has gained a rapid momentum. An important reason for such a positive development is boom in the economy which made possible an increase in the disposable and discretionary incomes of common people. The emergence of corporate culture paved copious avenues for the creation of job opportunities and credibility for the same goes to the process of globalisation which changed the concept and percept of economic transformation. When you have money in your pockets and each and everyday you witness people enjoying modern amenities and facilities for an opulent lifestyle; it is quite natural that you cannot regulate your temptation and find yourself floating in the tidal wave of material culture. This has happened during the yester years and this will happen even in the years to come. This is naturally to improve the demand position and professionals bear the responsibility of diagnosing the emerging trends and developing a prescription to optimise the supply position.

The institutionalisation of services becomes essential when the requirements of users are found multi-pronged. We are aware of the fact that during the yesteryears, there has been a considerable increase in the required personal score of an individual particularly serving the corporate sector. It is quite natural that at an individual level, the enrichment process would be much more difficult and therefore organisational support is necessitated. Delivering services commensurate with the organisational culture cannot be possible unless we institutionalise them with a professional touch. Corporatisation injects new life to the process of institutionalisation and keeps on moving the process of qualitative transformation. All the concerned personal care organisations have to work and serve with the motto of defining and re-defining service quality.

It is a general observation that during the yester years, there has been at least a three-fold increase in the demand position and in the coming years, it may go upto at least five-fold. This is due to the fact that process of corporatisation is found conceptualised even in the public sector. What to talk of the MNCs, when we find even domestic large and small players conceptualising it. They should perceive things in a right fashion which would help them in writing a new definition of service quality. We cannot negate that day-by-day the users have developed sophistication which has been impacting the product innovation process. The earlier concept of a general beautician is changed. Today, we find people looking for the specialised services. Apart from the popular area of skin and hair care, there are ample opportunities for pedicurists, manicurists and nail technicians. Making use of the services of specialists and generalists depend on the specific conditions for service processing and delivery. People now understand the difference between beauty clinics and the beauty parlours. The field of dermatology has taken a new turn and the techniques of cosmetology are now more developed. The providers need to have an in-depth study of the changing requirements of users so that the process of satisfaction and retention gain a rapid momentum.

The small as well as the big; the domestic as well as the global players have an opportunity to business the services concerned with personal care. The services may be specialised or of general nature keeping in view the requirements of users. The services, may be personal or institutional or organisational and therefore the personal care organisations need to study the areas where they have to locate the business. Some of the services may be processed and delivered manually whereas for some of the services we need supporting infrastructural facilities. When we talk about managing the wardrobe, accessorising, investment dressing, managing the hairstyle, grooming and etiquette, oral hygiene, managing stress, promoting yoga, creating civic and aesthetic sensibility and developing leadership skills; the services are found of specific nature. In all the areas, we find scope for an increase in the demand position and therefore the supply position is also to be increased.

The providers need to make it sure that they have skilled and professionally sound people; new generation of technology and the service ambience or environment to have service culture. Activating the process of quantitative transformation cannot be underrated to keep the demand and supply side at an optimal point. The Business Schools as well as the Finishing Schools cannot be spared from the responsibility of developing people to be productive to the corporate world. At this stage, it is pertinent that personal care organisations have devices for developing the monitoring mechanism. But our focus is here on the quality of services.

An improvement in the supply position makes it essential that personal care organisations know about their customers and markets in depth. By undertaking such studies, they may be potentially sound for the existing conditions. Since some of the services are found of significant nature, we need to promote the participation of government, religious organisations or even social and cultural organisation to come forward and resolve the problem. Actually, it is a time for developing the personal care organisations and improving the supply position.

The MNCs in general do not prefer to promote the dress-down policy. They are found very selective and work with this motto that employees are just an extension of the corporate brand and therefore the dress policy of an organisation remains the same globally, nationally and even regionally. Since the MNCs are dominating the corporate world, there will be a significant increase in the demand position. This necessitates a sizable increase in the supply position. It is not to be possible unless we find a large number of personal care organisations strengthening their participation in the different tiers of cities and design a packaged service for the varied segments making use of the services with diversified motives.

The important tasks before the personal care organisations are to be innovative, cost-effective and competitive. Actually, they need qualitative as well as the quantitative improvements in the supply position The future of personal care organisations will remain bright as long as the demand position shows an upward trend.

◈ Personal Care Business: The Strategic Areas

During the yester years, there has been a significant increase in the number of personal care organisations in different tiers of cities. The users of services come from different segments but our main focus is here on the corporate users serving domestic as well as the MNCs. The small and big players working at small and large scale need to identify the strategic areas to make their services much more competitive. Since we find the future of personal care organisations looking bright, it is imperative that they are strategically and tactically sound to capitalise on the opportunities. In an age of investment dressing, the youths as well as the upcoming and budding youths keep on nurturing their temptation to the material culture and for which they have no option but to enrich their personal score. Because the personal care organisations may fulfil their requirements; they depend on the service quality offered to them. If the personal care organisations have to thrive, it is pertinent that they identify the strategic areas which help them in activating the process of qualitative-cum-quantitative transformation. It is quite natural that while initiating the development process, the personal care organisations cannot confine themselves to the corporate segment. Of course, they may be specific to the policy decision making areas specially for the corporate people. If we talk about the business of personal care services, the maximisation of profit cannot be undermined. This necessitates identification of personal care services which may help users to be much more hireable and promotable. In this context, they also need to focus on the development of a package which must be cost-effective. The accessibility and availability are also considered important areas to provide comforts to the users. Making the personal care business much more prosperous is the target for which we need the following strategical measures in different areas of services.

Focus on Beautycare: Westernisation followed by corporatisation has changed our life styles. A majority of the people particularly youths and upcoming youths, evince interests in looking attractive and impressive. Dr. G.S. Kochar, Director. VLCC Institute also agrees that wellness boom in the society is giving fillip to the trade. It is against this background that we find growth with high intensity in Tier 2 and Tier 3 cities compared to the smaller cities. The towns and cities in general are becoming much more beauty conscious. The cosmetic industry has been prospering cosmetic surgery and body carving have also been found in big demand. The field of dermatology has taken a new turn specially after globalisation. People are now found more conscious of their looks and appearance. The spending capacity and behaviour show the positive trends. The cosmetology is also in big demand. The beauty clinics, hair cutting and dressing and skincare pave avenues for the development of a number of areas where we find opportunities to jump and prosper. We cannot negate that with the increasing demand for looking attractive and impressive, it is quite natural that the multi-billion dollar industry offers a whole array of opportunities specially to the youngsters.

The important thing is development of expertise in the concerned area. A number of government and private institutions are found engaged in developing people in the various areas. Apart from government affiliated vocational training institutes across the country, private training centres run by Shahnaz Hussain, Habibs, Blossom Kochchar, Bharti Taneja, Vandana

Luthra have become a brand in themselves and they also offer specialised courses. A course in cosmetology or beauty therapy paves the ways for openings in beauty clinics, hospitals, spas and health clubs where one can join as a consultant or therapists. Big brands also hire their own team of beauty consultants, product analysts, lab assistants, beauty advisors and other technical and managerial staff. Five star hotels and cruise liners too have their in-house salons and spas where professionals are much in demand. Apart from the popular areas, or skin and hair care, there are ample opportunities for pedicurists, manicurists and nail technicians.

The facts outlined above make it clear that with the development of corporatisation, we find a general shift in the lifestyles of common people then what to talk of the people serving the corporate sector. This is to create tremendous opportunities in the field of beauty care for both the genders, men or women.

Consciousness of Personal Hygiene: Today, we find common people realising, the relevance of personal hygiene but due to inadequate sensitivity and accessible; they fail in availing the services. This makes it essential that healthcare institutions or even educational institutions activate the sensitisation process. With the increasing awareness of personal hygiene, the personal care organisations would be required to extend the institutional support. There are a number of areas where we find opportunities such as children personal hygiene, personal hygiene education and training, personal hygiene guidelines. Corporatisation is based on attraction and therefore the corporate professionals need due attention on creating hygienic conditions particularly at the workplace. Besides, they also need to respect personal hygiene. We consider it an essential part of work etiquette. Handshake is an essential part of work etiquette and this also focuses on handcare. The nail care requires due attention because we find them acting as a carrier for germs. Oral hygiene requires proper care because mouth is found to be prone to the collection of bacterias. The problem of body odour cannot be undermined and for that we need awareness of daily shower. We also need proper hair care for the management of scalp, problem of lice and dandruff. The clothes that we wear also need due attention. The toilets, kitchens, floors need priority attention. The potable water plays an important role. We need to regulate the problem of obesity and awareness of medical hygiene. The personal hygiene training is found essential in the very context.

It is right to mention that in the coming years, the people are likely to be much more sensitive to the problem of personal hygiene which would create tremendous opportunities for the personal care business for hygiene.

Wardrobe creating a big area of business: Of late, we find wardrobes emerging as an important area for the development of personal care business. The corporate people in particular are hired and fired due to their poor wardrobes. This consists of business attire, ties, shoes helping you in looking smart and impressive. Powerful looking dresses impact our attitudes and mindset. The dress-code policy makes ways for professional mode whereas the dress-down policy paves avenues for the relaxed mode. Better wardrobe helps us in getting high bucks. The appearance factors make a place right from the time, we make preparations for entering the corporate world. Our large or shabbily dresses or scruffy or old or worn clothes project our negative image. Actually, it is an age of investment dressing where giving an extra edge to our personality appears to be a crying need of the hour. Etiquette and grooming experts have been found making a strong advocacy in favour of transformation in the whole package of attitude, body language, behaviour, communication and etiquettes. These facts are a staunch testimony to the proposition that in the coming years, the attractions for quality wardrobes would gain a rapid momentum. Hence, we find accessorising an important dimension of wardrobe management in which a number of areas are to emerge for making business. We cannot deny that an important reason for the development of look culture is the emergence of corporate culture which is considered another edition of western culture. The MNCs in general feel that employees are considered just an extension of the corporate brand and therefore the dress-policy adopted at one place would remain equally applicable even for other places which may be a nation or even a region. This makes it clear that day-by-day, the emergence of new business areas in the field of wardrobe management is quite natural.

It is a professional compulsion for the people serving the corporate sector that they are sincere to the wardrobes and respect the organisational culture. We cannot deny that the way in which we groom ourselves and the way in which we dress carry important meaning for the desired facial appearance. We need to make it sure that our outfits have a fair match with the corporate image. The MNCs in general feel that corporate people cannot overlook the professionalised management of their wardrobes.

The facts outlined above make it clear that in the coming days, there will be a significant increase in the items or articles to be instrumental in magnifying the look culture. This will bring a sizable increase in the demand position. Since we find corporate culture also affecting other segments of society; the demand position would considerably increase.

Hence, the personal care organisations need to diagnose the demand position and to promote the areas where we find tremendous business opportunities. Business in corporate apparel, shoes, socks, ties and accessories would increase further and therefore the concerned organisations have to study the trend and to improve the supply position in the face of changing requirements. The providers have to ensure quality for satisfaction and retention.

Business potentials in Yoga, Aerobics and Exercises: With the passage of time, we find people becoming much more health-conscious. The environment at the workplace makes them much more stressed. We cannot negate that the first form of happiness is sound health and therefore we need awareness of nutritious and balanced food to keep the body healthy. But healthy body is not to be possible unless we sincerely care for the health of our mind. So, it is essential that we care for both, the mind and body simultaneously. This draws our attention on yoga, aerobics and exercises. During the yester decades, we have found people of west developing their temptation for yoga because the stressed mind has made their task of stress-free life much more difficult. Corporatisation is another edition of westernisation which opens new vistas for materialistic gains and stress *pari passu* or with equal pace. This makes it essential that we take support of different postures of yoga. Besides, we also find physical health of an individual playing an important role particular in the corporate world. Yoga has the potential of keeping us physically and mentally healthy. In addition, we find aerobics, gym and jogging gaining much more popularity. These facts mate it clear that corporatisation has made ways for the promotion of yoga. It is in this context that we find demand side moving upward which makes it essential that the supply position is increased. Hence, the business opportunities existent in the yoga, aerobics and exercises are to be tapped optimally by the personal care organisations.

During the yester decades, there has been a significant increase in the institutions or organisations, promoting and marketing yoga, aerobics and exercises, however we find the supply position non-optimal to the demand position. This necessitates concerted efforts for opening more institutes at small and large scales who can educate and train people to keep them physically fit and mentally sound. It is not possible to seal doors of stress because we find the levels of expectations of common people which in a majority of the cases remain unfulfilled and result into stress. We find ourselves not in a position to clean the accumulated complexes and negative feelings which multiply the intensity of stress. The different postures of yoga are found instrumental in combating stress. Besides, the aerobics and exercises are also effective in keeping us physically fit.

In addition to the opening of institutes for yoga and holistic treatment of mind with commercial motives, we may also think in favour of promoting yoga by the religious and non-governmental organisations so that the general masses are found accessible to the services. So far as the corporate people are concerned, they may use the services of even leading organisations because they do not face the problem of affordability. What to talk of the big towns and cities when we find justifications for promoting yoga even in the small towns and cities.

The facts outlined above make it clear that we have tremendous business opportunities even in the field of yoga, holistic treatment and physical exercises, gym, jogging and aerobics.

Business in improving Civic and Aesthetic Sensibility: The emergence of an indisciplined and uncivilised society may harm the nation in different ways. We are aware of the fact that our laws and regulations are becoming ineffective in making the society sensible . The curative as well as the preventive measures may be practised to generate civic and aesthetic sensibility. It is also well known that the authorities responsible for implementing the laws or punishing for violating the laws have not been found sincere and honest while maintaining the provisions. We have sufficient examples to quote that even in the developed countries of the globe, the civic sensibility could not be possible unless the administration opted for the punitive measures. Thus as a curative measure we may think over the punitive devices and as a preventive, we may think in favour of institutional or organisational support for sensitising and educating the people that without civic and aesthetic sense; they cannot survive and thrive. We should not forget that softness, tenderness and politeness are the properties which can significantly help us in the corporate world.

Besides, it is also pertinent that corporate people assign due weightage to aesthetic sensibility. If we turn our eyes on the Indian civilisation, we find there copious avenues for the development of aesthetic sense. Our ancient traditions, art, poetry, literature, dance, drama, paintings, music, customs and culture are rich enough to refine our taste. It is significant that we love nature and link our relationships with art and culture and nurture zest for happy living.

Institutional support for civic and aesthetic sense is considered essential. The Business and Finishing Schools have enough opportunities to educate and sense their students in tune with the corporate culture. Around the globe, we find corporatisation gaining a rapid momentum. This has been opening new avenues for aesthete. A number of areas have developed to champion their cause. Amidst hustle and bustle, stress and tension, the life of common people is becoming too much complex and boring. Aesthetically refined people develop love for music. All these areas open ways for the organisation having the potentials to educate sense and influence people. Creating love for beauty and nature is found essential in the very context.

Either we talk about the rural folks, or our focus is on the city folks, we find both the segments lacking civic sensibility. Since we find family not making available to the citizen the required civic sense, we consider institutional support essential. In the process, we may involve educational institutions in general and the Business Schools in particular. There are a number of areas for generating civic sensibility and it is imperative that the concerned organisations or institutions make available to the concerned students or persons detailed knowledge of all.

Thus, in the face of facts outlined above, it is right to say that awareness of civic and aesthetic sensibility is essential and failing the family support, we may think in favour of the institutional or organisational support. The corporate world makes place for the best and therefore corporate people are required to prove themselves to be the best.

Inculcating Etiquette and Manners: Our outward behaviour, etiquette and manners, soft skills need due attention to get the competitive advantages in the business world of today. Etiquette is found concerned with the conventional laws of courtesy. It is decorum in which we find place for polite and socially acceptable behaviour observed between the members of same profession. If we talk about manners, our focus is on the outward behaviour or attitude towards others. It is also personal style of acting or bearing or a way in which something is done. In every educated society to be civilised, the etiquette and manners became a part and parcel of relationships. Social graces and polish are considered essential for the corporate people. It is against this background that the corporate society of today has been assigning due weightage to etiquette and manners. Our predilection towards education cannot be wrong but at the same time it is also pertinent that we do not undermine etiquette and manners.

The Business and Finishing Schools have realised the significance of etiquette and manners and therefore we find them taking help of corporate trainers for educating to their products the etiquette and manners. It cannot be denied that soft skills are as important as the hard skills to get an edge in the present competitive environment. The educational institutions in general and the business and finishing schools in particular need to address everything from voice and accents to dining etiquette to dressing up basics. Lack of social graces and communication skill prove to be a major factor for our failures specially in the corporate world. The youths and budding youths need to strengthen their realisation that they cannot do anything without knowledge of etiquette and manners.

The Global Education Centre in Mysore, opened by Infosys has been found educating more than 50,000 students leadership and corporate manners. Like this, we find a number of finishing schools in the leading towns and cities of the country educating students the leadership and manners. The Etiquette and Grooming experts are now in big demand. The whole package of attitude, body language, behaviour, communication and etiquette and manners account for our professional growth because a study makes it clear that technical skills account for 15% whereas the business and social graces account for 85%. We are least aware of the international workplace etiquette when the present corporate world assigns top priority to it.

The Business Schools today need to change their perceptions, priorities and strategies. They have to develop students in tune with the corporate requirements. Professional excellence cannot be possible in absence of professional growth and if we undermine corporate etiquette and manners, the professional growth of an individual is difficult.

We cannot deny that in the emerging cross-cultural society, the employees are considered an extension of the corporate brand and therefore the personal score of corporate people need due attention of institutions and organisations involved in the process of developing corporate professionals. The enrichment process thus paves avenues for the development and growth of modern B-Schools.

Building Character: The first decade of 21st century was dominated by knowledge power and the remaining decades are to be dominated by character power. We cannot negate that philanthropy comes from the heart of the people. In an age of societal globalisation, we find ethics, as a major determinant of individual or institutional success. Ethics matter because it makes good business and sense to do the right thing. Good corporate ethics result in attracting better talent, retaining customers and employees, creating new customers, making return on investments profitable and projecting of a fair image. Again, it is your image that recycles the development process. Hence, it is imperative that we assign top priority to the building of character which opens doors for all the positive developments. Practising ethics make the business whereas breaching ethics break the business.

When we find corporate people conceptualising business ethics, it is meant that they have remained successful in adding new dimensions in their personal score. Because they are ethical, we find their conduct good and character sizably different from others. Actually, this proves to be the strength of an individual. Ethics is the science of morality and that branch of philosophy which is concerned with human character and conduct. Character focuses our attention on strength and originality in the nature of an individual when conduct throws light on the way of our behaving with others. In a true sense, conduct is behaviour. It is in this context that we find organisation preferring morally-sound and behaviourally-decent people. People having a right conduct succeed in having a magnetic and charismatic personality. This makes it essential that corporate world makes concerted efforts to build character. Actually character is power.

A brick-by-brick process, no doubt, consumes more time but shows the desired results. Building an ethical climate in an organisation is the main thing which requires involvement of all. How and in what way the institutional support may be effective in this brick-by-brick process of building character is the main thing that we need to think over. Right from the primary stage to the higher stage of learning, the process of inculcating ethical values and building character keep on moving. In the process, the educational institutions need to play a catalytic role. The motivational forces inject new life to the process of increasing the number of ethically sound and value-based people in an organisation.

To keep alive the process of budding character, it is imperative that the Indian business tycoons change their attitudes which will make the ways for the development of personal philanthropy, the, most important dimension for respecting ethics and building character. If they motivate good people, the bad people would naturally be demotivated. Training Programme may be a positive step to create a conducive environment. To activate the process, the organisations may also think in favour of organising the spiritual sessions for employees working there which would engineer a sound foundation for generating ethics and building character. If people make themselves aware of the ethics and character and perceive their significance to the organisational development process; the avenues are paved for further development.

Developing leadership Skill: Having leadership skill is found significant to counter the sky rocketing volatility in the business world. Strong management with strong leadership may be an effective prescription because we have the bitter experiences of strong leadership with weak management, often proving worse than the reverse. The changes and challenges in the business world are but natural and it is upon a leader to constitute a team, inject team spirit, make possible team culture, and with the help of sound strategical and tactical decisions to achieve the target. Of late, we find the corporate world looking for leaders because they are considered potentially sound to successfully cope with the emerging changes and challenges. Strong leadership with strong management may be very much effective in excelling competition. We cannot deny that leadership trait of an individual is an important dimension of our personality. It is against this background that we find corporate world looking for a captain of the football team or leader at an orchestra party. The hiring experts advocate that successful leaders are found potentially sound to counter the risks. Since they have a high level of tolerance usually they are a performer and behaviourally sound to handle the crisis and we find them productive to the organisation. It is due mainly to the fact that they know the art of learning from the triumphs and failures. The people having leadership skills try to lead, take a risk, and accept the challenges, counter the threats, initiate and penetrate things and ultimately get a success in excelling competition. Institutionalising a leadership-centred culture is found to be a crying need of the hour for the creation of a sound corporate culture where working people realise the weight of strong leadership and further strive to create and continue it as an ongoing process. The corporate trainers, often, focus on the relevance of leadership for the development of personality in tune with the changing requirements of the business world.

In view of the mounting significance of leadership skills, it is imperative that concerted efforts are made by the concerned institutions and organisations to inculcate leadership skills. In the process of developing leadership skills, it is imperative that required traits are inculcated. The corporate world is looking for creative leaders. The concerned organisations need to develop their product in the face of changing requirements of the corporate world. The leaders should have efficacy of setting direction, aligning people, motivating people, creating a leadership culture, identifying the adaptive challenges, regulating distress and developing humanised leadership. The Business and Finishing Schools and even other educational institutions may be successful in developing quality leaders to be productive for the corporate world. We can negate that business leaders of today need much more empathy and personal philanthropy. We cannot deny that during the yester decades, the business tycoons of India could not take lessons from Warren Buffets, Bill Gates, Paul Allens and Azim Premji and resulting from which we find lack of personal philanthropy in a majority of the leaders of the business world. The providers need to strengthen their realisation that by developing leadership skills, they can increase the performance level of their employees.

◈ The Tactical Decisions for Personal Care services

Planning for gaining a specific end, of course, requires professional excellence of world class specially in the corporate world where the business environment is found much more competitive. The target is to promote the personal care business in such a fashion that users are created, satisfied and retained. The tactical decisions focus our attention on the promotional measures that we adopt for informing, sensing, sensitising, persuading and transforming the potential users into the actual and habitual users. The personal care services play an incremental role in enriching our personal score. A high level of insensitivity found amongst the potential users appears to be a prime reason for a deficient condition in which unawareness prevails and we find ourselves personally handicapped to be hireable or promotable in the corporate world. We cannot think about getting a respectable position in the business world of today, if we are unaware of the relevance of investment dressing and are not sincere and professional while managing our wardrobes. Our awareness of having a decent and elegant corporate looks would help us in getting the high bucks. A majority of the persons are yet to strengthen their realisation that the unawareness of the various dimensions of personal care may deprive on individual of getting the competitive advantages in the business world. If we are not aware of the relevance of personal hygiene, we suffer in different ways. Our civic and aesthetic insensibility prove to be an important reason for our face loss. If we are not aware of the soundness of our body, we fail in having a rock star personality which proves to be a negative score of our personality. If we do not discharge the accumulated complexes, we do not make place for positive feelings and minimise our potentials to counter the odds which make place for stress. If we undermine ethics and do not make efforts to build character, we invite a number of problems on that account. If we underrate etiquette and manners we suffer. If we do not have the required leadership skills, we fail in anticipating the changes and challenges to emerge in future. Like this, we find a number of adverse conditions making us potentially deficient for the present corporate world.

Believe it or not, the corporate world is full of wonders where an individual is hired due to his rock star personality and another individual is fired due to his unimpressive looks. Since we find both the genders nurturing a high level of temptation to serve the corporate world, it is imperative that at the outset, we develop our awareness of the organisational culture, the dress code policy of the organisation where we serve or plan to serve and the attitudes of high echelon of people regarding the dress-down policy. We should not forget that MNCs consider employees just an extension of the corporate brand and they prefer professional mode which cannot be possible unless we enrich our personal score. Our predilections need a shift. Of course, the thematical competition of an individual is significant but here we have also to remember that non-verbal communication has a strong edge over the verbal communication. The prevailing conditions necessitate a high level sensitisation process.

If we succeed in sensitising them; our task of influencing them is considerably simplified. Creativity makes the ways for sensitivity which we need to store it in our memory. Such a sensitisation is also to be done by the educational institutions in general and the Business and Finishing Schools in particular. The creation of customers is an ongoing process; we should not forget. Whatsoever the measures we adopt for sensitisation need to have a high level of acceptability. Since the users of services come even from the rural areas, it is imperative that we assign due weightage to creativity. Right from the primary stage to the advanced stage; awareness programme requires due focus.

The corporate culture is considered to be another edition of western culture. The cultural influences play an incremental role in shaping our lifestyles. The emergence of a cross-cultural society is a staunch testimony to this proposition. We find material culture an important by-product of the corporate culture. The materialistic gains and opulent lifestyles addict us to such an extent that we find it difficult to come out. More addiction, much more creation of new customers and tapping of niche markets which the corporate professionals need to remember. The increasing domination of MNCs in the corporate world has been successful in promoting westernisation. It is the gift of globalisation and we have to accept it without any option.

The corporate professionals need to remember that employees serving the corporate sector have no option but to welcome the expectations of the MNCs. They have to make it sure that their tactical decisions not only generate the desire but in addition also strengthen the realisation of people that if they have to climb the ladders of the corporate world, the only option left in their hands is to respect the organisational culture. They have to view even small things in detail. They have to remain optimistic. They have to adjust themselves with the changes and challenges of the corporate world. In a true sense, they need an attitudinal transformation in tune with the changing levels of expectations of the corporate world. They have to be a visionary and to regulate their behaviour.

The corporate professionals bear the responsibility of initiating and activating the process of attitudinal transformation that enrichment of personality would make employees hireable and promotable. Uniqueness and distinctness provide to us the competitive advantages. Our efforts for establishing an edge over others would determine the intensity of success. If we think for ourselves, we think for others. If we nurture zest for life, we explore avenues. The people serving the corporate world need to nurse zeal and zest which makes them optimistic and creative. The corporate world looks for people found to be optimistic. Making ways for survival is not the only thing expected from the corporate people. Indeed, your temptation for climbing and reaching to the peak of the corporate ladders is the real thing which helps you in many ways. If you keep on moving the process of enrichment, your task is considerably simplified. Joining the corporate world is, of course, easier but surviving is difficult and thriving is much more difficult. It is optimism that helps you in many ways.

◆ The Future of Personal Care Business is Prosperous

We need to business where our customers know us. We need to business where we know our customers. It is almost clear that the users of personal care services may depend on the domestic players, if they are ensured quality services at an affordable price. Whatsoever the trends, we have identified during the yester decades make it clear that with the growing impact of corporate culture the users have now started realising the relevance of personal care services to be delivered by reputed personal care organisations. It is high time that domestic players keep themselves engaged in identifying the opportunities and tap them with a personal and professional touch. Both in quantitative and qualitative terms, the demand side is to gain a rapid momentum and therefore it is imperative that all the concerned organisations make professionalised efforts to improve the supply position. For this, they can take help of new generation of technology and quality skilled people. They should not forget that marketing was found easier yesterday, marketing is difficult today and marketing is surely to be much more difficult tomorrow or a day after tomorrow. Because, we cannot regulate the entry of global big players and the moment they start dominating the markets the task would be much more difficult for the domestic players.

With the expanding ambit of personal care services and with the increasing levels of expectations of users; it is quite natural that the providers would be required to think about product uniqueness and distinction. This necessitates product innovation so that new quality of services or products are made available to the users. Like other organisations, the personal care organisations also need to intensify the research activities and to innovate the information system. This will simplify their task of studying and understanding the changing levels of expectations of users vis-a-vis the fluctuating organisational requirements. Because in the context of personal care, the users have no option but to depend on the changing organisational culture which considerably influences the personal traits for the people serving the corporate sector. If they assign due weightage to their looks, it is only due to the organisational culture. If they adopt the concept of investment dressing, it is also due to the dress code policy of the organisations where they work. Hence, the techno-driven information system will help personal care organisations in the policy decision making process.

The process of corporatisation is sizably dominated by the MNCs. Almost all the sectors and by and large almost all the areas are now dominated by them. With the development of beauty industry, we find a substantial increase in the demand for the beauty products. With the development of health care sector, we find a big increase in the demand of healthcare products. Since we find corporatisation another edition of westernisation, it is quite natural that the personal care services and the concerned organisations cannot keep themselves spared from the products promoting westernisation. Moreover, when MNCs consider employees just an extension of the corporate brand; the process of westernisation is surely to gain a rapid momentum.

However, it is also to be made clear that of late we find users in general developing a high level of temptation for herbal products. This necessitates due attention on the product innovation which would be easier with the co-operation of MNCs.

Any industry growing consistently gets an opportunity to strengthen its base and moreover when the average rate of growth is 20 to 25%, we can easily imagine the future of that industry. The Indian Retail Survey 2010 clarifies that the current size of beauty care industry is about ₹ 10,000 crores and in the second decade of 21st century it may reach even up to ₹ 20,000 crores. Like this, we find positive trends even in either areas of personal care such as beauty consultants product analysts, beauty advisors, chemical engineers, perm specialists and many others. The wellness boom and attitudinal transformation make it clear that personal care sector has a· prosperous future. Euromonitor dot based on a nationwide survey makes it clear that in the year 2011, there has been 17% increase in the demand for beauty products which is visible not only in the big towns and cities but also in the small towns and cities where we find job opportunities. The demand side will continue to gain a rapid momentum and it is upon the personal care organisations to momentise and intstrumentalise the supply side. The process of creation of wealth is considered an important dimension to accelerate the pace of economic transformation and a large-scale investment in the personal care sector can make it possible.

Of course, we witness much more fluctuations in economy due to recession and its continuance for the long time may invite even economic depression but at the same time, it is also right to say that living in a sophisticated condition ultimately turns into habits and a majority of the people find it difficult to bid a goodbye to the same. The spending patterns once adopted continue for the long time and during the first decade of the 21st century, we have witnessed a significant increase in the spending patterns of people in general and the corporate people in particular. The emergence of a large market even in the Indian perspective will invite small as well as the big domestic as well as the global players to take part in the process of development.

Mental elevation, physical invigoration and spiritual rejuvenation are the three considerations gaining a rapid momentum specially in the Indian perspective and therefore all the parameters indicate positive developments in the field of personal care sector. It is against this background that we find emergence of personal care sector as an industry specially during the yester years and do not find any sign that there will be a reversal in the trend. Emergence of a multi-billion dollar industry has been offering a whole array of opportunities to the youths in general and the upcoming or budding youths in particular. The Tier-2 and Tier-3 cities have witnessed a radical transformation in the standard of living and lifestyles of people.

Almost all the educational institutions have now no option but to bring a fundamental change in their attitudes because willingly or unwillingly they are governed by the attitudes of users and the emerging trends in the economy. They have to explore avenues that how and in what way they can make their products much more hireable and promotable in the corporate world. By educating, training and developing them in the face of changing corporate requirements, they can make their products much more productive to the corporate world. They have to ensure personality in totality making people efficacious of facing life in totality.

SUMMARY

In this chapter you have gone through the future of personal care business. While closing, make it sure that the following facts are well versed.

Emerging Positive Trends in the Personal Care Business: The growth and business indicators testify that emerging trends in the personal care business is of positive nature because the national economy is growing fast and the beauty sector has been witnessing a growth of 20 to 25%.

Improving the Supply Position: The personal care organisations need to identify the demand position and in the face of increasing demand, they have to improve the supply position. Hence, the small as well as the big players may be engaged in the business of personal care services. An existent increase in demand is not only amongst the corporate users but also amongst other users of personal care services. Hence, the providers have to make efforts for qualitative and quantitative improvements in the supply position. The different tiers of cities specially Tier 2 and Tier 3 need priority attention where we find a big increase in the demand position.

The Personal Care Business Strategic Areas: The service providers need to identify the thrust areas where they can identify opportunities and initiate professionalised effort to capitalise on the thrust areas are beauty care personal hygiene wardrobe management of mind, management of body, civic and aesthetic sensibility, etiquette and manners, ethics and building character, development of leadership skills. All the concerned areas have tremendous opportunities for business because the corporate users in particular prefer services of best quality which is possible only by the leading personal care organisations. The corporate professionals need to formulate a sound strategy to tap them in an optimal fashion.

The Tactical Decisions for Personal Care Services: It is significant that personal care organisations make professionalised efforts to inform, sense, sensitise, persuade and transform the potential users into actual and habitual users. They need to the successful in developing brand loyalty which requires increased rate of retention of users and in the process the tactical measures may be effective. Since the users come from almost all the segments, it is imperative that the personal care providers make use of creative promotional measures.

The Prosperous Future: The indicators reveal that the personal care services have a prosperous future. It is due mainly to the fact that corporatisation has paved avenues for westernisation, where we find a fundamental change in the organisational culture. The providers of service have to make innovative efforts to meet the expectations of users vis-a-vis they will also be required to respect the dress culture and the dress-code policy of the organisations where people work. Quality and affordability are the two important considerations which the providers have to take care.

KEY TERMS

- Personal Care Business
- Cosmetic Surgery
- Pedicurists
- Manicurists
- Chemical Engineers
- Photo Stylists
- Perm Specialists
- Personal Hygiene
- Wardrobe
- Powerful Looking
- Yoga
- Aerobics
- Hustle and Bustle
- Hurry and Worry
- Philanthropy
- Strategical Decisions
- Tactical Decisions
- High Bucks
- Material Culture
- Beauty Products
- Corporate World
- Obese
- Rock-star Personality
- Herbal Products
- Investment Dressing
- Product Analysts
- Scalp
- Shabbily Dresses
- Outward Behaviour
- Social Graces
- Niche Market

EXPECTED QUESTIONS

1. Throw light on the emerging positive trends in the personal care business mainly after the increasing domination of material culture due to globalisation.
2. Explain the measures to be adopted by personal care organisations to improve the supply position of quality and affordable services to the users.
3. Focus on the thrust areas of personal care services where we find tremendous opportunities for promoting the business.
4. Do you find beauty care emerging as an industry specially in the Indian perspective? Justify your arguments.
5. Discuss the opportunities that you find in the management of looks specially for the corporate professionals.
6. Do you find Yoga an important area where we find tremendous business opportunities? Defend your arguments.
7. Focus on the strategic decisions helping personal care organisations making the business much more lucrative.
8. Throw light on the relevance of tactical decisions for making the personal care business profitable
9. Do you find the business in personal care services to be prosperous in the coming years? Justify your arguments.

APPLICATION EXERCISES

1. "Globalisation is another edition of westernisation which has considerably influenced our lifestyles and paved avenues for the development of personal care organisations". Comment on the statement with a special reference to the corporate culture.

2. "The emerging trends in the consumer spending patterns is due mainly to the increasing growth rate of economy". Discuss this statement and explain the impact of recession on the personal care business.
3. There are a number of beauty products in which we find tremendous business opportunities. Focus on the development of beauty care industry in the Indian context mainly after globalisation.
4. "It becomes very difficult to believe the wonders of the corporate world. The growing popularity of corporate trainers, particularly in the second decade of the 21st century is a staunch testimony to this proposition that style and status, distinctiveness and elegance of our personality and looks have helped corporate professionals in getting big bucks and therefore we find a significant increase in the demand position". Explain this statement in the capacity of a corporate professional.
5. Beauty World India 2010 has cited the promising markets based on a survey which reveals that in the Indian markets, we find return of confidence a positive sign for the personal care business. Comment on this statement.
6. "It is a general observation that during the yester years, there has been at least a three-fold increase in the demand of personal care services and in near future it may go up five-fold. This is due to the fact that process of corporatisation is found practised even in the public sector organisations." Do you agree with this view? Justify your arguments.
7. "In an age of investment dressing, the youths as well as the upcoming youths keep on nurturing their temptation to the material culture and for which they have no, option but to enrich their personal scores. Because the personal care organisations fulfil their requirements; they depend on the service quality offered by them." In the light of this statement, focus on the strategic areas where personal care organisations may help them.
8. "It is a professional compulsion for the corporate people to be careful to their wardrobes and respect the dress-code policy of the organisation." Do you agree with this view? Defend your arguments in the capacity of a corporate professional.
9. For keeping us physically fit and mentally sound, we find yoga an effective device where we find tremendous business opportunities. Comment on this statement.
10. "We have sufficient examples to quote that even in the developed countries of the globe the civic sensibility cannot be possible unless the authorities bearing the responsibility start adopting the punitive measures." Do you recommend it in the Indian condition? Justify your arguments.
11. The Business and Finishing Schools have realised the significance of etiquette and manners and therefore we find them taking help of corporate trainers and the etiquette and grooming experts for this purpose. Do you find it an essential step? Justify your opinion.
12. "Character-building is a brick-by-brick process." Comment on this statement and focus on the relevance of character as a power specially the context of corporate world.
13. "Honing leadership skill is found significant to counter the sky rocketing volatility in the business environment. Strong management with strong leadership is an urgent requirement of the corporate world." Comment on this statement as a corporate professional.
14. "The tactical decisions may be helpful in informing, sensing, sensitising, persuading and transforming the potential users into actual and habitual users." Comment on this statement.
15. The future of personal care business is prosperous." Throw light on this statement as a corporate professional.

BACK-UP MATERIALS

1. spas.about.com.
   Business of Beauty.

2. www.wikihow.com.
   www.carrfitness.com.

   Business of Beauty Parlour.
   Value to Your Clinic.

3. www. bplans.com.
   www.ehow.com.
   www.ibisworld.com.

   Beauty Salon Industry Analysis.

4. www.beautybebavours.com.
   Hair style.

5 www.fibre2fashion.com.
   www.articleshmartcile.com.
   www.abacus.caree.com.

   Investment Dressing.

6. Jha, S.M.: Marketing of Personal Care Services; Planned Selling, Annual Volume, 1989 New Delhi.

7. Jha, S.M. & Singh, L.P.: Marketing Management in Indian Perspective; HPH, Mumbai, 1988 Chap. 34, pp.1083-1126.

8. Jha, S.M.: Services Marketing; HPH, Mumbai 2011, Chap.15, pp. 470-91.

◆ ◆ ◆

BIBLIOGRAPHY

BOOKS:

Abraham Zaleznik : *Managers and Leaders: Are they Different?* Harvard Business Review on Leadership; HBR Press, 1998

Argyle M. : *The Psychology of Inter-personal Behaviour*, Penguin 1984

Charles M. Farkas & Suzy Wetlaufer : *The Ways Chief Executive Officers Lead*; Harvard Business Review on Leadership; HBR Press, 1998

David Murray : *Ethics in Organisations*; Coopers and Lybrand, 1997

D.C. Feldman & H.J. Arnold : Managing Individual and Group Behaviour; Tata McGraw-Hill, 1983

Donald W. Cowell : *The Marketing of Services,* Heinemann, London, 1984

George D. Chryssides & Johan H. Kaler : *An Introduction to Business Ethics*; Chapman and Hall, London, 1993

Hartman Laura, P. : *Perspectives in Business Ethics;* Tata McGraw-Hill, Mumbai, 1999

Jha, S.M. : *Marketing Management in Indian Perspective,* Himalaya Publishing House Pvt. Ltd., Mumbai, 1988

Jha, S.M. : *Services Marketing,* Himalaya Publishing House Pvt. Ltd., Mumbai, 2011

Jha, S.M. : *Hospital Management,* Himalaya Publishing House Pvt. Ltd., Mumbai, 2011

John P. Kotter : *What Leaders Really Do;* Harvard Business Review on Leadership; HBR Press, 1998.

John Donaldson : *Key Issues in Business Ethics;* Academic Press, London, 1989

Joseph L. Badaracco, Jr. : *The Discipline of Building Character;* Harvard Business Review on Leadership; HBR Press, 1998.

Kotler Bloom : *Marketing Professional Services;* Prentice Hall, 1984

Lovelock : *Managing Services;* Prentice Hall, 1988

Lovelock : *Services Marketing;* Prentice Hall, 1984

Ralph M. Stogill : *Handbook of Leadership:* The Free Press, New York, 1974

Robert J. House & Terence R. Mitchell : *Path Goal Theory of Leadership*

Robert T. & Fred M. : *Leadership: A Frame of Reference in Leadership and Organization;* McGraw-Hill, 1961

Ronald A. Heifetz & Donald L. Laurie : *The Work of Leadership:* Harvard Business Review on Leadership; HBR Press, 1998

Ronald M. Green : *The Ethical Manager;* Macmillan College Publishing Company, New York, 1993

Swami Sivananda : *Easy Step to Yoga;* A Divine Life Society Publication; Garhwal, UP, India, 1994

Theophand A. Mathias : *Corporate Ethics;* Allied Publishers Ltd., New Delhi.

Thomas Toal : *The Human Side of Management;* Harvard Business Review on Leadership; HBR Press, 1998

Tripathi, A.N. : *Human Values;* New Age International Publisher; 2010

Walter A.N. Henry : *Cultural Values do correlate with Consumer Behaviour;* 1976

Zeithmal & Bitner : *Services Marketing;* Tata McGraw-Hill, New Delhi, 2003.

WEBSITE:

www.minoritycareernet.com
www..mindingmanners.com

Corporate Manners

www.watch=wiki.net ask.metafilter.com
www.brandedwatchesonline.com
Best Watch Brands

www.mentalhealth.about.com
www self-improvement-success.com

Building Self-esteem
Negative and Positive Thoughts

www.nos.org
www.webhealthcentre.com.

Healthy-india.org
Medical Hygiene
Home Hygiene
Hand Hygiene
Kitchen Hygiene
Bathroom Hygiene
Laundry Hygiene
www.economictimes.com
en.wikipedia.org

www.naaree.com
Saree is Way to Go for Indian Women CEOs

www.beautybehaviour.com
www.articlesbase.com
www.infobih.com
Hair Styles Personality

www.hindu.com
blogs.oneindia.in

Civic sense Document Transcript
Pure Civic Sense of City Folks

www.mindtools.com
www.sosuave.com
www.askmen.com

First Impression Power
Tips for Building your Professional Wardrobe

www.karencheng.com
www..pierss.com

artofmanliness.com
Building a Wardrobe
Dress for Success
The Well-Groomed Man
The Well-Groomed Woman

spas.about.com
Business of Beauty
Beauty Salon
Beauty Salon Products

www.webhealthcentre.com
en.wikipedia.org
www.statefundca.com

Personal Hygiene Resources
Handwash
Good Hygiene
Kids Hygiene

www.fibre2fashion.com
www.articleshmarticle.com
www.abacus-caree.com

Investment Dressing
Corporate Apparel
Choosing Corporate Wear
Tencel Clothing
Bamboo Fabric

www.scu.edu/ethics
www.business-ethics.com

Unethical Behaviour
Corporate Ethics
Business Ethics and Business Etiquette
Attributes for Ethical Decisions

www.missattymaam.wardrobe.com
www.essortmut.com
www.citygirlstyle.com

Wardrobe Essentials for the Young Professionals
Workplace Dress Codes in Big Law
Grooming and Appearance

www.tradeindia.com
www.suits/menonline.com
www.the guidetomenssuits.com

Wardrobe Essentials
Pick Solid Colours
Blazers

www.wikihow.com
www.carryfitness.com

Business of Beauty Parlour
Beauty Treatments
Hydrafacial

www.leatherfree.com

The Leather Briefcase
Handbags, Purses and Briefcases for women in the corporate world

www.citehr.com
www.corporategurukul.com

Adapting to Corporate Life
First Impression
Clothing Styles

www.Indianetzone.com
www.yogaforums.com
www.indianexpress.com

Diet and Meditation
Human Personality
Character vs. Personality

www.ties.scasues.co.in
www.indiamart.com

Corporate Ties
Casual Dress Policies
Dress for Success
Corporate Dress Code

www.yogacards.com
www.yogajournal.com
www.yogawiz.com

Yoga Postures
search/beauty.blogspot.com
Goodness, Truth and Beauty
Requirements for Charm and Beauty
Holistic Health and Disease
Path of Meditation

www.bplans.com
www.ehow.com
www.ibisworld.com

Beauty a World of Perfection
Beauty Salon Industry
Therapeutic spa
en.wikipedia.org.runway culture.net
Human Beauty
Inner Beauty
The Meaning and Purpose of Yoga

www.hindu.com
www.healthyeatingworld.com
www.healthyforms.com

Healthy Body
The Alkaline Diet Strategy
Health Problem by acidosis

www.frontierlaw.com
www.thehindubusinessline.com
legalservicesindia.com

Corporate Personality
Physical Appearance and Personality

JOURNALS AND NEWSPAPERS:

Jha, S.M., Planned Selling; Marketing Mix of Personal Care Services Annual Volume, New Delhi, 1989

The Economic Times: Wearabouts: A Smooth Finish, 24, October, 2010

The Times of India: Hired Young; February 13, 2011

The Times of India: Rejuvenate and Reenergise; June 5, 2011

The Times of India: What's age got to do with it; July 24, 2011

The Times of India: Contentment is Spirituality; April 17, 2011

The Times of India: Summer Indulgence? Mind it!; May 31, 2011

The Times of India: How to take a decision; May 22, 2011

The Times of India: Buy me Beauty; July 10, 2011

The Times of India: Damage Therapy; June 26, 2011

The Times of India: I do my Daily Karma; June 31, 2011

The Times of India: Laugh Out Loud; December 12, 2010

The Times of India: Eat with Awareness; December 5, 2010

The Hindustan Times: Potable Water for All; January 30, 1999 (Jha, S.M.)

The Hindustan Times: Too busy to Sleep; June 14, 2011

The Hindustan Times: Looks Make a Man; April 17, 2000 (Jha, S.M.)

The Hindustan Times: Hazardous Bio-Medical Waste (Jha, S.M.)